World Survey of Climatology Volume 10

CLIMATES OF AFRICA

World Survey of Climatology

World Survey of Climatology Volume 10

Climates of Africa

edited by J. F. GRIFFITHS

Texas A and M University
College Station, Texas (U.S.A.)

ELSEVIER PUBLISHING COMPANY Amsterdam-London-New York 1972

ELSEVIER PUBLISHING COMPANY
335 Jan van Galenstraat
P.O. Box 211, Amsterdam, The Netherlands

AMERICAN ELSEVIER PUBLISHING COMPANY, INC.
52 Vanderbilt Avenue
New York, New York 10017

Library of Congress Card Number: 72-135485
ISBN 0-444-40893-2.
With 205 illustrations and 368 tables

Printed in The Netherlands

World Survey of Climatology

Editor in Chief: H. E. LANDSBERG

List of Contributors to this Volume

F. BULTOT
The Royal Meteorological Observatory
Uccle
Brussels (Belgium)

J. F. GRIFFITHS
Department of Meteorology
Texas A and M University
College Station, Texas (U.S.A.)

R. RANAIVOSON
Meteorology Department
Tananarive (Malagasy)

B. R. SCHULZE
Formerly with S.A. Weather Bureau
Pretoria (South Africa)

K. H. SOLIMAN
Meteorology Department
Cairo (United Arab Republic)

J. D. TORRANCE
Department of Meteorological Services
Salisbury (Rhodesia)

Contents

VII

Chapter 3. THE NORTHERN DESERT

by J. F. Griffiths and K. H. Soliman

Chapter 4. THE HORN OF AFRICA
by J. F. Griffiths

Chapter 5. NIGERIA
by J. F. Griffiths

Chapter 12. MOZAMBIQUE

by J. F. GRIFFITHS

Chapter 13. MALAWI, RHODESIA AND ZAMBIA

by J. D. TORRANCE

Chapter 14. MADAGASCAR

by J. F. GRIFFITHS and R. RANAIVOSON

Contents

Chapter 15. SOUTH AFRICA
by B. R. SCHULZE

Chapter 1

General Introduction

J. F. GRIFFITHS

> I am ready to revoke my saying, if anythings
> have passed my mouth for want of learning, and
> to submit myself to correction and my book to
> reformation.
>
> Fitzherbert, 1534. *Book of Husbandry.*

History

Africa is the second largest continent in the world, ranking only behind Asia. In ancient times the continent was referred to by the Greeks as Libya and it was not until the Romans began exploring the area between Cyrenaica and Mauritania that the area received the name of Africa, derived from the word Aourigha (pronounced Afarica) that applied to the Berber inhabitants of the region.

Archaeologists now believe it was in Africa that a differentiation between man's ancestors and other primates first occurred. *Proconsul,* an erect ground dwelling creature whose fossilized remains were found on an island in Lake Victoria, has been dated to 25 million years ago. The earliest toolmaker (an accepted criterion for the distinction of man from beasts) is *Zinjanthropus,* studied in northern Tanzania and dated to about 1.75 million years ago. It would appear, as OLIVER and FAGE (1965) express it, that "Africa remained at the centre of the inhabited world for all but the last small fraction of this long development of the human form... all the true pebble tools yet found have been discovered in or very near Africa. The sites extend from the Vaal River in the south to Morocco and southern Palestine in the north, and the centre of their distribution appears to be the woodland savanna of tropical Africa."

In historical times ancient civilizations waxed and waned around the coasts of the Mediterranean while the north coast of Africa has been settled from time immemorial. However, penetration into the continent had been minimal for hundreds of years. The deepest assaults on the continent had taken place almost exclusively down the Nile, the life blood of the Egyptian civilization. Records covering thousands of years show no instance of the mighty river ever failing completely and the "mystery" of its rise and flood in September and October, hot and dry months along the Mediterranean littoral, while flowing through vast rainless areas, was surely the earliest meteorological problem of the African continent. Naturally, the Egyptians sought to explain this phenomenon and there are indications that explorers penetrated as far as the southern Sudan on their journeys. Around 600 B.C. the Pharaoh Necho dispatched a fleet, manned by Phoenician sailors, from the Red Sea specifically to explore the coast of Africa. Their journey took three years and they returned to the Mediterranean coast, thus completing the first recorded circumnavigation of Africa.

There is evidence that about 2,000 years ago the Roman legions penetrated certain routes across the Sahara with some semblance of regularity, garrisons being relieved and replaced. It is likely that some even went as far as the Niger for there were tales of a great river flowing from west to east. One of Africa's most intriguing legends, however, refers to the eastern area. It tells of a Greek merchant, named Diogenes, who landed in eastern Africa while on a journey home from India in the first century A.D. From the port of Rhapta, perhaps modern Pangani, he is said to have travelled 25 days inland arriving in the vicinity of two great lakes and a snowy range of mountains from whence the Nile derived its source. The story, recorded by Marinus of Tyre, was used by Claudius Ptolemy in his *Geography* when inserting "Mountains of the Moon" on his famous map. Even the first century guide for sailors *Periplus of the Erythrean Sea* indicates knowledge of Mount Kilimanjaro and inland great lakes.

It is now believed that there was appreciable intercommunication among the various groups spread across Africa for at least the past 2,000 years, routes existing in both the east–west and the north–south directions. Nevertheless, as far as Europeans were concerned the next steps in the exploration occurred when Portuguese sailors rounded the Cape of Good Hope and reached as far as Mombasa and Malindi during the 15th century. For experiences during the period between 100 and 1400 A.D. history is dependent upon some of the intrepid Arab explorers, such as Ibn-Batuta who visited the great mediaeval empires of the western Sudan. Hence, the origin of the phrase "forgetful of the world and by the world forgot" as a comment upon Africa.

The period from about 1770 to 1900 A.D. is the time of European exploration of Africa. The tales of Barth, Bruce, Burton, Caillie, Livingstone, Park and Stanley, among many, weave a fascinating story of challenging times and places across the continent. This was the period when scientific observations were begun, often in the face of tremendous personal hardship .Data collected by a handful of men offered more challenging problems to the mind and led eventually to the inauguration of the networks of observatories from which came the information such as is to be discussed in detail in this book.

Geography

Africa covers an area of over 30 million km², approximately 20% of all the earth's land surface. From east to west it stretches 7,200 km, very comparable with the north–south extent of 8,000 km. It is the most symmetrically placed of all the continents with respect to the equator; the most northerly point, Cape Blanc, being at 37°N and the extreme southerly point, Cape Agulhas, at 35°S. The coast line is remarkably smooth and extends for 36,000 km, less than that of Europe, which has only one third the area of Africa.

In the early days cartographers had a hard time obtaining details of the continent and Jonathan Swift's remark, made in the 18th century, was particularly apt, "Geographers in Afric maps, make savage pictures fill the gaps, and o'er inhabitable downs place elephants in place of towns". During the past decade many changes have taken place in political boundaries and names, there are now 40 independent countries on the continent compared with four in 1955. These countries range in size from the mighty Sudan, with over 2.5 million km², to the tiny Gambia of 10,000 km². The population of Africa is estimated at about 261 million, for an overall density of only nine persons per km² compared with Europe's 85 per km². Nigeria is the most populous country with over 55 million inhabitants, while the Territory of the Afars and the Issas (originally French

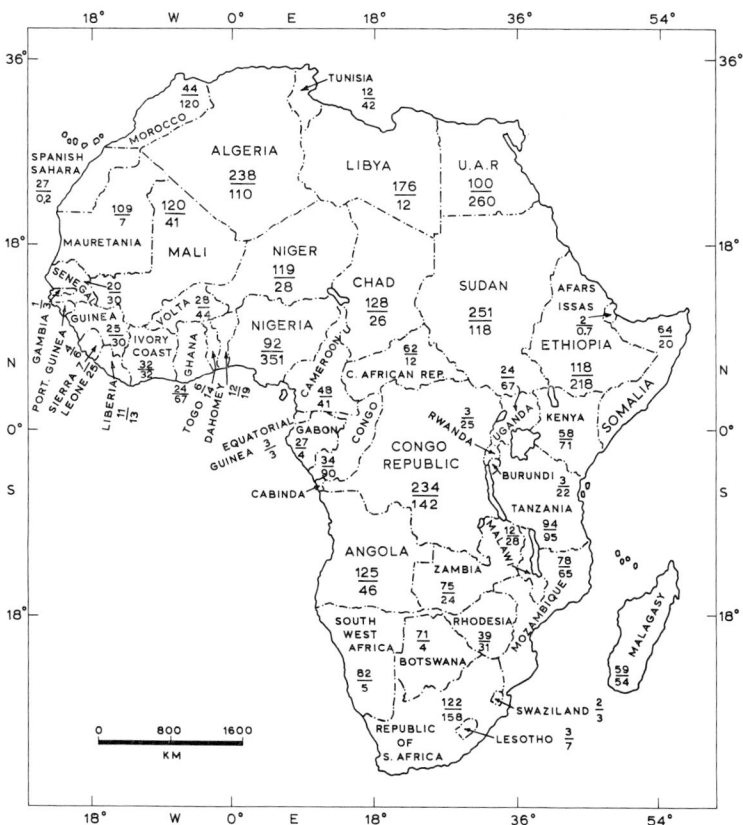

Fig.1. Political divisions, area and population. Numbers denote area in km² × 10⁴ (upper) and population × 10⁵ (lower).

Somaliland) has less than 70,000. The greatest population density is found in the mountainous republics of Burundi and Rwanda, about 88 persons per km², and the least is in the Spanish Sahara with some 13 km² per person. In Fig.1 locations, sizes and populations of the various territories are given. The only cities with an excess of a million inhabitants are Cairo (3.3 million), Alexandria (1.5) and Johannesburg (1.1) although both Casablanca and Algiers are approaching this total.

Geologically it is stated that Africa consists largely of a single rigid block of marine origin laid down perhaps 200 million years ago and later uplifted. It is essentially a giant plateau, very stable since Precambrian times. Volcanic activity has, however, been prevalent, occurring down to the present. Much of this activity has taken place along the 6,400 km crack known as the Great Rift Valley. This rift also contains most of the great lakes. One of the striking features of the vast continent is the relative lack of pronounced topography. The highest point is Kilimanjaro (5,894 m), while the Qattara Depression reaches 132 m below sea level. The vast plateau is broken by only a few mountain ranges of which the outstanding ones are the Atlas, Ahaggar, Cameroons, Tibesti, Ethiopian and East African highlands. In the East African area there are, in addition to Kilimanjaro, Mount Kenya (5,199 m), the Ruwenzoris (5,120 m) and Mount Elgon (4,321 m).

The eastern branch of the Great Rift Valley stretches from the Dead Sea to Rhodesia, meeting the West Rift in northern Malawi. Lake Tanganyika, lying in the West Rift, is

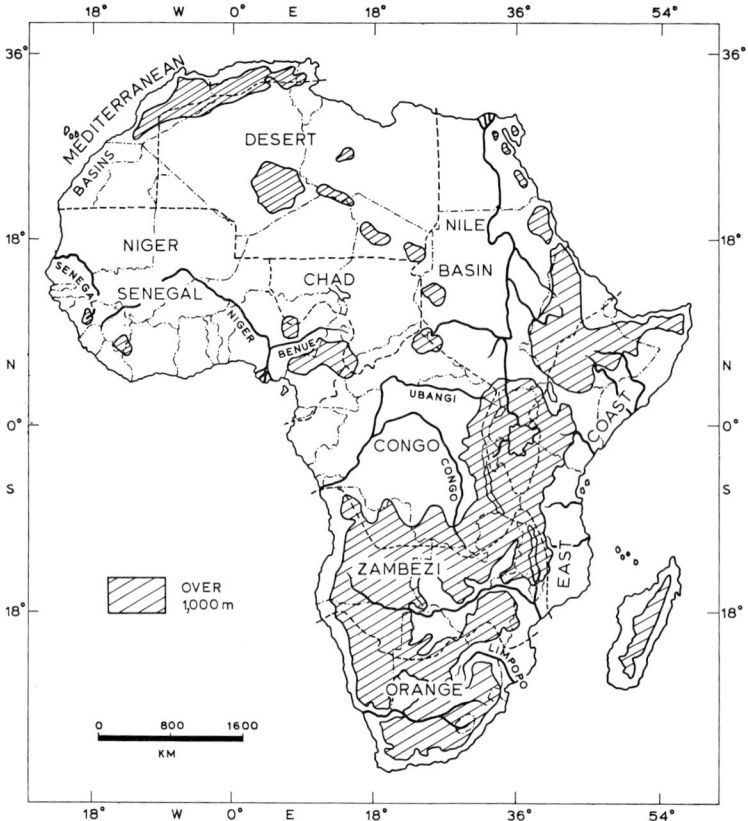

Fig.2. General hydrology and topography.

over 600 km in length and, with a depth of 1,420 m, is second only to Lake Baikal in Asia. Lake Victoria covering an area of 70,000 km² is exceeded in size only by Lake Superior in the world's fresh water lakes.

Mention has already been made of the Nile, Africa's longest river, but, in spite of its vast deserts, the continent supports other great rivers, the Congo, Limpopo, Niger, Orange and Zambezi. It is on the Zambezi that Africa's largest waterfall, the Victoria Falls, is found. The Falls are wider than Niagara (1,700 m) and twice the height (105 m), with a potential hydroelectric power of 2,600 million horsepower. In Fig.2 the major topographical features are noted.

Vegetation

Vegetation and climate are very closely related, a fact that has been well amplified by many climatic classifications. In Africa the basic vegetation types are characteristic of the tropical, sub-tropical and montane regions. It is possible to divide the continent into fifteen vegetation types, as shown in Fig.3.

The tropical rain forest of Africa is the smallest of three similar areas (Africa, Asia and South America). It appears in two main regions, the upper Guinea forest, occupying the area from Liberia to eastern Ghana, and the Congo forest, stretching from eastern Nigeria across the Cameroons, Gabon and the great Congo Basin to the slopes of the

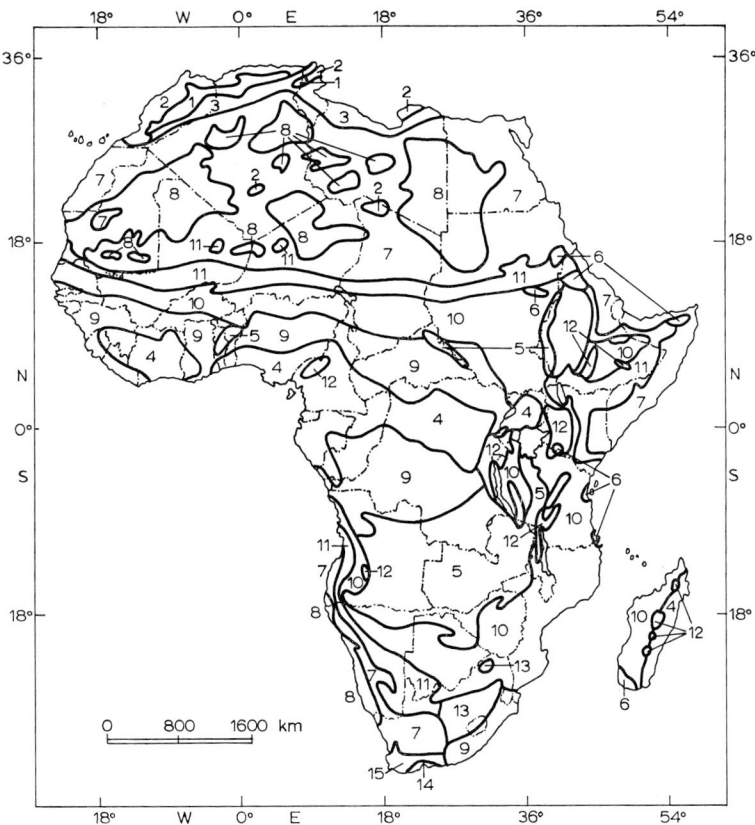

Fig.3. Basic vegetation types (generalized). *1* = cedar forest; *2* = maquis; *3* = garrigue and desert grass; *4* = tropical rain forest; *5* = tropical semi-evergreen and deciduous forest; *6* = thorn woodland and scrub; *7* = semi-desert and scrub; *8* = desert; *9* = broad-leaved tree savanna; *10* = thorn tree, tall grass savanna; *11* = thorn tree, desert grass savanna; *12* = tropical montane forest; *13* = veld; *14* = evergreen mixed forest; *15* = Cape sclerophyllous scrub.

East African Plateau. It is a vegetation type found where the temperature is always high and rainfall is in excess of about 1,500 mm/year, with no drought period. The forest consists of several stories of trees with the highest ranging from 50 to 80 m.

Savannas, the landscape intermediate between desert scrub and forest, are typical of the tropical areas experiencing droughts of from about three to eight months with heavy rains at other times. Although favouring the growth of grasses this climate nevertheless allows the development of scattered trees, generally small leafed and thorny and often of an acacia (mimosa) species, although the cactus-like euphorbia or the bulbous baobab may result.

The scrub land, with nine or ten months of near-drought, gives way to the desert areas where rainfall averages less than about 200 mm/year. In the Sahara, Africa's greatest desert, there are three distinct sub-divisions, namely, the areas of shifting sand dunes (erg), the bare rocky desert pavements (hammada) and the extensive plains of loose gravel and boulders (reg).

In the montane regions, where temperatures are reduced, an increase in rainfall will often give rise to a rainforest in the belt from about 1,500 to 2,300 m. In this type tree ferns, lianas and wild bananas can grow in abundance around and beneath the luxuriant, dense canopy. At the timberline the rapid growing bamboo is found, gradually giving way to heath land, Alpine land and finally snow.

At the extreme poleward ends of the continent the Mediterranean brushland thrives. The vegetation often consists of woody, evergreen plants with thick, leathery leaves, a factor helping the plants to withstand the long, hot, summer drought.

Soils

Many of the soils of Africa are agriculturally poor. Some are immature, or azonal, soils formed from recent rocks which have had insufficient time to acquire a good humus content. On the other hand, some soils are very old, badly leached and often infertile. In much of Africa the warm rain, which holds more chemicals in solution than cold water, has been very effective in eluviating the soil. Over a great percentage of Africa, frost, which is so beneficial in breaking up the soil, is absent. In the humid tropics soils are of four main types. The laterites, the oldest soils, are agriculturally unproductive. The laterized red earths are younger and less leached and occur in regions of heavy rainfall, being quite productive. The non-laterized red earths, found in drier regions, the savannas, are good agricultural soils. The upland red earths are an immature group that is occasionally intensively farmed.

In the regions of moderate rainfall the prairie soils, the most fertile, are located in the highveld of South Africa and parts of West Africa. The black soils, the chernozems, are very fertile but become adhesive during the rains and almost rock-like in the drought period. In the arid regions soil moisture is often drawn upwards by capillarity and, on evaporation, deposits the dissolved minerals in a crust at the surface. The humus content is very low in these areas. In the Mediterranean regions the summer drought, the absence of frost and the small degree of chemical weathering lead to poorly formed soils.

Recent developments

At the end of the 1870's only little of Africa was under European rule, the traditional government of African tribal rulers being in the majority, but by the mid-eighteen nineties half of the continent was under European influence. At the start of World War I all of the continent was under protectorates or colonies save Liberia, Ethiopia and the Union of South Africa. Cecil Rhodes remarked "Give yourself to Africa, you will never regret it" but the European approach appeared to be "give Africa to yourself".

During this period continuous meteorological observations were begun in many areas. Scientific data were being accumulated which, perhaps only after decades, were put to efficient use for the benefit of the land and the occupants. Development of population centres often took place along waterways and the newly constructed railways. Thus, the location of climatological stations is not ideally patterned for analysis. New centres would grow up in atypical areas, for instance, Marsabit in Kenya is situated on a hill in the scrub land, a relative oasis, the climate of which is not representative of its surroundings.

In the past 20 years dozens of independent nations have blossomed in Africa. Occasionally this political event has resulted in a complete collapse in data collecting services, either immediately or at a later date. However, most countries exhibit a good continuation of services, for some of the new rulers have been farsighted enough to appreciate the importance of the observations to applied fields such as agriculture, architecture, engineering, human physiology and hydrology.

The sensible application of climatological knowledge can be of very real benefit to major aspects of African economy and it is to be hoped that some of the shortsighted policies that have ignored climatological facts in the past will not persist and thereby cause further detriment to the African economy. It will be sufficient here to cite just two important examples of the ignoring of useful climatological information both of which have resulted in the loss of millions of pounds sterling, money that this emerging and developing continent can ill afford.

The East African Groundnut Scheme began operations in the colony of Tanganyika as an attempt to alleviate the shortage of oils and fats after World War II. The reasons for the almost abject failure of the scheme are many, but one of fundamental importance was the inadequate attention given to the climatic conditions in the selected areas. The naturally great variability in tropical rainfall from year to year was ignored and a series of "dry" (below normal) years helped to deal a death blow to the grandiose scheme in which, it has been estimated, at least 50–100 million dollars was invested.

The second example concerns the Aswan High Dam and the Jonglei Canal. The great seasonal fluctuations in the Nile are not desirable characteristics for the rapidly developing agricultural schemes of the United Arab Republic, and a method of controlling the flow is highly desirable. The High Dam Scheme has been to build a huge dam that will yield a large reservoir (Lake Nasser) covering at least 2,000 km². This lake will have very large-scale siltation problems (the High Dam has no sluices) and will suffer from huge evaporation losses in this the sunniest region of the world's surface. The Jonglei Canal Scheme (the Equatorial Nile Project) was to construct a canal between Jonglei and Malakal in the Sudan to provide a direct passage, unhampered by the sudd, in which control of the water level would keep the Nile level reasonably constant. At present less than half the water entering at Mongalla leaves at Malakal due to overspilling into the swamps and evaporation, while in addition, all the rainfall on the catchment area is lost.

As JARRETT (1966) expresses it "... the extra amount of water which could have been available to Egypt as a result of the saving in evaporation expected through the Jonglei scheme would have been more than she will gain through the High Dam project, but the Jonglei scheme would have been less spectacular ..."

General weather conditions

It is not the intent in this section to enter into a discussion of the various forecasting techniques used in Africa, but it is necessary to have some appreciation of the main weather features experienced over the continent.

The climatic feature of most significance in Africa is undoubtedly rainfall. Temperature is a rather conservative element showing a relatively small annual range, save at the extreme poleward edges of the continent, while wind speed is generally low compared with the temperate regions.

Within tropical Africa there is little or no synoptic evidence of the existence or persistence of moving areas of rainfall (JOHNSON, 1962). The exceptions that may be cited are the revolving storms and the West African disturbance lines. There is no apparent continuity in the rainfall pattern from day to day and even within the affected area the rainfall is seldom consistent. Thus, it is believed that rainfall results not from the travelling systems but from developments that take place in situ.

For rainfall to occur two conditions must be satisfied: (*1*) an adequate supply of water vapour must be available within the atmosphere; and (*2*) a cooling process must be initiated.

The latter condition is generally obtained by ascent of the air which, in turn, leads to higher moisture content (raised dew points) within the lower and middle troposphere. A major feature in such uplifting of air is horizontal convergence, and if this is noted within an appreciable depth of the atmosphere the vertical ascent becomes significant and, providing condition (*1*) is satisfied, rainfall must result. For a discussion of how the various forms of horizontal convergence may come into existence the reader is referred to the paper by JOHNSON and MÖRTH (1960).

No synoptic discussion concerning the tropics would be complete without mention of four specific phenomena: (*1*) the easterly wave; (*2*) the Equatorial Trough; (*3*) the Inter-Tropical Front; (*4*) tropical cyclones.

Easterly waves, the wave-like perturbations in the easterly current on the equatorial sides of the subtropical belts of high pressure, are still, at present, an unproven phenomenon over Africa. While their existence in the Pacific and elsewhere is well substantiated their existence as independent significant features in African meteorology is doubtful. The Equatorial Trough, the zonal pressure trough, is detectable up to a height of about 500 mbar over Africa and has a mean position near to the equator at that height. At lower levels a seasonal shift is well in evidence, the surface position often being beyond the equatorial limits.

The Inter-Tropical Front, or Inter-Tropical Convergence Zone (I.T.C.Z.), as a surface discontinuity separating northeasterly winds from southeasterly winds, can easily be identified on climatic charts. As a dividing line or zone between the generally warm, dry and cooler, moist air masses it appeared to fit well into the concept of frontal analyses in vogue in temperate zone forecasting. A seasonal migration related to the sun's movements was traced and since the "appearance" of this front occurred at the season of maximum rainfall a cause and effect relationship was assumed. THOMPSON (1965) points out the difference between the temperate and tropical frontal concepts when he notes that in the temperate zones fronts are a concept of the synoptic (daily) pattern; they are not identifiable on climatological mean charts. In the tropics the "front" appears on the climatological charts and not, generally, in the daily patterns.

January

Over central Africa a broad low pressure exists north of the equator (Fig.4A). Air flows into this are very weak and these light and variable winds mean that the I.T.C.Z. can rarely be detected. There is little rainfall associated with this pattern as it is overlaid by divergent northeasterlies. In West Africa the surface trough is parallel to the Guinea coast, coinciding with the highest mean surface temperature. This system is very shallow and little rainfall occurs. The axis of the surface equatorial trough in Central and West Africa is wholly north of the rain belt. In southern Africa, where the surface level chart has little meaning, troughs in the upper levels (850 and 700 mbar) give rise to heavy rains over the Angolan Plateau but the subsidence of the South Atlantic anticyclone causes an abrupt termination of these towards the coast.

April

The equatorial troughs have moved northwards from the January positions (Fig.4B). Over the coast of East Africa the trough appears as a duct between the diminishing Arabian high and the intensifying sub-tropical anticyclone of the South Indian Ocean. The Southern Hemisphere trough dies out in the vicinity of the equator and the thermal low over Arabia leads to a monsoonal drift. The equatorial trough in West Africa, moving northwards, has not elongated in structure but becomes gradually more identifiable on the daily surface charts. THOMPSON (1965) identifies this as the centre of the transition season with rainfall a result of complex interplays among many different synoptic processes, so that the idea of a continuous zonal rain belt progressing northwards is both unreal and incorrect.

July

The surface equatorial trough (Fig.4C) is now near 20°N, extending across the continent. The isobars indicate a meridional pressure gradient from the anticyclonic belt of the Southern Hemisphere to the well developed heat lows of North Africa and Arabia. Subsidence at the southern edge of the Saharan anticyclone at 700 mbar restricts rainfall. THOMPSON (1965) suggests that the coincidence of the axis of the 850-mbar trough with the disturbance line zone (squall line) in West Africa indicates some connection between the two phenomena. The transequatorial ridges in East Africa give rise to frequent periods of convergence at the 700- and 500-mbar levels but subsidence at 850 mbar. Thus, below 850 mbar (1,900 m) this is the month of lowest rainfall while above this level it is the wettest month. The appearance of a long, north-pointing ridge at the 850-mbar level that extends from the South Atlantic anticyclone to the West African coast (near Ghana) is suggested as a reason for the low rainfall over this area at this time (see Chapter 6).

In comparing the rainfall of the northern and southern summers THOMPSON (1965) writes "In the northern summer the dominant quasi-permanent anticyclone over the Sahara both damps out the vertical motions and prevents drift situations in depth from reaching far northwards, with the result that significant rainfall is restricted to southern areas. In southern Africa (plateau Africa), on the other hand, the equatorial trough has a vertical extent during the southern summer to almost 500 mbar and the absence of a damping anticyclone in the lower troposphere permits various synoptic processes, though principally the drift, to occur in depth over a wide range of latitude; the result is a much greater amount and extent of rainfall."

October

The axis of the rain belt has moved southwards (Fig.4D). The equatorial trough is still

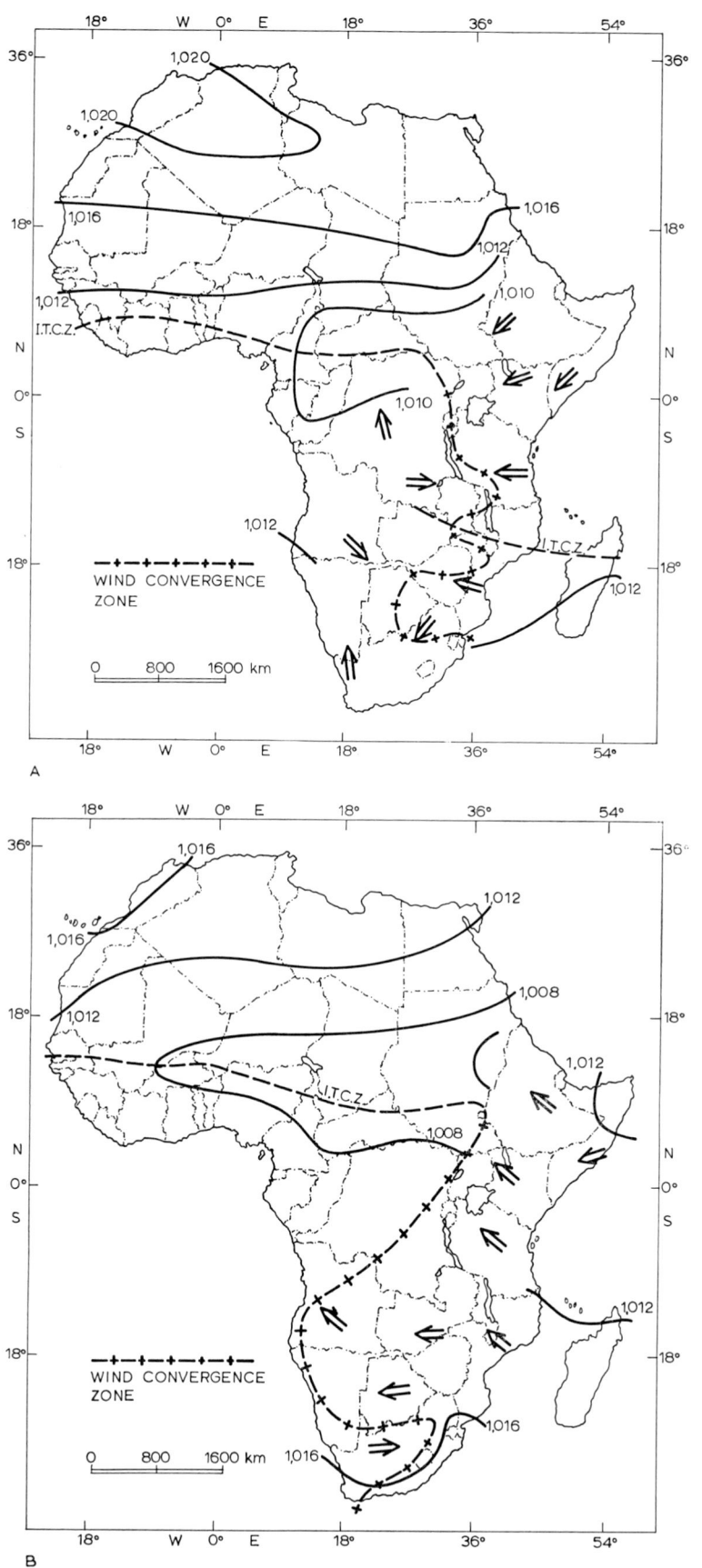

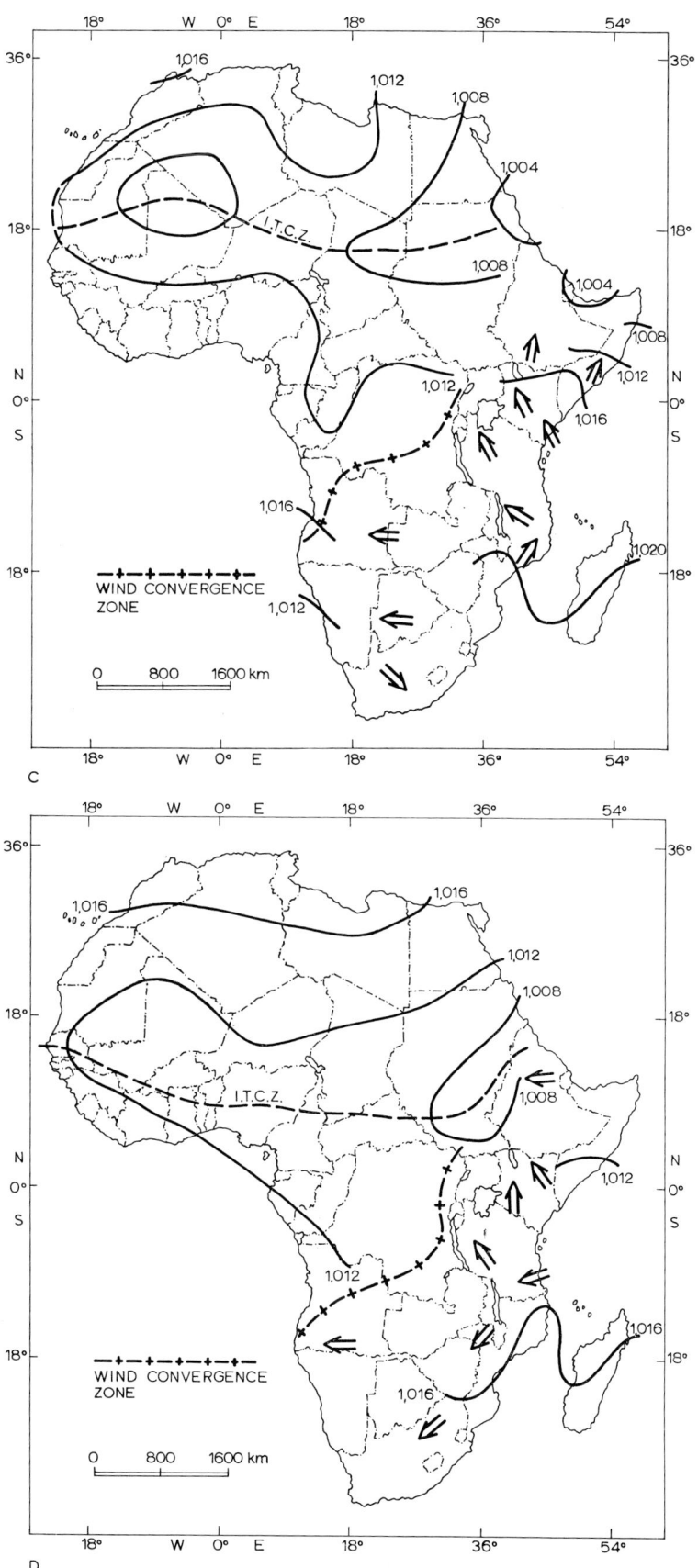

Fig.4. Mean pressure and air flow patterns for: A. January; B. April; C. July; D. October.

north of the main rain areas and a new trough is developing across the Arabian Sea and Somalia. This is another transition season, similar to that of April.

Climatic zones

In this section attention is focussed on period analyses or patterns, not the synoptic, the daily, patterns. It is necessary to study the climatic zonation of the continent so as to show the basic patterns that exist and to be made aware of those areas in which analogous climates may be experienced. A climatic zone should be a region in which a significant uniformity of the climatic elements is observed. However, two definite limitations have to be applied to this idealized definition. First, it is not possible to analyse all the meteorological elements at all stations either singly or in relation to each other. Secondly, within any region a large number of microclimates are likely to exist, each showing some very real differences from the macroclimatic pattern in one or more elements.

To extract some order from the excessive amount of climatic data recourse is often had to the use of climatic classifications. These are simply means by which a grouping of similar climatic areas can be accomplished, generally using the elements of temperature and precipitation because these are the most readily available. It must be appreciated that any climatic classification is limited in use because the method in which it was derived is usually not aimed at the practical problem on hand. A climatic classification can, nevertheless, be a good starting point for future analyses.

Climatic classifications

It is intended here to mention just two of the many climatic classifications that have been advocated, namely those due to Köppen and Thornthwaite. The classical work of Köppen has had, over the past decades, more ascribed to it than originally intended by its compiler. A vast number of letter indices has developed which makes memorizing difficult and it has been shown what vast variations in temperature and rainfall may exist within the same climatic zone (GRIFFITHS, 1966). A presentation of Africa using Köppen's classification is given so that those conversant with its usefulness and limitations may be made aware of the zonation resulting (Fig.5).

Thornthwaite's classification, like Köppen's, attempts to define climatic boundaries, based ultimately on vegetation, by means of mathematical expressions using measured meteorological elements. In the construction Thornthwaite used the ideas of temperature efficiency (*TE*) and precipitation effectiveness (*PE*) (also called the precipitation–evaporation ratio).

These are given by:

$TE = \Sigma \, (5T/36)$, summed over the twelve months
$PE = \Sigma \, 11.5 \, [2R/(9T + 110)]^{10/9}$, summed over the twelve months

where *R* is the mean monthly rainfall (cm) and *T* the mean monthly temperature (°C). Thornthwaite then determined temperature and humidity provinces as in Table I. In addition four subdivisions according to the seasonal distribution are introduced: *v*—

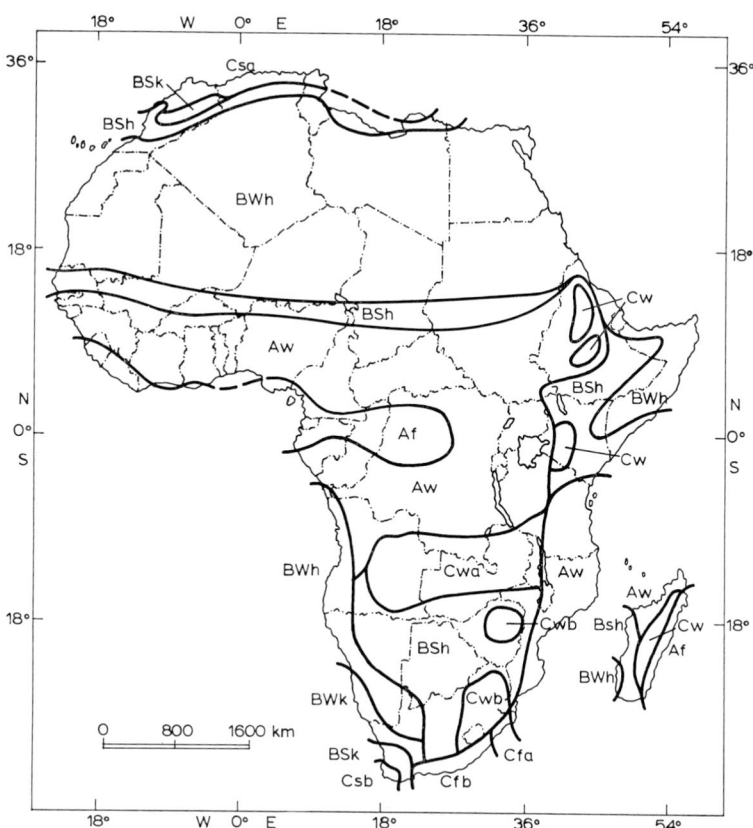

Fig.5. Africa, according to Köppen's classification (generalized). The meaning of the symbols used is as follows: A = Mean temperature of coldest month at least 18°C. C = One or more months with mean temperature less than 18°C. $BS = R < 2T$ (winter rains); $R < 2(T + 14)$ (summer rains); $R < 2T + 14$ (other patterns). $BW = R < T$ (winter rains); $R < T + 14$ (summer rains); $R < T + 7$ (other patterns). R is the mean annual rainfall (cm), and T is the mean annual temperature (°C).

For A climates: f = every month more than 6 cm rainfall; w = mean annual rainfall $< 100 + 10(6 -$ amount in driest month).

For B climates: h = mean annual temperature above 18°C; k = mean annual temperature below 18°C.

For C climates: a = hot summer, mean of hottest month more than 22°C; b = warm summer, mean of hottest month below 22°C; w = winter dry, rainfall in winter season's driest month less than one tenth of wettest summer month; s = summer dry, rainfall in summer's driest month less than one third of wettest winter month; f = uniform rain, neither w nor s.

TABLE I

CLIMATIC CLASSIFICATION IN TERMS OF TEMPERATURE EFFICIENCY (TE) AND PRECIPITATION EFFECTIVENESS (PE)

Temp.	Name	*TE*	Humid.	Name	*PE*
A′	tropical	>127	A	wet	>127
B′	mesothermal	64–127	B	humid	64–127
C′	microthermal	32–63	C	sub-humid	32–63
D′	taiga	16–31	D	semi-arid	16–31
E′	tundra	1–15	E	arid	<16
F′	frost	0			

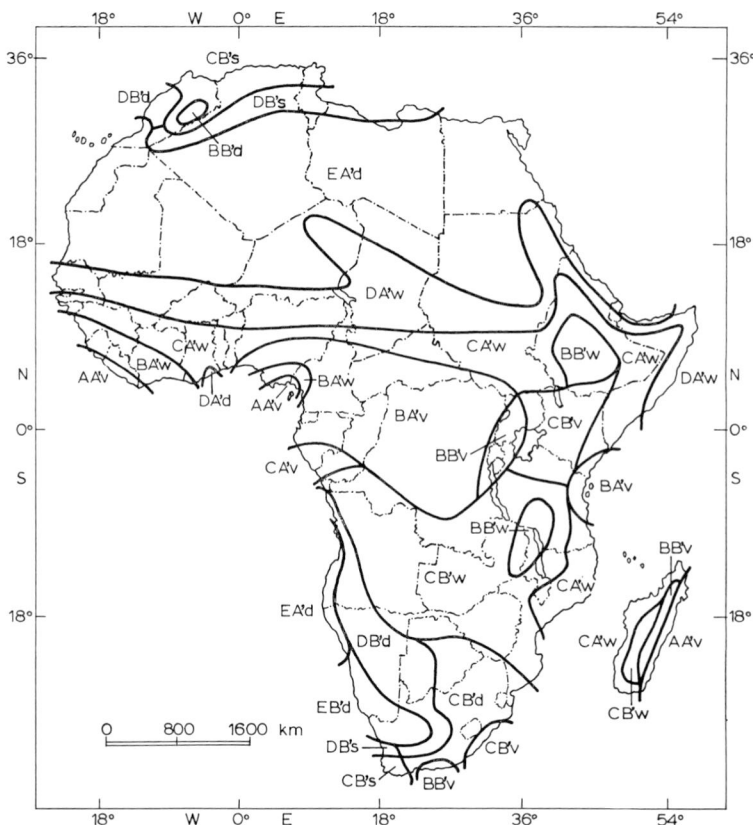

Fig.6. Africa, according to Thornthwaite's classification (generalized).

rainfall adequate in all seasons; *s*—rainfall deficient in summer; *w*—rainfall deficient in winter; *d*—rainfall deficient in all seasons.

The zonation resulting from the use of these criteria is shown in Fig.6.

As this book is concerned with the climate of an area of over 30,000,000 km², it is essential to subdivide the area into zones of roughly similar climatic characteristics and to treat of these individually. It is clear that such a subdivision will, in detail, be a function of the actual classification used. However, a secondary subdividing criterion appears—political boundaries. The climates of a few countries have been studied and written by different authors while, in addition, it must be realised that many countries process and publish their data differently so that strict comparisons are made difficult if not, occasionally, impossible. With these factors in mind the zonation shown in Fig.7 has been developed. This appears to be a compromise with the above limitations and yet will not cross any significant climatic boundaries.

The boundaries used are as follows: (*a*) between I and II—the 125 mm annual isohyet; (*b*) between II and III—a rainfall/temperature relationship; (*c*) between IIa and VI, VIa—a rainfall/temperature relationship; (*d*) between III and IV—less and more than six wet months; (*e*) between IV and V—less and more than nine wet months; (*f*) zone VIa—land above 1,000 m elevation; (*g*) zones VI, VII, VIII, IX and X—mainly political boundaries. With these divisions the areas covered by each zone, expressed as a percentage of the continental area, are as shown in Table II.

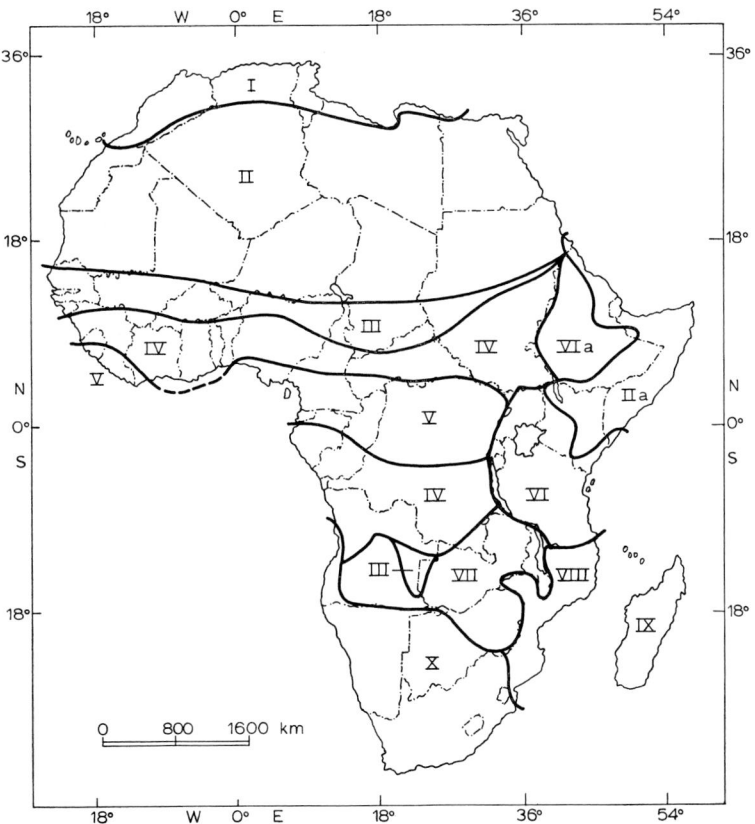

Fig.7. Basic zonation.

It is proposed, throughout this text, to use the basic zonation pattern decided above and leading to the chapter headings. Then, within each chapter, climatic elements will be considered in turn. This is believed to be better than attempting a further climatic break-down via a special classification since the boundaries of a subdivision of one climatic element will not coincide with those of another element so that the resultant regions,

TABLE II

PERCENTAGE AREA OF AFRICA COVERED BY THE CLIMATIC ZONES

Zone	Region	Percentage area
I	Mediterranean	2.6
II	northern desert	33.0
IIa	Horn of Africa	5.2
III	semi-arid	7.2 (6.6 in north, 0.6 in south)
IV	tropical wet-dry	17.5 (11.5 in north, 6.0 in south)
V	equatorial wet	6.8
VI	East Africa	6.4
VIa	Ethiopian highlands	2.3
VII	south Savanna Plateau	5.7
VIII	Mozambique	1.9
IX	Malagasy	2.2
X	southern Africa	9.2

after a combination of elements is considered, will become unusably small. No two places have identical climates and, in a detailed study, an analysis of one thousand stations could result in an undesirable outcome of one thousand climatic regions.

Radiation, sunshine and cloud

Short wave radiation is fundamental to all meteorological (atmospheric) processes. The patterns of pressure are decided by heat balance considerations and they, in turn, control wind flow. Temperature is directly influenced by radiation and, in conjunction with wind flow, leads to a control on rainfall, humidity and evaporation. It is unfortunate that so few measurements are available for the continent of Africa.

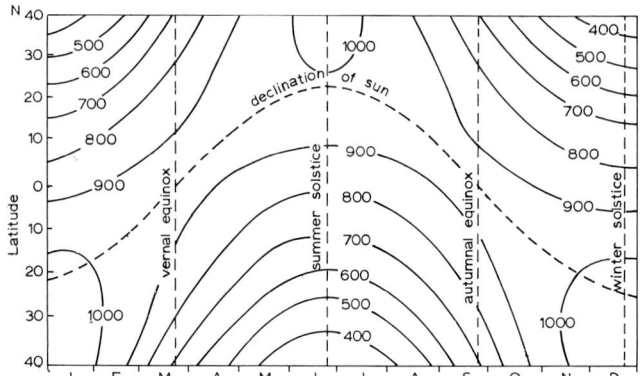

Fig.8. Daily variation of solar radiation at the top of the atmosphere in Ly/day (after SELLERS, 1965).

Normal astronomical considerations lead to the calculated values of solar radiation which would reach the earth in the absence of an atmosphere. This distribution is given in Fig.8.

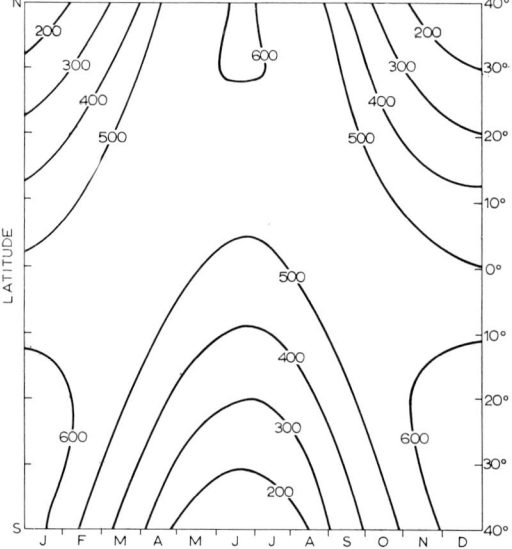

Fig.9. Daily variation of direct solar radiation, transmission coefficient 0.7, in Ly/day.

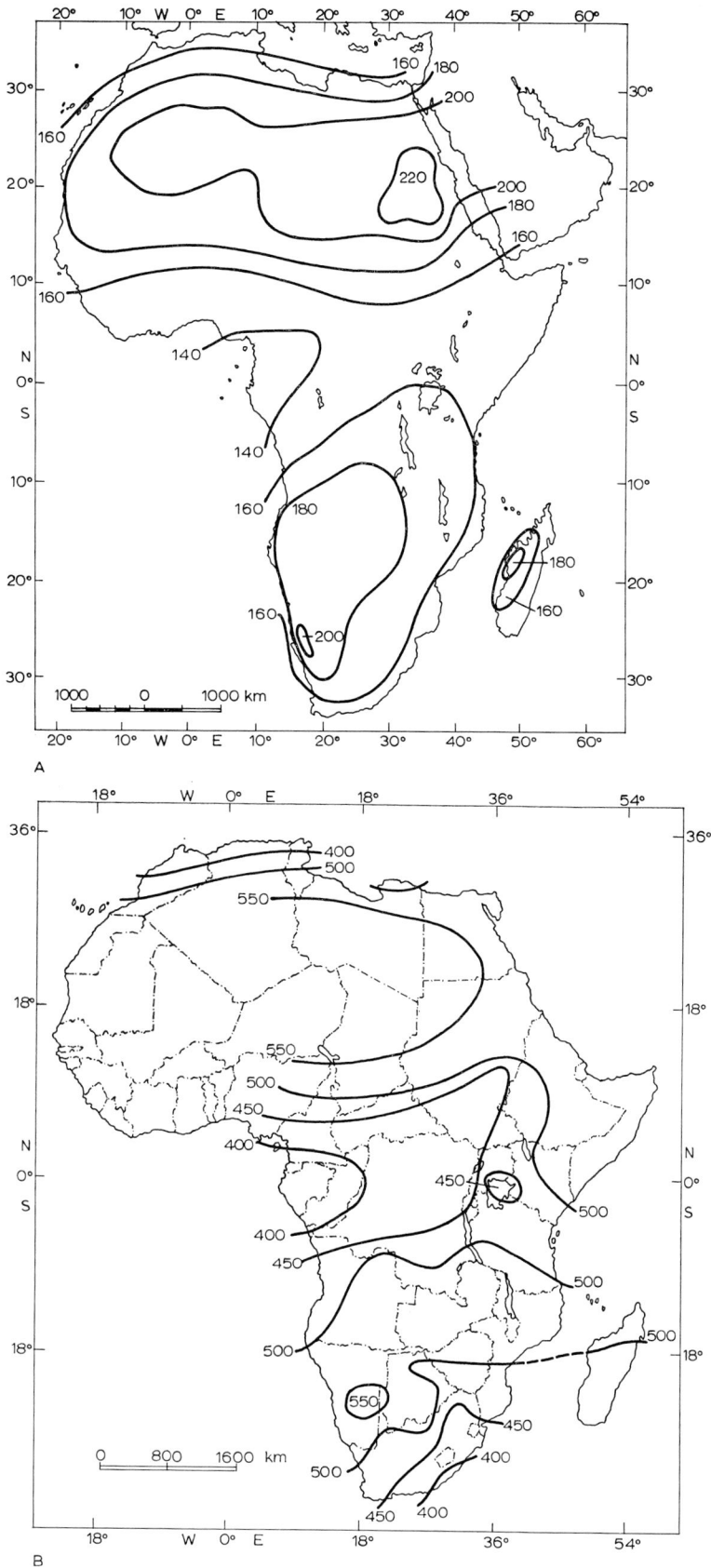

Fig.10. A. Mean annual global radiation (kLy). (After LANDSBERG, et al., 1963.)
B. Annual radiation (Ly/day) (after THOMPSON, 1965).

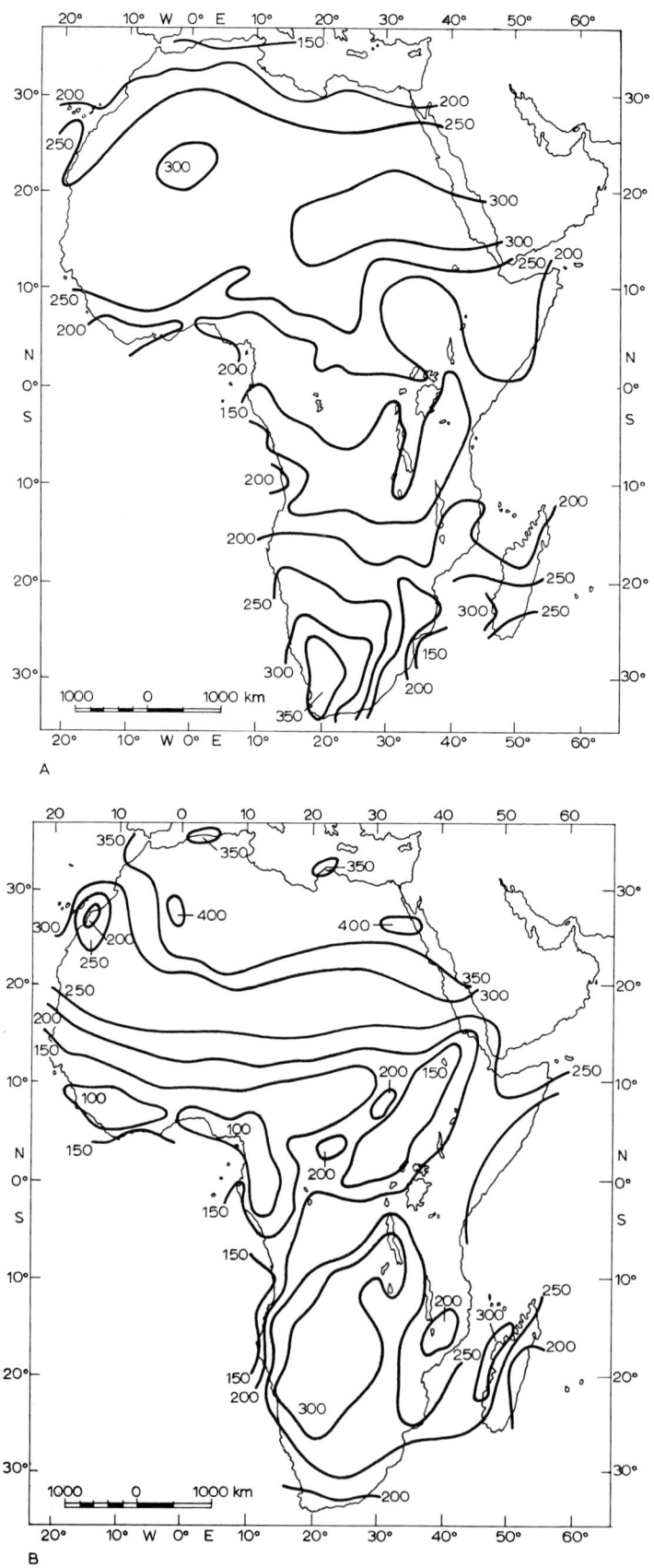

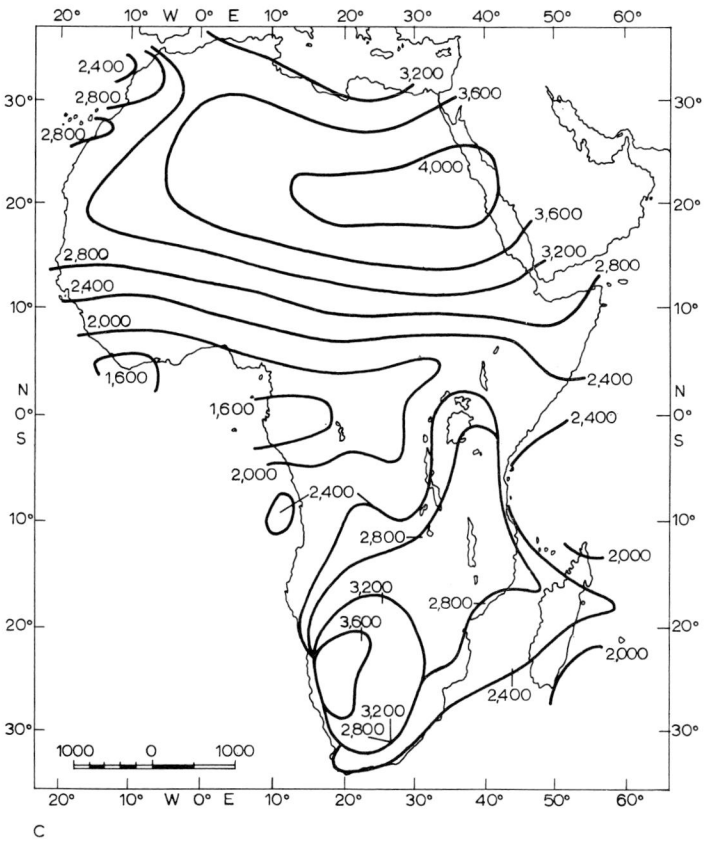

Fig.11. A. Mean monthly sunshine hours for January.
B. Mean monthly sunshine hours for July.
C. Mean annual sunshine hours.

With an atmospheric transmission coefficient of 0.7 this pattern becomes that shown in Fig.9.

It is apparent that, on a yearly total basis, Africa receives a very high radiation load. This load, varying from about 320 kLy to 260 kLy at the extreme poleward edges, compares with 200 kLy at 55°N.

The *World Maps of Climatology* (LANDSBERG et al., 1963) have presented a mean annual pattern for Africa, given in Fig.10A, which does not accord too well with THOMPSON (1965; Fig.10B). Discrepancies are bound to occur due to the dearth of stations. In order to improve the construction of such maps the authors have had to use empirical relationships between sunshine and radiation, often rather inaccurate. The high radiation in areas of mainly subsiding, dry air is clearly shown in Fig.10, especially in southwest Africa and the western Mediterranean.

Many more sunshine measuring stations are available than for radiation. However, a problem arises due to the use of different instruments with different sensitivity and methods of chart analysis. In spite of this, reasonably accurate maps can be produced and Fig.11 shows the values for January, July and the year (LANDSBERG et al., 1963). The January pattern illustrates the effect of the Canaries current in increasing the cloud amount as well as the cloud hanging over the sudd area of the Sudan. In July a cold upwelling off western Morocco is evident, as is the belt of cloud around the Guinea coast.

In the annual pattern the effect of the cold Benguela and Canaries currents are obvious. The sunshine data have been utilized to obtain estimates of radiation values. It is logical to look for a high correlation between these two elements and work by GLOVER and McCULLOCH (1958) has substantiated this hypothesis. They obtained the equation:

$$Q/Q_0 = 0.29 \cos \varphi + 0.52 \, n/N$$

where Q = global radiation on a horizontal surface; Q_0 = global radiation on a horizontal surface with no atmosphere; φ = station latitude; n/N = percentage of possible sunshine measured.

This equation yielded a correlation coefficient of 0.86, that is, 75% of the variance is explained.

Recently a paper by DAVIES (1967) has suggested an empirical relationship between net and solar radiation, of the form:

$$R_N = 0.617Q - 24 \quad (R_N \text{ is net radiation}; \ R_N \text{ and } Q \text{ in Ly/day})$$

This has a very high correlation coefficient ($r = 0.99$) but, naturally, only applies to daytime net radiation. For West African stations the equation was:

$$R_N = 0.612Q - 28 \qquad (r = 0.93)$$

Temperature

Temperature is intimately connected to radiation and elevation so that in Africa, with its relatively small annual variation in radiation, there is likely to be only a small annual range of temperature. This fact is well illustrated in Fig.12A where it is seen that about one-third of the continent experiences an annual range of less than 6°C. The small area wherein the range is below 3°C does not extend fully across the continent, terminating in the highlands of Kenya. This area of larger annual range is unusual in equatorial regions and is mainly due to the pronounced annual variation in cloud cover and precipitation, characteristics that do not apply in the western section. In this eastern portion Mombasa exhibits the smallest annual range, 3.5°C.

In contrast, the continent has large areas in which the diurnal range is great, often exceeding 15°C with a maximum of 19°C in southwest Libya (Fig.12B). In fact, most of the continent has a diurnal range far in excess of the annual range, giving credence to the statement that "night is the winter of the tropics". The large diurnal fluctuation leads to a daily freeze-thaw cycle in some of the highland areas, and vegetation and soils show a distinct relationship with this phenomenon. The broad parallelism of the isotherms and the coastline is expected as it is an illustration of climatic continentality.

To depict the practically important range of temperature over the continent two maps are necessary, one of the highest mean monthly maximum temperature (H) and another of the lowest mean monthly minimum (L) (Fig.13). High values of H (greater than 32°C) are found over much of the continent with about 30% experiencing values in excess of 38°C and a maximum of 47°C in southwest Algeria. The increase of H with distance from the sea (continentality effect) is very marked, the only outstanding deviations being in the plateau and highland areas of the east and in the northwest where the Atlas Mountains of Morocco shield effectively a small area from marine or oceanic influences.

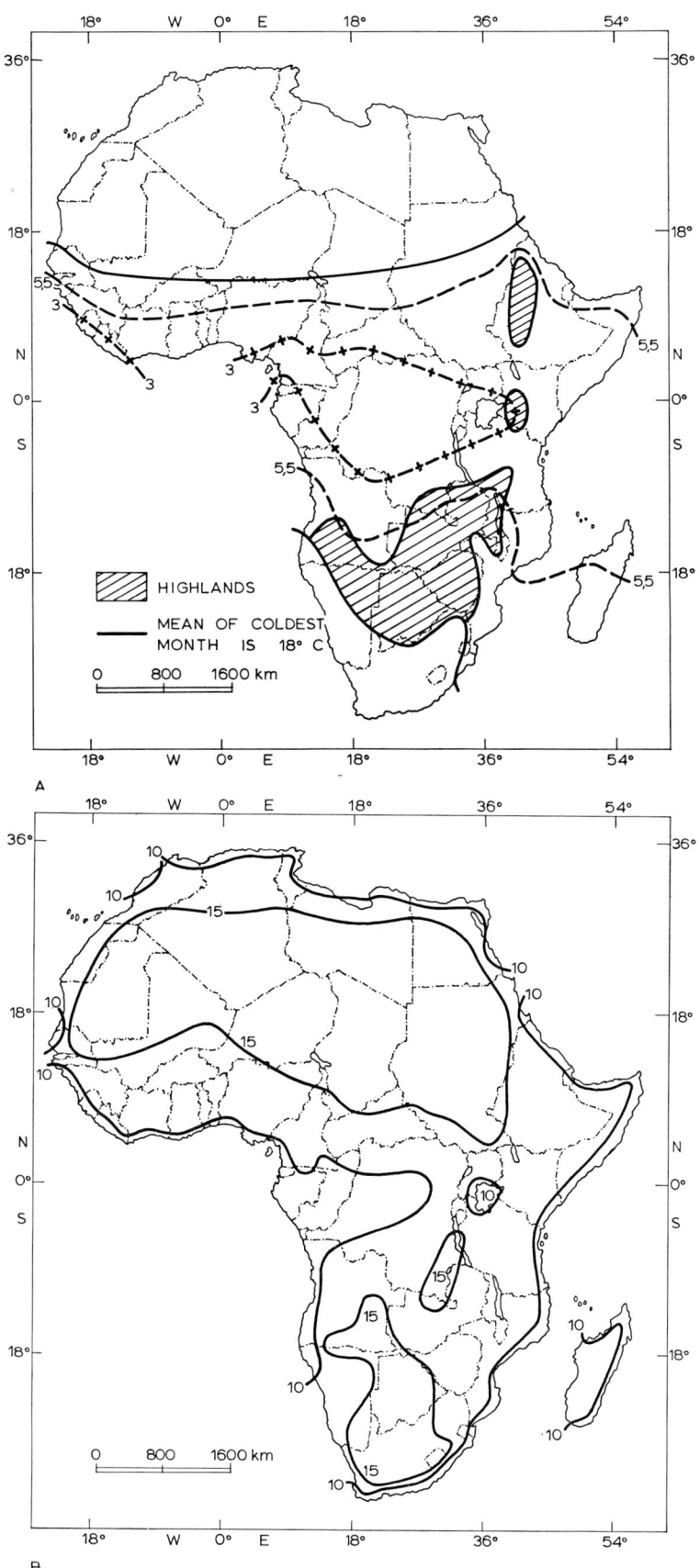

Fig.12. A. Annual temperature range (°C).
B. Mean annual diurnal temperature variation (°C).

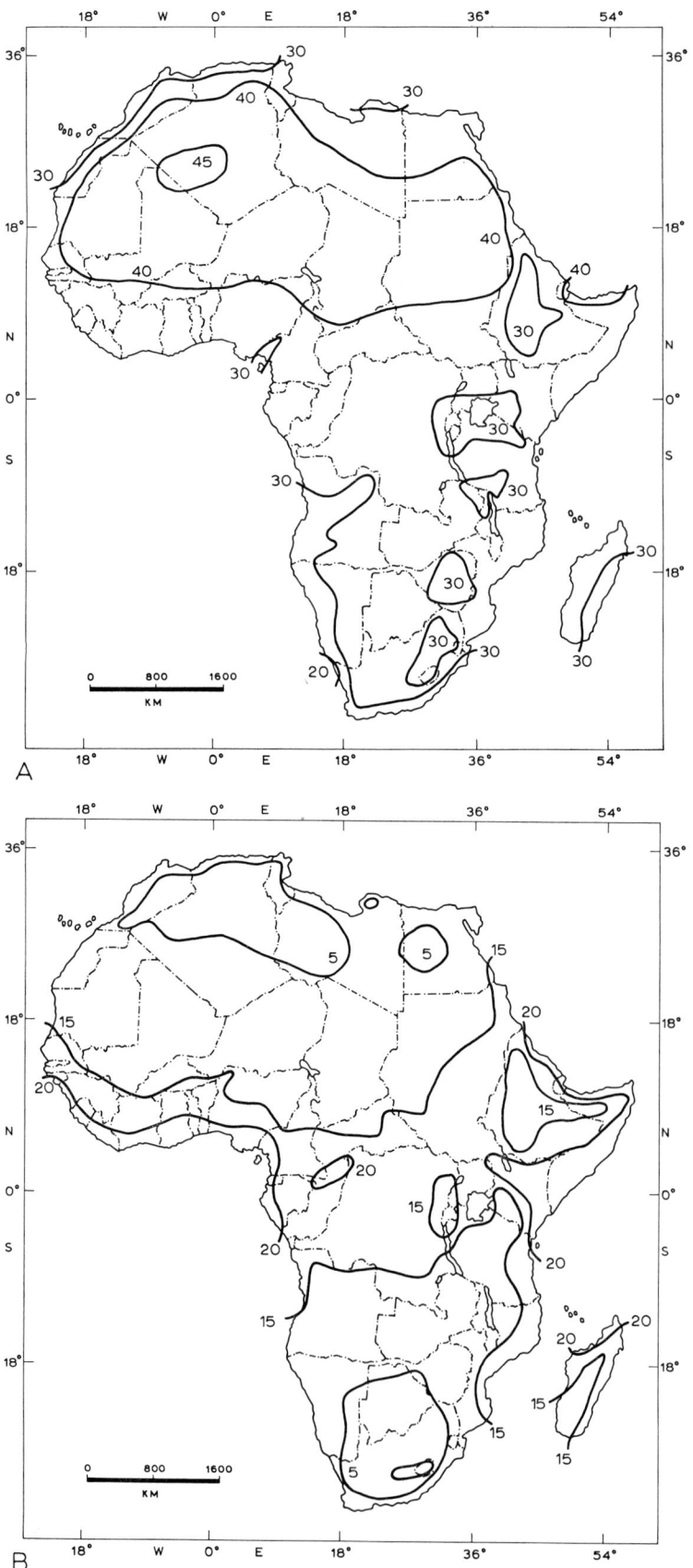

Fig.13. A. Highest monthly maximum temperature (*H*, in °C).
B. Lowest mean monthly minimum temperature (*L*, in °C).

The values of L show more the effect of latitude and elevation than of continentality. Very small areas have L values below 5°C and only in Algeria, Morocco and the Republic of South Africa, at elevations above about 1,000–1,500 m, will L fall below 0°C. Dallol, Ethiopia, has an L value of 26°C. In Fig.14 the range $H–L$ is depicted; this is a measure of combined annual and diurnal range. Because of this fact the isopleths show a relationship with both continentality and latitude. The maximum value is reached at Adrar (western Algeria) with 42°C while along the coast of Sierra Leone and Liberia the range is only 8°C.

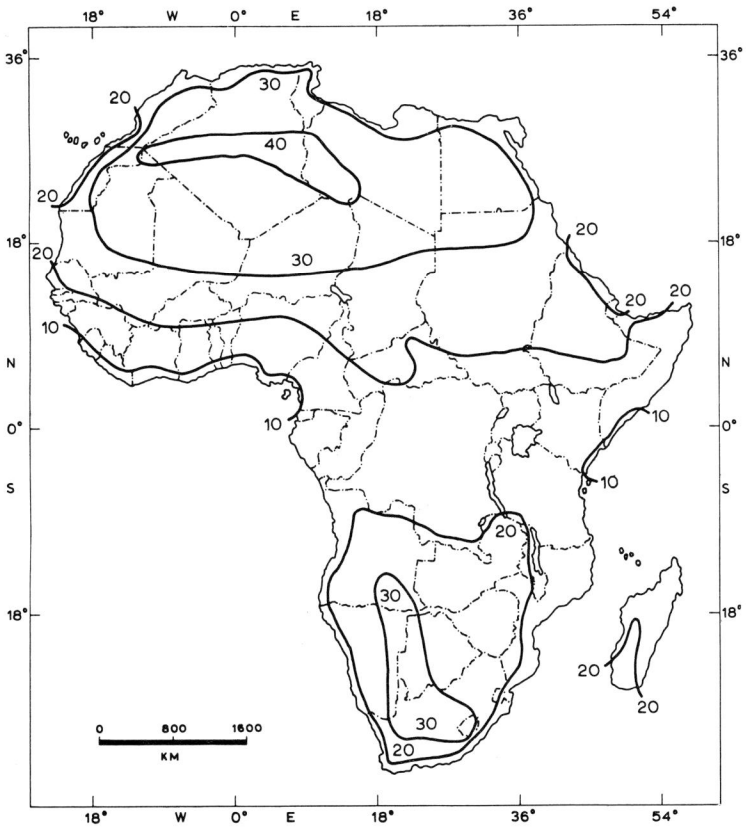

Fig.14. The range $H–L$. For explanation see text.

Mean monthly temperatures exhibit one rather unusual characteristic in that the lowest temperature is recorded in July or August over a region extending from Cape Town to as far as 12°N, in extreme West Africa. This is due to the fact that the area with a "low sun" (small radiation potential) minimum is contiguous with the area of low radiation due to heavy cloud and moist air.

In northern Africa the boundary of a winter (December–February) minimum of mean monthly temperature extends down to about 12°N and even as far as 6°N in the Somali Republic (Fig.15). The cool outbreaks from the north plus the clearer air and radiational cooling lead to the mean monthly minima being recorded during this period almost as far as the West African coast and even into the Congo Republic.

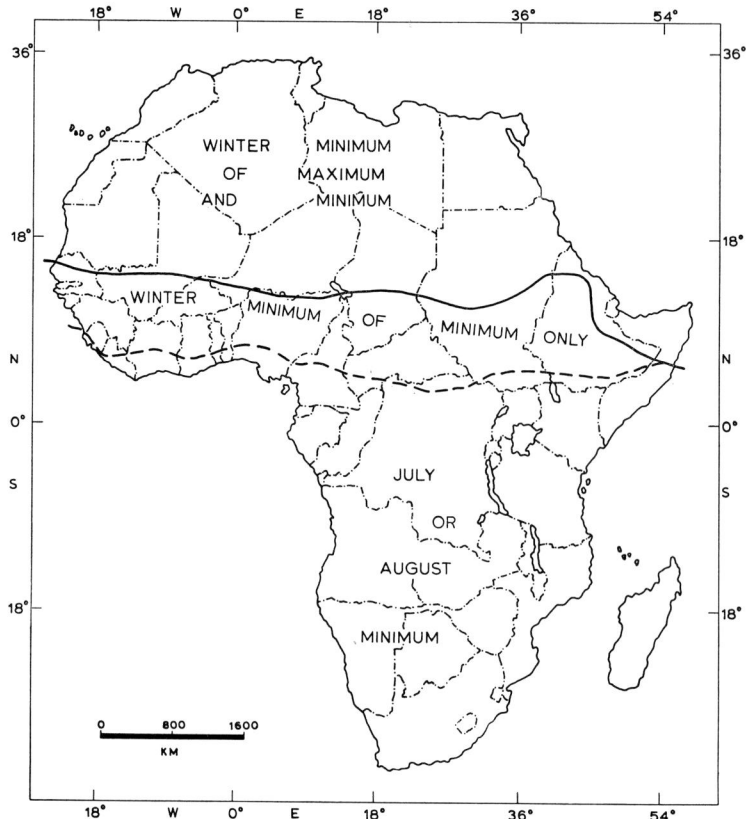

Fig.15. Month of minimum temperature.

Precipitation

From the viewpoint of vegetation most of Africa has sufficient warmth for good growth at all seasons. The climatic element that is essential is rain. Man and his wellbeing are truly at the whim of the rain in vast areas of Africa and only great irrigation and water control schemes can help overcome this dependence on the elements. For many regions such an outlook is generations away from fulfillment.

The major causes of rain in Africa are detailed later in relevant chapters but the dominant causes are the temperate zone type depressions (especially for the Mediterranean regions both north and south) and the convergence of the trade winds. The overall picture is clearly understood and appreciated but the subtle complexities due to ocean currents, topography, inland large lakes and upper air conditions are only now beginning to be studied in depth, let alone explained and detailed. Nevertheless, both the depressions and the convergence area (I.T.C.Z.) follow broad seasonal movements so that a basic pattern can evolve. The difficulty arises in the vast variations in rainfall that can occur at one station through the years. There is hardly a better example of this than Makindu, Kenya, which has experienced totals ranging from 67 mm to 1,964 mm.

A set of "rainfall rules" to apply in Africa have been suggested by some cynic, perhaps a tropical meteorologist but certainly a person with experience in the tropics. These rules are: (*a*) the rainfall is seasonal in nature; (*b*) the amount increases as one approaches the equator; (*c*) do not put too much faith in (*a*) and (*b*).

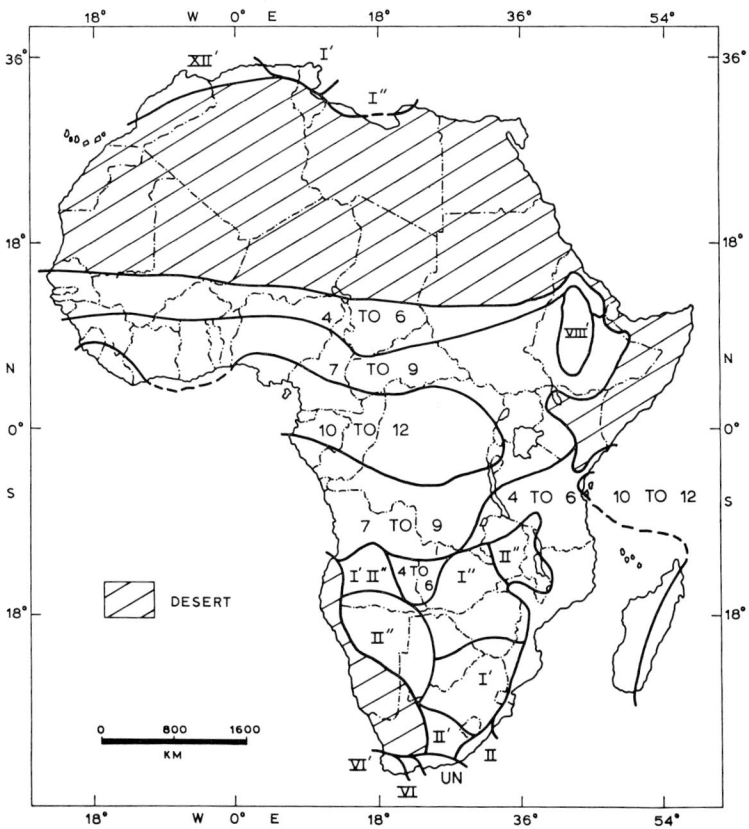

Fig.16. Rainfall distribution. Arabic numerals refer to number of months receiving at least 50 mm of rain. Roman numerals denote central month of wettest quarter. ' indicates 40–60% annual total received in wettest quarter; " indicates over 60%.

It is necessary to appreciate more concerning the rainfall than just the yearly total; some idea of the seasonal distribution is essential. The presentation of such information is complicated by the fact that whereas in tropical latitudes, with little annual variation in the temperature, the time of year at which the rain falls is relatively unimportant, this is not so in the temperate or subtropical zones. Hence, in the tropical zones (every month with mean temperature above 18°C) it suffices to record the number of wet months while in other areas the season must be indicated. With these criteria in mind Fig.16 has been derived. The choice of a 50-mm threshold is based on vegetation considerations but if another threshold were chosen the zones would show mainly a change in the Arabic numerals and not in the boundary positions. The very real and practical concentration of rainfall in short periods is indicated in the 4–6 zones and the I', I'', II', II'', VI', XII' areas. This concentration causes great stress to be placed on these short seasons and failure of the rain inevitably leads to crop failure and extreme hardship since a whole year must elapse before rain can be expected again in sufficient quantities. This important fact is better illustrated in Fig.17, where it is shown that more than two-thirds of Africa experiences over half its annual rainfall in a period of 3 months.

As mentioned earlier, Africa is an area of very definite rainfall seasons. Nevertheless, there is some degree of uniformity with regard to the time of these seasons, for two periods of maximum fall predominate, namely June–August and December–February. These

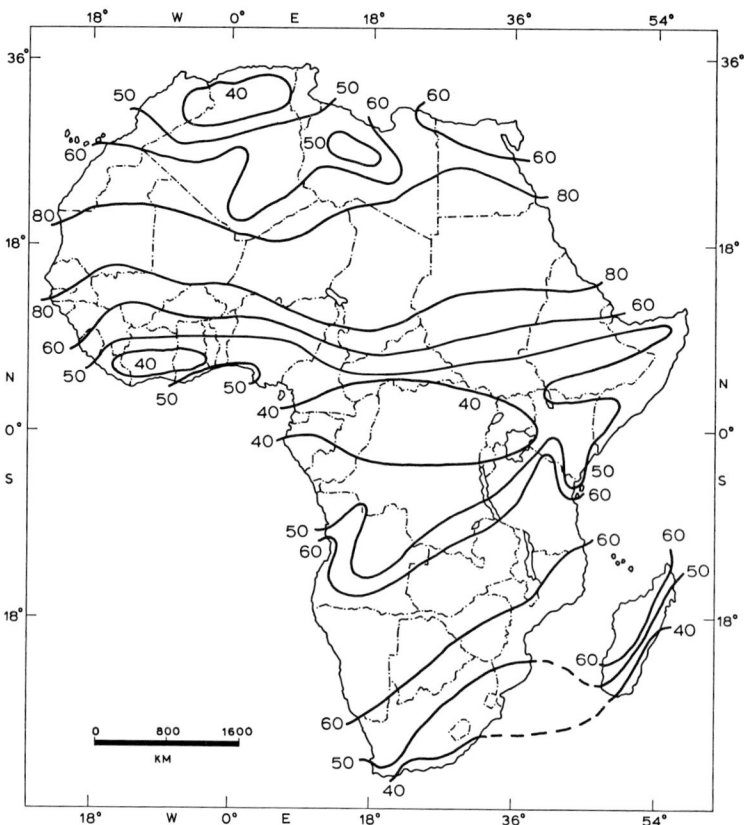

Fig.17. Percentage rainfall in wettest quarter.

correspond to the times of maximum rainfall activity associated with the I.T.C.Z. and the distribution is illustrated in Fig.18, showing the rainfall concentration during these seasons. From Fig.18 the very clear division of the continent into seven areas is made obvious. In the extreme north and south at least 30% of the annual total falls in December–February, this is the zone of Mediterranean type climate; next, a band of desert area (Sahara in the north and Namib in the south) with very little precipitation appears, then, centered on about 18°N and 18°S are regions of "high sun" rainfall; finally, along the equator is the belt of either dual peaked or of uniform rainfall. Two small exceptions to this simplified pattern occur, one along the Red Sea with a "low sun" maximum and the other along the coastal strip of equatorial East Africa with the June to August maximum induced by effects from the Asiatic monsoonal flow patterns.

Allied with this concentration pattern is the nature of the rainfall distribution during the year. Most stations show only one maximum and one minimum in the "amount vs. month" diagram, these are the areas marked "single" in Fig.19. But, in a wide band across the continent, double maxima and minima occur. However, only in two areas are these peaks significant. Expressed mathematically these are where:

annual mean < 20 (secondary maximum − secondary minimum)

A unique area exists in the Horn of Africa where the annual mean is less than ten times the above difference but much of the area is semi-arid. The double peak pattern is,

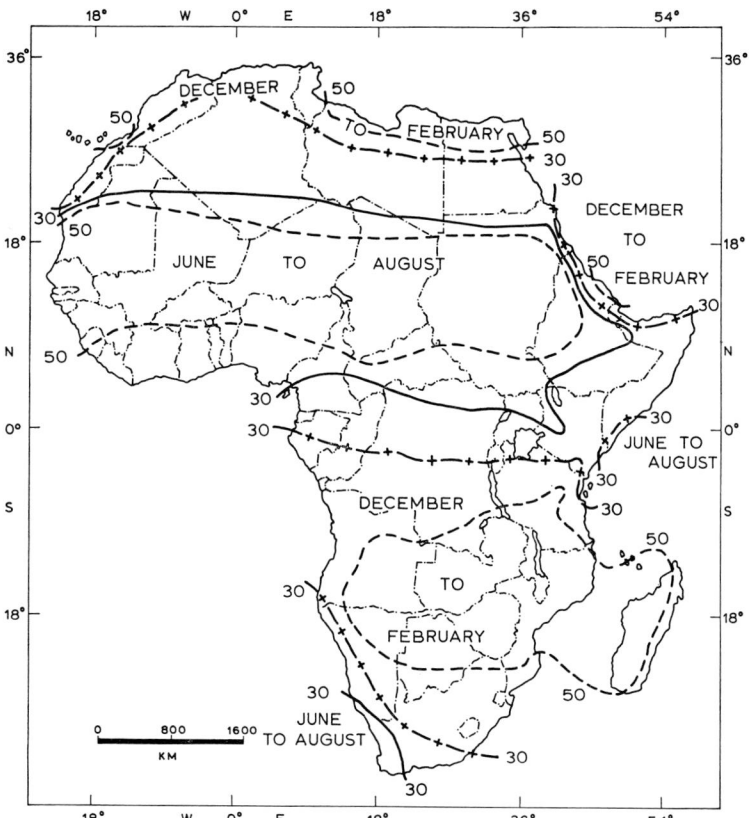

Fig.18. Period and amount (%) of rainfall concentration.

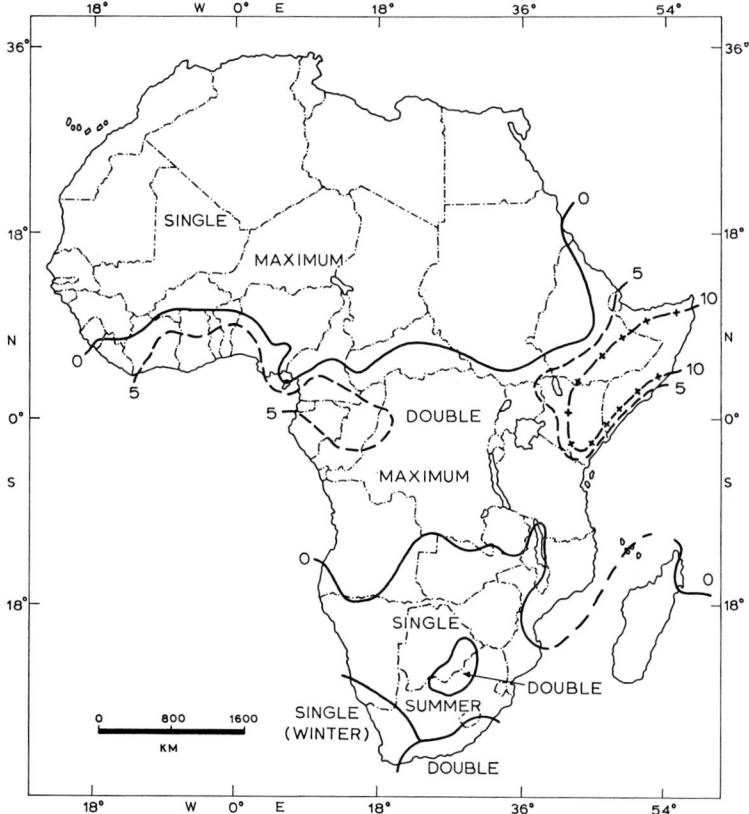

Fig.19. Nature of annual rainfall distribution. Values of $\dfrac{\text{secondary max.} - \text{secondary min.}}{\text{annual total}}$ given as a percentage.

generally, broadly associated with the annual movements of the I.T.C.Z. but in South Africa it is the interplay between the winter depressions and the summer convective rains that gives a coastal strip of double maxima.

Hail

In general, hail is not a common phenomenon in Africa. The report of FRISBY and SANSOM (1966) shows that little of the continent experiences more than five incidences per year. The distribution of annual hail frequency is shown in Fig.20. In contrast, however, the area around Kericho, astride the equator in western Kenya, reports as many as 80 hail storms per year, a frequency that may not be exceeded anywhere in the world, save perhaps in a region of the Peruvian mountain chain.

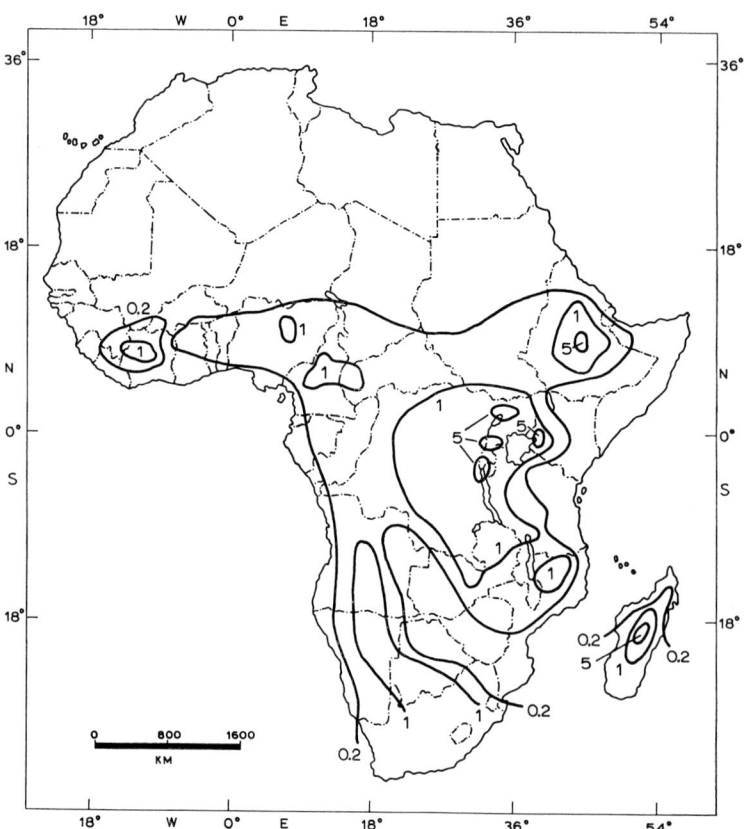

Fig.20. Mean annual frequency of hail over Africa (10-year record).

Hail is very unusual on the coast of tropical Africa although there is regular incidence in Malagasy (Madagascar) and Mozambique, especially along the Mozambique Channel. Stations situated on high land naturally report more hail than lowland stations. For instance, Jos, Nigeria, has an average of three falls per year compared with about one fall every 2 years as an average for the country. An interesting occurrence was in Senegal, a country with no reports for 30 years, when St. Louis experienced a 4-min hailstorm with stones of 10 mm in diameter.

Q C 983 B78 hear

Thunderstorms

The distribution of thunderstorm days per year is given in Fig.21. This diagram and the following statistics are taken from a publication of the WORLD METEOROLOGICAL ORGANIZATION (1953).

About 20% of the continent experiences more than a 100 thunderstorm days each year while the smallest frequency, less than five, is reported from northwestern Cape Province, South Africa, and Cape Guardafui, Somali Republic.

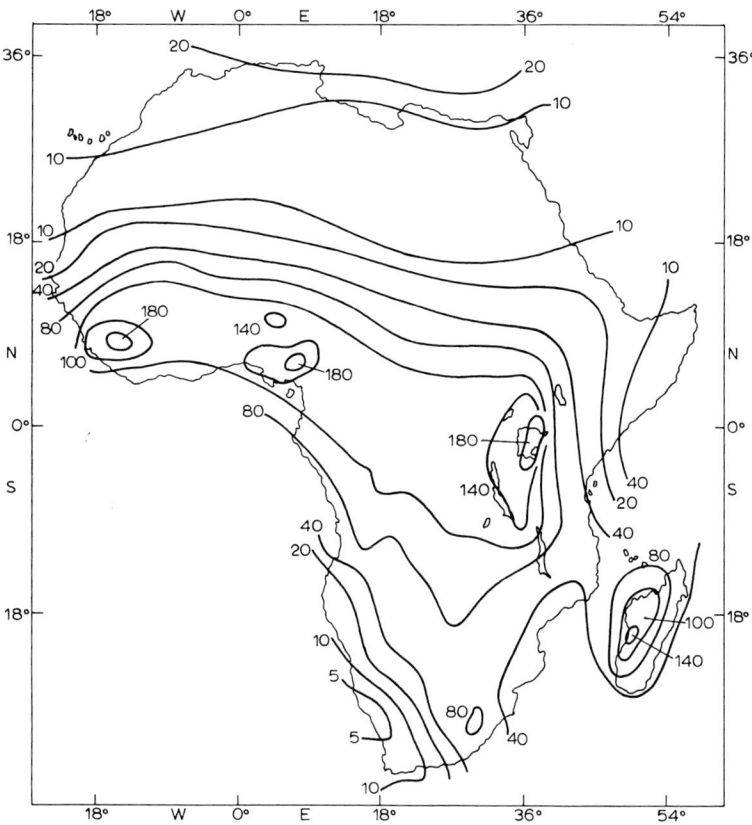

Fig.21. Mean annual frequency of thunderstorms.

Areas of very marked convective instability can have values in excess of 200, for instance, Kampala (Uganda) 242, Costermansville (Congo Republic) 221, Calabar (Nigeria) 216 and Entebbe (Uganda) 206. The importance of large bodies of warm water as sources for the thunderstorm activity is clearly evident while in Costermansville (Bukavu) the local relief accentuates the effect.

Atmospheric humidity

Over most of the continent the only element of atmospheric moisture for which climatological normals exist is relative humidity. Unfortunately, for other than first order stations, this measurement is only made once or twice a day, in the early morning and

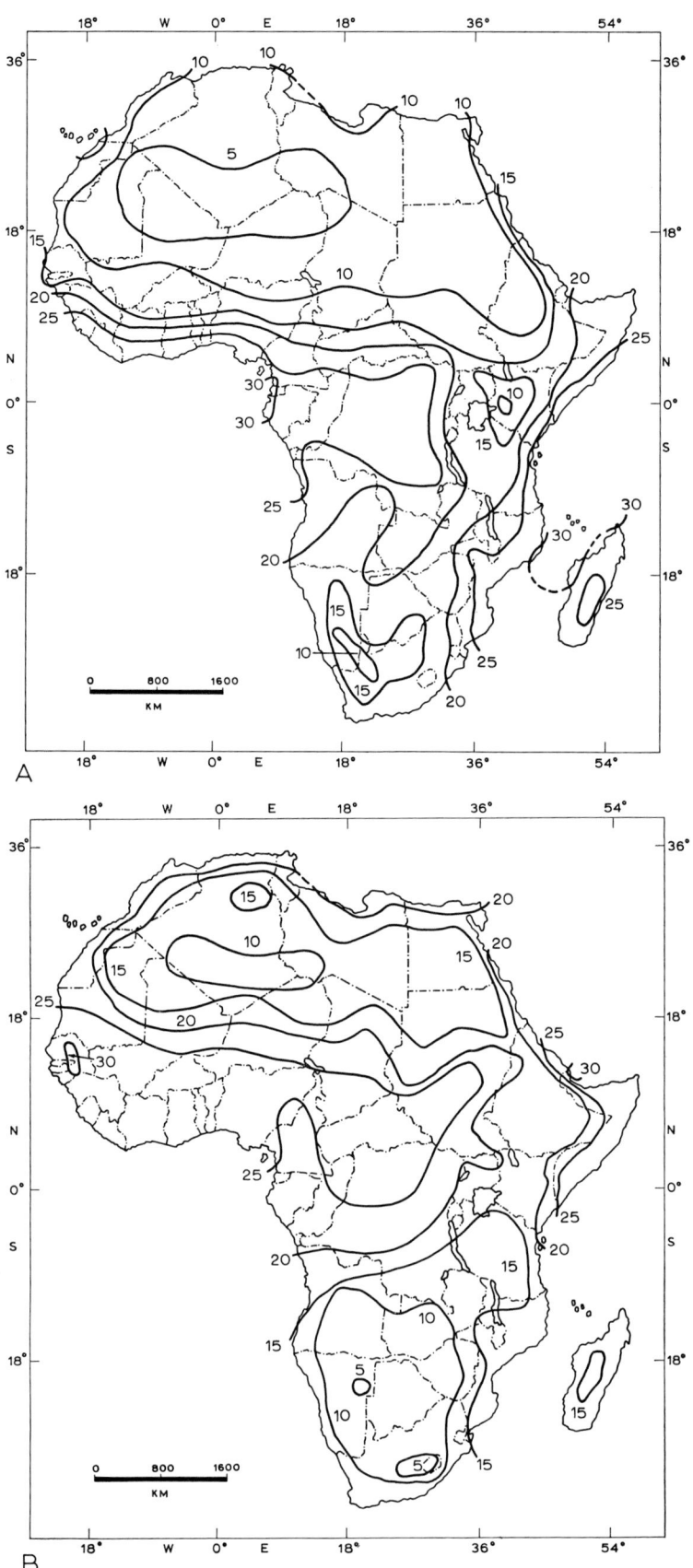

Fig.22.A. Mean water vapour pressure (mbar) for January.
B. Mean water vapour pressure (mbar) for July.

mid-afternoon. The times are not uniform across the continent and the early morning observation is taken at a time when the relative humidity is changing rapidly. As is well known, relative humidity at a specific station has a very close inverse correlation with air temperature and a corresponding temperature is needed for each relative humidity record if the state of the atmosphere is to be specified completely. For the afternoon reading the maximum temperature can usually be applied with sufficient accuracy but the morning value has no readily available simultaneous temperature. For this reason it is highly desirable to consider some other parameters of atmospheric humidity such as the dew point or the absolute humidity. These two parameters do not show the large diurnal fluctuation typical of the relative humidity curve while there are few of the temperate type of frontal passages to induce rapid changes. This means that, in most places, the daily dew point temperature stays constant to within a couple of degrees.

In Fig.22, taken from a paper by LANDSBERG (1964), the mean absolute humidity is given for January and July. It is seen how the pattern moves with the solar declination, reflecting the movement of the rainfall areas associated with the I.T.C.Z. The illustrations also bring to mind the reasonably high values of absolute humidity, for even in the Sahara and Namib deserts they are on a par with those for Oregon and Scotland.

Human comfort

Africa is generally pictured as a continent in which an unpleasant combination of the climatic elements, as judged from the human viewpoint, is often experienced. Any index of a physio-climatic nature should take cognizance of the four elements of temperature, radiation, wind speed and humidity, plus a realisation of the role played by age, clothing, health, work load and other conditions. However, no such comprehensive index exists at present but an initial investigation has been undertaken by TERJUNG (1967) to map four selected indices for the whole of Africa in January and July. The indices chosen are the effective temperature, the predicted 4-h sweat rate, the relative strain and the still-air temperature. The author's general findings are that "the Northern Hemisphere summer is by far the most severe, physiologically, over vast areas of northern Africa. Regions of greatest stress are located along the southern Red Sea, interior southern Somalia and, to a lesser degree, the Djouf Basin and Bodele Depression. The year-round mildest areas occur most frequently in parts of the eastern highlands and Atlantic coast (those influenced by cold currents). Few really oppressive conditions during nighttime could be observed."

Recent information

Interest in Africa is growing at a rapid rate, the newly independent countries as well as the older established ones are fully aware of the fundamental role of agriculture in their economy, a realization that brings with it the acceptance of climate as one of the nation's resources. It is hoped that this book will assist readers in obtaining an understanding of the climates existing in each region and that the references will be sufficient to allow one seeking more data to embark on his own studies.

Information is constantly accruing and, even in the time since this volume was completed, a number of new and important papers have come to my notice. It is necessary to refer to a few of these because of their special relevance and comprehensiveness.

A Russian publication (LEBEDEV, 1968) on the climate of Africa has recently been translated and part I consists of data for 749 temperature and 1,564 rainfall stations. The temperature information consists of mean monthly mean, maximum and minimum values, absolute maxima and minima, mean diurnal range and mean degree-days above 10°, 15°, 20° and 25°C. The rainfall data are of mean monthly amounts, number of days with over 0.1, 1.0, 10 and 50 mm end the 24-h maximum total. Standard deviations and confidence limits are also given for the rainfall values. The importance of rainfall and its variation to the continent of Africa is further accentuated by a work on desert areas (HOWE et al., 1968), where the authors use a new classification system to show that Africa has 26% of its land area extremely arid (10–12 months with less than 1 day of rain—rain day > 0.25 mm rain); 15% is arid (10–12 months with less than or equal to 3 rain days); 29% is semi-arid (6–9 months with less than or equal to 3 rain days); 2% as demi-arid (4–5 months with less than or equal to 3 rain days and 10–12 months with less than or equal to 6 rain days). Thus, little more than a quarter of Africa is not classified arid.

Although Africa has much arid area it also has large regions of high temperature and humidity. The problem of sultriness has been studied by TROLL (1969). The author relates his criterion of "sultriness" to four stations and discusses their hourly variation patterns. The data used are mostly old and of short period. Studies of atmospheric circulation have not been neglected recently (STRUNING and FLOHN, 1969). Their investigations show that over East and Central Africa there is a seasonal displacement of the low-level equatorial westerlies and the high tropospheric easterlies while the belt of easterlies and low-level westerlies persist throughout the year in the 0°–8°N belt. These findings have been illustrated by the work of FINDLATER (1968), in his paper on the month to month variation of low-level winds, and also by NAKAMURA (1968) who suggests that equatorial westerly waves exist and that, in East Africa, all regional differences of wheather are related to the westerlies.

Another first-class study in agroclimatology (BROWN and COCHEME, 1969) has been published by the F.A.O./UNESCO/W.M.O. agencies. This report is directed towards the highland of East Africa and Ethiopia and deals with the causes of the climate and studies the climatic requirements of barley, coffee, maize, pyrethrum, tea, tef (*Eragrostis tef*—a cereal) and wheat. The problems of rainfall and water budgets are discussed at some length. Still in East Africa a recent article by RODWELL (1969) suggests that in April, 1872, a "hurricane" was experienced in Zanzibar (7°S). The storm was of devastating proportions and brought with it very heavy and intense rainfall. It is a pity that the meteorological records are not available to substantiate this "equatorial" hurricane's existence.

Finally, the danger of statistical deductions was unfortunately illustrated in Tunisia recently. Reports indicate that on 24–25th September, 1969, up to six times the average rainfall for September total were recorded with heavy flooding resulting. In Algeria and Libya also extremes were noted, with 3-day totals yielding 18–20 times the monthly mean. A recent paper by WINSTANLEY (1970) shows that the most intense falls over a large area were associated with a cyclonic storm that developed southeast of Malta and moved westwards. The phosphate mines at Gafsa were flooded and Roman bridges were destroyed. Winstanley quotes rainfall figures for Biskra, 299 mm in September (210 mm on 27 and 28), compared with a mean of 17 mm and an annual 150 mm. The heavy rains caused loss of life, destruction of homes, damage to roads, wells and cultivated land. In Algeria alone nearly half a million date-palms were lost.

The aim of the presentation in this volume has been to specialize in giving details of and explaining the climate of Africa; no attempt has been made to apply the data to specific, real and pressing, problems. It is hoped, nevertheless, that such applications will be facilitated by this book for the fact that problems with a meteorological facet exist in Africa has been made very clear by a W.M.O. publication recently (1969). As is pointed out in the report "the purpose of the seminar was to highlight the ways in which meteorology can contribute to economic development in Africa". In addition, the seminar recommendations included the following statement: "that natural resources including human resources, plant and animal resources, agriculture, animal husbandry and hydro-electric resources are closely related to meteorological processes. It was stressed that, as climate is one of the basic causes of other natural resources, it must be taken into account in the rational exploitation of these other resources. In particular, the intensive exploitation of the climate by agriculture would open the way to substantial socio-economic growth in Africa.

It was unanimously agreed that economic development in African countries depends on the proper use of their natural resources with the help of modern science and technology. Furthermore, it was realized that all human activities are dependent on weather and climate. As the population in Africa will at least double in the next 30 years, the seminar stressed the need for accelerating the exploitation of natural resources on the basis of sound scientific knowledge, especially in the field of meteorology."

The most rewarding work of a scientist is when the practical results benefit mankind. It is to be hoped that the meteorologists will heed the words of R. K. A. Gardiner, Executive Secretary of the Economic Commission for Africa,

"Now that there is a growing understanding of the weather and climatic resources of Africa, the time has arrived for planners and meteorologists to come together and examine carefully the ways in which these resources can best be used to advance economic and social development. I hope that the seminar will be able to explain in clear terms, understandable to planners, the contributions the science of meteorology can make to Africa's further economic development."

Acknowledgements

It is obvious that, in the compilation and preparation of a work such as this, a number of persons have provided assistance and it is a pleasure to acknowledge their help.

Specifically I wish to thank the following for supplying data used in the text: G. Allorent (Senegal), P. Antignac (Chad), M. Ayadi (Tunisia), B. Azmy (Morocco), S. R. Barrani (Libya), Pierre Baudry (Ivory Coast), J. O. Belford (Sierra Leone), A. Bessemoulin (France), Abdou Boukary (Niger), M. Clerebaut (Congo-Kinshasa), P. Cohade (Togo), I. O. Emore (Nigeria), W. Mandengue Epoy (Cameroon), H. Amorim Ferreira (Portugal), A. Gaddar (Libya), A. Kabre (Upper Volta), Nama Keita (Mali), E. F. Lawes (Kenya), T. Limaiem (Tunisia), L. Loemba-Maidou (C. African Republic), I. Madani (Morocco), G. Mankedi (Congo-Brazzaville), K. Mostefa-Kara (Algeria), G. Mustafa (Sudan), J. M. Pruvost (France), D. A. Rijks (Kenya), Lorna Rogerson (Kenya), A. Sene (Mauretania), F. Suranol (France), A. Tchibozo (Dahomey), Emile Thievet (Gabon), B. W. Thompson (Kenya), Jessie E. Tomsett (Kenya), I. Toure (Guinea), Mohamed Traore (Mali), Godana Tuni (Ethiopia).

My particular thanks are due to Mike Welsh and Jack Grant for their drafting help, to Dorothy Mallett and Carolyn Hugo for secretarial assistance, to my father, John H. Griffiths, for indexing aid, and to my wife Joan for her patience and understanding while "living with a book" once again.

References

BROWN, L. H. and COCHEME, J., 1969. *A study of the Agroclimatology of the Highlands of Eastern Africa—FAO/UNESCO/WMO Interagency Project, Tech. Rept. FAO, Rome*, 330 pp.

DAVIES, J. A., 1967. A note of the relationship between net radiation and solar radiation. *Quart. J. Roy. Meteorol. Soc.*, 93:109–110.

FINDLATER, J., 1968. The month to month variation of mean winds at low level over Eastern Africa. *E. African Meteorol. Dept., Tech. Mem.*, 12:29 pp.

FRISBY, E. M. and SANSOM, H. W., 1966. *Hail Incidence in the Tropics*. U.S. Army Electronics Command, Ecom. 02105-F, 45 pp.

GLOVER, J. and McCULLOUGH, J. S. G., 1958. The empirical relationship between solar radiation and hours of sunshine. *Quart. J. Roy. Meteorol. Soc.*, 84:172–175.

GRIFFITHS, J. F., 1966. *Applied Climatology, An Introduction*. Oxford University Press, London, 118 pp.

HOWE, G. M., REED, L. J., BALL, J. T., FISHER, G. E. and LASSOW, G. B., 1968. Classification of world desert areas. *U.S. Army, Natick Lab., Tech. Rept.*, 69-38-ES, 104 pp.

JARRETT, R. H., 1966. *Africa*. MacDonald and Evans, London, 510 pp.

JOHNSON, D. H., 1962. Rainfall in East Africa. *Quart. J. Roy. Meteorol. Soc.*, 88:1–19.

JOHNSON, D. H. and MÖRTH, H. T., 1960. Forecasting research in East Africa. In: D. J. BARGMAN (Editor), *Tropical Meteorology in Africa*. Munitalp Foundation, Nairobi, pp.56–137.

LANDSBERG, H. E., 1964. Die mittlere Wasserdampfverteilung auf der Erde. *Meteorol. Rundschau*, 17(4):102–103.

LANDSBERG, H. E., LIPPMANN, H., PAFFEN, K. H. and TROLL, C., 1963. *World Maps of Climatology*. Springer, Berlin, 5 maps, 28 pp.

LEBEDEV, A.V. (Ed.), 1970. *The Climate of Africa, I. Air Temperature, Precipitation*. Israel Program for Scientific Translations, Jerusalem, 482 pp.

NAKAMURA, K., 1968. Equatorial westerlies over East Africa and their climatological significance. *Geograph. Rept. Tokyo Metropolitan Univ.*, 3:43–46.

OLIVER, R. and FAGE, J. D., 1965. *A Short History of Africa*. Penguin Books, Harmondsworth, 284 pp.

RODWELL, E. E., 1969. The day of the great hurricane. *E. African Standard*, December 5, p.8.

SELLERS, W. D., 1965. *Physical Climatology*. Univ. of Chicago Press, Chicago, Ill., 272 pp.

STRUNING, J. O. and FLOHN, H., 1969. Investigations on the atmospheric circulation above Africa. *Bonner Meteorol. Abhandl.*, 10:55 pp.

TERJUNG, W. H., 1967. The geographical application of some physio-climatic indices to Africa. *Intern. J. Biometeorol.*, 11(1):5–19.

THOMPSON, B. W., 1965. *Climate of Africa*. Oxford University Press, London, 132 pp.

TROLL, C., 1969. The spatial and temporal distribution of sultriness and its geophysical representation (with special reference to Africa). In: *Erdkunde*, Vol. XXIII. Bonn, pp.183–192.

WINSTANLEY, D., 1970. The Nort African flood disaster, September 1969. *Weather*, 25:390–403.

WORLD METEOROLOGICAL ORGANIZATION, 1953. World distribution of thunderstorm days. *World Meteorol. Organ., Tech. Publ.*, 21(6); I: 204 pp.; II: 71 pp. + 18 maps.

WORLD METEOROLOGICAL ORGANIZATION and ECONOMIC COMMISSION FOR AFRICA, 1969. *The Role of Meteorological Services in Economic Development in Africa* (Seminar). W.M.O., Geneva, 145 pp.

Other sources

Angola, Boletin Meteorológico para a Agricultura. Servicio Meteorológico de Angola, Lourenço Marques, April, 1967 – December, 1969 (published monthly).

Annales des Services Météorologiques de la France d'Outre Mer, I. Territoires françaises de l'Afrique noire. Sécretariat Général à l'Aviation Civile et Commerciale, Paris, 1951–1959 (published annually).

Anuario Climatologico de Portugal, II. Territorios Ultramarinos. Servicio Meteorologico Nacional, Lisbon, Volume I (1947) – Volume XXI (1967) (published annually).

Climatological Atlas of Africa, S. P. JACKSON. Univ. of Witwatersrand, Johannesburg, 1961, 73 maps.

Climatological Normals for Climat and Climat Ship Stations for the Period 1931–1960. World Meteorological Organization, 1962, Tech. Publ. 52.

Climatologie de la Tunisie, Normales et Statistiques diverses. Ministère des Travaux Publics, Tunis, 1952, 34 pp.

Contributo alla Climatologia dell'Etiopia. A. FANTOLI. Ministero degli Affari Exteri, Roma, 1965, 558 pp.

Contributo alla Climatologia della Somalia. A. FANTOLI. Ministero degli Affari Esteri, Roma, 478 pp.

Solar Radiation and Radiation Balance Data. Glavnaia Geofizicheskaia Observatoria, Leningrad, 1964–1970 (published monthly).

Tables of Temperature, Relative Humidity and Precipitation for the World, IV. Africa. H.M. Stationery Office, London, 1958.

World Weather Records:

until 1920, *Smithsonian Miscellaneous Collections,* Vol. 79. Washington, D.C., 1927.

1921–1930, *Smithsonian Miscellaneous Collections,* Vol. 90. Washington, D.C., 1934.

1931–1940, *Smithsonian Miscellaneous Collections,* Vol. 105. Washington, D.C., 1947.

1941–1950, U.S. Weather Bureau, Washington, D.C., 1959.

1951–1960, Vol. 5. *Africa.* U.S. Dept. of Commerce, ESSA, Washington, D.C., 1967.

Chapter 2

The Mediterranean Zone

J. F. GRIFFITHS

Introduction

Along the northern coast of Africa, in a narrow belt stretching from the Spanish Sahara to the Suez Canal, is an area that experiences the classical Mediterranean type of climate of warm or mild, wet winters and hot, dry summers—perhaps the most desirable of yearly climatic patterns. This area, while showing many local variations, can nevertheless be considered as one climatic zone, a zone that is here delimited by the sea to the northern edge and the 125-mm annual isohyet to the south. Few parts of the zone are more than 300 km from the coast while in Libya and the United Arab Republic the band is only about 30 km wide at its maximum extent. Included in this zone is the Atlas mountain range, with peaks rising above 4,000 m, most of Morocco and Tunisia, northern Algeria and the coastal belts of Libya and the United Arab Republic.

The highland chain forms a very effective barrier. It divides the seaward slopes, which have the benefit of a climatic pattern that is considered very favourable for the development of mankind, from the Sahara, with its relatively extreme temperatures and intense aridity. In the eastern section, from Tunisia to the Suez Canal, no such highland exists and the Saharan influence extends northwards to the coast. Only in a narrow, often fragmented band does the rainfall reach amounts much in excess of 125 mm/year.

In the whole zone, with one minor exception, the maximum rainfall coincides with the period of lowest temperatures. The rainfall excess is therefore of a potential nature, the water generally being stored in the soil for use during the spring. In very few areas is the spectre of aridity absent, especially during the summer months. For the economic development of this zone irrigation is an essential feature.

Four countries have the greater part of their population in this Mediterranean zone, Morocco, Algeria, Tunisia and Libya (Fig.1). The United Arab Republic will be considered separately in the northern desert zone. The parts of the first three countries within this zone are often called the Barbary States or the Djezira el Maghrib (the Western Isle).

The kingdom of Morocco, covering some 450,000 km², comprises the old colonial territories of French and Spanish Morocco and the International Zone of Tangier. The majority of its 12 million people live on the Atlantic coastal plains and the plateaux, where much of the arable land is located. On the edges of the Atlas Mountains oak and conifers grow, the remnants of once vast forests, while the middle Atlas supports the famous cedar forests. The prime vegetation is the evergreen scrub, or maquis, a degraded or replaced forest. Cereals and citrus crops are of prime importance to the agriculture while sheep are grazed in many areas. The economic crops are the citrus fruits, tobacco

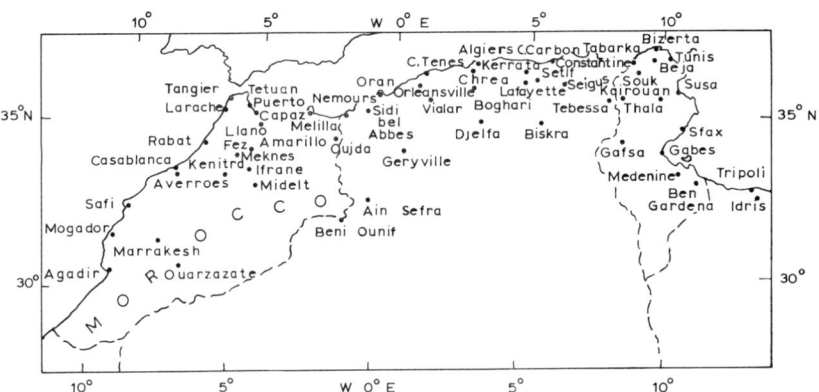

Fig.1. Stations in the western Mediterranean zone.

and grapes. Mining, especially of rock phosphates, coal and iron, brings in a sizeable income.

The northern strip of the Republic of Algeria contains most of the important cities, with the coastal lowlands and the Tell Atlas (Tell from Latin, is fertile earth) being home for three quarters of the 11 million inhabitants. It is mainly an agricultural community with crops such as cereals, grapes, figs, market vegetables, oranges, olives and appreciable sheep grazing. The forested areas contain oaks (cork, holm and zen), Aleppo pine, juniper and cedar. Phosphates are the main mineral commodity in this region.

The Republic of Tunisia covers 125,000 km² and is divided by the High Tell Mountains into northern and southern sections. In the northwest cork oak forests are found, while in the north central area wheat and barley are grown and sheep and goats grazed. Here the principal agricultural activities centre on grains, grapes, citrus and livestock. In the region between Susa and Sfax olives abound, while the oases of the south export tons of dates. Much agriculture is based around the Medjerda, the country's only perennial river, fed by water from the high land that was once heavily forested.

Libya covers 1.75 million km², but only a small area, mainly within this climatic zone, is fertile and here are found about 80% of the 1.25 million inhabitants. The highest land, about 1,200 m, is located in the south central area but the Barce Plateau, reaching 900 m, in Cyrenaica, is the most economically important highland and here some forest remnants are to be found. Otherwise, the vegetation, where it exists, consists mainly of shrubs, scrub and palms. Around Tripoli market gardening is possible but generally citrus, olives and dates are the rule. Livestock are grazed over most of the steppe land. Salt from the interior forms an important export item but in recent years the discovery of oil has rejuvenated the Libyan economy.

Before beginning the climatic description of this zone brief mention must be made of the possibility of climatic change having taken place within historic times, fluctuations of longer periodicity are beyond the scope of this presentation. During the past 50 years many publications have purported to produce evidence confirming the fact that over the past 2,000 years the rainfall has declined sufficiently to make the type and degree of agriculture practised in the Roman occupation no longer possible (CARPENTER, 1969). Perhaps the most reasoned account in summary of the arguments for and against this idea is given by MURPHEY (1951). In this paper he suggests that Ptolemy's weather journals are based on indirect reports with no quantitative measurements while the works of Herodotus and Diodorus "both describe the climate of Egypt in their day in terms which fit the Present". Murphey suggests in summary that "there is no reliable evidence of important changes in the climate of Egypt or Libya[1] since Roman times, there are ample indications that the decline in productivity of the oases has been profoundly affected by non-climatic or human factors, and that much of the Roman prosperity could even now be regained by an equally effective utilization of the groundwater resources."

Primary pressure features

Cool season

In winter the eastward moving cyclones crossing Europe bring frequent outbreaks of cold northwest air which penetrate into this area and meet with warmer, moist air. The resultant vertical instability then leads to the development of active depressions which result in relatively heavy rainfall and frequent gales in the Mediterranean. In addition, cold air outbreaks from the north or northeast may occur at any time between October and May. If these manage to penetrate sufficiently far south the pronounced thermal contrast can spawn vigorous depressions that then move into the Mediterranean.

Spring and summer

During the spring period this zone continues to be affected by depressions and troughs related to the air mass movements over Europe. This is a windy time around the coast-line but, perhaps because of the small temperature differential between land and sea, there is relatively little rain and cloud, except where orographic influences intervene.

In summer, when the Azores high intensifies, a period of calm, sunny weather predominates. Heat lows develop over the southwest Asia Peninsula and the Sahara and the resulting subsidence over the cooler, large sea area supplies the reason for the northwest to northeast winds that prevail at this time.

Perhaps the most important type of depression affecting this zone is the Saharan (occasionally called "sirocco" or "khamsin"). These cyclones can form in the lee of the Atlas Mountains at any time of the year, but generally show a maximum frequency in the spring (April, May) and a secondary maximum in October. In the latter period, when the sea is warm, they give rise to appreciable rainfall but their most pronounced effects during the spring are on wind and temperature. A very detailed discussion of these depressions, with relevant examples, is given in *Weather in the Mediterranean* (METEOROLOGICAL OFFICE, 1962).

In Fig.2 the tracks of depressions affecting this zone are depicted. It is clearly illustrated that for this zone the Saharan depression forms the major contributor although the depressions moving southeast from the northwestern Mediterranean also play a prime role, especially along the Algerian and Tunisian coast.

---

[1] Libya in this instance being the term applied to the remainder of North Africa. (Editor.)

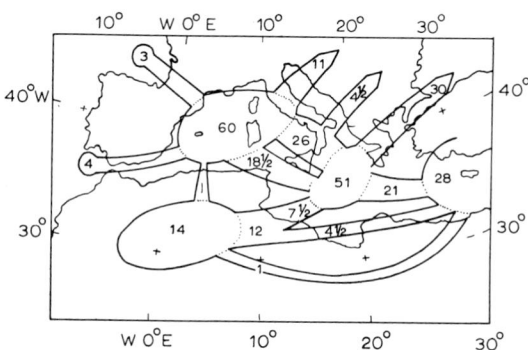

Fig.2. Tracks of depressions. (After METEOROLOGICAL OFFICE, 1962.)

Radiation and sunshine

Radiation data for this zone are rather scarce and therefore much of the information contained in this section relates to sunshine records. However, from the *World Maps of Climatology* (LANDSBERG et al., 1963) it is found that, in general, the zone experiences about 150–180 kLy/year. (410–490 Ly/day) reaching, perhaps, as high as 190 kLy/year in southern Morocco.

Global (sun and sky) radiation data are only available over a representative period for two stations (Table I).

In Tunis over 700 Ly/day have been recorded in May, June and July with a maximum of 770 in June. In *Le Climat d'Algerie* SELTZER (1946) has presented the diurnal pattern

TABLE I

MEAN MONTHLY GLOBAL RADIATION (Ly/day)

	Jan.	Feb.	Mar.	Apr.	May	June	July	Aug.	Sept.	Oct.	Nov.	Dec.	Year
Algiers	185	237	392	426	470	553	545	456	405	263	185	145	355
Tunis	194	253	361	476	579	630	630	566	452	313	226	176	405

of global radiation at Algiers (Fig.3). From this it appears that around midday from April to July the atmospheric transmission coefficient is appreciably reduced, for the isopleths lose their elliptical pattern and become circular. The almost perfect symmetry is also rather surprising.

TABLE II

MAXIMUM DIRECT RADIATION (Ly/min)

	Jan.	Feb.	Mar.	Apr.	May	June	July	Aug.	Sept.	Oct.	Nov.	Dec.
Algiers	1.48	1.47	1.54	1.56	1.53	1.47	1.43	1.41	1.39	1.48	1.49	1.47
Ariana	1.54	1.59	1.61	1.57	1.60	1.54	1.56	1.57	1.64	1.70	1.62	1.51
Casablanca	1.49	1.50	1.52	1.55	1.52	1.53	1.48	1.47	1.48	1.49	1.52	1.51
Ifrane	1.60	1.61	1.70	1.67	1.70	1.59	1.63	1.61	1.60	1.66	1.69	1.60

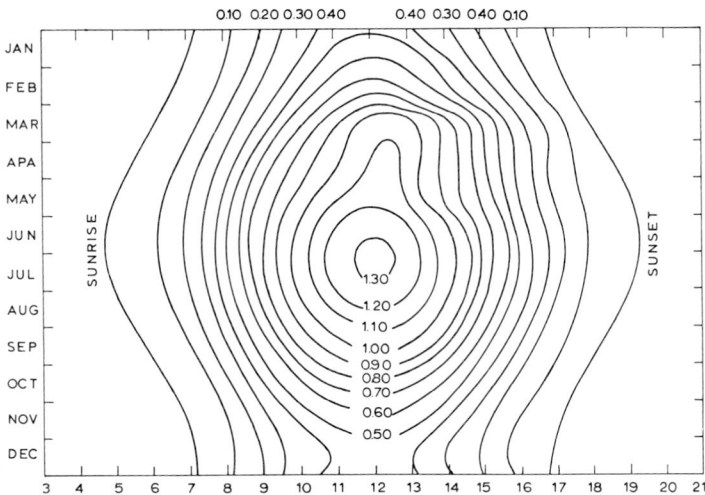

Fig.3. Mean global radiation (Ly/h), Algiers.

Direct radiation has been measured for periods of about four years at Algiers, Ariana, Casablanca and Ifrane. In Table II the maximum value recorded in each month is given. This zone is well known for its high total of sunshine hours. Most of the area, except for Morocco, experiences from 3,000 to 3,500 h each year, or 70–80% of possible. In western Morocco, especially along the coast, the influence of the Canaries Current is evident by an increase in cloud amount and a related reduction in sunshine hours, reaching only 2,500 (less than 60% of possible) at Casablanca.

TABLE III

MEAN MONTHLY HOURS SUNSHINE

Station	Jan.	Feb.	Mar.	Apr.	May	June	July	Aug.	Sept.	Oct.	Nov.	Dec.	Year
Agadir	236	232	285	298	301	289	289	266	256	248	228	228	3,156
Algiers	170	180	210	258	285	314	356	324	247	225	170	156	2,895
Casablanca–													
Anfa	165	180	228	269	292	294	310	300	268	224	175	166	2,871
Djelfa	164	200	235	234	316	330	358	340	300	236	188	137	3,028
Fez	156	181	222	228	287	287	339	315	247	219	164	157	2,802
Gabes	235	232	254	261	285	303	369	360	286	241	222	209	3,257
Geryville	180	220	250	264	328	346	359	341	306	254	180	183	3,211
Ifrane	158	171	209	241	279	301	351	317	257	214	163	148	2,809
Kairouan	213	207	247	279	322	344	383	347	282	252	213	199	3,288
Kenitra	149	181	224	269	295	308	340	319	273	221	161	135	2,875
Marrakesh	215	212	252	269	290	322	358	330	281	242	216	206	3,193
Meknes	164	183	220	245	301	313	363	338	276	232	180	157	2,972
Oujda	179	196	233	271	312	324	372	344	288	246	196	184	3,145
Rabat-Sale	167	185	221	263	298	300	336	318	268	231	184	170	2,941
Safi	190	202	253	281	307	303	333	321	260	236	196	184	3,066
Sidi bel													
Abbes	185	145	225	238	291	285	327	300	222	196	179	148	2,741
Souk el Arba	159	177	222	218	290	323	387	338	265	212	163	148	2,902
Tangier	155	167	215	264	308	325	366	346	284	237	168	144	2,979
Tetuan	161	157	173	213	276	290	314	289	227	191	161	161	2,613
Vialar	154	148	250	242	266	291	353	284	249	205	155	133	2,730

Long period sunshine records are not common in this zone but Table III gives some of the data available. Amounts in excess of 10 h/day are the rule in most regions during June, July and August, the only exception being Agadir (Canaries Current). In winter the stations at high elevations or along the Mediterranean coastal belt experience fewer hours of sunshine than other sites.

Temperature and mean

Temperatures in this zone are affected mainly by the factors of distance from the sea, altitude, the Canaries Current and the proximity to air flow from the Sahara. Stations influenced by the sea show a markedly smaller diurnal and annual range than the inland areas. In western Morocco the cool Canaries Current causes a most marked decrease in temperature, especially during the summer.

Minimum

In this zone it is rather rare for a coastal station to report a freeze but in the highlands (above 1,500 m) minima around –10°C have been recorded, while Ifrane has reached –20°C. This station has reported freezes every month from September to May.

Along the Atlantic coast the Canaries Current is the dominant factor responsible for the relatively low summer temperatures. For example, at Agadir the mean temperature of the warmest month is 22.8°C while at Ouarzazate, at a height of 1,135 m, in the same latitude, it is 30.0°C; also, at Rabat a 23.1°C mean compares with 27.2°C at Fez (410 m), and at Mogador a 21.7°C mean contrasts with 28.9°C at Marrakesh (465 m). In this narrow belt the annual ranges are also very small, being 6°C at Mogador and 8°C at Agadir.

Maximum

Most of the lowland stations have recorded extreme maxima above 45°C, with 50°C being common. Al Azizia, Libya, has recorded 57°C but the exposure of the thermometer is in doubt. As high as 55°C has been noted at Ben Gardene in Tunisia. Coastal stations, especially in the Nemours–Algiers area, hardly ever exceed 43°C. At higher elevations these maxima are reduced so that at about 1,500 m it is unusual to reach even 38°C.

Progressing eastwards the summer temperatures become higher, especially in Libya and Egypt where there is no mountain barrier to hinder the Saharan influence and the hot, dry winds move northwards unchecked. Temperatures also increase southwards but the effect of the high ranges, extending over 4,000 m in some places, must be considered. January is generally the coldest month, mean temperatures at the coast being about 10°C in the western section and 13°C in the eastern. The maxima at this time are about 15°–18°C at the coast, decreasing to below 10°C in the mountains but reaching 20°C in southern Morocco. The coastal minima are about 7°–8°C with readings below zero in the highlands.

Precipitation

The whole of this Mediterranean zone, about 85,000 km², experiences low amounts of precipitation, totals in excess of 600 mm/year being confined to very small regions. Most of the precipitation is in the form of rain but snow is not unknown, even at coastal stations. In most instances the precipitation is associated with north or west winds so that it is natural to find the exposed north and west slopes wetter than the sheltered south and east slopes. However, rain shadow areas exist, for example, Setif and Constantine are sheltered by the Kabylie Mountains. Some rains are related to northeast flow over the Mediterranean, for instance, in Tunisia during late winter this can occur, giving rise to the saying "rain in March is pure gold". It is possible to consider many aspects of the precipitation when defining sub-divisions but attention will be focussed here on just two, amount and distribution. Because of the lack of original data the distribution aspect will be limited to monthly patterns.

Amount

Under a quantitative sub-division four areas may be identified; (*1*) moist regions with over 800 mm/year; (*2*) humid regions with 400–800 mm/year; (*3*) steppe regions with 200–400 mm/year; and (*4*) semi-arid regions with 125–200 mm/year.

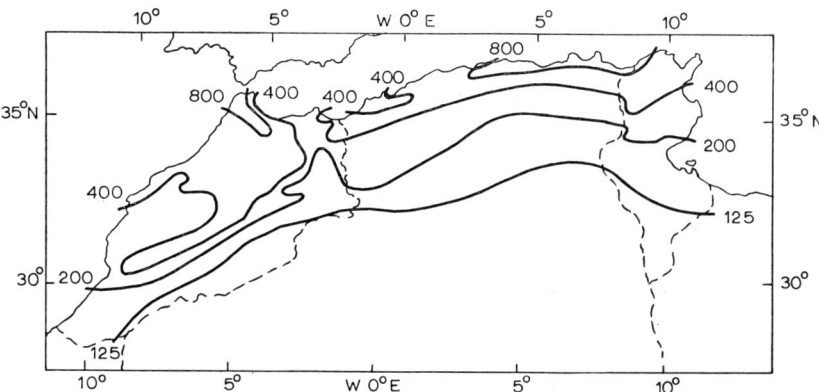

Fig.4. Mean annual isohyets (mm).

Except in (*4*) all stations exhibit a strong maximum in the cool season. The rainfall regions are shown in Fig.4.

(1) Moist regions (over 800 mm/year)

These regions occur in three distinctly separate parts of the zone, a narrow coastal belt extending from near Algiers to Cape Serrat (just west of Bizerta), a tongue of land pointing southeastwards from Tangier for about 250 km and an area south of Meknes. The first two regions are separated by about 800 km. In all three regions the heaviest rainfall is received at higher altitudes, reaching over 1,000 mm at Ifrane (1,635 m), 900 mm at

Rhafsai (350 m) and 1,500 mm at Ain Drahan (740 m). Tabarka is the only coastal station with an annual mean in excess of 1,000 mm. Details are given in Table IV.

A dominant feature of these rainfall patterns is their marked similarity, about 70% of the annual totals being concentrated in the cooler months (October–March) and very low rainfall in June to August (about 8%).

TABLE IV

MEAN MONTHLY RAINFALL (mm)

	Jan.	Feb.	Mar.	Apr.	May	June	July	Aug.	Sept.	Oct.	Nov.	Dec.	Year
Ifrane	112	127	125	117	82	38	8	11	40	137	152	163	1,112
Rhafsai	108	131	114	85	60	17	T	1	17	78	140	152	903
Ain Drahan	250	195	159	124	80	25	6	9	66	139	204	275	1,512
Tabarka	167	132	87	71	42	17	4	9	53	115	144	198	1,039

(2) Humid regions (400–800 mm/year)

The regions designated as moist cover about one third of the zone and, except for a rain shadow break of about 80 km, stretch from the Atlantic coast to the Tunisian coast, north of Susa. An isolated, small region in Cyrenaica, to the east of Benghasi, records over 700 mm near Cyrene. In this and the moist region most of the population of Morocco and Algeria are concentrated.

Although the dryness of the summer months is still the rule it is interesting to note that the season has some rain, while amounts in excess of 25 mm/day have been recorded from severe thunderstorms on occasional days in summer (Table V).

TABLE V

RAINFALL DATA (mm) FOR SOUK EL ARBA (36°29′N 8°48′E, 140 m), 30 YEARS

	Jan.	Feb.	Mar.	Apr.	May	June	July	Aug.	Sept.	Oct.	Nov.	Dec.	Year
Mean fall	65	49	47	45	33	16	3	10	33	56	47	73	477
24 h max.	49	36	36	45	48	58	14	25	61	85	45	50	85
Max.	196	145	144	124	90	91	17	36	165	143	111	242	709

(3) Steppe region (200–400 mm/year)

This region occupies a belt from the Atlantic to near the Egyptian border with breaks along the coast in the Gulf of Sidra and the Gulf of Gabes. The region, for as far east as Sfax, generally occupies higher land but does reach the coast around Agadir and Melilla. Sfax, right on the boundary between steppe and semi-arid, shows how every month may receive reasonable amounts of rain, with the exception of July (Table VI).

TABLE VI

rainfall data (mm) for sfax (34°43′N 10°41′E, 20 m), 30 years

	Jan.	Feb.	Mar.	Apr.	May	June	July	Aug.	Sept.	Oct.	Nov.	Dec.	Year
Mean fall	18	18	25	21	12	5	1	5	26	38	26	15	210
24 h max.	34	47	49	71	34	41	3	65	95	51	88	37	95
Max.	67	87	112	118	44	49	17	90	120	144	147	51	391

It is seen that in every month it is possible to have a daily fall in excess of the monthly mean, August giving the supreme example with a 1,300% fall. During the 30-year period each month has been completely dry at least once.

(4) Semi-arid region (125–200 mm/year)

This is the most southerly region, a continuous band across the zone. The Saharan influence is maximal and great variation within each month is the rule (Table VII).

TABLE VII

rainfall data for gafsa (34°25′N 8°49′E, 310 m), 30 years

	Jan.	Feb.	Mar.	Apr.	May	June	July	Aug.	Sept.	Oct.	Nov.	Dec.	Year
Mean fall	15	14	20	18	11	6	2	6	12	21	20	15	160
24 h max.	50	21	38	48	28	32	20	38	36	67	34	30	67
Max.	76	55	94	82	47	37	27	50	36	126	78	54	289

Distribution

Rain seasons

It was pointed out earlier that the rainfall in this zone can be attributed to three main causes, the winter cyclonic depressions, topography and convection. These causes, especially the great variation in relief features, give rise to the rather complex pattern of rainfall seasons experienced over the zone. Broadly speaking the coastal areas receive their maximum fall during December or January while inland the wettest months are November, December or January. This pattern is illustrated by the monthly rainfall data in Table VIII. The inland region tends to show double maxima, due to the dual season pattern of the Saharan depressions. It is seen that as the border with the desert is approached there is an increasing tendency for a summer maximum to occur until, at an extreme situation such as Bou Denib, there is a winter drought.

For the purposes of general illustration a simple pattern of seasonal analysis has been adopted. In a region where the monthly amounts show a gradual rise to a maximum then a gradual fall (minor fluctuations of only a few millimetres have been ignored) then

TABLE VIII

PRECIPITATION PATTERNS (mm)

Station	Ht. (m)	Lat. (N)	Long.	Jan.	Feb.	Mar.	Apr.	May	June	July	Aug.	Sept.	Oct.	Nov.	Dec.	Ann.	Pattern	No. of years
Mogador	8	31°31′	9°47′W	39	37	33	26	11	4	0	0	5	25	*54*	52	286	Nov.	24
Apollonia	6	32°54′	21°59′E	102	61	34	10	6	0	T	T	5	29	42	*115*	404	Dec.	19
Alexandria	30	31°12′	29°53′E	50	25	10	3	2	0	0	0	1	6	33	*56*	186	Dec.	46
Philippeville	70	36°52′	6°54′E	*169*	108	72	50	50	10	4	7	34	84	92	149	829	Jan.	12
Tabarrant	high	34°56′	4°29′W	*260*	220	160	154	53	13	T	6	26	58	125	210	1,285	Jan.	9
Marrakesh	470	31°37′	8°02′W	24	27	*39*	26	16	9	2	5	11	20	35	21	235	Nov., Mar.	34
Bouarfa	1,302	32°34′	1°58′W	11	13	*21*	19	12	5	1	8	21	24	25	21	181	Nov., Mar.	13
Cabao	645	31°50′	11°20′E	27	28	*50*	6	3	2	T	T	8	5	*31*	26	186	Nov., Mar.	12
Djerba	5	33°53′	10°51′E	28	19	22	11	8	1	T	1	13	34	*43*	27	207	Nov., Jan., Mar.	50
Bab Tazza	875	35°03′	5°14′W	207	*242*	220	120	62	21	T	2	20	90	127	222	1,333	Dec., Feb.	11
Safi	45	32°17′	9°14′W	44	35	*40*	24	13	5	0	0	6	56	56	*64*	327	Dec., Mar.	24
Orleansville	110	36°18′	1°21′E	55	45	39	32	37	9	1	1	20	35	60	*66*	400	Dec., May	25
Dar Drius	195	35°59′	3°23′W	40	28	22	*48*	19	3	T	2	*18*	*19*	12	24	235	Jan., May	10
Cabo Tres Forcas	40	35°28′	3°01′W	*36*	20	11	22	16	2	1	2	4	19	14	27	174	Jan., May	8
Setif	1,075	36°11′	5°25′E	*60*	45	43	36	*51*	28	11	13	37	39	53	52	468	Jan., May	25
Susa	6	35°49′	10°39′E	43	34	30	23	18	6	1	5	*51*	43	37	38	*329*	Sept., Jan.	50
Tebessa	860	35°24′	8°07′E	*33*	26	38	30	38	29	10	10	*33*	29	30	29	335	—	24
Ain-Mimoun	1,335	35°23′	6°57′E	*60*	51	*89*	47	56	35	12	23	31	48	66	57	575	—	13
Ain Sefra	1,075	32°45′	0°36′W	10	10	*14*	9	15	28	8	7	15	29	*29*	18	192	Mar.,June, Nov.	15
Bou Denib	920	31°57′	3°35′W	T	3	6	9	15	18	*23*	22	18	12	5	1	132	July	11

Numbers in italics denote maxima.

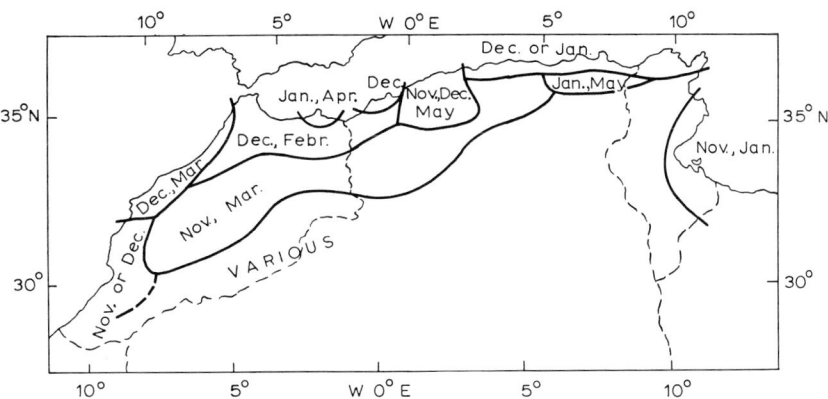

Fig.5. Months of rainfall maxima.

the single maximum month is considered. If, however, a secondary maximum appears this is also shown. Fig.5 is a representation of such primary and secondary maxima.

Rainiest quarter

Over most of the zone December is the centre of the wettest three consecutive months period. Nevertheless, some stations show a marginal maximum in January. A regular pattern for November becomes apparent in the mountains of Morocco with a January maximum persisting in eastern Algeria and northern Tunisia. In the Sfax–Susa area the maximum becomes October but proceeding westwards this is more diffuse until finally at the Saharan margin the rainfall is so light that this form of analysis is meaningless. The October maximum is likely to be due to instability convective formations over the relatively warm sea drifting inland on the northeast winds in the early autumn period while a rainshadow effect reduces winter rains.

Maximum daily rainfall

In this predominantly dry zone heavy falls are rare and many regions have never experienced falls in excess of 60 mm in a day, a fact especially true in southern Morocco. In contrast, in northern Morocco in the area between Tangier and Melilla, falls of over 150 mm in a day have been recorded. Llano Amarillo has reported daily falls in excess of 85 mm for all months from October to April while Tangier has noted 80 mm for each month from September to June, with the exception of May. Most of the maximum falls have been recorded in December or November but every month, save July, is represented in Table IX that gives the two highest daily amounts for a selection of stations. In fact November appears 13 times, December 12, October 7, January 5, September and April 3, February, March, May, June and August once.

If a day of heavy rainfall is defined as one in which over 30 mm is recorded then it has been shown (SELTZER, 1946) that in the Algerian littoral most stations experience the greatest number of heavy rainfalls in December, while amounts in excess of 100 mm/day have occurred at most stations east of the Greenwich meridian. In the Tell the maximum occurs in January or May and over half the stations have received more than 100 mm in a day, with Ain Feen recording 277 mm in 24 h. In the high plains the time of heavy

TABLE IX

<small>TWO HIGHEST DAILY RAINFALLS (mm)</small>

Station	Maxima		Station	Maxima	
Agadir	76 (Dec.),	66 (Oct.)	Jedebya	28 (Dec.),	18 (Feb., Sept.)
Ain Sefra	33 (Aug.),	25 (Apr.)	Kairouan	112 (Oct.),	66 (Nov.)
Alexandria	63 (Nov.),	56 (Dec.)	Larache	145 (Dec.),	89 (Nov.)
Algiers	135 (Oct.),	81 (Nov.)	Llano Amarillo	198 (Jan.),	193 (Nov.)
Avarroes	63 (Nov.),	58 (Oct.)	Marrakesh	41 (June),	38 (Nov.)
Beja	74 (Dec.),	51 (Sept., Mar.)	Medenine	51 (Oct., Nov.),	49 (Mar.)
Benghasi	43 (Nov.),	38 (Oct.)	Melilla	221 (Jan.),	168 (Nov.)
Bizerta	135 (Oct.),	89 (Dec.)	Mersa Matruh	99 (Dec.),	76 (Oct.)
Boghari	49 (Jan.),	41 (Oct.)	Midelt	53 (Dec.),	31 (Apr., May)
Bone	81 (Sept.),	56 (Dec.)	Misurata	78 (Oct.),	31 (Feb., Sept.)
Cape Carbon	66 (Jan.),	63 (Nov.)	Mogador	81 (Nov.),	56 (Sept.)
Cape Tenes	53 (Apr.),	49 (May)	Oran	81 (Feb.),	72 (Nov.)
Casablanca	41 (Nov.),	38 (Mar.)	Puerto Capaz	94 (Dec.),	78 (Mar.)
Constantine	58 (Dec.),	32 (Apr.)	Rabat	49 (Nov.),	41 (Jan.)
Cyrene	89 (Nov.),	41 (Jan.)	Sfax	89 (Mar.),	69 (Oct.)
Derna	61 (Nov.),	51 (Sept., Dec.)	Sirte	66 (Sept.),	43 (Nov.)
Fez	38 (Jan., Nov.),	36 (Feb.)	Susa	154 (Sept., Oct.)	117 (Nov.)
Gabes	105 (Oct.),	102 (Nov.)	Tangier	122 (Dec.),	112 (Oct.)
Gafsa	46 (Apr.),	41 (Mar.)	Tebessa	33 (Apr.),	28 (Sept.)
Gaza	78 (Nov., Dec.),	71 (Mar.)	Thala	66 (May),	64 (Apr.)
Idris	94 (Dec.),	74 (Feb.)	Tripoli	129 (Nov.),	125 (Feb.)
Ifrane	163 (Dec.),	152 (Nov.)	Tunis	86 (Nov.),	81 (Dec.)

rainfall varies from November to June with a maximum likelihood in January; falls of more than 100 mm/day being noted only at Sigus. Short period falls (15–40 min) at a rate of 100 mm/h or more have been measured at a few stations with a 4-h fall at an intensity of 49 mm/h reported from Chrea (1,550 m) in September, 1931.

Snow and hail

Snow is not a common occurrence in this zone but at elevations above about 1,000 m it is likely to be reported during the winter. On the peaks of the High and Middle Atlas in Morocco snow may be seen during early October while at heights of 1,000–2,000 m it may lie for a week or so in the winter. Occasional snow is noted down to about 500 m but it is a very rare phenomenon at the coast. In the High Atlas winter blizzards are frequent and the snow can lie a metre or more in depth, while some north or west facing slopes can retain a snow cover for 6–9 months. Snow is never seen at Rabat or Casablanca but it occurs about one year in five at Tangier, once in two years at Algiers and nearly every year at Oran, usually December. Fez, Meknes and the highland stations experience snow almost every year. In the eastern part of the zone snow is extremely rare beyond Susa but in the Tunisian highlands, above 1,000 m, snow is reported about 10 days in each year. Soft hail is more frequent than snow. In Morocco hail occurs often above about 1,000 m being associated mainly with local cyclonic storms during middle and late spring.

Snow is very uncommon in Libya, except on the higher ground, but in February, 1949, three days of snow left a cover of 1 m depth over most of the Gebel. Hail of small size occurs more frequently while large sized stones doing considerable damage have been reported, for example, in 1955.

Humidity

It is an unfortunate fact that most of the information for this zone is given in the form of relative humidity at specific times of the day. In addition to the omission of the corresponding dry bulb temperature the actual times of observation vary over a few hours, a period during which the relative humidity is often changing quite rapidly.

Nearly all stations exhibit a mean daily relative humidity maximum in January and a minimum in July but the pattern is often masked by observations taken at a fixed hour which thereby misses the times of maximum or minimum readings. The relative humidity patterns for sunrise and midday (approximately) in January and July are given in Fig.6. The Atlantic coast, with its cooler temperatures, exhibits the greatest relative humidity in this zone, over 90% in January and over 80% in July at the time of sunrise. Most coastal stations record about 80% in January and 75% in July while inland stations experience about 75% and from 40 to 60%, respectively. Naturally, the lowest relative humidity is noted at the semi-arid locations, often below 15% during the afternoon. In the early afternoon the coastal relative humidity is about 70% but this falls rapidly inland to about 50% in January and 20% in July. Fogs, high humidity and heavy dews are characteristic of the Atlantic coast in the summer.

The use of dew point values is better for the interpretation of measurements as it is a more conservative value than relative humidity and does not show the great inverse dependence on temperature. Some representative values are given in Table X.

TABLE X

MEAN MONTHLY DEW POINT (°C)

Station	Jan.	Feb.	Mar.	Apr.	May	June	July	Aug.	Sept.	Oct.	Nov.	Dec.
Melilla	11.4	11.9	12.9	16.1	17.3	20.9	23.1	24.5	22.9	13.7	15.1	12.3
Algiers	7.4	7.4	8.2	9.8	12.9	16.1	18.7	19.4	18.1	14.1	10.5	7.7
Bone	7.4	7.6	8.6	10.5	13.7	17.3	19.9	20.5	19.0	15.1	11.1	8.1
Tunis	7.6	7.8	9.4	11.9	13.5	17.3	19.1	20.2	19.3	16.0	12.5	8.7
Gabes	4.3	4.9	7.8	11.1	14.9	18.2	20.0	20.3	19.4	15.7	10.4	6.6
Gafsa	2.9	3.2	5.2	7.9	11.0	13.1	14.3	16.6	15.7	13.2	8.3	4.9
Tripoli	6.8	7.7	9.0	11.2	14.0	17.2	19.5	19.9	18.7	16.4	12.1	8.2
Sirte	7.1	8.8	9.5	12.0	16.0	19.3	22.0	22.8	21.2	18.0	12.7	8.0
Benghasi	7.7	7.4	6.5	8.8	11.4	15.4	18.7	19.6	17.6	13.9	11.2	9.2
Sollum	4.8	5.9	7.6	9.7	13.1	15.5	18.9	20.1	18.1	15.6	14.3	7.3

Air flow

It is a disappointing fact that few reliable measurements of wind speed and direction are available in publication for this zone, save for a few coastal stations. Much of the information has been obtained from visual estimates of the wind velocity.

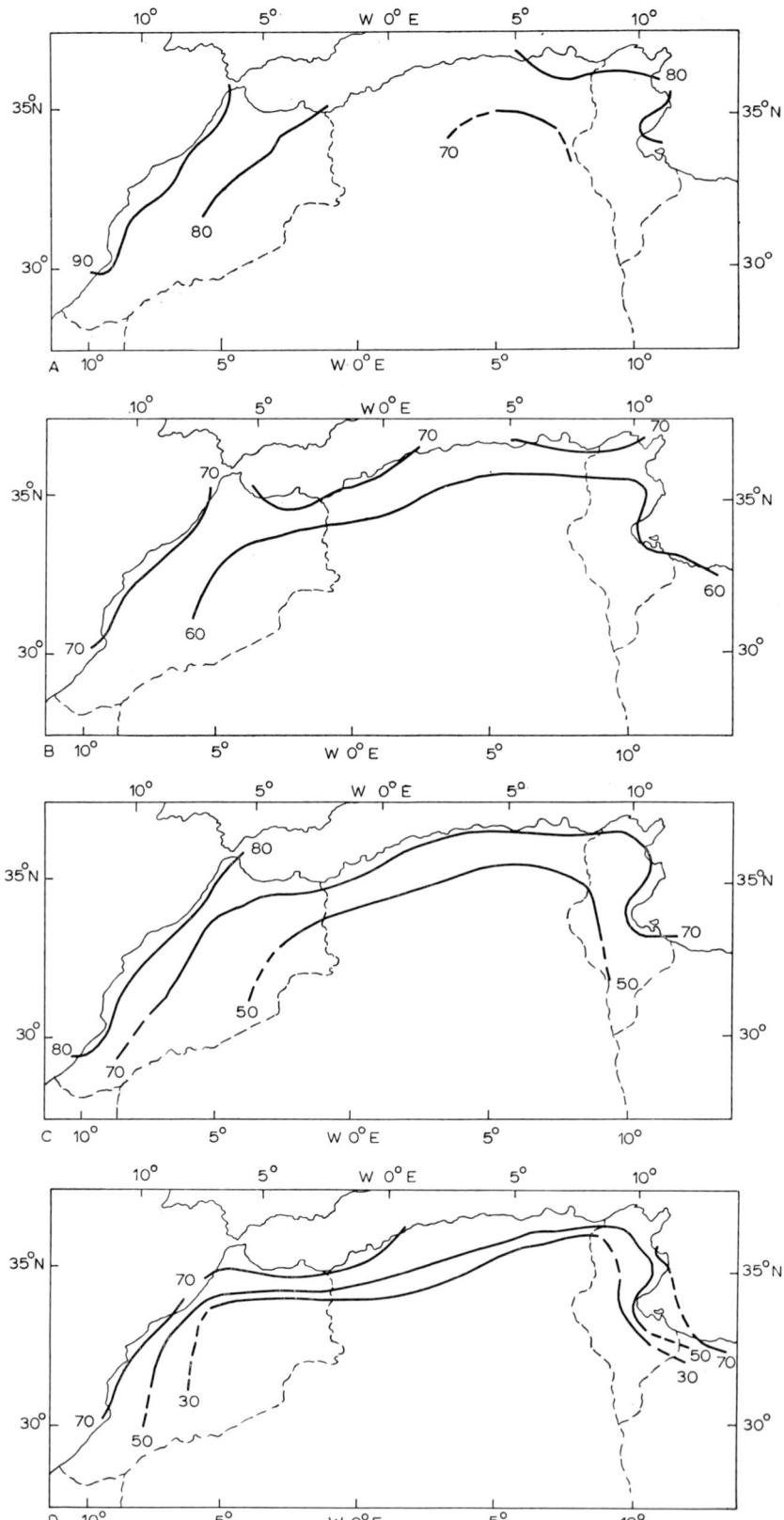

Fig.6. Mean relative humidity (%). A. January, sunrise. B. January, mid-day. C. July, sunrise. D. July, mid-day.

From a climatological viewpoint the most important winds are the rain-bearing ones, mainly westerlies, associated with depressions moving eastwards through the Mediterranean, and the sirocco, the hot, dry, dust-laden wind blowing out of the Sahara Desert region. The sirocco can bring with it very dramatic changes in the space of a few minutes, especially in the maritime areas which normally experience the cooler, more humid, sea breezes.

The land–sea breeze cycle is, of course, fundamentally important in the coastal areas of this zone and gives rise to very different mean wind speeds and directions for the various times of observation. For instance, Nemours has a predominantly south wind every month at 07h00 (local time) but this changes to northeast or northwest at 11h00 and 18h00. Further evidence of these changes can be seen in Table XI.

TABLE XI

SOME PREVAILING WIND DIRECTIONS

Time	Bizerta	Gabes	Gafsa	Kairouan	Sfax	Souk	Tunis
Summer:							
00h00	—	C(E)	NE	C(N)	C(N)	C(NW)	C(NW)
06h00	C(W)	C(NE)	NE	C(N)	C(N)	C(NW)	C(W)
12h00	N	NE	NE/SW	N/S	SE	C(NW)	N
18h00	N	E	S	E	E	NW	N
Winter:							
00h00	—	C(SW)	NE	C(SW)	W	C(SW)	W
06h00	C(W)	C(SW)	NE	C(SW)	W	C(SW)	W/SW
12h00	NW	SW	SW	C(W)	V	C(SW)	W
18h00	NW	C(W/E)	SW	C(NW)	SW	C(SW)	W

V = variable; C(W) = mainly calm but, if sufficient flow, W.

Gales appear to be most frequent in the region around Tripoli where an average of 23 per year is recorded (four in March). At Misurata the average is zero while at Melilla, Oran and Sirte it is only one.

As mentioned earlier the winter air flow is dominated by the eastward moving depressions so that winds tend to have a westerly component at most stations. In summer, when there is less pressure variation, the winds become more variable and are dominated by local conditions. These can bring considerable differences, as shown by SELTZER (1946) in the case of Algiers and Maison Carrée, some 10 km southeast of Algiers. Fig.7 shows some of their typical wind roses and illustrates the real difference between the air flows at the two stations. At 07h00 Maison Carrée is experiencing cold air gravity flow from the Mitidja Plain at each season of the year but such a land breeze is not present at Algiers with anywhere near the same intensity. The afternoon wind directions, both sea breezes, reflect the different orientation of the coast at these locations.

The sirocco is, fundamentally, just a wind of continental tropical origin blowing over the Mediterranean Sea and coast. The source of such a wind is the desert area of North Africa or Arabia and the wind is given various local names, chili in Morocco and Algeria, chebili in Tunisia, ghibli in Libya and khamsin in Egypt. The violent dust storms general-

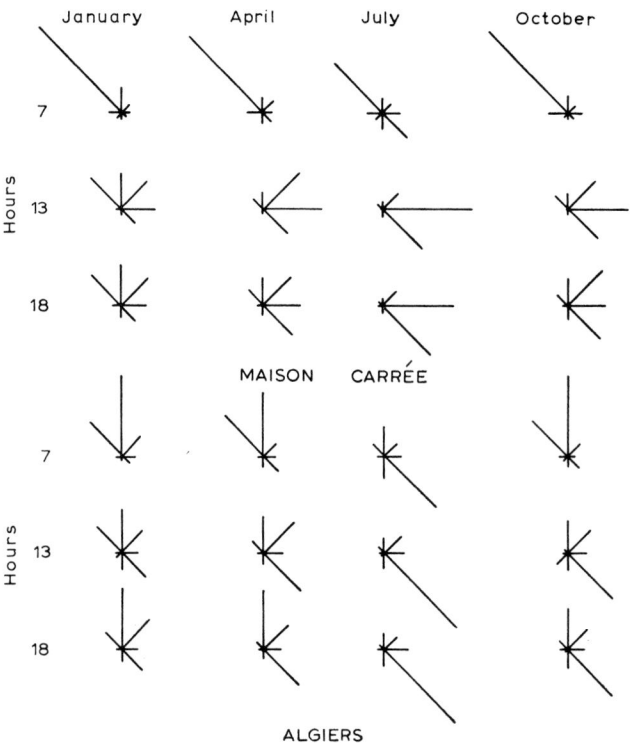

Fig.7. Typical wind roses at Maison Carrée and Algiers.

ly associated with this wind are called simoon. The sirocco reaches the coast at its hottest and driest state but rapidly picks up moisture and experiences some degree of cooling. A slow moving sirocco will become very humid and can give rise to heavy, dense, low stratus and sea fogs. The "dry" sirocco can bring such low humidities that vegetation can be damaged, due to both dessication and the "scouring" effect of the sand particles. From Tangier to Tunis there is an average of four or five sirocco days per month (a slight maximum occurs in May and June). In summer the wind brings high temperatures (in excess of 40°C or even 45°C) and low humidities (below 20%). If the wind is strong then the resulting dust may reduce visibility to a few metres. The Libyan ghibli can be prolonged in duration and gives rise to oppressive conditions. The commonest season for ghibli is in spring when the Saharan depressions frequently pass near the region and cause the advection of air masses with a long trajectory over the desert.

Evaporation

One of the problems associated with a climatological study of evaporation in this zone is the wide variation in instrumentation. Piche evaporimeters, pans and Wild evaporigraphs have all been utilized and comparison is thereby rendered almost impossible. Pan evaporation figures (mm/month) are given in Table XII. It is interesting to note the very large range at Souk (70–319) and Gafsa (90–325) compared with the much smaller variation at Sfax (105–195) and Gabes (119–181). It is likely that the winds, predominantly easterly, with a long fetch over the seas contribute to this fact because of the ad-

TABLE XII

MEAN MONTHLY PAN EVAPORATION (mm)

	Jan.	Feb.	Mar.	Apr.	May	June	July	Aug.	Sept.	Oct.	Nov.	Dec.	Year
Tunis	79	80	97	109	157	190	221	209	152	112	83	80	1,568
Souk	70	79	74	104	162	244	319	315	221	124	84	72	1,868
Sfax	110	105	126	129	160	184	195	191	154	127	109	107	1,691
Gabes	126	132	150	133	153	164	181	154	149	136	119	120	1,717
Gafsa	98	119	170	188	264	308	362	325	234	167	115	90	2,452

vection of a cooler, moister air mass, although this reasoning does not apply in the case of Tunis.

In Table XIII values of Piche evaporimeter readings for five stations in Algeria are given for comparison. These represent stations in the coastal belt, the lower hills, high mountains and a desert station.

Regardless of the evaporation apparatus used the pronounced excess of evaporation over rainfall during the year is evident and the need for efficient and controlled irrigation very obvious.

TABLE XIII

MEAN MONTHLY PICHE EVAPORATION (mm)

	Jan.	Feb.	Mar.	Apr.	May	June	July	Aug.	Sept.	Oct.	Nov.	Dec.	Year	Ht. (m)
Algiers	55	63	78	86	83	85	94	99	87	81	67	61	937	20
Orleansville	25	35	57	83	112	158	218	185	131	72	37	28	1,141	112
Kerrata	47	56	90	126	138	186	236	256	189	123	76	46	1,569	470
Lafayette	70	80	136	150	154	208	257	268	228	168	114	86	1,919	886
Beni-Ounif	128	175	241	269	320	370	532	450	338	195	157	118	3,293	825

References

CARPENTER, R., 1969. Climate and history. *Horizon*, 11 (2): 48.

LANDSBERG, H. E., LIPPMANN, H., PAFFEN, K. H. and TROLL, C., 1963. *World Maps of Climatology*. Springer, Berlin, 5 maps, 28 pp.

METEOROLOGICAL OFFICE, 1962. *Weather in the Mediterranean, I*. Meteorological Office, London, 362 pp.

MURPHEY, R., 1951. The decline of North Africa since the Roman occupation. *Ann. Assoc. Am. Geographers*, 41 (2): 116–132.

SELTZER, P., 1946. *Le Climat d'Algérie*. Univ. of Algiers, Algiers, 260 pp.

TABLE XIV

CLIMATIC TABLE FOR AGADIR, MOROCCO
Latitude 30°23'N, longitude 9°34'W, elevation 48 m

Month	M.s.l. press. (mbar)	Temperature (°C) mean max.	mean min.	extreme max.	extreme min.	Relative humidity (%) 06h	12h	18h	Precipitation mean (mm)	max. (mm)	min. (mm)	days ≥0.1 mm	max. in 24 h (mm)	Wind av. speed (m/sec)	preval. direct.	calm (%)	Averages cloud-iness (oktas)	sun-shine (h)	clear days
Jan.	1,018	20	9	31	0	85	60	72	48	155	0	5	71	2.7	E	36	3.2	236	12
Feb.	1,017	22	9	38	2	82	59	66	32	190	0	4	75	3.3	W	27	3.2	232	9
Mar.	1,014	22	11	38	2	85	60	66	24	147	0	5	51	3.3	W	24	3.4	285	9
Apr.	1,012	22	12	36	6	89	67	69	16	86	0	3	43	3.5	W	24	3.4	298	8
May	1,012	24	15	42	8	84	64	69	5	78	0	2	50	3.5	W	25	3.8	301	7
June	1,013	24	16	43	11	90	72	71	1	2	0	1	2	3.3	W	28	3.7	289	4
July	1,012	26	18	46	13	92	76	72	0	<1	0	0	<1	2.6	W	34	3.2	289	4
Aug.	1,011	27	18	47	12	91	71	72	<1	12	0	<1	12	2.9	W	32	3.9	266	4
Sept.	1,013	27	17	44	11	87	68	72	6	46	0	1	44	2.9	W	31	3.5	256	6
Oct.	1,014	26	15	40	9	84	63	72	22	128	0	4	65	2.7	W	33	3.6	248	7
Nov.	1,015	23	12	35	4	84	59	73	29	111	0	4	52	2.3	W	35	3.2	228	9
Dec.	1,017	20	8	29	2	85	59	75	41	193	0	6	123	2.2	E	37	3.0	228	12
Annual	1,014	24	13	47	0	86	65	71	224	430	84	35	123	2.9	—	30	3.4	3,156	
Rec. (yrs.)	21	10	10	10	10				30	30	30	30	30			21			

54

TABLE XV

CLIMATIC TABLE FOR SIRTE, LIBYA
Latitude 31°12'N, longitude 16°35'E, elevation 20 m

Month	M.s.l. press. (mbar)	Temperature (°C)				Dew point (°C)	Precipitation					Wind						Averages		
		mean		extreme			mean (mm)	max. (mm)	min. (mm)	days ≥1 mm	max. in 24 h (mm)	av. speed (knots)		preval. direct.		calm (%)		cloudiness (oktas)		sunshine (h/day)
		max.	min.	max.	min.							07h	13h	07h	13h	07h	13h	07h	13h	
Jan.	1,018	18	8	26	3	7.1	40	95	2	4	11	8	9	SW	W	4	<1	3	4	6.4
Feb.	1,019	19	9	37	4	8.8	23	65	0	4	19	8	8	S	NW	3	0	4	3	8.1
Mar.	1,017	22	11	38	4	9.5	16	79	0	4	24	7	8	S	NW	7	<1	3	3	7.6
Apr.	1,016	23	14	41	7	12.0	2	24	0	2	4	7	8	S	N	1	<1	3	3	7.5
May	1,013	26	17	42	11	16.0	3	20	0	1	5	6	8	SE	N	10	1	4	2	9.0
June	1,016	28	19	46	13	19.3	<1	3	0	<1	2	6	7	N/S	N	7	0	2	1	10.9
July	1,015	29	22	46	16	22.0	0	0	0	0	0	6	7	N	N	9	0	3	2	11.5
Aug.	1,015	31	23	45	18	22.8	0	0	0	0	0	5	7	V	N	14	0	3	2	11.2
Sept.	1,016	31	21	43	16	21.2	15	41	0	1	9	6	6	S	N	9	<1	3	2	8.2
Oct.	1,017	28	18	40	12	18.0	16	67	0	2	67	6	7	S	N	6	<1	3	3	6.5
Nov.	1,018	24	14	36	6	12.7	33	122	0	4	43	7	7	S	NW	2	2	3	4	6.8
Dec.	1,018	19	10	31	4	8.0	38	101	0	6	37	7	8	SW	W	5	1	3	4	5.4
Annual	1,017	25	15	46	3	15.7	187	349	66	28	67	7	7	—	—	6	<1	3	3	8.2
Rec. (yrs.)	7	7	7	7	7	9	12	17	17	12	12	6	6	6	6	6	6	9	9	2

TABLE XVI

CLIMATIC TABLE FOR MARRAKESH, MOROCCO
Latitude 31°36′N, longitude 8°01′W, elevation 460 m

Month	Mean press. (mbar)	Temperature (°C)				Relative humidity (%)			Precipitation					Wind			Averages		
		mean		extreme		06h	12h	18h	mean (mm)	max. (mm)	min. (mm)	days ≥0.1 mm	max. in 24 h (mm)	av. speed (m/sec)	preval. direct.	calm[1] (%)	cloud-iness[1] (tenths)	sun-shine[1] (h)	clear days
		max.	min.	max.	min.														
Jan.	1,021	18	7	29	0	88	64	60	28	89	0	7	33	2.5	W,E	53	3.5	215	8
Feb.	1,019	20	8	34	0	83	62	51	29	99	0	6	33	3.0	E,W	45	3.5	212	7
Mar.	1,016	22	10	34	2	85	55	47	32	99	0	6	36	3.6	W	39	3.9	252	5
Apr.	1,015	24	12	34	4	86	54	43	31	139	0	6	63	3.5	W	32	3.7	269	8
May	1,015	28	15	38	8	81	49	38	17	81	0	4	42	3.1	W	34	3.6	290	7
June	1,015	31	17	41	12	81	48	33	7	47	0	2	40	2.7	W	33	2.5	322	12
July	1,014	36	20	44	14	73	42	27	2	26	0	<1	26	3.0	N,W	32	1.7	358	15
Aug.	1,013	36	20	45	14	71	41	28	3	23	0	1	23	3.1	N,W	33	1.9	329	14
Sept.	1,015	32	18	42	12	76	47	34	10	49	0	1	29	2.7	W	42	2.6	281	9
Oct.	1,016	27	15	35	7	76	50	43	21	60	0	4	43	2.5	W	46	3.3	242	6
Nov.	1,018	21	10	30	4	86	60	57	28	89	0	6	37	2.3	W	50	3.4	216	5
Dec.	1,021	18	7	26	−1	86	62	62	33	131	<1	8	52	2.3	W,E	58	3.2	206	10
Annual	1,017	26	13	45	−1	81	53	43	241	(462)	(126)	51	63	2.8	—	41	3.1	3,192	
Rec. (yrs.)	10	10	10	10	10	10	10	10	30	30	30	30	30	10	20	20			

[1] Mean of 06h00, 12h00 and 18h00.

TABLE XVII

CLIMATIC TABLE FOR BENINA, LIBYA
Latitude 32°06'N, longitude 20°04'E, elevation 25 m

Month	M.s.l. press. (mbar)	Temperature (°C)				Dew point (°C)	Precipitation					Wind					Averages		
		mean		extreme			mean (mm)	max. (mm)	min. (mm)	days ≥1 mm	max. in 24 h (mm)	av. speed (km/h)	preval direct. 09h	15h	calm (%) 09h	15h	cloud-iness[1] (tenths)	sun-shine (h)	number of gales (≥Be 8)
		max.	min.	max.	min.														
Jan.	1,018	17	8	26	2	7.7	65	257	7	14	34	5	SE	NW	10	2	5	201	0.1
Feb.	1,017	18	10	32	0	7.4	35	141	0	8	27	6	SE	NW	6	2	6	219	0.8
Mar.	1,016	21	11	38	1	6.5	22	90	0	7	38	6	SE	NW	8	2	5	245	0.9
Apr.	1,015	24	13	38	4	8.8	5	29	0	2	23	6	SE	NW	10	3	4	264	0.6
May	1,015	28	16	45	6	11.4	7	46	0	2	5	6	NW	NW	6	1	4	325	0.6
June	1,015	29	19	45	10	15.4	<1	5	0	<1	3	5	NE	N	6	2	2	336	0.4
July	1,013	29	22	42	15	18.7	0	4	0	0	4	5	N	N	9	3	1	391	0
Aug.	1,013	30	22	44	14	19.6	<1	4	0	<1	1	4	N	N	8	1	2	366	0.1
Sept.	1,016	27	18	41	10	17.6	4	45	0	1	30	4	N	N	8	1	2	291	0.1
Oct.	1,017	26	17	38	11	13.9	21	91	0	4	40	5	SE	NW	13	1	4	248	0.1
Nov.	1,018	24	14	37	6	11.2	32	200	1	7	43	5	SE	NW	11	2	5	222	0.3
Dec.	1,018	20	11	30	4	9.2	67	250	1	12	30	5	SE	NW	6	3	6	171	0.5
Annual	1,016	24	15	45	0	12.3	258	426	106	57	43	5	—	—	8	2	4	3,279	4.6
Rec. (yrs.)	30	20	20	20	20	12	60	60	60	30	15	8	8	8	8	8	5	4	8

[1] Mean of 09h00 and 18h00 local time.

57

TABLE XVIII

CLIMATIC TABLE FOR MISURATA, LIBYA

Latitude 32°25'N, longitude 15°06'E, elevation 6 m

Month	Mean sta. press. (mbar)	Temperature (°C) mean max.	mean min.	extreme max.	extreme min.	Dew point (°C)	Precipitation mean (mm)	max. (mm)	min. (mm)	days ≥1 mm	max. in 24 h (mm)	Wind av. speed (m/sec)	preval. direct. 07h	13h	calm (%) 07h	13h	Averages cloud-iness[1] (oktas)	sun-shine (h)	number of gales ≥Be 8
Jan.	1,018	18	8	26	1	5.0	61	180	3	8	37	3	W	W	22	0	5	183	0
Feb.	1,019	18	9	32	3	6.7	22	74	1	5	32	4	W	NW	21	1	5	218	0.1
Mar.	1,018	21	11	39	4	8.0	17	45	0	3	14	3	W	NW	18	3	5	239	0
Apr.	1,017	24	14	39	7	11.3	15	60	0	2	12	3	V	V	21	1	4	255	0
May	1,014	27	17	41	11	14.7	5	35	0	1	25	4	NW	V	16	1	4	316	0
June	1,016	31	20	45	14	17.6	<1	21	0	<1	3	3	NW	E	21	1	2	303	0
July	1,015	32	23	46	18	19.1	0	0	0	0	0	3	W	NW	26	1	2	378	0
Aug.	1,015	34	23	51	17	19.8	<1	6	0	<1	3	3	V	NE	32	1	2	353	0
Sept.	1,017	32	22	45	15	19.2	5	80	0	1	30	2	V	NE	35	1	3	273	0
Oct.	1,017	29	19	40	13	16.1	27	222	0	4	78	3	W	NW	27	3	5	239	0
Nov.	1,017	24	14	37	6	12.5	21	111	0	6	36	3	W	NW	24	3	5	213	0
Dec.	1,017	19	10	29	3	5.8	76	138	1	7	28	3	W	NW	22	4	5	180	0
Annual	1,017	26	16	51	1	13.7	250	465	90	37	78	3	—		24	2	4	3,150	0.1
Rec. (yrs.)	8	10	10	10	10	9	30	38	38	10	7	9	9	9	9	9	9	5	10

[1] Mean of 07h00 and 13h00.

TABLE XIX

CLIMATIC TABLE FOR DERNA, LIBYA
Latitude 32°49'N, longitude 22°38'E, elevation 7 m

Month	M.s.l. press. (mbar)	Temperature (°C) mean max.	mean min.	extreme max.	extreme min.	Dew point (°C) 08h	14h	Precipitation mean (mm)	max. (mm)	min. (mm)	days ≥1 mm	max. in 24 h (mm)	Wind av. speed (knots) 08h	14h	preval. direct. 08h	14h	calm (%) 08h	14h	Averages cloud-iness (oktas) 08h	14h	sun-shine (h/day)	number of gales ≥Be 8
Jan.	1,017	18	11	31	4	7.7	9.2	46	143	5	8	40	12	11	SW	NW	1	1	5	5	4.9	1
Feb.	1,017	18	10	33	4	7.6	9.1	34	143	<1	5	23	12	12	S	NW	4	3	4	4	6.7	1
Mar.	1,017	18	13	41	5	8.4	10.6	28	107	<1	5	23	12	11	S	NW	6	3	5	4	6.6	<1
Apr.	1,016	22	14	38	7	11.3	12.8	5	56	0	1	14	10	10	W	NW	9	2	3	3	7.7	<1
May	1,014	24	16	44	9	14.7	16.7	10	40	0	1	25	7	9	W	NW	12	2	3	3	9.1	1
June	1,015	27	19	44	8	18.0	19.5	0	3	0	0	1	8	9	NW	NW	7	1	2	1	9.9	0
July	1,012	28	22	42	10	21.0	22.0	<1	1	0	0	1	9	10	NW	NW	4	1	2	1	10.2	0
Aug.	1,012	29	24	41	18	21.5	22.7	1	11	0	<1	11	11	11	NW	NW	4	1	2	1	9.6	0
Sept.	1,015	28	22	41	15	19.3	20.8	9	61	0	1	50	9	8	NW	NW	5	3	3	2	7.9	0
Oct.	1,017	26	19	39	10	16.0	17.4	11	189	0	4	60	8	7	S	NW	10	5	4	4	7.2	0
Nov.	1,017	23	16	38	8	12.5	14.1	57	173	0	5	62	10	9	S	NW	5	3	4	5	6.3	0
Dec.	1,016	19	12	33	7	9.3	10.6	55	164	0	8	50	12	11	S	NW	3	2	5	5	4.7	1
Annual	1,015	23	17	44	4	14.6	16.1	256	455	125	38	62	10	10	—	NW	6	2	3	3	7.7	4
Rec. (yrs.)	9	9	9	20	20	9	9	10	20	20	10	10	6	6	6	6	6	6	9	9	4	6

TABLE XX

CLIMATIC TABLE FOR TRIPOLI, LIBYA

Latitude 32°54′N, longitude 13°11′E, elevation 20 m

Month	M.s.l. press. (mbar)	Temperature (°C) mean max.	mean min.	extreme max.	extreme min.	Dew point (°C)	Precipitation mean (mm)	max. (mm)	min. (mm)	days 0.1 mm	max. in 24 h (mm)	Wind av. speed (m/sec)	preval. direct. 07h	15h	calm (%) 07h	15h	Averages cloud-iness (oktas)	sun-shine (h/day)	number of gales ⩾Be 8
Jan.	1,018	17	8	28	−1	6.8	62	205	<1	11	53	6	SW	NW	1	4	4	5.5	3
Feb.	1,018	18	9	35	−1	7.7	38	162	0	7	125	7	SW	NW	1	4	3	6.8	3
Mar.	1,016	20	10	40	1	9.0	19	98	0	4	52	6	S	NW	3	3	3	7.3	4
Apr.	1,014	23	13	44	3	11.2	14	81	0	1	50	7	S	NE	7	1	3	8.5	2
May	1,015	25	16	46	5	14.0	3	34	0	1	20	7	E	NE	9	0	3	9.9	2
June	1,015	29	19	47	7	17.2	1	17	0	<1	11	6	E	NE	12	0	1	9.9	1
July	1,015	30	21	48	13	19.5	<1	9	0	0	4	7	SE	NE	19	1	<1	11.5	<1
Aug.	1,015	31	22	48	14	19.9	1	28	0	<1	28	6	SE	NE	18	0	<1	10.9	<1
Sept.	1,016	30	21	47	12	18.7	10	109	0	1	78	7	SE	NE	10	0	1	8.6	3
Oct.	1,017	28	18	41	7	16.4	32	196	0	4	81	6	S	NE	5	2	3	7.3	1
Nov.	1,017	23	13	37	3	12.1	41	293	0	6	130	6	SW	NW	3	4	3	6.2	<1
Dec.	1,018	18	9	31	0	8.2	65	378	1	10	71	6	SW	W	3	5	4	5.3	2
Annual	1,016	24	15	48	−1	14.0	286	758	114	45	130	6	—		8	2	3	8.7	23
Rec. (yrs.)	30	34	34	34	34	12	34	85	85	34	34	8	8	8	8	8	5	12	8

60

TABLE XXI

CLIMATIC TABLE FOR IFRANE, MOROCCO
Latitude 33°31'N, longitude 5°07'W, elevation 1,640 m

Month	Mean sta. press. (mbar)	Temperature (°C) mean max.	min.	extreme max.	min.	Relat. humid. (%) 06h	12h	Precipitation mean (mm)	max. (mm)	min. (mm)	days >1 mm	max. in 24 h (mm)	Wind av. speed (m/sec)	preval. direct.	calm[1] (%)	Aver. sunshine (h)
Jan.	837	9	−5	19	−22	83	58	112	379	28	8	127	3	W	31	157
Feb.	836	11	−3	21	−21	84	57	127	353	5	8	73	4	W	19	171
Mar.	835	13	−1	26	−15	85	58	125	324	22	10	66	5	W	16	209
Apr.	834	16	3	27	−8	83	55	117	159	19	8	66	4	W	18	241
May	836	18	4	32	−5	82	54	82	196	14	7	71	3	W	20	279
June	837	24	9	33	1	75	46	38	90	3	5	45	3	W	21	301
July	839	31	12	37	3	58	28	8	46	<1	1	23	3	W	21	351
Aug.	839	30	12	36	2	63	30	11	42	1	2	30	3	W	20	317
Sept.	838	25	8	34	0	76	42	40	98	6	5	42	4	W	21	257
Oct.	837	18	5	29	−5	85	54	137	218	2	8	98	4	W	19	213
Nov.	834	14	1	30	−17	88	59	152	344	59	7	86	4	W	24	163
Dec.	835	9	−3	20	−20	89	63	163	524	7	9	145	4	W	31	148
Annual	836	18	3	37	−22	79	50	1,112	1,793	654	78	145	4	—	22	2,807
Rec. (yrs.)	10	16	16	16	16	8	8	10	10	10	10	10	10	10	10	9

[1] Mean of 06h00, 12h00 and 18h00.

TABLE XXII

CLIMATIC TABLE FOR CASABLANCA, MOROCCO
Latitude 33°34'N, longitude 7°40'W, elevation 49 m

Month	M.s.l. press. (mbar)	Temperature (°C) mean max.	mean min.	extreme max.	extreme min.	Relat. humid. (%) 06h	12h	Precipitation mean (mm)	max. (mm)	min. (mm)	days ≥0.1 mm	max. in 24 h (mm)	Wind av. speed (km/h) 06h	12h	preval. direct.	calm[1] (%)	Aver. cloudiness (tenths) 06h	12h
Jan.	1,021	17	9	31	2	91	72	80	179	7	12	50	3	3	S,NE	26	3.8	4.7
Feb.	1,019	18	9	35	0	89	68	68	198	0	10	42	3	4	SW	18	4.0	4.8
Mar.	1,017	19	11	34	5	89	68	68	125	6	10	50	3	5	W	14	4.1	4.6
Apr.	1,017	20	12	33	6	90	68	37	115	0	6	53	2	5	N	14	4.2	4.1
May	1,017	22	15	39	9	89	68	22	76	0	5	72	2	5	N	17	5.0	3.9
June	1,017	24	17	36	12	88	70	5	11	0	2	10	2	5	N	18	5.3	3.1
July	1,017	26	19	33	14	90	72	0	1	0	<1	1	1	5	N	20	5.1	2.2
Aug.	1,016	26	20	41	15	91	72	1	11	0	<1	11	1	5	N	20	5.0	2.2
Sept.	1,017	26	19	37	14	91	69	3	31	0	2	24	1	5	N	20	4.7	3.0
Oct.	1,017	24	15	32	7	88	66	25	139	1	7	59	2	4	NE	20	3.9	3.9
Nov.	1,018	20	12	28	6	89	67	77	188	0	11	45	3	4	SW,NE	28	3.7	4.5
Dec.	1,021	18	10	27	2	91	72	125	234	7	12	58	3	4	SW	23	3.8	4.5
Annual	1,818	21	14	41	0	90	69	511	666	227	77	72	2	4	—	19	3.4	4.4
Rec. (yrs.)	10	10	10	10	10			10	30	30	10	30				21		

[1] Mean of 06h00, 12h00 and 18h00.

TABLE XXIII

CLIMATIC TABLE FOR GABES, TUNISIA
Latitude 33°53'N, longitude 10°06'E, elevation 4 m

Month	M.s.l. press. (mbar)	Temperature (°C)				Humidity		Precipitation					Wind						Averages	
		mean		extreme		dew point (°C)	relat. (%)	mean (mm)	max. (mm)	min. (mm)	days ≥0.1 mm	max. in 24 h (mm)	av. speed (knots)		prevalent direction		calms (%)		sun-shine (h)	evap. (mm)
		max.	min.	max.	min.								08h	14h	08h	14h	08h	14h		
Jan.	1,017	16	6	27	−3	4.3	65	17	96	0	3	34	7	11	W	W	28	11	235	126
Feb.	1,016	17	7	32	−2	4.9	61	17	65	0	3	57	8	11	W	W	37	13	232	131
Mar.	1,015	20	10	41	1	7.8	64	16	67	0	4	32	7	14	W	E	35	9	253	150
Apr.	1,013	22	13	42	5	11.1	67	17	122	0	3	59	7	11	E	E	31	5	261	133
May	1,013	25	17	43	6	14.9	70	9	86	0	2	86	8	11	E	E	20	2	285	153
June	1,015	28	20	48	12	18.2	70	2	9	0	1	7	6	10	E	E	38	8	303	164
July	1,014	32	22	49	15	20.0	69	0	5	0	0	4	5	8	E	E	39	7	369	181
Aug.	1,013	32	23	50	16	20.3	67	1	5	0	0	4	4	9	E	E	44	3	360	154
Sept.	1,015	30	21	46	13	19.4	70	14	143	0	3	72	4	7	E	E	48	9	285	149
Oct.	1,015	26	17	40	7	15.7	69	41	320	0	4	98	4	9	E	E	49	12	241	136
Nov.	1,016	22	12	36	2	10.4	67	30	128	0	4	57	6	8	W	W	41	20	222	119
Dec.	1,017	17	8	28	0	6.6	69	19	93	0	4	73	7	9	W	W	28	13	209	120
Annual	1,015	24	15	50	−3	12.8	67	183	489	94	31	98	6	10	−	−	36	9	3,255	1,716
Rec. (yrs.)	30	30	30	30	30	10	10	30	30	30	30	30							6	15

TABLE XXIV

CLIMATIC TABLE FOR RABAT, MOROCCO
Latitude 34°03'N, longitude 6°40'W, elevation 75 m

Month	M.s.l. press. (mbar)	Temperature (°C)				Relat. humid. (%)		Precipitation					Wind			Averages		
		mean		extreme		06h	12h	mean (mm)	max. (mm)	min. (mm)	days ≥0.1 mm	max. in 24 h (mm)	av. speed (m/sec)	preval. direct.	calm (%)	cloud-iness[1] (tenths)	sun-shine (h)	number of gales ≥16 m/sec
		max.	min.	max.	min.													
Jan.	1,010	17	9	29	2	91	73	66	194	21	9	56	2.6	S–W	26	4.4	166	2
Feb.	1,010	18	9	36	1	91	70	64	183	2	8	40	3.2	W	22	4.5	185	2
Mar.	1,007	19	10	34	4	92	70	66	227	7	10	42	3.7	W	14	4.6	221	2
Apr.	1,006	20	11	33	6	92	66	43	153	9	7	151	4.0	W–N	10	4.1	263	1
May	1,006	23	14	39	8	91	66	28	34	0	6	23	3.6	NW	14	4.0	298	<1
June	1,006	26	16	41	10	92	67	8	31	0	2	23	3.6	NW	16	3.9	300	<1
July	1,006	26	17	40	12	93	67	<1	4	0	<1	10	3.5	NW	20	2.6	336	<1
Aug.	1,005	27	18	44	13	93	66	1	21	0	<1	21	3.3	NW	21	2.9	318	<1
Sept.	1,006	26	17	40	11	93	65	1	60	0	2	38	3.4	NW	19	3.4	268	<1
Oct.	1,007	24	14	36	6	88	62	49	144	0	6	55	3.3	N–W	19	3.5	231	<1
Nov.	1,008	20	11	29	4	88	67	84	212	0	9	69	3.1	W–S	21	4.5	184	3
Dec.	1,010	17	9	26	2	90	71	86	263	12	10	54	3.2	W–S	25	4.4	170	4
Annual	1,007	22	13	44	1	91	67	496	808	259	70	151	3.4	—	19	3.9	2,840	14
Rec. (yrs.)	20							20	20	20	20	20			20			

[1] Mean of 06h00, 12h00 and 18h00.

TABLE XXV

CLIMATIC TABLE FOR GAFSA, TUNISIA
Latitude 34°25'N, longitude 8°49'E, elevation 313 m

Month	Temperature (°C)				Humidity		Precipitation					Wind					Averages	
	mean		extreme		dew point (°C)	relat. (%)	mean (mm)	max. (mm)	min. (mm)	days ≥0.1 mm	max. in 24 h (mm)	av. speed (knots)	preval. direct.[1]		calm[1] (%)		sun-shine (h)	evap. (mm)
	max.	min.	max.	min.														
Jan.	14	4	25	−6	2.9	68	15	76	0	3	50	5					211	98
Feb.	17	5	29	−4	3.2	62	14	55	0	3	21	5					224	119
Mar.	20	8	37	1	5.2	56	20	94	0	4	38	5	NE	NE	5	8	249	170
Apr.	24	11	35	3	7.5	54	18	82	0	3	48	6					258	188
May	28	15	40	8	11.0	51	11	47	0	2	28	6					315	263
June	34	19	45	11	13.1	44	6	37	0	1	33	5	NE	SE	4	9	307	308
July	37	21	44	15	14.3	41	2	27	0	1	20	5					366	362
Aug.	36	22	46	16	16.6	48	6	50	0	1	38	5					359	325
Sept.	32	19	42	11	15.7	54	12	36	0	2	36	5	NE	SW	15	15	286	234
Oct.	26	15	39	5	13.2	65	21	126	0	3	67	4					245	167
Nov.	20	9	30	−1	8.3	68	20	78	0	3	34	4					219	115
Dec.	15	5	25	−4	4.9	72	15	54	0	3	30	4	NE	SW	13	10	213	90
Annual	25	13	46	−6	9.6	57	160	289	71	29	67	5					3,252	2,449
Rec. (yrs.)	30	30	30	30	10	10	30	30	30	30	30	10	10		10		10	15

[1] First column mean of 00h00 and 06h00; second column mean of 12h00 and 18h00.

TABLE XXXVI

CLIMATIC TABLE FOR SFAX, TUNISIA
Latitude 34°43'N, longitude 10°41'E, elevation 21 m

Month	Temperature (°C)				Humidity		Precipitation					Wind				Aver. evap. (mm)
	mean		extreme		dew point (°C)	relat. (%)	mean (mm)	max. (mm)	min. (mm)	days ≥1mm	max. in 24 h (mm)	av. speed (knots) 06h 12h	preval. direct.[1]	calm[2] (%)	
	max.	min.	max.	min.											
Jan.	16	6	26	−2	4.9	67	18	67	0	3	34	5 8	W V	10 0	110
Feb.	18	7	30	−1	5.4	66	18	87	0	3	47	4 7	W V	10 0	104
Mar.	19	9	35	0	7.5	66	25	112	0	4	49	4 8	N E	28 1	125
Apr.	21	12	32	3	9.7	68	21	118	0	3	71	4 8	N E	28 1	130
May	24	15	39	6	12.2	65	12	44	0	3	34	4 7	N E	28 1	160
June	28	19	43	11	15.4	63	5	49	0	1	41	4 7	N E	40 3	184
July	30	20	47	14	17.6	61	1	17	0	0	3	3 7	N E	40 3	195
Aug.	31	21	47	15	19.2	65	5	90	0	1	65	2 7	N E	40 3	191
Sept.	29	20	42	14	18.7	70	26	120	0	3	95	3 6	W V	18 0	154
Oct.	26	17	36	8	15.5	71	38	144	0	4	51	3 6	W V	18 0	127
Nov.	22	12	32	3	10.6	69	26	147	0	4	88	4 6	W V	18 0	109
Dec.	18	8	28	−1	6.8	69	15	51	0	3	37	4 7	W V	10 0	107
Annual	23	14	47	−2	12.0	67	210	391	93	32	95	4 7			1,696
Rec. (yrs.)	30	30	30	30	8	8	30	30	30	30	30	10 10	10 10	10	5

[1] First column: 00h00–08h00; second column: 12h00–18h00. V = variable.
[2] Double values mean that the first holds for 06h00, the second for 12h00.

TABLE XXVII

CLIMATIC TABLE FOR OUJDA, MOROCCO

Latitude 34°47'N, longitude 1°56'W, elevation 470 m

Month	Mean sta. press. (mbar)	Temperature (°C)				Relative humidity (%)		Precipitation					Wind			Averages	
		mean		extreme		06h	12h	mean (mm)	max. (mm)	min. (mm)	days ≥1mm	max. in 24 h (mm)	av. speed (m/sec)	preval. direct.	calm (%)	cloudiness[1] (tenths)	number of gales ≥16 m/ sec
		max.	min.	max.	min.												
Jan.	964	16	5	25	—5	83	65	43	110	1	7	57	3.4	W	37	4.2	4
Feb.	963	17	5	33	—4	76	55	31	109	0	7	70	3.5	W	32	4.3	5
Mar.	966	19	7	32	—2	85	55	52	176	0	9	59	4.0	W	32	4.4	5
Apr.	960	25	8	31	1	86	54	45	133	<1	8	66	3.3	N	33	4.5	2
May	961	25	11	37	3	85	51	31	122	<1	6	53	3.3	N	32	3.8	1
June	962	28	14	42	8	84	49	15	48	0	5	29	3.5	N	30	3.4	2
July	962	33	17	43	10	75	39	4	13	0	2	13	3.6	N	30	1.9	1
Aug.	961	33	18	41	10	78	42	1	23	0	1	13	3.5	N	32	2.4	1
Sept.	962	31	16	41	8	80	43	13	80	<1	4	56	3.2	N	34	3.1	2
Oct.	963	25	11	34	0	85	50	15	80	tr.	5	52	2.9	N–W	40	3.6	2
Nov.	963	19	8	30	0	85	54	29	120	tr.	8	51	3.0	W	44	3.9	3
Dec.	963	16	6	26	—3	82	59	58	117	6	10	63	4.3	W	34	4.0	7
Annual	962	24	10	43	—5	82	51	337	570	110	72	70	3.5	—	34	3.6	3
Rec. (yrs.)	21							30	30	30	30	30			21		

[1] Mean of 06h00, 12h00 and 18h00.

TABLE XXVIII

CLIMATIC TABLE FOR BISKRA, ALGERIA

Latitude 34°51′N, longitude 5°44′E, elevation 122 m

Month	M.s.l. press.[1] (mbar)	Temperature (°C) mean max.	min.	extreme max.	min.	Relative humidity (%) 07h	13h	Precipitation mean (mm)	max. (mm)	min. (mm)	days ≥0.1 mm	max. in 24 h (mm)	Wind av. speed (km/h)	preval. direct.	cloud- iness (oktas)	Averages sun- shine (h/day)	evap. (mm/ day)
Jan.	1,009	16	6	24	−1	69	52	13	79	0	4	13	2.2	NW	2	7.1	3.0
Feb.	1,009	18	8	28	0	62	44	11	92	0	3	19	2.3	NW	3	8.4	3.7
Mar.	1,006	22	11	31	1	58	40	19	82	0	5	60	2.4	NW	3	9.2	5.4
Apr.	1,005	26	14	33	6	47	32	15	50	0	2	23	2.4	NW	3	10.1	7.0
May	1,003	31	19	40	8	47	32	9	59	0	3	24	2.3	NW	2	10.9	9.1
June	1,004	36	24	46	16	42	27	4	48	0	2	38	2.1	SE	2	11.1	11.3
July	1,005	40	27	48	20	36	20	1	10	0	1	6	1.9	SE	1	12.2	12.4
Aug.	1,004	39	26	49	19	38	25	6	48	0	1	9	1.9	SE	1	11.2	11.6
Sept.	1,006	35	23	43	12	50	24	17	124	0	3	46	2.2	SE	2	10.6	8.9
Oct.	1,007	28	17	38	8	57	39	18	66	0	3	53	2.1	NW	2	8.6	5.9
Nov.	1,008	21	12	30	2	64	45	19	90	0	4	69	2.3	NW	3	7.1	3.8
Dec.	1,008	17	7	27	−1	69	49	16	54	0	3	20	2.4	NW	2	6.8	2.8
Annual	1,002	27	16	49	−1	53	37	148	299	31	34	69	2.2	−	2	9.5	7.1
Rec. (yrs.)	15							30	30	30	30	10			10	4	9

[1] Mean of 06h00, 12h00 and 18h00.

TABLE XXIX

CLIMATIC TABLE FOR TANGIER, MOROCCO
Latitude 35°43′N, longitude 50°54′W, elevation 15m

Month	Temperature (°C)				Relative humidity (%)		Precipitation					Wind				Average cloudiness (tenths)	
	mean		extreme		06h	12h	mean (mm)	max. (mm)	min. (mm)	days ≥1 mm	max. in 24 h (mm)	av. speed (m/sec) 06h 12h	preval. direct.	calm[1] (%)	06h	12h
	max.	min.	max.	min.												
Jan.	16	9	23	−1	88	73	114	304	22	10	104	5 7	E	14	3.9	4.8
Feb.	17	9	25	0	86	70	106	208	11	10	109	5 7	E	10	3.8	4.8
Mar.	18	11	26	3	86	70	120	229	7	10	84	5 8	E	15	4.5	5.0
Apr.	20	12	28	4	86	67	90	187	9	8	111	5 8	E,W	14	4.2	4.4
May	23	14	31	8	85	64	42	72	1	5	49	5 8	E,W	16	3.8	3.7
June	26	17	36	10	85	62	15	39	0	3	94	5 8	E,W	15	3.5	2.9
July	29	19	39	11	85	60	1	2	0	<1	7	4 8	E,W	18	2.2	1.3
Aug.	29	19	39	14	84	60	1	11	0	<1	5	4 8	E,W	18	2.4	1.4
Sept.	28	18	31	11	87	63	23	66	0	3	81	4 7	E	11	3.3	3.0
Oct.	24	16	32	7	84	62	99	193	0	8	112	5 7	E	22	3.1	3.6
Nov.	20	12	28	3	84	67	147	269	24	10	96	5 7	E	22	3.7	4.7
Dec.	17	10	24	2	87	72	137	374	33	10	122	6 7	E	20	3.9	5.0
Annual	22	14	39	−1	86	66	895	1,249	439	78	122	5 7	—	16	3.5	3.7
Rec. (yrs.)	10	10	10	10	10	10	35	18	18	7	24	10 10	10	19	10	10

[1] Mean of 06h00, 12h00 and 18h00

TABLE XXX

CLIMATIC TABLE FOR ORAN, ALGERIA
Latitude 35°44'N, longitude 0°39'W, elevation 11 m

Month	M.s.l. press. (mbar)	Temperature (°C) mean		Temperature (°C) extreme		Dew point (°C)		Precipitation					Wind				Averages		
		max.	min.	max.	min.	07h	13h	mean (mm)	max. (mm)	min. (mm)	days >1 mm	max. in 24 h (mm)	av. speed (m/sec)	preval. direct.[1]	calm (%) 07h 13h		cloud-iness (oktas) 13h	sun-shine (h)	number of gales >Be 8
Jan.	1,019	16	9	26	1	7.6	9.3	70	163	0	8	63	2	SW	54	28	4	173	0
Feb.	1,019	17	10	28	3	7.5	9.2	54	175	0	6	81	4	SW	48	12	4	183	0.4
Mar.	1,016	18	11	30	6	8.8	10.3	35	124	2	4	25	3	SW	42	5	3	251	0.2
Apr.	1,015	21	13	34	7	10.2	11.5	33	110	1	3	30	4	SW N	54	5	3	258	0.4
May	1,015	23	16	31	9	11.1	14.0	19	81	0	4	33	4	SW N	46	3	3	312	0
June	1,016	25	18	38	14	16.2	17.1	7	32	0	1	20	5	SW N	39	1	3	300	0
July	1,015	28	21	38	17	18.7	20.4	1	8	0	<1	5	5	SW N	38	0	2	343	0
Aug.	1,014	29	22	41	18	19.4	21.0	3	23	0	<1	23	4	SW N	60	1	2	340	0.2
Sept.	1,016	27	20	36	13	17.4	19.5	16	67	0	2	27	3	SW N	68	0	2	278	0
Oct.	1,017	23	16	37	11	14.1	16.2	43	168	0	3	43	3	SW N	71	6	3	238	0
Nov.	1,018	19	13	29	7	11.9	12.1	46	125	0	6	70	3	SW	60	15	4	169	0.2
Dec.	1,018	17	9	26	2	8.2	9.7	67	199	2	7	52	2	SW	51	21	4	160	0
Annual	1,016	22	15	41	1	13.3	14.8	394	554	288	44	81	3	—	53	8	3	3,005	1
Rec. (yrs.)	30	25	25	25	25	25	25	30	30	30	14	15	5	5	5	5	26	10	5

[1] The two values indicate measurements at 07h00 and 13h00.

TABLE XXXI

CLIMATIC TABLE FOR SETIF, ALGERIA
Latitude 36°11'E, longitude 5°25'E, elevation 1,080 m

Month	Mean sta. press.[1] (mbar)	Temperature (°C)				Relative humidity (%)		Precipitation					Wind		Averages	
		mean		extreme		07h	13h	mean (mm)	max. (mm)	min. (mm)	days ≥0.1 mm	max. in 24 h (mm)	av. speed (Be)	preval. direct.	cloud-iness (tenths)	sun-shine (h/day)
		max.	min.	max.	min.											
Jan.	901	9	1	21	−7	86	66	60	288	1	12	88	2.9	NW	5.4	5.3
Feb.	901	11	1	24	−6	86	57	45	82	3	10	10	3.1	NW	5.5	6.8
Mar.	900	14	3	26	−6	78	52	43	102	<1	10	47	3.1	NW	5.5	7.3
Apr.	899	18	6	29	−2	70	40	36	109	4	9	38	3.1	NW	4.6	8.3
May	900	22	9	33	−2	69	43	51	102	1	8	31	2.9	NE	4.6	10.1
June	903	28	13	38	3	64	34	28	104	1	6	36	2.9	NE	3.7	10.1
July	904	33	17	41	7	56	26	11	27	<1	3	14	2.7	NE	2.1	11.8
Aug.	903	32	17	39	8	56	26	14	120	1	4	26	2.8	NE	2.4	10.4
Sept.	904	27	14	37	5	71	36	37	110	1	7	46	2.7	NE	3.7	9.0
Oct.	903	21	9	30	−1	80	47	39	163	5	8	61	2.8	NW	4.3	7.0
Nov.	902	14	4	26	−3	83	65	53	102	6	11	34	2.8	NW	5.6	5.5
Dec.	901	10	1	21	−9	88	66	52	161	12	12	46	2.8	NW	6.3	4.9
Annual	902	20	8	41	−9	74	47	469	636	265	100	73	2.9	—	4.4	8.1
Rec. (yrs.)	30	26	26	26	26	26	26	30	30	30	30	10			10	5

[1] Mean of 06h00 and 12h00.

TABLE XXXII

CLIMATIC TABLE FOR SOUK EL ARBA, TUNISIA
Latitude 36°29'N, longitude 08°48'E, elevation 143 m

Month	Temperature (°C)				Humidity		Precipitation					Wind					Averages	
	mean		extreme		dew point (°C)	relat. (%)	mean (mm)	max. (mm)	min. (mm)	days ≥1 mm	max. in 24 h (mm)	av. speed[1] (knots)	preval. direct.[2]		calm[2] (%)		sun-shine (h)	evap. (mm)
	max.	min.	max.	min.														
Jan.	15	5	25	−4	6.0	79	65	196	4	11	49	2.9					160	70
Feb.	16	5	31	−4	6.1	75	49	145	3	8	36	2.9					177	79
Mar.	19	6	36	−5	7.8	74	47	144	5	9	36	2.9	W	NW	55	20	222	74
Apr.	22	8	36	0	10.7	75	45	124	8	8	45	3.0					218	104
May	26	12	43	3	13.0	68	33	90	2	6	48	3.2					290	162
June	33	16	48	4	15.5	58	16	91	0	4	58	3.2	NW	NW	62	20	323	245
July	37	18	49	10	15.5	48	3	17	0	1	14	3.3					387	319
Aug.	37	19	52	12	17.0	51	10	36	0	2	25	3.6					338	315
Sept.	33	17	46	9	16.4	60	33	165	3	5	61	2.5	SW	NW	50	40	265	221
Oct.	26	13	39	5	14.2	72	56	143	0	7	85	2.5					212	124
Nov.	20	9	32	−1	10.3	77	47	110	8	9	45	2.2					163	84
Dec.	16	6	27	−4	7.8	80	73	244	4	11	50	2.9	SW	NW	48	37	148	72
Annual	25	11	52	−5	11.7	68	477	709	255	81	85	2.9					2,903	1,869
Rec. (yrs.)	30	30	30	30	9	9	30	30	30	30	30	10	10		10		10	21

[1] Mean of 06h00, 12h00 and 18h00.
[2] First column mean of 00h and 06h; second column mean of 12h and 18h.

TABLE XXXIII

CLIMATIC TABLE FOR ALGIERS, ALGERIA
Latitude 36°46'N, longitude 3°03'E, elevation 60 m

Month	M.s.l. press. (mbar)	Temperature (°C) mean max.	mean min.	extreme max.	extreme min.	Dew point 07h (°C)	Precipitation mean (mm)	max. (mm)	min. (mm)	days ≥1 mm	max. 24 h (mm)	Wind[1] av. speed (m/sec)	preval. direct.	calm (%)	Averages cloud-iness[2] (oktas)	sun-shine (h)	radi-ation (Ly/day)	evap. (mm)
Jan.	1,018	15	9	24	1	7.4	116	245	6	11	56	3	W	23	6	141	185	58
Feb.	1,018	16	9	20	1	7.4	76	192	3	9	48	3	W	20	4	159	237	61
Mar.	1,016	17	11	29	3	8.2	57	139	11	9	62	3	W	19	4	207	392	81
Apr.	1,015	20	13	37	6	9.8	65	195	6	5	48	3	W	20	4	227	426	86
May	1,015	23	15	38	7	12.9	36	104	0	5	66	3	NE	21	3	300	470	80
June	1,016	27	18	38	13	16.1	14	78	0	2	22	3	NE	23	3	301	553	85
July	1,015	28	21	41	17	18.7	2	21	0	<1	9	3	NE	20	2	353	545	94
Aug.	1,014	29	22	42	18	19.4	4	76	0	<1	26	3	NE	25	2	324	486	99
Sept.	1,016	27	21	39	12	18.1	27	73	0	4	73	2	NE	34	3	268	405	88
Oct.	1,017	23	17	38	7	14.1	84	350	7	7	59	3	W	24	4	197	263	81
Nov.	1,017	19	13	31	4	10.5	93	284	13	11	147	3	W	22	4	153	185	67
Dec.	1,018	16	11	24	0	7.7	117	281	30	12	119	3	W	21	5	146	145	62
Annual	1,016	22	15	42	0	13.1	641	1,087	500	76	147	3	—	23	4	2,776	360	937
Rec. (yrs.)	30	25	25	25	25	25	30			17	17	10	10	10	25		3	

[1] Mean of 07h00 and 17h00 local time.
[2] Mean of 07h00 and 13h00 local time.

TABLE XXXIV

CLIMATIC TABLE FOR TUNIS, TUNISIA
Latitude 36°50'N, longitude 10°14'E, elevation 3 m

Month	M.s.l. press. (mbar)	Temperature (°C) mean max.	mean min.	extreme max.	extreme min.	Humidity dew point (°C)	relat. (%)	Precipitation mean (mm)	max. (mm)	min. (mm)	days ≥1mm	max. in 24 h	Wind av. speed[1] (knots)	preval. direct.	calm[2] (%)	Averages sun-shine (h)	radi-ation (Ly/day)	evap. (mm)
Jan.	1,016	15	7	24	0	7.6	81	70	177	4	13	63	5	W	14	161	194	78
Feb.	1,016	16	8	30	0	7.8	78	47	130	4	9	101	5	W	14	166	253	80
Mar.	1,015	18	9	35	0	9.4	77	43	104	3	9	37	4	W V	30 3	202	361	97
Apr.	1,015	21	11	32	3	11.9	77	42	131	3	7	60	5	W V	30 3	239	476	109
May	1,014	23	14	40	7	13.5	72	23	96	0	5	41	5	W V	30 3	299	579	157
June	1,015	29	18	41	12	17.3	69	10	66	0	3	52	5	W NE	40 2	319	630	190
July	1,015	32	20	46	15	19.1	67	1	7	0	1	6	5	W NE	40 2	379	630	221
Aug.	1,014	32	21	47	11	20.2	69	11	47	0	2	34	5	W NE	40 2	351	566	209
Sept.	1,016	29	20	43	13	19.3	74	37	155	0	5	81	4	W	22	259	452	152
Oct.	1,015	25	16	37	7	16.0	77	52	215	2	8	83	4	W	22	205	313	112
Nov.	1,015	20	12	31	3	12.5	81	57	234	15	10	62	4	W	22	174	226	83
Dec.	1,015	16	8	25	2	8.7	80	68	276	2	13	134	4	W	14	153	176	80
Annual	1,015	23	14	47	0	13.6	75	461	913	248	85	134	5	—	—	2,907	405	1,568
Rec. (yrs.)	30	30	30	30	30	10	10	30	30	30	30	30	10	10	10	30	3	5

[1] Mean of 06h00, 12h00 and 18h00.
[2] Figures for March–August are percentages at 06h00 and 12h00 respectively.

Chapter 3

The Northern Desert (Sahara)

J. F. GRIFFITHS AND K. H. SOLIMAN[1]

Introduction

The name "Sahara" is derived from an Arabic word meaning "wilderness", an apt term that is applied here to zone II although, in strict geographical sense, the zone includes other areas beyond the Sahara, such as the Nubian, the Western and the western side of the Arabian deserts (west of the Red Sea). The whole area is one of extreme aridity and is the world's largest desert, stretching about 4,500 km from west to east and 1,500 km from north to south. This "negative" region has little potential for development, save perhaps oil, and thus, throughout historical times, has formed a vast and very effective barrier between the Mediterranean cultures of the Hamitic and Semitic peoples and the Sudanese culture of the negro race. Not all of the zone is true desert, on some high areas, such as the Ahaggar and Tibesti plateaus, there is enough rainfall to support an open grassland and a sparse, nomadic population.

It is likely that any chosen limitation of the area would be open to criticism and discussion for, except at the coastal boundaries, the desert shades almost imperceptibly into the semi-arid regions. The boundaries that have been chosen for this text are: (*1*) in the north, the 125-mm isohyet; (*2*) in the south, the isopleth $R < 5T$, where R is the mean annual rainfall (inches) and T is the mean annual temperature (°F).

The northern boundary is chosen because, with irrigation and good management, many areas of very low rainfall have been made to support crops and a moderate density of population; it is hardly a "wilderness". The southern boundary follows the suggestion of MILLER (1961) based on a world study of deserts and can be said to correspond, roughly, to the 400-mm isohyet. Since a desert is attributed, strictly, to a (rainfall–evaporation) relationship and not directly to rainfall it is clear that, over a latitudinal change of some 20°, boundary definitions will alter. A popular misconception is that the Sahara Desert (and, for that matter, most deserts) is a region of soft sands. In fact the "erg", or sandy desert, occupies only about 15% of this zone, the remainder being either "reg" (stony desert) or "hammada" (rocky desert). These types originate from the weathering of the rocks and dispersion of the particles. It is presently believed that the desert landscape is due to weathering occurring in past ages when the zone was more humid than it is now.

With such a vast area, about 10 million km², it is convenient to study various sections separately and four sub-divisions have been chosen, namely, the United Arab Republic,

---

[1] Dr. K. H. Soliman is the author of the section "The climate of the United Arab Republic", p. 79.

the Sudan, Libya, southern Algeria and the southern Saharan republics (Mauritania, Mali, Niger and Chad).

General pressure distribution and wind circulation[1]

The whole of this arid zone is characterised by the general absence of moist air masses. Although the zone has some long boundaries with the sea it rarely experiences the wind patterns necessary to bring the moist air over the land. Of course, the mere presence of moist air is not sufficient, by itself, to produce precipitation, there is need for some extra, triggering mechanism, such as topographic ascent, convection or frontal (or convergence) activity. It must not be inferred that, because the air masses over the Sahara have generally low relative humidity, there is little moisture in the air. In fact, air with a 30% relative humidity at 40°C contains more water vapour (absolute humidity) than saturated air at 19°C, while saturated air at 5°C has an absolute humidity equivalent to only 9% relative humidity at 45°C.

The northern and southern edges of the Sahara show very different annual distributions of their scanty rainfall, the former having winter period rains the latter having summer rains. Therefore, it is convenient to consider two distinct plus two intermediate seasons when discussing the climatic causes. The seasons will be referred to as the winter season (December–February), the summer season (June–September), the advancing I.T.C.Z. season (March–May) and the retreating I.T.C.Z. season (October–November). The terms winter and summer are justifiable in this zone (mainly north of 15°N) since thermal seasons are well in evidence.

Winter season

At this period six important features can be identified, each of which can play a significant role in the weather over the northern desert:
(*1*) the Sahara high, an extension of the Azores anticyclone;
(*2*) the Arabian high, another part of the sub-tropical high pressure belt;
(*3*) the Balkan high in conjunction with the great anticyclone over central Asia;
(*4*) a low pressure area over the central and eastern Mediterranean;
(*5*) the equatorial trough over central Africa;
(*6*) the I.T.C.Z.
As can be seen from Fig.1, the only winds affecting the area that give rise to air mass trajectories over a sea surface sufficient to impart significant amounts of water are along the northern boundary and on the Red Sea coast. The other parts of the zone are influenced by the large scale subsidence caused by the Saharan high, a condition giving rise to dynamically heated, desiccated air. In the northern section DUBIEF (1943) identifies incidence of rainfall at this season with either cyclonic perturbations of a Mediterranean or a Saharan source or, rarely, a combination of both. The difference between the two types is mainly whether their trajectory commences at or passes north or south of the Atlas Mountains. This situation has been described earlier while the incidence of break-away de-

---

[1] After BHALOTRA (1963).

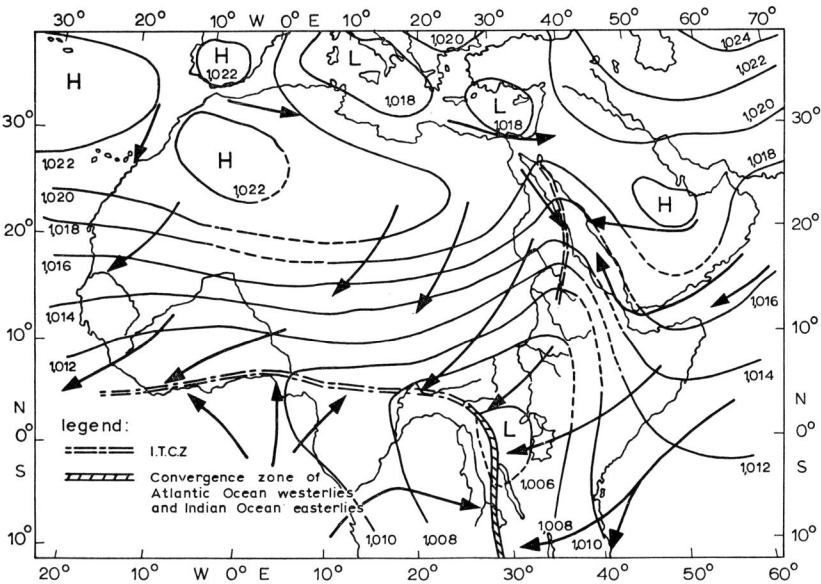

Fig.1. Mean daily pressure pattern (mbar) and air flow for January.

pressions in the Red Sea (which, on average, bring only a little rain) is discussed in Chapter 4. It must be noted that these occasions can sometimes give rise to intense falls of 100–150 mm/day.

Summer season

At this season (Fig.2), an approximate inverse of the winter situation, the main features are: (*1*) a low over the Arabian Peninsula; (*2*) a low over the southern Sahara; (3) the high pressure ridge over central Africa; (*4*) the I.T.C.Z.

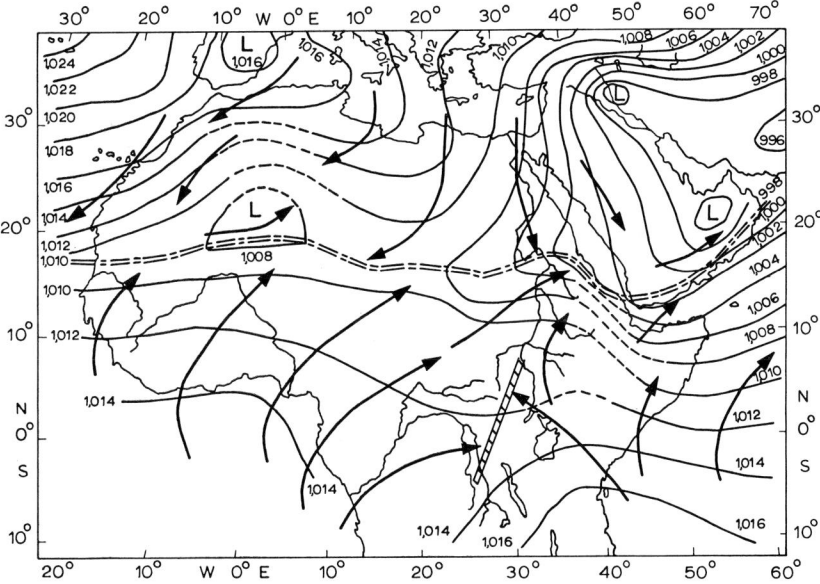

Fig.2. Mean daily pressure pattern (mbar) and air flow for July (legend see Fig.1).

The wind circulation is now such that air masses reaching most of the Sahara have experienced reasonably long trajectories over the sea. However, the extremely high temperatures over the land at this time bring about a reduction in the relative humidity and a corresponding need for greater impetus (ascending currents) before rainfall results. This is especially true in the north where the Mediterranean, although warm, cannot give either a sufficient trajectory to the south-flowing air mass or an adequate temperature rise compared with the air masses entering the zone from the south, over the southern Atlantic Ocean. The source region of moist air penetrating from the sub-tropical anticyclone in the Indian Ocean hardly affects this zone. The earlier cooling of the area to the south, due to the wide belt of clouds often associated with the I.T.C.Z. and the intense convective activity (either isolated or mesoscale or of the "line storm" type), combine to give the summertime showers so characteristic of the southern Sahara. It must be noted that some of the stations in the north (especially mountain areas) can experience summer falls for reasons obvious from Fig.2 and detailed above.

Intermediate

These seasons are transitional between the two definite periods described earlier. They have many similarities to each other, as is evident from a comparison of Fig.3 and 4, but they exhibit some interesting and significant differences. In general, the northward movement of the I.T.C.Z. tends to be slower than the southward movement. Because of this the southern Sahara generally records the highest temperatures immediately before the onset of the rains, for long periods of cloudless skies, and the resultant intense insolation, precede the I.T.C.Z. Of course, from the point of view of human comfort, the slightly cooler, much more humid, periods may be the more exhausting. At the "advancing" season duststorms, mirages and dust devils are of common occurrence.

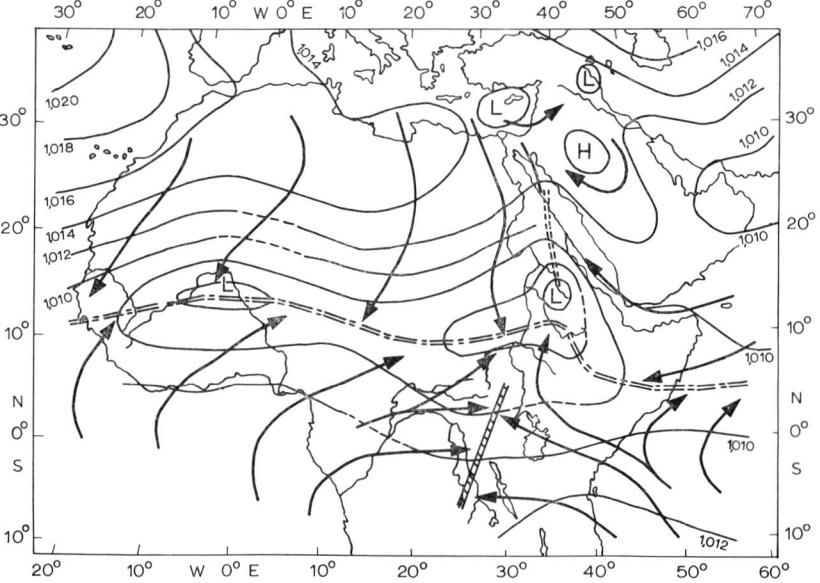

Fig.3. Mean daily pressure pattern (mbar) and air flow for April (legend see Fig.1).

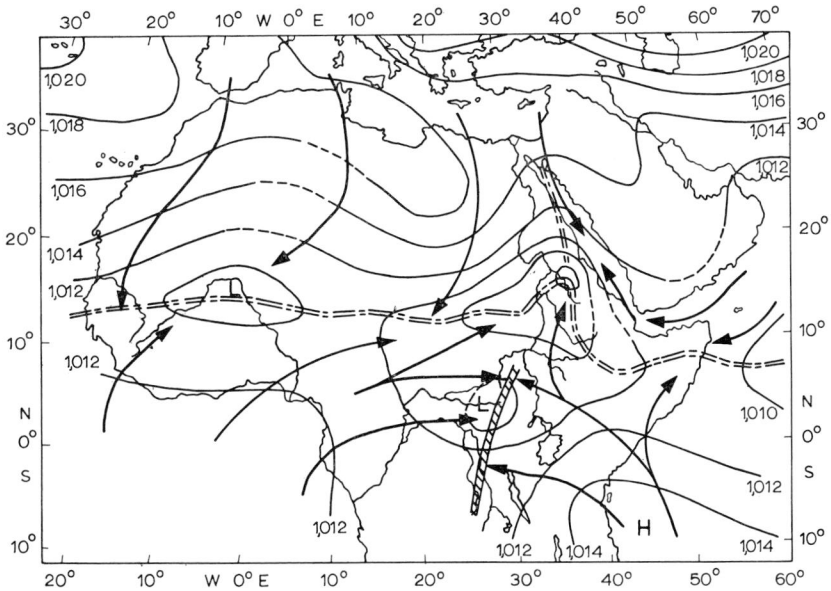

Fig.4. Mean daily pressure pattern (mbar) and air flow for October (legend see Fig.1).

The climate of the United Arab Republic

Introduction

The United Arab Republic occupies the extreme northeastern corner of Africa and has the continent's only land border with Asia. The country covers about one million km² but so much is desert that the inhabited and cultivated territory is less than 4% of this total. The population is more than 30 million and the country has the two largest cities in Africa, Cairo (about 4.5 million) and Alexandria (about 2 million). The chief exports are centred around cotton and textiles but rice, fruit and vegetables are also important.

Causes of the climate

The climate of Egypt is determined basically by the following factors:
(*1*) The semi-permanent pressure systems in each season, such as the cold Siberian anti-cyclone in winter, the heat lows of Africa in spring and autumn, and the huge low over southwest Asia in summer. These systems are air mass source regions in their respective season.
(*2*) The travelling depressions and associated weather in winter and the transitional seasons.
(*3*) The Mediterranean and, to a much lesser extent, the Red Sea as sources of water vapour, in addition to their being positive or negative thermal sources (warm surface to cold polar air masses and cool surface to tropical masses). The Mediterranean has a pronounced influence on the northern areas (Lower Egypt) but the effect of the sea diminishes to a large extent towards Upper Egypt.
(*4*) Orography plays a small role in the general climate but has local effects.

The above factors (as well as other minor ones) will be taken into consideration when discussing the climate in each season.

Winter (December–February)

The climate of Lower Egypt is mild with some rain showers, mainly over coastal areas. Upper Egypt is practically rainless with warm sunny days but rather cool nights.

Air masses

The Siberian anticyclone is the source region for genuine Pc air masses. The coldest spells experienced in Egypt are on the arrival of such air masses. The synoptic conditions that favour the invasion of this Pc air occur when a deep depression with tight pressure gradient (usually centred over Cyprus) covers the Mediterranean at the time that the Siberian anticyclone extends westwards to cover the Balkans. The Pc air starts as a northeasterly current in the rear of the depressions over the east Mediterranean but reaches Egypt as a cold northwesterly wind. When, in addition, the Balkans have been covered with snow for a long time, conditions are such that snow, which is practically unknown in the U.A.R., may occur. This situation arises perhaps once in 10 years. The Siberian Pc air mass is generally colder than either Pc air from Europe or the Pm air arriving as northwesterly currents over the Mediterranean.

A source of hot Tc air is the thermal low above the land mass of Africa. This air mass $(Tc)_h$ is much warmer than the Tc air above North Africa. There is a large difference in temperature (amounting to 10–15°C) between the two air masses [$(Tc)_h$ and Tc] from the ground to about 500 mbar (6 km). The two air masses are separated by a quasi-stationary surface of discontinuity, the sub-tropical discontinuity (STD). In this winter season, however, the $(Tc)_h$ air is too far south to be drawn northwards by Mediterranean depressions and therefore rarely affects Egypt in winter (Fig.5A). It will be seen later that this air mass plays an important role in other seasons, when the STD lies further north, within the scope of interaction of moving desert or Mediterranean depressions. It is to be noted that Tm air from the South Atlantic is changed to Tc on its trajectory over North Africa.

Travelling Mediterranean depressions

In winter the Mediterranean becomes the theatre for the consecutive passage of depressions, some of which are single centred and others are complex. They are the main cause of the weather in this season.

In front of these depressions south–southwesterly winds blow across Egypt, with clear skies (only patches of high cloud) and low relative humidity occurring. With the approach of the depressions towards the eastern Mediterranean cold, dry southwesterly winds are experienced. These winds are, in fact, modified polar air, originally from a west–northwesterly direction but they have turned around the centre of the low to blow as southwesterlies over Egypt. This fact makes for a differentiation between the structure of these depressions and those of middle latitudes, where the southwesterlies are warm (forming the warm sector).

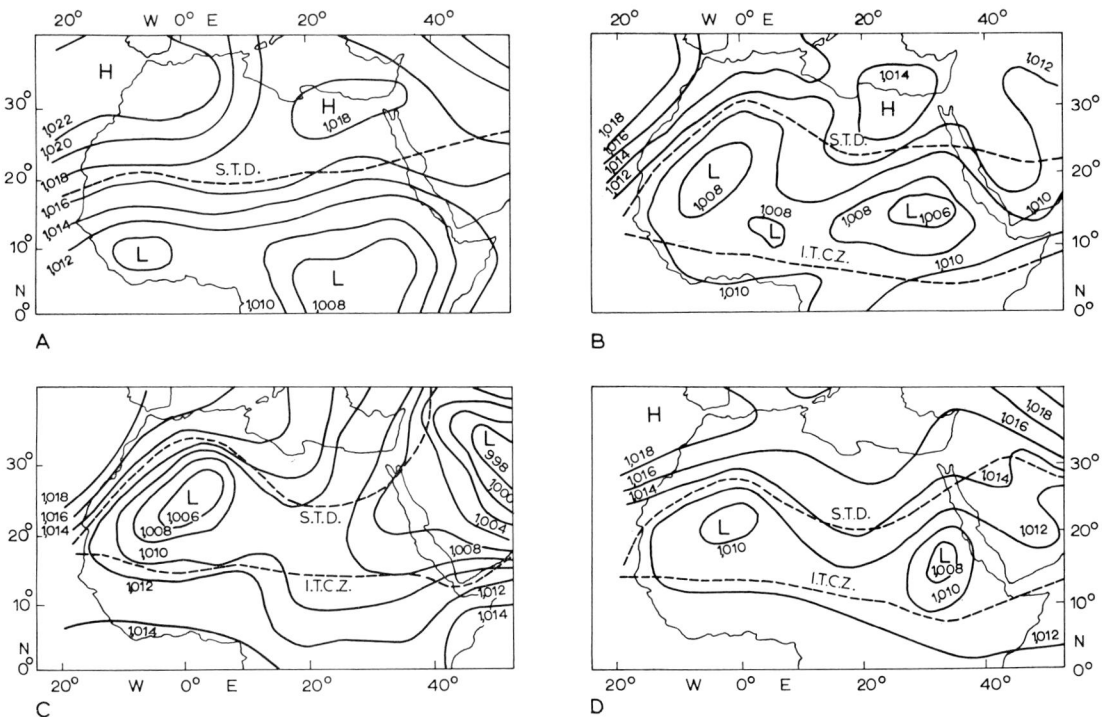

Fig.5. Mean seasonal pressure patterns (mbar). A. winter; B. spring; C. summer; D. autumn.

When the depression reaches the eastern Mediterranean cold, moist, northwesterly winds blow over Egypt and convection clouds appear during the daytime. When an upper cold low or steep trough exists above the depression much cloud and rain result over Lower Egypt by both day and night. The rain is sometimes heavy and accompanied by thunder. The depression may stay an average of two or three days over the eastern Mediterranean during which time Egypt experiences its worst winter weather. The warm Mediterranean waters play an important part in supplying enormous amounts of water vapour to the polar air masses moving south towards Egypt. The process of supplying heat and moisture in the lower layers is continuous and leads to instability and heavy showers. When the depressions are deep the southwest winds may reach gale force and cause severe sandstorms. The north–northwesterly winds in the rear of these depressions may also reach gale force, especially at the coast, but the dust raised is much less than with southwesterly winds.

Mediterranean depressions mainly affect Lower Egypt, Upper Egypt remaining practically untouched. However, the cold northwesterly winds in the rear of depressions over the eastern Mediterranean continue their journey southwards to Upper Egypt and cause both a reduction in the temperature and rising sand; they are not associated with any precipitation.

Between the passage of consecutive depressions high pressure covers the eastern Mediterranean. This situation is responsible for the flow of northeasterly winds over Lower Egypt, a condition that favours the formation of radiation fog in the early morning, dispersing a few hours after sunrise. In extreme Upper Egypt the dryness of the air does not favour such fog formation.

Spring (*March–May*)

The main feature in this season is the southward shift of the tracks of depressions. The centres of the depressions move either along the coast line of North Africa or further south, where they are known as desert or "khamsin" depressions. The average frequency of these latter depressions is three or four per month but may vary between two and six per month. Differentiation between khamsin "depressions" and khamsin "conditions" should be made clear, the latter being the warm, dry, dust laden, southerly winds that usually occur in front of khamsin depressions.

These depressions are smaller in area than the winter Mediterranean depressions and may be associated with more high and medium clouds but much less rain. The depressions can be vigorous and cause severe sandstorms. The sand is raised by the strong southerly winds in front of the depression, especially at the passage of the cold front or even a few hours ahead. When these depressions have become cold upper lows (cut-offs from troughs further north) they are often associated with large amounts of high and medium clouds as well as with thunderstorms which can give very heavy showers of rain and hail. Clouds and precipitation are also attributed to the jet stream, which oscillates in close and intimate relationship with the STD in all seasons, occupying a position a little further to the north.

The role played by the Mediterranean waters in this season in producing instability and supplying moisture to cold air masses is obviously less pronounced than in winter. Many of the rain showers in this season originate from mid-tropospheric instability clouds. This fact explains why some of the showers are characterized by very large water drops, they are actually melted hail. Most of the rain drops evaporate during the 3 km path they usually have to travel from the base of the cumulonimbus cloud to the ground. Some of the thunder clouds do not give more than a beautiful display of lightning that continues for many hours and, perhaps, a few scattered, large rain drops. It is only when thunderstorms have humid air in the lower layers that they yield heavy showers. The moisture in this case is mainly supplied by the Mediterranean waters. Except in its immediate area the Red Sea does not play a role in the aspect of thunderstorms over Egypt because it is enclosed by a high chain of mountains which, however, play a part in the lifting of air masses as well as being a high level heat source.

In spring, as in autumn, the Sudan trough sometimes extends northwards to cover Egypt. The hot, southeasterly current of Arabia turns northeastwards over Egypt and moderate or severe heat waves are then experienced. The air is hot and dry, except in the surface layers where it picks up moisture from the Mediterranean, a feature that sometimes leads to the formation of early morning radiation fog over Lower Egypt. The Sudan trough may extend northward to cover not only the Red Sea but also the east Mediterranean Basin. In such cases there is usually an upper cold trough or low over the eastern Mediterranean area. Thunderstorms which may occur in such situations are due to this cold low aloft. In this season the STD is located appreciably north of its winter position and comes within the field of interaction of the khamsin depressions (Fig.5B). After the formation of the depression the STD experiences northward movement so that the very hot $(Tc)_h$ air forms the warm sector of the depressions. Severe heat waves are then experienced in regions affected by these hot winds. All record maximum temperatures are caused by this $(Tc)_h$ air which is, at the same time, the reason for record low relative humidities (often less than 5%).

When the depression is west of Egypt the eastern Mediterranean is covered by high pressure thereby causing frequent northeasterly winds over Lower Egypt.

Summer (*June–September*)

The spring conditions may extend a week or 10 days into June but afterwards, practically to the end of September, summer conditions prevail. The general climate is hot, dry and rainless. Clear skies prevail, except for some coastal fair weather cumulus or early morning stratus clouds which form over Lower Egypt and disperse a few hours after sunrise. In this season depressions cease to move across Egypt and the weather becomes settled. The steady Etesian winds (north or northwest) blow persistently for they are part of the circulation around the huge Asiatic low centred over northwestern India.

The climate of Lower and Middle Egypt, being affected by the cool Mediterranean waters, is warm during the daytime and rather cool by night. The maximum effect is obviously in coastal areas where the weather is pleasant. As the STD moves further northward in summer extreme Upper Egypt lies to the south of it and experiences a hot, very dry climate (Fig.5C).

In contrast to the spring, heat waves at this season are caused by the westward (not northward) oscillation of the STD. The $(Tc)_h$ air of west Syria and Iraq invades Egypt and very high temperatures are then recorded. When travelling over the Mediterranean this air picks up moisture in the lower layers and becomes most oppressive. Such heat waves are worse than those of spring because, although the temperature may not be as high, there is this increased humidity. Northeasterly winds in this season again favour the formation of early morning fog or very low stratus in Lower Egypt.

Autumn (*October, November*)

The climate in this season is similar to that in spring for it is another transitional season. Khamsin-like depressions begin to cross Egypt during late October and cause a breakdown of the settled summer regime. Early depressions in September are infrequent and usually die out on arriving in Egypt from the west. The depressions at this time are much less vigorous than in spring and are slower in their eastward movement. On the other hand, the higher humidity in this season favours greater frequency of thunderstorms and heavier precipitation, a fact especially true in November.

As in spring northeast winds and early morning radiation fog are frequent. Heat waves are less common and less severe than in spring. This is because the depressions are weaker and, since the STD is further south, the $(Tc)_h$ air is not easily drawn northwards to affect Egypt (Fig.5D).

Radiation

Radiation measurements were only recently begun in the U.A.R. There are two stations, Giza (just south of Cairo) and Tahrir (west of the Nile delta). Table I gives data con-

TABLE I

GLOBAL RADIATION DATA FOR GIZA AND TAHRIR (Ly/day)

	Jan.	Feb.	Mar.	Apr.	May	June	July	Aug.	Sept.	Oct.	Nov.	Dec.
Giza												
Mean	290	375	498	576	635	667	663	610	533	420	319	266
Max. daily	417	510	662	722	754	743	751	714	632	543	410	365
Min. daily	46	85	172	185	109	410	564	457	183	156	123	48
Tahrir												
Mean	293	401	489	568	659	684	682	627	538	413	325	282
Max. daily	404	513	628	715	742	755	747	692	602	497	405	380
Min. daily	52	136	261	196	366	378	606	541	337	231	99	96

The length of record is 10 years at Giza and 3 years at Tahrir.

cerning the global radiation at these two stations. The difference between the mean values at the stations is rather small since, unfortunately, they are only about 100 km apart and lie in the same climatic region.

Sunshine

The U.A.R. lies in the sub-tropical high pressure belt, with clear skies for most of the time, so that sunshine recorders have only been installed in Lower Egypt, an area with a reasonable amount of cloudiness, especially in the cool season. Table II gives details for seven stations, three along the coast of the Mediterranean, one in the middle of the Nile delta and three in the Cairo area. As the stations are all in the same climatic area variation is quite small. The table shows a marked decrease in the percentage sunshine in November when there is a rather rapid change from the summer regime, with clear skies most of the time, to the relatively cloudy winter regime.

TABLE II

MEAN DAILY PERCENTAGE OF POSSIBLE SUNSHINE

Station	Jan.	Feb.	Mar.	Apr.	May	June	July	Aug.	Sept.	Oct.	Nov.	Dec.
Sallum	67.3	67.6	75.0	67.2	71.7	83.1	90.7	91.7	87.9	85.0	68.9	66.7
Mersa Matruh	62.5	65.8	65.0	70.8	79.7	82.4	87.8	89.5	83.8	77.2	78.3	64.4
Alexandria	69.2	67.6	72.5	73.6	75.9	79.4	87.8	82.7	83.9	81.6	72.6	61.8
Port Said	66.3	69.4	70.0	69.0	75.9	80.1	82.3	84.2	83.9	82.4	79.2	70.6
Qurashya	67.6	70.2	73.3	79.0	81.0	90.0	87.0	85.6	85.4	85.0	76.7	70.6
Cairo (Almaza)	70.5	72.0	74.0	76.0	78.8	81.4	82.7	84.1	84.6	84.2	80.4	73.5
Giza	67.6	77.5	73.3	74.4	81.0	85.0	85.6	84.0	83.7	80.7	77.6	70.6

Cloudiness

As would be expected in a sub-tropical, semi-arid country, the mean monthly total cloud amount does not exceed 4 oktas. The cloudiness is greater in Lower Egypt (especially on the Mediterranean coast) than in Upper Egypt and reaches a maximum in winter and a minimum in the summer. In general there is a noticeable diurnal variation of cloudiness, there being more cloud by day than by night, not only in convective type clouds but also, to some extent, in medium and high clouds. The diurnal variation is rather small in Upper Egypt where the cloud is mainly medium or high.

In summer there is a particular pattern of diurnal variation in Lower Egypt. On many days early morning low stratus forms, especially over places in the Nile delta and the canal zone, frequently reaching 8/8 with a height of 300–600 m. This formation is due to radiation loss and turbulence in the humid, surface layer and usually disperses from two to four hours after sunrise, leaving a clear sky until the next morning.

A recent paper by KHALIL (1968) gives the following division for cloud.

General pattern for most of the year

Maxima occur over: (*1*) an area extending from the northeast coasts to Cairo and which reaches Middle Egypt; (*2*) an area from the northwest coast reaching into the northern part of the western desert.

Minima occur over: (*1*) the north coast, the delta area and into the western desert; (*2*) the eastern desert between the Suez Gulf and the Nile Valley.

Pattern in November, December and sometimes in February, March, June and October

Maxima occur over: (*1*) the northwest coast to Cairo area reaching Middle Egypt; (*2*) the northeast coast to the canal zone.

Minima occur over: (*1*) the delta and eastern desert between Suez and the Nile Valley; (*2*) Cairo, the southwest and Fayoun.

Temperature

A study of the temperature data reveals the following general characteristics:

(*1*) The change from the Mediterranean depressions of the winter to the khamsin depressions of spring causes a rather sudden rise in temperature.

(*2*) The sudden change from the summertime regime to the winter regime, often occurring in late October, gives rise to a very drastic alteration in mean monthly temperatures, maxima, minima and mean.

Mean and absolute maximum temperatures

The highest values of the mean maximum temperature occur in July or August, except in the most southerly part of the country where the combination of high sun and the arrival of hot $(Tc)_h$ air south of the STD leads to a June maximum.

The extreme maximum temperatures exceed 40°C in most places when there is an influx of the $(Tc)_h$ air mass during the period March to October. This fact does not, however, apply in the eastern part of the Mediterranean coast, an area least affected by heat waves. On many occasions the pressure distribution favours this area with cool northeasterly winds from over the Mediterranean while the rest of the country is suffering a severe heat wave.

Mean and absolute minimum temperatures

The lowest minimum temperatures are encountered in winter in the heart of the western desert, approximately in the area between 25°N and 29°N and west of 31°E. This area comprises the oases and that part of the Nile protruding into the western desert near Minya. The intensive nocturnal radiation, under a high pressure cell, is due to clear skies, dry air and a bare, sandy soil. The area is too far south to be affected by the warm Mediterranean and too far north to be influenced by the warm east–northeast winds forming a part of the Sudan trough.

Extreme minima vary greatly with locality and reach between 0°C and –4°C in the Cairo area. Values below –5°C have not been recorded.

Interdiurnal variation of temperature

The mean monthly values vary between 1°C and 3°C in most places. The highest values occur in spring with the alternating hot and cold spells while the lowest values occur in the settled summer months.

In exceptional cases individual daily values may reach 20°C and this usually takes place in coastal areas when the passage of khamsin depressions causes the cool, northerly winds from over the Mediterranean to be replaced by the excessively hot, southerly winds. Similar values occur in the reverse process, after the passage of a cold front.

Precipitation

Nature

Rain in the U.A.R. falls in the form of showers and its amount may vary considerably from year to year in the same place and may also differ widely in two neighbouring localities in the same season or year. Furthermore, owing to the low frequency of occurrence and high intensity of the rain, a single heavy shower may affect the average of a certain locality for many years. For instance, 41 mm of rain fell in Hurghada (a station on the Red Sea) on the 8th November, 1939, yet the station has an annual mean of only 3 mm. The highest values of rainfall in one day occur on the Mediterranean coast (50–100 mm) and decrease southwards to Upper Egypt (5–10 mm). On the other hand the values increase, for the same latitude, for Red Sea stations (30–40 mm) due to the humidity and orographic effects. The highest two values on record during the period 1918–1967 are 120.8 mm at Sallum (November, 1947) and 142 mm at El-Themed in the eastern Sinai (November, 1925).

At all stations it is possible for any month to be almost dry. Alexandria, the rainiest city, may have values as low as 5 mm during the winter months while in other years it may receive over 100 mm in a month. Sallum recorded the highest monthly total, 227.5 mm, in November, 1947. Years of marked rainfall deficiency can cause disastrous effects on the crops along the Mediterranean coastal strip which depend on rain for irrigation.

It should be noted that, owing to the dryness of the air in the warm sector of depressions, warm front rain does not occur and cold front rain forms only a minor part of the total amount and frequency of the precipitation. Cold upper troughs and lows (cut-offs from deep troughs further to the north) are responsible for most of the rain and thunderstorms experienced.

Distribution

The distribution of the mean annual total of rain (Fig.6) shows a maximum over the Mediterranean coast with a rapid decrease inland. The area south of 28°N is practically rainless. This pattern is explained by the fact that most of the rain is associated with upper cold troughs which only affect Lower Egypt, and in particular the coastal areas. The uneven distribution along the coast is explained by the configuration of the coast line. The decrease from 180 mm at Alexandria to only 80 mm at Port Said is very striking.

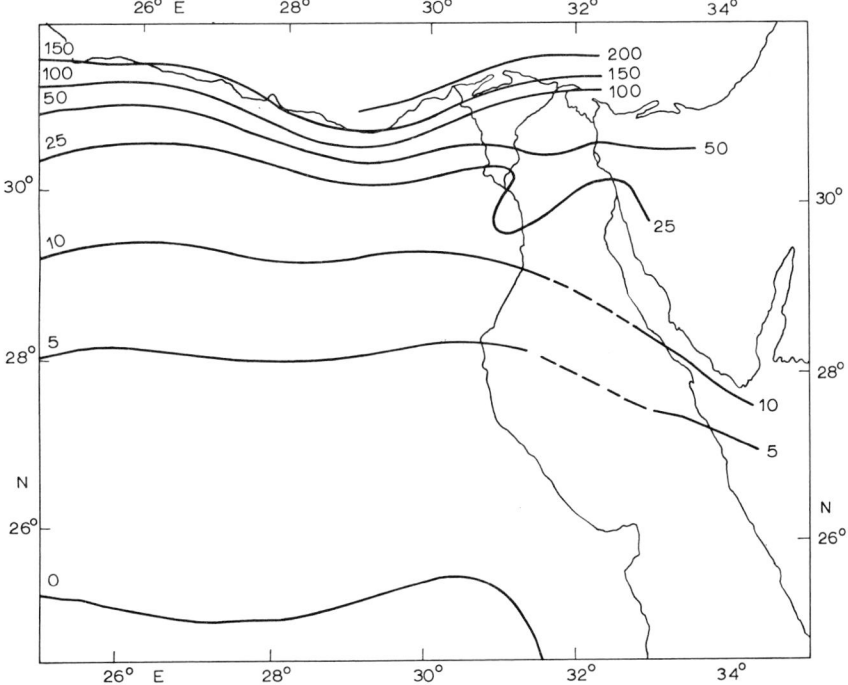

Fig.6. Mean annual rainfall (mm).

Annual variation

Rain occurs in the cold season. In Lower Egypt December and January are the rainiest months, half the annual total falls during these months. In Upper Egypt, in spite of the rarity of rain, May and October represent the rainiest months.

In exceptional cases the conditions of the transitional seasons may occur in summer giving thunderstorms with heavy, squally showers of rain and hail. These abnormal conditions usually occur late in August (early unseasonal autumn conditions) but generally affect only coastal areas and the north of Lower Egypt. Rainfall amounts can reach 10–20 mm and, sometimes, 40 mm.

Diurnal variation

An examination of the diurnal variation curves for Sallum, Mersa Matruh, Alexandria, Port Said and Cairo shows a marked tendency for two maxima, one in the early morning and the other in the afternoon. In Alexandria the early morning maximum is more pronounced than the one of the afternoon, the reverse of the findings for each of the other stations.

Snow

Except for the mountain peaks in Sinai snow is an extremely rare phenomenon in Egypt. It occurs about once in ten years, mainly on the coast, and is very rare inland. In the 50 years 1918–1967 snow fell on six occasions, five in February and one in late January. The localities affected were along the Mediterranean coast, the only inland stations being Suez and Cairo. On the summits of the Sinai Mountains snow falls every year during the period November–April. The depth of snow there may reach 1 m and can remain for a long time.

Thunderstorms

Thunderstorms are most frequent in the area of Alexandria, where an average of seven days of thunderstorms occur every year. This value decreases westwards to 2.5 at Sallum, eastwards to 4 at El-Arish, and southwards to 1.8 at Cairo then further to only 0.1 at Aswan. On the Red Sea coast the average is 1.2. Although the frequency of thunderstorms is small they are sometimes very violent and accompanied by heavy precipitation of rain and hail. The rate of rainfall may be of the order of 2 mm or more per minute. For instance, Cairo has recorded 12 mm in five minutes and Alexandria 30 mm in 15 min.

Diurnal variation of thunderstorms

Thunderstorms show a distinct tendency to occur during certain periods of the day. An examination of the diurnal variation at Sallum, Mersa Matruh, Alexandria and Port Said (coastal stations) and at Cairo and Helwan (inland stations) showed the following facts:

(*1*) All stations exhibit three maxima, the times of which are early morning, afternoon and evening.

(*2*) There is a common minimum of occurrence during the forenoon (08h00–12h00 local time) for all stations.

(*3*) Not all coastal stations show the same pattern, Port Said had a marked maximum in the afternoon while Mersa Matruh had maxima that were nearly equal.

(*4*) Inland stations showed afternoon and evening maxima stronger than the morning value.

Annual variation of thunderstorms

In coastal areas the maximum frequency occurs in November and December while in inland stations and the Red Sea area there are two marked maxima, in October and in May.

Hail

The formation of hail requires certain favourable conditions, such as instability to great heights, violent convection, high moisture and reasonably low temperatures between the cloud base and the ground. It has been mentioned earlier that in the transitional seasons, when the freezing level and the base of the cloud are high and the air below the cloud is warm, the hailstones melt and reach the ground as large scattered water drops.

The most favourable conditions for hail are found over Lower Egypt during late autumn and early winter (November and December). In Upper Egypt hail is an extremely rare phenomenon, occurring only once in Aswan in the period 1918–1967.

The average size of the hail varies between 0.5 and 2 cm in diameter but, in rare cases, the hailstone can reach much larger size. The following are instances of abnormally large hailstones that have been reported in the last 50 years: (*a*) 21st and 22nd October, 1907—Cairo area, diameter 4 cm; (*b*) 21st and 22nd October, 1907—Port Said area, diameter 8 cm; (*c*) October, 1923—Alexandria—large hailstones; (*d*) 8 November, 1966—Cairo area—large hailstones.

The average annual frequency of hail in Lower Egypt is very small at all stations (0.2–0.7) except at Alexandria where it reaches 4.6.

Evaporation

The amount of evaporation is highly dependent upon the station location. Values for a station in a town will be different from those taken only a few kilometres away in the outskirts. The difference will be due mainly to a variation in wind speed. For instance, the mean annual value of evaporation from a Piche instrument located inside the city of Cairo (Ezbakia) is 4.6 mm/day, while at the Cairo Airport the value is 11.2 mm/day. In Table III values are given for certain stations chosen to give representation to different areas.

On the Mediterranean coast the annual variation of mean monthly values is rather small with the highest values occurring in summer. On the Red Sea coast the values are larger, due to the effect of greater wind speed and lower humidities. At inland stations the variation is large, especially in the southernmost areas (south of 27°N) where monthly means vary from 8 mm (January) to about 24 mm (June).

Table IV gives the maximum daily values and illustrates what high evaporation can take place within 24 hours. Values of 30 mm can, in general, occur anywhere in the U.A.R. with a high for the country of 56.9 mm at Matruh. Individual large values such as this are a result of long duration of the hot, dry, southerly gale winds. The relatively low values at Alexandria and Port Said are due to their location between the Mediterranean and lakes Mariut and Manzala, respectively. On the coast winter is the season of strong, dry southwesterly winds which blow in front of the Mediterranean depressions and high individual values may occur in winter as well as in spring.

TABLE III

MEAN DAILY AMOUNT OF EVAPORATION (mm)

Station	Jan.	Feb.	Mar.	Apr.	May	June	July	Aug.	Sept.	Oct.	Nov.	Dec.
Sallum	7.5	8.1	8.4	8.2	8.7	10.0	10.6	9.4	8.5	8.1	7.6	7.4
Mersa Matruh	4.6	4.8	4.9	5.0	5.3	5.1	5.7	5.7	5.8	5.1	4.4	4.5
Alexandria	4.2	4.6	5.2	5.4	5.8	5.7	5.5	5.6	5.8	5.4	4.4	3.8
Port Said	4.7	5.4	6.5	6.4	6.8	7.4	7.5	7.3	7.8	6.9	5.9	4.5
El Arish	3.5	4.0	4.4	4.6	4.9	4.9	4.8	4.9	5.2	4.8	4.0	3.6
Cairo (Almaza)	5.6	7.0	8.7	10.6	13.1	13.0	11.2	10.0	8.9	8.5	6.6	5.5
Minya	4.5	5.8	7.7	10.2	14.0	15.0	13.6	11.7	9.1	7.9	6.0	4.6
Asyout	7.3	9.3	12.6	17.6	22.2	23.2	19.8	18.8	17.8	12.6	8.9	7.2
Luxor	4.8	6.2	8.9	12.6	15.4	16.9	16.6	16.5	13.4	9.7	6.8	5.1
Aswan	8.9	10.5	14.3	17.5	18.0	22.2	20.6	20.5	19.4	17.4	12.1	9.6
Hurghada	10.2	11.5	12.1	14.4	17.0	18.9	18.0	17.9	16.5	12.7	10.9	9.9
Siwa	5.4	6.9	9.4	12.1	14.1	15.5	15.5	14.2	11.5	8.9	6.3	5.2
Bahariya	5.3	7.8	8.5	11.0	13.2	13.9	13.0	12.2	10.2	8.4	6.2	5.1
Farafra	7.3	9.8	13.3	17.8	21.5	24.4	22.3	21.2	18.4	14.0	9.5	7.3
Dakhla	7.7	10.0	13.4	17.7	21.8	23.8	22.4	21.3	19.5	15.4	10.9	7.7
Kharga	7.7	9.6	13.2	18.3	20.4	23.9	21.5	19.7	18.5	14.7	10.3	7.3
Suez	5.1	5.8	7.6	10.1	12.5	13.7	13.2	12.4	10.8	8.8	6.5	5.2
Tor	7.1	7.8	9.0	9.9	10.6	12.6	11.7	11.4	9.8	7.8	7.5	7.0
Quseir	10.7	11.9	12.8	13.8	15.5	17.3	15.1	15.6	15.1	12.8	11.7	10.5

TABLE IV

HIGHEST DAILY AMOUNT OF EVAPORATION (mm)

Station	Jan.	Feb.	Mar.	Apr.	May	June	July	Aug.	Sept.	Oct.	Nov.	Dec.
Sallum	23.8	19.8	30.0	33.7	36.5	35.0	23.5	20.7	17.1	33.1	20.2	22.8
Mersa Matruh	17.0	52.2	32.6	28.5	27.6	27.0	26.2	23.3	27.8	25.8	20.1	56.9
Alexandria	12.7	12.2	15.0	14.7	17.0	16.4	11.2	9.3	9.5	10.0	11.3	12.0
Port Said	15.4	16.6	16.4	15.4	13.5	15.5	14.5	14.5	12.8	10.5	12.9	19.3
Cairo (Almaza)	21.3	23.9	27.7	32.2	42.5	41.0	23.9	32.6	28.3	29.0	23.8	29.6
Minya	11.6	10.0	17.0	21.3	25.0	26.4	20.0	18.0	14.4	14.8	11.2	14.2
Asyout	20.5	20.0	29.5	35.0	33.5	32.5	26.0	27.4	25.0	23.3	23.7	18.5
Aswan	21.8	25.5	38.3	34.7	34.5	40.5	32.4	32.5	32.7	38.0	24.5	20.2
Hurghada	30.0	21.7	32.4	36.2	37.0	36.7	35.0	33.6	33.0	30.0	26.4	28.0
Dakhla	17.0	28.9	29.0	46.0	35.0	47.7	39.7	34.8	30.2	30.0	20.4	17.3

Extreme minimum daily values exceed 10 mm at some stations, Asyout (May, June, July, August and September), Aswan (June, July) and Dakhla (June, July, August and September). At other stations this value may be less than 1 mm, Mersa Matruh (December), Alexandria (December), Port Said (December and January) and Cairo (January).

Relative humidity

Distribution

In the Mediterranean coastal areas the mean monthly values of relative humidity increase eastwards. However, they decrease rapidly southwards. For example, the mean annual value is 69% at Alexandria and 29% at Aswan. It should be noted that the mean values for stations on the Mediterranean coast are appreciably higher than those on the Red Sea.

Annual variation

The annual variation of the mean monthly values is very small, especially in the eastern part of the Mediterranean coast. In the west the occurrence of the hot, dry khamsin conditions in spring lowers the mean values slightly.

At inland stations the annual variation is more pronounced, with a maximum in January and a minimum in May or June, the difference being about 20 to 25%.

Extreme values

Values of around 100% can occur in Lower and Middle Egypt in any month of the year due to intense nocturnal cooling. In Upper Egypt the extreme dryness of the air does not admit of this occurrence.

Except on the Red Sea, exceptionally low values of relative humidity (below about 5%) can occur anywhere, even in the coastal areas of the Mediterranean when excessively hot, southerly winds blow across the desert.

Surface wind

In winter the Mediterranean depressions affect Lower Egypt directly, causing surface winds to become variable, both in speed and direction. Since the tracks of the depressions are north of the coast line the prevailing directions are, as expected, south and southwesterly in front of the depressions and west or northwesterly in the rear. Upper Egypt and the northern Red Sea area are practically unaffected by these depressions and are, for most of the time, under the eastern flank of the sub-tropical high pressure cell that covers the western desert of Egypt. The prevailing winds are, therefore, northerlies. The cold north to northwesterly winds in the rear of depressions usually become fresh or strong when reaching Upper Egypt, due to the tightening of the pressure gradient. Orographic effects in the northern Red Sea can cause these winds to reach gale force.

Winter and early spring are the seasons of strong and gale winds in Lower Egypt, usually blowing from the western quadrant. It is to be noted that the frequency of strong and gale winds decreases considerably in Upper Egypt. Northeasterly winds become more frequent in the spring and autumn months over Lower Egypt because of the passage of the centre of khamsin depressions south of the Mediterranean coast line. This fact leads to the eastern Mediterranean becoming an area of relatively high pressure. In Upper Egypt northerly winds prevail during this period for they are interrupted only temporarily by the passage of these depressions. Autumn, especially October, is the time of lowest wind speed.

Aswan exhibits a feature peculiar for Upper Egypt; autumn (and to a lesser extent spring) is the season of high winds. These occur as heavy squalls with small instability systems, sometimes with thunderstorms or merely light rain showers. These systems belong more to the Sudanese pattern as they extend northwards.

91

In summer steady northerly winds prevail over all of Egypt. Gales do not occur during this season, except on the Red Sea. In this area the strong northwesterly winds are products of the local topography and the shallow, small centres of low pressure that appear over the northern Red Sea.

The mean annual values of wind speed are highest on the western side of the Mediterranean coast (Fig.7). (In this region the wind is utilized for power.) The value decreases from about 20 km/h in the extreme west (Sallum) to about 8 km/h in the extreme east (El-Arish). The north Red Sea is also a relatively windy area but regions inland are notably less windy although local topography plays an important role.

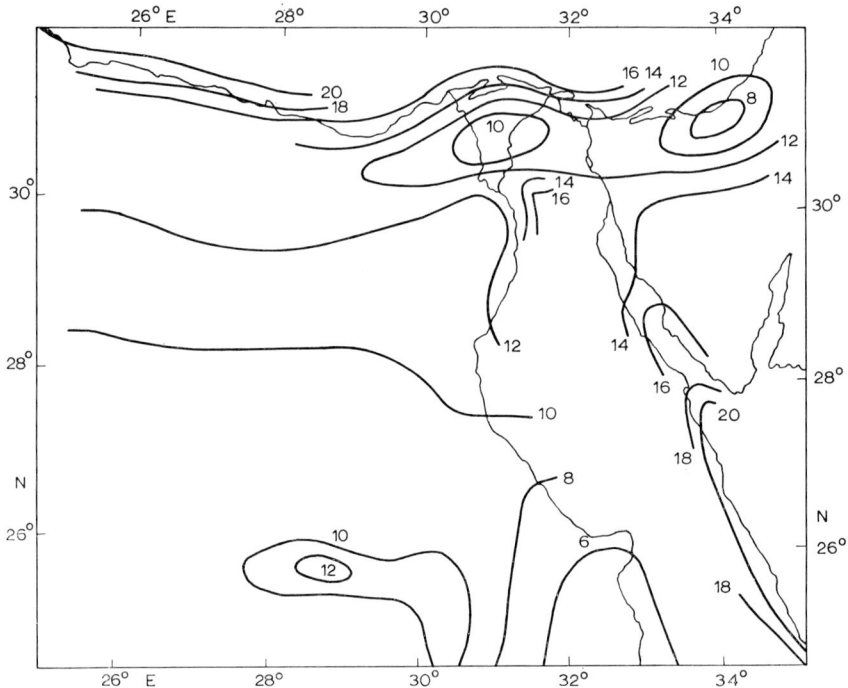

Fig.7. Mean annual wind speed (km/h).

Climate regions

The general climate of the U.A.R. is "dry, hot, desert type". The country, however, can be classified into four climatic sub-regions:

(*1*) Lower Egypt comprises the northern part (north of about 30°N) and has a rather "Mediterranean climate" with a mild winter and some rain and a dry, warm, rainless summer.

(*2*) Upper Egypt, comprising the area south of 30°N and including the western desert, has a sub-tropical, hot, very dry, desert climate. The Nile and adjacent narrow cultivation belts have very limited local modifications on the climate.

(*3*) North Red Sea and coastal areas (including the Gulf of Suez), having a hot, but rather humid, and rainless climate.

(*4*) Mountains of Sinai which, owing to their altitude, belong more to the temperate climates but have very little precipitation.

The Sudan

The Republic of the Sudan is the largest country in Africa, having an area of more than 2.5 million km². Its population is about 12.5 million with the only really large concentration being Khartoum–Omdurman with 300,000 inhabitants. The chief exports, mainly from the southern half of the country, are cotton, gum arabic, groundnuts and sesame. The area included in this zone is that of the northern Sudan, north of about 15°N. The brief rainy season, at best lasting from July to September, decreases rapidly northwards until it vanishes near the U.A.R. border. The only vegetation is along the banks of the Nile. Northerly winds prevail during most of the year. The summers are invariably hot (mean maximum 41°C, mean minimum 25°C) with the large diurnal variation and low relative humidity (average 25%) giving the only relief to the heat. Winters can be quite cool, temperatures around and below zero occurring fairly frequently in the extreme north of the region while in the south relatively low temperatures of 5 or 6°C have been recorded. The impact of these temperatures, together with the low relative humidity, makes for great discomfort of the local population at such times. Strong winds blow sand from the north most mornings while cold fronts from the northern Sahara and outbreaks stemming from eastern Europe and central Asia do occur, occasionally bringing appreciable rain to the far north. Mean maximum and minimum temperatures are about 10°C lower than in the summertime.

Sunshine is very prevalent in this region, ranging from about 80 to 90% of the possible hours, on an annual basis. Wadi Halfa is one of the sunniest places on the earth's surface with about 4,000 h/year. Even during the cloudy months in the south of the area the average is about 8 h/day (60% of possible).

No description of the climate of this area would be complete without reference to the duststorm, a rapidly moving mass of air containing large amounts of dry, opaque particles which reduce visibility to less than 1,000 m. Three types have been distinguished in the northern Sudan:

(*1*) the instability type associated with thunder activity and related to advancing or early monsoon (I.T.C.Z.);

(*2*) the pressure gradient kind caused by southerly winds and also occurring about the same time as (*1*);

(*3*) the pressure gradient variety caused by northerly winds and most prevalent in February to May.

The term "haboob" (Arabic word meaning "to blow") is often used indiscriminately with reference to high winds, sandstorm, duststorm, rising sand, and the like, but it is applied by the Sudanese meteorologists only to type (*1*). The average number of duststorms reaches a maximum around Khartoum (18–20 per year) with averages 4, 6, 4 for May, June and July, respectively. At Atbara the maximum of five occurs in August.

Radiation figures are available for 4 years at Wadi Halfa (21°52′N 31°32′E), 10 years at Shambat (15°40′N 32°32′E) and 4 years at El Fasher (13°35′N 25°21′E). The mean values are given in Table V.

These figures do not give as high values as would be deduced from the *World Maps of Climatology* (LANDSBERG et al., 1963), only about 200kLy/year compared to 220. It is likely that dust in the atmosphere is the cause of the "relatively" low summertime values at Wadi Halfa. There is a great increase over the values given in Table I.

TABLE V

MEAN VALUES OF GLOBAL RADIATION (Ly/day)

	Jan.	Feb.	Mar.	Apr.	May	June	July	Aug.	Sept.	Oct.	Nov.	Dec.	Year
Wadi Halfa	483	557	612	648	622	589	571	563	562	522	488	455	556
Shambat	457	525	588	640	667	656	638	609	582	525	461	426	562
El Fasher	480	550	590	600	610	560	540	520	570	530	490	470	543

Libya

Part of Libya has been discussed in the chapter on the Mediterranean zone (Chapter 2) but, unfortunately, the larger area of the country falls into the arid zone. The Republic of Libya comprises three provinces, Cyrenaica in the east, Tripolitania and Fezzan in the west. South of about 30°N the country is almost entirely desert, except for a few oases, such as Ghat, Murzuk and the famous Kufra, home of the Senussi tribe. Hammada, reg (called "serir" in Libya) and erg are all well represented in the area and the only source of wealth is from mineral oil in the region southeast of Sidra. Recently a fine publication by KANTER (1967) has given an interesting introduction to this country, concerning itself with the geology, geography, climate and human aspects.

In the southern areas rainfall can stem from small depressions moving from the north (northwest–northeast) and, if convergence takes place, heavy rainfall in the Hammada (south of Tripoli, north of Fezzan) can occur, producing large rain lakes (October, 1937). Heavy rainfall from thunderstorms in November have caused extensive damage, destruction of villages and treacherously rapid flooding of wadis. In 1841 Vogel reported a week of rain near Murzuk. Even in the extreme southwest extensive and localised rains occur, an event often missed by the sparse network of observing stations, and virga are frequent. These sporadic falls are very important to the pasturing patterns and the rain-agriculture of the people of the region. In the summer months winds from the Gulf of Guinea can bring moist air masses to this region.

As is typical of such arid areas rainfall shows pronounced variation, as Table VI (KANTER, 1967) illustrates.

TABLE VI

DETAILS OF ANNUAL RAINFALL (mm)

	Aujila	Ghadames	Ghat	Kufra	Murzuk	Sebha	Ubari
Max.	42.0	145.6	37.5	2.5	30.9	30.3	39.3
Av.	11.7	29.0	13.1	0.7	8.4	8.3	11.9
Min.	0.2	6.0	0.1	0.0	0.0	0.0	0.5

Temperatures are normally pleasantly cool at night in the Sahara Desert. In some regions temperatures below freezing occur often in winter (–6°C east of Ghadames, January, 1962). In summer northeasterly–easterly air flow maintains days with maxima of 35–40°C and minima of 18°–22°C, but with the onset of the ghibli minima rise to an uncomfortable 30°C, blowing dust is evident and an enervating sultriness occurs.

Central and western Sahara

Southern Algeria

This part of Algeria comprises the territory to the south of the Atlas Mountains and covers over 2 million km², but has a population of less than 600,000. The chief exports are mineral oil, natural gas and dates. The major administrative centres are Colomb Bechar and Laghouat. There are scattered oases, such as Biskra, Figuig, In Salah, Tamanrasset and Tessalit, but the Tassili and Ahaggar plateaus have the best watered areas. Rivers can flow deep into the heart of the desert, as much as 700 to 800 km at times, as the Wadi Saoura proves, but mostly water is found only in isolated spots.

Mauritania

A very arid country covering over 1 million km² has a population of about 640,000. In the north of the territory there are large areas of erg but in the extreme south a small region has more than 500 mm of rain per year and some agriculture is carried out on the flood plain of lower Senegal, the Chemana. The chief exports are fish, cattle, salt and gum arabic. The capital, Nouakchott, has only 6,000 inhabitants.

Mali

Mali is another dry territory, of over 1,200,000 km², supporting a population of nearly 4.5 million. Most of these are centred around and dependent upon the inland delta of the Niger, a very fertile area. Bamako is the only large town, with 120,000 inhabitants. During the brief rains the nomadic pastoralists move to the ergs of El Djoufa and Tanezrouft. The chief exports are groundnuts, dried fish, live animals and cotton.

Niger Republic

This is a country of more than 3 million people with an area just a little larger than Mali. The northern and central portions are mainly erg but in the south there is excellent pastoral country during and after the short rainy season, for about a quarter of the country has over 400 mm rain per year. Niamey (23,000 inhabitants) is the capital and the principal exports are groundnuts and live animals.

Chad

More than half of this country, which in size and population is very similar to the Niger Republic, falls in the desert zone. The major export is cotton and Fort Lamy (88,000) is the capital.

Spanish Sahara

A little-known, desolate area of over 250,000 km² with a population of only 24,000 nomads. Villa Cisneros (5,300) is the capital town but most administration is effected from the Canary Islands.

General survey

As may be imagined, the climatic elements most commonly measured in the Saharan zone are precipitation and temperature, and for such a vast area even these elements are not recorded at many stations. Because of this fact attention must be focussed on these two aspects, as has been the case in the mammoth works by DUBIEF (1959, 1963).

Rainfall

In an area such as this life revolves around the occurrence or non-occurrence of rainfall and its resultant distribution patterns. Fig.8 shows a slightly simplified map of the mean

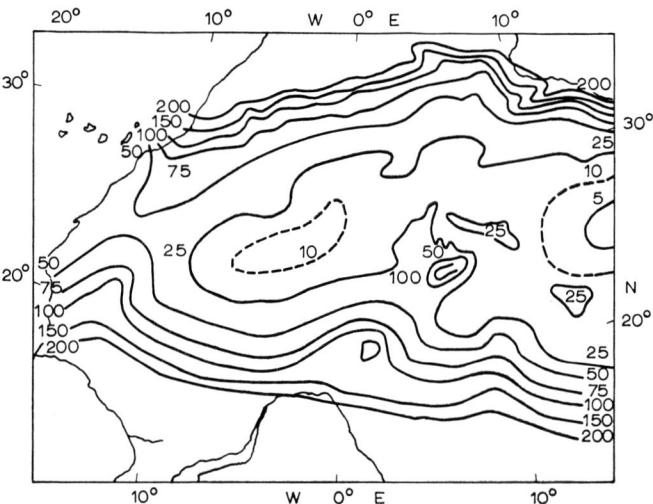

Fig.8. Mean annual rainfall (mm) (1926–1960).

annual rainfall (based on the period 1926–1960) for most of the area. The isohyets are, as expected, seen to parallel roughly the coastal configuration except where high plateaus, such as the Ahaggar and the Tibesti, intervene. Even on this high ground desert conditions prevail. In an area subject to the vagaries of complex air circulation patterns great variations occur in annual totals and most regions have experienced zero or very little rainfall during one year. Fig.9 gives an idea of the maximum falls ever recorded and, as can be noted, most of the zone has never had sufficient rainfall during the time of climatic records to be considered other than arid. Table VII gives an idea of maximum and minimum annual rainfall totals at a selection of stations.

Some stations are not strictly within the Sahara zone boundaries but are marginal and presented here for comparison only.

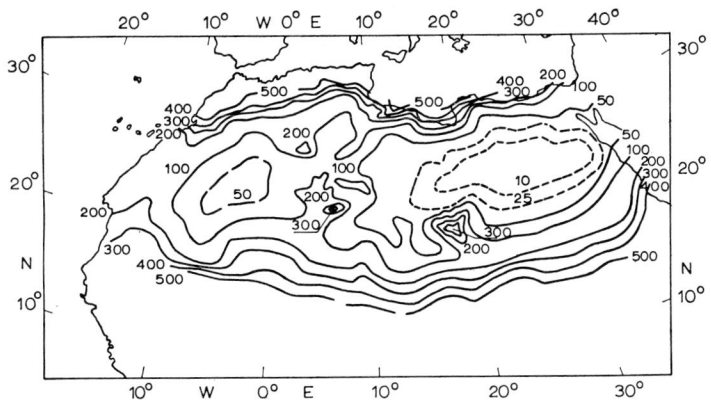

Fig.9. Maximum annual rainfall (mm).

TABLE VII

MAXIMUM AND MINIMUM ANNUAL RAINFALL AT CHOSEN STATIONS

Station	Ann. rainfall (mm)		Station	Ann. rainfall (mm)	
	max.	min.		max.	min.
Cyrene	963	208	El Themed	191	0
Misurata	465	126	Damietta	187	50
Zuara	439	60	El Adem	178	38
Sirte	430	7	Port Said	154	29
Kamaran	367	12	Ismailia	126	8
Agedabia	325	25	Jalo	94	0
Nalut	287	41	Helwan	91	1
Hon	267	4	Giarabub	41	0

Owing to the skewed nature of the annual totals DUBIEF (1959, 1963) has had recourse to the use of the interquartile variability factor, $100(Q_3 - Q_1)/Q_2$, and a map of this factor is given in Fig.10. The isopleths actually are similar to the annual isohyetal pattern because of the dominance of Q_2 in this type of analysis of rainfall. The great variation is

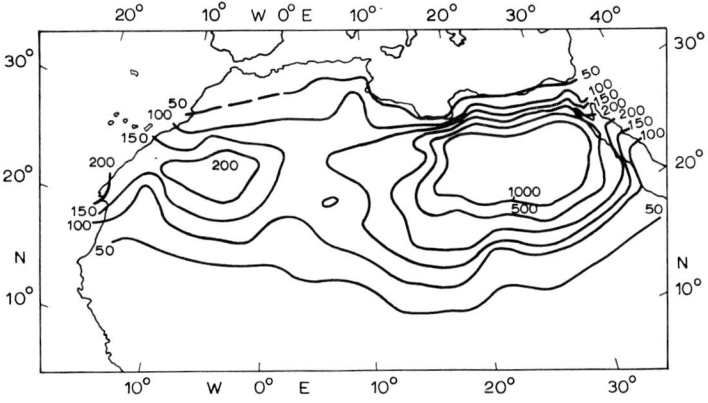

Fig.10. Interquartile variability of annual rainfall (mm).

very obvious, most of the zone has values in excess of 100, while some areas have such a large variation that average values are meaningless.

Seasonal distribution is also of interest and importance in rainfall studies and well illustrates the distinct division between the north and south regions of the Sahara. It is seen from Table VIII that Ouallen is the changing point, the node, of the rainfall in the western Sahara. Amounts increase away from Ouallen, very slowly to the northeast (due to the difficulty in advecting moist air to the region) and more rapidly to the south. At Ouallen there is some little rain associated both with the "winter" cyclones and the "monsoon" convergence rains. To the north (Adrar, Fort Flatters, Ouargla, Tabelbala) the "winter" pattern predominates while to the south (Tidjikja, Tin Zaouaten) the "monsoon" rains are all-important. The autumn rains of the western area (Tindouf, Villa Cisneros) also just affect Ouallen.

Fig.11 gives the pattern of the wettest month(s) while Fig.12 illustrates the wettest quarter of the year. Fig.11 shows very distinctly the regions which experience rainfall associated with the "monsoon" (I.T.C.Z.) (south of the northern limit of August area) and those with "winter" rainfall (north of southern limit of December or January areas). In the Red Sea the winter rain is due to the convergence between the southeast (Indian Ocean) and the northwest (Atlantic) air masses. The large area of May rains (actually very rare and of small amounts) is associated with upper air troughs moving overland causing a

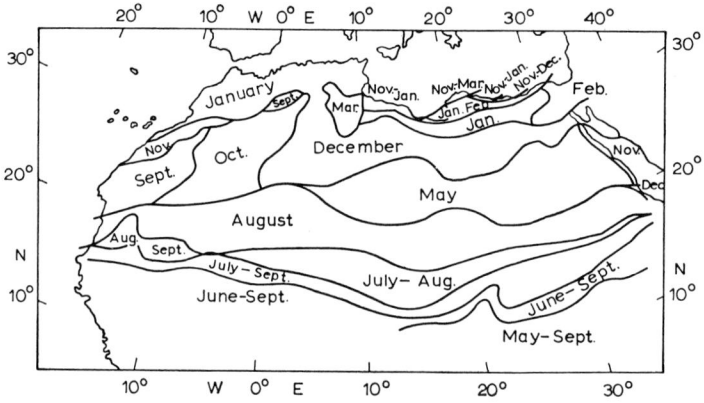

Fig.11. Wettest months.

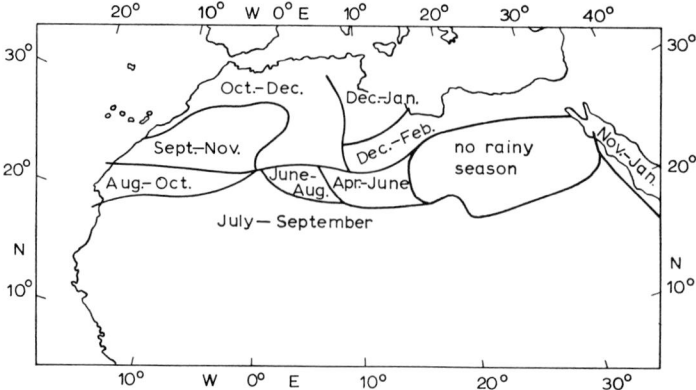

Fig.12. Wettest quarter of the year.

TABLE VIII

PRECIPITATION PATTERNS (mm)

Station	Latit. (N)	Longit.	Ht. (m)	Record (yrs)	Jan.	Feb.	Mar.	Apr.	May	June	July	Aug.	Sept.	Oct.	Nov.	Dec.	Year
Tindouf	27°42'	8°08'W	600	32	0	0	6	0	0	0	1	11	7	4	1	3	33
Adrar	27°52'	0°17'W	286	14	0	1	2	0	1	0	1	1	1	5	5	1	15
Ft. Flatters	28°06'	6°42'E	373	28	7	3	2	4	1	1	0	0	1	1	5	4	28
Ouallen	24°36'	1°14'E	346	12	1	1	2	0	0	0	1	4	1	0	4	0	13
Tin Zaouaten	19°57'	2°55'E	720	64	0	1	1	0	1	1	0	37	26	0	0	0	65
Ouargla	31°54'	5°20'E	135	39	5	4	5	3	2	0	0	0	1	3	9	8	39
V. Cisneros	23°42'	15°52'W	10	77	1	1	1	1	3	0	1	5	35	2	5	25	78
Tidjikja	18°33'	11°26'W	400	47	0	7	1	0	7	15	23	53	25	10	5	1	148
Tabelbala	29°27'	3°10'W	570	21	0	2	5	0	0	0	1	2	0	1	8	2	21

type of cold front rain. In the northwestern area of the Sahara the autumn rains are related to instability showers moving in from the Atlantic, still warm at this time of year. The small pocket of March rains stems from a tendency for a northeast flow over the Mediterranean that meets the higher land and gives rise to thunderstorms. Fig.12, a simplified pattern due to smoothed averaging, tells the same story. Fig.13 shows the air flow patterns over the zone that eventually lead to the areas of specific rainfall seasons illustrated in Fig.11 and 12.

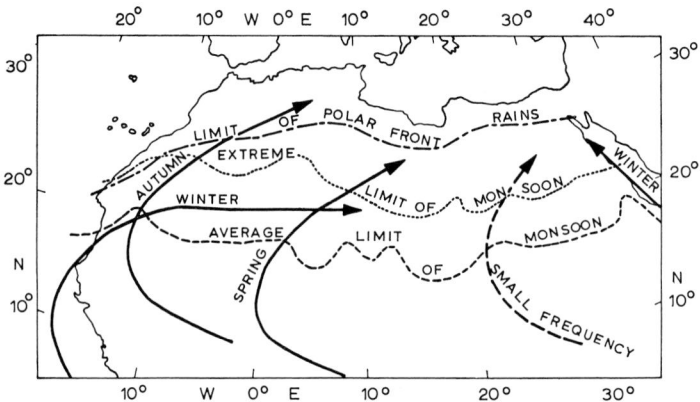

Fig.13. Most frequent trajectories of Sudan–Saharan disturbances.

Fig.14 gives the number of rainy days per year, and again the Wadi Halfa region shows an extreme value, of less than one day each year. In this area many years can pass before a fall of a few millimetres is recorded, and Fig.15 shows how a year or more may pass in most of the zone before a rain day is recorded. The rather fragmented nature of this pattern is partly due to the varying length of the records used in the analysis.

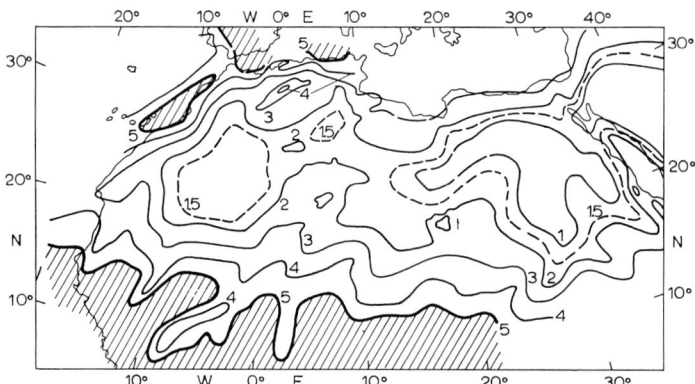

Fig.14. Annual number of rain days.

Although rain days are unusual it must not be inferred that heavy falls are impossible. More than half of the zone has measured at least 40 mm in a day, and only the Wadi Halfa region fails to report some days with at least 10 mm (Fig.16). Snow, while being uncommon, is not such a rare event in parts of the Sahara, as reference to DUBIEF's (1959, 1963) work will show; especially interesting are some outstanding photographs of heavy falls in certain oases. Fig.17 gives the extreme southerly limit of recorded snowfall.

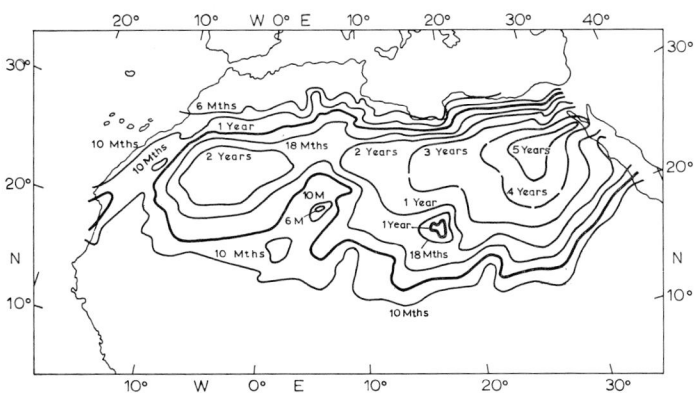

Fig.15. Maximum duration of period without at least 0.1 mm in 24 h.

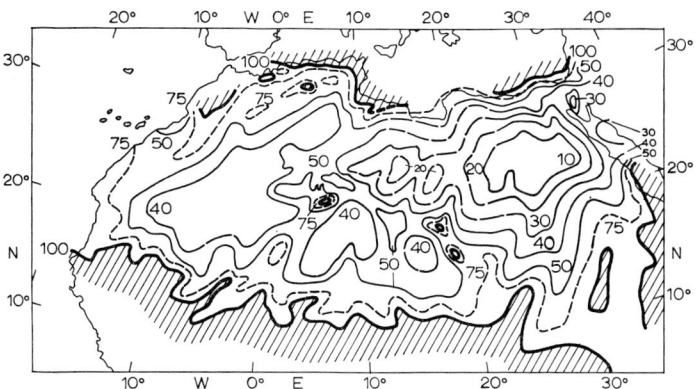

Fig.16. Maximum rainfall in 24 h (mm).

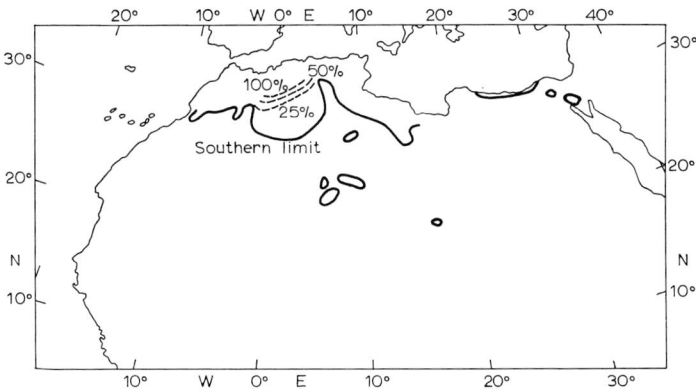

Fig.17. Saharan regions reached by snow.

Rainfalls of extremely high intensity have occurred in this zone but their discovery is made difficult due to the paucity of recording raingauges. For rainfalls of a duration of an hour or more an intensity of 15–20 mm/h has been recorded with a high of 46 mm/h for a period of 63 min, at Tamanrasset. Short period falls of a few millimetres have given rates in excess of 60 mm/h, with maxima of 174 mm/h (8.7 mm in 3 min) at Golea and 92.4 mm/h at Beni Abbes (38.5 mm in 25 min). The latter is the most sustained high intensity fall.

Temperature

Temperatures are normally considered to be very high in the Sahara but earlier references to snow will show that such is not always the case. However, about half of the zone has recorded temperatures in excess of 50°C, as depicted in Fig.18. It appears likely that 60°C could occur, or has occurred, in an area around Ogdetel Biar (23°30′N 7°45′W). The month of highest maximum temperature, given in Fig.19, shows, as would be expected, a gradual delay northwards, becoming as late as August, September and even October, in areas where the maritime influence is so great that the large water mass must become heated before maximum readings can be obtained.

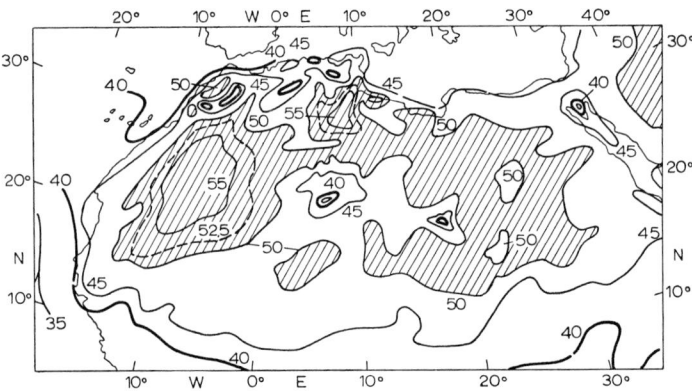

Fig.18. Extreme maximum temperature (°C), 1926–1950.

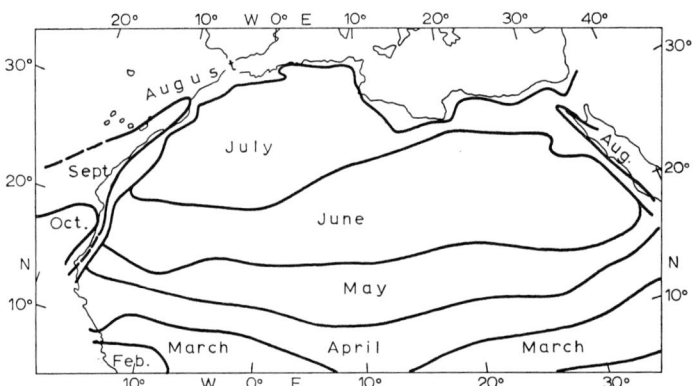

Fig.19. Month of highest monthly maximum temperature.

Minimum temperatures are more a function of the microclimate than the macroclimate but Fig.20 proves how two-thirds of the zone has experienced freezing temperatures and that, even in non-mountainous areas, −5°C is possible. With such an extreme continental climate large diurnal variation is to be expected, the dry air being excellent for both the gain and loss of heat by radiative processes. Fig.21 illustrates how values of more than 15°C are the rule and even 20°C occurs over a large area, a very high value for an annual mean diurnal variation.

The annual range of temperature (the difference between the mean temperatures of the

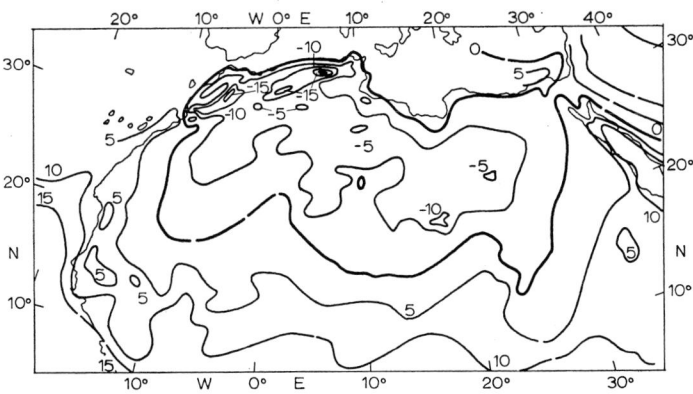

Fig.20. Extreme minimum temperature (°C), 1926–1960.

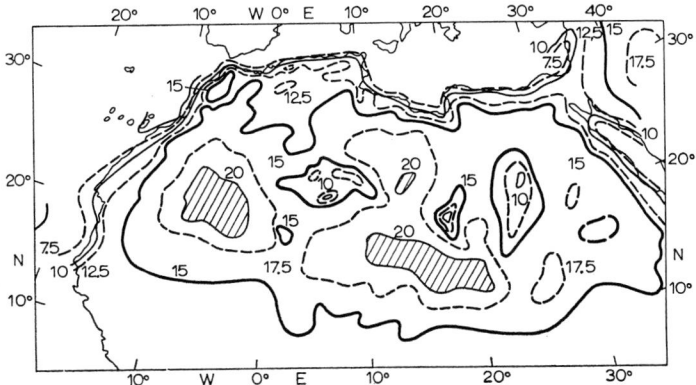

Fig.21. Mean annual diurnal temperature range (°C).

hottest and the coldest months) exhibits a similar high value, except along the Moroccan coast where the cool current has an ameliorating effect of great magnitude (Fig.22).

Soil temperatures are available for very few stations. Values obtained at Gao (Mali), measured at 06h00 local time in the morning show a range from about 28°C to 38°C at both 30 cm and 60 cm. Minima are reached in January with maxima in May (30 cm) and June (60 cm). At Tessalit, at the same times of observation, the range at 30 cm was from

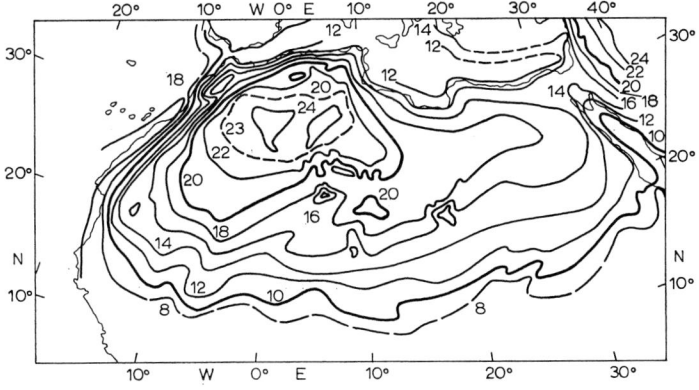

Fig.22. Mean annual temperature range (°C).

38.4°C (June and July) to 22.9°C (January) while at 60 cm it was from 37.1°C (July) to 23.7°C (December).

Cloud, sunshine and radiation

The Sahara is a region in which upper air subsidence occurs during most of the year so that cloud amounts are small and the number of sunshine hours is great. Fig.23 shows

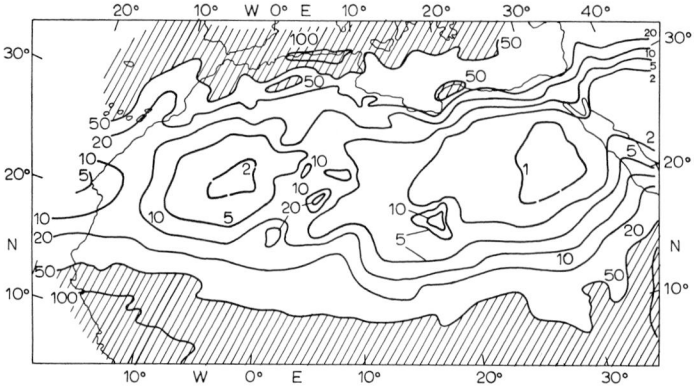

Fig.23. Mean annual cloudiness (tenths).

how the mean annual cloud amount (in tenths of sky covered) ranges from less than one in southern Egypt to four in the Timbuktu area. The number of completely clear days per year shows two isolated maxima, one in excess of 250 in the Wadi Halfa region and the other of more than 200 around the Algeria–Mauritania border. This pattern is reflected in the hours of sunshine (Fig.24). The cloudiness and reduced sunshine along the Moroccan coast, due in part to the upwelling of cold water, is also made obvious.

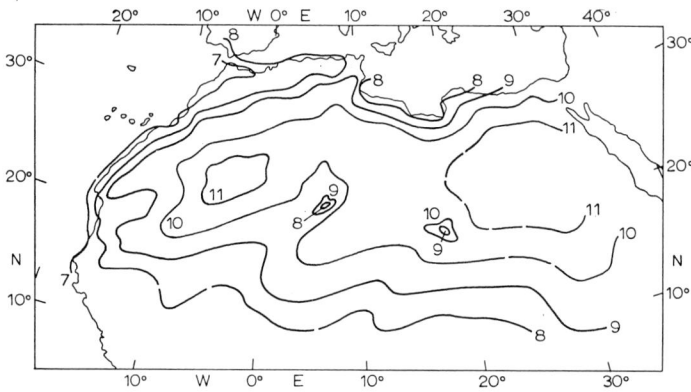

Fig.24. Annual mean of daily sunshine (h).

Radiation is measured at only a few stations and must be calculated from the number of sunshine hours, using empirical formulas. Nevertheless, Fig.25 gives an idea of the global radiation (short wave) received on a horizontal surface, in kLy/year (200 corresponds roughly to 550 Ly/day). The proximity of the heat equator (dotted line) to the

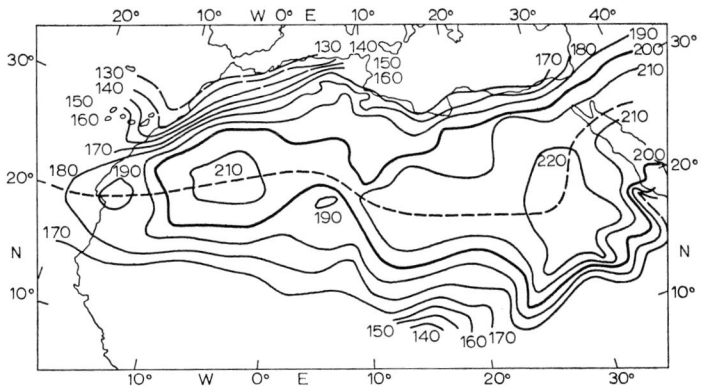

Fig.25. Global radiation; annual total (kLy/cm²).

Tropic of Cancer is an interesting phenomenon, nowhere do the two separate by more than about 3.5° of latitude (400 km) in the whole 6,000 km distance.

Humidity

As would be expected, relative humidity over the Sahara is low at most times. The maximum relative humidity is generally noted about sunrise and, as shown by Fig.26 and 27, is still quite low even then. July (Fig.26) is the driest month with most values below 40%, but even in the most humid month, December (Fig.27) values are still only around 60%.

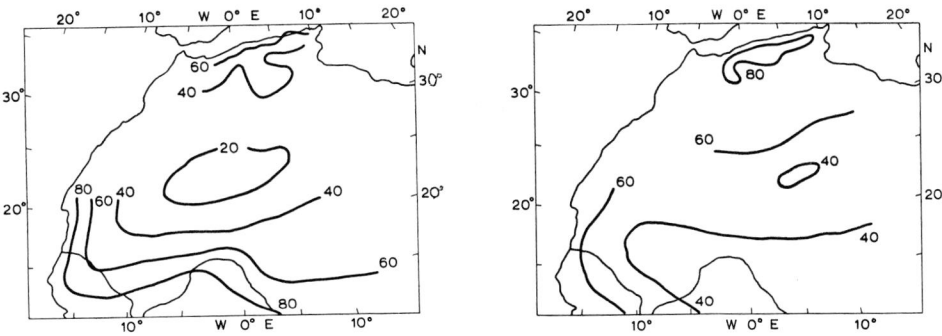

Fig.26. Mean relative humidity (%) at 07h00 G.M.T. for July.

Fig.27. Mean relative humidity (%) at 07h00 G.M.T. for December.

In the afternoon, when relative humidity is minimal, Fig. 28 and 29 illustrate the averages to be nearer 20% and 40% respectively. These very low values make the high temperatures at least tolerable for human existence, high humidities allied to the intense heat would lead to heat prostration and death.

A better way of expressing the humidity of the air is by use of the absolute vapour pressure and Fig.30 gives the mean annual values and the corresponding dew points. The minimum around Ouallen corresponds to a dew point of only 0°C, and for comparison the relative humidity at Ouallen is given in Table IX (cf. with rainfall centre, p. 98).

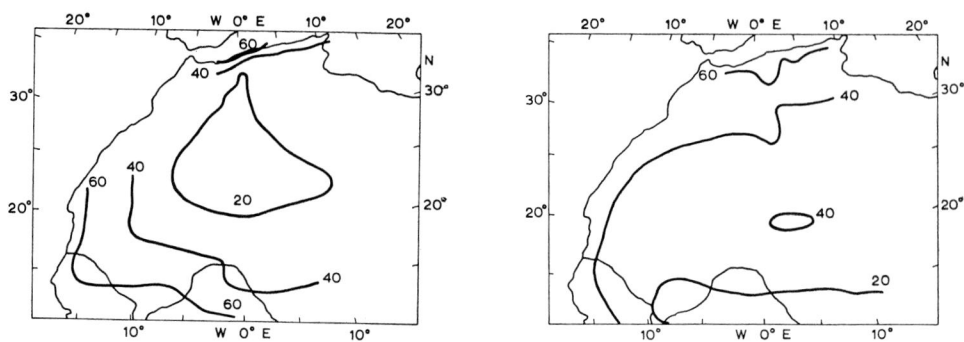

Fig.28. Mean relative humidity (%) at 13h00 G.M.T. for July.

Fig.29. Mean relative humidity (%) at 13h00 G.M.T. for December.

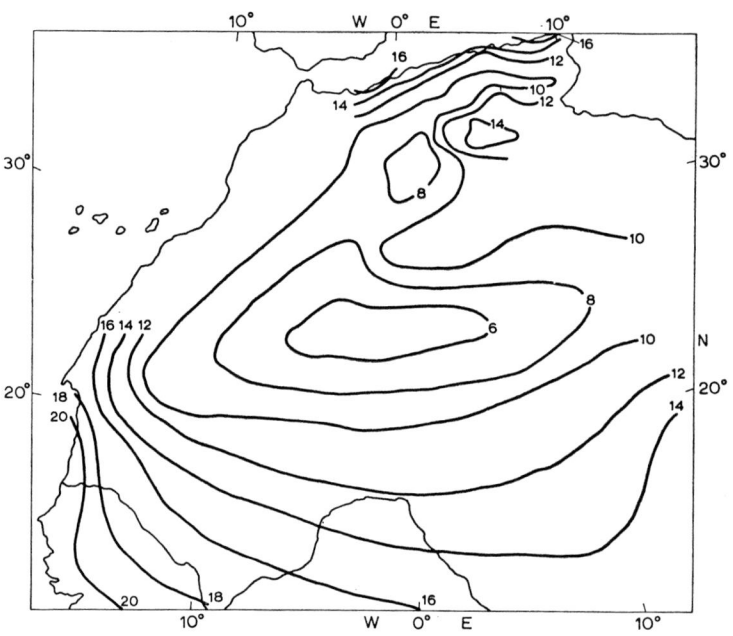

Fig.30. Mean annual vapour pressure (mbar).

TABLE IX

RELATIVE HUMIDITY AT OUALLEN (%)

Hour	Jan.	Feb.	Mar.	Apr.	May	June	July	Aug.	Sept.	Oct.	Nov.	Dec.	Year
07h00	33	35	24	24	16	11	15	24	23	36	41	47	27
13h00	14	15	10	11	8	7	7	15	13	19	24	30	14

July (Fig.31) is about the most humid month with many areas reaching 10 to 15 mbar and some even 20 mbar water vapour pressure. In December (Fig.32) and January, however, very few stations record as high as 10 mbar.

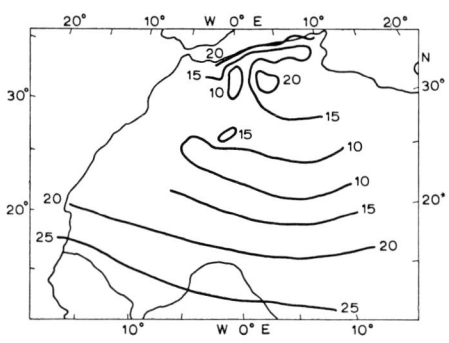 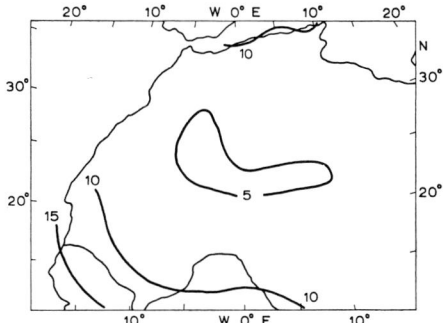

Fig.31. Mean vapour pressure, July (mbar).

Fig.32. Mean vapour pressure, December (mbar).

Evaporation

Most measurements of evaporation in this zone have been made by use of the Piche evaporimeter exposed in an instrument shelter. Fig.33 shows the annual mean evaporation can reach as great as 5 m, or about 14 mm/day, in the central Sahara, values comparable

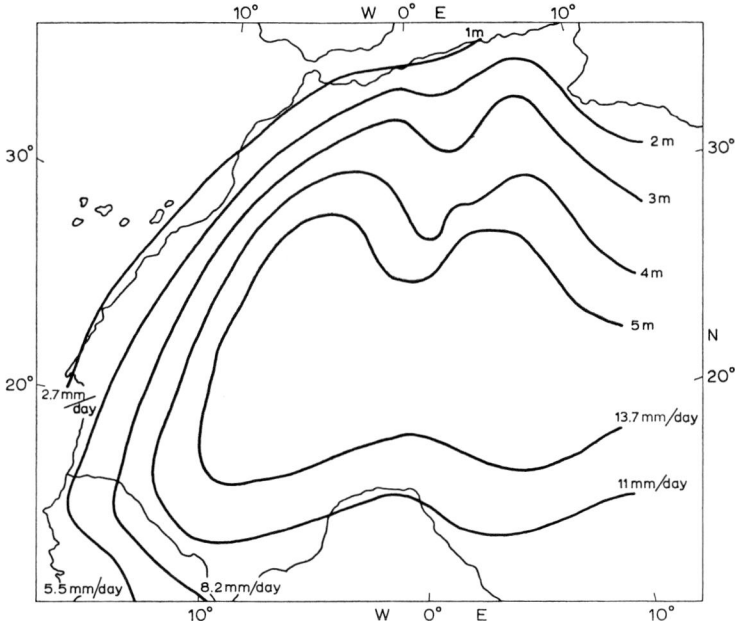

Fig.33. Mean annual "Piche" evaporation.

with Aswan and Asyout in Egypt. It is likely that about 6 m/year represents the maximum Piche evaporation recorded at the earth's surface under natural conditions. Fig.34 showing the June values (the month of maximum values) is given for reference, figures of 24 mm/day for the monthly mean have been reported from In Salah for June and July.

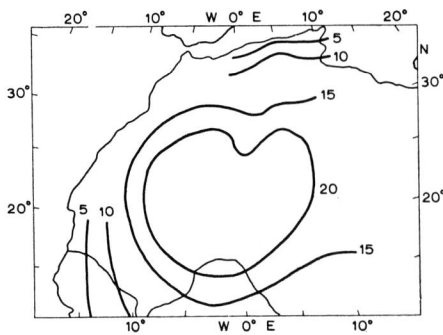

Fig.34. Mean "Piche" evaporation, June (mm/day).

Wind

In the section on pressure and wind circulation a description of wind flow has been given but local variations give rise to certain important modifications.

Over the southern Algerian section the surface winds at 07h00Z are predominantly from the northeast during November to February with a slight veering to the east in the other months. Calm conditions prevail much of the time (about 30%) except in the Adrar–Timinoun–In Salah triangle (often about 10%) and the Laghouat–El Oued region (below 10%). On the border of the Atlas Mountains winds are frequently northwesterly or westerly at this time.

At 13h00Z winds are usually from the eastern quadrant throughout the year with a smaller percentage of calms. Again northwesterly winds prevail near the Atlas in winter with variable conditions in summer.

The flow at 18h00Z is similar to the 07h00Z pattern. At the 1,000-m level easterly or northeasterly winds are general throughout the year, except in the Laghouat–Biskra area and there is a tendency for some southeasterly flow in August in the whole of southern Algeria.

Tamanrasset

This station was, for many years, a principal observatory and possesses valuable records. For instance, soil temperature was taken at 07h00, 13h00 and 18h00 local time for eight years (1933–1940) both on the soil surface and at depths of 38 and 59 cm (the reasons for the choice of these depths are unknown). At the soil surface values below freezing were noted from November to May with a record –13.8°C in January. The 13h00Z readings (corresponding roughly to the maxima) reached 69.5°C in August and over 65°C in the period May to September. The mean temperature (calculated) varied from 32.8°C in June and July to 12.8°C in January. Within the soil the annual mean at both depths was about 24.7°C but the fluctuation at 38 cm was 14.1°C compared with 12°C at 59 cm.

Tamanrasset also has many years (1939–1951) of global radiation measurements. The monthly variation of these values is given in Table X.

The mean monthly values for 2 or 3 years at El Oued are 354, 457, 482, 712, 760, 675, 714, 618, 635, 467, 363 and 336 but the quality of these records is suspect.

TABLE X

MEAN MONTHLY GLOBAL RADIATION (Ly/day) AND SUNSHINE VALUES (h/day), TAMANRASSET

	Jan.	Feb.	Mar.	Apr.	May	June	July	Aug.	Sept.	Oct.	Nov.	Dec.	Year
Radiation	437	508	589	639	656	636	654	606	517	480	427	394	545
Sunshine	9.6	9.5	10.4	10.9	10.6	10.2	11.5	10.7	9.6	10.0	9.5	8.8	10.1
% possible	88	83	87	85	80	76	86	83	77	86	85	80	83

Fig.35 gives the diurnal variation of global radiation and shows the maximum intensity being reached in late April and early May, while a slight build up of cloud, or a dusty atmosphere, occurs in the afternoons in late May, June and early September.

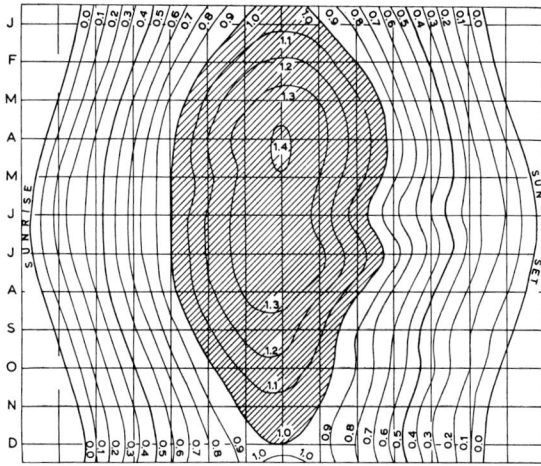

Fig.35. Isopleths of global radiation in Ly/min at Tamanrasset.

Direct radiation has been measured to reach as high as 1.71 Ly/min in January and in excess of 1.5 in each month. The transmission coefficient of the atmosphere has ranged from a mean of 0.67 in June and July to 0.81 in January, calculated from a noonday observation.

The recording raingauge analyses have shown variations in the number of rain hours per year from a minimum of 7.4 h (8.6 mm) in 1931 to 79.9 h (159 mm) in 1933. Average intensities have varied from 4 mm/h (134 mm in 34 h) to 0.3 mm/h (10 mm in 30 h).

Fig.36. Station locations in the northern desert.

References

BHALOTRA, Y. P. R., 1963. Meteorology of Sudan. *Sudan Meteorol. Serv., Mem.,* 6: 113 pp.

DUBIEF, J., 1943. Note au sujet de la climatologie du Sahara. *Univ. Algerie, Inst. Météorol. Phys. Globe Algérie, Fasc.,* 4: 22 pp.

DUBIEF, J., 1959. *Le Climat du Sahara.* University of Algeria, Algiers, 1: 275 pp.

DUBIEF, J., 1963. *Le Climat du Sahara.* University of Algeria, Algiers, 2: 313 pp.

KANTER, H., 1967. *Lybien: eine geographische-medizinische Landeskunde.* Springer, Berlin, Heidelberg, 163 pp.

KHALIL, A. S. A., 1968. Clouds over U.A.R. *U.N. Conf. Exploration Peaceful Uses Outer Space, Vienna.* Presented paper.

LANDSBERG, H. E., LIPPMANN, H., PAFFEN, K. H. and TROLL, C., 1963. *World Maps of Climatology.* Springer, Berlin, 5 maps, 28 pp.

MILLER, A. A., 1961. *Climatology.* Methuen, London, 320 pp.

TABLE XI

CLIMATIC TABLE FOR KASSALA, SUDAN
Latitude 15°28'N, longitude 36°24'E, elevation 500 m

Month	Mean sta. press. (mbar)	Temperature (°C) mean max.	mean min.	extreme max.	extreme min.	Dew point (°C) 06h	12h	Precipitation mean (mm)	max. (mm)	min. (mm)	days ≥1 mm	max. in 24 h (mm)	Wind av. speed (km/h)	preval. direct.	calm (%)	Averages cloud-iness[1] (oktas)	sun-shine (h/day)	evap. (Piche) (mm/day)
Jan.	1,009	35	16	41	5	13.7	11.5	0	<1	0	0	tr.	5	NNE	6	1	10.1	9.3
Feb.	1,007	36	16	43	6	13.6	10.5	1	9	0	<1	8	5	NNE	6	1	10.4	10.6
Mar.	1,005	39	19	45	9	13.1	9.3	1	12	0	<1	12	5	NNE	6	3	10.2	13.6
Apr.	1,004	41	22	45	12	13.3	9.8	5	38	0	1	16	5	N	7	2	10.8	15.4
May	1,004	42	25	46	15	14.2	11.9	14	64	0	2	39	5	S	12	2	10.5	15.4
June	1,006	40	25	47	18	17.0	14.6	27	104	0	3	56	6	S	9	3	10.2	13.6
July	1,007	36	23	42	18	19.5	18.3	100	274	8	8	78	8	S	3	5	8.4	9.1
Aug.	1,008	34	22	40	18	20.2	20.2	124	232	47	10	96	6	S	5	5	8.4	6.3
Sept.	1,008	36	23	42	18	20.0	18.9	60	160	5	5	91	5	S	9	3	9.7	7.6
Oct.	1,006	39	23	43	13	17.3	14.4	7	29	0	1	25	3	S	12	2	10.3	11.0
Nov.	1,007	38	21	41	10	15.7	12.3	2	20	0	<1	15	3	NNE	8	1	10.1	11.2
Dec.	1,009	35	17	40	7	14.7	12.0	0	<1	0	0	tr.	5	NNE	7	1	10.0	9.5
Annual	1,007	37	21	47	5	16.2	13.9	341	488	131	30	96	5	—	7	2	9.9	10.9
Rec. (yrs.)	24	30	30	30	30	30	30	30	30	30	30	30	10	10	10	28	28	30

[1] Mean of 06h00, 12h00 and 18h00.

TABLE XII

CLIMATIC TABLE FOR KHARTOUM, SUDAN
Latitude 15°36'N, longitude 32°32'E, elevation 380 m

Month	Mean sta. press. (mbar)	Temperature (°C)				Dew point (°C)		Precipitation					Wind			Averages		
		mean max.	mean min.	extreme max.	extreme min.	06h	12h	mean (mm)	max. (mm)	min. (mm)	days ≥1 mm	max. in 24 h (mm)	av. speed (km/h)	preval. direct.	calm (%)	cloud- iness[1] (oktas)	sun- shine (h/day)	evap. (Piche) (mm/day)
Jan.	1,012	32	16	40	7	3.4	6.0	0	0	0	0	0	16	N	<1	1	10.6	14.1
Feb.	1,010	34	17	43	8	1.5	3.4	tr.	<1	0	0	tr.	16	N	<1	1	10.7	16.4
Mar.	1,008	37	19	45	12	1.3	3.1	tr.	<1	0	0	tr.	15	N	1	2	9.9	19.5
Apr.	1,006	40	23	47	14	3.8	5.0	1	21	0	<1	21	14	N	1	2	10.4	21.3
May	1,005	42	26	47	19	10.0	8.8	5	15	0	1	10	16	N	2	2	10.3	20.5
June	1,006	42	27	48	20	14.6	10.6	7	60	0	1	26	14	S	2	3	9.9	19.9
July	1,007	38	26	46	19	19.1	15.8	48	159	2	5	70	16	S	1	4	8.6	15.3
Aug.	1,008	36	25	43	18	20.8	18.6	72	175	7	7	80	15	SSW	2	5	8.7	11.6
Sept.	1,007	38	25	45	17	18.8	16.0	27	96	1	3	66	11	S	3	4	10.0	13.6
Oct.	1,007	40	25	45	19	13.6	11.6	4	23	0	1	19	13	N	1	2	10.3	16.2
Nov.	1,009	36	21	42	13	8.4	8.9	tr.	3	0	<1	3	14	N	0	1	10.8	16.0
Dec.	1,011	33	17	40	6	6.0	7.6	tr.	<1	0	0	0	16	N	0	1	10.6	13.8
Annual	1,008	37	22	48	6	11.4	10.3	164	382	76	18	80	15	—	1	2	10.1	16.5
Rec. (yrs.)	30	30	30	30	30	30	30	30	30	30	30	30	6	6	6	30	20	30

[1] Mean of 06h00, 12h00 and 18h00.

TABLE XIII

CLIMATIC TABLE FOR GAO, MALI
Latitude 16°16′N, longitude 0°03′W, elevation 270 m

Month	M.s.l. press. (mbar)	Temperature (°C) mean		extreme		Relative humidity (%)		Precipitation					Wind			Averages		
		max.	min.	max.	min.	06h	12h	mean (mm)	max. (mm)	min. (mm)	days ≥1 mm	max. in 24 h (mm)	av. speed (km/h)	preval. direct.	calm (%)	cloudiness[1] (oktas)	sunshine (h/day)	number of gales >34 knots
Jan.	1,013	28	14	44	7	35	16	<1	15	0	0	8	7.1	ENE	37	4	9.4	0
Feb.	1,012	33	17	43	7	31	13	0	1	0	0	1	6.2	N	40	3	9.6	0
Mar.	1,009	36	22	45	9	30	10	<1	8	0	<1	8	7.8	N	32	4	9.6	0.3
Apr.	1,007	41	25	47	15	31	12	<1	25	0	<1	20	6.3	N	36	4	9.9	0.2
May	1,007	41	27	47	18	41	19	8	61	0	1	38	7.6	SW	24	4	9.7	1
June	1,009	39	28	48	18	54	29	23	73	0	4	33	10.1	SW	22	4	8.7	4
July	1,009	36	27	46	19	63	41	71	159	10	8	76	8.8	SW	25	5	9.2	5
Aug.	1,010	34	25	42	17	83	53	127	259	5	8	120	5.8	SW	28	6	9.1	3
Sept.	1,009	37	26	44	18	78	43	38	154	0	4	35	6.5	SW	20	5	9.4	3
Oct.	1,009	38	26	44	15	54	22	3	23	0	1	10	4.8	NE	48	4	9.7	1
Nov.	1,011	34	21	42	11	39	15	<1	7	0	<1	2	6.0	N	43	4	9.8	0.5
Dec.	1,013	31	17	39	8	35	15	<1	5	0	0	2	6.0	N	40	4	9.3	0
Annual	1,010	36	23	48	7	48	24	270	431	134	26	120	6.9	—	34	4	9.4	18
Rec. (yrs.)	30	15	15	15	15	9	9	33	30	30	33	33	8	8	8	10	10	6

[1] Mean of 06h00, 12h00 and 18h00.

TABLE XIV

CLIMATIC TABLE FOR NEMA, MAURITANIA
Latitude 16°36'N, longitude 7°16'W, elevation 265 m

Month	Mean sta. press. (mbar)	Temperature (°C) mean max.	min.	extreme max.	min.	Relative humidity (%) 06h	12h	Precipitation mean (mm)	max. (mm)	min. (mm)	days ≥1 mm	max. in 24 h (mm)	Wind av. speed (km/h)	preval. direct.	calm (%)	Averages cloudiness[1] (oktas)	number of gales ≥34 knots
Jan.	983	30	17	39	8	28	19	<1	18	0	<1	10	10.8	SE	30	3	0.4
Feb.	981	33	19	42	11	27	19	<1	5	0	0	5	10.4	NE	30	3	0
Mar.	980	37	23	44	15	22	15	1	5	0	<1	3	9.0	NE	36	2	0
Apr.	979	40	26	46	15	21	15	3	23	0	<1	10	7.3	ENE	60	3	0
May	978	42	29	49	20	41	18	10	92	0	1	38	9.5	ENE	34	4	0
June	980	42	28	47	17	50	30	30	117	0	3	81	7.0	E	35	3	1
July	980	38	26	46	12	72	48	63	185	15	7	46	5.5	SW	40	4	0.5
Aug.	980	35	24	43	18	81	56	111	312	38	7	125	6.9	SW	30	5	0.2
Sept.	980	37	25	43	18	77	47	55	117	10	5	33	4.3	SW	39	4	0.4
Oct.	981	39	26	45	16	45	27	15	58	10	2	25	5.7	SE	40	3	0.3
Nov.	981	36	23	44	15	32	22	<1	16	0	<1	8	10.0	NE	22	3	0.2
Dec.	983	31	18	40	9	35	24	<1	25	0	<1	18	9.9	NE	18	3	0.2
Annual	981	37	24	49	8	44	28	288	507	184	25	125	8.0	—	35	3	3
Rec. (yrs.)	6	23	23	23	23	10	10	30	30	30	30	30				10	6

[1] Mean of 05h00, 11h00 and 17h00.

TABLE XV

CLIMATIC TABLE FOR FAYA-LARGEAU, CHAD
Latitude 18°00'N, longitude 19°10'E, elevation 233 m

Month	Mean sta. press. (mbar)	Temperature (°C)				Relative humidity (%)		Precipitation					Wind		Aver. cloud- iness (oktas)
		mean		extreme		06h	12h	mean (mm)	max. (mm)	min. (mm)	days ≥0.1 mm	max. in 24 h (mm)	av. speed (km/h)	preval. direct.	
		max.	min.	max.	min.										
Jan.	986	25	14	39	4	31	19	0	0	0	0	0	7.3	NE	2
Feb.	984	30	15	42	5	28	16	tr.	0	0	0	0	7.2	NE	2
Mar.	983	34	18	44	8	25	13	0.1	0	0	<1	0.1	6.8	NE	2
Apr.	981	39	21	50	11	23	12	tr.	0	0	0	0	5.5	NE	2
May	981	41	24	50	18	27	14	0.6	2	0	<1	1.5	5.3	NE	2
June	981	42	26	50	16	28	15	1.5	48	0	<1	48	4.6	NE	1
July	980	41	25	47	16	43	22	2.7	13	0	1	13	4.1	NE	2
Aug.	981	40	26	46	15	54	23	11	35	0	2	35	3.5	NE	3
Sept.	982	39	25	46	17	32	18	1	23	0	<1	23	5.2	NE	2
Oct.	984	37	23	46	12	29	16	0.1	3	0	<1	2	5.7	ENE	1
Nov.	985	33	19	41	8	32	18	0	1	0	0	0	6.5	NE	2
Dec.	987	28	15	38	6	35	20	0	0	0	0	0	6.1	NNE	2
Annual	983	36	21	50	4	32	17	17	48	tr.	4	48	6.6	—	2
Rec. (yrs.)	7	26	26	26	26	31	31	30	30	30	30	30	10	10	15

TABLE XVI

CLIMATIC TABLE FOR NOUAKCHOTT, MAURITANIA

Latitude 18°07′N, longitude 15°36′W, elevation 21 m

Month	Mean sta. press. (mbar)	Temperature (°C) mean max.	mean min.	extreme max.	extreme min.	Relative humidity (%) 07h	13h	Precipitation mean (mm)	max. (mm)	min. (mm)	days ≥1 mm	max. in 24 h (mm)	Wind av. speed (km/h)	preval. direct.	calm (%)	Averages cloud-iness¹ (oktas)	number of gales >34 knots
Jan.	1,014	29	13	38	5	51	32	<1	5	0	<1	1	10.1	NE	4	3	0
Feb.	1,013	30	14	39	7	53	28	<1	18	0	<1	18	10.3	NE	9	3	0
Mar.	1,012	33	16	43	5	65	34	<1	15	0	0	15	12.8	N	4	2	0
Apr.	1,011	33	18	45	12	68	31	1	10	0	0	10	11.7	NW	1	2	0
May	1,011	35	20	46	13	72	35	1	16	0	0	13	11.9	NW	10	2	0
June	1,012	34	22	46	16	79	48	1	13	0	<1	8	16.2	NW	3	4	0.2
July	1,011	32	24	45	15	85	62	18	46	0	2	23	15.7	NW	5	4	0
Aug.	1,011	32	24	44	17	87	66	81	386	3	4	249	12.8	WNW	9	5	0
Sept.	1,012	34	24	45	17	84	58	38	190	0	4	51	12.3	WNW	16	4	0
Oct.	1,012	35	22	43	13	73	41	10	42	0	1	38	13.1	NW	11	4	0
Nov.	1,012	33	18	42	9	65	33	5	28	0	<1	23	11.7	N	7	3	0
Dec.	1,014	29	14	40	5	57	34	<1	25	0	<1	8	12.8	NE	8	4	0
Annual	1,012	32	19	46	5	84	50	156			12	249	12.6	—	7	3	0.2
Rec. (yrs.)	6	21	21	21	21	10	10	25	25	25	25	25	10	10	10	10	6

¹ Mean of 05h00, 11h00 and 17h00.

TABLE XVII

CLIMATIC TABLE FOR BILMA, NIGER
Latitude 18°39′N, longitude 13°23′E, elevation 355 m

Month	Mean sta. press. (mbar)	Temperature (°C)				Relative humidity (%)		Precipitation					Wind			Averages		
		mean		extreme		07h	13h	mean (mm)	max. (mm)	min. (mm)	days >1 mm	max. in 24 h (mm)	av. speed (km/h)	preval. direct.	calm (%)	cloud-iness (oktas)	sun-shine (h)	number of gales >34 knots
		max.	min.	max.	min.													
Jan.	974	27	7	37	−3	41	17	<1	4	0	0	4	7.8	NE	60	1	290	0
Feb.	973	30	9	40	0	34	14	0	2	0	0	0	7.4	NE	66	1	279	0.6
Mar.	970	35	13	45	1	29	13	0	0	0	0	0	6.0	NE	63	1	300	0.2
Apr.	969	38	17	46	8	23	9	<1	2	0	0	1	5.0	E	55	1	296	0.3
May	968	42	21	47	13	28	13	1	12	0	<1	8	4.6	E	58	1	322	0.3
June	968	43	23	49	14	31	13	1	15	0	<1	10	6.0	E	56	1	317	0
July	968	42	23	47	15	40	18	3	23	0	<1	10	4.5	E	59	2	335	0.3
Aug.	968	40	23	48	16	55	27	10	62	0	1	30	3.5	W	65	2	320	0.5
Sept.	970	41	21	45	12	36	17	5	33	0	<1	33	3.6	E	63	1	305	0.2
Oct.	971	38	16	43	7	33	15	2	49	0	0	49	2.3	E	67	<1	320	0.3
Nov.	973	33	11	41	3	39	17	0	<1	0	0	0	2.7	E	64	1	305	0
Dec.	975	27	8	37	−1	43	19	0	0	0	0	0	3.2	NE	58	1	292	0.2
Annual	970	36	16	49	−3	36	16	22		0	2	49	4.7	—	61	1	3,681	3
Rec. (yrs.)	20	20	20	20	20	10	10	27	27	27	27	37	10	10	10	9	11	6

TABLE XVIII

CLIMATIC TABLE FOR DONGOLA, SUDAN
Latitude 19°10'N, longitude 30°29'E, elevation 225 m

Month	Mean sta. press. (mbar)	Temperature (°C) mean max.	mean min.	extreme max.	extreme min.	Dew point (°C) 06h	12h	Precipitation mean (mm)	max. (mm)	min. (mm)	days ≥1 mm	max. in 24 h (mm)	Wind av. speed[1] 1-3	4-7	preval. direct.	calm (%)	Averages cloud-iness[2] (oktas)	evap. (Piche) (mm/day)
Jan.	988	28	9	37	3	2.3	4.8	0	0	0	0	6	97	2	NE	1	<1	7.9
Feb.	987	29	10	40	3	1.3	2.9	tr.	1	0	<1	0	96	3	NE	<1	<1	9.5
Mar.	985	34	14	45	4	2.5	3.1	0	tr.	0	0	tr.	92	8	NE	<1	1	11.8
Apr.	983	38	18	47	10	3.8	3.4	0	tr.	0	0	tr.	93	5	NE	2	1	14.5
May	982	42	22	48	14	6.5	7.1	1	20	0	<1	16	94	4	NE	<1	1	17.0
June	981	43	24	48	17	8.8	9.7	tr.	tr.	0	0	tr.	95	4	NE	1	<1	17.8
July	980	42	25	47	19	12.9	12.3	9	50	0	1	32	94	4	NE	2	1	15.7
Aug.	980	42	26	47	19	16.1	14.7	13	56	0	2	36	94	4	NE	2	2	14.5
Sept.	981	41	25	47	15	11.8	11.3	tr.	3	0	<1	3	95	5	NE	<1	1	15.1
Oct.	983	39	21	45	10	10.5	9.5	tr.	3	0	<1	3	96	4	NE	<1	<1	13.7
Nov.	986	33	15	40	6	7.6	9.7	0	2	0	<1	2	94	6	NE	0	<1	10.0
Dec.	988	29	11	38	4	5.8	8.5	0	tr.	0	0	tr.	96	4	NE	<1	<1	7.8
Annual	984	37	19	48	3	8.1	8.5	23	60	0	3	36	95	5	—	1	1	13.0
Rec. (yrs.)	16	16	16	16	16	30	30	30	23	23	30	30	6	6	6	6	16	16

[1] Mean of 06h00 and 12h00; intervals are in km/h.
[2] Given as percentages in the Beaufort scales shown.

TABLE XIX

CLIMATIC TABLE FOR TESSALIT, MALI
Latitude 20°12′N, longitude 0°59′E, elevation 520 m

Month	M.s.l. press. (mbar)	Temperature (°C) mean max.	mean min.	extreme max.	extreme min.	Relative humidity (%) 06h	12h	Precipitation mean (mm)	max. (mm)	min. (mm)	days ≥1 mm	max. in 24 h (mm)	Wind av. speed. (m/sec)	preval. direct.[1]	calm (%)	Averages cloud-iness[1] (oktas)	sun-shine (h/day)	number of gales >34 knots
Jan.	1,015	27	12	34	4	30	17	<1	1	0	0	1	3	NE	18	3	9.6	0
Feb.	1,013	30	14	38	4	24	14	<1	2	0	0	2	3	NE	18	3	9.5	0
Mar.	1,011	32	18	41	8	23	14	<1	3	0	1	3	3	NE	17	3	10.3	0.2
Apr.	1,009	37	22	44	12	21	13	<1	1	0	0	1	3	NE	15	2	10.5	0.3
May	1,008	40	25	45	17	23	13	1	8	0	1	8	3	NE	20	3	10.2	0
June	1,008	43	28	46	21	28	15	2	27	0	2	15	3	SW	21	2	9.2	0.5
July	1,007	42	27	46	18	43	22	15	53	0	4	25	3	SW	17	3	9.6	0.7
Aug.	1,008	40	26	45	16	59	30	51	165	12	5	63	2	SW	34	4	9.4	3
Sept.	1,009	40	26	43	18	45	23	23	61	0	4	38	2	SW	33	3	9.3	0.7
Oct.	1,010	37	24	42	11	30	17	2	3	0	<1	3	3	NE	27	3	9.6	0
Nov.	1,012	33	19	38	7	28	17	1	4	0	<1	2	3	NE	18	3	9.2	0
Dec.	1,015	28	14	35	3	31	18	<1	1	0	0	<1	3	NE	17	4	9.0	0
Annual	1,010	37	21	46	3	32	18	96			17	63	3	—	21	3	9.6	5
Rec. (yrs.)	30	10	10	10	10	5	5	20	10	10			5	5	5	8	10	6

[1] Mean of 06h00, 12h00 and 18h00.

TABLE XX

CLIMATIC TABLE FOR ATAR, MAURITANIA
Latitude 20°31'N, longitude 13°04'W, elevation 225 m

Month	Mean sta. press. (mbar)	Temperature (°C) mean max.	Temperature (°C) mean min.	Temperature (°C) extreme max.	Temperature (°C) extreme min.	Relative humidity (%) 05h	Relative humidity (%) 17h	Precipitation mean (mm)	Precipitation max. (mm)	Precipitation min. (mm)	Precipitation days ≥1 mm	Precipitation max. in 24 h (mm)	Wind av. speed (km/h)	Wind preval. direct.	Wind calm (%)	Averages cloudiness[1] (oktas)	Averages number of gales ≥34 knots
Jan.	990	27	12	38	4	50	30	1	15	0	<1	13	10.9	NE	28	3	0
Feb.	989	29	14	39	5	49	25	1	18	0	<1	3	10.1	N	30	2	0
Mar.	988	34	17	45	9	47	24	<1	21	0	<1	13	11.3	N	18	2	0
Apr.	986	36	20	45	11	39	21	<1	5	0	0	5	10.1	N	18	2	0
May	985	39	23	47	11	35	19	1	21	0	<1	5	12.0	N	16	3	0
June	986	42	27	48	17	34	18	8	98	0	<1	13	13.9		13	3	0.2
July	984	42	27	48	17	51	24	8	48	<1	1	35	14.4	W–N	14	3	0
Aug.	985	41	27	49	14	58	29	33	86	0	4	28	16.0	N	21	3	1
Sept.	986	40	27	49	12	56	31	35	121	0	3	69	16.2	N	20	3	1
Oct.	987	37	23	45	12	50	28	8	119	0	1	46	12.6	N	13	4	0
Nov.	988	33	18	40	7	51	31	10	56	0	<1	15	11.3	N	22	4	0.2
Dec.	990	28	14	40	4	53	31	1	16	0	1	8	11.1	N	25	4	0.3
Annual	987	37	21	49	4	48	26	106			10	69	12.5	—	20	3	3
Rec. (yrs.)	8	29	29	29	29	10	10	33	33	33	33	33				10	6

[1] Mean of 08h00 and 18h00.

TABLE XXI

CLIMATIC TABLE FOR ETIENNE, MAURITANIA
Latitude 20°56′N, longitude 17°03′W, elevation 4 m

Month	Temperature (°C)				Relative humidity (%)		Precipitation					Wind			Averages	
	mean		extreme				mean (mm)	max. (mm)	min. (mm)	days >1 mm	max. in 24 h (mm)	av. speed (km/h)	preval. direct.	calm (%)	cloud-iness[1] (oktas)	number of gales ≥34 knots
	max.	min.	max.	min.	07h	13h										
Jan.	26	13	31	7	74	55	2	33	0	0.3	15	7	NE	2	3	0
Feb.	26	13	37	8	78	52	1	13	0	0.3	10	9	N	5	2	1
Mar.	26	14	36	8	84	53	2	28	0	0.2	28	9	N	1	2	1
Apr.	27	14	43	8	85	54	1	18	0	0	18	9	N	0	2	0.5
May	28	16	39	9	87	48	<1	3	0	0	2	10	N	3	2	0
June	29	17	46	10	86	49	<1	18	0	0	18	10	N	2	2	0
July	27	18	39	13	89	51	<1	1	0	0.3	1	9	N	5	2	0
Aug.	29	19	40	12	93	52	3	15	0	0.5	10	8	N	4	2	0
Sept.	31	20	42	14	83	47	8	58	0	0.9	53	7	N	4	3	0.2
Oct.	30	18	40	11	84	45	5	83	0	1	83	7	N	1	3	0
Nov.	28	16	38	11	85	47	5	61	0	0.4	10	6	N	3	3	0.8
Dec.	25	14	36	8	74	46	2	66	0	0.8	66	6	NE	0	2	0.3
Annual	28	16	46	7	83	50	27	33	0	5	83	8	—	2	3	4
Rec. (yrs.)	13	13	13	13	10	10	33	33	33	33	33	5	5	5	10	6

[1] Mean of 05h00, 11h00 and 17h00.

TABLE XXII

CLIMATIC TABLE FOR WADI HALFA, SUDAN
Latitude 21°50'N, longitude 31°18'E, elevation 160 m

Month	M.s.l. press. (mbar)	Temperature (°C) mean max.	mean min.	extreme max.	extreme min.	Dew point[1] (°C)	Precipitation mean (mm)	max. (mm)	min. (mm)	days ≥1 mm	max. in 24 h (mm)	Wind av. speed (km/h)	preval. direct.	calm (%)	Averages cloudiness[1] (oktas)	sunshine (h/day)	rad. (Ly/day)	evap. (Piche) (mm/day)
Jan.	1,018	25	8	38	1	0.7	0	4	0	0	tr.	14	N	5	1	10.2	457	11.3
Feb.	1,017	27	9	41	1	−0.5	0	<1	0	0	<1	15	N	4	1	10.4	525	13.7
Mar.	1,015	31	13	43	3	−0.7	0	<1	0	0	<1	16	N	3	1	10.3	588	18.1
Apr.	1,012	36	17	47	8	0.7	0	<1	0	0	<1	16	N	6	1	10.0	639	22.4
May	1,010	41	22	49	11	4.1	1	9	0	0.1	9	16	N	5	1	11.3	667	25.7
June	1,009	42	23	49	17	5.1	0	0	0	0	0	15	N	6	<1	11.9	686	25.2
July	1,007	41	24	48	18	7.4	1	29	0	0.2	19	14	N	10	1	11.0	638	24.0
Aug.	1,008	41	25	47	20	10.4	0	1	0	0.1	1	13	N	9	1	11.1	609	24.2
Sept.	1,010	39	23	47	17	8.9	0	tr.	0	0	tr.	14	N	4	1	10.0	582	24.8
Oct.	1,012	37	20	44	12	7.4	1	14	0	0.1	12	14	N	3	<1	10.7	525	21.7
Nov.	1,015	31	15	41	5	5.9	0	2	0	0.1	2	13	N	4	1	10.4	461	15.1
Dec.	1,018	26	10	38	2	4.3	0	6	0	0	4	11	N	6	1	9.8	426	11.4
Annual	1,013	35	17	49	1	4.8	3	33	0	<1	19	14	—	5	1	10.6	567	19.8
Rec. (yrs.)	30	30	30	30	30	30	30	24	24	30	24	9	9	9	30		4	20

[1] Mean of 06h00, 12h00 and 18h00.

TABLE XXIII

CLIMATIC TABLE FOR TAMANRASSET, ALGERIA
Latitude 22°42'N, longitude 05°31'E, elevation 1,405 m

Month	Mean sta. press. (mbar)	Temperature (°C) mean max.	mean min.	extreme max.	extreme min.	Relative humidity (%) 07h	13h	Precipitation mean (mm)	max. (mm)	min. (mm)	days ≥1 mm	max. in 24 h (mm)	Wind preval. direct. 07h	13h	calm (%) 07h	13h	Averages cloud-iness[1] (oktas)	sun-shine (h/day)
Jan.	865	19	4	26	−7	37	21	4	55	0	1	7	NE	NW	14	4	2	9.3
Feb.	865	22	6	28	−4	34	27	1	16	0	1	3	NE	NW	5	1	2	9.6
Mar.	864	26	9	32	0	31	20	1	5	0	1	5	NE	NW	9	1	2	10.4
Apr.	863	30	13	36	3	35	18	2	33	0	1	20	NE	NW	8	0	2	10.4
May	864	33	17	38	4	34	23	6	95	0	2	48	NE	NW	6	0	3	10.7
June	866	35	21	38	15	27	20	4	35	0	3	19	NE	SE	2	0	3	10.0
July	865	35	22	39	17	25	17	3	18	0	2	5	NE	SE	2	1	2	10.4
Aug.	865	34	21	38	17	29	20	10	73	0	3	35	NE	SE	5	1	3	10.3
Sept.	866	33	19	37	14	29	23	7	96	0	3	48	NE	SE	5	2	3	8.5
Oct.	866	29	15	34	8	37	21	2	19	0	2	17	NE	SE	8	0	2	9.0
Nov.	866	26	11	30	−1	40	24	2	34	0	1	29	NE	NW	10	0	2	9.0
Dec.	865	21	6	27	−3	40	21	2	26	0	1	21	NE	NW	9	2	2	7.9
Annual	865	28	13	39	−7	33	21	44	159	6	21	48	—	NW	7	1	2	9.7
Rec. (yrs.)	19	35	35	35	35	15	15				10						10	

[1] Mean of 06h00, 12h00 and 18h00.

TABLE XXIV

CLIMATIC TABLE FOR KUFRA, LIBYA
Latitude 24°13′N, longitude 23°20′E, elevation 381 m

Month	M.s.l. press. (mbar)	Temperature (°C) mean max.	Temperature (°C) mean min.	Temperature (°C) extreme max.	Temperature (°C) extreme min.	Relat. humid. (%)	Precipitation mean (mm)	Precipitation max. (mm)	Precipitation min. (mm)	Precipitation days ≥0.1 mm	Precipitation max. in 24 h (mm)	Wind av. speed (knots)	Wind preval. direct.	Wind calm (%)	Averages cloudiness (oktas)	Averages sunshine (h/day)	Averages evap. (Piche) (mm)
Jan.	1,021	21	5	32	−3	47	0	<1	0	0	0	4	N,E	25	1	8.9	225
Feb.	1,020	23	7	34	−2	41	0.5	7	0	<1	4	5	N	19	1	9.1	269
Mar.	1,017	27	10	39	1	33	0	1	0	0	1	5	N	18	1	9.5	406
Apr.	1,014	33	15	42	7	28	0	<1	0	0	0	6	N	14	1	9.5	516
May	1,013	37	20	48	10	27	0.2	3	0	0	3	6	N	11	1	11.2	627
June	1,013	39	22	50	16	24	0	<1	0	0	<1	6	N	9	<1	11.4	646
July	1,012	38	23	43	17	26	0	0	0	0	0	7	N	5	<1	12.2	681
Aug.	1,012	38	23	46	18	26	0.5	11	0	<1	11	6	N	7	<1	12.1	592
Sept.	1,015	36	21	42	15	31	0.3	7	0	<1	5	6	N	10	<1	10.3	576
Oct.	1,017	32	16	42	8	35	0.1	2	0	0	1	5	N,E	14	<1	9.9	437
Nov.	1,019	27	11	38	4	43	0	1	0	0	1	4	E	24	<1	9.7	278
Dec.	1,021	22	6	33	−1	48	0.2	2	0	0	2	4	N,E	29	1	8.4	241
Annual	1,016	31	15	50	−3	34	2	13	0	1	11	5	—	15	1	10.2	5,494
Rec. (yrs.)	22	22	22	11	11	22	22	22	22	22	22	5	5	5	22	4	4

TABLE XXV

CLIMATIC TABLE FOR DAKHLA, U.A.R.
Latitude 25°29'N, longitude 29°00'E, elevation 110 m

Month	M.s.l. press. (mbar)	Temperature (°C)				Dew point (°C)	Precipitation					Av. wind speed (m/sec)	Averages	
		mean		extreme			mean (mm)	max. (mm)	min. (mm)	days ≤1 mm	max. in 24 h (mm)		cloud-iness (oktas)	evap. (mm/ day)
		max.	min.	max.	min.									
Jan.	1,019	22	4	36	−3	0.5	0	0.3	0	0	0.3	2	1	7.7
Feb.	1,018	24	5	39	−4	−0.2	0.3	10	0	<1	8	2	2	10.0
Mar.	1,016	28	9	43	0	−1.3	0	0.1	0	0	0.1	2	1	13.4
Apr.	1,013	33	14	47	2	−0.6	0	tr.	0	0	tr.	2	1	17.7
May	1,011	37	19	48	7	2.5	0.1	3.4	0	<1	3.4	2	<1	21.8
June	1,010	38	23	50	13	5.2	0	tr.	0	0	tr.	2	<1	23.8
July	1,008	38	23	49	16	7.2	0	0	0	0	0	2	<1	22.4
Aug.	1,008	39	23	46	16	7.6	0	0	0	0	0	2	<1	21.3
Sept.	1,012	36	20	44	11	8.6	0	0	0	0	0	2	<1	19.5
Oct.	1,014	33	17	44	8	6.3	0	1	0	0	1	2	<1	15.4
Nov.	1,016	28	11	42	2	4.2	0	tr.	0	0	tr.	2	<1	10.9
Dec.	1,019	23	6	35	−3	2.1	0.1	1	0	<1	1	1	1	7.7
Annual	1,014	32	14	50	−4	3.9	0.5	11	tr.	<1	8	2	1	16.0
Rec. (yrs.)	30	25	25	25	25	25	25	35	35	25	25	5	5	10

TABLE XXVI

CLIMATIC TABLE FOR LUXOR, U.A.R.
Latitude 25°40'N, longitude 32°42'E, elevation 95 m

Month	M.s.l. press. (mbar)	Temperature (°C) mean max.	min.	extreme max.	min.	Dew point (°C)	Precipitation mean (mm)	max. (mm)	min. (mm)	days ≥1 mm	max. in 24 h (mm)	Wind av. speed (m/sec)	preval. direct.[1]	calm[1] (%)	Averages cloud-iness (oktas)	evap. (mm/day)
Jan.	1,017	23	6	32	0	3.8	0.1	2	0	0	2	2	N	28	1	4.8
Feb.	1,016	25	7	35	−2	2.8	0.2	3	0	0	3	2	N	28	1	6.2
Mar.	1,013	29	11	42	2	3.6	tr.	0.3	0	0	0.3	2	NW	14	1	8.9
Apr.	1,011	35	16	46	6	4.5	tr.	tr.	0	0	tr.	3	NW	14	1	12.6
May	1,009	39	20	48	11	6.3	0.5	6	0	<1	6	2	NW	14	1	15.4
June	1,007	41	23	49	17	8.9	0	0	0	0	0	2	NW	13	<1	16.9
July	1,005	41	24	48	20	10.4	0	0	0	0	0	2	NW	13	<1	16.6
Aug.	1,005	41	24	47	17	10.6	0	0	0	0	0	2	NW	13	<1	16.5
Sept.	1,008	38	21	45	16	11.8	0	1	0	0	1	2	N	19	<1	13.4
Oct.	1,012	35	18	43	10	12.8	0.1	1	0	<1	1	1	N	19	<1	9.7
Nov.	1,015	30	12	38	3	10.7	0.1	1	0	<1	1	2	N	19	1	6.8
Dec.	1,017	25	8	35	0	7.1	0.1	1	0	<1	1	2	N	28	1	5.1
Annual	1,011	34	16	49	−2	7.8	1	6	tr.	<1	6	2	—	18	1	10.1
Rec. (yrs.)	30	18	18	18	18	18	18	35	35	18	18	19	14	14	18	10

[1] From hourly observations.

126

TABLE XXVII

CLIMATIC TABLE FOR QUSEIR, U.A.R.
Latitude 26°08′N, longitude 34°18′E, elevation 10 m

Month	M.s.l. press. (mbar)	Temperature (°C) mean max.	mean min.	extreme max.	extreme min.	Dew point (°C)	Precipitation mean (mm)	max. (mm)	min. (mm)	days ≥1 mm	max. in 24 h (mm)	Wind av. speed (m/sec)	preval. direct.	calm (%)	Averages cloud-iness (oktas)	evap. (mm/day)
Jan.	1,016	22	14	33	4	7.6	0	1	0	0	1	5	W	4	2	10.7
Feb.	1,016	23	14	35	6	6.3	0	tr.	0	0	tr.	5	W	5	2	11.9
Mar.	1,013	25	16	38	7	8.5	0.4	9	0	<1	9	5	N	6	2	12.8
Apr.	1,011	27	19	43	13	11.3	0.2	2	0	<1	2	5	N	9	1	13.8
May	1,009	30	23	41	16	13.1	0	1	0	0	1	5	N	9	<1	15.5
June	1,007	32	25	48	21	15.4	0	tr.	0	0	tr.	5	N	7	<1	17.3
July	1,005	33	26	42	21	17.8	0	0	0	0	0	4	N	11	<1	15.1
Aug.	1,005	34	27	41	21	17.9	0	0	0	0	0	4	N	13	<1	15.6
Sept.	1,008	32	25	38	19	17.3	0	tr.	0	0	tr.	5	N	9	<1	15.1
Oct.	1,012	30	23	39	17	15.6	1	11	0	<1	11	4	N	7	1	12.8
Nov.	1,014	27	19	34	11	13.0	2	20	0	<1	20	5	N/W	3	1	11.7
Dec.	1,017	24	16	31	9	10.0	0.2	4	0	0	4	4	W	2	1	10.5
Annual	1,011	18	21	48	4	12.8	4	34	tr.	1	20	5	—	7	1	13.6
Rec. (yrs.)	25	25	25	25	25	25	25	35	35	25	25	5	5	5	5	10

127

TABLE XXVIII

CLIMATIC TABLE FOR CAIRO, U.A.R.
Latitude 30°08′N, longitude 31°34′E, elevation 95 m

Month	Mean sta. press. (mbar)	Temperature (°C) mean max.	Temperature (°C) mean min.	Temperature (°C) extreme max.	Temperature (°C) extreme min.	Dew point (°C)	Precip. mean (mm)	Precip. max. (mm)	Precip. min. (mm)	Precip. days >0.1 mm	Precip. max. in 24 h (mm)	Wind av. speed (m/sec)	Wind preval. direct.[1]	Wind calm[1] (%)	Avg. cloudiness (oktas)	Avg. sunshine (h/day)	Avg. evap. (mm/day)
Jan.	1,009	19	9	30	2	5.6	4	22	0	3	9	4	NE/SW	5	3	7.4	5.6
Feb.	1,009	21	9	35	1	5.2	5	21	0	2	11	4	NE/SW	5	3	8.0	7.0
Mar.	1,006	24	11	40	4	6.5	3	15	0	2	11	4	N	1	2	8.9	8.7
Apr.	1,005	28	14	42	7	8.7	1	5	0	<1	3	4	N	1	2	9.7	10.6
May	1,004	33	18	47	10	10.6	1	17	0	<1	10	4	N	1	2	10.8	13.1
June	1,002	35	20	46	14	14.5	0	tr.	0	0	tr.	3	N	1	1	11.4	13.0
July	1,000	35	22	46	18	17.5	0	tr.	0	0	tr.	3	N	1	1	11.5	11.2
Aug.	1,000	35	22	42	16	18.4	0	<1	0	0	<1	3	N	1	1	11.1	10.0
Sept.	1,004	32	20	41	15	17.1	0	tr.	0	0	tr.	3	NE	3	1	10.4	8.9
Oct.	1,006	30	18	43	11	14.7	1	6	0	<1	4	3	NE	3	2	9.6	8.5
Nov.	1,008	26	14	40	5	12.0	1	13	0	<1	12	3	NE	3	2	8.6	6.6
Dec.	1,009	21	10	32	4	7.6	8	54	0	3	44	3	NE	4	3	7.5	5.5
Annual	1,005	28	16	47	1	11.5	24	63	3	10	44	3	—	2	2	9.6	9.9
Rec. (yrs.)	10	25	25	25	25	25	25	35	35	25	25	25	14	14	21	11	10

[1] From hourly observations.

TABLE XXIX

CLIMATIC TABLE FOR GHADAMES, LIBYA
Latitude 30°08′N, longitude 09°40′E, elevation 360 m

Month	M.s.l. press. (mbar)	Temperature (°C) mean max.	mean min.	extreme max.	extreme min.	Relative humidity (%) 05h30	11h30	Precipitation mean (mm)	max. (mm)	min. (mm)	days ≥0.1 mm	max. in 24 h (mm)	Wind av. speed (knots)	preval. direct.	calm (%)	Aver. cloud-iness (oktas)
Jan.	1,020	18	3	32	−7	72	45	5	41	0	1	8	8.0	W	22	2
Feb.	1,017	21	4	34	−3	63	36	3	35	0	1	4	7.0	W	21	1
Mar.	1,016	26	8	41	−1	61	32	5	21	0	1	17	6.4	W,N	14	2
Apr.	1,010	32	13	48	4	51	26	2	22	0	<1	11	9.0	E	15	2
May	1,011	37	18	52	7	42	19	2	10	0	<1	10	8.8	E	10	2
June	1,010	42	22	55	14	38	17	1	8	0	<1	0	8.6	NE	11	1
July	1,011	43	22	53	15	37	17	0	0	0	0	<1	8.0	NE	12	<1
Aug.	1,011	42	22	52	13	45	21	<1	4	0	0	4	7.2	NE	10	<1
Sept.	1,013	38	19	50	10	46	21	1	20	0	<1	5	8.0	NE	14	1
Oct.	1,015	32	15	48	3	59	30	2	23	0	1	17	6.8	NE	19	2
Nov.	1,017	24	9	39	2	62	33	5	35	0	2	5	6.6	SW	25	2
Dec.	1,017	19	4	31	−3	65	36	1	26	0	1	4	8.0	W	21	2
Annual	1,014	31	13	55	−7	54	28	27	79	6	7	17	7.7	—	16	1
Rec. (yrs.)	7							18	18	18	18	7	10		10	6

TABLE XXX

CLIMATIC TABLE FOR ALEXANDRIA, U.A.R.
Latitude 31°12'N, longitude 29°51'E, elevation 7 m

Month	M.s.l. press. (mbar)	Temperature (°C) mean max.	mean min.	extreme max.	extreme min.	Dew point (°C)	Precipitation mean (mm)	max. (mm)	min. (mm)	days ≥0.1 mm	max. in 24 h	Wind av. speed (m/sec)	preval. direct.[1]	calm[1] (%)	Averages cloud-iness (oktas)	sun-shine (h/day)	evap. (mm/day)
Jan.	1,018	18	9	26	2	8.1	49	101	1	11	48	4	NW	6	4	7.2	4.2
Feb.	1,017	19	9	36	2	7.9	31	91	6	7	28	4	NW	6	4	7.5	4.6
Mar.	1,015	21	11	40	6	9.4	12	48	tr.	6	13	5	N	4	4	8.7	5.2
Apr.	1,014	24	13	42	7	11.7	3	18	0	2	13	4	N	4	3	9.5	5.4
May	1,013	27	16	45	10	15.0	2	10	0	1	9	4	N	4	3	10.4	5.8
June	1,012	28	20	44	12	18.4	tr.	<1	0	0	<1	4	N	5	2	11.2	5.7
July	1,009	30	23	38	17	20.6	0	tr.	0	0	tr.	4	N	5	2	12.2	5.5
Aug.	1,009	31	23	40	17	21.0	<1	9	0	0	9	4	N	5	2	11.0	5.6
Sept.	1,013	29	21	40	15	19.0	<1	4	0	0	4	4	N	8	2	10.4	5.8
Oct.	1,016	28	18	39	12	16.4	9	34	0	3	24	3	N	8	3	9.3	5.4
Nov.	1,017	24	15	36	7	13.8	29	100	0	7	32	3	N	8	4	7.7	4.4
Dec.	1,020	20	11	29	4	10.2	56	154	5	10	37	4	NW	6	4	6.3	4.5
Annual	1,014	25	16	45	2	14.3	191	316	33	47	48	4	—	6	3	9.3	5.2
Rec. (yrs.)	30	24	24	24	24	24	24	34	34	24	24	9	14	14	24	16	10

[1] From hourly observations.

TABLE XXXI

CLIMATIC TABLE FOR SALLUM, U.A.R.
Latitude 31°53'N, longitude 25°11'E, elevation 170 m

Month	M.s.l. press. (mbar)	Temperature (°C) mean max.	Temperature (°C) mean min.	Temperature (°C) extreme max.	Temperature (°C) extreme min.	Dew point (°C)	Precipitation mean (mm)	Precipitation max. (mm)	Precipitation min. (mm)	Precipitation days ≥0.1 mm	Precipitation max. in 24 h	Av. wind speed (m/sec)	Averages cloudiness (oktas)	Averages sunshine (h/day)	Averages evap. (mm/day)
Jan.	1,019	19	9	27	3	6.1	12	67	tr.	7	38	5	4	7.0	7.5
Feb.	1,017	20	10	33	3	4.2	12	37	tr.	5	17	5	3	7.5	8.1
Mar.	1,017	21	11	41	4	7.2	12	59	0	4	30	5	3	9.0	8.4
Apr.	1,015	24	13	42	6	9.6	1	10	0	1	8	4	3	9.9	8.2
May	1,015	26	17	43	9	12.6	3	23	0	2	16	4	2	9.9	8.7
June	1,014	30	20	46	14	16.5	0	1	0	0	1	4	1	12.3	10.0
July	1,012	31	21	44	16	18.7	0	tr.	0	0	tr.	5	<1	12.7	10.6
Aug.	1,012	30	22	43	16	19.6	0	0	0	0	0	4	<1	12.2	9.4
Sept.	1,015	29	20	42	14	17.2	1	9	0	<1	6	4	1	10.9	8.5
Oct.	1,017	27	18	40	12	15.2	5	73	0	3	58	3	3	9.7	8.1
Nov.	1,018	25	15	36	7	11.8	28	227	tr.	2	121	3	3	7.3	7.6
Dec.	1,019	20	11	32	5	7.7	21	70	tr.	6	33	5	4	6.8	7.4
Annual	1,016	25	16	46	3	12.2	95	324	4	30	121	4	2	9.6	8.5
Rec. (yrs.)	30	20	20	20	20	20	20	35	35	20	20	9	10	9	10

Chapter 4

The Horn of Africa

J. F. GRIFFITHS

Introduction

The vast Sahara Desert meets two natural barriers on its eastern border, the Red Sea and the high mountains of Ethiopia. Here the Sahara proper terminates but, in a boomerang-shaped strip, at first narrow and then very wide, another arid or semi-arid area is located, pushing its way south towards and even beyond the equator. In this large region of more than 1,000,000 km² the average annual rainfall only exceeds 500 mm on a few high ranges and vegetation is everywhere quite sparse, save on the Erigavo escarpment in the Somali Republic. This arid zone, comprising the coastal belt of the Eritrean province of Ethiopia, the territory of the Afars and the Issas (French Somaliland), the Somali Republic, the Ogaden (southeastern Ethiopia) and parts of northeastern Kenya, is often referred to as the Horn of Africa, due to its prominent protrusion on the eastern seaboard.

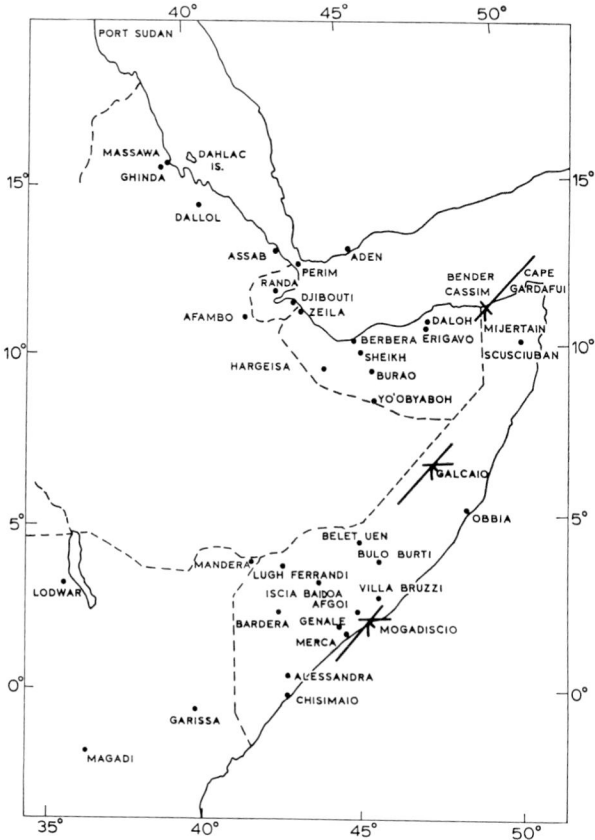

Fig.1. The Horn of Africa (with three wind roses).

The zone is a strange climatological phenomenon—a desert (the Somali–Chalbi) on the eastern coast in tropical latitudes. The extreme aridity is caused, in the main, by the fact that the prevailing winds, during most months of the year, have a northeasterly or south-westerly direction, thus making moist air masses over the land an exception rather than the rule (Fig.1).

The Somali Republic is the largest country within this zone, covering about 640,000 km² and with an estimated population of 2 million persons. It has been formed from the federation of what were previously the Somaliland Protectorate and Italian Somaliland. The population is almost entirely nomadic and the few small towns are mainly along the coast or the lower courses of the Juba and Webi Shebili rivers. The capital, Moga-discio, has only 77,000 inhabitants. The elevated plateau areas support reasonable pastures while hides, skins, livestock and fresh fruit comprise the major exports.

The territory of the Afars and the Issas has an area of only 22,000 km² and a population of less than 70,000 of which about half live in Djibouti, the seaward terminus of the Ethiopian railway. The exports from the port are all items in transit from Ethiopia.

Along the Eritrean coast some salt flats are located, as much as 100 m below sea level, and salt, potash and pearls (from the Dahlac Islands) are important commodities. Some crops are grown on the coastal plain on irrigation from the streams originating in the highland plateau. The northeastern corner of Kenya, covering about a half of the country, bears a great resemblance to the Somali Republic and the Ogaden. Livestock, hides and skins form the major economic exports of the area.

General pressure patterns and wind flow

In a zone so large, extending 2,500 km in a north–south direction and 1,500 km in the east–west, it is natural that the various synoptic situations with which precipitation is often associated occur at very different times of the year. Nevertheless, it is generally possible to identify four main seasons, the northeast monsoon, the southeast monsoon and the two transition periods.

Reference to the figures in Chapter 1 (p. 10) is necessary to gain full appreciation of the pressure and wind patterns obtaining over this zone. In January the high over Arabia and the low over central Africa combine to give rise to an air flow over the zone which is everywhere parallel to the coast. Only in the northern corner, from Port Sudan to Massawa (depending upon the air flow), is there convergence of different air masses. In this case the Indian Ocean easterlies (appearing as southeasterly flow) and the Atlantic westerlies (appearing as northwesterly flow) meet, with resultant ascent and precipitation. More will be given later on this aspect in the section on rainfall patterns.

In April the development of the Ethiopian low brings some convergence to much of the area while the extreme south is being affected by the I.T.C.Z. In spring a marked upper air trough is often evident, extending from the eastern Mediterranean to the Red Sea. The upper divergence of the winds and the lower convergent winds ahead of the trough lead to convective changes, a kind of upper cold front. These fronts are most pronounced where the lowest stratum consists of warm, humid air with high conditional instability, the normal for tropical oceanic areas. Upper troughs extend further south in spring than in winter and can lead to showers over areas as far north as the northern Sahara and Arabia.

In July there is marked divergence over the whole zone and the only rainfall takes place either over high ground or as a "spilling" effect over the Ethiopian Plateau or the Red Sea escarpment. The unusual aridity of this area has caused Flohn to ask the question "why are the summer rains missing?". In a most interesting paper (FLOHN, 1964) he arrives at the answers as: (*1*) directional divergence produced by overheating at the Ethiopian highlands; (*2*) speed divergence produced by the northerly increase of the pressure gradient; (*3*) frictional divergence in coast-parallel winds; (*4*) deflection of wind-driven ocean surface current and cold upwelling along the coast.

In October I.T.C.Z. rains can occur over much of the zone, perhaps triggered or supplemented by the upper trough condition mentioned in the spring period.

Rainfall

As was the case with the Mediterranean zone (Chapter 2), there has been much speculation and study as to whether climatic changes have taken place in recent times in the Horn of Africa. HEMMING (1966) cites specific investigations that have purported to show evidence of a reduction in the rainfall together with an increase in the temperature. One of the examples quoted is the reduction in the 30-year mean annual rainfall for Aden, from 55 mm (1881–1910) to 36 mm (1911–1940). Unfortunately, the zone considered here has very few long period stations but the reliable observatory at Serpent, Djibouti, does not confirm this idea. The 10-year averages, beginning with 1901 are 121, 122, 133, 144, 139, 131, and 134 mm per year—a small variation and well within the limits expected from a homogeneous population of rainfall data.

In most of this zone the seasons, defined by the rainfall patterns, are called the Jilal, Gu, Hagar (Harat) and Der (Dhair). As general statements the following comments pertain to these seasons:

(*1*) Jilal—December to March, the northeast monsoon is in dominance and conditions are dry and relatively hot.

(*2*) Gu—April and May, the transition period, relatively wet and hot.

(*3*) Hagar—June to September, the southwest monsoon dominates, bringing relatively cool conditions with showers along the coast but dry inland.

(*4*) Der—October and November, the transition period, similar to the Gu but there is the important rainy season in the north.

Naturally, with a zone extending so far in the north–south direction, the times of these seasons will vary but the above is a reasonable guide.

The wet months (mean values in excess of 50 mm) are shown in Fig.2. These diagrams illustrate the distinct differences between the northern area and the southern area, the 10°N parallel being the approximate boundary. The zone can be said to be divided into two regions, according to the rainfall season: (*a*) winter rains; (*b*) two peaked, summer dominant. The terms summer and winter are meant in their context as June to August and December to February, not with a thermal connotation.

Winter rains

If the rain falling in the six-month period October to March is expressed as a percentage

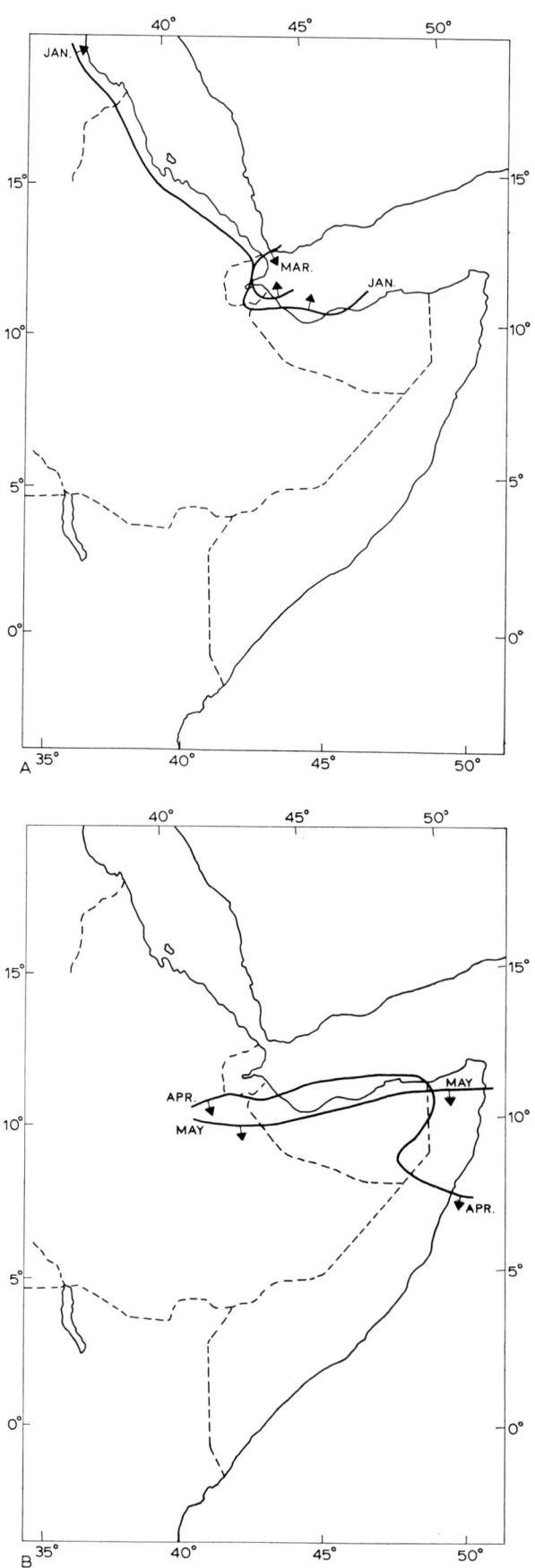

Fig. 2. A and B (legend see p. 138).

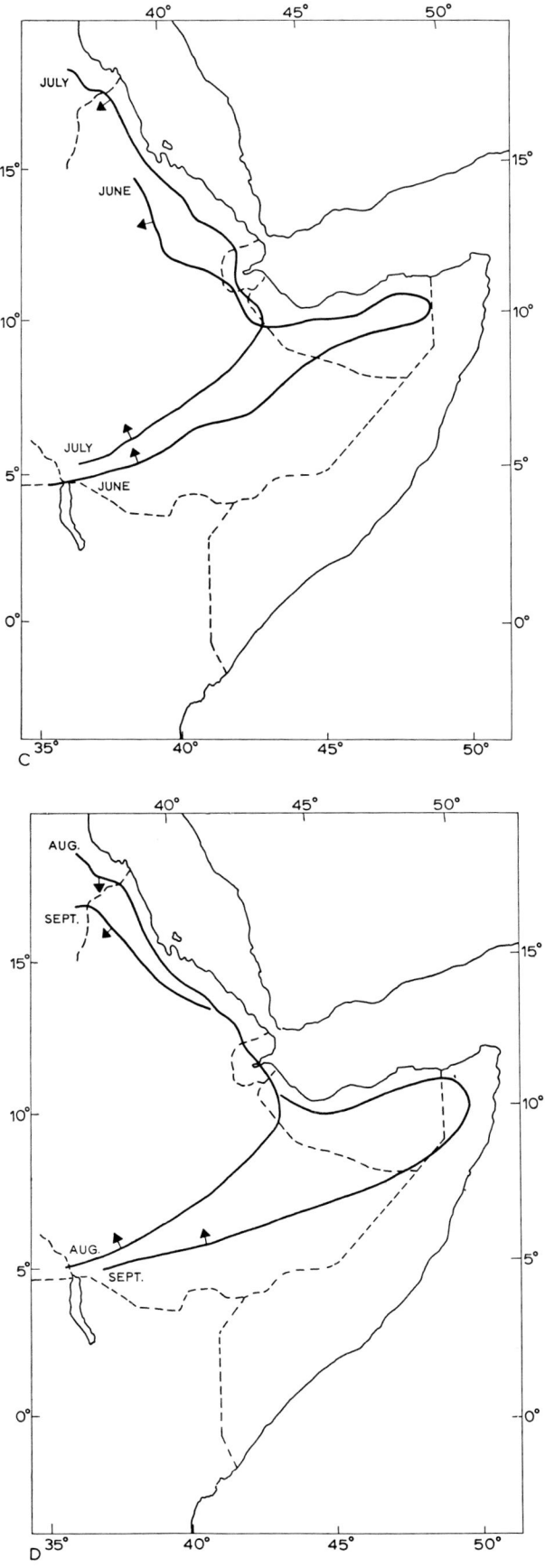

Fig.2. C and D (legend see p.138).

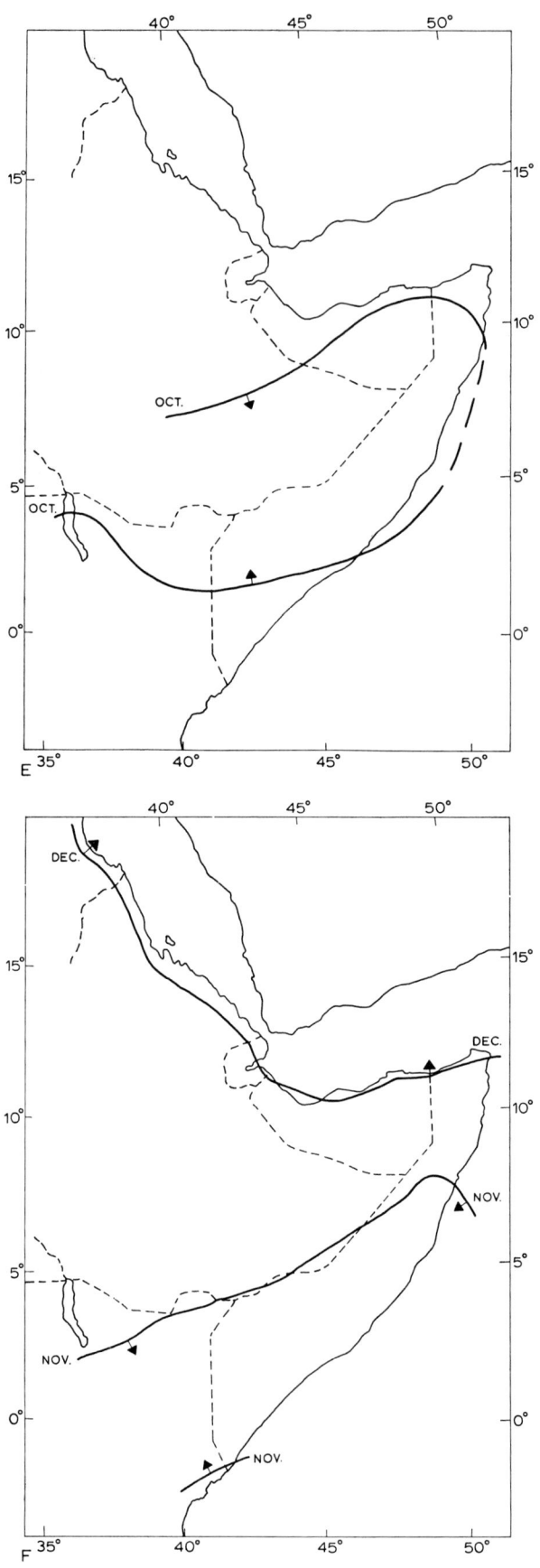

Fig.2. 50-mm isohyets. A. January, March; B. April, May; C. June, July; D. August, September; E. October; F. November, December.

of the annual total one finds the following values: Port Sudan, Dongonab, Zeila—90%; Assab, Massawa, Socotra—80%; Bender Cassim, Djibouti—70%; Berbera—55%. In these stations the rainfall is associated with the aforementioned convergence area. The wettest period gets progressively later as one moves southwards, from October to December in the Port Sudan region to March to May at Berbera.

Summer dominant

In Table I it is noted that much of the zone exhibits two peaks of rainfall, or twin maxima. Their occurrence is generally around April and October, with the former dominant. In this region the Jilal, Gu, Hagar and Der pattern holds. The seasonal distribution illustrates the influence of the I.T.C.Z. and the absence of its effect in the summer months

TABLE I

MEAN MONTHLY RAINFALL (mm)

Station	Jan.	Feb.	Mar.	Apr.	May	June	July	Aug.	Sept.	Oct.	Nov.	Dec.	Year	Wettest quarter[1]
Dongonab	1	2	0	0	2	0	0	1	0	8	13	11	38	XI
Port Sudan	4	1	1	1	2	1	9	3	1	12	52	25	110	XI
Massawa	26	36	15	21	3	1	8	1	2	18	21	42	195	I
Assab	0	1	0	0	0	0	5	0	0	0	6	16	27	XII
Djibouti	10	13	25	12	5	1	2	8	8	10	22	13	129	III
Berbera	8	2	5	12	8	1	1	2	1	2	5	5	49	IV
Bender Cassim	0	0	1	2	3	0	0	0	0	2	7	3	18	XI
Ghinda	152	89	80	74	58	15	48	52	30	77	52	22	826	XII
Randa	18	4	2	46	6	6	23	32	31	12	30	61	271	XII
Erigavo	18	13	33	38	81	63	10	41	114	8	13	2	434	V
Galcaio	0	3	1	24	60	2	0	2	1	41	14	1	148	V
Obbia	12	0	8	21	32	0	0	1	2	38	26	25	165	XI
Lugh Ferrandi	2	4	28	113	40	1	3	0	1	47	56	15	309	IV
Mogadiscio	1	0	9	58	56	82	58	40	23	27	36	9	399	V
Hargeisa	3	8	25	61	61	58	42	81	58	10	8	1	416	VII
Garissa	10	6	27	59	16	5	1	6	6	21	77	64	298	XI
Magadi	32	43	66	89	55	8	1	3	5	15	34	47	398	IV

[1] The Roman numerals indicate the central month of the wettest quarter.

is noticeable in all but two small areas. These areas are the high lands (Ghinda, Randa, Erigavo and Hargeisa) and along the coast near Mogadiscio, where the Indian monsoon circulation is felt. Randa is a wet spot in the dry country of the Afars and the Issas for it has an annual mean rainfall of 320 mm and a maximum of 606 mm in 1964. HEMMING (1966) shows that at the coastal stations of northern Somaliland there is no predictable seasonal pattern but on the plateau there is a definite seasonal distribution. In the northern part (Hargeisa and Sheikh) there is a two-season rainfall, not separated by a summer dry spell; rainy seasons are more clearly separated in the centre (Burao) and the south (Yo'obyaboh) (Fig.3). The wettest area is around Daloh (2,060 m) with an annual mean of 725 mm while Gan Libah (1,660 m) has 660 mm. It is generally necessary to reach 1,500 m to receive over 500 mm/year.

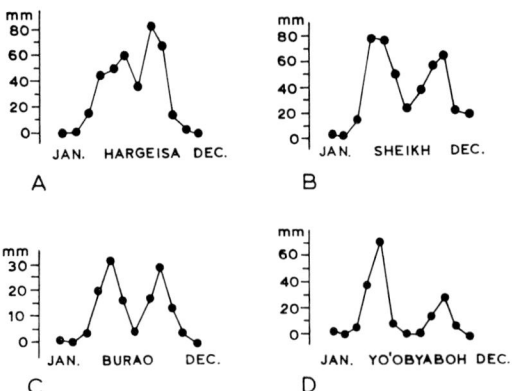

Fig.3. Rainfall patterns, North Somali Republic (after HEMMING, 1966). A. and B. Northern plateau; C. Central plateau; D. Southern boundary.

Rainfall variation and intensity

In Fig.4 the average annual isohyets are given (GRIFFITHS and HEMMING, 1963). This map does not, however, tell the whole story for this is a zone in which even annual amounts show a pronounced variability. Table II gives the annual rainfall amounts at Djibouti for 64 years, an example of amazing fluctuations. Values less than 30 mm have been recorded five times while readings of 250 mm or more occurred four times.

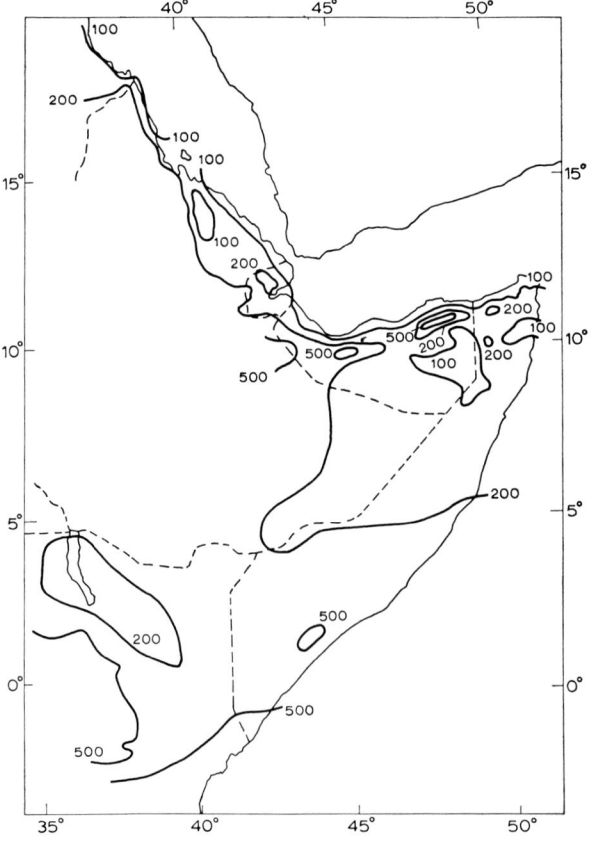

Fig.4. Annual rainfall (mm).

TABLE II

ANNUAL RAINFALL AT DJIBOUTI, SERPENT OBSERVATORY (mm)

Decade \ Year:	0	1	2	3	4	5	6	7	8	9
1900–	—	193	73	92	153	153	119	58	105	46
1910–	241	250	110	94	109	26	232	36	10	116
1920–	123	42	125	—	140	241	245	203	87	89
1930–	205	25	218	119	182	109	67	282	53	183
1940–	191	137	45	102	62	194	168	86	114	289
1950–	41	160	25	67	237	56	121	300	155	52
1960–	161	114	205	88	213	22				

Monthly fluctuations in this zone are also very pronounced, as Table III shows.

The rapid and outstanding change from May to June at Obbia is most unusual and would indicate a rapid termination of the rain-bearing easterly winds as the Asian monsoon southwesterly flow becomes dominant. The unreliable nature of the rains at any season is very obvious from the minimum values.

TABLE III

MONTHLY RAINFALL VARIATIONS (mm)

Station		Jan.	Feb.	Mar.	Apr.	May	June	July	Aug.	Sept.	Oct.	Nov.	Dec.	Year
Djibouti	max.	89	155	211	181	43	21	79	60	65	79	224	83	300
	av.	10	13	25	12	5	1	2	8	8	10	22	13	129
	min.	0	0	0	0	0	0	0	0	0	0	0	0	10
Chisimaio	max.	16	15	55	174	336	243	255	71	154	166	96	46	621
	av.	1	1	21	23	92	96	52	17	13	20	7	4	326
	min.	0	0	0	0	0	1	0	0	0	0	0	0	90
Mogadiscio	max.	9	3	257	245	324	349	240	182	239	192	179	76	997
	av.	1	0	9	58	56	82	58	40	23	27	36	9	399
	min.	0	0	1	5	7	13	13	10	5	4	4	1	57
Obbia	max.	67	33	180	177	210	0	5	2	5	72	258	131	596
	av.	9	2	26	21	46	0	1	1	1	24	49	21	200
	min.	0	0	0	0	0	0	0	0	0	0	0	0	48
Berbera	max.	66	57	145	89	66	21	19	19	18	31	47	69	178
	av.	8	2	5	12	8	1	1	2	1	2	5	5	59
	min.	0	0	0	0	0	0	0	0	0	0	0	0	2
Hargeisa	max.	69	120	229	188	121	189	121	179	135	64	72	17	812
	av.	3	8	25	61	61	58	42	81	58	10	8	1	416
	min.	0	0	0	0	4	18	12	13	17	0	0	0	259

Maximum daily rainfall varies greatly across the zone. Scusciuban has a high of only 36 mm (April) while Bardera (220 mm, April) and Djibouti (211 mm, March) have recorded more than five times this amount. Falls in excess of 150 mm have been noted at Chisimaio (May and June), Mogadiscio (May) and Djibouti (February, April and November), while over 100 mm has been reported from Berbera (March), Port Sudan (November and December) and Mogadiscio (June, July, September and October). Massawa's maximum is 90 mm (December), Perim's 74 mm (March), Obbia's 70 mm (March and December) and Hargeisa's 61 mm (March and August).

Temperature

This zone almost certainly contains the place with the world's highest mean annual temperature. Until recently Lugh Ferrandi was generally accorded the "honour" with a mean of 30.3°C, the same value as that of Afambo, a station in the east of Ethiopia. However, the "hot pole" is now identified as Dallol, a station in northeastern Ethiopia on the edge of the Danakil Depression at 75 m below sea level (PEDGLEY, 1967). Over a period of seven years (1960–1966), with some missing months, the temperature data yield an annual mean maximum of 41°C and an annual mean minimum of 28°C for a mean value of 34.5°C, well in excess of the previous record. During the period of observations (58 months) every month reported at least one day in excess of 38°C while some days the thermometer never went below 30°C. The extreme temperatures recorded were 21° and 49°C (Table IV).

TABLE IV

TEMPERATURES AT DALLOL (°C)

	Jan.	Feb.	Mar.	Apr.	May	June	July	Aug.	Sept.	Oct.	Nov.	Dec.
Absolute max.	39	42	48	46	49	48	49	48	48	46	44	41
Mean max.	36	36	39	41	44	47	46	45	43	42	39	37
Mean min.	26	26	26	27	28	31	32	31	32	30	27	27
Absolute min.	22	22	21	21	23	25	24	24	27	26	24	24

Although data are not available it is likely that Dallol does, at least, have a relatively low humidity so that perhaps the most uncomfortable stations are Massawa, with a mean annual temperature of about 29.5°C and a location on the Red Sea with resultant high relative humidity (mean annual about 70%), and Perim Island with mean maxima in June to September of 37°C and corresponding relative humidity of over 60%.

In Table V values are given for the mean monthly maximum temperatures and the extremes. In southern Somalia March and April are the warmest months but in the north central region this shifts to May, June or July, while in the area previously known as the Somaliland Protectorate maxima occur inland in June to September and as late as October or November along the coast.

In Table VI readings are given of the mean monthly minimum temperatures and the extreme minima. The coldest spot in the zone appears to be Daloh where readings below zero have been recorded. In contrast, some stations have reported only one or two nights below 18°C, these include Chisimaio, Mogadiscio and Perim. Dallol with an extreme minimum of 21°C has been mentioned earlier. In southern Somalia the coldest month is generally July, but in the northern region and the Mijertain it is December or January.

TABLE V

MAXIMUM TEMPERATURE DATA (°C)

Station		Jan.	Feb.	Mar.	Apr.	May	June	July	Aug.	Sept.	Oct.	Nov.	Dec.
Alessandra	mean max.	35	36	36	35	33	32	31	31	32	33	34	35
	abs. max.	40	39	41	40	39	35	35	35	37	38	38	40
Bardera	mean max.	38	39	41	38	36	34	32	33	35	36	36	37
	abs. max.	45	45	49	46	45	46	42	39	43	44	43	43
Belet Uen	mean max.	34	35	37	37	35	34	33	34	35	34	35	34
	abs. max.	41	42	43	43	41	39	39	39	40	45	40	42
Burao	mean max.	27	29	31	31	33	32	31	32	32	31	28	27
	abs. max.	32	32	34	34	37	38	37	36	35	34	31	32
Chisimaio	mean max.	30	30	31	32	30	28	28	28	29	30	31	31
	abs. max.	32	33	34	38	34	34	32	32	30	32	32	33
Obbia	mean max.	29	30	31	33	31	30	29	28	29	30	31	30
	abs. max.	32	35	36	38	38	33	32	32	32	34	34	33
Perim	mean max.	29	29	31	32	35	37	37	37	36	33	31	29
	abs. max.	32	33	34	36	39	41	41	41	41	38	34	32
Scusciuban	mean max.	30	30	34	36	40	39	38	39	39	36	33	31
	abs. max.	32	36	40	42	46	44	41	42	41	41	40	40
Sheikh	mean max.	21	24	27	28	29	31	29	29	30	27	23	22
	abs. max.	28	29	32	33	33	33	33	33	32	31	29	26
Socotra	mean max.	28	28	30	32	34	33	32	32	32	30	29	28
	abs. max.	30	32	33	37	38	37	33	34	36	34	33	31

The annual range of temperature varies from about 3°C (Belet Uen, Lodwar and Mandera) to 12°C (Berbera). Values of 8°–11°C are usual for the winter rains area, the region most distant from the equator. Most of the southern region exhibits annual ranges of only 4°–6°C. Diurnal temperature ranges are mainly a function of the distance inland and vary from 5°–15°C.

Soil temperatures are available for very few stations. Table VII gives some relevant data.

Humidity and evaporation

Table VIII presents the relative humidity data for ten stations in this zone. It is noted that relative humidity is high (70–80%) in both morning and afternoon at coastal stations and those near large rivers. In many areas afternoon values, especially in the summer, may fall below 10%. The onset of the sea breeze at Bender Cassim is reflected in the increased afternoon relative humidity.

Mean annual dew points in the south region of the Somali Republic are about 23°C at

TABLE VI

MONTHLY MINIMUM TEMPERATURES (°C)

Station		Jan.	Feb.	Mar.	Apr.	May	June	July	Aug.	Sept.	Oct.	Nov.	Dec.
Alessandra	mean min.	22	22	22	23	23	21	21	20	20	21	22	22
	abs. min.	17	18	19	20	19	17	17	16	16	17	19	19
Bardera	mean min.	21	22	23	23	23	21	20	21	22	22	22	22
	abs. min.	16	17	18	18	18	17	15	12	16	18	14	16
Belet Uen	mean min.	22	23	23	24	23	23	23	22	23	23	22	22
	abs. min.	16	17	17	16	18	17	17	16	17	17	15	15
Burao	mean min.	12	13	15	17	19	19	19	19	19	15	13	12
	abs. min.	7	6	11	13	14	17	17	18	16	8	7	7
Chisimaio	mean min.	24	25	25	26	25	24	23	23	23	24	25	24
	abs. min.	21	22	23	21	20	21	19	21	22	22	23	22
Obbia	mean min.	22	23	24	25	24	23	22	22	22	23	23	23
	abs. min.	17	18	18	19	20	19	17	17	18	18	19	18
Perim	mean min.	24	24	25	26	28	29	30	30	29	27	26	24
	abs. min.	16	20	21	22	22	22	23	23	23	23	21	18
Scusciuban	mean min.	18	18	20	23	24	25	25	25	25	21	19	19
	abs. min.	13	12	12	16	20	21	21	22	22	16	14	14
Sheikh	mean min.	9	11	13	15	17	18	17	17	17	13	11	10
	abs. min.	3	3	8	11	12	14	14	14	14	7	6	5
Socotra	mean min.	21	21	22	23	26	26	25	26	25	22	22	22
	abs. min.	18	18	19	21	23	23	22	24	22	19	19	19

TABLE VII

SOIL TEMPERATURES (°C)

Station:	Genale			Alessandra			Villabruzzi		
Depth(cm):	20	40	60	30	50	70	20	25	35
Mean monthly	27.5	27.7	28.2	28.2	28.9	29.2	30.0	30.4	30.6
Maxima	29.6	29.4	29.9	30.8	31.2	31.3	32.6	32.5	34.0
Minima	26.0	26.1	26.6	25.7	26.8	27.6	27.2	27.8	28.0

the coast, reducing rapidly to 19°C inland. The mean monthly values vary by about 1.5–2°C either side of the annual mean.

Evaporation values are available for only a few stations. The figures in Table IX are taken from Wild evaporimeters and it is unlikely that they are strictly comparable with the pan values appearing in the main tables.

TABLE VIII

AVERAGE RELATIVE HUMIDITY (%)

Station	Local time	Jan.	Feb.	Mar.	Apr.	May	June	July	Aug.	Sept.	Oct.	Nov.	Dec.	Year
Djibouti	06h00	82	82	83	84	83	62	57	62	73	77	79	82	75
	12h00	69	71	73	74	70	53	43	44	60	65	67	71	63
Bender Cassim	09h00	65	67	59	55	53	35	33	35	44	68	74	70	55
	15h00	66	68	69	72	71	61	46	61	67	73	74	71	67
Berbera	06h00	87	87	86	89	80	51	45	44	52	78	81	84	72
	08h00	76	77	77	79	71	52	46	45	49	69	73	71	65
	15h00	69	70	71	73	66	46	43	46	50	65	66	68	61
Sheikh	08h00	74	70	64	59	64	67	71	67	66	64	67	68	67
Burao	08h00	53	54	53	54	52	49	48	46	45	48	47	46	49
Hargeisa	06h00	86	82	79	78	78	73	72	71	72	74	80	89	78
	09h00	69	62	55	55	58	57	50	56	53	47	56	64	57
	15h00	36	32	31	34	32	32	37	37	34	30	36	42	34
Galcaio	08h00	70	76	77	77	77	74	76	77	76	79	80	75	76
	14h00	51	57	56	61	63	56	58	61	56	58	63	63	59
Belet Uen	08h00	71	74	74	75	78	74	75	75	74	77	75	76	75
	14h00	52	54	54	53	58	56	59	57	52	57	53	54	55
Bardera	08h00	80	79	79	83	85	83	81	83	82	84	83	82	82
	14h00	67	64	61	64	70	68	66	67	68	72	76	71	68
Mogadiscio	08h00	80	78	78	78	82	83	84	85	84	82	81	81	81
	14h00	78	75	75	75	77	79	80	80	80	78	78	78	78

TABLE IX

VALUES OF EVAPORATION IN SOMALIA (mm)

	Annual total	Highest monthly	Lowest monthly
Genale	949	96 (Mar.)	60 (Aug.)
Mogadiscio	1,752	177 (Jan.)	130 (Aug., Oct.)
Iscia Baidoa	1,971	260 (Feb.)	110 (Nov.)
Villabruzzi	2,263	300 (Mar.)	130 (Oct.)

Radiation, sunshine and cloud

Radiation data are available for only two stations in this zone, at Mogadiscio and Iscia Baidoa. The monthly data are given in Table X.

Unfortunately these values do not accord too well with the *World Maps of Climatology* (LANDSBERG et al., 1963) which give about 400 Ly/day for Mogadiscio. This same source gives a maximum figure of around 500 Ly/day for Massawa.

TABLE X

MEAN GLOBAL RADIATION (Ly/day)

	Jan.	Feb.	Mar.	Apr.	May	June	July	Aug.	Sept.	Oct.	Nov.	Dec.	Year
Mogadiscio Iscia	606	615	613	581	558	492	503	567	613	615	588	570	577
Baidoa	529	569	518	417	414	430	354	434	496	469	529	554	471

Sunshine data are more plentiful but still do not yield a good coverage. Table XI gives some of the pertinent information.

Supplementary estimates from the world maps for the months of January and July give Djibouti 240 and 250 h, respectively, Cape Guardafui 190 and 270, Massawa 310 and 210, Obbia 200 and 200, the Ogaden 225 and 225. In the extreme south of the zone a maximum occurs in December or January but around Mogadiscio this shifts to March. The minima are usually recorded in June or July, except in the area of winter rains.

TABLE XI

MEAN SUNSHINE HOURS

Station	Jan.	Feb.	Mar.	Apr.	May	June	July	Aug.	Sept.	Oct.	Nov.	Dec.	Year
Alessandra	285	253	310	229	236	206	210	246	255	232	202	234	2,924
Afgoi	275	288	312	252	222	209	275	281	288	260	228	229	3,117
Bulo Burti	290	283	293	249	287	261	216	238	262	230	246	268	3,124
Genale	291	265	293	246	240	198	195	235	256	237	220	256	2,931
Iscia Baidoa	288	271	276	228	238	206	161	208	208	194	238	277	2,802
Lodwar	319	280	282	279	307	297	279	310	321	316	282	310	3,582
Merca	280	252	279	250	293	247	251	253	263	276	265	289	3,197
Mogadiscio	268	251	282	260	273	218	226	253	265	267	261	259	3,082
Port Sudan	208	229	276	312	331	309	301	298	300	300	249	237	3,350
Villabruzzi	273	270	285	213	218	176	183	219	244	215	239	258	2,794

The connection between cloud and rainfall would lead one to suspect a wide variation in mean monthly cloud amounts from year to year. This fact is well substantiated by a consideration of Table XII, based on 35 years of records.

Cloud amounts show, in general, very little practical diurnal variation when considering

TABLE XII

VARIATION IN MEAN MONTHLY CLOUD AMOUNTS, MOGADISCIO (tenths)

	Jan.	Feb.	Mar.	Apr.	May	June	July	Aug.	Sept.	Oct.	Nov.	Dec.	Year
Maximum	5.4	5.0	6.6	7.3	7.4	7.4	7.7	7.7	6.6	6.7	6.1	5.6	6.0
Average	3.2	3.3	3.7	4.4	4.7	5.5	5.7	5.2	4.4	4.4	4.1	3.8	4.4
Minimum	0.7	2.0	1.6	1.9	3.1	3.6	3.1	3.0	2.6	2.8	2.6	2.4	3.0

TABLE XIII

MEAN MONTHLY CLOUD AMOUNTS (TENTHS)

Station	Local Time	Jan.	Feb.	Mar.	Apr.	May	June	July	Aug.	Sept.	Oct.	Nov.	Dec.	Year
Bardera	08h30	3	3	4	5	6	7	6	6	6	6	5	5	5.2
	14h30	3	3	5	5	6	6	6	5	5	5	5	4	5.0
Belet Uen	08h30	3	4	4	6	5	4	5	5	4	5	5	4	4.6
	14h30	2	3	3	5	5	5	5	5	4	5	4	3	4.2
Bender Cassim	08h30	3	3	2	2	2	2	3	3	2	2	3	3	2.5
	20h30	3	2	2	1	2	1	2	1	1	2	2	3	1.7
Berbera	09h00	3	3	2	2	1	1	2	1	1	1	1	2	1.7
	15h00	2	2	2	2	2	1	2	1	1	1	1	2	1.3
Cape Guardafui	07h00	6	5	4	3	2	2	4	3	2	2	4	5	3.5
	17h00	5	4	4	3	2	3	4	2	3	2	4	5	3.5
Djibouti	06h00	4	3	4	4	3	4	4	4	3	3	4	4	3.5
	18h00	3	2	2	3	2	2	3	3	3	2	2	2	2.4
Hargeisa	09h00	3	2	2	3	3	2	3	3	1	2	2	3	2.4
	15h00	2	2	3	5	5	4	4	5	5	3	2	2	3.6
Chisimaio	08h30	5	5	4	5	5	5	5	5	5	5	5	5	4.9
	14h30	3	3	3	3	5	5	5	5	4	4	5	4	4.1
Massawa	09h00	6	7	6	5	3	4	5	6	5	3	3	5	4.9
	15h00	5	7	5	4	3	2	5	5	4	3	3	4	4.2
Mogadiscio	08h30	4	4	4	5	5	5	6	6	5	5	6	5	4.8
	14h30	3	2	3	4	4	5	5	5	4	4	4	3	3.8

the monthly averages. Table XIII illustrates that differences between morning and afternoon amounts rarely exceed about one-tenth.

The close relationship between the annual variation and rainfall is evident, while the driest areas (Berbera and Bender Cassim) report the lowest annual means.

Wind

Details of the overall wind pattern have been given and explained at the beginning of the chapter. However, owing to the importance of local, secondary circulations to many of the population centres in this zone it is necessary to give more data for specific stations. Generally, the winds are from the northeast with a change to southwest as the "monsoon" sets in. Obbia is a fine example of this simple pattern with northeast flow dominant from November to April and southwest from May to October. Since Obbia is a coastal station only a small percentage (less than one) of the readings were calms. Villabruzzi shows the same basic pattern but April, October and November are transition months, with a large percentage of calms, as high as 36% in November. At the extreme southern end of the zone (Magadi) southwesterly flow is reported all the year while in the extreme north (Port Sudan) southwesterly flow is only noted in the early morning readings during July and August, becoming swamped by the dominant east or northeast winds (sea-breeze) later in the day.

TABLE XIV

DIRECTION AND DURATION (%) OF PREVAILING WINDS

Direction	Duration											
	Jan.	Feb.	Mar.	Apr.	May	June	July	Aug.	Sept.	Oct.	Nov.	Dec.
Djibouti												
06h00:												
NW	—	—	—	—	3	15	18	13	13	—	—	—
W	—	—	—	6	12	16	48	46	17	7	1	—
SW	20	6	13	12	8	7	16	18	12	29	16	20
S	32	29	8	22	13	2	4	5	11	15	40	26
SE	12	10	3	9	4	6	—	3	6	12	8	18
E	20	31	43	22	11	11	1	1	10	12	13	8
NE	8	18	30	9	11	10	2	5	5	11	9	10
N	1	3	4	2	8	17	5	3	4	3	—	1
Calm	7	3	9	18	30	16	6	6	22	11	13	17
12h00:												
NW	—	—	—	—	3	9	25	22	12	1	—	—
W	1	—	—	—	—	8	37	39	17	—	—	—
SW	—	—	—	—	—	—	6	11	2	1	—	—
S	—	—	—	—	—	—	—	—	1	—	1
SE	2	2	1	1	2	—	1	1	—	—	6	1
E	65	53	38	45	28	22	3	7	26	31	54	59
NE	28	40	55	50	53	39	14	13	33	51	32	34
N	4	5	6	4	12	12	4	8	10	11	8	4
Calm	—	—	—	—	2	—	—	1	—	1	—	1
Bender Cassim:												
08h30												
NW	7	5	1	3	6	2	2	5	7	8	19	15
W	2	—	—	—	3	4	—	2	2	2	9	1
SW	1	3	2	1	1	—	1	4	2	2	1	1
S	17	14	18	39	39	48	51	47	28	7	5	5
SE	11	16	20	25	20	39	44	39	35	6	1	3
E	9	8	7	3	—	1	1	—	5	3	3	4
NE	28	35	32	21	18	2	—	—	9	27	18	36
N	15	9	19	7	11	1	1	—	9	38	38	30
Calm	9	9	2	2	2	3	—	2	3	7	7	5
14h30:												
NW	7	5	6	8	13	51	61	62	28	6	10	15
W	—	—	—	—	1	4	12	14	5	—	—	1
SW	—	—	—	—	—	—	1	1	—	—	—	—
S	—	—	—	—	—	—	3	—	1	—	—	—
SE	—	—	—	—	2	—	4	1	—	1	—	—
E	1	2	2	—	1	—	—	2	—	—	2	3
NE	55	53	61	50	39	15	2	6	18	19	17	35
N	38	40	31	42	45	30	15	13	48	74	71	46
Calm	—	—	—	—	—	—	2	2	—	—	—	—

TABLE XIV *(continued)*

Direction	Duration											
	Jan.	Feb.	Mar.	Apr.	May	June	July	Aug.	Sept.	Oct.	Nov.	Dec.
Berbera												
08h00:												
NW	—	—	2	6	2	—	—	—	—	2	2	—
N	7	5	11	11	7	—	—	1	2	2	1	4
SW	3	8	7	14	16	80	97	97	53	6	3	2
S	12	7	8	1	2	4	2	1	1	9	9	13
SE	22	9	4	1	2	—	—	—	4	17	26	24
E	6	2	1	—	2	—	—	—	4	3	4	3
NE	2	5	2	2	2	1	—	—	2	2	1	7
N	—	2	1	4	2	—	—	—	1	1	1	—
Calm	47	62	64	61	65	14	1	2	33	58	53	47
14h00:												
NW	3	1	1	1	9	19	24	30	26	3	2	1
N	—	1	—	1	1	10	21	20	7	—	—	—
SW	—	—	—	2	3	25	44	19	4	—	—	—
S	—	—	—	1	—	—	—	—	—	—	—	—
SE	—	—	—	1	—	—	—	—	4	—	1	—
E	—	1	4	5	2	—	—	—	—	—	—	1
NE	78	80	73	73	61	21	1	5	29	71	76	74
N	18	16	21	15	22	22	9	24	29	24	20	23
Calm	—	—	—	1	2	2	1	1	1	—	—	—

In the region around the Straits of Bab el Mandab the topography and changes in direction of the coast line make for a complicated picture. For instance, from Table XIV it is noted that easterly winds, and even southerlies, occur at Djibouti during the winter. This is due to the high ground deflecting the air flow. At this time northerly winds, called "shamal", can blow for periods of 3–4 days. From December to March winds are light southerly at night, north or northeasterly in the afternoon, but in January the northeasterly monsoon is at its height and afternoon winds are sometimes of gale force. In April and May the northeasterly winds weaken (the khalil lull) and the land/sea circulation dominates the coastal regions. From June to September the area experiences the "kharif", "khamsin" and "saba". The "kharif" is a hot, dry, off-shore wind that reaches its maximum strength near dawn. The "khamsin" blows from the northwest, setting in about midday and abating at dusk. It frequently raises dust, is squally and has high speed gusts. The "saba" is a westerly wind that occurs around midday with an onset that may be accompanied by drops of rain. The "saba" begins and ends abruptly and is very

TABLE XV

NUMBER OF DAYS WITH GALE (BEAUFORT 8 OR MORE)

	Jan.	Feb.	Mar.	Apr.	May	June	July	Aug.	Sept.	Oct.	Nov.	Dec.	Year
Bender													
Cassim	0	0	0	0	0	0	1	0.3	0	0	0	0	1
Berbera	0.4	0	0	0.1	0.8	11	19	17	5	0	0	0	53

squally by nature and gale force winds are common. The frequent occurrence of gales is illustrated in Table XV at Berbera and Bender Cassim. These gale force winds are generally south to southwesterly and bring high temperatures, blowing sand and no ameliorating effect of the sea breeze. Sandstorms, with a visibility of less than 1,000 m occur about three times per year at Djibouti, mainly in June and July.

Climatic zones

In Fig.5 a rough sub-division of the zone into five regions is depicted. The main features corresponding to these regions are given below.

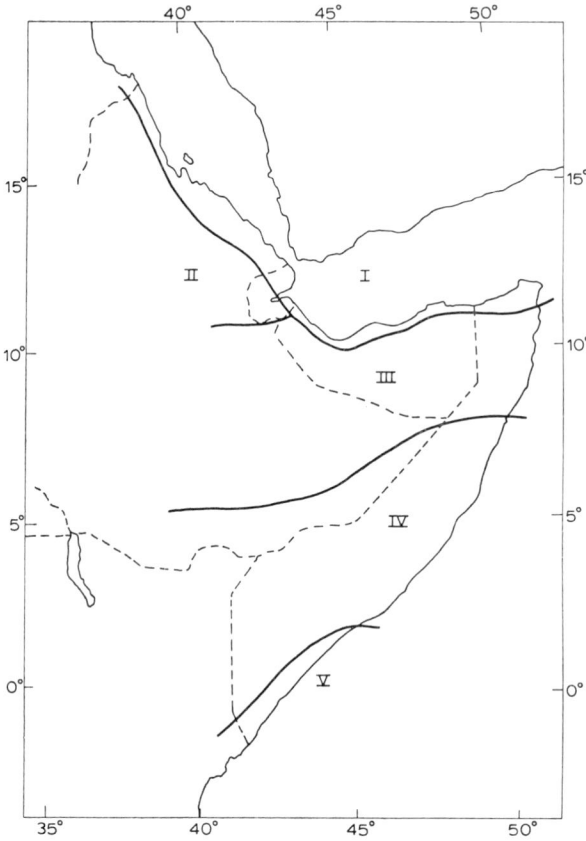

Fig.5. Climatic zones.

Region I

The northern coastal strip is identified by the incidence of definite winter rainfall and almost complete summer drought. The temperatures are affected greatly by the land–sea breeze circulation and show small diurnal variation together with high humidity throughout the year.

Region II

The northwestern corner of this zone shows a single maximum of rainfall, during the summer months. It is near the extreme northern location of the I.T.C.Z. There are very few stations in this region, most of the country being very inhospitable with high temperatures, little rainfall and small benefit from cooling winds.

Region III

This central portion has the double-peak of rainfall distribution but amounts may vary widely, from about 50 mm to 750 mm/year. A common characteristic of the temperature pattern is that the winter season (usually December and January) is the time at which the lowest temperatures are recorded.

Region IV

Like region III this area has the double-peak of rainfall distribution with amounts from 150 mm to over 500 mm/year. The difference between the two regions is that here the coolest temperatures are recorded in the summer season (July or August) due to the characteristics of the I.T.C.Z.

Region V

This very small area along the southern coast of the zone is very definitely affected by the circulation from the Indian monsoon. Some heavy rainfalls in June and July are often associated with this effect but even a few tens of kilometres inland this influence is not noticeable.

References

FLOHN, H., 1964. On the causes of the aridity of northeastern Africa. *Würzburger Geograph. Arb.*, 12: 17 pp. (English translation by East African Meteorological Dept., Nairobi, 1966.)

GRIFFITHS, J. F. and HEMMING, C. F., 1963. A rainfall map of eastern Africa and southern Arabia. *Mem. E. African Meteorol. Dept.*, 111 (10): 42 pp.

HEMMING, C. F., 1966. The vegetation of the northern region of the Somali Republic. *Proc. Linnean Soc., London*, 177 (2): 173–250.

LANDSBERG, H. E., LIPPMANN, H., PAFFEN, K. H. and TROLL, C., 1963. *World Maps of Climatology.* Springer, Berlin, 5 maps, 28 pp.

METEOROLOGICAL OFFICE, 1962. *Investigations Division Climatological Report.* Meteorological Office, London, 60: 66 pp.; 61: 102 pp.

PEDGLEY, D. E., 1967. Air temperature at Dallol, Ethiopia. *Meteorol. Mag.*, 96: 265–271.

TABLE XVI

CLIMATIC TABLE FOR GARISSA, KENYA
Latitude 0°29'S, longitude 39°38'E, elevation 128 m

Month	Temperature (°C)				Dew point (°C)		Precipitation					Wind			Average cloudiness (oktas)	
	mean		extreme		09h	15h	mean (mm)	max. (mm)	min. (mm)	days >1 mm	max. in 24 h (mm)	av. speed¹ (km/h)	preval. direct.	calm (%)	09h	15h
	max.	min.	max.	min.												
Jan.	35	22	38	16	20.9	19.3	10	55	0	2	32	5	SE	7	6	4
Feb.	36	23	39	19	21.1	19.8	6	39	0	1	36	6	S	7	7	4
Mar.	37	24	41	20	22.2	20.3	27	251	0	3	116	5	S	1	6	5
Apr.	36	24	44	21	22.8	21.0	59	251	3	5	82	7	S	1	6	5
May	35	23	46	19	21.5	20.1	16	91	0	2	58	9	S	1	5	5
June	33	22	42	17	20.1	18.2	5	26	0	1	23	9	S	0	5	5
July	32	21	42	16	19.2	17.1	1	6	0	1	6	10	S	0	6	5
Aug.	32	21	38	16	19.1	17.0	6	39	0	1	35	10	S	0	6	5
Sept.	34	21	37	14	19.6	17.4	6	58	0	2	14	9	S	0	6	5
Oct.	35	23	38	19	20.7	18.3	21	169	0	3	50	8	SE	0	6	5
Nov.	34	22	38	19	22.1	20.3	77	419	1	7	127	5	SE	4	7	5
Dec.	34	23	37	19	22.1	20.9	64	181	1	7	69	5	E	10	7	5
Annual	34	23	46	14	20.9	19.1	298	757	69	35	127	7	—	3	6	5
Rec. (yrs.)	23	23	23	23	23	23	32	32	32	32	32	21	21	21	22	22

¹ Mean of 09h00 and 15h00.

TABLE XVII

CLIMATIC TABLE FOR MAGADI, KENYA
Latitude 1°53'S, longitude 36°17'E, elevation 613 m

Month	Mean sta. press. (mbar)	Temperature (°C) mean max.	mean min.	extreme max.	extreme min.	Dew point (°C) 09h	15h	Precipitation mean (mm)	max. (mm)	min. (mm)	days ≥1 mm	max. in 24 h (mm)	Wind av. speed (km/h)	preval. direct.	calm (%)	Average cloudiness (oktas) 09h	15h
Jan.	942	37	24	41	19	16.7	14.5	32	150	0	5	41	5	SW	0	3	4
Feb.	941	37	24	42	18	16.5	14.0	43	155	0	5	73	6	SW	0	3	4
Mar.	941	37	24	42	19	17.6	15.5	66	274	1	10	91	7	SW	0	4	5
Apr.	943	35	24	40	19	19.0	17.7	89	271	13	12	58	5	SW	0	5	5
May	944	33	23	38	19	18.2	17.6	55	209	1	11	74	4	SW	0	5	5
June	946	33	22	37	18	15.4	15.1	8	47	0	2	34	5	SW	0	5	4
July	946	32	22	36	18	13.9	13.8	1	11	0	1	11	5	SW	0	5	4
Aug.	946	33	22	37	17	14.2	13.8	3	24	0	1	21	5	SW	0	5	4
Sept.	945	35	23	40	20	14.8	14.2	5	24	0	2	12	5	SW	0	4	4
Oct.	943	36	24	40	19	15.5	14.2	15	47	0	3	28	6	SW	0	4	4
Nov.	944	36	24	40	19	17.4	15.7	34	196	1	8	59	6	SE	0	5	4
Dec.	943	35	23	41	19	17.6	15.6	47	176	1	7	64	5	SW	0	4	5
Annual	944	35	23	42	17	16.4	15.1	398	621	153	67	91	5	—	0	4	4
Rec. (yrs.)	10	21	21	21	21	21	21	32	32	32	32	32	19	19	19	20	20

TABLE XVIII

CLIMATIC TABLE FOR MOGADISCIO, SOMALIA
Latitude 2°02'N, longitude 45°21'E, elevation 17 m

Month	Mean sta. press. (mbar)	Temperature (°C) mean max.	mean min.	extreme max.	extreme min.	Dew point (°C)	Precipitation mean (mm)	max. (mm)	min. (mm)	days ≥1 mm	max. in 24 h (mm)	Wind av. speed (m/sec)	preval. direct. 08h30	14h30	calm (%) 08h30	14h30	Averages cloudiness (oktas)	sunshine (h)	rad. (Ly/day)
Jan.	1,013	30	23	39	19	22,3	1	9	0	0	8	5	NE	E	1	0	3	268	606
Feb.	1,012	30	23	40	19	22.1	0	3	0	0	3	4	E	E	0	0	3	251	615
Mar.	1,012	31	25	37	20	23.6	9	258	0	1	65	4	E	E	0	0	3	282	614
Apr.	1,012	32	26	40	18	24.4	58	245	0	5	95	3	SE	S	0	0	4	260	581
May	1,013	31	25	35	18	24.1	56	324	1	7	150	4	SW	SW	0	0	4	273	558
June	1,014	30	24	34	20	22.6	82	349	0	13	133	4	SW	SW	0	0	4	218	492
July	1,015	29	23	34	17	21.6	58	240	1	13	134	4	SW	SW	0	0	5	226	503
Aug.	1,015	29	23	36	18	21.7	40	182	0	10	82	4	SW	SW	0	0	4	253	567
Sept.	1,015	29	23	36	18	22.0	23	239	0	5	100	3	SW	SW	0	0	4	265	613
Oct.	1,014	30	24	37	17	22.9	27	192	0	4	110	3	S	S	0	0	4	267	615
Nov.	1,014	31	24	39	16	23.1	36	179	0	4	74	3	E	E	1	0	3	261	588
Dec.	1,013	31	23	37	17	22.7	9	76	0	2	38	4	NE	E	0	0	3	259	570
Annual	1,014	30	24	40	16	22.7	399	997	57	64	150	4	—		0	0	4	3,082	580
Rec. (yrs.)	7	48	48	48	48	6	46	46	46	46	46	8	6	6	6	6	44	13	5

TABLE XIX

CLIMATIC TABLE FOR LODWAR, KENYA
Latitude 3°07'N, longitude 35°37'E, elevation 506 m

Month	Temperature (°C)				Dew point (°C)		Precipitation					Wind				Averages			
	mean		extreme		09h	15h	mean (mm)	max. (mm)	min. (mm)	days ≥0.1 mm	max. in 24 h (mm)	av. speed (km/h)		preval. direct.	calm (%)	cloud-iness (oktas)		sun-shine (h)	evap. (mm)
	max.	min.	max.	min.								09h	12h			09h	15h		
Jan.	36	22	39	17	15.7	14.3	8	111	0	1	101	5	12	E	0	3	4	319	412
Feb.	37	23	40	18	15.7	14.2	5	28	0	1	21	5	13	E	1	3	3	280	370
Mar.	36	24	40	19	17.9	16.0	20	149	0	3	74	6	13	E	1	4	4	282	402
Apr.	35	24	40	19	20.1	18.1	41	141	0	5	47	7	11	E	2	5	5	279	380
May	35	25	38	20	19.8	18.1	27	114	0	3	52	8	10	E	3	4	5	307	351
June	34	24	38	21	18.5	17.0	8	116	0	1	102	8	9	E	2	4	4	297	352
July	33	24	37	20	17.8	16.4	13	86	0	3	51	8	8	NE	1	5	4	279	319
Aug.	33	24	38	18	17.6	16.5	9	63	0	1	42	9	9	NE	1	4	4	310	345
Sept.	35	24	37	20	17.4	15.5	3	57	0	1	56	9	10	NE	0	3	4	321	400
Oct.	35	24	38	19	17.5	15.5	8	89	0	1	83	9	11	E	0	4	4	316	423
Nov.	35	24	38	19	17.7	15.6	10	107	0	1	37	6	12	E	1	4	5	282	398
Dec.	35	23	37	18	17.4	16.0	13	198	0	2	51	4	12	E	0	4	4	310	389
Annual	35	23	40	17	17.8	16.1	165	498	19	23	102	7	11	—	1	4	4	3,582	4,541
Rec. (yrs.)	17	17	17	17	17	17	44	44	44	44	44	17	17	17	17	17		6	6

TABLE XX

CLIMATIC TABLE FOR LUGH FERRANDI, SOMALIA
Latitude 3°45'N, longitude 42°35'E, elevation 193 m

Month	Temperature (°C)				Dew point (°C)	Precipitation					Wind			Aver. cloudiness (oktas)
	mean		extreme			mean (mm)	max. (mm)	min. (mm)	days ≥ 1 mm	max. in 24 h (mm)	av. speed (m/sec)	preval. direct.	calm (%)	
	max.	min.	max.	min.										
Jan.	39	24	49	16	16.4	2	12	0	1	11	1	NE	18	1
Feb.	40	25	50	18	14.6	4	15	0	1	15	1	NE	25	1
Mar.	41	25	50	16	17.5	28	108	0	3	68	1	SE	20	2
Apr.	38	25	50	17	20.8	113	272	16	9	136	1	SE	28	4
May	36	25	47	17	20.0	40	168	0	3	94	1	S	19	3
June	35	24	42	15	17.7	1	10	0	0	8	1	SW	10	3
July	34	23	42	19	17.5	3	23	0	1	10	1	SW	6	4
Aug.	34	23	42	19	17.8	0	3	0	0	2	1	SW	7	4
Sept.	36	24	49	18	17.8	1	13	0	0	7	1	SW	7	3
Oct.	37	24	46	17	18.5	47	260	0	4	134	1	SE	13	4
Nov.	37	24	50	18	18.1	56	290	0	5	110	1	SE	16	3
Dec.	38	23	49	18	16.8	15	122	0	2	64	1	NE	10	2
Annual	37	24	50	15	17.8	310	553	59	29	136	1	—	15	3
Rec. (yrs.)	36	36	36	36	6	39	39	39	39	39	15	15	15	20

TABLE XXI

CLIMATIC TABLE FOR MANDERA, KENYA
Latitude 3°57'N, longitude 41°52'E, elevation 331 m

Month	Mean sta. press. (mbar)	Temperature (°C) mean max.	mean min.	extreme max.	extreme min.	Dew point (°C) 09h	15h	Precipitation mean (mm)	max. (mm)	min. (mm)	days ≥1 mm	max. in 24 h (mm)	Wind av. speed (km/h)	preval. direct.	calm (%)	Averages cloudiness (oktas) 09h	15h	evap. (mm)
Jan.	985	35	22	38	15	17.8	16.4	1	17	0	1	12	7	NE	0	2	2	332
Feb.	984	36	24	40	15	18.6	16.9	4	69	0	1	36	8	NE	0	2	2	344
Mar.	984	37	25	40	15	20.1	18.6	23	161	0	3	54	7	E	0	3	3	366
Apr.	985	35	25	40	17	21.8	20.7	86	186	0	6	116	5	V	4	5	5	253
May	986	34	24	38	21	21.1	20.3	27	87	0	3	54	7	SW	1	6	5	263
June	987	33	24	37	18	18.8	18.1	0	3	0	0	3	10	SW	0	5	5	346
July	989	33	23	37	20	17.7	17.2	0	5	0	0	5	11	SW	0	5	5	374
Aug.	988	33	23	38	20	17.2	16.7	1	3	0	0	3	10	SW	0	5	5	398
Sept.	988	34	23	38	21	18.0	17.4	2	26	0	1	26	9	SW	0	5	4	396
Oct.	987	34	24	38	19	20.2	19.8	42	125	1	4	75	6	SW	1	6	5	278
Nov.	986	33	23	37	18	21.1	19.9	34	191	3	4	38	5	NE	1	6	5	236
Dec.	986	34	23	37	16	19.7	18.7	8	104	0	1	43	6	NE	0	3	3	282
Annual	986	34	24	40	15	19.3	18.4	228	443	42	24	116	7	—	1	4	4	3,868
Rec. (yrs.)	3	27	27	27	27	27	27	27	27	27	27	27	26	26	26	27	27	6

157

TABLE XXII

CLIMATIC TABLE FOR GALCAIO, SOMALIA
Latitude 6°46'N, longitude 47°25'E, elevation 240 m

Month	Mean sta. press. (mbar)	Temperature (°C) mean		extreme		Dew point (°C)	Precipitation mean (mm)	max. (mm)	min. (mm)	days	max. in 24 h (mm)	Wind preval. direct.	calm (%)	Aver. cloudiness (oktas)
		max.	min.	max.	min.									
Jan.	978	32	18	39	11	17.9	0	1	0	0	1	NE	4	2
Feb.	978	33	19	40	13	17.5	3	43	0	0	23	NE	7	2
Mar.	977	35	20	43	13	18.4	1	10	0	0	10	E	5	3
Apr.	977	36	22	47	17	19.8	24	111	0	2	53	E	23	4
May	976	35	23	47	17	20.7	60	368	0	5	160	SW	16	4
June	977	34	23	40	16	20.0	2	19	0	0	19	SW	1	3
July	978	33	22	37	19	19.4	0	2	0	0	2	SW	0	4
Aug.	977	33	22	42	17	18.8	2	34	0	0	34	SW	0	4
Sept.	976	34	22	40	18	19.2	1	19	0	0	12	SW	2	3
Oct.	978	34	22	43	15	19.9	41	179	0	3	75	SW	30	4
Nov.	979	34	20	40	12	19.7	14	98	0	1	60	NE	13	3
Dec.	979	33	19	38	13	18.8	1	5	0	0	4	NE	2	3
Annual	978	34	21	47	11	19.2	149	448	33	11	160	—	8	3.5
Rec. (yrs.)	10	26	26	26	26	5	26	26	26	26	20	13	13	10

TABLE XXIII

CLIMATIC TABLE FOR HARGEISA, SOMALIA

Latitude 9°31'N, longitude 44°06'E, elevation 1,370 m

Month	Temperature (°C)				Relative humidity (%)		Precipitation					Wind						Aver. cloud-iness[1] (oktas)
	mean		extreme				mean (mm)	max. (mm)	min. (mm)	days ≥1 mm	max. in 24 h (mm)	preval. direct.			calm (%)			
	max.	min.	max.	min.	06h	15h						09h	15h	21h	09h	15h	21h	
Jan.	24	12	29	7	86	36	3	69	0	<1	46	N	N	N	3	2	2	2
Feb.	27	13	32	9	82	32	8	120	0	<1	43	N	NE	N	7	9	0	3
Mar.	29	16	33	10	79	31	25	229	0	2	61	SE	NE	NE	5	6	4	2
Apr.	29	17	33	13	78	34	61	188	0	4	58	S	V	NE	4	9	12	3
May	31	18	34	14	78	32	61	121	4	6	49	SW	V	NE	3	6	23	4
June	31	18	34	14	73	32	58	189	18	8	51	SW	SW	SW	0	8	6	3
July	30	17	34	16	72	37	42	121	12	5	51	SW	SW	SW	0	3	4	4
Aug.	29	18	33	14	72	37	81	179	13	9	61	SW	SW	SW	0	1	2	4
Sept.	31	17	33	14	72	34	58	135	17	8	49	SW	SW	SW	0	5	8	3
Oct.	28	15	31	7	74	30	10	64	0	3	33	NE	NE	N	5	0	15	2
Nov.	28	13	29	4	80	36	8	72	0	<1	38	N	N	N	0	1	2	2
Dec.	25	12	28	6	89	42	1	17	0	<1	15	N	N	N	0	1	7	2
Annual	28	15	34	4	78	34	416	812	259	47	61	—	—	—	2	4	7	3
Rec. (yrs.)	30	30	30	30	3	12	30	40	40	30	30	5	5	5	5	5	5	5

[1] Mean of 09h00, 15h00 and 21h00.

TABLE XXIV

CLIMATIC TABLE FOR BERBERA, SOMALIA
Latitude 10°26'N, longitude 45°02'E, elevation 8 m

Month	Temperature (°C)				Relative humidity (%)		Precipitation					Wind						Aver. cloudiness[1] (oktas)
	mean		extreme		06h	15h	mean (mm)	max. (mm)	min. (mm)	days >1 mm	max. in 24 h (mm)	preval. direct.			calm (%)			
	max.	min.	max.	min.								08h	11h	20h	08h	11h	20h	
Jan.	28	21	31	16	87	69	8	66	0	<1	46	SE	NE	NE	47	0	1	2
Feb.	29	22	32	16	87	70	2	57	0	<1	38	V	NE	NE	62	0	4	2
Mar.	31	23	33	20	86	71	5	145	0	<1	132	W	NE	NE	64	0	6	2
Apr.	32	25	36	21	89	73	12	89	0	1	59	SW	NE	NE	61	1	18	2
May	36	28	43	23	80	66	8	66	0	1	67	SW	NE	NE	65	2	36	2
June	42	31	46	25	51	46	1	21	0	<1	23	SW	SW	V	14	2	55	1
July	42	32	46	27	45	43	<1	19	0	<1	21	SW	SW	SW	1	1	52	2
Aug.	42	32	46	24	44	46	2	19	0	<1	16	SW	NW	SW	2	1	68	1
Sept.	39	29	44	23	52	50	<1	18	0	<1	18	SW	N	NE	33	1	51	1
Oct.	33	24	38	20	78	65	2	31	0	<1	28	SE	NE	NE	58	0	24	1
Nov.	30	22	33	19	81	66	5	47	0	<1	48	SE	NE	NE	53	0	6	1
Dec.	29	22	31	17	84	68	5	69	0	<1	33	SE	NE	NE	47	0	2	1
Annual	34	26	46	16	72	61	49	178	2	5	132				42	1	27	1
Rec. (yrs.)	30	30	40	40	4	9	30	40	40	40	40	12	12	12	12	12	12	17

[1] Mean of 09h00, 15h00 and 21h00.

TABLE XXV

CLIMATIC TABLE FOR ERIGAVO, SOMALIA
Latitude 10°37'N, longitude 47°22'E, elevation 1,730 m

Month	Temperature (°C)				Relative humidity (%)		Precipitation					Wind	
	mean		extreme				mean (mm)	max. (mm)	min. (mm)	days ≥1 mm	max. in 24 h (mm)	preval. direct.	calm (%)
	max.	min.	max.	min.	08h	14h							
Jan.	24	6	31	−3	42	34	18	102	0	1	30	NE	1
Feb.	26	7	33	1	55	35	13	51	0	3	32	NE	1
Mar.	26	8	32	1	59	42	33	126	0	6	61	NE	1
Apr.	27	10	33	2	69	56	38	102	0	5	48	SE	1
May	27	12	32	2	67	51	81	152	0	8	76	SW	1
June	26	13	31	4	70	48	63	102	10	9	51	SW	0
July	26	13	31	5	64	43	10	25	0	1	23	SW	0
Aug.	26	13	30	4	65	49	41	152	0	5	18	SW	0
Sept.	26	12	30	3	70	55	114	177	25	15	35	SW	1
Oct.	25	8	29	0	53	43	8	23	0	1	8	NE	0
Nov.	24	7	29	−3	37	34	13	76	0	2	25	NE	0
Dec.	23	6	28	−3	43	37	2	10	0	<1	10	NE	<1
Annual	25	9	33	−3	58	44	434	550	224	56	76	—	1
Rec. (yrs.)	14	14	14	14	3	3	18	18	18	18	14	9	9

TABLE XXVI

CLIMATIC TABLE FOR BENDER CASSIM, SOMALIA
Latitude 11°17′N, longitude 49°11′E, elevation 6 m

Month	Mean sta. press. (mbar)	Temperature (°C)				Humidity		Precipitation					Wind				Aver. cloud-iness (oktas)
		mean		extreme		dew point (°C)	relat. (%)	mean (mm)	max. (mm)	min. (mm)	days ≥1 mm	max. in 24 h (mm)	preval. direct.		calm (%)		
		max.	min.	max.	min.								08h30	14h30	08h30	14h30	
Jan.	1,017	29	20	38	12	20.6	70	0	2	0	0	2	NE	NE	9	0	2
Feb.	1,016	30	20	37	14	20.7	71	0	0	0	0	0	NE	NE	9	0	2
Mar.	1,014	31	21	39	15	21.7	68	1	6	0	0	5	NE	NE	2	0	1
Apr.	1,013	34	23	42	17	23.5	66	3	31	0	0	20	S	NE	2	0	2
May	1,010	37	25	45	19	24.6	64	3	22	0	0	22	S	N	2	0	2
June	1,007	41	29	45	21	23.9	52	0	1	0	0	1	S	NW	3	0	2
July	1,006	41	30	45	23	23.1	47	0	0	0	0	0	S	NW	0	2	2
Aug.	1,006	40	29	45	24	22.3	48	0	0	0	0	0	S	NW	2	2	2
Sept.	1,008	39	28	45	21	25.1	56	0	0	0	0	0	SE	N	3	0	2
Oct.	1,013	33	23	45	14	23.7	69	2	19	0	0	19	N	N	7	0	2
Nov.	1,016	30	20	36	12	22.1	76	7	32	0	1	23	N	N	7	0	2
Dec.	1,017	29	20	36	11	21.2	73	3	22	0	0	13	NE	N	5	0	2
Annual	1,012	35	24	45	11	22.8	63	19	58	0	2	23	—		4	0	2
Rec. (yrs.)	7	12	12	12	12	6	6	12	12	12	12	10	5	5	5	5	2

TABLE XXXVII

CLIMATIC TABLE FOR DJIBOUTI
Latitude 11°36′N, longitude 43°09′E, elevation 7 m

Month	Mean sta. press (mbar)	Temperature (°C) mean max.	mean min.	extreme max.	extreme min.	Relative humidity (%) 06h	12h	Precipitation mean (mm)	max. (mm)	min. (mm)	days ≥1 mm	max. in 24 h (mm)	Wind preval. direct. 06h	12h	calm (%) 06h	12h	Aver. cloudiness[1] (oktas)
Jan.	1,015	29	23	34	19	82	69	10	89	0	3	71	S	E	7	0	3
Feb.	1,014	29	24	34	18	82	71	13	155	0	2	155	S	E	3	0	3
Mar.	1,012	31	25	36	21	83	73	25	211	0	2	211	E	NE	9	0	3
Apr.	1,010	32	26	38	21	84	74	12	181	0	1	181	E	NE	18	0	3
May	1,007	34	28	44	21	83	70	5	43	0	1	43	V	NE	30	2	3
June	1,004	38	30	47	23	62	53	1	21	0	<1	21	NW	NE	16	0	3
July	1,003	41	31	47	22	57	43	2	79	0	1	25	W	W	6	0	3
Aug.	1,003	39	29	47	22	62	44	8	60	0	1	60	W	W	6	1	3
Sept.	1,006	36	29	44	23	73	60	8	65	0	1	64	W	NE	22	0	3
Oct.	1,011	33	27	39	21	77	65	10	79	0	1	79	SW	NE	11	4	2
Nov.	1,014	31	25	36	18	79	67	22	224	0	2	156	S	E	13	0	2
Dec.	1,015	28	23	34	17	82	71	13	83	0	2	83	S	E	17	1	3
Annual	1,009	32	27	47	17	75	63	129	300	10	17	211	—		13	1	3
Rec. (yrs.)	30	16	16	11	11	6	6	64	64	64	64	64	3	3	3	3	9

[1] Mean of 06h00, 12h00 and 18h00.

TABLE XXVIII

CLIMATIC TABLE FOR MASSAWA, ETHIOPIA
Latitude 15°37'N, longitude 39°27'E, elevation 20 m

Month	Temperature (°C) mean max.	mean min.	extreme max.	extreme min.	Relative humidity (%) 09h	21h	Precipitation mean (mm)	max. (mm)	min. (mm)	days ≥1 mm	max. in 24 h	Wind preval. direct. 09h	15h	calm (%) 09h	15h	Aver. cloudiness[1] (oktas)
Jan.	29	20	37	11	76	74	26	213	0	4	76	W	NE	11	3	5
Feb.	29	21	38	12	75	73	36	169	0	6	31	NW	NE	6	0	6
Mar.	30	22	39	12	73	68	15	31	0	3	23	NW	NE	9	1	5
Apr.	33	24	41	13	76	78	21	78	0	2	23	NW	NE	14	0	3
May	36	25	45	18	73	75	3	53	0	<1	12	NW	NE	19	0	2
June	39	27	45	19	59	60	1	4	0	<1	2	NW	NE	19	1	3
July	39	29	47	17	56	59	8	82	0	1	61	NW	NE	16	0	4
Aug.	39	29	48	16	56	63	1	69	0	<1	38	W	NE	18	1	4
Sept.	37	27	44	17	57	66	2	31	0	<1	25	NW	NE	20	0	3
Oct.	33	25	43	19	67	67	18	80	0	2	69	NW	NE	26	0	3
Nov.	33	23	40	17	72	69	21	158	0	2	63	NW	NE	12	0	2
Dec.	30	21	37	13	76	76	43	190	0	3	90	W	NE	7	2	4
Annual	34	25	48	11	68	69	195	561	50	23	90	—		15	1	4
Rec. (yrs.)	15	15	15	15	10	10	26	26	26	18	18	5		5		6

[1] Mean of 09h00 and 15h00.

TABLE XXIX

CLIMATIC TABLE FOR PORT SUDAN, SUDAN
Latitude 19°35'N, longitude 37°13'E, elevation 5 m

Month	Mean sta. press. (mbar)	Temperature (°C)				Dew point (°C)		Precipitation					Wind					Averages			
		mean		extreme				mean	max.	min.	days	max. in 24 h	av. speed	preval. direct.		calm (%)		clou-diness[1]	sun-shine	rad.	evap. Piche
		max.	min.	max.	min.	06h	12h	(mm)	(mm)	(mm)	≥1 mm	(mm)	(knots)	07h	13h	07h	13h	(oktas)	(h/day)	(Ly/day)	(mm/day)
Jan.	1,014	27	20	32	10	17.5	20.0	4	41	0	1	17	10	NW	NE	2	0	3	6.9	354	8.4
Feb.	1,013	27	19	32	12	17.0	19.7	1	6	0	<1	5	10	NW	NE	3	0	3	8.2	450	8.6
Mar.	1,011	29	20	35	13	17.9	20.2	1	24	0	<1	22	9	NW	NE	9	0	2	9.1	539	9.0
Apr.	1,010	32	21	40	14	18.9	21.2	1	10	0	<1	8	9	NW	NE	15	0	1	10.4	613	10.1
May	1,008	35	24	44	17	20.4	22.8	2	20	0	<1	19	8	NW	NE	23	0	1	10.9	625	12.0
June	1,005	38	26	47	20	19.7	22.3	Tr	6	0	<1	6	7	NW	NE	33	1	1	10.3	577	15.1
July	1,004	41	28	47	22	21.1	23.6	9	55	0	1	48	8	SW	E	30	1	2	9.9	564	16.4
Aug.	1,004	41	29	48	21	21.5	24.4	3	28	0	<1	21	7	SW	E	23	0	2	9.6	552	16.0
Sept.	1,007	38	27	46	22	22.3	24.0	Tr	2	0	0	1	7	NW	NE	33	0	2	10.0	547	11.8
Oct.	1,010	34	25	39	20	23.5	24.8	12	156	0	1	78	7	NW	NE	6	0	2	9.9	486	7.8
Nov.	1,012	31	24	36	18	22.6	23.7	52	182	0	4	112	8	NW	NE	1	0	3	8.3	383	7.9
Dec.	1,014	29	22	32	14	19.3	21.3	25	145	0	3	106	9	NW	NE	4	0	2	7.6	340	8.2
Annual	1,009	34	24	48	10	20.3	22.4	110	422	19	11	112	8	—		15	0	2	9.3	505	10.9
Rec. (yrs.)	30	30	30	30	30	30	30	30	30	30	30	30	9	9	9	9	9	30	20	10	30

[1] Mean of 06h00, 12h00 and 18h00.

Chapter 5

Nigeria

J. F. GRIFFITHS

Introduction

Nigeria is situated in the southeastern sector of West Africa between latitudes 4° and 14°N and covers an area in excess of 900,000 km². The country, the most populous in Africa (36 million people), extends about 1,000 km from north to south and slightly more from east to west. The land, rising gently from the coast, is traversed by the Niger and Benue rivers. Most of the country is below the 600-m contour and very little exceeds 1,500 m in elevation (Fig.1).

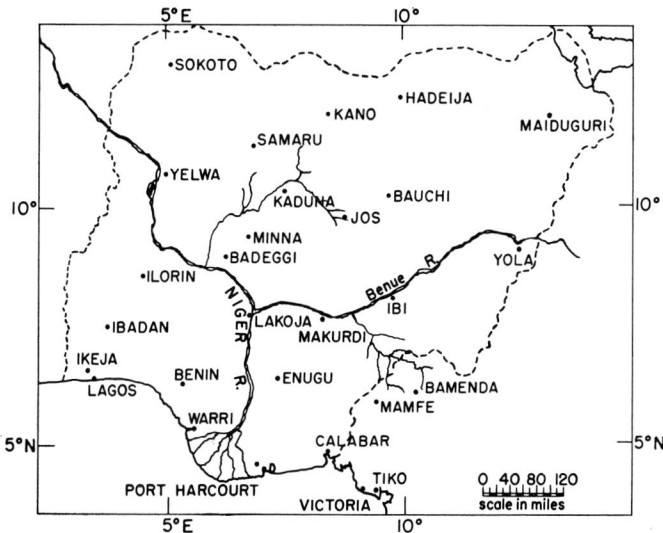

Fig.1. Stations in Nigeria.

Lagos, the capital with 700,000 inhabitants, and Ibadan (600,000) are by far the largest cities. The chief exports are cocoa, palm oil and kernels, and groundnuts, each about 20% of the total, with cotton and rubber also important. For local consumption yams, cassava, maize, sugar cane and bananas are raised and in the Fulani area of the north large herds of cattle are grazed.

The geographical location, size and shape of Nigeria allow the country to experience most of the West African climates and weather within its boundaries. In other words, this country is climatically a microcosm of West Africa from central Africa to the Atlantic. Because of this situation it is a logical step to devote a chapter to a special study of Nigeria in order to obtain and understand a good cross-section of the West African climate. As is true for any region of the world, a study of the weather conditions is absolutely essential to any appreciation of the climate. This fact necessitates a realization of the overall picture of the atmospheric circulation in West Africa.

West African weather

In this section of West Africa the weather exhibits very definite seasons. In the nomenclature of tropical climatology this really means contrasts between wet and dry periods. The belts of distinctive weather have been observed to show a pronounced migration across the region, a migration strongly associated with the north–south movements of a zone of discontinuity between humid maritime (Atlantic) air and dry continental (Sahara) air. As pointed out earlier in the book, this discontinuity has received various names but here, following GARNIER (1967), the term surface discontinuity (S.D.) will be used to denote a zone in which the two air masses meet near ground level. The usual identifiers of the S.D. are the dew point and the surface wind. The moist air has a dew point in excess of 14°C with winds exhibiting a southerly or westerly component, while the drier air generally has a dew point below 14°C and winds with northerly or easterly components. ADEJOKUN (1966) notes that "owing to the low density of radiosonde stations over West Africa only the wind field is used to determine the position of the inter-tropical discontinuity (I.T.D.) on upper air charts".

In Fig.2 the average position of the S.D. in January and July is given. This illustrates, roughly, the extreme geographical situations of the S.D. and is used only to depict some general facets of West African meteorology. The diagrams make clear the representativeness of Nigeria as an example of the weather experienced by this section of the continent. In Fig.2A it is seen that the southward migration of the pressure and wind belts in January results in the whole area experiencing outbreaks of dry, continental air nearly as far as the coast. In July (Fig.2B), however, with the S.D. near 20°N a flow of moist maritime air covers the area.

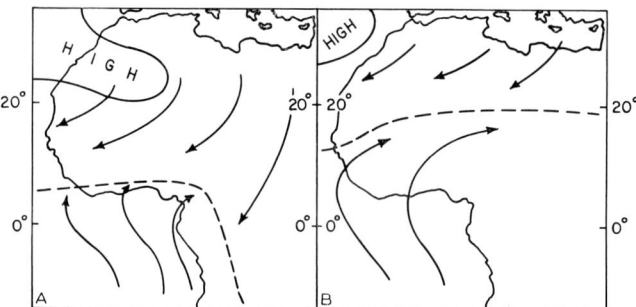

Fig.2. Average position of S.D. A. January; B. July.

The afore-mentioned distinctive weather zones are found to be associated with the S.D. in a manner that is illustrated in Fig.3, a rather schematic and idealized cross-section through the atmosphere in proximity to the S.D.

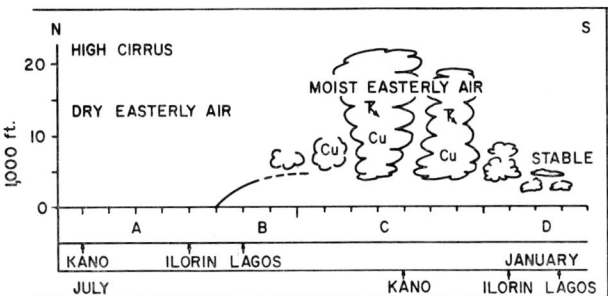

Fig.3. Weather zones of West Africa.

Zone *A*, situated immediately north of the S.D., is a region of dry air and little cloud, save perhaps for some high cirrus and local medium cloud. Much dust is often associated with this zone, especially in the winter months when, as seen in Fig.2, there has been a lengthy trajectory over the Sahara. It is often possible to relate strong Harmattan conditions during late December to early February with the occurrence of a cold front in Spain or Italy.

Zone *B*, immediately south of the S.D., extends for 200–300 km. The air is moist in the lower layers but dry above (Fig.3) with a surface wind from the southwest and an upper flow from the north or northeast. The existence of the lower, moist air is noticeable in two ways—early morning mists or stratus, and scattered, small cumulus later in the day. In the northern part of Nigeria the mists or stratus conditions are often absent but small cumulus is still characteristic of afternoon conditions. In this zone the dome-shaped nature of the protrusion of moist air can often be well identified by cloud formations. Except for isolated showers, rain is not evident here but high night-time temperatures and humidities are typical of the zone, unlike the clear, cooler nights of zone *A*.

In zone *C*, extending for 700–1,000 km south of *B*, the air is mainly moist to a height of 6,000 m or more. Therefore, the growth of cumulus is almost unrestricted in this unstable atmosphere. However, this zone does not exhibit continuous rain or even daily falls, it is short-lived rainfall with high radiation (little cloud) at other times. GARNIER (1967) notes specifically three atmospheric situations with which the rainfall is associated:

(*1*) disturbance lines, a line of thunderstorms moving east–west along a 150–600 km line (these will be described in more detail later);

(*2*) an ill-defined region of local thunderstorm activity giving widespread, variable and sporadic rainfall;

(*3*) a region in the extreme southern part of the zone where widespread and often quite steady rains occur.

Humidity is generally high in the zone and the diurnal temperature range is small.

Zone *D*, 1,000–1,300 km south of the S.D., is a region of much stratus (base about 300 m), high humidity and relatively low and constant temperature. An inversion or stable conditions above the stratus inhibits upward movement of the air so that very little rain results but mists and fogs are quite common. This is the zone of the "little dry season" and only occurs along the coast.

ADEJOKUN (1966) identifies a fifth zone south of zone *D*. This is a region of decreasing stratocumulus and stratus with increasing altostratus, altocumulus or cirrus. Drizzle and rain are frequent occurrences. There is again high humidity and low diurnal range of temperature. Since these zones move in conjunction with the position of the S.D. each station exhibits an apparent geographical shift in relation to the S.D. For instance, in Fig.3 the relative positions of Lagos, Ilorin and Kano are shown for the January and July locations of the S.D. Because of this, as pointed out by GARNIER (1967), "the movement of the S.D. controls both the number and duration of the weather types experienced in different parts of Nigeria". He illustrates this statement with the example of Ibadan which shows the following sequence: zone *A*—late December and part of January; zone *B*—February and part, or all, of March; zone *C*—April (or late March) to about mid or late July; zone *D*—late July and part, or all, of August; zone *C*—late August to end of October or early November; zone *B*—part of November and early December; zone *A*—end of December and early January.

It must not be construed from the above discussion and analyses that the resulting pattern is very simple for all the stations. The S.D. unfortunately does not move generally at a steady rate or even in a constant direction for a long period of time. Two diagrams given by GARNIER (1967) (Fig.4, 5) illustrate well the complex movement of the S.D.

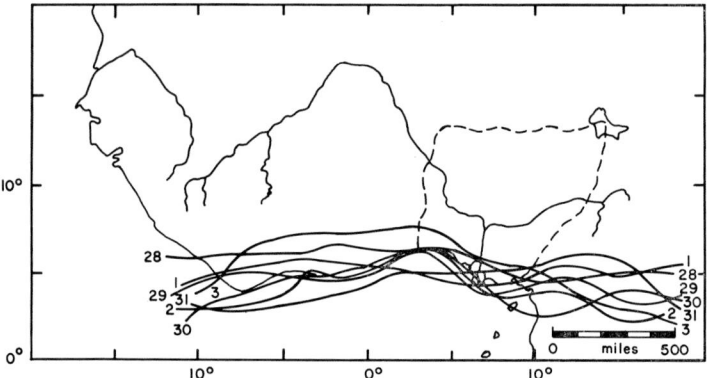

Fig.4. Location of the surface discontinuity over West Africa, December 28, 1955–January 3, 1956.

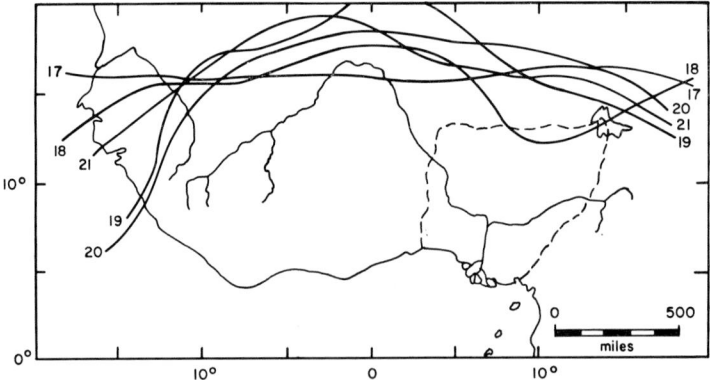

Fig.5. Location of the surface discontinuity over West Africa, May 17–21, 1959.

when studied on a day to day basis. Work by Adejokun suggests an average rate of movement of the S.D. ranging from 1.9° latitude to 4.9° latitude per month with the southward movement faster than the north. A fact well substantiated by the average monthly positions of the S.D. shown in Fig.6. Another method of depicting the variation

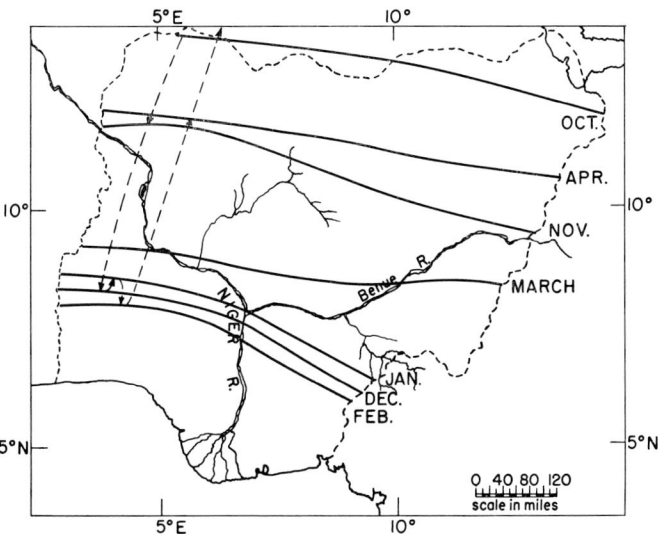

Fig.6. Average monthly positions of the surface discontinuity.

in location of the S.D. is given in Fig.7. Although a rather general kind of progression is evident the wide variation is obvious. The S.D. appears to move in a series of latitudinal steps rather than in a steady manner. Even when considered from year to year the S.D.

Fig.7. The location of the surface discontinuity at 06h00Z at 3°E each day of 1956.

displays a wide deviation. Fig.8 indicates how some days this position may range over 10° latitude during a 5-year spell while other days give a range of less than 2° latitude.

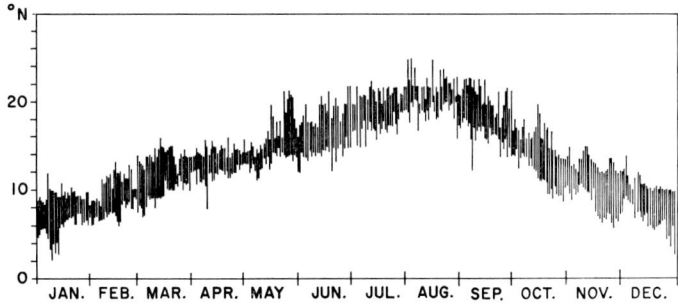

Fig.8. The range of location of the surface discontinuity at 06h00Z at 3°E, 1956–1960.

171

Zonal analysis of climate

The method of analysing the yearly climatic patterns according to the characteristics of the various zones and the position of the S.D. can be illustrated by the example of Kano (12°N). The climatic statistics given in Fig.9 can be utilized for zone identification for the year 1956. During January the low vapour pressure, relatively low maxima and minima

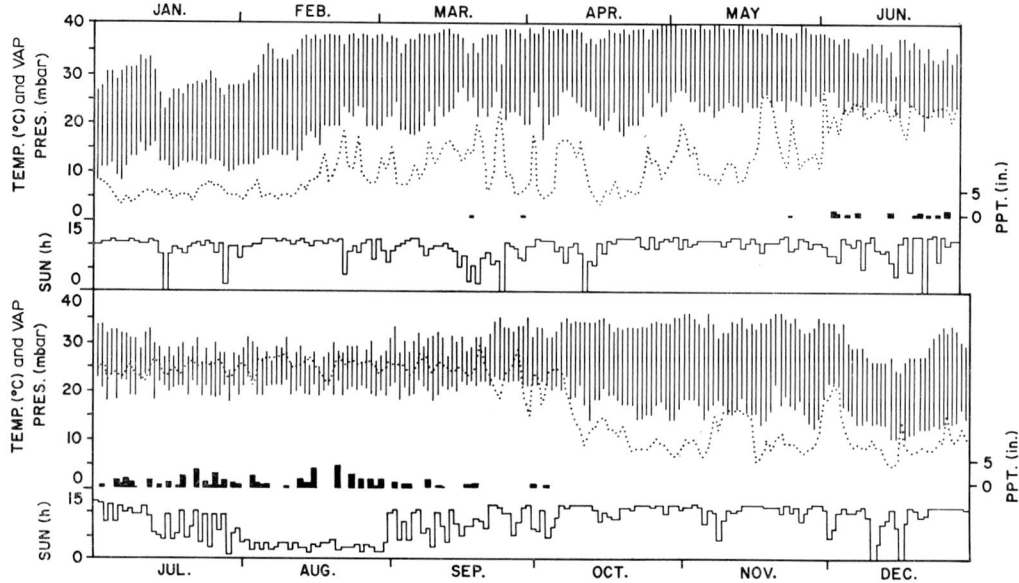

Fig.9. Selected daily statistics for Kano, 1956.

and high sunshine hours indicate zone *A*. In early February a change occurs and from mid-February to late May higher temperature and fluctuating vapour pressure suggest a period of interplay between zones *A* and *B*. In June through September, zone *C*, with rain, smaller sunshine amounts and small diurnal temperature variation, dominates. October and November show the zone *A–B* variation once again while in December zone *A* dominates. Using this method of analysis Garnier has compiled probability maps of the frequency of occurrence of the various zones, using the period 1958–1960. The resulting patterns are given in Fig.10. From a composite of these twelve maps he has suggested a regional classification shown in Fig.11. Region I experiences zone *A* conditions for at least half the year, has little zone *B* weather and about four months of zone *C*. Region II experiences a definite spell of zone *B* weather, especially during the northward movement of the S.D. Region III, while experiencing only limited periods of zone *A* conditions, nevertheless is the only area of Nigeria wherein the effects of all four zones are felt. In region IV, zone *C* dominates while zone *A* is seldom experienced.

The weather pattern of Nigeria, in the light of Garnier's work, indicates a simple form. However, pronounced individuality does exist, due in part to the local topography and to the mesoscale atmospheric systems, especially the disturbance lines. As Garnier concludes, "the weather zones provide no more than a framework within which variability occurs to the extent made possible by the prevailing or dominating weather zones". It is likely that, when further data become available, much of the weather of West Africa could be interpreted by the use of the zonation technique.

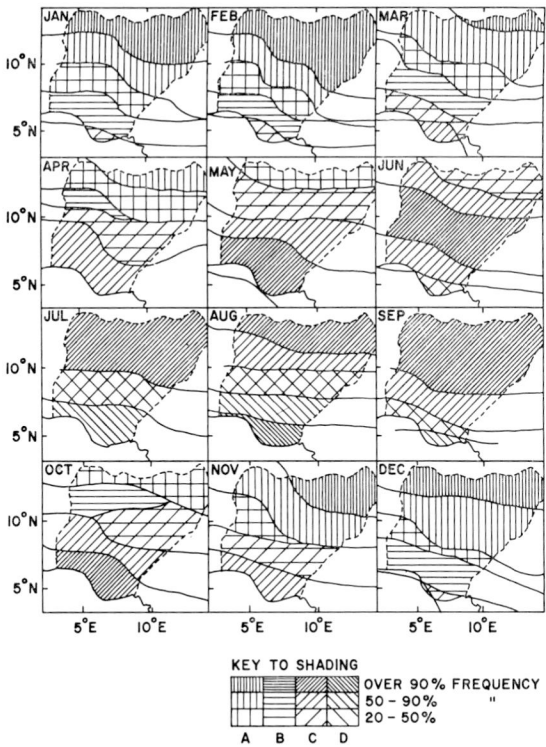

Fig.10. The percentage frequency distribution of weather zones in Nigeria, 1958–1960. For further explanation see text.

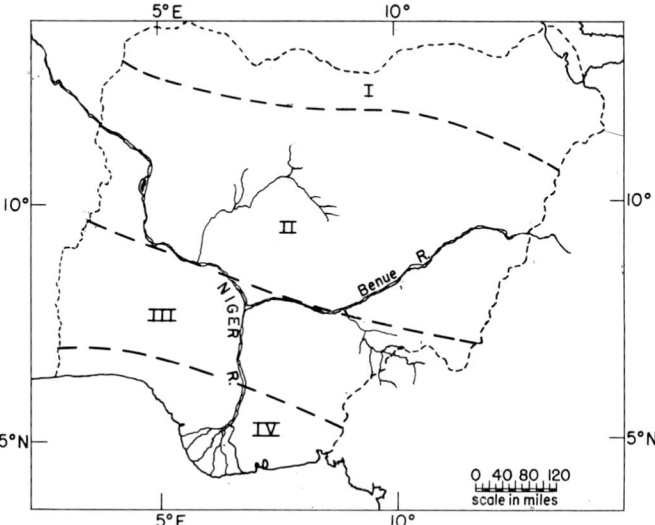

Fig.11. The weather regions of Nigeria.

Disturbance lines

Sometimes called squall lines, these atmospheric phenomena usually begin about 3°–5° south of the S.D. They extend for about 300 km on average and travel as an arc-shaped entity, convex to the west, with a speed of about 30–50 km/h in a roughly westerly direction. An interesting article by ELDRIDGE (1957) shows that they often form just east of Nigeria and that there is some relationship between their length and the distance traversed, which is often over 1,000 km and may exceed 3,000 km.

The thunderstorms so characteristic of a disturbance line are often generated when there are topographic effects to be added to the atmospheric instability. A period of calm usually presages the storm that advances as a menacing front of cumulo-nimbus cloud. When overhead an onrush of easterly wind is experienced, followed by heavy rain lasting up to half an hour with an intensity of as much as 10 cm/h. This is followed by a period of light drizzle with much low or medium cloud. ELDRIDGE (1957) has suggested that in Ghana much of the rainfall in some months is associated with such disturbance lines.

Rainfall

In the introduction the association of rainfall with the S.D. has been explained but, strictly, the incidence of rainfall can be linked with one or more of four causes. This gives rise to the concept of classifying rainfall according to the types of rain:

(*1*) Coastal—occurring in a strip about 30 km in width where the oceanic regime influence is strong.

(*2*) Monsoon—widespread and occurring from stratiform cloud.

(*3*) Local thunderstorms—a sporadic pattern, widely experienced inland during the main rainy season, often exhibits afternoon maximum.

(*4*) Disturbance lines—the belts of intense thunderstorms moving east–west with heavy rain of short duration.

Nigeria exhibits a very wide variation in mean annual totals of rainfall, some areas receiving less than 700 mm and others in excess of 5,000 mm. Debundscha, now in the Cameroons, has an annual mean of over 10,000 mm—one of the three stations in the world with a reliable average of over 10,000 mm. The mean annual pattern is shown in Fig.12. The isohyets are seen to run roughly parallel to the lines of latitude but with

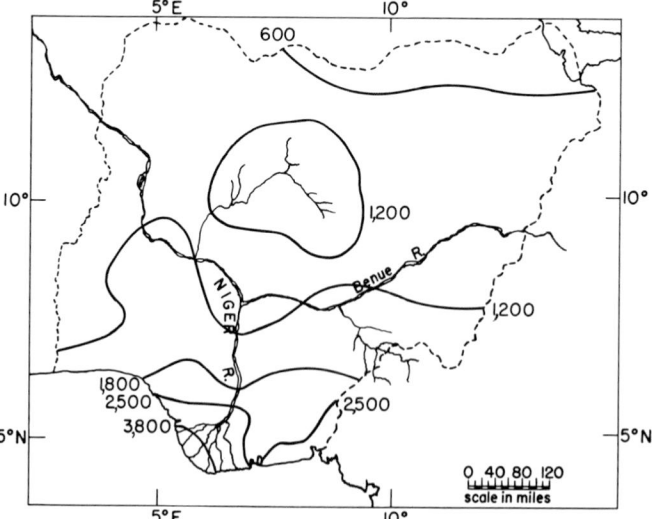

Fig.12. Generalized mean annual rainfall map (mm).

wetter pockets where there is highland (Jos Plateau) or where a change in coastline direction brings warm moist air over the heated land. It is essential to consider the monthly variation in rainfall in all tropical regions, for a single value, such as the annual total, can be extremely misleading. Some idea of the various patterns experienced in Nigeria is given in Fig.13, where data for Jos, Kano, Lagos and Makurdi are presented. These

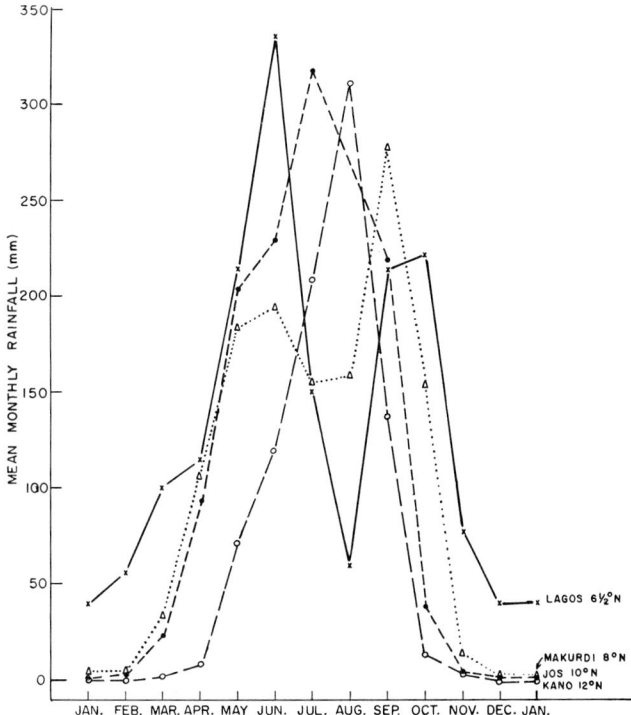

Fig.13. Rainfall patterns for selected stations.

represent a reasonable north–south cross-section of the country and the incidence of the "little dry season" can be seen extending as far as Makurdi at 8°N. As pointed out by IRELAND (1962) this "dry season" is not detectable in the averages, either of amounts or of rainy days (Fig.14). This drier spell also disappears beyond longitude 5°E when considered as amount (Fig.15). The minimum appears to occur in the second week of August at all stations. This phenomenon is rather similar to that of the Verranillo in Central America. The seasonal distribution of rainfall is given in more detail in Table I. These fifteen stations, extending from 4° to 13°N and within 150 km of the 7°10'E longitude, illustrate both by amount and the number of raindays how the double peak in rainfall extends to about Bida (9°N), but is unimportant even at 4°N in the eastern section of the country. It is interesting to observe that of many stations examined nearly all south of 5°30'N had at least 25 mm every month, while south of 9°N very few had completely dry months. The pronounced reduction in rainfall as latitude increases is admirably illustrated in Fig.16, showing the number of months receiving more than 50 mm of rainfall. A few isolated stations near the coast receive twelve months but the large areas exhibit values from 3 to 11. The break in the "6 belt" is certainly due to the Jos Plateau where

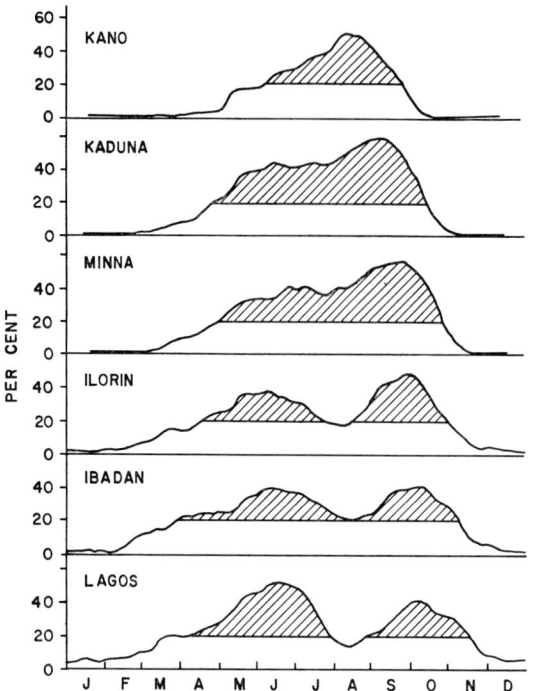

Fig.14. Percentage occurrence of rain days (more than 0.04 mm).

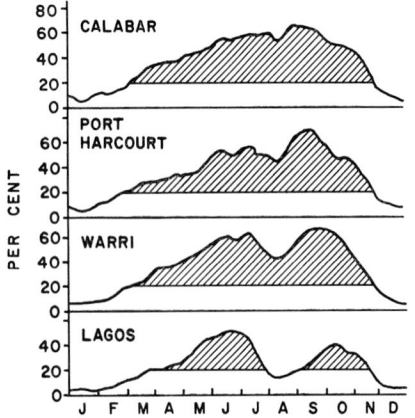

Fig.15. Percentage occurrence of rain days (more than 0.04 mm).

orographic influences increase the number of wet months. This type of bunching of wet months is typical of the whole of West Africa south of the Sahara.

The month of maximum rainfall exhibits a most unusual pattern (Fig.17). The northern half of the country receives most rainfall during August, when the S.D. is at about 20°N or up to 1,100 km away. As the convergence zone travels southwards so does the month of maximum rainfall so that, except for the coast and a few isolated areas, a September high is recorded. Again (see Fig.6), the S.D. is over 1,000 km north of parts of this zone. The coastal strip, influenced greatly by the oceanic regime of land and sea breezes, has maxima during June or July, dependent upon the direction of the coast to the slightly veering wind at this season of the year.

TABLE I

MEAN RAINFALL AMOUNT (MM) AND DAYS[1]

Station	Lat. (N)	Long. (E)	Elev. (m)	Jan.	Feb.	Mar.	Apr.	May	June	July	Aug.	Sept.	Oct.	Nov.	Dec.	Ann.	Record (yrs.)
Isongo	4°04'	9°01'	45	269	361	338	452	668	1,359	1,509	1,539	1,610	1,130	538	292	10,066	11
				10	12	15	16	19	23	26	27	26	23	17	10	224	
Moliwe	4°03'	9°16'	300	25	56	127	191	211	432	851	709	399	241	97	23	3,360	12
				2	4	7	10	12	18	23	23	19	16	7	2	143	
Idenau	4°13'	8°59'	3	109	145	287	285	538	1,189	1,542	1,425	1,516	1,057	373	155	8,621	11
				9	12	18	19	25	27	28	30	28	28	21	12	257	
Brass	4°19'	6°14'	3	76	104	165	251	411	665	211	297	528	432	206	91	3,739	26
				6	7	11	14	18	20	19	10	25	20	14	9	179	
Ndian	4°57'	8°51'	100	119	142	290	452	513	864	955	947	823	584	353	160	6,203	10
				10	12	15	16	19	23	20	27	26	23	17	10	224	
Oleh	5°29'	6°10'	15	30	64	157	244	338	391	411	302	513	335	89	18	2,893	10
				2	4	9	11	15	20	21	18	24	19	7	1	151	
Agbor	6°16'	6°11'	150	15	41	117	165	213	269	272	183	328	218	53	13	1,897	46
				1	3	7	7	9	12	14	12	18	13	4	1	101	
Okene	7°34'	6°13'	400	7	18	71	107	163	188	165	170	190	157	18	20	1,275	21
				1	2	5	8	9	10	11	9	17	12	3	2	89	
Ahuji	8°33'	6°13'	120	0	2	30	86	135	168	234	232	226	102	23	8	1,245	15
				0	0	3	5	8	9	13	10	12	7	1	1	69	
Bida	9°12'	6°03'	170	5	5	32	66	147	180	191	201	239	99	8	0	1,173	25
				0	0	2	5	8	11	12	10	15	8	1	0	72	
Kaduna	10°29'	7°25'	630	0	2	15	69	142	216	224	279	292	84	5	0	1,328	45
				0	0	2	6	12	14	16	18	20	8	1	0	97	
Maigana	11°02'	7°56'	660	0	2	10	38	130	150	218	335	213	38	0	0	1,135	35
				0	0	1	4	10	12	17	20	18	6	0	0	88	
Kafinsoli	12°32'	7°45'	540	0	0	0	8	56	97	206	287	145	15	0	15	813	26
				0	0	1	1	5	9	15	17	13	2	0	0	63	
Katisina	13°01'	7°41'	515	0	0	0	5	56	84	185	274	127	10	0	0	742	37
				0	0	0	1	5	8	15	17	13	2	0	0	61	

[1] First line: amount in mm; second line: number of days.

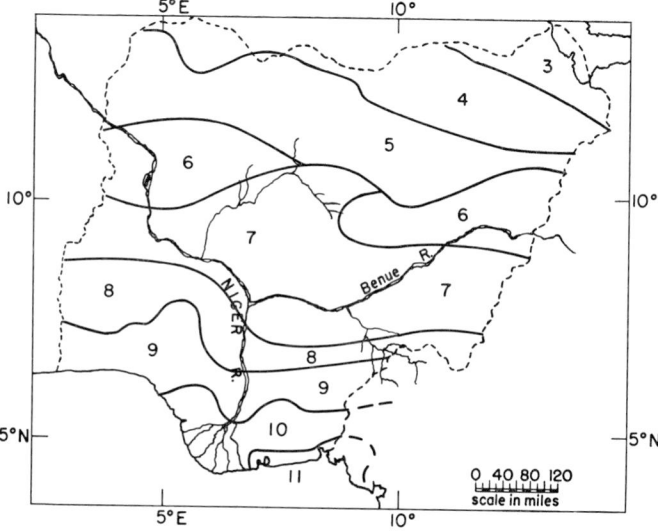

Fig.16. Number of months with 50 mm mean rainfall.

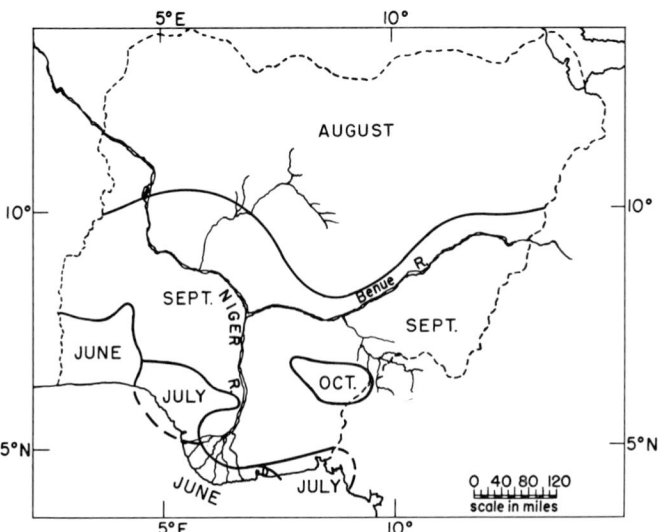

Fig.17. Month of maximum rainfall.

The maximum 24 h precipitation amount, recorded during a period of about 40 years, rarely exceeds 150 mm north of 7°N, falling in July and August. Nearer the coast, however, falls in excess of 250 mm are noted, the record being 513 mm in July in Victoria. At this station falls of over 150 mm have been measured in every month from January to October. Enugu experienced a very unusual 310 mm during one September day, although it is over 200 km inland. Bamenda (5°56′N), the station with highest elevation (1,700 m), has a unique December maximum of 154 mm.

The diurnal variation of rainfall can only be studied at those stations possessing a recording raingauge but the six centres mentioned here give a reasonable picture of the overall pattern. Data have been extracted from a report of the BRITISH WEST AFRICAN METEOROLOGICAL SERVICE.

The stations show the following facts:

(*1*) Tiko (4°06′N 9°21′E, 50 m)—coastal belt, diffuse early morning maximum, in August 36% chance of rain in 01h00Z–09h00Z, reducing to a minimum of 22% at 17h00Z.

(*2*) Port Harcourt (4°51′N 7°01′E, 15 m)—outside the coastal belt, marked afternoon maximum caused by local thunderstorms and young line-squalls, in September 30% chance of rain at 15h00Z–17h00Z, with the minimum of 12% between 23h00Z and 02h00Z.

(*3*) Enugu (6°28′N 7°33′E, 140 m)—diffuse night and early morning maximum in rainy season, perhaps due to southern Cameroons line-squall source-area, in September the maximum is 16% (22h00Z–03h00Z) with a minimum of 6% (10h00Z–12h00Z).

(*4*) Minna (9°37′N 6°32′E, 260 m)—evening and early morning maxima, the former may be due to line-squalls, the latter from monsoon rain or distant source-area line-squalls to the east, in September the maximum is 18% at 20h00Z–21h00Z and the minimum 6% between 12h00Z and 14h00Z.

(*5*) Jos (9°52′N 8°54′E, 1,260 m)—marked afternoon maximum characteristic of line-squall source-area, a minor early morning maximum may be of the monsoon type, in July the maximum is 28% chance of rain between 15h00Z–17h00Z and the minimum is 8% (09h00Z–11h00Z).

(6) Sokoto (13°01′N 5°15′E, 345 m)—marked night and early morning maxima associated with source-areas to the east, in August the maximum chance of rain is 8% between 01 h00Z and 09h00Z with the minimum 5% from 12h00Z to 14h00Z.

The month selected for each station is that in which the greatest probability of rain occurs.

Temperature

The mean annual temperature for most stations in Nigeria is about 27°C. Many of the other temperature characteristics are dependent upon distance from the coast, as Table II illustrates.

TABLE II

TEMPERATURE ASPECTS FOR CHOSEN STATIONS (°C)

Station	Distance from coast (km)	Annual range	Diurnal range	Highest mean monthly max.	Lowest mean monthly min.
Lagos	2	3	6	32	23
Enugu	200	4	8	33	21
Bauchi	620	6	8	37	13
Maiduguri	900	9	16	40	12

The annual range is very small in all save the far northern areas, confirming the position of Nigeria on the thermal equator. The diurnal range also illustrates the role of latitude on increased continentality. Although the mean annual temperature remains remarkably constant over the whole country, the maximum mean monthly temperature varies greatly,

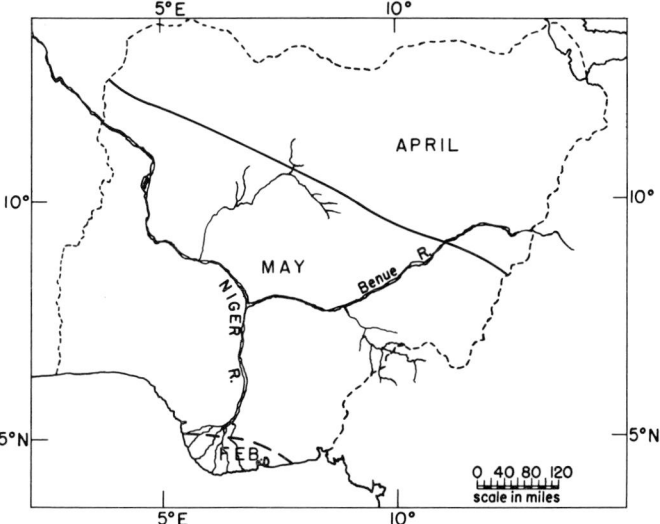

Fig.18. Month of highest mean monthly maximum temperature.

from 31°C at Victoria to 42°C at Hadeija. The time of maximum afternoon temperatures occurs either in March or April, with a very few stations showing a February maximum (Fig.18). Mean monthly maxima below 27°C are only found in the plateau area, Jos records 25°C in August.

The lowest mean monthly temperatures show an interesting pattern (Fig.19). In the south the lowest mean is reached about the time of maximum rainfall but in the north the continentality (latitude) effect predominates and the coldest month is in the northern winter (December or January). Stations in this region do nevertheless show a secondary minimum at the time of heaviest rains. Mean monthly minima range from about 12° to 24°C in the north, 18°–24°C in the central area, and 21°–25°C at the coast. Very few temperatures below 5°C have been recorded but, except for a few coastal stations, most areas have been below 10°C.

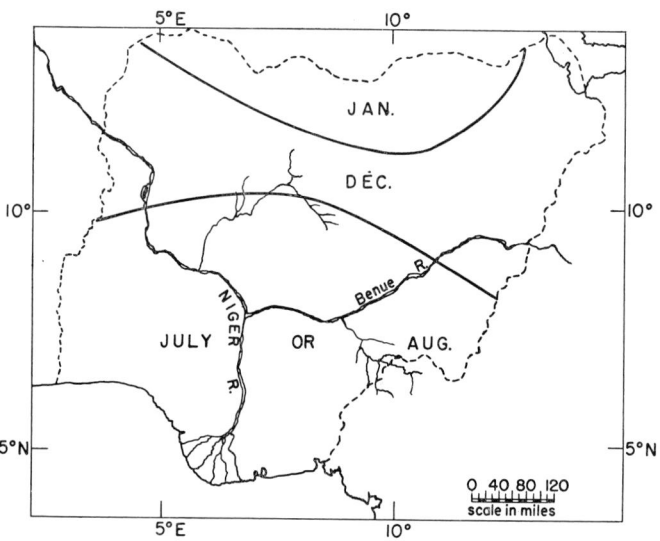

Fig.19. Month of lowest mean monthly temperature.

The hourly temperature variation makes for an interesting presentation and one, for Kano, is given in Fig.20. The cooling effect due to the rains is evident in May to September, the cloudy conditions almost halving the diurnal range at this time.

Soil temperature variation shows a distinctly geographical pattern, a primary maximum at the 30-cm depth occurs in February at the coast but the time gets progressively later as one moves north until at Kano the maximum occurs in May. A secondary maximum appears in October or November at most stations. South of 10°N the stations have a minimum in July, August or September only, but north of this latitude the primary minimum occurs in January with a secondary in August. These latter stations are far enough away from the southern sun for this to dominate the effect due to cloud and rainfall associated with the movement of the I.T.C.Z. This pattern is repeated, broadly, at the 120-cm depth. Stations, except in the highland, also exhibit an increase northwards in the amplitude of both maximum and minimum soil temperature ranges, from about 2°C at the coast to 9°C for the maximum and 6°C for the minimum in the north.

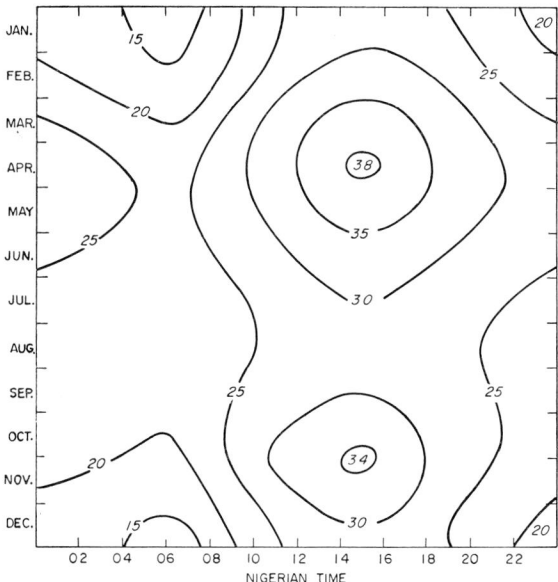

Fig.20. Air temperature, Kano (°C).

Humidity

Relative humidity shows very large variations over Nigeria. In the coastal regions the months June to October have monthly means of over 90% while in the north, during January to April, mean values are close to 20 or 25%. Of course, such fluctuations are also reflecting the temperature changes taking place and it is preferable to study humidity patterns through vapour pressure or dew point measurements.

Vapour pressure tends to show a minimum value during January (16h00Z readings) with only very few exceptions of a marginal value. Fig.21 shows the isopleths at this time and illustrates clearly the rapid change from moist maritime to dry continental air, with a remarkable gradient of some 2 mbar/10 km in many areas. The closed low is reflecting the elevated Jos Plateau.

For maximum vapour pressures the constancy lies not in the time of occurrence but more in the value reached, which is from about 25 or 26 mbar in the extreme north, to 28 in the south, reaching 30 right at the coast. These values are modified at highland stations. It must be remembered that these figures refer to the surface layer and so generally coincide with the period of arrival and stabilization of the southerly flow. The modifying effect of the Jos Plateau is again in evidence but the over-riding of the "predicted" July maximum by a September maximum in certain areas is rather strange (Fig.22), and may be due to the increase occasioned by the heavy rains (often 25% of the annual fall) which occur on many days (about 20 or more).

Daily variation in vapour pressure is generally about 2 mbar only but in the period March–May can average as high as 5 mbar, the 6 mbar variation (such as Kano in April) is unusual. The hourly variation throughout the year is presented in Fig.23 for Ibadan, Ikeja, Kaduna and Kano.

Ibadan illustrates a typical, slightly inland, pattern with maxima occurring in the mid morning and late evening as instability showers occur and the moist air of the land/sea

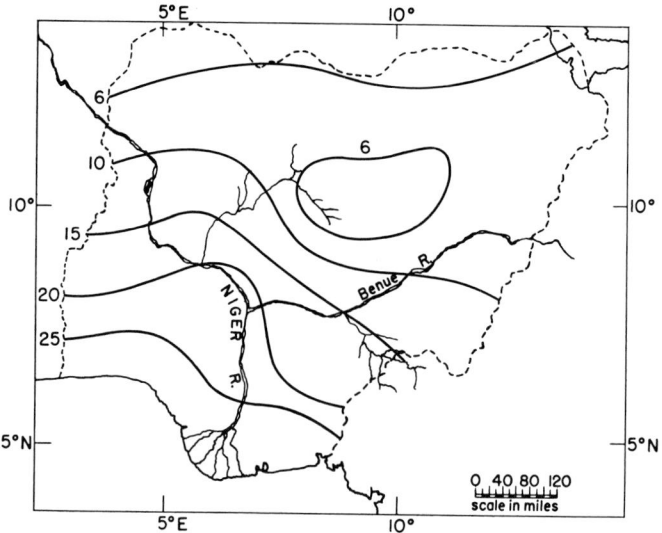

Fig.21. Vapour pressure (mbar) at 16h00Z, January.

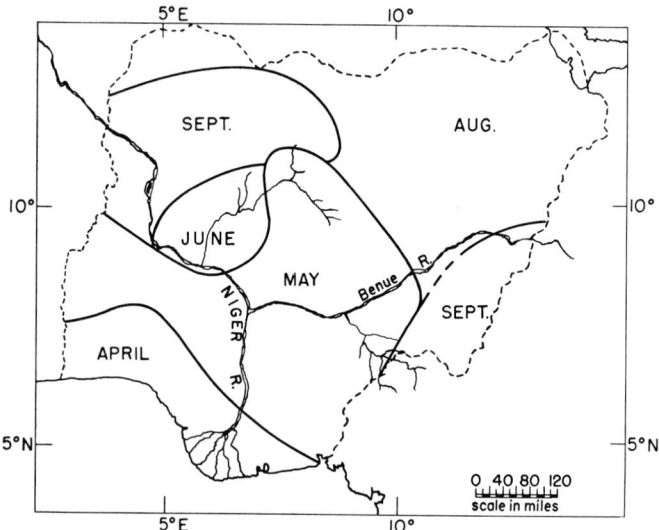

Fig.22. Month of maximum mean vapour pressure.

circulation reaches the littoral. Ikeja, nearly on the coast, has a high incidence of the sea breeze.

Kaduna and Kano, far inland, show very little diurnal fluctuation, but the tightness of the gradient illustrates the rapid onset of the moist, maritime air.

Evaporation

Evaporation increases markedly away from the coast, the mean annual value at Sokoto (mean relative humidity 50%) being three times that at Benin (mean relative humidity about 80%). Values in excess of 500 mm/month (16 mm/day) are recorded in the northern areas just prior to the onset of the rains. Maiduguri's measured 18 mm/day in March is the country's highest (Table III). August and September, the rainiest months generally

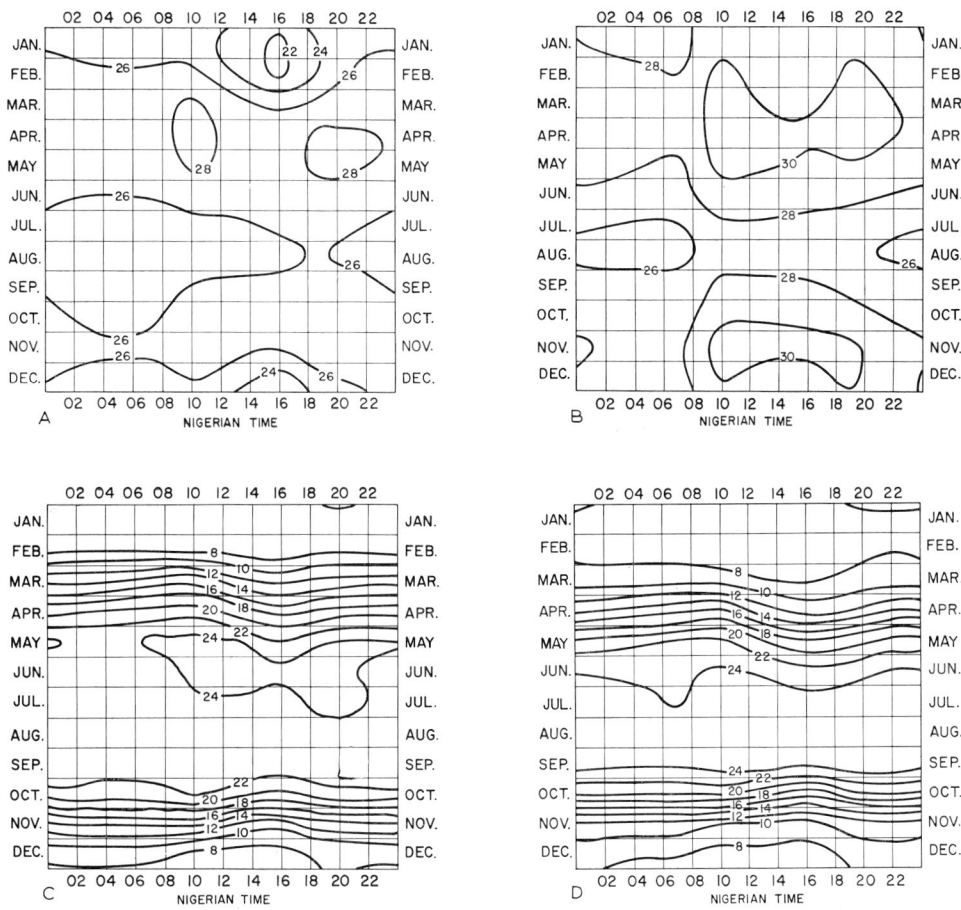

Fig.23. Average vapour pressure (mbar), 1951–1960. A. Ibadan; B. Ikeja; C. Kaduna; D. Kano.

TABLE III

PAN EVAPORATION (mm) FOR SELECTED STATIONS

Station	Jan.	Feb.	Mar.	Apr.	May	June	July	Aug.	Sept.	Oct.	Nov.	Dec.	Ann.	Record (yrs.)
Jos	307	335	368	272	236	201	163	142	183	254	295	302	3,058	7
Kano	277	307	386	404	384	292	218	183	206	282	290	277	3,506	7
Maiduguri	320	396	559	526	500	295	216	165	185	251	279	282	3,974	6
Makurdi	185	221	300	246	218	224	157	132	163	178	178	183	2,385	3
Sokoto	406	429	518	465	460	368	290	185	231	302	345	366	4,365	3
Enugu	201	206	259	236	213	231	175	178	152	155	175	178	2,359	3
Pt. Harcourt	130	152	170	160	150	114	104	114	119	142	127	122	1,604	6
Benin	117	135	152	142	137	119	99	91	102	122	127	114	1,457	5
Ibadan	130	160	191	163	150	122	91	99	99	127	127	130	1,589	7
Yelwa	231	274	328	325	297	218	183	180	178	185	191	185	2,775	6
Samaru	264	267	340	284	257	198	173	135	170	180	206	236	2,710	3
Yola	272	325	396	307	287	196	170	165	175	201	218	244	2,956	5
Badeggi	165	201	254	246	206	157	130	112	142	157	165	160	2,095	3

give the lowest evaporation rates, as little as 4 mm/day in some areas. The annual variation in the coastal strip is very much less than that in the northern region, a range of about 60 mm/month compared with 390 mm. Measurements of evapotranspiration from grass, with non-limiting soil moisture supply, showed good agreement with the amount of evaporation measured from a standard British Meteorological Office evaporation tank (STANHILL, 1963).

Radiation, sunshine and cloud

The *World Maps of Climatology* (LANDSBERG et al., 1963) suggest mean annual values of about 140 kcal./cm² near Port Harcourt, increasing to 160 kcal./cm² near Kano. Unfortunately, there are very few stations recording radiation data; two sets are given in Table IV.

TABLE IV

MEAN MONTHLY GLOBAL RADIATION (Ly/day)

Station	Jan.	Feb.	Mar.	Apr.	May	June	July	Aug.	Sept.	Oct.	Nov.	Dec.	Year
Benin	340	360	390	400	420	380	300	300	310	360	380	370	360
Samaru	500	570	600	560	510	520	450	390	480	550	520	500	510

The solar radiation is not high (about equal to that at Denver, New Orleans or Athens) due to two causes, the high moisture content of the air and the cloud cover during the wet season, and the dust and smoke (grass fires) during the dry season.

The coastal area receives about 2,000 h of sunshine per year (45% possible). In the north this improves to 2,800 h (65%) and reaches a maximum near Lake Chad of 3,200 h (75%). In the rainy season (July and August) coastal areas receive less than 100 h per month and in August it is rare for any station to record more than 50% of the possible sunshine hours. In the northern dry season (November–February) monthly means in excess of 80% possible are the rule, with certain months reaching 90% or more (Table V). There is very high cloud amount over the whole country in August (Table VI), the average being in excess of 7 oktas. At coastal stations, such as Port Harcourt, there is much cloud throughout the year, but further north there is a marked annual variation, often from 2 to 7 oktas.

Wind and sandstorms

Gales (wind speeds of over 34 knots) are relatively frequent at some stations. Jos experiences about ten occasions per year, with an average of three in May, while Kano records nine per year, two in each month June to September. Yelwa (8), Minna (5) and Lagos, Enugu and Sokoto (2) also have regular incidences of gales.

TABLE V

PERCENTAGE OF POSSIBLE SUNSHINE

Station	Jan.	Feb.	Mar.	Apr.	May	June	July	Aug.	Sept.	Oct.	Nov.	Dec.	Year
Bamenda	66	71	45	38	44	31	19	18	22	36	54	61	42
Bauchi	78	82	73	61	65	62	48	41	61	75	85	84	68
Benin	49	53	46	48	46	38	26	40	22	40	54	58	43
Enugu	57	61	51	52	52	42	32	27	32	47	60	63	48
Ibadan	56	59	53	49	49	41	24	19	25	45	58	59	45
Ibi	73	77	68	60	64	52	44	39	49	66	75	76	62
Ikeja	50	57	53	52	45	32	23	24	25	41	55	56	43
Ilorin	64	67	63	56	55	49	34	29	34	51	64	68	53
Jos	85	83	70	58	54	53	39	33	47	66	84	88	63
Kaduna	78	79	72	66	62	55	39	32	47	67	81	83	63
Kano	77	78	72	68	70	68	59	48	65	80	84	80	71
Lokoja	67	69	62	54	55	47	39	33	41	54	69	70	55
Maiduguri	82	85	77	71	71	69	54	48	60	79	86	84	72
Makurdi	67	71	62	56	57	46	38	31	40	54	61	64	54
Mamfe	53	59	48	45	46	34	26	20	27	42	50	53	42
Minna	73	74	71	63	62	53	33	31	46	71	79	78	61
Pt. Harcourt	45	51	39	40	40	27	20	20	17	29	39	47	35
Sokoto	79	82	76	69	71	73	58	51	66	83	86	84	73
Yola	78	82	72	63	69	62	51	43	52	73	85	84	68

TABLE VI

MEAN MONTHLY CLOUD AMOUNTS (oktas)

Station	Hour	Jan.	Feb.	Mar.	Apr.	May	June	July	Aug.	Sept.	Oct.	Nov.	Dec.	Ann. mean	Record (yrs.)
Enugu	10h00	4	4	6	7	7	7	7	7	7	7	6	4	7	13
	16h00	4	4	6	6	6	6	7	7	7	6	5	3	5.5	13
Jos	10h00	2	3	5	5	6	6	7	7	7	5	4	2	5	13
	16h00	3	3	5	6	6	6	7	7	7	5	4	3	5	13
Kano	10h00	2	2	3	5	5	5	6	6	6	4	3	2	4	15
	16h00	2	3	4	5	5	5	6	6	5	4	3	2	4	15
Maiduguri	10h00	2	2	4	4	5	5	6	7	6	5	3	2	4	10
	16h00	3	3	4	5	5	5	6	7	6	4	4	3	5.5	13
Port Harcourt	09h00	6	5	7	7	7	7	7	8	7	7	7	5	7	13
	15h00	5	6	7	7	7	7	7	7	7	7	7	5	7	13
Sokoto	09h00	2	2	4	4	5	5	7	7	6	5	3	3	4.5	10
	15h00	2	3	5	5	5	5	6	7	6	4	3	3	4.5	10
Yola	10h00	2	3	4	5	6	6	7	7	7	5	4	3	5	10
	16h00	3	3	5	5	6	6	6	7	6	5	4	3	5	10

During the daytime hours winds are predominantly north to northeasterly at the time of the northern winter, changing to south or southwesterly in the summer. The period of northerly flow is short near the coast, mainly November to February, extending to about six months (November–April) further north. During the day calm conditions are not common (1–3%) but the 03h00 local time observations note calms about 10–30% of the time. At Lagos the percentage of calms reaches about 50–60 with light winds from the west.

Sandstorms, with visibility below 1,000 m, are recorded most frequently at Maiduguri in May with an average of three. Two per month are recorded at Sokoto in July and Maiduguri in June. There is a marked secondary minimum of sandstorms in March.

A paper by McCormack (1958) shows a useful relationship between the maximum gust speed (G) experienced at the time of a disturbance line and the drop in temperature (dT °C). The expression is:

$$G \text{ (knots)} = 12.5 \, dT - 4.2$$

with a correlation coefficient of 0.75.

References

ADEJOKUN, J. A., 1966. The three-dimensional structure of the inter-tropical discontinuity over Nigeria. *Nigerian Meteorol. Serv., Tech. Note*, 39:9 pp.

BRITISH WEST AFRICAN METEOROLOGICAL SERVICE. Diurnal variation of rainfall. *Brit. W. African Meteorol. Serv., Meteorol. Note*, 9:20 pp.

ELDRIDGE, R. H., 1957. A synoptic study of West African disturbance lines. *Quart. J. Roy. Meteorol. Soc.*, 83(357):303–314 pp.

GARNIER, B. J., 1967. Weather conditions in Nigeria., *McGill Univ., Dept. Geograph., Climatological Res. Ser.*, 2:163 pp.

IRELAND, A. W., 1962. The little dry season of southern Nigeria. *J. Geograph. Assoc. Nigeria*, 5(1):7–21 (also in: *Nigerian Meteorol. Serv., Tech. Note*, 24).

LANDSBERG, H. E., LIPPMANN, H., PAFFEN, K. H. and TROLL, C., 1963. *World Maps of Climatology*. Springer, Berlin, 5 maps, 28 pp.

McCORMACK, J. G., 1958. Relation between peak gusts and associated temperature falls. *Brit. W. African Meteorol. Serv., Tech. Note*, 9:2 pp.

OBASI, G. O. P., 1965. Atmospheric, synoptic and climatological features over the West African region. *Nigerian Meteorol. Serv., Tech. Note*, 28:45 pp.

STANHILL, G., 1963. The accuracy of meteorological estimates of evapotranspiration in Nigeria. *Nigerian Meteorol. Serv., Tech. Note*, 31:7 pp.

TABLE VII

CLIMATIC TABLE FOR LAGOS, NIGERIA
Latitude 6°27'N, longitude 3°24'E, elevation 3 m

Month	M.S.L. press. (mbar)	Temperature[1] (°C) mean		extreme		Dew point (°C)		Precipitation					Preval. wind direct.		Calm (%)		Averages cloud-iness (oktas)		sun-shine[1] (h/day)
		max.	min.	max.	min.	07h	16h	mean (mm)	max. (mm)	min. (mm)	days ≥0.1 mm	max. in 24 h (mm)	09h	15h	03h 21h	09h 15h	09h	15h	
Jan.	1,011	31	22	35	14	22.5	23.3	40	155	0	4	123	W	SW	60	3	5	2	5.9
Feb.	1,010	33	23	36	16	23.0	23.4	57	180	0	4	95	W	SW	54	2	5	3	6.8
Mar.	1,010	33	23	36	19	23.0	24.0	100	286	5	8	105	SW	S	48	1	6	4	6.4
Apr.	1,010	32	23	36	20	23.0	24.2	115	325	34	10	133	SW	S	55	4	7	4	6.3
May	1,012	31	22	35	20	22.0	24.1	215	549	90	18	158	W	S	53	4	7	5	5.6
June	1,014	29	22	32	18	22.0	23.7	336	763	138	23	254	W	SW	51	3	7	5	4.0
July	1,014	27	22	31	17	21.9	22.5	150	786	2	15	177	SSW	SSW	41	1	7	5	2.9
Aug.	1,014	27	21	31	16	21.0	22.1	59	580	2	10	108	SSW	SSW	40	0	7	5	3.0
Sept.	1,013	28	22	31	19	22.0	23.2	214	424	10	17	158	SSW	SW	44	2	7	5	3.1
Oct.	1,012	29	22	33	19	22.0	23.8	222	450	75	15	163	W	SW	59	2	7	5	4.9
Nov.	1,011	31	23	33	20	22.8	24.5	77	183	4	8	107	NW	S	53	3	6	4	6.5
Dec.	1,011	32	22	34	17	22.2	23.6	41	150	0	3	109	NW	S	56	2	6	2	6.6
Annual	1,012	30	22	36	14	22.2	23.5	1,625	2,934	1,039	135	254	—	S	51	2	6	4	5.2
Rec. (yrs.)	30	10	10	10	10	10	10	60	60	60	60	60	5	5	5	5	15	15	10

[1] Records from Ikeja (6°35'N 3°20'E, 35 m).

TABLE VIII

CLIMATIC TABLE FOR ENUGU, NIGERIA
Latitude 6°28'N, longitude 7°33'E, elevation 140 m

Month	M.S.L. press. (mbar)	Temperature (°C)				Dew point (°C)		Precipitation					Averages		
		mean		extreme		07h	16h	mean (mm)	max. (mm)	min. (mm)	days ≥1 mm	max. in 24h (mm)	cloud-iness[1] (oktas)	sun-shine (h/day)	evap. (mm)
		max.	min.	max.	min.										
Jan.	1,011	32	22	36	13	19.0	16.2	18	124	0	1	125	4	6.7	201
Feb.	1,011	33	23	37	16	19.6	16.5	25	106	0	2	80	4	7.3	206
Mar.	1,010	33	24	37	20	22.4	20.7	68	201	0	5	104	6	6.2	259
Apr.	1,010	33	23	37	19	22.8	22.7	154	336	34	9	158	6	6.4	236
May	1,011	31	23	35	19	22.7	23.1	260	494	94	13	125	6	6.5	212
June	1,013	29	22	33	19	22.0	22.4	267	601	138	13	137	6	5.3	230
July	1,014	28	22	32	19	21.5	21.8	192	384	43	13	108	7	4.0	175
Aug.	1,013	27	22	32	19	21.3	21.6	175	584	6	14	115	7	3.4	177
Sept.	1,013	29	22	32	18	21.8	22.4	305	714	104	19	313	7	3.9	152
Oct.	1,012	31	22	34	19	21.9	22.4	252	398	98	16	122	6	5.6	154
Nov.	1,011	32	22	35	16	21.8	21.7	53	155	2	4	83	5	7.1	175
Dec.	1,011	32	21	34	13	19.9	19.0	15	109	0	1	68	3	7.4	177
Annual	1,012	31	22	37	13	21.4	21.0	1,784	2,300	1,266	110	313	6	5.9	2,352
Rec. (yrs.)	30	11	11	12	12	5	5	43	50	50	43	43	14	9	3

[1] Mean of 10h00, 16h00 and 22h00.

TABLE IX

CLIMATIC TABLE FOR JOS, NIGERIA
Latitude 9°52′N, longitude 8°54′E, elevation 1,260 m

Month	M.S.L. press. (mbar)	Temperature (°C) mean max.	mean min.	extreme max.	extreme min.	Dew point (°C) 07h	16h	Precipitation mean (mm)	max. (mm)	min. (mm)	days ≥0.1 mm	max. in 24 h (mm)	Averages cloud-iness[1] (oktas)	sun-shine (h/day)	evap. (mm)
Jan.	872	28	14	32	4	−0.9	−3.5	2	34	0	<1	25	2	9.9	307
Feb.	873	29	15	33	7	0.6	−4.1	4	68	0	1	68	3	9.8	335
Mar.	872	31	18	34	12	10.0	1.5	24	112	0	3	70	4	8.4	368
Apr.	872	30	18	34	13	15.8	10.4	93	196	21	11	63	5	7.1	271
May	873	28	18	33	14	17.7	16.0	205	351	35	16	87	6	6.7	237
June	874	26	17	31	14	17.3	16.7	229	389	105	17	98	6	6.7	200
July	874	24	17	28	14	16.9	17.2	318	569	185	23	140	7	4.9	162
Aug.	873	24	17	29	14	16.9	17.3	274	500	122	22	79	7	4.1	142
Sept.	873	26	17	29	12	16.8	16.3	219	334	80	21	83	6	5.7	182
Oct.	873	27	16	31	10	15.2	12.1	39	139	0	11	69	5	7.8	254
Nov.	873	28	15	32	9	7.3	2.9	5	46	0	1	46	4	9.8	295
Dec.	873	27	14	31	7	1.5	−1.5	2	34	0	<1	32	2	10.1	305
Annual	873	27	16	34	4	2.5	10.3	1,414	1,760	1,080	126	140	5	7.5	3,058
Rec. (yrs.)	10	10	10	10	10	10	10	30	40	40	40	40	14	10	7

[1] Mean of 10h00, 16h00 and 12h00.

TABLE X

CLIMATIC TABLE FOR MAIDUGURI, NIGERIA

Latitude 11°51'N, longitude 13°05'E, elevation 350 m

Month	M.S.L. press. (mbar)	Temperature (°C) mean max.	Temperature (°C) mean min.	Temperature (°C) extreme max.	Temperature (°C) extreme min.	Dew point (°C) 07h	Dew point (°C) 16h	Precipitation mean (mm)	Precipitation max. (mm)	Precipitation min. (mm)	Precipitation days ≥0.1 mm	Precipitation max. in 24 h (mm)	Averages cloudiness (okta) 10h	Averages cloudiness (okta) 22h	Averages sunshine (h/day)	Averages evap. (mm)
Jan.	1,015	32	12	39	6	3.8	3.2	1	13	0	0	13	2	2	9.4	323
Feb.	1,014	34	14	42	9	3.6	2.7	<1	8	0	0	8	2	2	10.0	396
Mar.	1,011	38	18	43	9	6.5	4.5	1	10	0	<1	10	4	3	9.2	558
Apr.	1,010	40	22	44	13	12.9	8.9	4	42	0	2	25	4	3	8.8	525
May	1,010	38	25	44	17	19.6	16.2	34	86	1	7	54	5	4	8.9	500
June	1,012	36	24	41	16	21.2	18.9	78	198	7	9	94	5	5	8.8	295
July	1,013	32	23	39	18	21.7	21.6	180	336	53	16	104	6	6	6.9	215
Aug.	1,013	30	22	37	16	22.0	22.5	227	373	16	19	117	7	6	6.1	165
Sept.	1,013	33	22	39	18	21.9	21.9	112	233	11	10	95	6	5	7.4	185
Oct.	1,013	36	20	41	13	19.2	16.5	23	78	0	3	68	5	3	9.4	252
Nov.	1,014	35	15	40	9	10.6	8.5	<1	8	0	0	8	3	3	10.0	280
Dec.	1,016	32	12	38	6	6.1	6.2	0	0	0	0	0	2	1	9.6	282
Annual	1,013	35	19	44	6	15.5	14.2	659	886	394	67	117	4	4	8.7	3,976
Rec. (yrs.)	30	15	15	15	15	10	10	30	37	37	30	43	13	13	5	6

190

TABLE XI

CLIMATIC TABLE FOR KANO, NIGERIA
Latitude 12°03′N, longitude 8°32′E, elevation 470 m

Month	M.S.L. press. (mbar)	Temperature (°C) mean max.	Temperature (°C) mean min.	Temperature (°C) extreme max.	Temperature (°C) extreme min.	Dew point (°C) 07h	Dew point (°C) 16h	Precipitation mean (mm)	Precipitation max. (mm)	Precipitation min. (mm)	Precipitation days ≥0.1 mm	Precipitation max. in 24 h (mm)	Preval. wind direct.	Averages cloudiness (oktas) 10h	Averages cloudiness (oktas) 22h	sun-shine (h/day)	evap. (mm)
Jan.	1,015	30	13	41	6	2.1	1.1	0	1	0	0	1	NE	2	1	8.9	277
Feb.	1,013	33	15	43	9	2.3	1.3	1	7	0	0	7	NE	2	2	9.1	309
Mar.	1,011	37	19	44	10	6.2	3.1	2	35	0	1	35	NE	3	2	8.6	386
Apr.	1,009	38	24	46	13	13.9	8.2	8	61	0	2	55	NE/SW	5	4	8.4	403
May	1,010	37	24	44	17	19.3	15.9	71	224	7	8	162	SW	5	5	8.8	383
June	1,012	34	23	41	17	20.3	19.4	119	267	41	11	76	SW	5	5	8.7	292
July	1,013	31	22	37	17	20.4	20.8	209	369	39	17	91	SW	6	5	7.5	217
Aug.	1,012	29	21	36	16	20.6	21.3	311	499	135	21	112	SW	7	6	6.0	182
Sept.	1,012	31	21	38	17	20.6	21.0	137	276	31	14	84	SW	6	5	7.9	205
Oct.	1,012	34	19	41	13	18.0	15.2	14	115	0	2	45	SW	4	3	9.5	282
Nov.	1,013	33	16	42	11	8.9	5.9	1	4	0	<1	4	NE	3	2	9.8	290
Dec.	1,015	31	13	43	7	4.0	3.1	0	0	0	0	0	NE	2	1	9.2	277
Annual	1,012	33	19	46	6	14.5	13.1	873	1,234	488	76	162	—	4	3	8.5	3,503
Rec. (yrs.)	30	23	23	34	34	10	10	30	49	49	26	44	5	15	15	10	7

191

TABLE XII

CLIMATIC TABLE FOR SOKOTO, NIGERIA
Latitude 13°01′N, longitude 5°15′E, elevation 345 m

Month	Temperature (°C)				Dew point (°C)		Precipitation					Averages		
	mean		extreme		07h	16h	mean (mm)	max. (mm)	min. (mm)	days ≥0.1 mm	max. in 24h (mm)	cloud-iness[1] (oktas)	sun-shine (h/day)	evap. (mm)
	max.	min.	max.	min.										
Jan.	33	16	42	7	-0.5	-0.7	<1	2	0	0	2	2	9.0	406
Feb.	36	17	43	8	-1.5	-1.7	0	0	0	0	0	3	9.6	430
Mar.	39	22	46	12	5.0	4.0	2	25	0	<1	21	4	9.1	518
Apr.	41	26	47	16	13.9	9.9	10	107	0	1	93	4	8.5	466
May	39	26	46	16	20.1	16.4	42	153	0	5	114	5	9.0	461
June	36	24	43	16	20.8	18.7	93	180	10	9	86	5	9.4	368
July	33	23	39	17	21.3	20.9	152	315	61	11	88	6	7.4	290
Aug.	31	22	40	14	21.5	21.8	244	469	127	16	147	7	6.4	185
Sept.	33	22	40	16	21.4	21.6	132	322	37	10	81	6	8.1	231
Oct.	37	22	43	15	19.5	16.9	13	92	0	2	38	4	9.9	308
Nov.	36	19	43	13	8.8	5.5	1	2	0	0	2	3	9.9	348
Dec.	33	16	41	9	1.5	1.3	0	0	0	0	0	3	9.6	368
Annual	36	21	47	7	14.8	13.3	689	1,030	400	55	147	4	8.8	4,379
Rec. (yrs.)	41	41	31	31	10	10	41	37	37	30	41	10	5	4

[1] Mean of 09h00 and 15h00.

Chapter 6

Semi-arid Zones

J. F. GRIFFITHS

Introduction

Along the southern fringe of the great northern desert there lies a narrow belt of territory in which rain falls for a short period of the year with some regularity. It is a region that experiences a hot, desert climate for most of the year and a tropical, rainy climate for the rest. In the territories that were once French this is referred to as the "zone sahelienne" and the "zone soudanien". The comparable zone to the north of the desert (combining hot desert and the temperate rainy climates) is the Mediterranean region discussed in Chapter 2. In the south the zone experiences summer rains associated with the monsoon or I.T.C.Z. conditions.

This semi-arid zone is, naturally, near the northern limit of movement of the I.T.C.Z. and stretches from the west coast at Dakar in a belt across the continent, until it vanishes at the Ethiopian Massif. In order to give some definite limits to this zone the concept of vegetation belts and climate, due to Troll (LANDSBERG et al., 1963), has been utilized and this semi-arid zone is defined here as a region having from three to six months each with at least 50 mm of rain (Fig.1). In the southern part of the continent due to the high plateau existing, a semi-arid region with such a rainfall pattern and high temperatures (mean of each month greater than 18°C) hardly exists except as a small enclave in a remote region in southeast Angola.

The characteristics of the climate have been discussed in Chapter 5, for the northern Nigerian region is a very good example of this zone. The zone has great affinity to the northern desert with large diurnal variation of temperature, except on the narrow coastal strip, high radiation and sunshine and dust storms during the period from October to April. In the other months cloudy conditions prevail and the zone takes on the hot, humid aspect common to the wet tropics.

In the west, Senegal, Gambia and Portuguese Guinea lie within this zone. Senegal is the largest of these, covering nearly 200,000 km² and having a population of some three million. Dakar with 400,000 inhabitants is the only city in the region, having a population in excess of all Gambia, the tiny strip of land bordering the lower and middle reaches of the Gambia River for about 300 km. Portuguese Guinea is larger, 36,000 km² and a population of half a million, but its capital Bissau is, like Bathurst, only a small town of some 25,000 people. The economy of these three territories is dependent almost entirely upon groundnuts with a little trade in palm kernels. Along the coastal belt there is more rain than inland (rice is grown in Portuguese Guinea and southern Senegal), increasing to about 2,000 mm/year. However, as with the interior region, this rainfall is concen-

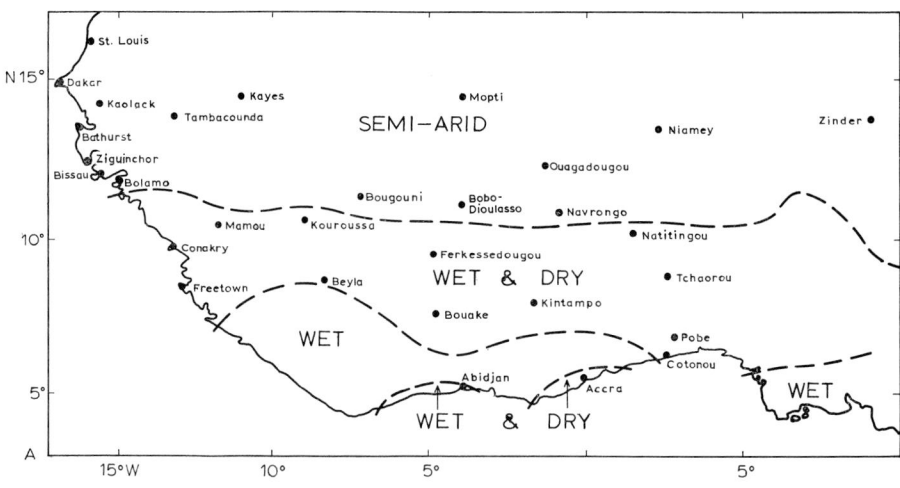

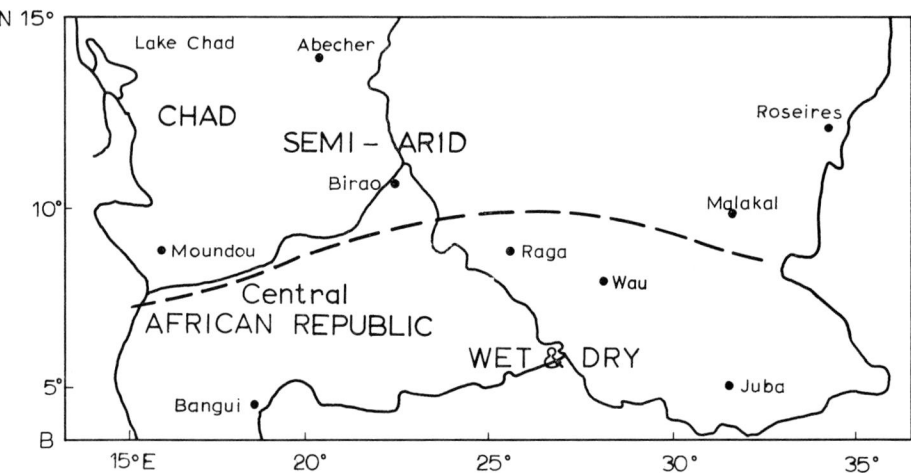

Fig.1. Station and zone locations.

trated in a few months of the year and many months are completely dry. The area is referred to as Casamance. North of the Gambia, in interior Senegal, rainfall is very light and little is grown in the Ferlo Desert but further north still the flood plain of the left bank of the Senegal River (the Fouta) supports many agricultural activities.

While parts of the territories of Mali, Niger, Chad and the Sudan are included in this zone the only other country falling almost entirely within it is Upper Volta, an area of 250,000 km² and a population of about 4,5 million. The capital, Ouagadougou, has only 65,000 inhabitants and the chief export is livestock. Unfortunately, much of the eastern area, especially the river valleys, is uninhabitable because of sleeping sickness. In southern Mali and Niger agricultural productivity is aided by flood plain cultivation in the inland Niger delta, where groundnuts, rice and cotton are grown. In the Chad republic the area south of Lake Chad is savanna country where cotton and groundnuts are generally grown in rotation. In southeast Angola, illustrated by Cangamba, there are few important centres and maize, sisal and wheat are the only crops of value, together with some ranching.

Causes of the climate

The factors of the pattern of seasons experienced in this zone are detailed in Chapter 5, specifically in regard to the northern section of Nigeria. The major variation that occurs is in the extreme west, where the proximity to the sea (moist air masses) causes a dramatic increase in the amount of rainfall with the onset of the westerlies (SERVICE MÉTÉOROLO-GIQUE, RÉPUBLIQUE DU SÉNÉGAL, 1963). The reasons for the climatic pattern are unaltered but, for rainfall, they give an exaggerated effect. In winter the north winds associated with the Azores high sometimes bring relatively cold air, at a medium level in the atmosphere, that gives rise to instability, extensive cloud and rain, the "Heug" weather.

Radiation, sunshine and cloud

Radiation measurements are not common in this zone but, fortunately, the stations available give a good cross-section of the region, ranging from Dakar and Bissau, on the west coast, to Navrongo (Ghana) in the interior and Malakal (Sudan) in the east. The relevant data are given in Table I.

TABLE I

MEAN MONTHLY AND GLOBAL RADIATION (cal./cm² day)

Station	Jan.	Feb.	Mar.	Apr.	May	June	July	Aug.	Sept.	Oct.	Nov.	Dec.	Year
Dakar	427	518	590	616	600	554	497	443	447	464	426	424	500
Bissau	428	511	576	594	557	495	470	400	433	482	447	414	484
Navrongo	586	583	571	586	581	554	502	426	465	552	562	549	543
Malakal	471	521	527	536	510	448	448	486	484	487	487	477	490

From these limited data (Navrongo has only one year of observations) it would appear that the annual average radiation is about 180 kcal./cm². Monthly totals reach a maximum in April, prior to the start of the rains, then fall to a minimum in July or August. The very high values in January and February at Navrongo do not accord well with the low sun angle and cloud amounts in that region then. This discrepancy was also noted by COCHEMÉ and FRANQUIN (1967).

The average hours of sunshine per year is about 3,000 h (7.5–8.2 h/day) but in the southern Chad these values can increase to 3,400 h (9.3 h/day), while on the west coast they decrease to only 2,600 h (about 7 h/day). Sunshine amounts usually reach a maximum in March or April in the west (about 300 h/month) but in the Sudan and the central area the period November–January is the sunniest season with 300–310 h/month. Bobo-Dioulasso (Upper Volta) only reaches 270 h for its maximum. The least sunny period is generally August (the rainy month), with about 150–160 h although some stations still record 200 h then. The 93 h in August at Ziguinchor is the zone's lowest and indicates the heavy cloud then prevailing.

Mean annual cloud amounts average 4 oktas over this zone, but to the extreme northern edges this increases to 5 oktas while on the southern boundary the value approaches 3 oktas. At most stations there is an average of 6–7 oktas during the rainiest months and about 2–3 oktas in the dry season. However, Bougoni, Roseires and Zinder have some months with only 1 okta of cloud cover recorded.

Temperature

The mean annual temperature over this zone is about 27°–28°C, with the exception of the coast where the oceanic influence keeps values down to about 24°–25°C. The annual range at the coast is small, about 6°–7°C, decreasing slightly inland to about 4°C (Kaolack and Ziguinchor), where the land/sea breeze circulation is less influential, and then increasing rapidly to 8°, 9° and even 10°C in the northern part of the interior. In the southern section, where there is more cloud, higher humidity and less radiation variation, the annual range is 5°–6°C.

This zone is almost delimited on its northern border by the isopleth shown in Fig.15 of Chapter 1 (p.24), the line dividing a winter minimum of maximum temperatures from the summer minimum of maximum temperatures. Again the coastal region is an exception for it is influenced by the flow of cool air from the north, over the cooler ocean current. All the zone experiences its minimum temperature during the winter period for with only a short rainy season at the time of overhead sun the period of low sun and dry air combined give an effect that dominates the seasonal pattern.

During the period from April to October the mean temperature shows an increase towards the north, from about 27° to 30°C, but in winter (November–March) this gradient is reversed and goes from 25° to 28°C. The isotherms generally run east–west but turn abruptly to run parallel to the coast on the western edge.

The highest temperatures are usually reached just prior to the onset of the rains, during March, April or May, and these extremes are in the range 43°–47°C, with values up to 50°C being reached near the Saharan border. The lowest minimum temperatures ever observed are from 7° to 9°C, but are a little higher near the coast and a few degrees less near the northern limit. Cangamba (Angola), at an elevation of over 1,300 m, has experienced frost and has an all-time low of −7°C.

Rainfall

The amount of rainfall received at stations within this zone varies considerably, from less than 400 mm at St. Louis to over 2,000 mm at Bolama, as shown in Table II. Nevertheless, the same pattern is identifiable at both stations, namely, the rapid increase and

TABLE II

VARIATION OF RAINFALL AT TWO STATIONS (mm)

Station	Jan.	Feb.	Mar.	Apr.	May	June	July	Aug.	Sept.	Oct.	Nov.	Dec.	Year
St. Louis	<1	5	<1	1	1	12	55	170	111	28	5	<1	388
Bolama	1	<1	<1	1	21	198	586	700	429	203	41	2	2,182

decrease in rainfall amounts in the transition periods. In other words, abrupt beginning and ending to the rainy season. In the whole zone July, August and September are the wettest months, giving from 70 to 90% of the annual total, save near the wetter fringes. In the southern sector December to February is the wettest quarter.

Rainfall gradients are very great for there is a rapid increase in amount from north to south. The concentration of the rainfall into certain months is amazingly definite in this zone. For example, Ziguinchor, with over 1,600 mm/year, has never had more than five wet months in the year and July, August and September have never been dry months. Such regularity of distribution, if not of amount, is hard to find in the tropical regions. Each station has, however, recorded as low as 50–60% of its annual total and as great as about 150% in certain years.

In central Sudan line squalls are recorded mainly in April, May, June and October in Malakal. There are 51 days of squalls there with the maximum likelihood being between 14h00 and 17h00 local time. These line squalls are usually spawned in the direction of the Ethiopian highlands and about 40% come from the south or southeast and 25% from the north or northeast, the directions for the really severe (winds over 80 knots) squalls. However, some 15% move from the north or northwest sector. Thunderstorms reach a maximum at 13h00–19h00 local time with a minimum between 01h00 and 11h00. These thunderstorms are often of long duration, 85% being over 1 h and one per year lasting over 8 h.

The northward and southward movement of the I.T.C.Z. has been studied via its relationship with rainfall by BHALOTRA (1963) and Fig.2 depicts an interesting correlation

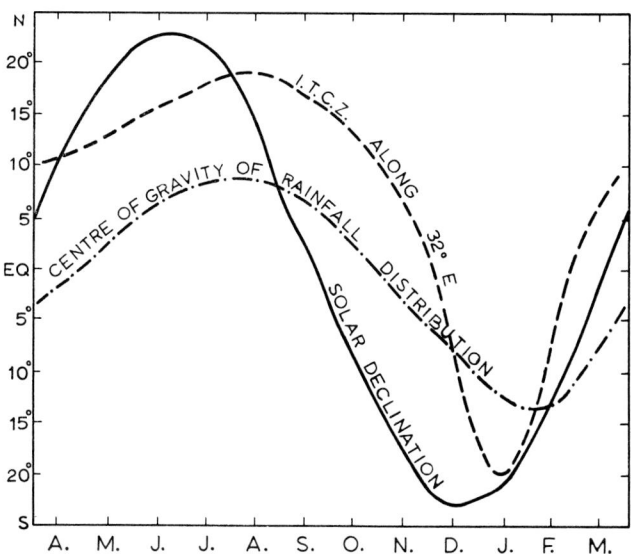

Fig.2. Relationships among I.T.C.Z., solar declination and centre of gravity of rainfall distribution.

among the I.T.C.Z., solar declination and rainfall. It is seen that the retreat (southward) movement of the I.T.C.Z. is very much more rapid in the Sudan than the northward journey. For instance, from 0° to 20°N takes 5.5 months whereas from 20°N to 0° takes only 3.5 months. This agrees with findings in western Africa (Chapter 5) and is a contributory factor in the rapid cessation of the rains.

The number of days of rain naturally increases with increasing rainfall, the average being about 7 days per 100 mm. The average amount of rain per rain day is approximately 14 mm (COCHEMÉ and FRANQUIN, 1967). A study by DELORME (1963) indicated that the mean intensity is approximately 4 mm/h.

The maximum daily rainfall is about 150 mm, but reaches over 200 mm along the southern section of the west coast, Bolama recording 280 mm on one July day. Near the zone's northern and drier border the value may reach 100 mm, generally in August when severe thunderstorms are evident. Maximum daily falls, expected once per year, increase towards the south and range from about 50 to 70 mm (BRUNET-MORET, 1963). At Dakar falls in excess of 10 mm/day are not recorded in December to May, over 100 mm/day is noted almost every other year during August and about once in ten years in July and September. Of the rain days about half report between 1 and 10 mm, a quarter between 10 and 30 mm and one in a hundred over 90 mm.

Humidity

The excellent publication by COCHEMÉ and FRANQUIN (1967) fortunately shows some data for water vapour pressure for the part of the zone west of the Sudan for, otherwise, this information is not readily available. In Fig.3 the annual pattern is presented.

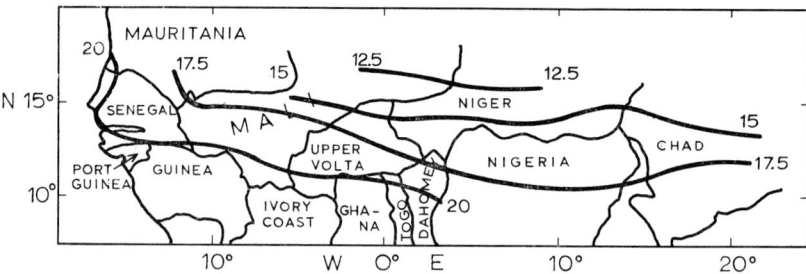

Fig.3. Mean annual vapour pressure (mbar).

It is seen that values range from about 15 mbar (dew point 13°C) to 21 mbar (dew point 18°C), increasing southwards at a rate of about 1 mbar (roughly 1°C in dew point) per 1° latitude, on average. The highest values are experienced in August at almost all stations, when daily means are around 26–29 mbar (dew points 21.5–23.5°C). The winter values range from 8 to 12 mbar (dew point 4–9°C) inland but near the coast the water vapour pressure increases rapidly, reaching 17 mbar (15°C dew point) near Dakar.

Relative humidity values reach their highest around sunrise during the rainy season, reaching 90–95% at most stations. At this period the afternoon relative humidity is around 50–60%, except near the coast where 70% is usual. The mean maximum values during the dry season are rarely above 45%, with readings below 30% on the northern limits. However, morning relative humidity measurements of about 70% are general near the coast and in the extreme southern part of Chad. In the dry season mean afternoon values are mostly below 20% except near the coast.

Evaporation

In this zone evaporation is very variable, being high during the pre-rainy season and low during the rains. For example, Ziguinchor varies from 1.4 to 5.8 mm/day, with a mean of 3.7, Malakal from 2.9 to 20.0 mm/day, mean of 10.6, and Roseires from 3.4 to 15.6 mm/day, mean 9.6. These ranges, from about one-third of the mean to five-thirds of the mean are characteristic.

Annual totals vary from about 1,000 to nearly 4,000 mm but it appears from the little data available that the highest rates are reached in the eastern section.

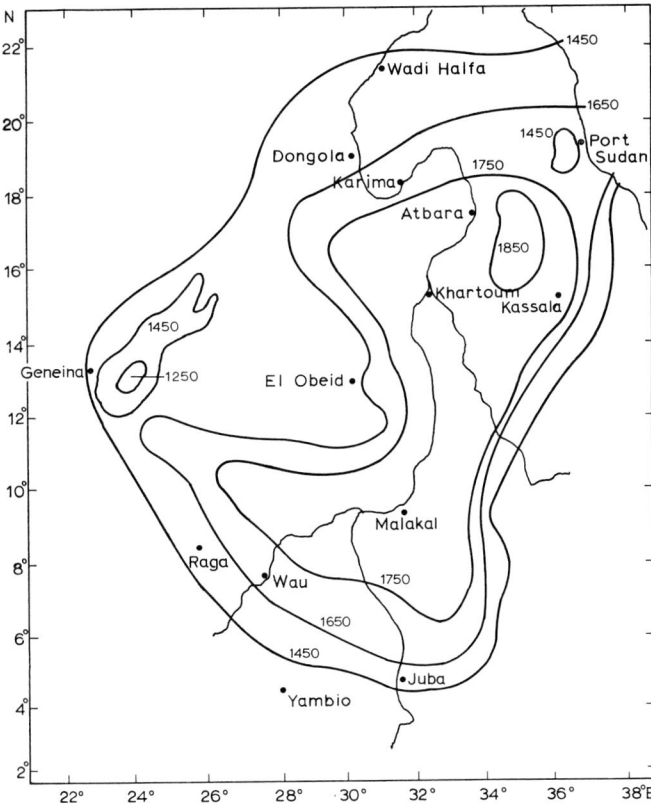

Fig.4. Mean annual potential evapotranspiration (mm), 1921–1950.

Applying the Thornthwaite method the pattern of potential evapotranspiration has been calculated for the Sudan and is given in Fig.4, showing that maximum values for the whole country occur around Malakal. As given in Table III (COCHEMÉ and FRANQUIN, 1967) potential evapotranspiration in the whole zone is seen to vary from about 1,600 mm to a little in excess of 2,000 mm with monthly values in the range from 100 to 200 mm.

Air flow

Most of the stations have a prevailing northeasterly air flow during the dry season (November–March), with a change to southwest or south occurring when the monsoon

TABLE III

MONTHLY AND ANNUAL AVERAGES OF EVAPORATION (mm)

Station	Jan.	Feb.	Mar.	Apr.	May	June	July	Aug.	Sep.	Oct.	Nov.	Dec.	Year
Senegal:													
Dakar, Yoff	142	134	155	173	166	165	159	141	142	149	149	151	1,827
St. Louis	131	128	170	155	147	141	145	140	138	141	127	126	1,690
Tambacounda	125	133	172	176	193	146	114	106	106	119	112	114	1,615
Mali:													
Kayes	134	139	185	197	216	178	144	118	124	139	122	121	1,819
Mopti	146	163	210	223	211	188	155	139	136	148	135	129	1,983
Ghana:													
Navrongo	142	145	178	172	165	139	120	114	118	145	138	126	1,702
Niger:													
Niamey	161	167	207	209	219	203	156	131	137	171	158	143	2,057
Zinder	138	153	184	192	198	184	157	128	146	167	144	130	1,922
Chad:													
Abecher	141	152	189	206	203	175	152	119	138	164	156	132	1,926
Moundou	122	132	152	149	142	114	103	97	99	118	121	116	1,464
Upper Volta:													
Ouagadougou	141	149	189	192	188	148	133	112	119	148	133	131	1,783
Bobo Dioulasso	148	157	188	171	163	130	118	114	116	137	133	166	1,712

sets in. The only slight exception to this pattern is near the west coast where the northerly flow of the winter season gives way to the summertime, wet season, westerlies.

The percentage of calms increases during the wet season (see climatic tables) and many stations experience a large percentage of observations of calms, 30–50% being usual but reaching 70–80% at Bougouni. However, calms are markedly less frequent in the Sudan and along the Senegal coast where the land/sea breeze cycle is always in evidence.

Mean annual wind speeds show a range from about 3 to 16 km/h, with maximum values occurring along the coast and inland towards the eastern section of the northern boundary. A minimum value exists in southern Chad (COCHEMÉ and FRANQUIN, 1967).

March and April are the windiest months on the coast, May and June just inland, and the winter months (December–February) in the northeastern sector. Winds of speeds greater than 25 km/h are common in the coastal regions, especially in January to May, and as far inland as Kaolack. Mopti also has a high incidence of strong winds, particularly in March to May when rapid heating is occurring. Most of the other areas have a low percentage (0–3%) of winds in excess of 25 km/h.

References

BHALOTRA, Y. P. R., 1963. Meteorology of Sudan. *Sudan Meteorol. Serv., Mem.*, 6:113 pp.

BRUNET-MORET, Y., 1963. *Étude Générale des Averses Exceptionelles en Afrique Occidentale*. Orstom, Paris, 5 volumes.

COCHEMÉ, J. and FRANQUIN, P., 1967. An agroclimatology survey of a semi-arid area in Africa south of the Sahara. *World Meteorol. Organ., Tech. Note*, 86:136 pp.

DELORMÉ, G. A., 1963. Répartition et durée des précipitations en Afrique Occidentale. *Monographies Météorol. Natl.*, 28:26 pp.

LANDSBERG, H. E., LIPPMANN, H., PAFFEN, K. H. and TROLL, C., 1963. *World Maps of Climatology.* Springer, Berlin, 5 maps, 28 pp.

SERVICE MÉTÉOROLOGIQUE, RÉPUBLIQUE DU SÉNÉGAL, 1963. *Aperçus de Climatologie Aeronautique du Sénégal.* Service Météorologique, Sénégal, 16 pp.

TABLE IV

CLIMATIC TABLE FOR MOUNDOU, CHAD
Latitude 8°37'N, longitude 16°04'E, elevation 420 m

Month	Mean sta. press. (mbar)	Temperature (°C) mean max.	mean min.	extreme max.	extreme min.	Relative humid. (%) 07h00	13h00	Precipitation mean (mm)	max. (mm)	min. (mm)	days ≥ 1 mm	max. 24 h (mm)	Wind av. speed (km/h)	preval. direct.	calm (%)	Average cloud-iness (oktas)	sun-shine (h)	evap. (mm)
Jan.	964	34	15	43	10	70	21	0	0	0	0	0	7	WNW		2	288	122
Feb.	962	37	17	45	11	62	19	4	9	0	4	6	9	WNW		3	258	132
Mar.	961	39	22	46	15	64	25	2	52	0	1	26	8	W		4	250	152
Apr.	961	37	24	46	17	71	32	40	119	0	4	61	8	SSW		4	213	149
May	963	35	23	44	19	85	51	118	295	19	9	81	8	SSW		4	239	142
June	965	33	22	45	19	89	63	171	293	85	11	107	1	S		5	198	114
July	965	30	21	43	18	92	23	244	612	101	15	140	6	W		6	183	103
Aug.	966	30	21	41	18	93	75	303	490	134	17	121	5	W		6	158	97
Sept.	965	30	21	37	17	92	72	250	441	93	15	79	4	S		6	177	99
Oct.	964	32	21	38	17	91	62	96	328	16	8	78	4	W		5	226	118
Nov.	964	35	19	39	13	88	38	4	35	6	1	31	4	N		3	285	121
Dec.	964	34	15	40	9	76	27	0	2	0	0	2	5	WNW		2	298	116
Annual	964	34	20	46	9	81	47	1,228	2,186	868	80	140	6	—	54	4	2,773	1,464
Rec. (yrs.)	7	13	13	13	13	13	13	30	30	30	30	30	10	10	—	15	10	9

TABLE V

CLIMATIC TABLE FOR MALAKAL, SUDAN
Latitude 9°33'N, longitude 31°39'E, elevation 385 m

Month	M.S.L. press. (mbar)	Temperature (°C) mean		extreme		Relative humid. (%)	Precipitation mean (mm)	max. (mm)	min. (mm)	days ≥ 1 mm	max. 24 h (mm)	Wind av. speed (km/h)	preval. direct.	calm (%)	Average cloudiness[1] (oktas)	sunshine (h)	radiation (Ly/day)	evap. (mm/day)
		max.	min.	max.	min.													
Jan.	1,008	36	19	41	12	29	tr.	4	0	0	tr.	14	NNE	2	2	302	421	18.1
Feb.	1,007	37	20	43	11	26	tr.	3	0	4	3	14	NNE	5	3	260	521	20.0
Mar.	1,006	39	22	43	15	26	3	39	0	1	19	10	N	6	3	279	527	19.1
Apr.	1,006	39	24	43	18	38	24	63	0	3	42	10	S	8	4	249	536	14.4
May	1,007	36	23	42	19	59	95	270	27	8	120	10	S	4	5	239	510	9.0
June	1,010	33	22	41	18	71	115	211	31	10	102	8	S	8	6	165	448	5.9
July	1,011	31	22	36	18	80	153	254	73	14	91	8	S	10	6	165	448	3.7
Aug.	1,010	31	21	36	16	82	167	312	74	16	107	5	S	13	6	183	486	2.9
Sept.	1,010	32	22	38	18	84	144	345	15	11	176	5	V	15	6	180	484	3.2
Oct.	1,008	34	22	39	17	75	77	245	18	7	117	5	V	14	5	226	487	4.4
Nov.	1,008	36	20	40	13	52	6	43	0	4	37	8	N	9	3	258	487	10.2
Dec.	1,008	35	18	41	12	36	1	21	0	4	21	12	NNE	5	2	313	477	13.3
Annual	1,008	35	21	43	11	55	783	1,175	508	70	176	9	—	8	4	2,824	490	10.6
Rec. (yrs.)	24	30	30	30	30	30	30	30	30	30	30	6	10	10	30	18	7	30

[1] Mean 06h00, 12h00 and 18h00.

TABLE VI

CLIMATIC TABLE FOR BIRAO, CENTRAL AFRICAN REPUBLIC
Latitude 10°17′N, longitude 22°47′E, elevation 465 m

Month	M.S.L. press. (mbar)	Temperature (°C)				Relative humid. (%)		Precipitation				
		mean		extreme				mean (mm)	max. (mm)	min. (mm)	days ≥ 1 mm	max. 24 h (mm)
		max.	min.	max.	min.	07h00	13h00					
Jan.	1,009	35	12	41	3	54	16	0	0	0	0	0
Feb.	1,008	37	15	42	7	43	14	0	0	0	0	0
Mar.	1,005	39	19	44	8	47	18	2	15	0	1	11
Apr.	1,005	39	21	43	11	57	23	19	66	0	2	34
May	1,006	37	23	42	15	74	37	97	234	35	8	59
June	1,008	34	22	40	18	86	55	112	159	47	11	58
July	1,009	31	21	36	18	93	66	217	289	124	15	97
Aug.	1,009	30	21	34	18	95	68	204	362	137	18	63
Sept.	1,008	32	21	36	18	95	63	171	245	112	13	65
Oct.	1,008	34	20	38	13	93	49	37	80	6	4	27
Nov.	1,007	35	14	39	7	80	26	1	12	0	0.2	12
Dec.	1,008	35	12	39	5	64	20	0	0	0	0	0
Annual	1,008	35	18	44	3	73	38	860	1,018	702	72	97
Rec. (yrs.)	4	11	11	11	11	11	11	30	10	10	10	10

TABLE VII

CLIMATIC TABLE FOR BOBO-DIOULASSO, UPPER VOLTA
Latitude 11°10′N, longitude 4°15′W, elevation 435 m

Month	M.S.L. press. (mbar)	Temperature (°C)				Relative humidity (%)		Precipitation					Wind			Average		
		mean		extreme														
		max.	min.	max.	min.	06h	12h	mean (mm)	max. (mm)	min. (mm)	days ≥1 mm	max. 24h (mm)	av. speed (km/h)	preval. direct.	calm (%)	cloud-iness (oktas)	sun-shine (h)	evap. (mm)
Jan.	1,012	33	14	39	8	43	16	1	21	0	0	21	4	SSE	57	3	272	148
Feb.	1,011	36	17	40	11	42	26	2	33	0	4	18	4	E	51	2	261	157
Mar.	1,009	38	20	46	12	53	28	17	137	0	2	121	9	S–E	25	4	267	188
Apr.	1,009	37	22	42	13	71	43	48	142	0	4	69	8	S	25	4	226	171
May	1,010	36	22	41	16	83	54	108	264	5	7	71	10	S	24	5	240	163
June	1,012	33	21	37	13	90	63	130	287	33	9	53	9	S	20	4	229	130
July	1,012	31	21	35	14	94	70	208	422	23	11	162	8	SSW	26	5	197	118
Aug.	1,012	29	21	40	15	96	74	308	610	56	16	157	7	S	31	6	147	114
Sept.	1,012	31	21	37	11	96	69	206	386	31	13	81	5	S	61	6	188	116
Oct.	1,011	32	21	38	15	91	55	74	254	5	7	49	4	S	63	4	259	137
Nov.	1,011	34	19	38	12	78	35	10	111	0	1	100	2	E	66	2	265	133
Dec.	1,012	33	16	39	9	56	19	1	33	0	0	17	1	NNE	73	2	272	166
Annual	1,011	34	20	46	8	74	45	1,113	1,552	672	71	162	6	—	44	4	2,823	1,712
Rec. (yrs.)	30	11	11	11	11	9	9	50	46	46	46	35	8	8	8	10	10	

TABLE VIII

CLIMATIC TABLE FOR BOUGOUNI, MALI
Latitude 11°25'N, longitude 7°30'W, elevation 370 m

Month	M.S.L. press. (mbar)	Temperature (°C) mean		extreme		Relative humid. (%)		Precipitation					Wind			Aver. cloudiness (oktas)
		max.	min.	max.	min.	06h	12h	mean (mm)	max. (mm)	min. (mm)	days ≥1 mm	max. 24 h (mm)	av. speed (km/h)	preval. direct.	calm (%)	
Jan.	1,010	36	17	40	11	46	19	<1	18	0	0	2	3	S	82	1
Feb.	1,009	36	20	43	10	44	19	1	23	0	0	21	3	S	85	1
Mar.	1,008	38	23	43	16	56	32	5	33	0	1	19	4	S	80	2
Apr.	1,007	38	25	45	20	69	44	17	152	1	3	81	5	S	66	4
May	1,009	36	24	42	18	73	55	68	229	3	6	93	5	S	67	4
June	1,011	33	22	39	18	90	65	140	371	71	11	76	3	S	75	3
July	1,012	31	22	39	16	95	74	231	640	132	14	140	2	S	72	5
Aug.	1,011	29	21	41	18	96	76	335	660	150	16	199	3	S	70	6
Sept.	1,011	31	21	36	18	96	68	210	691	93	14	170	1	S	83	4
Oct.	1,010	33	21	39	17	93	61	61	330	3	8	89	3	S	81	3
Nov.	1,010	35	20	39	14	83	41	10	187	0	1	28	1	N–S	86	2
Dec.	1,011	34	17	39	11	59	24	<1	21	0	<1	15	3	N	89	1
Annual	1,010	34	21	45	10	75	48	1,078	1,874	805	74	199	3	—	77	3
Rec. (yrs.)	30	22	22	22	22	9	9	34	35	35	34	18	5	5	5	7

TABLE IX

CLIMATIC TABLE FOR ROSEIRES, SUDAN
Latitude 11°51′N, longitude 34°23′E, elevation 465 m

Month	Mean sta. press. (mbar)	Temperature (°C)				Relative humidity (%) 08h30	Precipitation			Average	
		mean		extreme			mean (mm)	days ⩾ 1 mm	max. 24 h (mm)	cloud- iness (oktas)	evap. (mm/ day)
		min.	max.	min.	min.						
Jan.	956	37	17	42	10	41	0	0	0	1	11.6
Feb.	956	38	18	44	9	34	tr.	0	6	1	13.4
Mar.	954	40	20	45	12	27	1	<1	4	1	15.6
Apr.	954	41	24	46	13	31	11	2	35	2	15.6
May	955	38	24	44	17	48	58	7	70	3	12.4
June	957	35	22	43	16	66	126	13	69	4	8.0
July	958	32	22	38	18	79	166	15	116	5	4.7
Aug.	958	31	21	37	18	83	221	17	87	5	3.4
Sept.	958	32	21	40	18	80	152	11	112	4	4.0
Oct.	956	36	20	40	16	70	36	4	43	3	6.1
Nov.	955	38	18	41	11	49	5	<1	25	1	9.6
Dec.	957	37	16	42	10	42	0	0	1	1	10.9
Annual	956	36	20	46	9	54	770	75	116	3	9.6
Rec. (yrs.)	18	30	30	30	30	26	30	30	30	28	28

TABLE X

CLIMATIC TABLE FOR OUAGADOUGOU, UPPER VOLTA
Latitude 12°22′N, longitude 1°31′W, elevation 300 m

Month	M.S.L. press. (mbar)	Temperature (°C) mean max.	min.	extreme max.	min.	Relative humid. (%) 06h00	12h00	Precipitation mean (mm)	max. (mm)	min. (mm)	days >1 mm	max. 24 h (mm)	Wind av. speed (km/h)	preval. direct.	calm (%)	Average cloud-iness (oktas)	sun-shine (h)	evap. (mm)
Jan.	1,012	33	16	45	9	42	19	0	5	0	0.4	5	6	ENE	45	3	277	141
Feb.	1,011	37	20	45	12	38	19	2	25	0	1	25	6	ENE	44	3	252	149
Mar.	1,009	40	23	45	15	39	20	13	45	0	2	38	7	ENE	32	4	281	189
Apr.	1,008	39	26	47	15	51	28	16	63	0	3	31	9	SW	22	5	250	192
May	1,010	38	26	48	19	65	40	83	241	8	6	120	9	SW	14	5	264	188
June	1,012	36	24	44	17	73	49	122	203	48	9	56	8	SW	20	5	241	148
July	1,012	33	23	41	18	78	62	203	308	125	11	99	9	SW	26	6	227	133
Aug.	1,012	31	22	38	14	81	67	280	414	137	14	91	6	SW	40	6	177	112
Sept.	1,011	32	23	39	19	79	60	144	270	61	10	69	5	SSW	45	6	213	119
Oct.	1,011	35	23	41	18	72	44	33	141	0	4	42	6	SW	48	4	287	148
Nov.	1,011	36	22	42	16	58	30	1	10	0	1	5	3	NE	51	3	282	133
Dec.	1,012	35	17	45	11	46	23	0	0	0	<1	0	3	ENE	62	3	280	131
Annual	1,011	35	22	48	9	60	38	897	1,134	408	61	120	6	—	37	4	3,031	1,783
Rec. (yrs.)	30	10	10	10	10	10	10	15	15	15	15	15	6	6	6	10	11	10

TABLE XI

CLIMATIC TABLE FOR ZIGUINCHOR, SENEGAL
Latitude 12°35′N, longitude 16°16′W, elevation 10 m

Month	M.S.L. press. (mbar)	Temperature (°C)				Dew point (°C)	Precipitation					Wind			Average		
		mean max.	mean min.	extreme max.	extreme min.		mean (mm)	max. (mm)	min. (mm)	days ≥1 mm	max. 24 h (mm)	av. speed (km/h)	preval. direct.	calm (%)	cloud-iness (oktas)	sun-shine (h)	evap. (mm)
Jan.	1,012	33	15	39	8	15.6	<1	35	0	0	21	8	ENE	46	4	213	168
Feb.	1,011	35	17	42	8	17.7	1	13	0	0	12	7	var.	53	3	228	166
Mar.	1,010	37	18	44	12	19.2	0	0	0	0	0	10	var.	21	3	293	199
Apr.	1,010	37	19	45	15	19.5	<1	2	0	0	1	10	W	16	3	299	199
May	1,011	36	21	44	15	21.5	11	42	0	1	31	9	WNW	21	4	273	171
June	1,013	34	23	41	18	23.4	143	242	23	9	71	8	W	32	5	170	111
July	1,013	31	23	37	17	23.9	407	544	145	20	151	8	W	40	7	125	64
Aug.	1,012	30	23	37	18	23.8	558	887	196	22	216	9	W	35	7	93	47
Sept.	1,012	31	22	39	18	24.0	338	668	188	18	131	6	W	44	6	154	53
Oct.	1,012	33	23	38	17	23.6	159	346	43	9	119	5	N,NNW	50	6	206	65
Nov.	1,011	33	21	37	13	21.6	8	42	0	1	35	6	NE	42	4	234	97
Dec.	1,012	32	17	37	10	17.5	<1	21	0	0	3	8	NE	38	4	179	138
Annual	1,012	33	20	45	8	21.2	1,626	2,031	968	80	216	8	—	36	5	2,467	1,478
Rec. (yrs.)	30	30	30	30	30	14	30	30	30	30	14	9	9	9	16	12	10

TABLE XII

CLIMATIC TABLE FOR NIAMEY, NIGER
Latitude 13°30'N, longitude 2°07'E, elevation 220 m

Month	Mean sta. press. (mbar)	Temperature (°C) mean max.	Temperature (°C) mean min.	Temperature (°C) extreme max.	Temperature (°C) extreme min.	Relative humid. (%) 06h00	Relative humid. (%) 12h00	Precip. mean (mm)	Precip. max. (mm)	Precip. min. (mm)	Precip. days ≥1 mm	Precip. max. 24 h (mm)	Wind av. speed (km/h)	Wind preval. direct.	Wind calm (%)	Average cloudiness (oktas)	Average sunshine (h)	Average evap. (mm)
Jan.	986	34	14	39	8	33	14	0	1	0	0	1	5	E	49	3	280	161
Feb.	985	37	17	43	10	29	12	<1	5	0	0	2	5	E	63	3	264	167
Mar.	983	41	21	44	11	28	12	<1	53	0	<1	53	6	E	51	4	264	207
Apr.	982	42	25	46	17	40	19	7	64	0	1	35	6	VAR	51	5	251	209
May	983	41	27	46	19	61	35	36	140	0	4	46	7	WSW	42	5	257	219
June	985	38	25	46	19	75	46	87	170	14	6	61	7	WSW	44	5	251	203
July	986	34	23	40	18	84	58	138	328	28	9	61	7	SW	39	5	238	156
Aug.	986	32	23	38	17	91	69	206	490	76	13	173	5	SW	45	6	203	131
Sept.	986	34	23	41	19	89	61	88	231	18	7	54	4	SSW	50	5	228	137
Oct.	985	38	23	43	16	77	39	21	96	0	2	59	4	W	63	4	285	171
Nov.	985	38	18	43	12	52	17	1	16	0	0	10	4	E	61	3	285	158
Dec.	986	34	15	40	9	41	16	0	0	0	0	0	5	E	53	3	276	143
Annual	985	37	21	46	8	58	33	584	980	452	42	173	5	—	51	4	3,087	2,057
Rec. (yrs.)	8	10	10	10	10	10	10	37	35	35	25	19	6	6	6	8	8	7

TABLE XIII

CLIMATIC TABLE FOR CANGAMBA, ANGOLA
Latitude 13°41′S, longitude 19°52′E, elevation 1,325 m

Month	Temperature (°C)				Relat. humid. (%) 09h30	Precipitation		
	mean		extreme			mean (mm)	days ⩾ 1 mm	max. 24 h (mm)
	max.	min.	max.	min.				
Jan.	29	17	33	13	86	225	12	58
Feb.	29	17	38	12	85	187	13	51
Mar.	31	17	41	11	80	172	13	56
Apr.	32	14	43	5	75	46	6	30
May	32	11	42	1	26	1	1	2
June	30	9	41	−3	26	0	0	0
July	28	8	37	−7	28	0	0	0
Aug.	31	8	39	0	23	5	1	10
Sept.	32	13	37	4	68	5	1	8
Oct.	31	15	37	7	72	41	5	42
Nov.	29	16	37	9	75	130	12	71
Dec.	29	16	34	12	80	215	14	63
Annual	30	23	43	−7	77	1,027	83	71
Rec. (yrs.)	5	5	5	5	6	7	7	7

TABLE XIV

CLIMATIC TABLE FOR TAMBACOUNDA, SENEGAL
Latitude 13°46'N, longitude 13°38'W, elevation 55 m

Month	M.S.L. press. (mbar)	Temperature (°C)				Dew point (°C)	Precipitation					Wind			Average	
		mean		extreme			mean (mm)	max. (mm)	min. (mm)	days ≥1 mm	max. 24 h (mm)	av. speed (km/h)	preval. direct.	calm (%)	cloudiness (oktas)	evap. (mm)
		max.	min.	max.	min.											
Jan.	1,011	35	15	42	7	5.5	<1	15	0	<1	2	6	NE	20	4	125
Feb.	1,010	37	18	45	10	6.1	<1	8	0	<1	8	5	ENE	35	3	133
Mar.	1,009	39	21	45	13	8.9	<1	8	0	<1	8	7	NE	24	3	172
Apr.	1,009	41	23	46	14	11.4	1	28	0	<1	28	7	S	15	3	176
May	1,009	41	25	46	17	16.9	20	129	0	1	56	8	S	7	5	193
June	1,011	36	24	44	15	21.2	130	337	23	8	89	9	SSW	11	6	146
July	1,012	32	23	40	16	23.1	172	287	28	11	102	7	WSW	15	7	114
Aug.	1,012	32	22	37	15	23.4	257	495	56	17	147	6	S	25	7	106
Sept.	1,011	32	22	37	16	23.5	224	396	63	14	119	5	S	40	6	106
Oct.	1,011	34	22	40	15	23.2	71	185	2	5	96	6	VAR	35	4	119
Nov.	1,011	36	18	40	10	18.9	1	25	0	<1	21	5	ENE	24	4	112
Dec.	1,012	34	15	40	5	9.0	<1	0	0	0	0	6	NE	18	5	114
Annual	1,011	36	21	46	5	17.2	872	1,246	476	57	147	6	—	22	5	1,615
Rec. (yrs.)	30	25	25	25	25	17	35	35	35	35	35	7	—	7	10	8

TABLE XV

CLIMATIC TABLE FOR ZINDER, NIGER
Latitude 13°48'N, longitude 8°59'E, elevation 510 m

Month	Mean sta. press. (mbar)	Temperature (°C) mean max.	mean min.	extreme max.	extreme min.	Relative humid. (%) 07h00	13h00	Precipitation mean (mm)	max. (mm)	min. (mm)	days ≥1 mm	max. 24 h (mm)	Wind av. speed (km/h)	preval. direct.	calm (%)	Average cloud-iness (oktas)	sun-shine (h)	evap. (mm)
Jan.	958	31	14	41	4	33	18	0	1	0	0	<1	9	E	29	2	270	138
Feb.	957	34	17	42	5	29	15	<1	<1	0	0	1	6	ESE	54	1	253	153
Mar.	955	38	21	47	12	26	14	<1	<1	0	0	1	7	E	50	2	265	184
Apr.	955	41	25	47	17	29	15	1	21	0	<1	2	6	E	45	3	260	192
May	955	41	25	46	19	51	26	23	158	0	3	51	7	WNW	50	4	274	198
June	956	39	24	45	17	69	38	48	114	8	6	48	7	WNW	55	3	258	184
July	957	35	22	42	15	83	55	160	259	54	9	89	7	W	56	5	241	157
Aug.	957	32	22	40	17	91	66	218	418	81	12	119	4	W	71	6	213	128
Sept.	956	35	22	42	16	85	52	69	182	2	7	63	5	WNW	52	4	254	146
Oct.	956	38	22	43	17	55	26	10	89	0	<1	31	5	E	56	2	291	167
Nov.	958	36	19	41	11	36	17	<1	10	0	0	2	6	E	45	2	279	144
Dec.	958	32	15	40	8	37	20	0	0	0	0	0	6	E	44	2	274	130
Annual	956	36	21	47	4	52	30	529	662	330	38	119	6	—	51	3	3,132	1,922
Rec. (yrs.)	8	29	29	29	29	9	9	19	19	19	19	19	6	6	6	10	8	8

TABLE XVI

CLIMATIC TABLE FOR ABÉCHER, CHAD
Latitude 13°51′N, longitude 20°51′E, elevation 550 m

Month	Mean sta. press. (mbar)	Temperature (°C) mean		extreme		Relative humid. (%)		Precipitation					Wind			Average		
		max.	min.	max.	min.	07h30	13h00	mean (mm)	max. (mm)	min. (mm)	days ≥ 1 mm	max. 24 h (mm)	av. speed (km/h)	preval. direct.	calm (%)	cloud-iness (oktas)	sun-shine (h)	evap. (mm)
Jan.	949	35	15	45	8	33	17	0	0	0	0	0	12	NE		2	313	141
Feb.	948	36	18	49	9	29	16	0	0	0	0	0	13	NE		2	292	152
Mar.	946	39	22	50	11	25	17	<1	2	0	0	2	13	NE		3	295	189
Apr.	946	41	25	49	11	28	20	1	8	0	<1	8	11	E		3	297	206
May	947	40	25	50	11	49	29	24	74	0	3	40	11	E		4	307	203
June	948	38	24	48	15	60	34	26	69	4	6	31	10	S		4	258	175
July	948	34	23	45	14	79	53	141	273	28	12	68	9	S		6	236	152
Aug.	949	31	21	39	17	90	67	232	454	48	17	138	8	S		6	201	119
Sept.	949	34	21	45	15	83	49	67	171	0	7	62	7	E		5	261	138
Oct.	948	37	21	46	15	52	22	14	65	0	1	36	10	ENE		3	310	164
Nov.	949	36	20	46	11	36	20	0	0	0	0	0	11	NE		3	306	156
Dec.	948	35	17	43	10	38	19	0	0	0	0	0	11	ENE		2	316	132
Annual	948	36	21	50	8	50	30	505	898	335	46	138	10	—	31	4	3,392	1,926
Rec. (yrs.)	6	14	14	14	14	14	14	30	30	30	30	30	10	10	—	15	10	9

TABLE XVII

CLIMATIC TABLE FOR KAOLACK, SENEGAL
Latitude 14°08′N, longitude 16°04′W, elevation 6 m

Month	Mean sta. press. (mbar)	Temperature (°C) mean		extreme		Relative humid. (%)		Precipitation					Wind			Average	
		max.	min.	max.	min.	05h00	17h00	mean (mm)	max. (mm)	min. (mm)	days ≥ 1 mm	max. 24 h (mm)	av. speed (km/h)	preval. direct.	calm (%)	cloud- iness (oktas)	evap. (mm)
Jan.	1,012	34	16	40	9	52	27	<1	5	0	<1	2	5	NE	28	3	276
Feb.	1,011	36	16	43	11	53	26	<1	15	0	<1	5	4	N	49	2	289
Mar.	1,010	38	19	45	13	59	24	<1	1	0	0	1	6	NNW	35	2	354
Apr.	1,010	39	20	46	15	66	27	1	1	0	0	1	6	W	21	2	344
May	1,011	39	21	47	13	74	38	8	71	0	<1	69	7	W	19	3	264
June	1,012	36	24	44	19	84	51	61	200	5	6	102	10	W	23	4	173
July	1,012	33	24	40	20	90	67	165	360	67	11	127	9	W	33	5	107
Aug.	1,012	31	24	38	20	94	76	307	570	86	16	121	6	W	30	6	65
Sept.	1,012	33	24	39	20	94	74	268	575	51	13	124	4	W	40	5	52
Oct.	1,011	34	23	42	15	93	64	63	234	0	5	76	4	W	48	5	97
Nov.	1,011	35	20	42	13	81	43	2	40	0	<1	26	5	W	44	3	152
Dec.	1,012	34	17	40	9	65	33	<1	43	0	<1	2	4	W	51	4	222
Annual	1,011	35	21	47	9	75	46	875	1,276	525	53	127	6	—	35	4	2,395
Rec. (yrs.)	10	14	14	14	14	9	9	35	35	35	35	35	7	7	7	10	8

TABLE XVIII

CLIMATIC TABLE FOR KAYES, MALI
Latitude 14°26'N, longitude 11°26'W, elevation 30 m

Month	M.S.L. press. (mbar)	Temperature (°C) mean max.	mean min.	extreme max.	extreme min.	Relative humid. (%) 05h00	17h00	Precipitation mean (mm)	max. (mm)	min. (mm)	days ≥ 1 mm	max. 24 h (mm)	Wind av. speed (km/h)	preval. direct.	calm (%)	Average cloud-iness (oktas)	sun-shine (h/day)	evap. (mm)
Jan.	1,012	34	17	41	11	33	17	<1	18	0	0	18	7	NE	39	4	8.3	134
Feb.	1,011	37	19	44	13	30	15	<1	18	0	0	10	8	E	26	2	8.8	139
Mar.	1,009	40	22	47	16	26	13	1	3	0	0	3	9	NE	32	3	9.8	185
Apr.	1,008	43	26	48	19	28	13	1	31	0	<1	31	8	N	29	4	9.8	197
May	1,008	43	28	47	19	43	22	23	122	0	2	46	9	W	30	5	8.4	216
June	1,011	38	26	46	17	72	45	96	223	23	8	63	9	W	27	5	7.8	178
July	1,011	34	25	42	18	86	62	170	343	69	10	65	8	W	34	6	6.7	144
Aug.	1,011	32	22	39	18	92	71	244	516	56	14	122	7	SW	43	7	5.9	118
Sept.	1,011	33	23	39	18	94	72	160	370	54	11	68	5	W	53	6	7.0	124
Oct.	1,011	35	23	41	17	89	59	46	122	2	4	46	5	W	43	6	7.9	139
Nov.	1,011	36	21	41	15	62	34	5	84	0	<1	48	5	ENE	47	4	8.6	122
Dec.	1,012	34	17	41	10	41	24	<1	5	0	<1	2	7	ENE	39	4	7.4	121
Annual	1,011	37	22	48	10	58	37	746	1,127	494	50	122	7	—	37	5	8.0	1,819
Rec. (yrs.)	30	21	21	21	21	9	10	34	34	34	34	34	10	10	10	10	10	10

TABLE XIX

CLIMATIC TABLE FOR MOPTI, MALI
Latitude 14°30′N, longitude 4°12′W, elevation 280 m

Month	M.S.L. press. (mbar)	Temperature (°C)				Relative humid. (%)		Precipitation					Wind			Average		
		mean		extreme		06h00	12h00	mean (mm)	max. (mm)	min. (mm)	days ≥ 1 mm	max. 24 h (mm)	av. speed (km/h)	preval. direct.	calm (%)	cloud-iness (oktas)	sun-shine (h/day)	evap. (mm)
		max.	min.	max.	min.													
Jan.	1,012	30	14	38	7	52	18	<1	10	0	<1	5	7	NNE	37	4	8.1	146
Feb.	1,010	33	16	42	7	46	15	<1	0	0	<1	0	8	NNE	40	3	8.5	163
Mar.	1,009	37	20	44	11	39	13	1	10	0	<1	2	10	NE	24	3	9.1	210
Apr.	1,007	40	23	45	14	40	17	5	41	0	<1	10	9	NE	37	4	8.6	223
May	1,008	40	25	46	16	58	29	23	109	0	2	103	10	NE–SW	25	4	8.0	211
June	1,010	37	25	45	19	76	42	56	157	10	7	43	9	SW	33	5	8.2	188
July	1,010	34	23	43	17	86	60	147	292	46	11	90	10	SW	29	6	7.5	155
Aug.	1,010	31	23	37	19	91	71	198	441	74	12	127	8	SW	43	6	7.0	139
Sept.	1,010	32	24	38	19	91	66	94	206	31	8	74	7	SW	44	5	8.0	136
Oct.	1,010	34	24	40	18	82	51	18	78	0	2	23	7	SW	40	5	8.8	148
Nov.	1,010	33	20	41	12	61	27	1	5	0	<1	5	8	NE	40	3	8.9	135
Dec.	1,011	30	16	39	8	55	22	<1	5	0	<1	0	9	NE	31	4	7.3	129
Annual	1,010	34	21	46	7	65	36	543	964	360	43	127	8	—	35	4	8.2	1,983
Rec. (yrs.)	30	20	20	20	20	9	9	34	30	30	30	30	5	5	5	10	10	10

TABLE XX

CLIMATIC TABLE FOR DAKAR, SENEGAL
Latitude 14°44'N, longitude 17°30'W, elevation 23 m

Month	M.S.L. press. (mbar)	Temperature (°C) mean max.	mean min.	extreme max.	extreme min.	Dew point (°C)	Precipitation mean (mm)	max. (mm)	min. (mm)	days ≥ 1 mm	max. 24 h (mm)	Wind av. speed (km/h)	preval. direct.	calm (%)	Average cloud-iness (oktas)	sun-shine (h)	radi-ation (Ly/day)	evap. (mm)
Jan.	1,013	26	18	39	13	15.6	<1	10	0	0	2	14	N	12	4	219	427	103
Feb.	1,012	27	17	38	14	15.2	<1	21	0	<1	5	16	N	4	3	261	518	74
Mar.	1,012	27	18	43	15	16.1	<1	6	0	<1	3	17	N	6	3	282	590	82
Apr.	1,011	27	18	38	16	17.3	<1	8	0	0	2	22	N	4	3	295	616	85
May	1,012	29	26	38	16	19.4	1	16	0	0	2	15	N	9	3	247	600	79
June	1,013	31	23	38	16	22.1	17	94	0	2	56	12	W	10	4	195	554	86
July	1,013	31	24	37	21	23.1	88	290	3	7	150	11	W	13	5	216	497	89
Aug.	1,012	31	24	37	21	23.3	254	476	54	13	213	10	WNW	14	6	181	443	72
Sept.	1,012	32	24	38	21	23.8	132	330	56	11	103	11	NW	12	6	195	447	69
Oct.	1,012	32	24	38	21	23.6	38	249	0	3	96	11	N	11	5	209	464	84
Nov.	1,012	30	23	37	18	21.4	2	30	0	1	25	13	N	5	4	216	426	100
Dec.	1,013	27	19	35	12	16.5	8	98	0	<1	8	14	N	5	5	213	424	130
Annual	1,012	29	21	43	12	20.1	540	901	273	38	213	14	—	9	4	2,719	500	1,053
Rec. (yrs.)	30	20	20	20	20	12	32	54	54	32	24	10	10	10	14	9	5	8

TABLE XXI

CLIMATIC TABLE FOR ST. LOUIS, SENEGAL
Latitude 16°01'N, longitude 16°30'W, elevation 7 m

Month	M.S.L. press. (mbar)	Temperature (°C)				Dew point (°C)	Precipitation					Wind			Average		
		mean		extreme			mean (mm)	max. (mm)	min. (mm)	days ≥1 mm	max. 24 h (mm)	av. speed (km/h)	preval. direct.	calm (%)	cloud-iness (oktas)	sun-shine (h)	evap. (mm)
		max.	min.	max.	min.												
Jan.	1,013	28	16	36	10	12.8	<1	(40)	0	<1	8	18	NE	6	4	209	211
Feb.	1,013	26	16	39	10	14.0	5	89	0	<1	5	19	N	23	2	220	141
Mar.	1,012	27	17	41	11	15.1	<1	1	0	0	2	20	NNW	1	2	283	120
Apr.	1,011	25	17	42	11	16.6	1	2	0	0	3	18	NW	2	2	298	103
May	1,011	25	19	42	13	19.2	1	30	0	<1	8	16	NW	2	3	272	80
June	1,012	28	23	40	13	23.1	12	58	0	1	23	14	WNW	2	4	235	84
July	1,012	30	24	37	17	24.3	55	(130)	1	3	56	13	WNW	8	5	231	124
Aug.	1,011	31	24	38	15	24.7	170	290	5	9	84	12	W	13	6	214	113
Sept.	1,011	31	25	39	14	24.9	111	370	8	8	79	12	WNW	7	5	230	120
Oct.	1,012	31	24	39	13	23.2	28	185	0	3	72	14	NW	8	6	239	122
Nov.	1,012	29	20	37	13	19.7	5	22	0	<1	21	16	N	4	4	229	136
Dec.	1,013	28	17	38	11	14.6	<1	42	0	<1	2	14	NE	1	4	180	208
Annual	1,012	28	20	42	10	19.2	388	593	173	26	84	16	—	6	4	2,840	1,562
Rec. (yrs.)	30	21	21	21	21	11	35	35	35	20	20	8	8	8	12	8	6

Chapter 7

Wet and Dry Tropics

J. F. GRIFFITHS

Introduction

Between the semi-arid or highland regions and the equatorial rain forest regions of West Africa and the Congo Basin lies a belt of land often referred to as the wet and dry tropics. In this zone, separated into two distinct regions by the East African highlands, tropical temperatures prevail and from seven to nine months have a mean rainfall in excess of 50 mm, while some months have very much more than this amount. Basically it is a region over which the I.T.C.Z., with its associated rain, has a very dominant effect, but for part of the year the convergence zone moves away sufficiently for a dry spell to ensue.

In the northern belt lie the countries of Guinea, the Ivory Coast, Ghana, Togo, Dahomey, Central African Republic, plus the southern Sudan, central Cameroons and a large part of Sierra Leone and Nigeria.

Because of the greater rainfall amounts (from 1,000 to 4,000 mm/year) better agriculture than in the semi-arid zones is possible and less subsistence farming needs to be practised. The Republic of Guinea, an area of 250,000 km² with a population of three million, has three distinct regions: a coastal plain with heavy rainfall on which rice, bananas and palms are grown; the Futa Djallon and Guinea highlands support citrus fruit, pineapples and coffee; while the poorer lateritic plains of the interior with their smaller rainfall are used for grazing and growing millet. The Ivory Coast is about 330,000 km² with a population of 3.5 million and is a very agriculturally oriented country. In the south, rice, yams and cassava are grown for local consumption while coffee, cocoa, bananas and mahogany are the chief export crops. In the north, corn, millet, cotton and groundnuts are raised while cattle rearing is also important. Ghana, with the same area as Guinea, has over twice the population and relies heavily on cocoa and timber for cash exports. Accra, the capital, with 400,000 inhabitants, has an extremely low rainfall (700 mm/year) for these latitudes, about which more will be said later. Togo (57,000 km², 1.5 million people) and Dahomey (116,000 km², 2 million population) are two small republics completely within this climatic zone. Togo exports mainly coffee and cocoa but Dahomey depends largely on palm kernels and groundnuts. The Central African Republic is situated astride the highland ridge extending from the Cameroons to the Sudan. It has an area of 620,000 km² but less than one and a quarter million people. Cotton and coffee are the most important agricultural exports. Most of the 72,000 km² of Sierra Leone also lie in this zone. This is a country of over two million inhabitants whose chief exports are minerals (diamonds and iron ore) but with a good market in palm kernels, coffee and the fibre piassava.

In the southern belt the republic of Gabon, the southern portions of the Congo Republic

(Brazzaville) and the Republic of the Congo (Kinshasa) and the northern part of Angola are found. The Gabon has an area of over 250,000 km² but a population of less than 0.5 million. Timber is easily the most important export (especially okoumé, a wood excellently suited for plywood and veneers), but coffee and cocoa are becoming of economic value. The southern section of the Congo Republic (total area 350,000 km², population just under one million) has a narrow coastal plain with a steppe type vegetation giving way to savanna and then rain forest. Agriculture is still primarily on a subsistence level.

Weather patterns

This zone of approximately 5 million km² is unified by the causes of its climate. In both belts, northern and southern, moist air flow over the territory for much of the year gives rise to rains, usually of adequate amount for farming requirements. The source of the moist air masses may be the Gulf of Guinea (for most of West Africa), the Indian Ocean or the Congo Basin (for Central African Republic and the Sudan) or the South Atlantic (for Angola and the southern Congo) but the important aspect is that, for a short period each year (3–5 months), this air trajectory becomes altered or deflected so that the territory is under the influence of continental air masses, with their low humidities and consequently lower rainfalls.

As for the previous zone a detailed illustration of the climate of this zone is given for south Nigeria in Chapter 5, but in this case supplemental examples (including parts of Chapter 8) are necessary to show the spectrum of climatic conditions obtained in this large zone.

General climate of the northern belt

The mean annual temperature of this region is in the range 30°–32°C with a small variation of about ± 2°–4°C during the year. However, at some of the more continental stations this can increase to 5° or even 6°C. The mean annual minimum temperature is generally from 19° to 21°C with values up to 23° or 24°C on the coast. There is much less variation from month to month of minimum temperature than of the maximum, ± 2°C being normal. Extreme temperatures rarely reach 40°C except at the far interior stations, especially around Natitingou (northern Ghana) where as high as 45°C has been recorded. Coastal stations never reach 40°C. Absolute minima vary from 4°C at Kouroussa to 18°C at Cotonou, with 10°–15°C being the usual limit. The annual range is approximately 4°C, being as little as 2°C at Conakry and 5°–6°C inland. Average maximum temperatures reach their highest values in February or March with the lowest minima in December or January. The lowest maxima occur in July or August, whilst the highest minima are found in April or May. Near the coast the lowest minima also occur in July and August, paralleling the maximum temperature pattern.

Relative humidity is quite high throughout the year, reaching 85–95% in most months during the early morning hours. In the afternoons mean annual relative humidity averages from 50 to 75% at the coast. In the dry months some of the inland stations exhibit afternoon means as low as 25–30% whilst the marine stations may not go below 70%.

The incidence of the harmattan (dry air from the north) can drop the relative humidity from nearly 100% to 30–40% in the space of 2–3 h while the temperature remains sensibly constant.

Cloud amounts average about 5 oktas on an annual basis. At stations north of about 10°N the range is from 2 to 6 or 7 oktas but south of this the variation is generally less, especially in the Tchaorou–Pobe–Kintampo triangle. Sunshine records show a wide variation, from about 1,800 to 2,800 h/year, being related strongly to the continentality of the station. The sunniest months average over 200 h, usually in the period October–March, while the lowest values are reached in August and are very variable, from 70 to 150 h.

Winds are generally from the southwest but for the November–February period north-easterlies are dominant, except near the coast where north or northwest winds are usual. In the interior, especially the highland regions, a large percentage of calms is recorded (91% in Beyla). Along the coast this percentage is reduced appreciably, with wind speeds reaching as high as 19 knots at Cotonou in July, the windiest month at most stations.

Rainfall

While all the region experiences from 3 to 5 dry months (with less than 50 mm rainfall) amounts vary considerably. Some coastal stations experience over 4,000 mm in an average year, while in the vicinity of Accra totals are less than 1,000 mm (see Fig.3). The dry months are generally in the period November–February, but at the coast a "little dry season" (Chapter 5) is noted in the August rainfall in the area from Sassandra to Porto Novo—this phenomenon extends only a few score of kilometres inland.

In the single peaked pattern of rainfalls July, August and September are generally the wettest months; Conakry once had nearly 2,000 mm during July. In the double peaked areas June is the wettest month, except in a narrow band from Bouake to Kintampo where September rains are dominant. This may be due to the slowing up of the southward movement of the I.T.C.Z. as it meets the Jos Plateau and the Guinea highlands. The greatest 24 h falls have been measured at the coastal stations, often in excess of 300 mm; even Accra has received 303 mm in a day, about 40% of its annual total. Further inland these amounts decrease rapidly until values from 100 to 150 mm as maximum falls are common.

An interesting paper by GREGORY (1965) gives the following details concerning the rainfall seasons in Sierra Leone. In January the atmospheric stability is pronounced, due to the Saharan anticyclone and the harmattan, and there is little rainfall in the country, usually less than 25 mm. February to April is a period in which there is an increase in the number of disturbance lines, especially in the east. The disturbance lines are from 300 to 600 km south of the I.T.C.Z. where humid, hot air is sufficiently deep to allow development of the instability phenomena. In May the average rainfall is about 200–250 mm over the whole country, and in June this shows a slight increase, being wetter in the south than in the north with the coast having more rain than inland. In July and August there are no disturbance lines and the southwest "steady" monsoonal rains set in; there is a little suggestion of drying out in the extreme south. In September rainfall averages from 400 to 750 mm with the south coast having more than 750 mm; in the latter half of the month disturbance lines reappear to replace the I.T.C.Z. In October more disturbance lines occur and rainfall averages from 300 to 400 mm whilst November and December show a decrease in both the number of disturbance lines and the amount of rainfall.

During the period from January to March only a small percentage, ranging from less than 0.5% to 5% of the annual amount is recorded, while in the season July–September from 45%, in the east, to in excess of 70%, in the west, of the annual total is noted. In his paper Gregory uses the premise that rainfall in that country is due mainly to four causes, namely: (*1*) monsoonal air from the ocean; (*2*) disturbance lines; (*3*) the I.T.C.Z.; and (*4*) relief. These factors he expresses mathematically as: (*1*) the distance from the coast; (*2*) the longitude west; (*3*) the northern latitude; and (*4*) a ratio of station elevation to the distance from the sea. Then, for the annual pattern (Fig.1), using linear equations in the logarithms of the four factors, he obtains a correlation coefficient of 0.86; that is, about 75% of the variation of the annual amount is explained by regression on these four factors. For the individual monthly values some of these correlation coefficients are even higher, for instance in July when the main rainfall is usually associated with the monsoonal conditions and no disturbance lines are present, the explained variance increases to about 83% of the total.

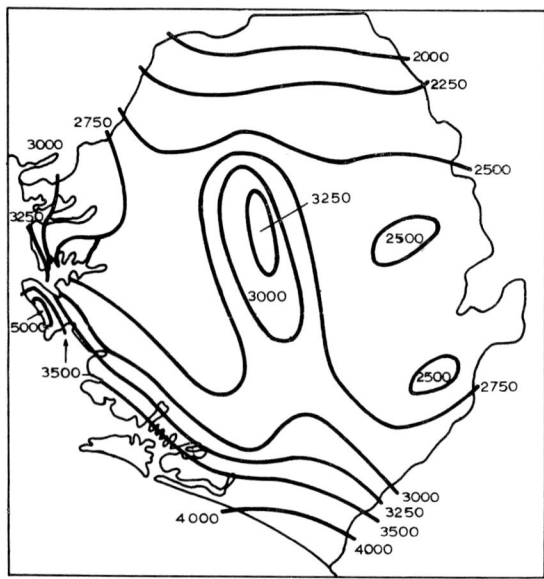

Fig.1. Mean annual rainfall (mm), Sierra Leone.

Some confusion has been occasioned in the past due to the change in location of the official Freetown gauge. The town is on the northern edge of the peninsula and about 3 km south of Freetown the hills rise to 300–500 m running in a ridge approximately northwest–southeast. Therefore, location is extremely important, for instance, along the coast for 20–30 km either side of Freetown the annual average is about 3,500 mm, but in the hills 6 km to the south, at Regent and Kongo and in the western foothills at Number Two River, exposed to the full force of the moist southwesterlies, amounts exceed 5,000 mm annually (Sierra Leone Meteorological Service, 1952). In the vicinity of Freetown port rainfall increases approximately 30 mm for each 100 m elevation.

In Sierra Leone the number of days per year with 50 mm or more of rain increases from about 6 in the drier north and east to more than 30 along the coast. The Freetown Hill station experiences 30 such falls, 10 in August and 9 in July; falls in excess of 125 mm/day are noted 5 times per year at this station.

In this whole western section the annual coefficient of variation is quite large, generally over 10% and up to 20%. At Bangui (Central African Republic) annual rainfall totals show a reasonably small variability of, at maximum, only some 20%—mean 1,560 mm, maximum 1,911 mm, minimum 1,252 mm. However, a very great fluctuation in the seasonal distribution has been noted (CHABRA, 1952). This is shown drastically in Fig.2 where it is seen that from one to four maxima may occur, compared with the normal three. Such a change in the distribution will clearly have great effect on the normal agricultural practices during these years. Nevertheless, such variation is no more than is to be expected and, by its lack of persistence from month to month, adds more weight to the idea of random fluctuations in monthly rainfall amounts.

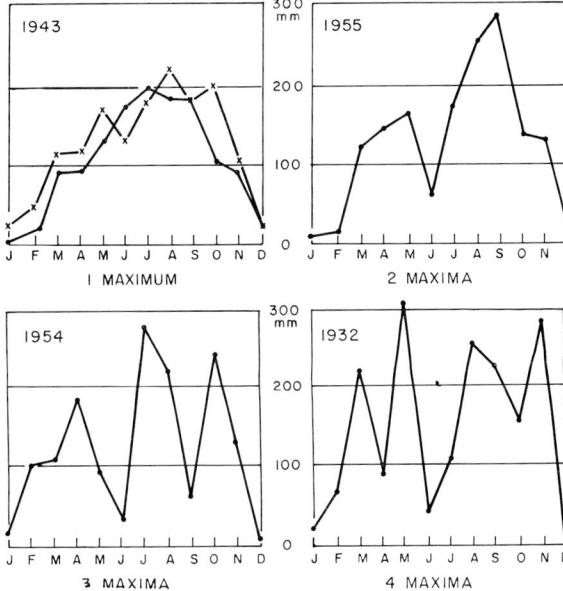

Fig.2. Variation in rainfall pattern, Bangui.

The Ghana dry belt

No discussion of this tropical zone would be complete without mention of the dry belt of the littoral of Ghana, Togo and Dahomey. To the east and west of this small region are the tropical humid areas with forest vegetation, but here is a semi-arid littoral with a wooded grassland cover.

Table I shows the sudden change in rainfall amounts and Fig.3 illustrates how the dry belt even penetrates inland for some distance.

From Axim to Takoradi the gradient is an amazing 15 mm/km on annual values and is even as high as 6 mm/km in the month of May. TREWARTHA (1962) suggests what the real causes of this dry area are: (*1*) the winds are parallel to the shore so that frictional divergence occurs; (*2*) there is a cool pool or current of water in the region, an idea borne out by the lower August temperatures here than along the rest of the Guinea coast.

TABLE I

MEAN MONTHLY AND ANNUAL RAINFALL (mm)

Station	Jan.	Feb.	Mar.	Apr.	May	June	July	Aug.	Sept.	Oct.	Nov.	Dec.	Year
Tabou	38	70	100	119	412	579	177	99	198	222	222	117	2,353
Sassandra	25	28	65	102	306	500	122	25	32	78	125	95	1,503
Abidjan	26	42	120	169	366	608	200	34	55	225	188	111	2,144
Axim	41	54	122	157	426	613	147	56	90	205	130	74	2,115
Takoradi	33	25	78	110	278	249	84	41	49	127	63	45	1,182
Accra	16	37	73	82	145	193	49	16	40	80	38	18	787
Akuse	20	41	129	107	167	152	69	32	94	197	115	36	1,159
Cotonou	36	51	104	134	201	338	120	22	82	164	68	19	1,339
Lagos	28	45	102	150	269	458	279	63	140	204	68	25	1,831

These reasons are very similar to those advanced for the arid area of the Horn of Africa. The dry belt here is alleged to be paralleled by conditions along the Liberian coast where the shoreline changes direction, but there are no reliable records to confirm or disprove this. The winter rains are due to a southwest flow at this time bringing warm, moist air direct to the area.

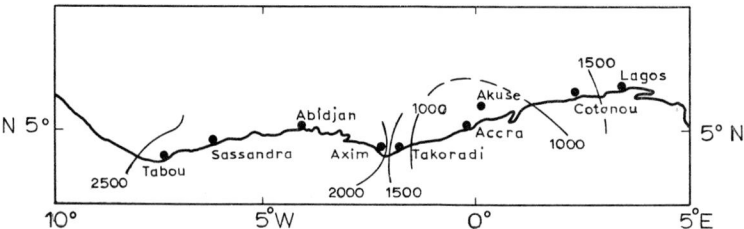

Fig.3. Mean annual isohyets (mm) along the coast of central west Africa.

The Togo Republic

Geographical situation

Togo is located on the coast of the Gulf of Benin and is a narrow band of land, very long, extending from 6° to 11°N, about 600 km, but at widest only 60 km. Crossing it from southwest to northeast there is a chain of mountains (less than 1,000 m) which is like a dorsal ridge, while a lower plain leads towards the coast and includes the valley of Mono in the east of the territory. The river Mono is the principal river of the south but in addition there are the Haho and the Sio which flow towards Lake Togo; in the north the Oti and its tributaries flow towards the Volta Basin. Along the coast there is a chain of lakes which includes Lake Togo, linked to the sea through the bay of Mono.

Climate

In view of the geographical situation Togo presents the following climatic characteristics.

The northern half (north of 8°N)

Climate of a Sudan type, which has a rainy season extending from March to the end of October and a dry season from November to March. The maximum rainfall is found in July and August. The major rains are due to convective showers. The organized and periodic perturbations only make their appearance during May and their frequency increases until August. The end of the rainy season is abrupt and occurs, on the average, during the third decade of October.

The mean annual value of the precipitation in the northern zone varies from about 1,200 to 1,300 mm in the south of the mountains and increases rapidly as one approaches them (the isohyets are aligned southwest–northeast, that is to say, parallel to the dorsal chain). On the mountains a maximum of about 1,600 mm is attained; it then falls rapidly to 1,200–1,300 mm to the north of the mountains and then decreases fairly regularly northward to around 1,000–1,100 mm (the isohyets are then orientated east–west). In the dry season fog is frequent in the mountains and haze is everywhere. The temperature (minimum in December–January with the east wind prevailing to within 100 km of the coast) varies within the following limits: in the mountains 17°–30°C in the dry season, 20°–35°C in April and May, 18°–26°C in July and August, 20°–30°C in October and November; the humidity is also high. Elsewhere temperature oscillates between 18° and 36°C in November to February, 26°–40°C in March to May, 22°–32°C during the rest of the year; the low humidity in the dry season becomes much higher in the rainy season.

The southern half (south of 8°N)

This climate is of the Guinea type with the following characteristics: (*a*) two dry seasons, from November to March and July to September; (*b*) two rainy seasons, from March to July and September to November; (*c*) small variation in pressure and temperature.

The main rainy season generally begins in March when showers, at the end of the day or during the night, are noted from convective clouds; the first are in the interior (afternoon showers), the second near the sea (night showers). Eventually squall lines appear with a growing frequency (maximum frequency, in May, once in approximately three days).

In June the storms decrease appreciably in intensity, giving place to monsoon rains which are characterized by low intensity of precipitation but of long duration. During the first half of July, the first rainy season ends in a little dry season which is then established until September. This season is often marked by an appreciable diminution and is very free of rainfall. In September, generally towards the end, the second rainy season begins which ends on average in mid-November. Often some monsoon rains are experienced at the start of the season; then storms and squall lines are generated of a frequency that is very variable from one season to another but of a generally high intensity. This second rainy season is much less marked than the first and the October maximum is less than that in June. During certain years it is even almost non-existent.

The long dry season begins in November and ends about March. Rainfall is rare and, if it occurs, is caused by convective cells. The mean annual rainfall in this region varies from about 750 to 800 mm at the coast, then increases rapidly to 1,000–1,200 mm in the interior and 1,500–1,700 mm on the mountain slopes. In the dry season the frequent fogs and mists of the mornings are followed by a cloudy sky of middle and upper level clouds with a cover of haze in December and February. The temperature varies between about 22° and 32°C and the humidity between 50 and 96%. In the wet seasons, in contrast, the temperature varies between 26° and 32°C in March, April and May (the warmest months of the year), between 23° and 31°C in September, October and November. The humidity is generally quite high. The characteristic clouds are cumulus that develop into local cumulonimbus or form a squall line which gives rise to storm showers in the afternoon.

The southwest regions exposed to the mountain winds

This area enjoys a pleasant climate but is quite humid when the little dry season is practically non-existent; the mean temperature and the lowest values are 2° to 4°C different from neighbouring areas.

Some observations on surface winds

On the coast the mean prevailing wind blows from the south-southwest. During the whole year, except during the harmattan and the monsoon, the land breeze from the north-northwest to the west-northwest at 5–10 km/h starts to be noticeable at 06h00; then little by little the influence of the sea breeze and the trade winds increases; the wind turns to west then southwest, 10–15 km/h. About 08h00–10h00 it goes to the south-southwest, 15–25 km/h, and 11h00–12h00 from the south at 25 km/h. During the July to September monsoon the wind blows throughout the day from the sector west-southwest to southwest at 15–30 km/h. From the end of December to the beginning of February the harmattan blows intermittently and sometimes for several days consecutively, from sector north-northeast at 10–25 km/h in the morning until about 14h00 and from the east to southeast, 10–15 km/h following. During and after squalls the wind oscillates between northeast and southeast with a possibility of gusts reaching 100 km/h.
In the interior of the territory the wind blows generally from south to southwest throughout the year except in November–March, during the harmattan, when it oscillates between east-northeast and east from Mango (10°25′N) to Atakpame (7°30′N).

Southern Sudan

During the winter season most of the southern Sudan is affected by tropical continental subsiding air. This air is thus very dry and stable, bringing northerly winds and large diurnal variation in temperature. In the rainy season the I.T.C.Z. moves northward through and beyond this region to bring moist, relatively cool maritime air. Sometimes a direct southeasterly flow from the Indian Ocean meets with a southwesterly flow from the Atlantic Ocean and especially heavy precipitation results.

Cloud, sunshine and radiation

During January the country is generally free from low and medium cloud. However, some thunderstorm activity over the Ethiopian Plateau may cause medium clouds to appear over this region. In July the cloudiness reaches a maximum at about 8°N, decreasing on either side. The Malakal–Rumbek–Tonj area, with a mean of 6 oktas, is the area of maximum cloudiness. A good cover of altocumulus is common on most mornings but it decreases rapidly.

TABLE II

PERCENTAGE OF POSSIBLE SUNSHINE

Station	Lat. (N)	Long. (E)	Jan.	Feb.	Mar.	Apr.	May	June	July	Aug.	Sept.	Oct.	Nov.	Dec.
Yambio	04°35′	25°26′	71	72	57	53	58	51	45	38	60	57	61	72
Juba	05°52′	31°36′	78	68	59	53	63	61	47	56	61	63	66	69
Wau	07°42′	28°01′	85	79	70	61	64	61	44	49	57	63	77	87
Malakal	09°33′	31°39′	85	79	75	67	62	43	40	45	49	61	73	87
Nahud	12°42′	28°26′	90	89	81	84	76	62	58	55	69	79	90	94
Kosti	13°10′	32°40′	90	87	83	82	80	67	58	56	69	81	89	90
El Obeid	13°10′	30°14′	91	91	82	83	76	65	57	54	68	79	92	93
Fasher	13°38′	25°20′	91	92	83	81	77	71	60	59	71	84	95	93
Geneina	13°29′	22°27′	93	93	83	78	77	67	56	48	71	86	95	93
Gedaref	14°02′	35°24′	84	87	77	80	79	77	67	63	71	81	87	91
Medani	14°23′	33°29′	93	91	87	86	79	72	60	62	73	85	93	93
Kassala	15°28′	36°24′	89	90	85	86	81	78	65	66	79	87	89	89
Khartoum	15°36′	32°32′	94	90	82	83	80	75	67	69	81	88	95	95
Atbara	17°42′	33°58′	91	92	87	95	85	79	76	75	81	87	91	91
Karima	18°33′	31°51′	89	93	87	87	87	81	85	75	79	87	95	95
P. Sudan	19°35′	37°13′	62	71	76	83	84	78	75	75	81	84	74	64
W. Halfa	21°50′	31°18′	93	91	86	86	86	90	89	86	88	91	94	91

TABLE III

AVERAGE GLOBAL RADIATION (cal./cm² day)

Station	Lat. (N)	Long. (E)	Jan.	Feb.	Mar.	Apr.	May	June	July	Aug.	Sept.	Oct.	Nov.	Dec.
Juba (1957–1966)	05°52′	31°36′	458	464	462	454	479	459	415	466	509	480	457	445
Malakal (1960–1966)	09°33′	31°39′	471	521	527	536	510	448	448	486	484	487	487	476
Ghazala Gawazat (1964–1966)	11°28′	26°27′	486	544	554	569	553	522	482	470	509	501	485	480
Tozi (1957–1962)	12°30′	34°00′	422	474	516	528	529	499	466	470	504	476	415	399
Abu Na'Ama (1963–1966)	12°44′	34°08′	483	545	574	595	589	536	482	481	497	466	451	426
Wad Medani (1957–1966)	14°23′	33°29′	483	433	576	602	584	459	474	484	562	533	489	466
Fasher (1957–1966)	13°38′	25°20′	457	534	579	594	592	550	532	534	563	529	486	456
Shambat (1957–1966)	15°40′	32°32′	483	557	612	648	622	587	571	563	561	522	488	455
Wadi Halfa (1961–1964)	21°50′	31°18′	457	524	588	639	667	655	638	609	582	525	461	426
Port Sudan (1957–1966)	19°35′	37°13′	354	449	539	612	625	577	564	552	547	486	383	340

Sunshine hours are very great over all of the Sudan, being 60% of possible even at Yambio, the minimum value. As can be seen from Table II the cloud belt ceases at about 6°N in December, retreats to about 5°N in January and does not reach 10°N except during the period April to October. This pattern is also reflected in the radiation measurements (Table III).

Temperature

Owing to the moist air mass in the southern Sudan, temperatures here show a smaller variation than in the arid belt. For instance, at Wadi Halfa the annual variation of maximum and minimum temperatures is 17° and 17.5°C respectively, at Khartoum 10° and 11°C, while at Juba only 7° and 3°C. In the winter season (January) maximum temperatures average 34°–36°C and minima 16°–20°C, at the time of the advancing monsoon (April) minimum temperatures are about 22°C while maxima range from about 32°C at Yambio to 38°C around Juba. In the wet season (July) minima are 20°–22°C while maxima go from about 30°C (Yambio) to 33°C (Juba.) In October minima are 20°–22°C and maxima 30°–35°C. In this region there is no maximum and minimum pattern corresponding to a "winter" and a "summer", only the fluctuations due to the dry and rainy season. The diurnal variation of temperature is also large, 17°C in July and 10°C in January in Juba being representative for the whole area.

Rainfall

In this area annual means from about 1,000 to 1,400 mm are recorded (Table IV). Wau and Raga, in the extreme north of the region, show a single peak pattern but the other stations show a secondary minimum in June or July, as the full rainfall effect of I.T.C.Z.

TABLE IV

MONTHLY AND ANNUAL MEANS OF RAINFALL (mm)

Station	Jan.	Feb.	Mar.	Apr.	May	June	July	Aug.	Sept.	Oct.	Nov.	Dec.	Year
Wau	0	4	20	69	132	170	199	234	179	130	8	0	1,145
Juba	5	10	43	107	157	116	136	154	105	101	35	13	982
Torit	5	21	46	102	132	122	157	142	113	99	41	15	1,005
Yubo	5	23	63	102	187	220	169	212	234	170	51	15	1,451
Raga	1	1	15	56	150	165	223	254	192	78	10	1	1,146

has passed northward. Maximum daily falls rarely exceed 100 mm. The pattern of the annual isohyets (Fig.4) illustrates well the part played by the Ethiopian highlands in spawning thunderstorms and also the influence of the moist Congo air flowing into the southwestern area giving, for instance, Wau, a much greater rainfall than Juba.

In Fig.5, of the position of the mean 10-mm isohyets, it is seen that about half the area experiences less than 10 mm only in January but some regions have three or four months with below 10 mm. It is very obvious how rapid is the southward movement (retreat) of the I.T.C.Z. as compared with its advance.

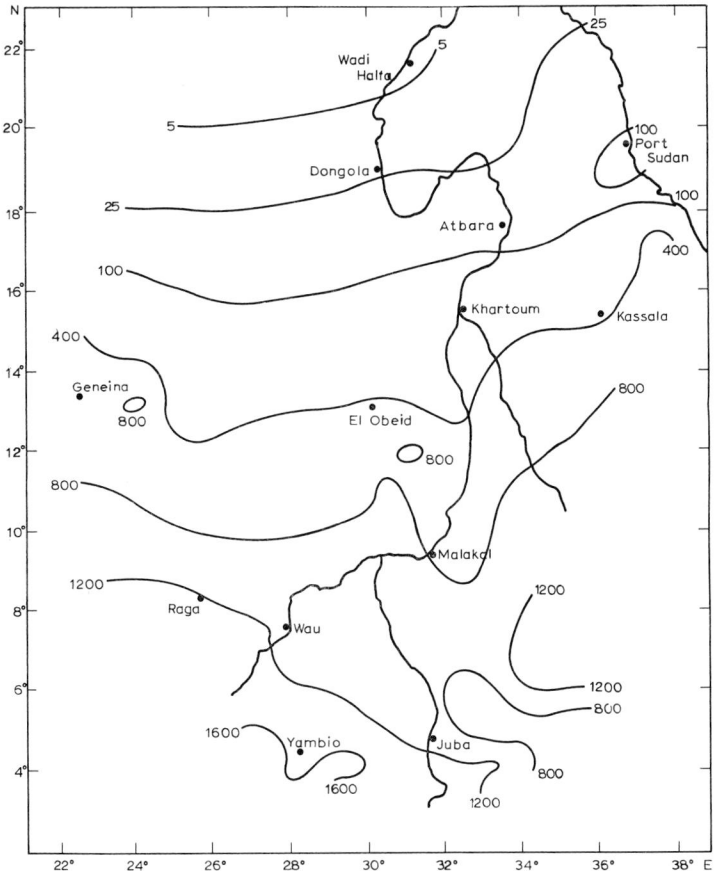

Fig.4. Mean annual rainfall (mm), Sudan.

Thunderstorms in Juba reach a maximum at 15h00–18h00 local time and threequarters of them last for only two hours or less. The maximum frequency is in May when 17 are recorded, but April, June, July and August each report 14. In Wau the maximum (14 per month) occurs in October, with September (13) being very close.

Relative humidity, evaporation and wind

Relative humidity in the southern Sudan is still quite low in spite of the greater rainfall. In January it ranges from about 25% (12h00 G.M.T.) to 50% (06h00 G.M.T.) but in July values of 90% are averaged at 06h00 near Juba, falling to 60% at 12h00. Extreme values may reach less than 10% in the northern part of this belt. Further south, during June to October, daily variation is quite small, from about 60 to 80%.

The normal evaporation closely follows the average temperature pattern month by month at each station. The values vary from 3.7 mm/day at Yambio to 6.6 mm/day at Juba, with the swamp areas recording about 4.7 mm/day. These readings are taken from a Piche evaporimeter. Calculated from the Thornthwaite method the annual potential evapotranspiration varies from about 1,750 mm in the north of the area to about 1,400 mm in the south.

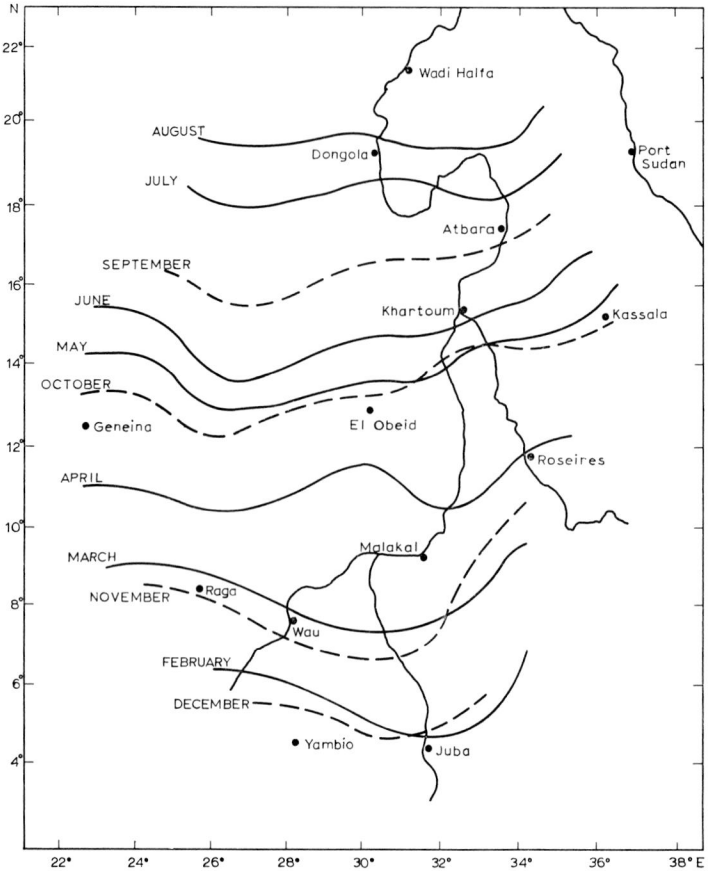

Fig.5. Mean 10-mm isohyets, 1931–1960.

In this region the average wind speed is about 7–10 knots but squalls associated with well-developed thunderstorm cells give gusts up to 100 knots. The prevailing directions are north-northeast in front of the I.T.C.Z. and south-southwest behind. At Juba the division of the percentage time according to the various sectors is given in Table V.

TABLE V

MEAN MONTHLY WIND DATA (%), JUBA

	Jan.	Feb.	Mar.	Apr.	May	June	July	Aug.	Sept.	Oct.	Nov.	Dec.
North-northeast	35	32	19	12	8	12	15	19	19	18	20	31
South-southwest	10	14	35	45	47	35	28	24	29	25	26	16
Calm or unrecorded	35	31	22	19	27	30	34	35	32	32	33	33

Climate of the southern belt

The southern belt comprises portions of Angola, Gabon, the Republic of the Congo (Brazzaville) and the Congo Republic (Kinshasa). The last of these regions is discussed in Chapter 8.

Angolan tropics

In northern Angola, on the Congo border, there exists a large area that must be considered as having a truly tropical climate with the mean temperature of every month in excess of 18°C and from seven to nine wet months (over 50 mm rainfall). June, July and August are always the driest months while in the southern section May and September are also generally dry. Rainfall amounts range from about 1,750 mm in the extreme northeast down to about 1,000 mm on the western edge of this zone. The enclave of Cabinda shows some values as low as 650 mm. (Fig.6, annual rainfall map of Angola). Falls in excess of 100 mm/day are rare but over 150 mm/day is occasionally recorded in the remote north-eastern corner. April is, invariably, the wettest month with a secondary maximum in November or, occasionally, December. On the southern edge of this region, in the transition belt to the plateau climate, Vila Luso shows the unusual pattern of a single peak distribution with a January maximum, a fact repeated at Gazambo nearer the Zambian border.

Temperatures are influenced both by altitude and latitude with the highest mean monthly

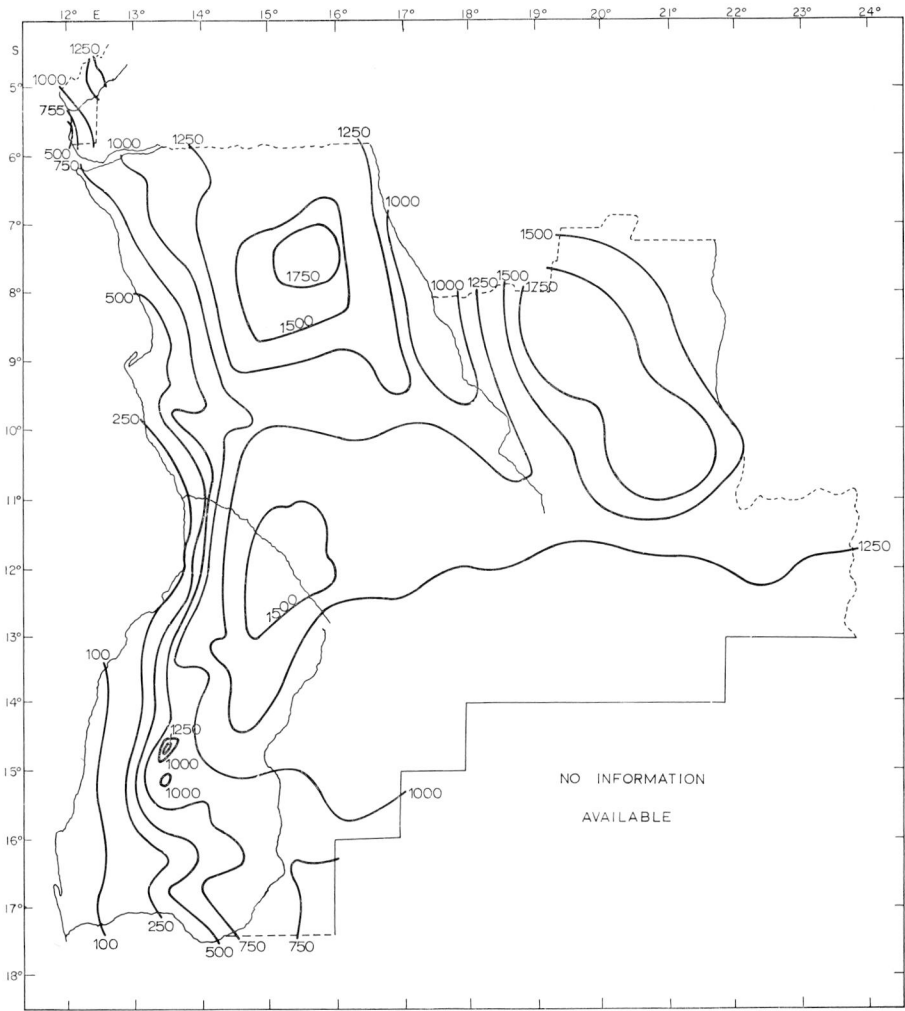

Fig.6. Mean annual isohyets (mm), Angola.

maximum around 30°C and the lowest mean monthly minimum about 15°–17°C. Extremes of over 38°C are very rare, as are minima below 3°C. Maximum temperatures occur during August–October. Diurnal variations are often quite large and Sunginge has a daily fluctuation of 26°C in June and July (from 32° to 6°C) and a yearly average of 18°C.

Morning relative humidities are high and show very little monthly variation nearer the coast. For instance, Noqui 72–78% and Sao Salvador 85–90%. Inland the fluctuation is about 25%, from 65 to 90%. Winds are mainly from the east at all seasons of the year.

Gabon and the Congo

In this small area in the west of these countries mean maximum temperatures average about 30°C and mean minima 20°C, except near the coast where 22°C is general. The variation from month to month is small (2°–3°C) and the annual range is small also, only from 3° to 5°C. Extreme temperatures are rarely in excess of 35°C or less than 13°C. The mean diurnal variation is very low at the coast, about 6°C, but increases to 10°–11°C inland. The thermal pattern is typical of the tropical areas with a monotonous regularity of variation related to a high level of relative humidity. Values of relative humidity are between 85 and 95% for early morning readings and even in midafternoon they are still around 70% at most stations.

Rainfall amounts vary greatly over this section, 650 mm at Cabinda (Angola) to 2,500 mm at Libreville. June–August are the driest months; generally less than 2% of the annual total falls in this quarter. November is usually the wettest month of the year but, nearer the coast, April dominates in the monthly totals. Daily falls of more than 125 mm are rare except in the extreme western Gabon where amounts of over 200 mm can occur in February through May.

Cloud amounts stay very constant from month to month with annual means from 5 to 7 oktas. The hours of sunshine vary from a low of 1,200 h (3.5 h/day) at Cabinda to about 1,800 h inland. September and October have less than 100 h on average. Winds are generally from the east in the morning and from the southwest during the afternoon although minor local variations are superimposed upon this flow in the immediate vicinity of the coast and near to some of the highland regions.

References

BHALOTRA, Y. P. R., 1963. Meteorology of Sudan. *Sudan Meteorol. Serv., Mem.*, 6:113 pp.
CHABRA, A., 1952. Aperçu sur le climat centrafricain. *A.S.E.C.N.A., Mem*,. 22 pp.
GREGORY, S., 1965. Rainfall over Sierra Leone. *Dept. Geograph., Univ. Liverpool, Res. Papers*, 2:58 pp.
SIERRA LEONE METEOROLOGICAL SERVICE, 1952. *Statistics Illustrating the Climate of Sierra Leone*. Government Printer, Freetown, 6 pp.
TREWARTHA, G. T., 1961. *The Earth's Problem Climates*. Univ. Wisc. Press, Madison, Wisc., 334 pp.

TABLE VI

CLIMATIC TABLE FOR LIBREVILLE, GABON
Latitude 0°27′N, longitude 09°25′E, elevation 12 m

Month	Mean sta. press. (mbar)	Temperature (°C) mean max.	mean min.	extreme max.	extreme min.	Relative humid.[1] (%)	Precip. mean (mm)	Precip. max. (mm)	Precip. min. (mm)	days ≥ 1 mm	max. 24 h (mm)	Wind av. speed (km/h)	preval. direct. 06h00	preval. direct. 12h00	calm (%)		cloud- iness[2] (oktas)	sun- shine (h)	evap. (mm)
Jan.	1,010	30	24	34	20	86	206	523	40	14	138	3	E	SW	61	28	6	174	70
Feb.	1,010	31	23	35	20	85	291	470	120	15	158	3	E	SW	55	19	6	170	69
Mar.	1,010	31	23	34	20	85	264	670	170	17	213	3	E	SW	52	18	6	170	70
Apr.	1,010	31	23	34	20	86	395	630	170	19	176	3	E	SW	55	26	6	171	69
May	1,011	30	24	34	20	84	244	550	10	15	248	3	S	SW	44	25	6	150	78
June	1,014	29	23	33	19	81	40	210	0	3	54	4	S	SW	27	24	6	122	91
July	1,015	28	22	31	17	79	<1	30	0	<1	2	4	S	SW	23	22	6	126	99
Aug.	1,014	28	22	33	16	80	11	41	0	5	12	4	S	SW	22	16	6	114	95
Sept.	1,013	29	23	31	19	83	106	370	10	13	181	5	S	SW	19	13	7	92	85
Oct.	1,012	29	23	32	20	87	359	670	92	22	108	4	S	SW	36	21	7	106	74
Nov.	1,011	30	23	32	20	88	416	722	150	21	132	4	E, S	SW	44	17	7	131	59
Dec.	1,010	30	24	32	18	86	260	771	25	16	158	4	E	SW	44	18	6	170	68
Annual	1,011	30	23	35	16	84	2,592	3,614	1,850	161	248	4	—	—	40	17	6	1,695	926
Rec. (yrs.)	10	17	17	17	17	15	18			18	16	8		10	10	14	14	10	10

[1] Mean of 06h00, 12h00 and 18h00.
[2] Mean of 06h00 and 12h00.

TABLE VII

CLIMATIC TABLE FOR MITZIC, GABON
Latitude 0°47'N, longitude 11°34'E, elevation 580 m

Month	Mean sta. press. (mbar)	Temperature (°C) mean max.	mean min.	extreme max.	extreme min.	Relative humid. (%) 07h	13h	Precipitation mean (mm)	max. (mm)	min. (mm)	days ≥1 mm	max. 24 h (mm)	Wind preval. direct.	calm (%) <1 m/sec	Average cloud-iness[1] (oktas)	evap. (mm)
Jan.	945	29	20	33	15	94	74	118	182	31	8	94	SW	75	6	49
Feb.	945	29	20	34	16	96	73	110	174	69	10	53	SW	59	6	51
Mar.	945	30	20	34	16	96	73	226	358	108	16	82	W	58	6	57
Apr.	945	30	20	34	17	96	72	207	423	80	16	75	W	58	6	52
May	946	29	20	33	16	97	74	222	397	134	18	123	SW	64	7	46
June	948	27	19	31	15	96	79	46	141	3	6	69	SW	64	7	39
July	948	26	18	31	13	96	78	10	38	0	3	34	SW	55	7	42
Aug.	948	26	18	31	13	95	76	14	41	0	5	37	SW	43	7	48
Sept.	947	28	19	32	16	95	75	150	215	51	14	86	SW	44	7	44
Oct.	946	29	19	33	16	96	74	346	505	154	24	92	SW	52	7	47
Nov.	946	28	19	32	17	96	74	247	318	118	19	80	SW	57	7	43
Dec.	945	28	20	32	16	96	73	146	328	31	11	102	SW	64	6	43
Annual	946	28	19	34	13	96	75	1,842	2,380	1,355	149	123	—	58	7	47
Rec. (yrs.)	6	15	15	15	15	5	5	30	15	15	15	15	15	15	15	14

[1] Mean of 07h00, 11h00 and 19h00.

TABLE VIII

CLIMATIC TABLE FOR KINSHASA, CONGO
Latitude 4°19'S, longitude 15°17'E, elevation 358 m

Month	Mean sta. press. (mbar)	Temperature (°C) mean max.	mean min.	extreme max.	extreme min.	Relative humid. (%)	Precipitation mean (mm)	max. (mm)	min. (mm)	days >1 mm	max. 24 h (mm)	Wind av. speed (km/h)	preval. direct.	Averages cloud-iness (oktas)	sun-shine (h)	radi-ation	diffuse rad. (cal./cm²)
Jan.	978	30	22	34	18	82	321	321	2	10	128	4	WSW	5	132	385	245
Feb.	978	31	22	35	19	80	139	330	49	10	105	5	WSW	5	134	427	248
Mar.	977	31	22	35	19	80	181	429	58	13	108	4	WSW	5	150	448	256
Apr.	977	32	22	34	20	82	209	379	59	15	131	4	WSW	4	166	445	235
May	978	30	22	34	19	83	134	280	22	11	111	4	WSW	5	140	374	220
June	980	28	19	33	15	81	5	38	0	1	29	4	WSW	5	139	332	198
July	981	27	17	32	13	76	1	34	0	0	34	5	WSW	5	125	319	198
Aug.	980	28	18	34	11	69	4	24	0	1	24	6	WSW	5	146	364	221
Sept.	979	30	20	36	16	69	33	100	2	4	73	5	WSW	5	129	375	234
Oct.	978	30	22	35	17	76	137	282	20	11	155	5	WSW	5	132	381	250
Nov.	977	30	22	34	19	81	236	348	84	16	147	5	WSW	5	142	418	245
Dec.	977	30	22	33	20	83	171	327	47	14	73	4	WSW	5	135	380	247
Annual	978	30	21	36	11	79	1,378	1,824	1,124	106	155	5	–	5	1,670	387	235
Rec. (yrs.)	6	10	10	10	10	3	30	30	30	30	30	1		9	9	7	7

TABLE IX

CLIMATIC TABLE FOR BANGUI, CENTRAL AFRICAN REPUBLIC
Latitude 4°22'N, longitude 18°34'E, elevation 385 m

Month	Mean sta. press. (mbar)	Temperature (°C) mean max.	Temperature (°C) mean min.	Temperature (°C) extreme max.	Temperature (°C) extreme min.	Relative humid. (%) 07h00	Relative humid. (%) 13h00	Precipitation mean (mm)	Precipitation max. (mm)	Precipitation min. (mm)	Precipitation days ≥1 mm	Precipitation max. 24 h (mm)	Average cloudiness (oktas)	Average sunshine (h)	Average evap. (mm)
Jan.	966	33	20	37	13	90	49	21	77	0	2	47	3	203	172
Feb.	965	34	20	39	13	88	47	47	106	0	5	59	4	201	196
Mar.	965	33	21	40	16	90	57	124	280	22	9	88	4	191	164
Apr.	966	33	21	38	18	92	62	128	235	44	10	89	5	184	125
May	967	32	21	39	16	92	65	173	315	65	14	98	6	193	116
June	968	31	21	36	17	94	68	135	296	32	12	86	5	158	90
July	968	29	20	34	15	94	71	185	324	94	14	129	6	138	73
Aug.	968	30	20	34	17	94	70	225	371	64	17	122	6	138	75
Sept.	967	31	20	35	17	94	69	185	314	62	16	107	6	143	76
Oct.	967	31	20	35	17	94	68	202	328	97	17	105	6	158	71
Nov.	966	31	20	37	17	94	66	101	239	30	10	63	4	171	97
Dec.	966	32	19	36	14	92	57	34	85	0	3	89	3	220	119
Annual	967	32	20	40	13	92	62	1,560	1,911	1,252	130	129	5	2,098	1,373
Rec. (yrs.)	10	31	31	31	31	11	11	30	30	30	30	30		11	11

TABLE X

CLIMATIC TABLE FOR JUBA, SUDAN
Latitude 4°52'N, longitude 31°36'E, elevation 460 m

Month	Mean sta. press. (mbar)	Temperature (°C) mean max.	Temperature (°C) mean min.	Temperature (°C) extreme max.	Temperature (°C) extreme min.	Relative humid. (%)	Precipitation mean (mm)	Precipitation max. (mm)	Precipitation min. (mm)	Precipitation days ≥1 mm	Precipitation max. 24 h (mm)	Wind av. speed (km/h)	Wind preval. direct.	Wind calm (%)	Average cloud-iness[1] (oktas)	Average sun-shine (h/day)	Average radi-ation (Ly/day)	Average evap. (mm/day)
Jan.	1,007	37	20	42	11	43	5	42	0	1	33	5	NNE	36	3	9.3	456	11.5
Feb.	1,006	38	21	43	12	41	10	72	<1	2	50	5	NNE	29	4	8.2	464	11.9
Mar.	1,006	37	23	43	16	50	43	211	3	6	55	5	S	21	5	7.1	463	10.1
Apr.	1,007	35	23	42	18	63	107	211	30	11	111	5	S	17	6	6.5	454	7.3
May	1,009	33	22	44	17	85	157	318	38	12	110	5	S	19	6	7.8	479	4.6
June	1,011	32	21	38	16	77	116	244	27	11	89	3	S	30	5	7.5	459	3.9
July	1,011	31	20	37	17	82	136	297	29	11	79	3	S	31	6	5.9	415	3.0
Aug.	1,011	31	20	36	16	83	154	286	46	12	92	3	S	26	5	6.9	466	2.9
Sept.	1,010	32	20	38	16	77	105	216	27	10	73	3	S	27	5	7.5	509	3.8
Oct.	1,008	34	20	40	14	71	101	194	22	9	80	3	S	23	5	7.6	480	4.7
Nov.	1,007	35	20	40	13	63	35	111	<1	5	55	3	S	29	5	7.9	457	6.5
Dec.	1,007	36	20	41	14	52	13	62	0	2	29	3	NNE	32	4	8.1	446	9.0
Annual	1,008	31	21	44	11	66	982	1,317	679	93	111	4	—	27	5	7.5	462	6.6
Rec. (yrs.)	24	30	30	30	30	30	30	30	30	30	30	7	7	7	30			30

[1] Mean of 06h00, 12h00 and 18h00.

TABLE XI

CLIMATIC TABLE FOR ABIDJAN, IVORY COAST
Latitude 5°15'N, longitude 3°56'W, elevation 7 m

Month	Mean sta. press. (mbar)	Temperature (°C) mean max.	mean min.	extreme max.	extreme min.	Relative humid. (%) 06h00	12h00	Precipitation mean (mm)	max. (mm)	min. (mm)	days ≥ 1 mm	max. 24 h (mm)	Wind av. speed (km/h)	preval. direct.	calm[1] (%)	Average cloud-iness (oktas)	sun-shine (h)
Jan.	1,009	31	23	34	15	96	73	26	110	0	3	48	8	SW	37	5	187
Feb.	1,009	32	24	35	18	95	71	42	177	0	4	152	9	SW	35	6	196
Mar.	1,009	32	24	36	19	93	70	120	230	20	7	71	10	SW	33	6	228
Apr.	1,009	32	24	35	20	93	71	169	279	45	9	73	10	SW	30	6	284
May	1,010	31	24	34	20	94	75	366	685	(76)	16	232	9	SW	33	7	184
June	1,012	29	23	34	20	94	82	608	1,036	200	19	222	10	SW	29	7	110
July	1,013	28	23	33	18	92	79	200	663	5	10	274	12	SW	20	7	130
Aug.	1,013	28	22	31	17	94	79	34	254	5	6	89	13	SW	12	7	116
Sept.	1,012	28	23	32	18	95	80	55	185	7	9	53	14	SW	10	7	130
Oct.	1,011	29	23	33	19	93	78	225	459	8	13	160	13	SW	16	7	189
Nov.	1,010	31	23	34	19	93	73	188	345	81	13	104	10	SW	29	6	214
Dec.	1,009	31	23	35	17	95	73	111	175	5	7	61	8	SSW	38	5	197
Annual	1,010	30	23	36	15	94	75	2,144	3,131	1,650	116	274	10	—	27	6	2,086
Rec. (yrs.)	8	13	13	13	13	10	10	24	24	24	16	15	10				5

[1] < 5 km/h.

TABLE XII

CLIMATIC TABLE FOR CABINDA, ANGOLA
Latitude 5°33'S, longitude 12°11'E, elevation 20 m

Month	Mean sta. press. (mbar)	Temperature (°C) mean max.	mean min.	extreme max.	extreme min.	Relative humid. (%) 09h00	15h00	Precipitation mean (mm)	max. (mm)	min. (mm)	days ≥ 1 mm	max. 24 h (mm)	Wind preval. direct.	calm (%)	Average cloudiness (oktas)	sunshine (h)	evap. (mm)
Jan.	1,008	30	23	32	20	85	74	59	233	4	5	70	SW	21	5	117	55
Feb.	1,008	31	23	33	19	86	76	109	236	1	6	76	SW	25	5	115	54
Mar.	1,008	31	23	33	18	85	74	85	371	46	7	81	SW	25	5	147	63
Apr.	1,008	30	23	33	19	86	77	117	301	46	8	103	SW	25	5	144	50
May	1,010	29	23	33	19	87	80	56	259	2	3	56	SW	22	5	105	49
June	1,012	26	21	30	17	88	76	0.6	3	0	0	2	SW	27	5	95	52
July	1,013	26	18	28	14	84	72	0.1	1	0	0	1	SW	25	4	97	58
Aug.	1,013	26	19	29	15	85	75	0.8	5	0	4	2	SW	26	5	69	63
Sept.	1,011	27	21	30	15	85	75	6	11	2	2	10	SW	21	5	61	58
Oct.	1,010	28	23	33	19	85	75	34	124	9	6	90	SW	23	5	62	61
Nov.	1,009	29	23	33	19	85	73	114	333	14	8	135	SW	25	5	99	52
Dec.	1,009	28	23	34	19	85	78	89	180	6	6	96	SW	32	5	105	49
Annual	1,010	28	22	34	14	86	75	670	1,331	332	52	135	—	30	5	1,217	663
Rec. (yrs.)	10	13	13	13	13				15	15							

TABLE XIII

CLIMATIC TABLE FOR ACCRA, GHANA
Latitude 5°36′N, longitude 0°12′W, elevation 65 m

Month	M.S.L. press. (mbar)	Temperature (°C) mean max.	mean min.	extreme max.	extreme min.	Relative humid. (%) 06h00	12h00	Precip. mean (mm)	max. (mm)	min. (mm)	days ≥1 mm	max. 24h (mm)	Wind av. speed (km/h) 07h	14h	preval. direct. 07h	14h	calm (%) 07h	14h	Aver. cloudiness (oktas)
Jan.	1,011	32	23	34	15	95	61	16	95	0	1	89	4	11	W	S	22	1	3
Feb.	1,010	32	24	38	17	96	61	37	158	0	2	106	3	12	W	S	25	0	4
Mar.	1,010	32	24	38	20	95	63	73	223	0	4	108	4	13	W	S	23	1	5
Apr.	1,010	32	24	34	19	96	65	82	223	0	6	137	4	12	W	S	21	0	6
May	1,012	31	23	35	21	96	68	145	346	7	9	150	4	11	W	S	29	3	6
June	1,013	29	23	33	20	97	74	193	606	2	10	303	4	10	W	S	28	2	6
July	1,014	27	22	32	19	97	76	49	197	0	4	103	3	12	N	SW	25	0	7
Aug.	1,014	27	21	32	18	97	77	16	106	0	3	94	4	13	W	SW	21	0	6
Sept.	1,013	28	22	32	20	96	72	40	224	0	4	114	4	14	W	S	17	0	6
Oct.	1,012	30	23	32	19	97	71	80	201	0	6	139	5	12	W	S	14	1	5
Nov.	1,011	31	21	33	21	97	66	38	139	0	3	94	4	12	W	S	15	1	4
Dec.	1,011	31	23	34	17	97	64	18	133	0	2	76	4	11	W	S	16	0	4
Annual	1,012	30	23	38	15	96	68	787	1,197	275	54	303	4	12	—		21	1	5
Rec. (yrs.)	30	30		17	17	9	9				45		6	6			6	6	

TABLE XIV

CLIMATIC TABLE FOR ALBERTVILLE, CONGO (KINSHASA)
Latitude 5°53'S, longitude 29°11'E, elevation 790 m

Month	Mean sta. press. (mbar)	Temperature (°C)				Relative humid. (%)	Precipitation			Aver. wind speed[1] (km/h)	Average		
		mean		extreme			mean (mm)	days >1 mm	max. 24 h (mm)		sun-shine (h)	radi-ation (Ly/day)	evap. (mm)
		max.	min.	max.	min.								
Jan.	923	28	20	33	17	82	110	13	80	1.5	158	212	80
Feb.	923	28	20	32	18	80	77	12	41	1.5	158	214	73
Mar.	923	28	20	33	17	81	137	14	59	1.5	183	222	79
Apr.	924	28	20	31	17	82	207	17	90	1.5	195	230	82
May	925	28	19	31	15	78	96	8	72	2	256	248	106
June	926	27	16	30	12	72	9	1	31	2	284	243	124
July	926	27	15	30	12	68	0.6	0.2	4	2	308	243	152
Aug.	925	28	17	32	11	65	7	1	22	2	286	236	142
Sept.	924	29	19	34	14	64	43	4	65	2	239	233	148
Oct.	924	30	20	34	15	68	51	6	61	2	219	226	147
Nov.	924	28	20	33	17	77	146	16	63	2	164	208	77
Dec.	924	27	20	32	17	82	181	17	59	1.5	149	216	76
Annual	924	28	19	34	11	75	1,064	108	90	2	228	2,598	1,285
Rec. (yrs.)	9	9	9	9	9	7	9	9	9	4	5	9	5

[1] Prevalent wind direction annual: W (nights); SE (days).

TABLE XV

CLIMATIC TABLE FOR COTONOU, DAHOMEY
Latitude 6°21′N, longitude 2°26′E, elevation 10 m

Month	M.S.L. press. (mbar)	Temperature (°C)				Relative humid. (%)		Precipitation					Wind			Aver. cloud-iness (oktas)
		mean		extreme		06h00	12h00	mean (mm)	max. (mm)	min. (mm)	days ≥1 mm	max. 24 h (mm)	av. speed (km/h)	preval. direct	calm (%)	
		max.	min.	max.	min.											
Jan.	1,010	29	24	33	19	92	72	36	59	0	2	84	9	SW	16	4
Feb.	1,010	30	25	35	21	91	70	51	130	0	2	86	12	SW	9	5
Mar.	1,010	30	26	35	20	89	71	104	278	18	5	76	16	SW	9	6
Apr.	1,010	30	25	35	21	90	71	134	304	30	8	118	14	SW	15	6
May	1,011	29	24	35	20	92	75	201	448	60	11	152	13	SW	17	5
June	1,014	27	23	33	18	94	81	338	691	103	13	170	15	SW	11	7
July	1,014	27	23	32	19	91	81	120	540	1	6	85	19	SW	3	7
Aug.	1,014	27	23	32	20	91	78	22	144	0	4	56	17	SW	2	6
Sept.	1,013	27	23	32	20	92	78	82	223	1	7	69	16	SW	7	6
Oct.	1,012	28	24	33	20	95	78	164	317	12	10	117	12	SW	13	6
Nov.	1,011	29	24	34	20	95	74	68	230	0	6	112	10	SW	16	5
Dec.	1,011	29	24	34	18	95	70	19	55	0	2	25	9	SW	20	4
Annual	1,012	29	24	35	18	92	75	1,339	1,565	1,114	76	170	14	—	11	6
Rec. (yrs.)	30	11	11	11	11	10	10	30	33	33	17	15				

TABLE XVI

CLIMATIC TABLE FOR POBE, DAHOMEY
Latitude 6°56′N, longitude 2°40′E, elevation 135 m

Month	Temperature (°C)				Relative humid. (%)		Precipitation					Wind			Aver. cloudiness (oktas)
	mean		extreme		07h00	14h00	mean (mm)	max. (mm)	min. (mm)	days ≥1 mm	max. 24 h (mm)	av. speed (km/h)	preval. direct.	calm (%)	
	max.	min.	max.	min.											
Jan.	34	21	38	14	93	49	13	152	0	0.9	78	5	WSW	43	5
Feb.	36	22	40	18	94	54	32	130	0	3	51	7	WSW	34	5
Mar.	35	23	42	19	96	62	96	224	20	7	69	8	WSW	24	5
Apr.	34	22	39	19	94	70	142	376	66	9	193	9	WSW	22	5
May	33	22	38	19	94	73	172	440	10	12	74	10	W	15	6
June	31	21	33	18	95	78	186	381	61	15	97	11	W	23	6
July	29	21	34	17	94	80	125	280	5	8	106	14	W	28	6
Aug.	29	21	34	16	92	78	58	190	1	5	62	12	W	35	7
Sept.	30	21	35	17	93	77	129	358	12	9	53	10	W	42	6
Oct.	32	21	40	18	95	75	147	254	23	13	69	7	W	52	6
Nov.	33	22	36	17	95	69	42	92	5	5	39	5	W	57	5
Dec.	34	21	36	16	95	58	10	46	0	1	41	5	WSW	54	5
Annual	33	22	42	14	94	69	1,252	—	—	88	193	9	—	37	6
Rec. (yrs.)	12	12	14	14	10	10	29	29	29	15	10				7

TABLE XVII

CLIMATIC TABLE FOR BOUAKE, IVORY COAST
Latitude 7°42'N, longitude 5°00'W, elevation 365 m

Month	Mean sta. press. (mbar)	Temperature (°C) mean		extreme		Relative humid. (%)		Precipitation					Wind			Average	
		max.	min.	max.	min.	06h	12h	mean (mm)	max. (mm)	min. (mm)	days ≥ 1 mm	max. 24 h (mm)	av. speed (km/h)	preval. direct.	calm (%)	cloud-iness (oktas)	sun-shine (h)
Jan.	971	33	20	37	15	85	51	13	65	0	0.8	56	6	E	81	4	194
Feb.	970	34	21	39	15	84	52	46	142	0	3	66	6	SW	68	4	196
Mar.	970	34	21	40	15	91	60	92	186	5	5	102	8	SW	54	4	202
Apr.	970	33	21	38	14	93	65	140	319	17	7	86	8	SW	59	5	185
May	972	33	22	38	16	96	68	154	306	51	9	125	7	S	63	6	187
June	973	31	21	37	15	97	74	135	400	48	10	118	7	S	62	6	116
July	974	29	20	37	16	97	78	99	298	2	8	156	9	SW	10	7	88
Aug.	973	29	20	36	16	97	78	108	249	5	8	74	8	SW	44	7	73
Sept.	972	30	20	37	16	98	77	225	398	53	12	137	7	SSW	55	7	113
Oct.	972	32	20	37	16	97	73	140	495	42	10	101	6	SW	61	6	165
Nov.	971	33	21	37	18	97	68	35	135	0	3	50	7	SW	47	5	169
Dec.	971	33	20	38	14	94	57	23	133	0	2	35	8	SW	44	4	167
Annual	972	32	21	40	14	94	67	1,210	1,673	784	78	156	7	—	54	6	1,855
Rec. (yrs.)	8	12	12	15	15	9	9	32	42	42	17	15	7	7	7	10	8

TABLE XVIII

CLIMATIC TABLE FOR WAU, SUDAN
Latitude 7°42'N, longitude 28°01'E, elevation 440 m

Month	M.S.L. press. (mbar)	Temperature (°C)				Relative humid. (%)	Precipitation					Wind			Average		
		mean		extreme			mean (mm)	max. (mm)	min. (mm)	days ≥1 mm	max. 24 h (mm)	av. speed (km/h)	preval. direct.	calm (%)	cloud-iness[1] (oktas)	sun-shine (h/day)	evap. (mm/day)
		max.	min.	max.	min.												
Jan.	1,008	36	18	41	10	35	0	6	0	0.2	17	5	NNE	34	2	9.7	14.7
Feb.	1,007	37	19	44	11	29	4	37	0	0.6	25	3	NNE	29	3	9.3	12.6
Mar.	1,006	38	21	43	12	36	20	75	0.1	3	63	5	V	28	4	8.4	12.1
Apr.	1,006	37	22	46	14	45	69	156	0.2	5	101	5	S	23	5	7.6	9.5
May	1,008	35	22	42	14	64	132	218	79	10	102	5	S	23	5	8.2	6.3
June	1,010	33	21	41	14	73	170	347	89	11	86	3	SW	28	5	7.9	4.3
July	1,010	32	21	40	14	78	199	331	70	13	92	3	SW	33	6	5.7	3.3
Aug.	1,010	32	21	40	15	80	234	397	83	14	102	3	SW	35	6	6.2	3.0
Sept.	1,009	33	21	39	15	76	179	297	62	12	86	3	V	35	6	7.0	3.6
Oct.	1,008	34	21	40	16	71	130	256	30	9	103	3	V	38	5	7.4	4.5
Nov.	1,007	36	19	40	12	55	8	33	0	2	71	3	NNE	43	4	8.9	7.8
Dec.	1,006	36	18	40	10	46	0	3	0	0.1	12	3	NNE	34	3	9.8	10.4
Annual	1,008	35	20	46	10	57	1,145	1,487	894	80	103	4	—	32	4	8.0	7.7
Rec. (yrs.)	30	38	38	38	38	30	30	30	30	30	33	10	10	10	29	29	29

[1] Mean of 06h00, 12h00 and 18h00.

TABLE XIX

CLIMATIC TABLE FOR KINTAMPO, GHANA
Latitude 8°02'N, longitude 1°52'W, elevation 320 m

Month	Temperature (°C) mean max.	mean min.	extreme max.	extreme min.	Relative humid. (%) 09h00	Precipitation mean (mm)	max. (mm)	min. (mm)	days ≥1 mm	max. 24 h (mm)	Wind av. speed (km/h)	preval. direct.	calm (%)	Aver. cloudiness (oktas)
Jan.	33	19	38	10	62	8	223	0	0.7	32	11	NE	0	5
Feb.	34	21	41	10	64	40	225	0	3	119	14	SW	0	5
Mar.	35	22	46	15	71	102	232	28	6	89	14	SW	0	5
Apr.	33	22	47	10	72	160	560	42	9	87	14	SW	0	5
May	32	21	41	10	76	186	394	103	11	152	11	SW	0	5
June	30	21	38	10	79	239	444	69	15	105	11	SW	1	6
July	29	20	35	14	81	144	427	20	11	87	11	SW	0	6
Aug.	28	20	37	10	79	117	415	15	7	87	11	SW	0	6
Sept.	30	20	38	10	83	277	879	63	18	92	7	SW	0	6
Oct.	31	20	38	14	79	213	466	8	15	82	7	SW	0	6
Nov.	32	20	41	10	76	68	216	0	5	56	7	SW	0	5
Dec.	32	20	38	10	72	13	42	0	0.9	69	7	SW, NE	0	5
Annual	32	21	47	10	74	1,567	—	—	102	152	10	—	0	5
Rec. (yrs.)	23	23	15	15	20	35	25	25	25	25				

TABLE XX

CLIMATIC TABLE FOR FREETOWN, SIERRA LEONE
Latitude 8°37'N, longitude 13°12'W, elevation 20 m

Month	M.S.L. press. (mbar)	Temperature (°C) mean max.	mean min.	extreme max.	extreme min.	Relative humid. (%)	Precipitation mean (mm)	max. (mm)	min. (mm)	days ≥ 1 mm	max. 24 h (mm)	Wind av. speed (km/h)	preval. direct. 07h	14h	calm (%)	Average cloud-iness[1] (oktas)	sun-shine (h/day)
Jan.	1,011	30	23	33	15	73	8	105	0	1	69	3	SW	W + E	8	3	8.1
Feb.	1,010	31	23	36	18	72	6	106	0	1	15	4	SW	W	3	3	8.2
Mar.	1,010	31	24	33	19	72	28	154	0	2	76	5	SW	W	3	4	7.7
Apr.	1,010	31	25	37	21	79	68	336	0	5	104	4	SW, E	W	3	4	7.0
May	1,011	31	24	33	21	81	214	723	67	13	177	3	E	W	6	6	6.3
June	1,013	29	23	32	20	85	522	1,219	128	20	101	3	SW, E	W	6	6	5.3
July	1,014	28	23	31	19	88	1,190	1,299	429	25	187	3	SW	SW	6	7	2.8
Aug.	1,013	27	23	30	19	86	1,078	1,553	293	24	256	4	SW	SW	2	7	2.2
Sept.	1,012	28	23	31	20	89	800	1,220	310	23	204	3	E	W+SW	2	6	4.0
Oct.	1,012	29	22	32	19	84	333	837	135	19	318	3	E	W	2	6	6.2
Nov.	1,011	30	23	34	20	82	148	333	1	11	78	2	E	W	7	5	6.6
Dec.	1,011	30	23	33	16	78	38	187	0	5	134	2	E	W+E	6	4	7.0
Annual	1,012	30	23	37	15	81	4,373	5,245	2,603	146	318	3	—	—	4	5	5.9
Rec. (yrs.)	30	14	14	14	14	15	30	87	87	23	12	4	4	4	4	10	10

[1] Mean of 02h00, 08h00, 14h00 and 20h00.

TABLE XXI

CLIMATIC TABLE FOR BEYLA, GUINEA
Latitude 8°41'N, longitude 8°39'W, elevation 690 m

Month	Temperature (°C)				Relative humid. (%)		Precipitation					Wind			Aver. cloudiness (oktas)
	mean		extreme		05h00	11h00	mean (mm)	max. (mm)	min. (mm)	days >1 mm	max. 24 h (mm)	av. speed (km/h)	preval. direct.	calm (%)	
	max.	min.	max.	min.											
Jan.	31	17	35	11	77	50	8	50	0	1	59	0	C	92	2
Feb.	32	19	36	15	79	50	38	147	0	3	76	1	S	78	3
Mar.	32	19	36	17	79	51	117	293	10	9	51	1	S, E	89	4
Apr.	31	19	34	17	83	57	154	360	42	10	65	1	S	86	4
May	31	19	36	17	76	52	187	631	23	13	86	1	S	92	5
June	29	19	34	16	80	56	216	555	63	15	80	1	E	95	4
July	28	18	33	15	79	55	234	392	93	15	96	3	N	90	5
Aug.	27	18	32	16	81	54	264	490	83	17	96	2	NE	91	6
Sept.	28	19	32	17	81	57	285	495	159	19	84	1	N	95	5
Oct.	28	18	32	16	84	58	178	290	43	13	68	0	C	93	4
Nov.	29	18	34	12	84	57	83	274	7	7	63	0	C	97	3
Dec.	30	16	34	10	83	55	25	122	0	2	65	1	N	94	2
Annual	30	18	36	10	81	54	1,789	2,389	1,172	124	96	1	—	91	4
Rec. (yrs.)	6	7	5	5	5	5	29	29	29	15	17	7	7	7	9

TABLE XXII

CLIMATIC TABLE FOR TCHAOROU, DAHOMEY
Latitude 8°52'N, longitude 2°23'E, elevation 330 m

Month	M.S.L. press. (mbar)	Temperature (°C)				Relative humid. (%)		Precipitation					Wind			Aver. cloudiness (oktas)
		mean		extreme		06h00	10h00	mean (mm)	max. (mm)	min. (mm)	days ≥ 1 mm	max. 24 h (mm)	av. speed (km/h)	preval. direct.	calm (%)	
		max.	min.	max.	min.											
Jan.	1,009	35	19	39	13	74	34	7	49	0	0.6	43	5	ENE, SW	55	4
Feb.	1,008	36	21	41	14	76	36	15	71	0	1	35	6	SW, ENE	46	4
Mar.	1,008	36	23	41	16	89	49	58	180	5	4	45	8	SW	30	5
Apr.	1,009	35	23	41	18	93	58	104	203	20	6	62	10	SW	21	6
May	1,010	33	22	38	18	95	63	141	280	41	10	92	9	SW	30	7
June	1,012	31	21	36	18	96	69	161	282	80	13	86	7	SW	40	7
July	1,013	27	21	33	18	96	77	165	387	8	12	112	8	SW	30	7
Aug.	1,012	28	21	34	17	96	79	163	415	49	11	97	7	SW	38	7
Sept.	1,012	29	21	37	16	96	75	214	391	93	16	112	6	SW	46	7
Oct.	1,011	29	21	35	18	96	68	161	354	49	11	92	5	SW	49	7
Nov.	1,010	33	20	37	14	94	54	16	76	0	2	51	5	SW	44	6
Dec.	1,010	34	18	37	12	82	36	7	62	0	0.7	57	6	SW, E	40	5
Annual	1,010	32	21	41	12	90	58	1,211	1,732	861	87	112	7	—	39	6
Rec. (yrs.)	30	18	18	18	18	9	9	30	18	18	10	15				10

TABLE XXIII

CLIMATIC TABLE FOR CONAKRY, GUINEA
Latitude 9°31'N, longitude 13°43'W, elevation 17 m

Month	Mean sta. press. (mbar)	Temperature (°C) mean max.	mean min.	extreme max.	extreme min.	Relative humid. (%) 05h00	11h00	Precipitation mean (mm)	max. (mm)	min. (mm)	days ≥ 1 mm	max. 24 h (mm)	Wind av. speed (km/h)	preval. direct.	calm[1] (%)	Aver. cloudiness (oktas)
Jan.	1,005	31	22	34	18	87	61	1	15	0	0.1	13	3	NW	20	3
Feb.	1,005	31	23	34	17	87	58	2	7	0	0.2	13	6	NW	20	2
Mar.	1,005	31	23	36	20	86	58	5	64	0	0.9	56	8	WNW	22	2
Apr.	1,005	32	23	35	20	85	80	17	108	0	3	43	7	NW	18	3
May	1,006	31	24	35	19	88	67	154	360	3	10	78	7	WNW	17	5
June	1,008	29	23	33	18	93	78	564	1,010	272	22	162	8	SW	24	6
July	1,008	28	22	32	19	96	85	1,321	1,940	793	29	313	8	SW	24	7
Aug.	1,008	27	22	31	20	96	87	1,057	1,626	725	27	259	8	SW	20	8
Sept.	1,007	29	23	32	18	95	83	713	1,130	257	24	300	7	SW	23	7
Oct.	1,006	30	23	33	18	94	76	330	667	129	18	154	5	SW	20	6
Nov.	1,006	31	24	33	19	93	74	122	301	18	8	96	4	SW	24	4
Dec.	1,005	31	23	34	19	88	64	10	76	0	0.9	56	4	NW	23	3
Annual	1,006	30	23	36	17	91	71	4,296	5,741	3,320	143	313	6	—	21	5
Rec. (yrs.)	7	13	13	12	18	10	10	23	28	28	15	18	5	5	5	10

[1] < 4 knots.

TABLE XXIV

CLIMATIC TABLE FOR FERKESSEDOUGOU, IVORY COAST
Latitude 9°37'N, longitude 5°05'W, elevation 350 m

Month	Mean sta. press. (mbar)	Temperature (°C) mean max.	mean min.	extreme max.	extreme min.	Relative humid. (%) 06h00	12h00	Precipitation mean (mm)	max. (mm)	min. (mm)	days ≥ 1 mm	max. 24 h (mm)	Wind av. speed (km/h)	preval. direct.	calm (%)	Average cloud-iness (oktas)	sun-shine (h)
Jan.	974	34	16	38	10	67	30	5	74	0	0.4	15	1	E	73	3	277
Feb.	973	35	20	40	11	66	33	25	108	0	1	71	2	SW	64	3	248
Mar.	972	35	23	41	13	76	46	41	110	0	4	76	4	SW	49	4	254
Apr.	973	34	23	41	15	81	55	81	221	28	6	102	5	SW	48	5	234
May	974	33	23	40	17	85	65	149	258	49	9	61	3	SW	65	5	248
June	976	31	22	37	17	87	69	152	289	74	11	81	5	SW	49	6	219
July	976	29	21	36	17	89	74	185	339	94	12	106	3	SW	42	7	181
Aug.	976	29	21	36	17	91	77	305	508	114	16	152	4	SW	56	7	149
Sept.	975	30	21	36	18	92	78	238	381	156	17	81	2	SW	72	7	172
Oct.	975	31	21	37	17	90	70	118	280	28	12	77	1	SW	69	5	248
Nov.	974	33	20	37	13	88	60	30	101	1	3	50	0	SW	72	3	263
Dec.	974	33	17	38	10	80	38	8	35	0	0.8	27	0	SW	77	2	258
Annual	974	32	21	41	10	83	58	1,237	1,972	927	92	152	2	—	61	5	2,750
Rec. (yrs.)	7	14	14	18	18	8	8	28	38	38	17	15	7	7	7	9	6

TABLE XXV

CLIMATIC TABLE FOR NATITINGOU, DAHOMEY
Latitude 10°16'N, longitude 1°20'E, elevation 460 m

Month	M.S.L. press. (mbar)	Temperature (°C) mean max.	mean min.	extreme max.	extreme min.	Relative humid. (%) 06h00	12h00	Precipitation mean (mm)	max. (mm)	min. (mm)	days ≥1 mm	max. 24 h (mm)	Wind av. speed (km/h)	preval. direct.	calm (%)	Aver. cloudiness (oktas)
Jan.	1,010	34	19	39	13	36	22	3	35	0	0.3	15	6	ENE	25	2
Feb.	1,009	36	20	42	15	41	25	8	75	0	0.5	17	7	ENE	34	3
Mar.	1,008	37	23	45	15	62	35	26	106	0	3	42	8	ENE	35	4
Apr.	1,008	35	23	43	17	81	50	75	231	8	6	50	9	E, WSW	34	5
May	1,010	33	22	41	17	90	61	126	309	38	10	89	6	WSW	45	6
June	1,011	31	21	38	17	94	69	162	332	76	12	86	5	WSW	53	6
July	1,013	28	21	40	16	96	76	221	420	42	14	110	5	SW	52	7
Aug.	1,012	28	21	34	18	96	78	254	476	120	15	85	5	SW, E	60	7
Sept.	1,011	29	20	35	17	96	72	311	497	170	18	105	6	SW, E	51	6
Oct.	1,011	31	20	37	15	94	61	118	272	5	10	66	5	E, NW	57	5
Nov.	1,010	33	19	37	14	75	37	33	127	0	3	59	3	ENE	57	4
Dec.	1,010	34	19	38	14	42	22	5	62	0	0.3	28	4	NE	52	3
Annual	1,010	32	21	45	13	75	51	1,340	1,898	1,023	92	110	6	—	47	5
Rec. (yrs.)	30	14	14	16	16	10	10	30	34	34	15	15				10

TABLE XXVI

CLIMATIC TABLE FOR MAMOU, GUINEA
Latitude 10°22'N, longitude 12°04'W, elevation 730 m

Month	Mean sta. press. (mbar)	Temperature (°C) mean max.	mean min.	extreme max.	extreme min.	Relative humid. (%) 05h00	11h00	Precipitation mean (mm)	max. (mm)	min. (mm)	days ≥ 1 mm	max. 24 h (mm)	Wind av. speed (km/h)	preval. direct.	calm (%)	Aver. cloudiness (oktas)
Jan.	925	31	16	37	7	73	33	5	35	0	0.4	35	2	E	63	3
Feb.	924	33	18	38	8	70	30	8	54	0	1	32	3	E, W	54	3
Mar.	924	33	19	38	11	86	40	23	99	0	4	42	4	W	57	3
Apr.	924	32	21	38	12	89	54	101	225	10	9	93	4	W	49	4
May	925	29	21	37	15	93	65	180	408	27	12	170	3	W	56	6
June	926	27	19	32	15	96	75	236	567	82	19	71	3	W	49	6
July	927	26	19	31	16	97	82	301	495	165	22	125	3	SW	49	7
Aug.	926	25	19	33	15	98	87	439	668	249	25	108	3	SW	49	7
Sept.	926	26	19	33	16	98	78	368	647	101	21	125	2	SW	67	7
Oct.	926	27	19	31	15	97	72	234	488	102	18	59	2	VAR	71	6
Nov.	925	29	19	34	10	94	57	58	185	0	6	52	2	E	69	5
Dec.	925	30	16	34	8	80	37	10	74	0	1	37	2	ESE	63	3
Annual	925	29	19	38	7	89	59	1,963	2,579	1,798	138	170	3	—	58	5
Rec. (yrs.)	10	10	10	14	14	7	7	34	34	34	15	15	8	8	8	10

TABLE XXVII

CLIMATIC TABLE FOR KOUROUSSA, GUINEA
Latitude 10°39′N, longitude 9°15′W, elevation 372 m

Month	Mean sta. press.[1] (mbar)	Temperature (°C) mean max.	mean min.	extreme max.	extreme min.	Relative humid. (%) 06h00	12h00	Precipitation mean (mm)	max. (mm)	min. (mm)	days ≥ 1 mm	max. 24 h (mm)	Wind av. speed (km/h)	preval. direct.	calm (%)	Aver. cloudiness (oktas)
Jan.	970	33	14	41	6	70	19	<1	68	0	0.6	1.5	5	ENE	49	2
Feb.	969	35	16	43	7	70	24	5	63	0	0.3	41	6	ENE	45	2
Mar.	967	38	20	42	10	72	34	20	72	0	2	32	7	ENE	29	3
Apr.	968	37	21	42	10	78	42	63	178	1	5	63	7	WSW	34	4
May	969	35	21	41	10	85	55	95	218	21	8	93	6	SW	42	5
June	971	31	20	39	10	91	67	205	364	65	14	116	7	WSW	44	5
July	972	31	20	39	7	94	71	264	493	69	15	119	7	SW	25	6
Aug.	971	30	20	38	11	95	73	331	598	129	17	124	6	SW	35	6
Sept.	971	31	20	37	14	95	71	339	518	121	17	137	4	SW	55	6
Oct.	970	32	20	39	11	94	64	152	417	39	12	104	4	VAR	62	5
Nov.	969	34	18	40	7	94	46	25	176	0	3	43	3	ENE	68	4
Dec.	970	33	14	40	4	88	31	5	78	0	0.4	78	4	ENE	60	3
Annual	970	33	18	43	4	86	50	1,506	2,043	944	94	137	5	—	46	4
Rec. (yrs.)	10	14	14	12	12	5	5	27	47	47	15	17	7	7	7	9

[1] Mean of 08h00, 13h00 and 18h00.

TABLE XXVIII

CLIMATIC TABLE FOR TEIXEIRA DE SOUSA, ANGOLA
Latitude 10°43′S, longitude 22°15′E, elevation 1,100 m

Month	Temperature (°C)				Relative humid.[1] (%)	Precipitation			Aver. cloud-iness[1] (oktas)
	mean		extreme			mean (mm)	days ⩾ 1 mm	max. 24 h (mm)	
	max.	min.	max.	min.					
Jan.	30	17	35	10	77	228	15	112	5
Feb.	30	17	36	10	77	218	14	97	5
Mar.	30	17	37	10	76	236	15	80	4
Apr.	30	16	35	9	69	112	10	58	3
May	31	14	35	4	54	11	1	50	2
June	29	11	35	2	44	0	0	0	1
July	30	11	33	4	42	<1	0	3	1
Aug.	32	14	36	5	38	4	0	26	1
Sept.	33	16	38	5	47	24	3	50	2
Oct.	32	16	37	10	62	89	8	91	2
Nov.	31	16	39	10	72	181	14	68	4
Dec.	30	17	39	10	76	232	16	78	5
Annual	30	15	39	2	61	1,335	96	112	4
Rec. (yrs.)	21	21	21	21	20	20	20	20	20

[1] At 09h00.

Chapter 8

The Equatorial Wet Zone

F. BULTOT AND J. F. GRIFFITHS

Introduction

This zone, defined as those areas with less than three months receiving no more than 50 mm rainfall, is divided into two distinct portions. For convenience in presentation the first section will deal with the climate of the whole of the Congo Republic (although not all of the country is within this zone). The second section will be concerned with the isolated region around Liberia and the remainder of the central African area. This latter includes coastal Nigeria (Chapter 5), the southern Cameroons, Equatorial Guinea and small portions of the extreme north of Gabon and the Republic of the Congo. In this zone the length of the dry season is generally insufficient for vegetation to be put under a severe moisture stress and luxuriant vegetation results.

The Congo

The factors of climate

Latitude

The territory of the Congo extends approximately between 5°N and 13°S; three quarters of the area, however, is located between 5°N and 8°S (Fig.1). The Congo Republic has an area of more than 2.25 million km² and a population in excess of 14 million. The capital, Kinshasa (Leopoldville), has 400,000 inhabitants, twice that of the next largest city, Lubumbashi. The most important economic crops are palm kernels and oil, peanuts, rubber and cotton, but these are secondary to the mining of copper, manganese, gold, zinc, diamond and tin.

The proximity of the equator has two important consequences from the point of view of climatology. Firstly, the total radiation balance at ground level reaches a high value throughout the year; and secondly, these regions are situated in the equatorial zone of low pressure and small pressure variation, a situa tionfavourable to the stagnation of air masses.

A large part of the heat energy available is used in the form of latent heat for evaporation from the soil or water and strong evapotranspiration from the luxuriant vegetation which covers these regions. The balance is diffused by turbulence in the lower layers of the atmosphere. This results in an important vertical flux of water vapour and sensible heat

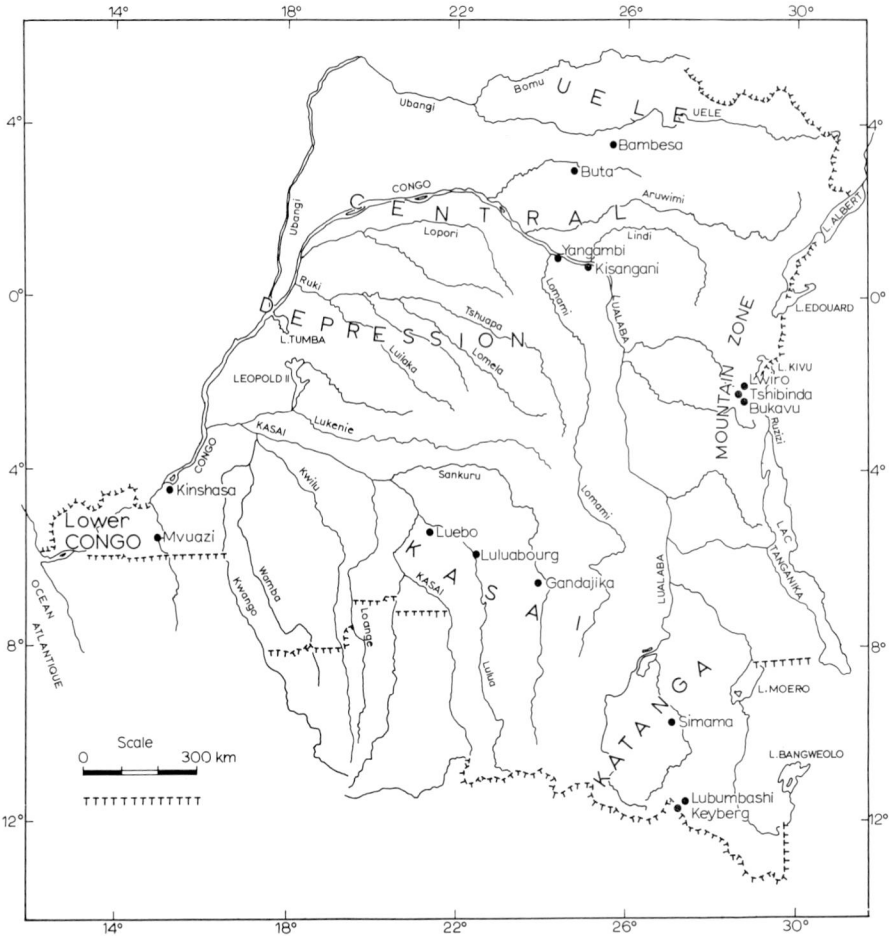

Fig.1. Stations and principal regions, Congo.

favouring convective instability of the air mass. In the midst of this mass of stagnant and unstable air there develop cloud formations of large vertical extent, giving rise to storm showers. They, on their part, supply the necessary moisture for evaporation. It follows that the regions now being considered have a hot, humid climate with frequent precipitation during most of the year.

The general circulation

On one side, the two sub-tropical anticyclones bring prevailing currents from the east to the middle and upper layers of the African equatorial regions (RIEHL, 1954; TSCHIRHART, 1959; QUOIDBACH and GOLBERT, 1969). On the other hand, the thermal contrast from ocean to continent produces, by the monsoon effect, a flow of humid air with a westerly component stemming from the anticyclonic centre of the south Atlantic. This humid air occupies the lower layers through a varying depth, but less than 2,000 m. It can extend far towards the east, even as far as the 30th meridian, that is to say, as far as the foot of the large mountain chain of the eastern Congo (height of more than 3,000 m) where its presence constitutes an obstacle to the direct invasion towards the west of the easterly currents in the lower layers of the atmosphere.

Where these high currents, always relatively dry (even when they make the long path over the Indian Ocean), are sufficiently diminished, the vertical structure of the atmosphere can produce the conditions required (absence of shear) for convective clouds to be formed during the warm hours of the day, while pronounced vertical development can produce precipitation. In the Congo the rains are then, in general, the convective type.

During the northern winter, the Saharan anticyclone is reinforced and directs towards the equatorial regions, both at ground level and in the free atmosphere, hot and dry northeasterly winds of directly continental origin. These winds impede the development of clouds and thereby give rise to a total cessation of precipitation in the northern part of the Congo. During the southern winter it is the South African anticyclone that strengthens and directs towards the equator dry and warm southeasterly winds causing the end of precipitation in Katanga, Kasai and the lower Congo (Fig.1).

The different regions of the Congo, except for the central basin, therefore experience a dry season as pronounced as those that are felt in regions further away from the equator. In Table I, mean dates of the beginning and end of the dry season are given together with the average duration for some stations considered representative of the principal climatic zones. These means are derived from a study of the period 1930–1959.

TABLE I

MEAN DATE OF START OF WET AND DRY SEASONS AND THE DURATION OF THE DRY SEASON (1930–1959)

Regions	Start of dry season	Start of wet season	Duration of dry season (days)
Uele (Bambesa)	9 December	8 February	61
Lower Congo (Kinshasa)	24 May	22 September	121
Kasai (Gandajika)	9 May	28 August	111
Katanga (Lubumbashi)	20 April	22 October	185
Mountain zone (Tshibinda)	17 June	27 August	71

If one now examines the fluctuations of the general circulation on an over-all scale it is possible to note that the centres of storms frequently appear in the zone of convergence of the two air masses (equatorial and Indian), in particular when this region is moving rapidly towards the east (TSCHIRHART, 1959). Moreover, one can observe displacements from west to east of the cloud system[1] as well as the large rainy zone (BULTOT, 1952).

The quasi-stationary zonal perturbations can also be spawned at the northern and southern limits of the equatorial Atlantic air mass when there is convergence in the lower layers (TSCHIRHART, 1959). These perturbations have a less marked daily evolution and give rise to rains of long duration.

There are, though, some currents with a strong meridional component which bring the cyclonic cells and as they approach the equator these fill up rapidly, thus increasing the instability and starting intense precipitation, sometimes accompanying cyclonic eddies of small size that are particularly violent (African tornadoes) (TSCHIRHART, 1959).

---

[1] A remark by W. Schuepp based on an interpretation of infrared radiation photographs (8–12 μ) from TIROS IV.

Finally one sees sometimes in regions near to the Atlantic coast perturbations accompanying rainfall of long duration which is produced during the night and the morning. These phenomena are present when a zone of high pressure in the Gulf of Guinea moves towards the interior of the land, starting in the northwest with hot and humid air that expands on rising over the chilled air of the continent (TSCHIRHART, 1959). Moreover it is only in the lower Congo that one can often observe fairly abundant precipitation at night and during the morning (BULTOT, 1956).

In summary, rainfall, even if of an essentially convective origin, is not distributed in a random manner in space or time. Except for certain days on which one only observes some precipitation scattered over the immense territory of the Congo, rains are generally concentrated each day in a zone of limited extent (BULTOT, 1954). In addition they are not necessarily found during the warmest period of the day. The rains in the interior of a "rainy" zone, are present as local showers of greater or less intensity (the density of rainfall stations recording rain is often less than 70%). On the other hand, the proportion of stations receiving precipitation in the centre of a rainy zone is not decided entirely by chance; the greater the percentage is, the greater the amount of rain noted by each station. It depends therefore on the convective activity of the air.

The components of the radiation balance

Short wave global radiation

In the central Congo Basin the global short wave radiation has an annual mean of approximately 410 cal./cm² day. The interannual variability of this parameter is extremely small; for instance, during the period 1955–1959 the values observed ranged only between 407 in 1959 and 413 in 1957. The annual regime of the short wave global radiation is determined by solar movement and cloud. It presents two maxima and two minima (see Table II). The principal maximum is found in March (454 cal./cm² day), the secondary maximum in November (422 cal./cm² day); the principal minimum is found in July (345 cal./cm² day), the secondary minimum in December (373 cal./cm² day). The interdiurnal variability of solar global radiation can be very high and a representative selection of maximum and minimum values is given in Table II. These important fluctuations can happen from one day to another resulting from rapid changes in the cloud and atmospheric turbidity.

It is in the lower Congo Basin that the solar global radiation is the least (387 cal./cm² day for mean annual value) and in Katanga it has the highest value (481 cal./cm² day). In the former region the cloud amount is very high throughout the year even in the dry season (see Table IV). In the latter, by comparison, the solar global radiation is increased very greatly during the dry season, there being very little cloud at this time (see Table IV). The annual regime appears, moreover, to be of the tropical type.

It is also observed that the mean annual deviation differs markedly from one region to the next (respectively 95 and 142 cal./cm² day) in the mountain region and in Katanga.

The diffuse solar radiation

In the Congo the heat component of the solar diffuse radiation is often larger than that

TABLE II

MONTHLY AND ANNUAL MEANS AND EXTREME VALUES OF GLOBAL RADIATION AND DIFFUSE RADIATION (cal./cm² day)

Regions		Jan.	Feb.	Mar.	Apr.	May	June	July	Aug.	Sept.	Oct.	Nov.	Dec.	Year
Global radiation (G)														
Central basin	mean	411	447	454	446	441	391	345	363	409	412	422	373	410
(Yangambi)	max.	563	658	656	638	617	557	516	560	652	638	623	576	658
1956–1959	min.	78	61	121	108	72	157	99	91	92	78	101	37	37
Lower Congo	mean	385	427	448	445	374	332	319	364	375	381	418	380	387
(Kinshasa)	max.	598	651	630	656	579	520	505	580	599	598	635	628	656
1954–1960	min.	121	106	91	114	108	70	96	76	75	107	55	54	54
Katanga	mean	451	413	449	465	480	468	477	523	555	554	493	445	481
(Lubumbashi)	max.	733	713	686	650	589	551	567	634	702	720	708	651	733
1955–1959	min.	173	141	195	194	92	281	327	297	258	255	105	196	92
Mountain zone	mean	442	452	492	463	399	397	404	421	481	454	484	465	446
(Lwiro)	max.	691	718	704	690	656	605	580	641	665	676	666	680	718
1956–1959	min.	152	117	110	193	186	126	116	101	213	148	225	209	101
Diffuse radiation (D)														
Central basin	mean	219	210	236	229	216	214	219	230	232	240	232	214	224
(Yangambi)	max.	302	315	364	366	337	295	316	349	354	352	308	296	366
1957–1959	min.	76	61	119	107	71	124	99	85	92	78	99	37	37
Lower Congo	mean	245	248	256	235	220	198	198	221	234	250	245	247	233
(Kinshasa)	max.	337	380	378	353	317	280	280	290	324	358	398	340	398
1954–1960	min.	116	107	92	107	107	70	96	76	75	108	55	54	54
Katanga	mean	252	247	234	181	115	103	96	119	155	189	207	255	179
(Lubumbashi)	max.	363	355	345	318	288	220	201	207	333	334	354	342	363
1955–1959	min.	124	129	103	67	45	56	58	60	78	102	86	144	45
Mountain zone	mean	238	245	234	232	225	188	195	213	220	238	240	243	226
(Lwiro)	max.	354	358	334	331	339	333	266	325	384	347	362	350	384
1956–1959	min.	80	115	93	106	95	105	104	98	127	116	110	109	80

due to the direct solar radiation (see Table II) especially during the mornings (DUPRIEZ, 1964; BULTOT, 1969). In the central basin the diffuse solar radiation reaches, in fact, 55% of the global solar radiation; in the lower Congo, 60%. In Katanga it reaches 50% in the wet season but then reduces to about 20% in July, that is to say, during the middle of the dry season. In the mountain zone these percentages are almost equal.

The balance of terrestrial radiation

The balance of terrestrial radiation (the upward flux minus the downward flux of long wave radiation) is relatively small during the course of the wet months because of the greenhouse effect which results from a strong absorption of water vapour and CO_2 in the atmosphere and also because of the relatively high temperature at the base of the cloud. The balance is about 90–120 cal./cm² day on the average (see Table III; BULTOT, 1969). In the dry season it increases considerably and can reach 190 cal./cm² day in Kasai and

TABLE III

MONTHLY AND ANNUAL MEANS OF GLOBAL RADIATION (G), TERRESTRIAL RADIATION BALANCE (N) AND TOTAL RADIATION BALANCE (B) OVER A COVER OF *Paspalum notatum* (cal./cm² day)

Regions		Jan.	Feb.	Mar.	Apr.	May	June	July	Aug.	Sept.	Oct.	Nov.	Dec.	Year
Central basin	G	411	447	454	446	441	391	345	363	409	412	422	373	410
(Yangambi)	N	108	113	102	98	99	98	97	96	98	98	97	97	100
1957–1959	B	208	231	248	245	241	203	169	184	217	219	228	190	215
Uele	G	440	475	464	468	470	427	384	422	466	458	465	441	448
(Bambesa)	N	129	134	105	100	99	102	99	97	102	103	100	114	107
1957–1959	B	210	232	252	260	263	227	197	228	257	250	258	226	238
Lower Congo	G	385	427	448	445	374	332	319	364	375	381	418	380	387
(Kinshasa)	N	91	93	91	96	90	103	110	116	107	96	92	90	98
1954–1960	B	205	236	254	247	198	153	132	161	178	194	230	203	199
Kasai	G	422	432	469	492	485	428	418	399	431	453	470	462	447
(Gandajika)	N	105	106	108	111	142	179	187	138	119	114	109	105	127
1957–1959	B	220	227	253	268	231	146	131	165	209	235	253	251	216
Katanga	G	451	413	449	465	480	468	477	523	555	554	493	445	481
(Lubumbashi)	N	105	106	116	142	176	199	218	226	215	199	125	107	161
1955–1959	B	242	212	230	216	189	157	145	171	207	222	250	236	206
Mountain zone	G	442	452	492	463	399	397	404	421	481	454	484	465	446
(Lwiro)	N	127	125	126	124	122	135	153	149	141	128	126	124	132
1956–1959	B	213	223	253	233	185	171	158	175	229	222	247	234	212

225 cal./cm² day in Katanga. In the mountain region to the east the mean monthly balance of terrestrial radiation is approximately constant at 120 cal./cm² day even in the rainy season, the greenhouse effect being less pronounced.

The balance of total radiation

The mean monthly values of the daily balance of total radiation over the surface of a stratum of *Paspalum notatum* (the lawn of the climatological station) is measured as being between 169 and 248 cal./cm² day in the central basin, 132–254 cal./cm² day in the lower Congo, 145–250 cal./cm² day in Katanga and 158–253 cal./cm² day in the mountain zone of the east (Table III). The monthly means of the daily total radiation balance vary relatively little in time and distance and this is in spite of the variation between the wet and dry seasons. Note that in the regions with a long and pronounced dry season the loss of terrestrial radiation energy is augmented at the same time by the solar global radiation and in such a proportion that the total radiation balance is even smaller in the course of the dry months than in the course of the wet months.

In the diurnal variation the balance of the total radiation follows a curve very similar to that of the solar global radiation (DUPRIEZ, 1964). It shows a maximum between 12h00 and 13h00 (true solar time) and reaches zero about 30 min after sunrise and 45 min before sunset. The cover of *Paspalum notatum* has an albedo of 0.23 (0.24 during the course of the dry months). The equatorial forest has an albedo of 0.13; the savanna of 0.18 in the wet season and 0.23 in the dry season (BULTOT, 1962).

As noted in the first paragraph, a large part of the total radiation balance is used up in the form of latent heat of vaporization. In the central basin, for instance, the evapo-transpiration actually consumes 80% of the available calories; in the lower Congo 85–90% in the wet season and 50–60% in the course of the dry season (July–September); in Katanga 80% in the wet season, 65–50% in the course of two months of the dry season (May–June) and 40–25% during the following four dry months (July–October). As the heat exchange between the air and the soil is very small on a scale of months (the temperature of the soil varies little from one month to the next), we can consider that the heat balance available is diffused into the air by turbulence.

Sunshine

In the central basin the mean monthly percentage of possible sunshine hours is between 35 and 55% (Table IV). In the lower Congo it reaches the least value, for even in the dry season the amount of sunshine remains very low. At this time the lower stable layer of relatively cool air from the Atlantic is generally surmounted by a dry and subsiding air mass. The thermal inversion which follows is propitious for the maintenance of strato-cumulus at the upper limit of the humid layer (1,500 m). In Katanga the mean monthly percentage possible sunshine is, in the rainy season, very much smaller than that in the central basin. We note that at this time, the rainfall is more abundant in Katanga than in the vicinity of the equator. In the dry season, in contrast, the mean monthly percentage of possible radiation exceeds 80%. In the mountain zone the mean monthly values are generally between 47 and 60%.

TABLE IV

MONTHLY AND ANNUAL MEANS OF SUNSHINE HOURS (PERCENTAGE OF POSSIBLE)

Regions	Jan.	Feb.	Mar.	Apr.	May	June	July	Aug.	Sept.	Oct.	Nov.	Dec.	Year
Central basin (Yangambi; 1950–1959)	55	56	50	50	49	45	41	36	42	42	45	47	47
Uele (Bambesa; 1950–1959)	63	65	52	50	54	48	43	38	48	50	56	61	52
Lower Congo (Kinshasa; 1951–1959)	35	39	40	46	38	39	34	39	36	35	38	35	38
Kasai (Gandajika; 1954–1959)	40	42	48	55	70	81	76	62	51	53	49	41	55
Katanga (Lubumbashi; 1954–1959)	37	37	50	71	83	87	89	87	82	76	54	37	65
Mountain zone (Lwiro; 1952–1959)	50	47	51	50	48	53	60	56	54	49	51	50	52

TABLE V

RELATIVE FREQUENCIES (MONTHLY) OF SUNSHINE (PERCENTAGE OF POSSIBLE)

Regions	Sunshine (%)	Jan.	Feb.	Mar.	Apr.	May	June	July	Aug.	Sept.	Oct.	Nov.	Dec.
Central basin	0	3	3	2	4	1	0	5	2	3	3	1	6
(Yangambi)	1– 30	13	12	29	17	16	21	28	37	32	27	31	25
1956–1959	31– 60	45	28	29	40	36	38	39	37	40	46	37	40
	61– 90	39	57	38	39	35	35	28	24	25	24	31	29
	91–100	0	0	2	0	12	6	0	0	0	0	0	0
Lower Congo	0	3	4	3	1	3	3	8	5	4	4	4	3
(Kinshasa)	1– 30	41	35	32	24	35	35	38	31	39	42	35	39
1951–1959	31– 60	40	38	37	46	42	38	30	34	36	38	32	42
	61– 90	15	23	28	29	19	24	24	30	21	16	19	16
	91–100	1	0	0	0	1	0	0	0	0	0	0	0
Katanga	0	0	2	0	0	1	0	0	0	0	0	1	1
(Lubumbashi)	1– 30	51	55	37	17	5	1	0	0	3	8	28	54
1954–1959	31– 60	33	35	39	24	15	3	2	1	6	17	28	35
	61– 90	15	8	23	49	45	49	47	52	77	69	36	10
	91–100	1	0	1	10	34	47	51	47	14	6	7	0
Mountain zone	0	0	1	2	0	2	0	2	2	0	0	0	1
(Lwiro)	1– 30	27	29	21	18	31	23	17	13	11	28	14	26
1956–1959	31– 60	45	35	32	47	43	35	29	35	37	38	55	44
	61– 90	26	32	43	34	23	39	46	45	51	34	31	28
	91–100	2	3	2	1	1	3	6	5	1	0	0	1

Table V shows that it is rare for the sky to be completely covered for the entire day. The maximum frequency of cloudy skies is found to be in July in the lower Congo, that is in the dry season, but even then the value is only 8%. In the same way it is rare to experience a completely clear sky for the entire day except in Katanga during the dry season.

Atmospheric turbidity and the spectral distribution of solar radiation

The turbidity of the atmosphere is generally high in the Congo because of the intense thermal convection; this gives a large depletion of the solar radiation.

In the central basin, for example, the extinction coefficient (α') of aerosols is, on average, from 1.7 to 1.8; the mean depth of precipitable water (w) is 4.8–5.4 cm (BULTOT, 1969).[1] In 33% of the cases the intensity of the solar radiation is less than 1 cal./cm² min (mean 0.89 cal./cm² min); in 45%, it lies between 1 and 1.2 cal./cm² min (mean 1.11 cal./cm² min); in 22% of the cases it is greater than 1.2 cal./cm² min (mean 1.25 cal./cm² min). For the three cases the coefficient of turbidity ($10^3 B'$) of Schuepp averages respectively 292, 169, and 82.

---

[1] The coefficient of turbidity B', the depletion α' of aerosols and the quantity of precipitable water w have been determined by the method of SCHUEPP (1953, 1956, 1959). The values of B' and α' are corrected to a vertical incidence of solar radiation and are therefore independent of the height of the sun. A constant correction has been applied in order to take account of the absorption by ozone of a thickness that has been estimated at some 1.6–1.7 mm.

The long wave radiation between 0.3 and 0.525 μ (blue and violet) has an intensity between 18 and 24% of the total; between 0.52 and 0.71 μ (yellow and red), from 26 to 27%; and above 0.71 μ (infrared) from 56 to 49%.[1]

In the lower Congo, values similar to those given have been observed in the rainy season. In contrast, in the dry season, the intensity of solar radiation falls below 1 cal./cm² min in 84% of the cases (mean 0.8 cal./cm² min). The coefficient of turbidity reaches then a value of 365 ($\alpha' = 1.6$ and $w = 3.1$ cm), whilst the intensity of the radiation in the various wave bands is respectively 14, 25, and 61% of the total intensity. In the dry season the infrared is increased to the detriment of the "blue–violet" radiation. It is seen, nevertheless, that due to the proximity to the ocean, the atmospheric conditions that prevail in the dry season in the lower Congo are very different from those which prevail in the dry season in other regions. For the latter, unfortunately, there are no data concerning the atmospheric turbidity and the spectral distribution of the solar radiation.

The components of the water balance

Rainfall

The amount of rain as well as the period of precipitation varies greatly from one region to another (Table VI). Over the major proportion of the country the amount of rainfall received during the year is, on the average, between 1,000 and 2,000 mm. Only the coast zone and the valleys of Rwindi and Ruzizi (in the eastern mountain region) record less than 1,000 mm whilst the sector situated immediately to the west of the central mountains of the Congo receives between 2,000 and 2,500 mm annually (BULTOT, 1969). The mean rainfall of the Congo is, therefore, relatively low compared with the values that one observes in many other equatorial regions. This results in the high degree of the continentality of the Congo Basin.

The mean monthly rainfall values are generally less than 250 mm everywhere, except in Katanga during the period December to February where they are slightly in excess of this value.

The annual rainfall regime is linked to seasonal changes in the general atmospheric circulation. Short period fluctuations of the general circulation are the causes of the relatively high variability which characterizes the rainfall (see Table VI). In the central basin, for example, one can see that on average once in ten times the annual rainfall is less than 1,535 mm; whilst once in ten it is greater than 2,110 mm. In the lower Congo it is less than 1,170 mm one year in ten and greater than 1,655 mm one year in ten. The ten and ninety percentiles of monthly mean rainfall values are even more extreme. In addition it is seen from Table VI that the extreme values observed during the period 1930–1959 deviate even more from the mean than these decennial thresholds.

The dry season, defined as a succession of days without precipitation (or with almost no precipitation), comes roughly at the same period during each year, with a mean duration of the order of 180 days in Katanga, 120 days in the lower Congo, 110 days in Kasai, 70 days in the mountain region, and 60 days in the Uele (see Table I). In the three former

---

[1] The intensity of the solar radiation as a function of the wavelength has been measured with the Michelson actinometer with Schott filters OG 1, RG 2, and RG 8.

TABLE VI

MONTHLY AND ANNUAL VALUES OF PRECIPITATION (1930–1959), MEANS, 10 AND 90 PERCENTILES AND EXTREMES (mm)

Regions		Jan.	Feb.	Mar.	Apr.	May	June	July	Aug.	Sept.	Oct.	Nov.	Dec.	Year
Central basin	min.	17.6	33.6	57.8	37.4	85.0	24.5	43.0	55.1	79.2	113.3	54.0	0.0	1,220.0
(Yangambi)	P_{10}	30.4	49.3	76.6	57.0	93.5	44.5	81.5	100.7	93.0	147.1	108.4	42.5	1,535.0
	mean	85.0	98.8	148.1	149.8	177.2	126.9	146.3	169.5	180.4	240.7	179.6	126.1	1,828.4
	P_{90}	151.0	157.5	274.1	229.2	297.2	183.7	229.7	273.9	302.6	327.8	260.0	192.4	2,110.0
	max.	228.7	187.9	361.9	264.0	341.7	341.9	265.8	291.4	318.5	381.1	317.3	217.0	2,629.0
Uele	min.	0.5	0.6	48.0	61.8	114.7	86.3	87.0	93.4	85.9	121.6	44.8	1.9	1,442.0
(Bambesa)	P_{10}	3.6	17.8	62.0	121.9	116.9	95.8	92.2	104.2	109.6	135.1	56.7	5.2	1,575.0
	mean	33.8	72.9	134.9	199.1	201.3	151.6	183.9	204.7	209.4	220.3	127.8	41.6	1,780.7
	P_{90}	68.5	168.9	210.5	256.2	298.4	235.2	260.7	298.4	308.3	283.2	199.1	83.5	2,097.0
	max.	75.2	210.6	299.6	323.6	324.5	255.1	297.5	381.6	380.9	358.3	243.4	111.2	2,396.0
Lower Congo	min.	1.7	48.6	58.0	58.9	22.2	0.0	0.0	0.0	1.6	19.5	84.3	47.4	1,124.0
(Kinshasa)	P_{10}	32.9	67.0	79.6	112.4	42.7	0.0	0.0	0.0	5.0	52.6	135.0	101.3	1,170.0
	mean	127.5	139.4	180.5	208.6	133.5	4.9	1.0	3.5	32.0	136.5	235.5	170.5	1,374.5
	P_{90}	227.1	234.2	317.3	326.9	217.8	22.7	1.1	17.8	76.3	206.8	334.8	275.8	1,655.0
	max.	320.6	329.8	428.9	378.6	280.0	37.6	34.0	24.4	100.4	281.6	347.7	326.6	1,824.0
Kasai	min.	32.0	26.4	52.3	71.7	0.0	0.0	0.0	0.0	40.5	29.2	99.0	109.0	1,155.0
(Gandajika)	P_{10}	73.1	51.8	93.2	87.9	2.4	0.0	0.0	4.2	51.2	73.5	122.5	123.5	1,178.0
	mean	157.2	131.2	181.4	173.5	50.8	3.6	5.7	34.8	100.1	139.2	200.4	217.0	1,394.9
	P_{90}	267.2	212.3	293.8	297.3	135.3	15.2	27.1	78.9	190.7	225.2	279.6	310.4	1,658.0
	max.	288.4	240.6	412.0	369.1	140.1	25.0	55.0	93.5	236.7	258.0	446.8	377.6	1,916.0
Katanga	min.	148.8	129.9	88.7	9.0	0.0	0.0	0.0	0.0	0.0	0.0	43.4	112.8	868.0
(Lubumbashi)	P_{10}	190.6	180.9	108.9	16.0	0.0	0.0	0.0	0.0	0.0	0.0	73.4	163.4	1,034.0
	mean	256.3	263.8	209.7	52.8	3.2	0.0	0.0	0.0	2.5	26.8	165.7	262.1	1,243.5
	P_{90}	391.1	362.9	328.3	113.0	11.6	0.0	0.0	0.0	15.7	58.4	290.1	364.9	1,512.0
	max.	471.7	421.5	378.4	155.2	40.9	3.6	0.0	14.5	30.8	71.5	395.9	479.3	1,554.0
Mountain zone	min.	51.5	50.2	112.6	121.5	61.4	0.0	0.0	0.0	32.5	98.6	92.4	33.4	1,352.0
(Tshibinda)	P_{10}	88.0	90.7	113.5	132.0	81.1	8.8	0.0	11.0	68.5	108.9	109.1	119.8	1,432.0
	mean	164.7	175.4	194.5	214.6	163.9	55.7	34.2	56.7	144.8	214.4	201.3	212.8	1,833.0
	P_{90}	250.8	303.9	277.9	325.3	270.1	95.4	74.1	110.0	232.2	309.6	332.8	332.6	2,165.0
	max.	301.1	354.2	311.0	364.1	295.4	111.6	169.6	165.4	251.8	424.3	398.4	358.0	2,306.0

regions the duration of the dry season varies relatively little from one year to the next; the interdecile interval is approximately of 30 to 40 days (see Table VII). At Bambesa and at Tshibinda, that is in the zone nearest to the equator, the influence of dry air masses coming from the Saharan and South African anticyclones is diminished and is very variable from one year to the next. It is for this reason that the length of the dry season is extremely variable; the interdecile interval is 52 days at Bambesa and 48 days at Tshibinda.

In Katanga the dry season begins, in eight cases out of ten, between the 8th of April and the 4th of May; it ends between the 9th of October and the 4th of November. In contrast, in Uele, it begins, in eight cases out of ten, between the 23rd of November and the 23rd of December, and ends between the 15th of January and the 4th of March. From one

TABLE VII

DATE OF START OF DRY AND WET SEASONS AND DURATION OF DRY SEASON (DAYS) (10TH AND 90TH PERCENTILES AND EXTREMES), 1930–1959

Regions	Start of dry season		Start of wet season		Length of dry season		Start of dry season (extremes)		Start of wet season (extremes)		Length of dry season (extremes)	
	P_{10}	P_{90}	P_{10}	P_{90}	P_{10}	P_{90}						
Uele (Bambesa)	23/11	23/12	15/1	4/3	36	88	21/11	6/1	1/1	10/3	23	103
Lower Congo (Kinshasa)	15/5	2/6	5/9	9/10	103	139	9/5	5/6	26/8	12/10	90	147
Kasai (Gandajika)	26/4	22/5	14/8	11/9	92	130	23/4	28/5	3/8	18/9	81	141
Katanga (Lubumbashi)	8/4	4/5	9/10	4/11	167	201	30/3	7/5	3/10	12/11	159	215
Mountain zone (Tshibinda)	29/5	4/7	13/8	10/9	48	96	16/5	25/7	3/8	19/9	35	106

year to the next the dates of commencement of the dry and wet seasons deviate very little from their mean values.

The movement, respectively towards the equator and towards the tropics, of the demarcation line between the dry and wet zones is essentially discontinuous. These discontinuities are linked to the short period fluctuations of the atmospheric circulation (BULTOT, 1954). It is as well to note here that in the vicinity of the ground surface the temperature and the humidity of the air do not show rapid changes when passing from the dry season to the wet season and vice versa (BULTOT, 1954).

The number of wet days (more than 0.1 mm) is greatest in the mountain region (185 days/year) and least in the lower Congo (107 days/year) (see Table VIII). Nevertheless it is in Katanga, during the rainy season, that the rainfall is most frequent (about 8 days out of 10).

In contrast, it is in the lower Congo that the maximum daily rainfall reaches the highest value, and in the mountain zone it is the lowest (see Table IX). In the lower Congo the one in ten year daily rainfall is 117 mm and in 50 years 143 mm. In the mountain region the corresponding values are respectively 91 mm and 112 mm.

It is likewise in the lower Congo and the central basin that the rainfall intensity is maximal (see Table X) (PIRE et al., 1960). The value decreases when one gets further from the equator and is minimal in the high regions of the territory towards the east. Notice especially that in the lower Congo and in the central basin rainfall intensities of 30 mm in 10 min, 60 mm in 30 min, and 90 mm in 90 min can be exceeded on average once in ten years.

Generally the rainfall intensity varies during the shower. It is maximal during intervals of 5–10 or 10–15 min. This fact is less accentuated in the night-time showers than those

TABLE VIII

MEAN NUMBER OF RAIN DAYS ($\geqslant$0.1 mm), MONTHLY AND ANNUAL, 1930–1959

Regions	Jan.	Feb.	Mar.	Apr.	May	June	July	Aug.	Sept.	Oct.	Nov.	Dec.	Year
Central basin (Yangambi)	7.9	8.4	12.9	13.7	14.1	11.3	12.8	13.2	15.1	17.9	16.4	12.1	155.8
Uele (Bambesa)	4.6	7.0	12.8	16.0	16.9	16.5	16.6	18.4	17.7	20.3	13.3	6.4	166.5
Lower Congo (Kinshasa)	10.1	10.2	12.8	15.4	10.7	0.9	0.2	0.7	4.4	11.2	16.0	14.2	106.8
Kasai (Gandajika)	13.8	12.7	15.1	14.3	5.4	0.6	1.0	3.9	9.0	11.8	15.4	16.6	119.6
Katanga (Lubumbashi)	23.7	23.1	21.0	9.3	1.6	0.0	0.0	0.1	0.6	4.9	16.6	24.1	125.0
Mountain zone (Tshibinda)	17.3	17.0	18.4	20.6	16.8	7.4	4.3	6.7	14.9	19.4	20.6	19.5	182.9

TABLE IX

MAXIMUM PROBABLE DAILY RAINFALL (mm)

Regions	10 years*	25 years	50 years
Central basin (Yangambi)	110	126	138
Uele (Bambesa)	98	109	117
Lower Congo (Kinshasa)	117	132	143
Kasai (Luebo)	111	126	138
Katanga (Lubumbashi)	102	117	128
Mountain zone (Tshibinda)	91	103	112

* Daily rainfall amount exceeded once, on average, in 10 years.

of the afternoon. After the first 45–60 min the rainfall intensity stabilizes usually to an amount of less than 0.4 mm in 5 min (BULTOT, 1956).

The duration of showers varies noticeably from one region to the other. In general, however, the rain showers in the afternoon are shorter than those of the evening, for reasons given earlier (BULTOT, 1956).

From the chemical point of view we find that the quantities of inorganic nitrogen brought to the soil by the rainfall vary with the degree of continentality; they are around 4 kg/ha year in the lower Congo, 6 in the central basin and as high as 11 in the eastern mountain region (DUPRIEZ and MEYER, 1959).

In 1958 the lower Congo, the central basin, and the mountain region of the east received respectively 1.4, 2.1 and 3 kg/ha year of potassium; 4.6, 3.9 and 4.1 kg/ha year of calcium; 0.9, 1.2 and 1.3 kg/ha year of magnesium. During 1958 the rainfall amounts in these three regions were 1,261, 1,584 and 1,364 mm respectively.

TABLE X

RAINFALL INTENSITY VALUES IN 10, 20 ... 90 MINUTES THAT ARE EXCEEDED, ON AVERAGE, ONCE IN 2 YEARS AND ONCE IN 10 YEARS (mm)

Regions	Years	10 min	20 min	30 min	40 min	50 min	60 min	70 min	80 min	90 min
Central basin	2	24.1	37.9	47.0	55.0	61.9	64.3	67.7	68.5	69.4
(Kisangani)	10	31.1	49.0	60.8	71.5	80.9	84.0	88.6	89.5	90.6
Uele	2	21.0	33.2	40.8	45.2	48.5	51.0	52.8	53.9	55.3
(Irumu)	10	26.9	42.8	52.9	58.7	63.0	66.3	68.8	70.2	72.1
Lower Congo	2	23.3	37.5	46.5	56.2	62.0	66.1	67.3	69.5	69.8
(Kinshasa)	10	30.6	49.3	61.2	74.4	82.4	87.9	89.5	92.5	92.7
Kasai	2	21.6	34.4	42.4	47.4	50.8	54.4	57.0	58.6	59.0
(Luluabourg)	10	27.9	44.4	54.9	61.5	65.9	70.7	74.1	76.1	76.5
Katanga	2	16.2	26.8	33.6	38.0	42.1	43.9	46.2	47.1	48.8
(Lubumbashi)	10	21.1	35.2	44.4	50.3	56.2	58.5	61.8	62.8	65.1
Mountain zone	2	17.1	25.1	29.1	31.4	33.6	36.4	37.3	38.2	38.4
(Bukavu)	10	22.1	32.4	37.6	40.6	43.6	47.7	49.0	50.1	50.3

Hail

To the west of the 23rd meridian there is, on average, less than one hail storm each year. Towards the east, in the region of the mountains (more precisely, in the vicinity of the 1,400-m contour) less than two showers of hail are noted annually. In the mountain region averages of from three to nine hail storms per year are noted, according to the local situation. In the volcanic region to the north of Lake Kivu the frequency is at a maximum (BULTOT, 1959).

Because of the generally high altitude of the level of freezing (BERRUEX, 1958) and the abundance of condensation nuclei, the hailstones do not grow very large; their diameter only rarely exceeds 13 mm. It is for this reason that, in the areas where the elevation is less than 800 mm, hailstones often melt during their fall and have little chance of reaching the ground (BULTOT, 1959).

Evaporation

Estimations of mean monthly potential evapotranspiration over a cover of *Paspalum notatum* (albedo of 0.23 or 0.24, depending upon the season) calculated by the energy balance method are given in Table XI (BULTOT, 1969). They generally lie between 60 and 120 mm. On the other hand, in the regions where there is a definite dry season the potential evapotranspiration is less during the dry months than during the rainy months because of the reduction of the radiation balance and in spite of the low humidity and increase in wind speed at this period. The annual potential evapotranspiration does not differ greatly from one region to the next (from about 1,100 to a little over 1,200 mm); the only exception is the humid high areas where a little less than 1,000 mm is recorded.

TABLE XI

MONTHLY AND ANNUAL MEANS OF POTENTIAL EVAPOTRANSPIRATION OF A COVER OF *Paspalum notatum* (mm)

Regions	Jan.	Feb.	Mar.	Apr.	May	June	July	Aug.	Sept.	Oct.	Nov.	Dec.	Year
Central basin (Yangambi)	90	96	107	103	101	87	72	80	90	94	96	79	1,095
Uele (Bambesa)	95	97	112	110	114	95	83	96	106	106	105	98	1,217
Lower Congo (Kinshasa)	97	97	118	112	89	70	62	73	97	96	101	98	1,110
Kasai (Gandajika)	100	94	114	116	113	78	72	90	103	110	110	111	1,211
Katanga (Lubumbashi)	109	87	106	104	91	75	75	90	98	111	114	101	1,161
Mountain zone (Tshibinda)	81	75	86	83	81	72	65	70	83	90	95	90	971

The potential evapotranspiration also varies little from one year to the next consequent upon the small changes in the factors which decide evapotranspiration (radiation balance, humidity, and wind).

The actual monthly evapotranspiration, which is dependent on rainfall that has a great variability, has been calculated separately for each of the years in the period of observation that is available. The median, and ten and ninety percentiles of the observed distribution of the monthly values are presented in Table XII.

TABLE XII

PERCENTILES (10, 90) AND MEDIANS OF MONTHLY VALUES OF ACTUAL EVAPOTRANSPIRATION (mm) OF A COVER OF *Paspalum notatum* (1930–1959)

Regions		Jan.	Feb.	Mar.	Apr.	May	June	July	Aug.	Sept.	Oct.	Nov.	Dec.	Year
Central basin	P_{10}	84	90	103	101	101	86	72	80	90	94	96	78	1,072
(Yangambi)	Med.	90	96	107	103	101	87	72	80	90	94	96	79	1,091
	P_{90}	90	96	107	103	101	87	72	80	90	94	96	79	1,095
Uele	P_{10}	65	58	84	110	114	95	83	96	106	106	102	85	1,122
(Bambesa)	Med.	80	89	112	110	114	95	83	96	106	106	105	92	1,176
	P_{90}	90	97	112	110	114	95	83	96	106	106	105	98	1,204
Lower Congo	P_{10}	79	95	111	112	82	45	28	26	32	61	101	98	932
(Kinshasa)	Med.	97	97	118	112	89	60	38	32	47	96	101	98	970
	P_{90}	97	97	118	112	89	64	43	44	83	96	101	98	1,025
Kasai	P_{10}	98	90	113	115	93	46	34	39	73	85	110	111	1,049
(Gandajika)	Med.	100	94	114	115	103	55	42	60	93	110	110	111	1,108
	P_{90}	100	94	114	116	113	70	55	85	103	110	110	111	1,149
Katanga	P_{10}	109	87	106	93	60	37	29	26	21	20	76	101	807
(Lubumbashi)	Med.	109	87	106	98	65	40	31	29	23	39	114	101	836
	P_{90}	109	87	106	104	80	50	39	36	35	60	114	101	896
Mountain zone	P_{10}	81	75	86	83	81	66	52	56	80	90	95	90	942
(Tshibinda)	Med.	81	75	86	83	81	72	61	68	83	90	95	90	962
	P_{90}	81	75	86	83	81	72	65	70	83	90	95	90	970

The actual evapotranspiration over a cover of *Paspalum notatum* was calculated by the method of Thornthwaite's water balance, taking into account the retention capacity of water in the soil. It has been shown that this retention generally lies between 200 and 300 mm (BULTOT, 1962). The result of these calculations is given in Table XII and the results show that everywhere in the wet season the actual evapotranspiration is, in eight cases of ten, equal to the potential evapotranspiration or very close to it. In spite of the great variation of rainfall the actual evapotranspiration varies little from one year to another. In contrast, in the dry season the actual evapotranspiration is considerably reduced. It is naturally limited by the quantity of rainfall and can, because of this reason, show important deviations from one year to another, particularly during the course of the transition months between the dry season and the rainy season. The annual median value of actual evapotranspiration of *Paspalum notatum* varies appreciably from one region to another (a little more than 800 mm in Katanga to a little less than 1,200 mm in Uele). It has been shown that the actual evapotranspiration from the principal natural vegetation cover is slightly more than that from *Paspalum notatum*. The radiation balance for the equatorial forest (albedo 0.13) and for savanna (albedo 0.18 in the rainy and 0.23 in the dry season) was higher than for the *Paspalum notatum* (albedo equal to 0.23). The evapotranspiration is maximum in the north of the central basin (the equatorial forest region) where it attains a value of 1,350 mm; in almost the whole of this zone it ranges between 1,250 and 1,350 mm. As one leaves the equatorial area or enters the higher regions of the eastern mountain zone (the savannas), the actual evapotranspiration is reduced. Nevertheless, it is below 1,000 mm only in the lower Congo (to the west of Kinshasa), in Katanga and in the lower regions of Graben (BULTOT, 1962).

As far as the large lakes are concerned, the mean annual evaporation is of the order of 1,400 mm for Kivu, 1,700 mm for Tanganyika and Mweru, 1,650 for Bangweulu, 1,350 for Leopold II and Tumba, and 1,900 mm for Edward (BULTOT, 1962). These values have been calculated by the energy balance method and corroborated, for Tanganyika, by the water budget method (BULTOT, 1965). Finally, it is clear that the values of actual evapotranspiration from natural surfaces, deduced from water balance calculation of the Congo Basin and its principal constituents, confirm the values found by the energy balance method. They show that on average the actual evapotranspiration generally measures between 75 and 85% of the annual precipitation (BULTOT, 1962). This shows that the mean net horizontal flux of water vapour over the Congo Basin is relatively restricted.

Temperature and humidity of the air; temperature of the soil

Temperature of the air

Temperature is the element that is most immediately dependent on the radiation climate. This is why it is generally very constant from one year to the next.

The mean daily temperature is approximately 25°C in Uele, the central basin, the lower Congo, and Kasai. In upper Katanga it is nearer to 20°C (see Table XIII). In the mountainous regions of the east it is reduced by about 0.65°C per 100 m of elevation; at around 2,000 m it is of the order of 17°C. At a constant altitude the temperature is

TABLE XIII

MEAN DAILY TEMPERATURES (MAXIMUM, MINIMUM AND EXTREMES)

Regions		Jan.	Feb.	Mar.	Apr.	May	June	July	Aug.	Sept.	Oct.	Nov.	Dec.	Aver.
Central basin	mean:	24.9	25.1	25.3	25.3	25.1	24.7	23.9	24.0	24.3	24.3	24.5	24.3	24.6
(Yangambi)	maximum:	30.2	30.8	30.6	30.3	30.1	29.5	28.5	28.4	29.2	29.1	29.3	29.0	29.6
1950–1959	minimum:	19.6	19.4	19.9	20.3	20.0	19.8	19.3	19.5	19.4	19.5	19.7	19.5	19.7
	extr. max.:	35.6	35.3	35.0	35.0	34.6	33.3	32.3	32.5	33.3	33.7	33.4	33.6	35.6
	extr. min.:	15.2	13.7	16.2	17.6	16.8	17.2	17.1	17.4	17.0	17.2	17.6	14.2	13.7
Uele	mean:	24.2	24.7	24.9	24.9	24.5	24.0	23.3	23.4	23.9	24.0	24.2	23.7	24.1
(Bambesa)	maximum:	31.4	32.5	31.3	30.6	29.9	29.1	28.2	28.2	29.3	29.5	29.9	30.1	30.0
1950–1959	minimum:	16.9	16.9	18.5	19.2	19.1	18.8	18.4	18.6	18.5	18.6	18.5	17.2	18.3
	extr. max.:	37.3	39.0	39.5	35.5	33.3	32.4	32.2	32.2	33.0	33.1	33.4	34.5	39.5
	extr. min.:	10.4	7.6	12.4	13.4	16.1	15.8	15.2	15.9	15.6	15.2	14.0	10.0	7.6
Lower Congo	mean:	26.0	26.3	26.7	26.9	26.0	23.6	21.9	23.2	25.2	26.1	26.0	25.7	25.3
(Kinshasa)	maximum:	30.1	30.7	31.3	31.6	30.4	28.3	26.7	28.4	30.1	30.4	30.2	29.6	29.8
1949–1958	minimum:	21.9	21.8	22.1	22.1	21.7	18.9	17.2	18.0	20.3	21.7	21.8	21.8	20.8
	extr. max.:	34.0	35.1	35.2	34.4	34.4	32.7	32.4	34.0	35.5	35.4	34.2	33.4	35.5
	extr. min.:	17.9	18.6	19.2	20.4	18.7	14.8	12.6	11.2	16.1	17.3	19.1	19.6	11.2
Kasai	mean:	24.1	24.2	24.6	24.5	24.5	23.5	23.3	24.3	24.5	24.1	24.1	24.0	24.1
(Gandajika)	maximum:	29.4	29.6	30.3	30.8	31.3	31.6	31.4	31.7	31.1	30.1	29.8	29.2	30.5
1950–1959	minimum:	18.7	18.8	18.9	18.3	17.6	15.3	15.2	16.8	17.8	18.0	18.3	18.8	17.7
	extr. max.:	35.0	34.0	34.1	34.3	34.7	34.3	34.1	36.5	36.5	34.0	33.5	33.5	36.5
	extr. min.:	16.2	16.1	16.4	16.2	13.1	10.5	9.5	12.1	15.0	15.5	15.6	15.1	9.5
Katanga	mean:	21.8	21.7	21.9	21.3	19.3	16.8	16.8	19.2	22.2	23.8	22.8	21.8	20.8
(Lubumbashi)	maximum:	26.7	26.6	27.1	27.4	26.8	25.0	25.2	27.7	30.7	31.7	28.8	26.8	27.5
1950–1959	minimum:	16.9	16.7	16.5	15.3	11.7	8.6	8.3	10.5	13.8	15.9	16.8	16.7	14.0
	extr. max.:	30.5	30.8	31.1	30.4	30.6	29.5	29.0	34.0	36.1	36.7	35.5	32.1	36.7
	extr. min.:	13.4	14.3	12.3	9.9	2.9	3.7	3.8	3.4	9.2	8.7	13.1	13.4	2.9
Mountain zone	mean:	16.6	16.7	16.6	16.4	16.3	15.6	15.2	16.1	16.5	16.5	16.3	16.5	16.3
(Tshibinda)	maximum:	21.8	21.7	21.7	21.1	20.7	20.6	21.0	22.0	22.2	21.8	21.5	21.5	21.5
1952–1959	minimum:	11.3	11.5	11.4	11.7	11.9	10.5	9.4	10.1	10.7	11.1	11.1	11.3	11.0
	extr. max.:	25.9	25.3	24.7	23.6	22.8	23.5	23.4	25.2	26.5	25.4	24.4	24.6	26.5
	extr. min.:	7.9	8.4	8.6	8.6	8.5	7.6	5.4	6.6	7.6	8.2	8.4	8.8	5.4

mainly dependent upon distance from the ocean, that is to say it is a measure of the degree of continentality (VANDENPLAS, 1943).

The mean daily temperature fluctuates little from one month to the other except in the lower Congo and Katanga where it changes significantly during the course of the first months of the dry season (see Table XIII).

During the rainy months the mean daily range is approximately 8–10°C. This low value is due to the greenhouse effect characteristic of equatorial and sub-tropical regions. This greenhouse effect, provoked by the high atmospheric value of water vapour and the CO_2, controls or reduces the nocturnal cooling by radiation and keeps minimum temperatures at a high value. On the other hand, in the regions where there is a definite dry season, the temperature falls considerably during the night in the dry months following an increase in the terrestrial radiation. This is why a lowering of the mean daily temperature is then observed, especially in the lower Congo and in Katanga during the first months of the dry season. In this season the diurnal temperatures decrease in relation to the reduction of the solar global radiation (stratus clouds and high atmospheric turbidity in the lower Congo, and noticeably lower position of the sun in Katanga).

From Table XIII it is seen that temperatures can rise to approximately 40°C in Uele and descend to around 3°C in upper Katanga. In this last region local frosts have been observed.

Everywhere in the Congo the temperature decreases rapidly between 16h00 and 20h00 (local mean time), then decreases more slowly to a minimum that is observed about 06h00. Between the minimum and the maximum the temperature increases approximately linearly, except in the dry season where the rise can be very rapid. The maximum is reached generally between 14h00 and 15h00, that is to say, approximately 2 h after the total radiation balance has attained its maximum. However, in the mountain region, the temperature maximum is often found between 13h00 and 14h00 (BULTOT, 1967). This change in time with respect to the maximum of the total radiation balance is less in the mountains due, most likely, to the greater turbulence of the air.

The humidity of the air

Humidity is essentially related to actual evapotranspiration and the advection of water vapour from the vicinity of neighbouring humid areas (the ocean and the great lakes). Comparison of the monthly values of the mixing ratio (see Table XIV), shows that in the central basin (the region where the actual evapotranspiration is maximal) the amount of

TABLE XIV

MEAN MONTHLY AND ANNUAL VALUES OF THE HUMIDITY MIXING RATIO, r (g/kg), WATER VAPOUR PRESSURE, e (mbar), AND OF RELATIVE HUMIDITY, U (%)

Regions		Jan.	Feb.	Mar.	Apr.	May	June	July	Aug.	Sept.	Oct.	Nov.	Dec.	Year
Central basin	r	16.4	15.7	16.6	17.2	17.1	16.7	16.6	16.4	16.4	16.4	16.9	16.9	16.6
(Yangambi)	e	24.5	23.5	24.9	25.7	25.6	25.0	24.9	24.5	24.6	24.6	25.3	25.4	24.9
1956–1958	U	84	81	84	86	86	87	88	88	87	87	86	88	86
Uele	r	14.4	14.0	16.4	17.1	17.0	16.4	16.4	16.4	16.4	16.3	16.9	16.0	16.2
(Bambesa)	e	21.4	20.7	24.2	25.2	25.1	24.3	24.3	24.2	24.3	24.1	25.0	23.7	23.9
1956–1958	U	80	76	83	86	85	87	89	89	87	87	86	85	85
Lower Congo	r	16.6	16.6	17.0	17.1	16.9	14.1	12.2	12.1	13.7	15.6	16.5	16.6	15.4
(Kinshasa)	e	25.4	25.3	26.0	26.2	25.9	21.6	18.8	18.6	21.1	24.0	25.3	25.4	23.6
1954–1956	U	82	80	80	82	83	81	76	69	69	76	81	83	79
Kasai	r	15.3	15.4	15.5	15.6	13.5	10.7	9.6	12.7	14.2	14.9	15.3	15.6	14.0
(Gandajika)	e	22.3	22.4	22.5	22.6	19.6	15.7	14.1	18.5	20.6	21.6	22.3	22.6	20.4
1956–1958	U	83	82	81	82	69	57	53	66	73	78	81	82	74
Katanga	r	14.1	14.2	14.3	13.0	10.6	8.2	6.9	7.0	7.8	8.7	13.2	13.9	11.0
(Lubumbashi)	e	19.4	19.5	19.6	17.9	14.6	11.3	9.6	9.7	10.8	12.1	18.2	19.1	15.2
1954–1956	U	83	85	81	75	68	62	54	45	42	44	74	83	66
Mountain zone	r	11.9	12.0	12.0	12.4	12.4	11.1	10.0	10.2	10.5	11.5	11.9	12.0	11.5
(Tshibinda)	e	14.9	15.2	15.2	15.6	15.6	14.0	12.6	12.8	13.2	14.5	14.9	15.2	14.5
1956–1958	U	84	86	84	88	89	84	76	75	74	83	85	87	83

water in the air is the highest (from 15.7 to 17.2 g/kg). As with the actual evapotranspiration the water vapour content of the air diminishes away from the equator. Nevertheless this reduction is not large in the rainy season (from 14 to 15.6 g/kg in Kasai and 13 to 14.3 g/kg in upper Katanga). In the dry season, on the contrary, the amount of water vapour decreases considerably (from about 10 g/kg in Kasai to 7 g/kg in upper Katanga). In the lower Congo this reduction is appreciably weakened because of the advection of water vapour from the Atlantic Ocean. In August, for example, the actual evapotranspiration median is 32 mm at Kinshasa and 29 mm at Lubumbashi, whereas the water vapour content is 12.1 g/kg at the first station (under the influence of the ocean) and only 7.0 g/kg in the second (a definite continental climate). It is noted elsewhere that, in the rainy season, the atmospheric humidity in the lower Congo is approximately the same as that in the central basin (15.0–17.1 g/kg). In the mountain zone the water vapour content decreases rapidly with elevation although the actual evapotranspiration remains high. In this sector the water vapour content is, in fact, limited by the temperature and to a certain measure by the turbulence of the air. By way of comparison, in July at Yangambi the actual evapotranspiration is 72 mm and water vapour content is 16.6 g/kg while in June at Tshibinda the actual evapotranspiration is also 72 mm but the water vapour content is only 11.1 g/kg.

In the rainy season the monthly values of the atmospheric humidity show little deviation from their mean values. The mean monthly water vapour pressure usually ranges between 23.5 and 25.7 mbar in the central basin, between 18.6 and 26.2 mbar in the lower Congo, between 9.6 and 19.6 mbar in Katanga, and from 12.6 to 15.6 mbar in the mountain region, at approximately 2,000 m altitude (see Table XIV).

The mean monthly relative humidity is between 81 and 88% in the central basin, 69–83% in the lower Congo, 42–85% in Katanga and between 74 and 89% in the mountain region (see Table XIV).

The mean daily curves of water vapour pressure are characterized by a period of very small variation, generally less than 4 mbar; the maxima about 09h00 and 18h00 (local mean time), and principal minimum around 05h00 to 06h00 with a secondary minimum around 14h00 to 15h00 (around 13h00 to 14h00 in the mountains). This secondary minimum is especially accentuated in the dry season. The decrease of the water vapour pressure during the night is due evidently to the cessation of evapotranspiration and formation of dew. As far as the low value recorded in the afternoon is concerned (at the time of highest temperature during the day) this results from the turbulent diffusion of the water vapour towards high levels brought on by the thermal instability of the air.

The mean daily relative humidity curves are characterized by a period of very large fluctuation, maximum around 06h00 (often in excess of 80%) and a minimum around 15h00 (rarely less than 50% except in Kasai and Katanga during the dry season).

The air is almost always completely saturated with water vapour when the temperature is less than 22°C in the central basin, in Uele, and in the lower Congo (in the rainy season); less than 20°C in Kasai (in the rainy season); 18°C in Katanga (in the rainy season) and in Kasai and the lower Congo (during the dry season); 14°C in the mountain zone (around 2,000 m in altitude); and 12°C in Katanga (during the dry season) (BULTOT, 1957).

The soil temperature

The mean annual temperature range at 10 cm depth is about 3°C in the central basin and Uele, about 6°C in the lower Congo, and 2°C in Kasai, 8.5°C in Katanga and only 1°C in the mountain region (DUPRIEZ, 1969; see Table XV). It is noticed that the annual temperature range decreases only slowly with depth. However, from one month to the next, the heat flux change in the soil is often less than 200 cal./cm²; it would appear that this is negligible (less than 5%) when compared with the monthly total radiation balance. The mean daily variation at 10 cm depth is generally around 5 to 10°C. It diminishes rapidly with depth; at 50 cm it is not more than a few tenths of a degree.

TABLE XV

MONTHLY AND ANNUAL MEANS OF SOIL TEMPERATURE AT 10, 20, 50 cm DEPTH (1954–1959)

Regions	cm	Jan.	Feb.	Mar.	Apr.	May	June	July	Aug.	Sept.	Oct.	Nov.	Dec.	Aver.
Central basin	10	28.7	29.0	29.6	29.2	29.0	28.2	27.1	26.6	27.2	27.2	27.7	27.1	28.1
(Yangambi)	20	28.4	28.6	29.3	28.9	28.7	28.1	27.0	26.5	27.0	27.0	27.5	26.9	27.8
	50	28.1	28.5	29.1	28.8	28.6	28.0	27.3	26.6	27.0	26.9	27.4	26.9	27.8
Uele	10	28.7	29.1	28.6	28.3	28.3	27.5	26.3	26.1	27.1	26.8	27.7	28.0	27.7
(Bambesa)	20	28.1	28.5	28.2	27.9	27.7	27.3	26.1	25.9	26.8	26.4	27.3	27.6	27.3
	50	28.1	28.5	28.4	28.2	27.9	27.6	26.6	26.2	26.9	26.7	27.4	27.7	27.5
Lower Congo	10	27.1	28.4	28.3	27.5	26.7	25.1	22.8	23.4	25.6	26.2	26.6	26.6	26.2
(Mvuazi)	20	26.8	27.9	28.0	27.2	26.5	25.1	22.9	23.2	25.3	25.9	26.3	26.3	25.9
	50	26.6	27.5	27.8	27.2	26.6	25.6	23.6	23.5	25.1	25.7	26.1	26.2	26.0
Kasai	10	25.9	26.3	27.2	26.9	27.0	25.8	25.3	26.1	26.3	26.4	26.2	26.0	26.3
(Gandajika)	20	25 9	26.1	27.0	26.7	26.8	25.6	25.0	25.7	26.0	26.1	26.1	25.9	26.1
	50	25.7	25.9	26.7	26.7	26.6	25.9	25.2	25.6	25.9	26.0	25.9	25.9	26.0
Katanga	10	24.0	23.8	24.6	24.7	22.5	19.5	19.1	21.5	25.3	27.5	25.8	23.8	23.5
(Keyberg)	20	23.7	23.5	24.2	24.4	22.4	19.9	18.9	21.0	24.6	26.8	25.4	23.6	23.2
	50	23.6	23.5	23.9	24.3	23.1	20.3	19.5	20.8	23.7	25.8	25.3	23.6	23.1
Mountain zone	10	19.0	18.8	19.4	19.1	19.0	19.5	19.3	19.7	19.5	18.7	18.8	18.7	19.1
(Tshibinda)	20	19.0	18.7	19.2	19.0	18.9	19.3	19.0	19.3	19.2	18.6	18.7	18.7	19.0
	50	19.3	19.0	19.3	19.3	19.2	19.5	19.2	19.5	19.4	19.0	19.0	19.0	19.2

The variability in monthly values of the soil temperature is very small. The mean monthly temperature at grass level is found to be very close to the mean monthly temperature of the air; the mean annual deviation between these two temperatures is often only between 0.1 and 0.5°C (DUPRIEZ, 1964).

The atmospheric pressure and surface wind

Atmospheric pressure

The mean daily curve of atmospheric pressure is the result of a semi-diurnal wave associated with the "tide" of the atmosphere, and with a daily wave highly correlated with the season and the temperature (VANDER ELST, 1955). The curve has a principal maximum around 09h00 (local mean time) and a secondary maximum around 21h00; a prime minimum at 15h00 and a secondary minimum at about 03h00. The daily barometric deviation is on average around 3 to 4 mbar. The mean monthly pressure usually reaches a maximum in June or July and a minimum in February to March; the variation between these two extremes is only some 2–4.5 mbar. The direction and value of the horizontal gradient of pressure varies markedly from one month to another; the value, however, is always very small (VANDER ELST, 1955).

Surface winds

In the Congo the mean monthly wind speed is everywhere very low (CRABBE, 1968). At 12h00, the time of day when the wind is generally strongest, the dominant directions are west, west-southwest and south in the central basin (see Table XVI); winds in excess of 3.5 m/sec are rare (11.5%). In Uele, the dominant directions are also west, west-southwest and south during both the dry and wet seasons; winds in excess of 3.5 m/sec are extremely rare (less than 5%). In the lower Congo the dominant directions are west and west-southwest in both seasons; winds in excess of 3.5 m/sec are principally observed in the dry season (26%). In Kasai the prevailing directions are west, north and north-northwest in the rainy season; west and northwest in the dry season. Winds greater than 3.5 m/sec are very frequent in the dry season (26%), more so than in the rainy season (15%); their prevailing directions are east and west in the dry season, west and north-northwest in the rainy season. In upper Katanga the prevailing directions are east-northeast, east

TABLE XVI

RELATIVE FREQUENCY (%) OF WINDS (12h00), 1954–1956*

Regions		m/sec	30°	60°	90°	120°	150°	180°	210°	240°	270°	300°	330°	360°	Total	Calm
Central basin	annual	≤3.5	2.6	4.4	5.5	2.9	8.9	11.5	4.6	11.0	12.3	4.7	7.8	7.0	83.2	5.3
(Kisangani)	values	>3.5	0.4	0.6	0.5	0.3	0.9	0.5	0.5	1.9	2.4	1.5	1.4	0.6	11.5	
Uele	rainy	≤3.5	2.0	3.6	8.6	2.6	5.1	13.9	2.5	13.3	19.6	4.8	8.7	4.6	89.3	6.0
(Buta)	season	>3.5	–	0.4	0.5	0.4	0.1	0.8	0.2	0.8	1.0	0.2	0.2	0.1	4.7	
	dry	≤3.5	3.8	8.0	10.2	5.9	9.6	12.9	2.2	11.2	12.9	2.2	4.2	5.9	89.0	6.0
	season	>3.5	–	–	0.5	0.6	1.1	–	0.6	1.1	0.6	0.5	–	–	5.0	
Lower Congo	rainy	≤3.5	10.0	10.2	3.9	0.7	2.1	4.0	2.9	12.0	22.6	1.7	4.4	11.3	85.8	4.0
(Kinshasa)	season	>3.5	1.2	0.7	0.4	–	0.4	–	0.5	1.2	3.4	1.0	0.3	1.1	10.2	
	dry	≤3.5	1.9	1.6	–	–	0.3	2.8	3.0	22.4	33.7	3.8	1.4	2.5	73.4	0.6
	season	>3.5	0.5	–	–	–	–	0.3	1.3	10.3	12.5	0.8	0.3	–	26.0	
Kasai	rainy	≤3.5	1.1	4.6	5.1	1.2	4.2	7.3	3.0	8.7	14.9	4.8	12.6	15.6	83.1	1.6
(Luluabourg)	season	>3.5	0.1	0.8	0.8	0.3	0.5	0.9	0.2	0.7	3.6	1.2	3.3	2.9	15.3	
	dry	≤3.5	1.4	5.1	7.3	3.0	5.8	6.5	2.5	7.9	13.8	2.5	11.1	4.7	71.6	2.3
	season	>3.5	–	2.2	5.5	1.1	4.0	1.1	–	1.8	5.4	1.8	1.4	1.8	26.1	
Katanga	rainy	≤3.5	5.5	10.6	10.3	8.4	7.1	4.6	1.9	3.7	5.3	5.1	8.1	7.0	77.6	7.2
(Lubumbashi)	season	>3.5	0.9	2.8	1.9	1.9	0.9	0.6	0.7	0.2	1.3	1.3	1.8	0.9	15.2	
	dry	≤3.5	1.5	7.4	14.8	13.7	15.0	4.9	0.5	0.3	–	–	0.3	1.5	59.9	1.0
	season	>3.5	–	3.1	14.0	10.5	10.5	0.8	–	0.2	–	–	–	–	39.1	

* 90° = east.

and east-southeast during the rainy season; nevertheless, at this period in 15% of the cases the winds also blow from north-northwest and north. In the dry season the prevailing directions are south-southeast, east-southeast and east. Winds greater than 3.5 m/sec are very much more frequent in the dry season (40%) than in the rainy season (15%); their prevailing directions are east in the dry season and east-northeast in the rainy season. Moist air with a westerly component reaches all the regions, except Katanga, at some time during both the dry and the rainy season. In Katanga the humid air from the Atlantic only reaches the zone sporadically and at the time of the rains. Actually Katanga is more often affected by winds with an easterly component, even in the rainy season. In the dry season these winds are intensified and have a more meridional component, due to the strengthening of the South African anticyclone. Although the mean wind speed may be low, nevertheless, some very high gusts of winds have been registered due to the turbulence of the air during the warm hours of the afternoon or the passage of a squall line (see Table XVII; CRABBE, 1968). This is the reason why violent gusts are generally

TABLE XVII

MEAN MONTHLY NUMBER OF WIND GUSTS EQUAL OR SUPERIOR TO 10, 13 AND 17 m/sec

Regions	Wet season			Dry season		
	$\geqslant$ 10 m/sec	$\geqslant$ 13 m/sec	$\geqslant$ 17 m/sec	$\geqslant$ 10 m/sec	$\geqslant$ 13 m/sec	$\geqslant$ 17 m/sec
Central basin (Yangambi) 1957–1960	6.0	2.4	0.6	–	–	–
Uele (Bambesa) 1956–1958	8.2	3.6	0.7	3.6	1.1	0.3
Lower Congo (Kinshasa) 1953, 1954, 1958	6.5	3.4	0.7	0.6	0.2	–
Kasai (Gandajika) 1956–1958	12.5	6.2	1.7	2.0	0.5	0.2
Katanga (Simama) 1958, 1959	14.7	7.1	2.1	1.4	0.7	0.4
Mountain zone (Bukavu) 1958, 1960, 1961	4.5	–	–	0.2	–	–

TABLE XVIII

EXTREME WIND GUST SPEEDS

Regions	Speed		Date	Time	Direction	Period of observation
	m/sec	km/h				
Central basin (Yangambi)	26.5	95.4	04-03-60	19h20	NNE	1950–1960
Uele (Bambesa)	25.8	92.9	22-02-58	14h50	NNW	1956–1958
Lower Congo (Kinshasa)	28.3	101.9	15-05-53	13h15	WSW	1953–1954, 1958
Kasai (Gandajika)	26.4	95.0	15-11-57	13h30	E	1956–1958
Katanga (Simama)	28.5	102.6	08-11-59	14h15	ENE	1958–1959
Mountain zone (Bukavu)	21.5	77.4	07-12-60	17h00	ENE	1952, 1960, 1961

only produced in the rainy season and are most often between 12h00 and 24h00. Their directions are frequently between 0 and 180° and often in opposition to the mean wind direction. The highest values that have been registered are about 25–30 m/sec, that is to say, from 90 to 110 km/h (see Table XVIII; CRABBE, 1968).

Climatic classification

Bioclimatic index

Referring now to the bioclimatic index G of LEE (1958) we find:

$$G = 2.5[\{M - W - 0.00033\ V\ (46 - e) - \{5.55(34 - T)\}(I_a + I_c)^{-1}\}/ (70 - e)(r_a + r_c)^{-1}]$$

where M is the rate of energy liberated (metabolic rate), W is the energy expended in external work, V is volume of respired air, e is the water vapour pressure, T is the air temperature, I_a and I_c are the resistivity of ambient air and clothing, respectively, to the outward passage of heat, r_a and r_c are the resistivity of ambient air and clothing, respectively, to the outward passage of water vapour. G is a measure of the strain on a human being. Values of the symbols. M, W, I_a, I_c, r_a, r_c and V proposed by Lee correspond to a normally clothed person working at a moderate rate in a moderate air flow. Lee states that most people are comfortable when G is between 4 to 4.5; none are comfortable when G is below about 1.5 to 3 or greater than 6 to about 8.5. Expressed in values of G, the zone of comfort for the tropics and inside dwellings has been found, after BROOKS (1950), to be between 3 and 6. From DEVROEY (1950), 26°C and 50% relative humidity during the day ($G = 5$), 21°C and 80% relative humidity at night ($G = 3$) would be recommendable in Congo dwellings. After LEBRUN and VANDER ELST (1958), an acclimatized person working only lightly during the warmest hours of the day can keep a reasonable efficiency, conserve his intellectual energies and his health only if the effective temperature (temperature corresponding to 100% relative humidity) does not exceed 26°C, that is $G = 9$.

In Mayumbe (western section of the lower Congo), during the rainy season, a value of G greater than 8 is imposed for a long time (a mean of 9.75 h/day; BULTOT, 1966). However, it is in the western part of the central basin that the highest values of the index G persist; here the values are greater than or equal to 12 during one hour per day, a value that is only reached for a quarter of an hour in Mayumbe. The climate is very monotonous everywhere in this latter region, since G does not go below 2, whilst in the west of the central basin it goes below this level during 1.25 h each day. This lack of contrast is general in the lower Congo during the rainy season.

In the central basin the strain imposed upon the body is reduced as one goes eastwards (G greater than or equal to 8 during eight hours of the day in the west, and only 3.5 h a day to the east; G greater than 10 during 4 h a day in the west and only 1 h/day in the east). In Uele, G is greater than or equal to 8 during 3.5 h of the day during the rainy season, during 5 h of the day during the dry season; it is equal to or greater than 10 during one hour a day in the rainy season and 2 h a day in the dry season; it is less than or equal to 2 during 3.25 h in the rainy season and during 2.25 h a day in the dry season.

In Kasai, *G* is as high as 8 or 9 during 2 or 3 h of the day during the rainy season, but only reaches the value 10 for less than 1 h/day; the climate is therefore less distressing than in the central basin, the lower Congo and Uele.

There is some evidence that the higher zones and south Katanga are more comfortable areas since *G* remains always below 8. In regions situated to the south of the equator and regions of marked alternate seasons it is during the course of the rainy months that the climate is the most unhealthy. This is normal since the temperature and humidity of the air is reduced considerably in the dry months. On the contrary, in Uele the temperature is raised in the dry season because of the advection of warm air from the northeast; this is why the strain imposed on the body is greater at this period than during the course of the rainy months.

Aridity index

The aridity index of BUDYKO (1958) is equal to the ratio *B/Lr*, where *B*, *L* and *r* are respectively the total radiation balance, the latent heat of vaporization, and the mean annual rainfall (in mm). The larger the index the more arid is the climate. The aridity index is between 0.65 and 0.70 in the central basin, 0.8–0.9 in Uele, 0.85 in the east of the lower Congo to 1.3 along the Atlantic Ocean coast, 0.8–0.9 in Kasai, and 0.9–1.3 in Katanga. In the mountain zone it varies considerably from one place to another; to the west of Lake Kivu, around 2,000 m elevation, it is between 0.6 and 0.7 (BULTOT, 1969). These values are based on measurements of the total radiation balance at the level of the surface of a cover of *Paspalum notatum* (albedo 0.23). It can be stated that, even in the less humid regions, Budyko's index is relatively low. We can see in this connection that the entire area of the Congo is included in the tropical humid zone (BULTOT, 1964). On one hand the mean monthly temperature is greater than 20°C during eight months or more (tropical climate); on the other hand the mean water deficit calculated by Thornthwaite's method is more than 25 mm during six months or more (humid climate).

The West African section

Almost the whole of this section is located in Liberia with small parts of Sierra Leone and Ivory Coast falling within its boundaries. Liberia is a rather remote country that does not possess a comprehensive network of meteorological stations. The few that do exist, and for which data are available, are located near to the coast. The country covers an area of about 110,000 km², and has a population estimated at one million people, of whom 50,000 live in Monrovia, the capital. The major exports are iron ore, rubber, gold, diamonds and palm kernels.

The climatic pattern is dominated by the I.T.C.Z., under the influence of which the section falls for the whole year. Warm, moist westerly to southerly flow for the major part of the year leads to high rainfall amounts everywhere. It is only when a drier, northeasterly flow dominates that the rainfall amounts are lower, below about 100 mm/month. The mean annual rainfall is high, ranging from nearly 5,000 mm to a low of 1,400 mm in the north (Fig.2). Rainfall variation is great, as is illustrated by the values for 29 years at Harbel, the Firestone Laboratories station (Table XIX).

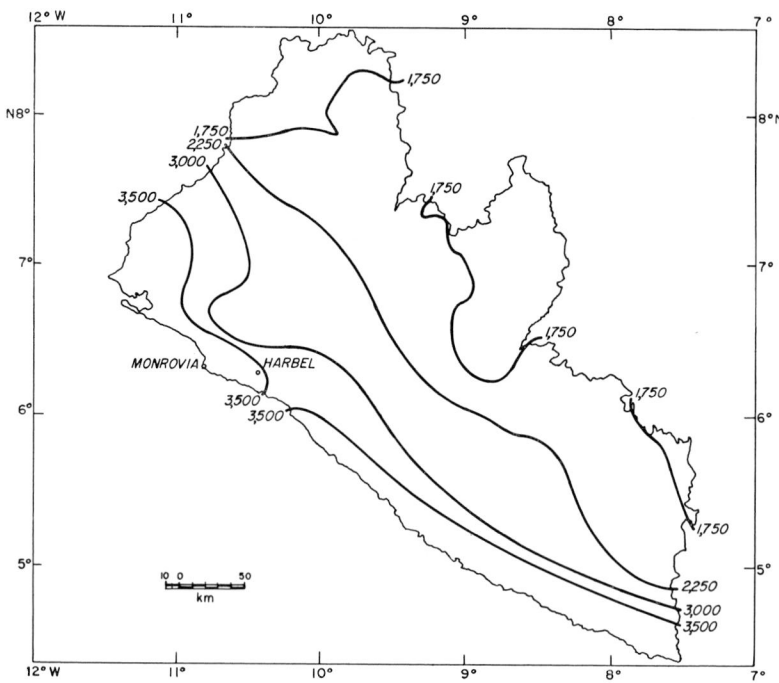

Fig.2. Mean annual isohyets (mm), Liberia.

TABLE XIX

RAINFALL VARIATION, HARBEL

	Jan.	Feb.	Mar.	Apr.	May	June	July	Aug.	Sept.	Oct.	Nov.	Dec.	Year
Maximum	140	196	364	249	466	681	1,203	910	932	650	325	178	4,313
Average	34	59	135	158	272	408	461	459	625	379	185	80	3,251
Minimum	0	2	29	71	98	138	123	192	420	143	100	11	2,321

Weekly totals over the period 1932–1939 at this station averaged less than 30 mm from mid-December until late March and then increased to maximum means of 204 mm (June 18–24) and 196 mm (September 10–16). Fig.3 shows a slight suggestion of a "little dry season" in late July. The highest amount recorded in one week was 383 mm and falls of

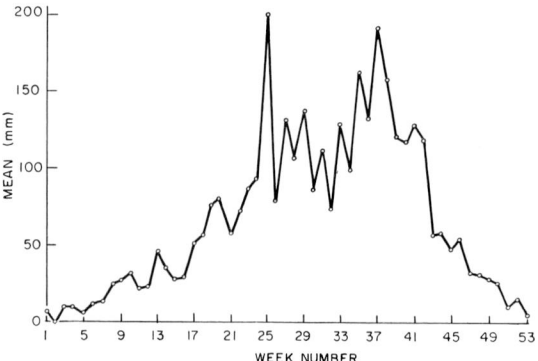

Fig.3. Mean weekly rainfall (mm), Harbel.

250 mm or more occurred, on average, once or twice per year. During the 416 weeks analysed (McINDOE, 1940) only 42 were dry, 36 of these occurring between mid-December and mid-February. There was no dry week from May to October. Daily rainfall in excess of 200 mm can occur during this period while rain falls on about 25 days during each month from June to October. As one moves inland (see the climatic tables at the end of the chapter) these values decrease.

Recording raingauge data for 4 years at Monrovia have shown that in a period of 2 h as much as 100 mm has fallen in every month from May to October. The record fall (March, 1954) gave 18 mm in 5 min, 43 mm in 15 min and 63 mm in 30 min. The diurnal variability at Harbel shows an interesting pattern. On the annual basis the percentage falls vary from 7% (13h00–14h00 and 14h00–15h00) to 3% (08h00–09h00, 09h00–10h00, 18h00–19h00 and 19h00–20h00). Most months show the classical afternoon maximum with the wet months having also a night-time secondary maximum.

Mean annual temperatures average about 26°C over the section with a low annual range of 2°C at the coast rising to a maximum inland of 6°C. Temperatures are rarely outside the range 20–34°C near the coast or 15–37°C inland. Soil temperatures at Harbel average from 16°C (August) to 18°C (March–April) at a depth of 30 cm and from 17°C (August–September) to 19°C (April) at 120 cm. The monotony of the temperature is extremely enervating.

Relative humidity is generally high, especially at or near the coast. The Harbel station has its lowest readings (below 70%) during the afternoon in January, while from 20h00 until 07h00 averages above 95% are the rule. The harmattan (dry, northeasterly wind) rarely reaches the coast in this section but its welcome arrival reduces the relative humidity very drastically, as Table XX illustrates.

TABLE XX

RELATIVE HUMIDITY, HARBEL[1]

	01h	03h	05h	07h	09h	11h	13h	15h	17h	19h	21h	23h	Aver.
June	99	100	100	95	91	87	85	87	89	95	96	98	94
Aug.	99	100	100	98	93	87	85	87	91	96	97	98	94
Oct.	100	100	100	99	91	84	84	87	95	97	99	99	95
Dec.	100	100	100	99	96	87	79	80	85	92	96	99	93
Feb.	98	99	100	99	95	80	73	75	80	89	93	97	90
Apr.	98	99	99	99	89	77	73	76	76	88	96	98	89
Jan. 8th[2]	98	99	100	96	86	81	57	51	64	82	87	95	83

[1] The values are only for one year.
[2] Harmattan.

Sunshine, along the coast, averages about 1,500 h/year, a little less than that at some of the inland stations. The seasonal variation and the monthly variability are shown in Table XXI for Harbel.

It is surprising to note that the highest average in a period of 348 months is only 7.4 h, while some months have recorded totals of only 12 h. In the coastal and inland areas early morning fogs are common from October to April, reaching a maximum occurrence of 15 in January.

TABLE XXI

DAILY SUNSHINE HOURS, HARBEL

	Jan.	Feb.	Mar.	Apr.	May	June	July	Aug.	Sept.	Oct.	Nov.	Dec.	Year
Maximum	6.8	7.4	7.1	6.5	6.4	4.7	3.7	2.7	3.5	5.6	6.0	6.6	1,784
Average	5.3	5.4	5.3	5.0	4.4	3.1	2.0	1.5	2.1	4.1	4.9	4.0	1,472
Minimum	3.3	3.1	3.2	3.0	1.4	1.2	0.4	0.4	0.7	2.2	2.8	3.2	1,252

As would be expected from the sunshine data, cloud amounts are very high in this section for much of the year. For most months the average is about 7 oktas and the lowest mean is 4, during the "dry" season, January and February.

Wind speed is very dependent upon local conditions, with the sea breeze often supplementing the prevailing southwesterly flow. Monrovia had a maximum wind speed of only 40 km/h during a five year period while Harbel records only five gale force gusts per year. Harbel has a wind flow of only 80 km/day during the windiest months (July, August and September) and as low as 40 km/day in January.

Equatorial Guinea (Rio Muni and Fernando Póo)

This small country of 28,000 km² recently became independent after years of Spanish rule. It comprises the mainland area of Rio Muni (26,000 km², population 180,000), with its capital of Bata (27,000 inhabitants), and the island of Fernando Póo (2,000 km², population 70,000), with its capital Santa Isabel (37,000 people). In addition there are the small islands of Annobon, Corisco and Elobey. The country exports timber (mahogany), rubber, cocoa, coffee and oil palm products but only the first is of real economic importance.

The territory is small, has little in the way of a meteorological service and only a small amount of climatological data. But, because of its important position in the Gulf of Guinea, it is worthy of some discussion here. The best publication concerning this area is the fine one by FONT-TULLOT (1951) and this has been drawn on quite extensively.

The climate of this area is dominated by two main factors, the I.T.C.Z. and the warm Guinea Current. The former brings the prevailing westerlies or southwesterlies throughout the year, warm and very moist air masses; the latter gives the islands and the coastal strip the "baño Maria" conditions of monotonously high relative humidity and temperature. Santa Isabel has mean monthly values as follows: relative humidity 88–92% (at 08h00 local time), minimum temperature 19–22°C, maximum temperature 29–32°C. These values are typical of conditions over the whole country but some regions (Ureka and Elobey) experience even higher humidities. The water vapour content averages annually about 21–22 g/m³ (dew point 24°C) in the coastal areas but decreases to 15 g/m³ (dew point 18°C) at 1,200 m. This height is the maximum in Rio Muni but on Fernando Póo the mountain of Santa Isabel reaches 3,000 m.

In this region of the Gulf of Biafra wind speeds can reach very high values. For Santa Isabel the maximum monthly speeds are all in excess of 60 knots/h with 115 knots/h (April) and 93 knots/h (January) being the greatest. On the continent the coast experiences

fairly constant westerly winds with an average speed of about 15 knots/h. Both areas
show winds with a strong easterly component at the time of the line squalls.

The most interesting climatological element for the region is rainfall. Available data for
monthly and annual totals are given in Table XXII. Ureka is shown to be one of the
"unfortunate" few stations around the world with an annual mean rainfall in excess of
10,000 mm, joining the select band of Mount Waialeale, Cherrapunji and Debundscha.
Fig.4 and 5 give the isohyets of mean annual rainfall. Fig.4, although it may be con-
jectural in places, illustrates the part played by the moist southwesterlies. In Fig.5 the
effect of a change in direction of the coastline is depicted.

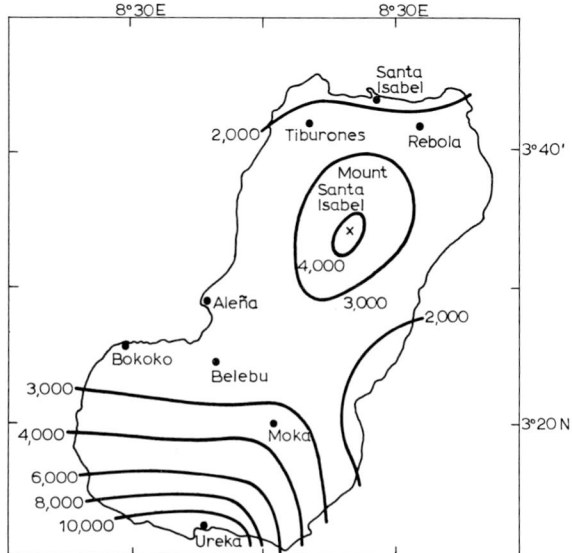

Fig.4. Mean annual rainfall (mm), Fernando Póo.

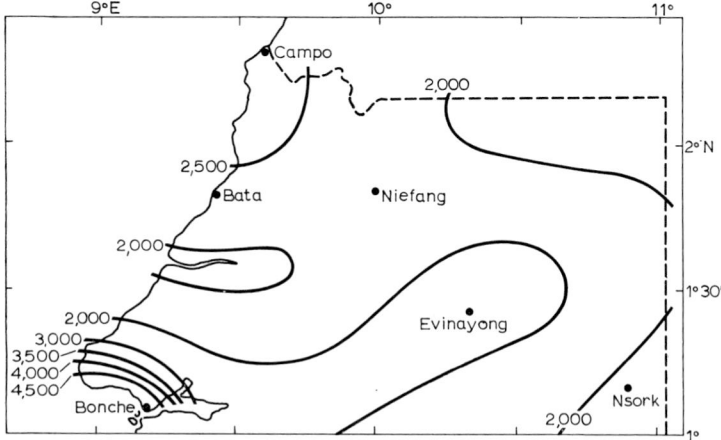

Fig.5. Mean annual rainfall (mm), Rio Muni.

It is seen from Table XXII that the island stations in the north of Fernando Póo exhibit
the double peak of seasonal distribution, with maxima in May–June and September–
October, with a pronounced minimum in December–January. This is the pattern typical
of an equatorial station with rainfall mainly associated with the I.T.C.Z. However, as

TABLE XXII

MEAN RAINFALL AMOUNTS (mm)

	Jan.	Feb.	Mar.	Apr.	May	June	July	Aug.	Sept.	Oct.	Nov.	Dec.	Year	No. of years
Ureka	206	129	293	243	962	2,032	2,205	1,867	1,348	560	410	191	10,450	7 (I)[1]
Bonche	326	269	392	438	474	202	49	111	417	923	675	429	4,705	2 (M)
Moka	82	60	234	236	405	312	638	513	661	376	131	31	3,680	7 (I)
Campo	104	154	188	274	360	175	88	156	480	501	220	96	2,796	17 (M)
Evinayong	132	324	235	330	279	156	5	31	239	367	299	163	2,558	10 (M)
Rebola	38	73	141	220	331	365	241	210	326	353	161	49	2,507	11 (I)
Tiburones	38	54	121	208	292	310	288	298	382	307	147	46	2,492	22 (I)
Bokoko	40	62	82	110	234	253	381	361	491	325	78	44	2,460	18 (I)
Belebu	28	65	125	144	186	279	252	416	362	298	91	32	2,270	13 (I)
Bata	153	151	190	276	295	67	4	44	277	372	218	125	2,172	10 (M)
Aleña	31	69	123	154	246	179	206	212	429	329	147	55	2,168	10 (I)
Niefang	50	99	228	264	255	126	21	42	269	369	292	97	2,112	13 (M)
Nsork	78	135	182	196	216	92	14	50	279	376	218	154	1,987	6 (M)
Santa Isabel	32	65	106	182	238	281	189	167	244	263	89	42	1,898	16 (I)
Annobon	98	177	253	165	99	1	0	4	4	39	142	113	1,094	9 (I)

[1] (I) denotes an island station (Fernando Póo except for Annobon), while (M) is a mainland station (Rio Muni).

the southern part of the island is approached the two maxima tend to merge until, at Ureka, a single maximum occurs. On the continent a complete reversal takes place; the dry season is July–August with maxima in July–August and October (primary). This is the classical pattern of tropical regions in the southern rainfall hemisphere where the I.T.C.Z. moves considerably north of the station in July–August and a dry period ensues. On Fernando Póo it is clear that the relatively heavy July–August rain is due to the island receiving the full brunt of the moist southwesterlies (cf. Chapter 5). This condition is obviously not met with on Annobon, 500 km to the south.

Daily maximum rainfalls in excess of 100 mm have been recorded at all stations, even Annobon, but Santa Isabel, in a rain shadow, has the lowest at 103 mm. Ureka has experienced over 100 mm/day in each month with 602 mm in July and 524 mm in June. Santa Isabel receives 63 days/year in which more than 10 mm fall and 19 days of over 30 mm. May records about one sixth of these values and December one-hundredth. Forty five times per year an hour records more than 10 mm of rain and ten hours have more than 30 mm. Santa Isabel has about two-thirds of its rainfall during the daylight hours, with monthly figures ranging from 48% in March to 75% in July and August, to 88% in December. Line squalls, called "tornados", are noted 28 times per year at Santa Isabel, five each in April and May and zero in July and August. The onset of the "tornado" is usually marked by a change in wind direction, a pronounced gust, a temperature drop of some 3°C and a pressure change of about 1.5 mbar, the classical "gancho do turbonada".

South Cameroons and north Gabon

In this region of about 300,000 km² live most of the population of the Cameroons

Federal Republic (4.5 million population) but only a small percentage of the Gabon's half a million inhabitants. The largest towns are Douala (130,000) and Yaounde (80,000), both in the Cameroons (Fig.6). The major exports from the area are cocoa, coffee, aluminium ore and timber. The topography of this region is very varied, ranging from sea level to over 4,000 m on Mount Cameroon.

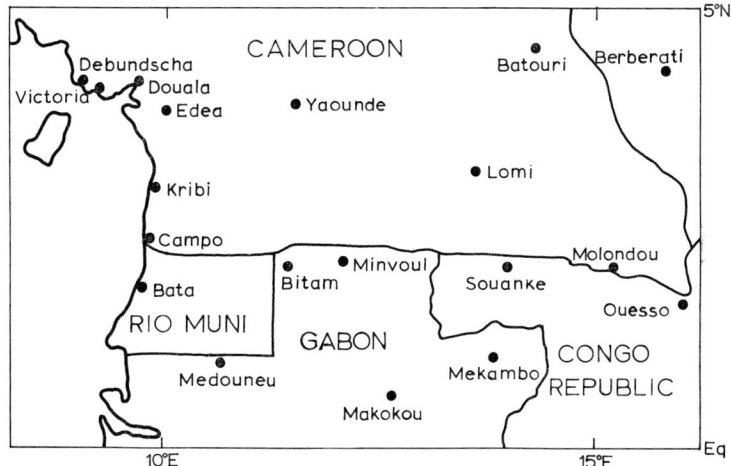

Fig.6. Station locations.

This section of the equatorial wet zone is subject to the advection of moist air masses throughout the year. The convergence zone (I.T.C.Z.) is rarely far removed from the area and some rainfall is recorded in every month. The amount can be very low (less than 10 mm) in the extreme southern portion but some coastal stations have never had a completely dry month (Kribi). Along the coast the west to southerly monsoon sets in during July and, together with local relief characteristics, can give rise to the maximum monthly rainfall being recorded then, although the I.T.C.Z. is far to the north.

Mean annual temperatures average about 24°C with mean maxima of 29°C and mean minima of 19°C, except very near the coast or at higher elevations (above about 600 m). Along the coastal belt maxima are nearly the same as mentioned above but minima are higher by some 2°C. The annual range is less than 3°C over the whole area. Absolute extremes of temperature (below the 500–600 m level) are generally about 35°C for maxima and 10–12°C for minima. On the slopes of the Cameroon mountains, above about 2,500–3,000 m, temperatures around freezing must be reached on most nights.

Relative humidity shows mean monthly values of about 86 ± 4% with, like the temperature, very little annual range. For example, in Makokou during the driest month (July, 5 mm rainfall) the average is 87% and in the wettest month (October, 331 mm rainfall) it is 85%. Afternoon means are about 65–75% but this is reduced to 55–65% at higher elevations during the "dry" season (December and January).

Sunshine averages about 1,300–1,400 h/year (3.5 h/day) near the coast but increases to 1,800 h (5 h/day) in the interior. In the latter region some months average nearly 200 h but normally the range is 50–150 h. Even stations with a markedly dry July and August show very little sunshine (50–70 h) at that time. As the above would suggest, cloud amounts are high, averaging about 6 oktas in Gabon and 5 oktas in Cameroons; maximum values of 6–7 oktas are reached in June to October and most stations show a diminution of cloud cover during the daylight hours.

By the limitation of a minimum of 10 months with in excess of 50 mm rainfall, annual totals are naturally high, being 1,600–1,800 mm over most of the region. (Table XXIII).

TABLE XXIII

MEAN MONTHLY AND ANNUAL RAINFALL (mm)

Station	Jan.	Feb.	Mar.	Apr.	May	June	July	Aug.	Sept.	Oct.	Nov.	Dec.	Year
Debundscha	271	319	545	510	757	1,232	1,460	1,372	1,588	1,204	658	383	10,299
Victoria	31	86	152	185	345	698	1,062	848	454	234	104	41	4,240
Douala	57	82	216	243	337	486	725	776	638	388	150	52	4,150
Kribi	102	128	203	264	378	257	117	234	512	540	197	96	3,017
Edea	37	42	178	249	311	284	234	304	450	403	168	50	2,712
Medouneu	155	163	235	199	160	59	4	14	168	337	301	172	1,969
Makokou	83	124	255	245	182	51	5	18	132	331	210	118	1,755
Bitam	49	72	182	191	231	101	26	37	277	297	208	75	1,747
Mekambo	77	130	182	174	178	88	28	70	153	268	209	104	1,661
Lomi	40	62	123	182	179	141	85	139	268	255	131	42	1,642
Batouri	31	50	119	153	184	173	112	161	217	274	117	34	1,625
Souanke	58	89	166	149	211	114	64	74	209	232	173	58	1,597
Ouesso	56	79	150	127	152	117	79	155	220	226	152	83	1,596
Berberati	21	53	90	134	163	153	137	192	215	268	90	23	1,539
Minvoul	45	71	128	134	202	116	37	60	194	272	181	63	1,503
Molondou	61	91	137	179	147	104	71	93	222	209	135	63	1,492

The quantity increases towards the coast where 2,500–4,000 mm is general. Debundscha with a mean of 10,300 mm is outstanding. In the stations near the centre of the Gulf of Biafra (Debundscha, Douala, Victoria) an effective single maximum occurs but elsewhere double maxima are noticeable. The minima occur at two distinctly different times in different parts of the region, either in December or January or in July. The sharp division over such a small area is repeated right across the continent, until the arid region of eastern Kenya is reached (Fig.7).

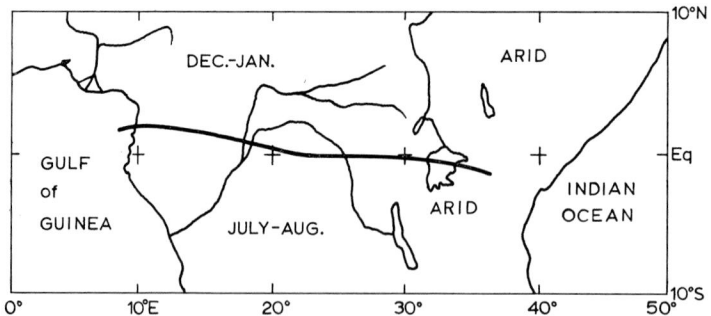

Fig.7. Line of demarcation for months with minimum rainfall.

In the areas with a July minimum the maxima are found in March to May and October, the latter being the dominant one. In the December/January minimum section the maxima are April or May and September or October, with the latter again being the greater. The rapid transition illustrates the great importance to the region of even small movements in the convergence zone that cause extreme changes in the trajectories of the moist air masses from off the Gulf of Guinea.

Daily rainfalls have reached 100–150 mm at all stations, with higher values along the coast—Kribi 205 mm, Douala 238 mm and Victoria 510 mm. Even during the "dry" season 50–100 mm/day is possible.

Annual evaporation is quite low, being about 500 mm at most stations, but reaches nearly 800 mm at Batouri. In the southern section there is little monthly variation but in the northern part July and August often have values about half that measured in February and March. No average values in excess of 100 mm/month have been noted for this area.

Wind speeds are generally low, especially in the interior, with a large percentage of calms quite common, as the climate tables at the end of the chapter show. The direction is dominantly southwesterly to westerly but, in the calmest periods, great variability is normal. With the incidence of line squalls the winds generally back to an easterly direction.

References

BERRUEX, M., 1958. Contribution à la connaissance de l'atmosphère équatoriale. Une année de radio-sondages à Léopoldville. *Acad. Roy. Sci. Outre-Mer (Brussels), Classe Sci. Tech., Mém.*, 5(5): 78 pp.

BROOKS, C. E. P., 1950. *Climate in Everyday Life*. Benn. London, 314 pp.

BUDYKO, M., 1958. *The Heat Balance of the Earth's Surface*. Weather Bureau, Washington, D.C., 259 pp.

BULTOT, F., 1952. Sur le caractère organisé de la pluie au Congo belge. *Publ. Inst. Natl. Etude Agron. Congo Belge, Sér. Tech.*, 6:16 pp.

BULTOT, F., 1954. Saisons et périodes sèches et pluvieuses au Congo belge et au Ruanda-Urundi. *Publ. Inst. Natl. Etude Agron. Congo Belge, Sér. Tech.*, 9:70 pp.

BULTOT, F., 1956. Etude statistique des pluies intenses en un point et sur une aire au Congo belge et au Ruanda-Urundi. *Publ. Inst. Natl. Etude Agron. Congo Belge, Sér. Tech.*, 11:90 pp.

BULTOT, F., 1957. Distribution conjointe de la température et de l'humidité de l'air au Congo belge. *Publ. Inst. Natl. Etude Agron. Congo Belge, Sér. Tech.*, 19:32 pp.

BULTOT, F., 1959. Etude statistique des chutes de grêle au Congo belge et au Ruanda-Urundi. *Publ. Inst. Natl. Etude Agron. Congo Belge, Sér. Tech.*, 17:43 pp.

BULTOT, F., 1962. Sur la détermination des moyennes mensuelles et annuelles de l'évaporation réelle et de l'écoulement dans le bassin congolais. *Bull. Séances Acad. Roy. Sci. Outre-Mer (Brussels)*, 4: 816–838.

BULTOT, F., 1964. Sur la délimitation de la zone tropicale humide. *Bull. Séances Acad. Roy. Sci. Outre-Mer (Brussels)*, 2:406–412.

BULTOT, F., 1965. À propos de l'évaporation du lac Tanganyika. *Bull. Séances Acad. Roy. Sci. Outre-Mer (Brussels)*, 4:1226–1241.

BULTOT, F., 1966. Comparaison des climats sous l'angle de l'effort imposé à l'organisme humain. *Bull. Séances Acad. Roy. Sci. Outre-Mer (Brussels)*, 6:1113–1125.

BULTOT, F., 1967. Estimation à partir d'un nombre limité de mesures des moyennes vraies journalières, diurnes et nocturnes de la température et de l'humidité de l'air au Congo, au Ruanda et au Burundi. *Publ. Inst. Natl. Etude Agron. Congo Belge, Sér. Tech.*, 20:97 pp.

BULTOT, F., 1969. *Atlas Climatique du Bassin Congolais*. In preparation.

CRABBE, M., 1968. Coups de vent et périodes de vent fort au sol au Congo. *Bull. Séances Acad. Roy. Sci. Outre-Mer (Brussels)*, 6:902-938.

DEVROEY, E., 1950. Habitations coloniales et conditionnement de l'air sous les tropiques. *Acad. Roy. Sci. Outre-Mer (Brussels), Classe Sci. Tech., Mém.*, 2(2):228 pp.

DUPRIEZ, G., 1964. Contribution à l'étude du bilan du rayonnement total et de ses composantes en région équatoriale africaine. *Bull. Séances Acad. Roy. Sci. Outre-Mer (Brussels)*, 3:568–616.

DUPRIEZ, G., 1969. La température du sol en région équatoriale africaine. *Acad. Roy. Sci. Outre-Mer (Brussels), Classe Sci. Tech., Mém.*, 16(7):60 pp.

DUPRIEZ, G. and MEYER, J., 1959. Quantités d'azote et d'autres éléments nutritifs apportés au sol par les eaux de pluie au Congo belge et leur intérêt agronomique. *Conf. Interafricaine Sols, 3ᵉ, Dalaba, 1959—Publ. Comm. Coopération Tech. Afrique,* 50:495–499.

FONT-TULLOT, I., 1951. *El Clima de las Posesiones Espanoles del Golfo de Guinea.* Instituto de Estudios Africanos, Madrid.

LEBRUN, A. and VANDER ELST, N., 1958. Le climat de habitation au Congo belge. *Acad. Roy. Sci. Outre-Mer (Brussels), Classe Sci. Tech., Mém.,* 8(2):51 pp.

LEE, D., 1958. Proprioclimats de l'homme et des animaux domestiques. *UNESCO—Arid Zone Res.,* 10.

McINDOE, K. G., 1940. A summary of the meteorological records, 1932–1939. *Firestone Plantation Co., Res. Dept., Rept.,* 11.

PIRE, J., BERRUEX, M. and QUOIDBACH, J., 1960. L'intensité des pluies au Congo et au Ruanda-Urundi. *Acad. Roy. Sci. Outre-Mer (Brussels), Classe Sci. Tech., Mém.,* 6(1):135 pp.

QUOIDBACH, J. and GOLBERT, G., 1969. Vents en altitude au Congo. *Meteorol. Serv. Kinshasa, Publ.,* 49: 13 pp.

RIEHL, H., 1954. *Tropical Meteorology.* McGraw-Hill, New York, N.Y., 392 pp.

SCHUEPP, W., 1953. *Measurement of Atmospheric Turbidity and Precipitable Water with Actinometers.* Meteorol. Serv., Kinshasa, 4 pp. (mimeogr.).

SCHUEPP, W., 1956. *Measurement of Atmospheric Turbidity and Precipitable Water with Actinometers.* Meteorol. Serv., Kinshasa, 5 pp. (mimeogr.).

SCHUEPP, W., 1959. Die Bestimmung der Komponenten der atmosphärischen Trübung aus Aktinometermessungen. *Arch. Meteorol. Geophys. Bioklimatol., Ser. B,* 1(3/4):257–346.

TSCHIRHART, G., 1959. Les perturbations intéressant l'A.E.F. méridionale. *Monograph. Méteorol. Natl.,* 13:32 pp.

VANDENPLAS, A., 1943. La température au Congo belge. *Mém. Inst. Roy. Meteorol. (Brussels),* 13:189 pp.

VANDER ELST, N., 1955. La pression au Congo belge. *Acad. Roy. Sci. Outre-Mer (Brussels), Classe Sci. Tech., Mém.,* 2(2):142 pp.

TABLE XXIV

CLIMATIC TABLE FOR EALA, CONGO
Latitude 0°03'N, longitude 18°18'E, elevation 350 m

Month	Mean sta. press. (mbar)	Temperature (°C) mean		Temperature (°C) extreme		Relat. humid. (%)	Precipitation					Wind		Averages			
		max.	min.	max.	min.		mean (mm)	max. (mm)	min. (mm)	days ≥ 0.1 mm	max. 24 h (mm)	av. speed (km/h)	preval. direct.	cloud-iness (oktas)	sun-shine (h)	radi-ation (Ly/day)	evap. (mm)
Jan.	973	30	21	35	15	87	107	339	8	9	113	2	SW	4	185	357	108
Feb.	973	31	21	37	18	84	125	230	25	8	91	3	SW	4	175	412	118
Mar.	973	31	21	36	18	85	144	279	54	13	103	3	WSW	4	182	442	144
Apr.	973	31	21	35	18	86	155	255	41	13	103	3	WSW	4	177	421	131
May	974	31	21	35	19	86	149	287	65	14	145	2	WSW	4	194	411	129
June	975	30	21	34	18	87	115	288	25	12	84	2	WSW	4	167	382	113
July	976	29	20	32	16	86	80	233	1	7	78	3	WSW	4	169	339	101
Aug.	975	29	20	34	16	84	139	328	33	11	90	3	WSW	5	160	348	105
Sept.	975	30	20	34	16	85	190	334	72	15	87	3	WSW	4	161	401	120
Oct.	975	30	20	34	18	87	203	307	96	16	106	3	WSW	5	163	440	140
Nov.	974	30	20	33	18	87	201	330	93	17	79	2	WSW	5	152	379	114
Dec.	974	30	21	34	18	87	141	233	37	13	79	2	SW	4	166	393	123
Annual	974	30	21	37	15	86	1,749	2,026	1,355	148	145	3	—	4	2,051	394	1,446
Rec. (yrs.)	5	10	10	10	10	3	30	30	30	30	30	2	2	6	6	3	3

TABLE XXV

CLIMATIC TABLE FOR YANGAMBI, CONGO
Latitude 0°49′N, longitude 24°29′E, elevation 487 m

Month	Mean sta. press. (mbar)	Temperature (°C) mean max.	mean min.	extreme max.	extreme min.	Relat. humid. (%)	Precipitation mean (mm)	max. (mm)	min. (mm)	days ≥ 0.1 mm	max. 24 h (mm)	Wind av. speed (km/h)	preval. direct.	Averages cloud- iness (oktas)	sun- shine (h)	radi- ation (Ly/day)	evap. (mm)	diffuse rad. (Ly/day)
Jan.	957	30	20	36	15	84	85	229	18	8	80	3	NE	4	207	411	121	219
Feb.	957	31	19	35	14	81	99	188	34	8	112	3	SW-SE	4	189	447	127	210
Mar.	956	31	20	35	16	84	148	362	58	13	89	4	SW-SE	4	186	454	141	236
Apr.	956	30	20	35	18	86	150	264	37	14	74	4	SW-SE	4	182	446	135	229
May	957	30	20	35	17	86	177	342	85	14	146	3	SW-SE	4	184	441	132	216
June	958	30	20	33	17	87	126	342	25	11	81	3	SW-SE	4	164	391	115	214
July	959	29	19	32	17	88	146	266	43	13	170	3	SW-SE	5	156	345	97	219
Aug.	958	28	20	33	17	88	170	291	55	13	104	4	SW-SE	5	135	363	107	230
Sept.	958	29	19	33	17	87	180	319	79	15	80	4	SW-SE	5	155	409	119	232
Oct.	958	29	20	34	17	87	241	381	113	18	134	4	SW-SE	4	157	412	124	240
Nov.	958	29	20	33	18	86	180	317	54	16	76	3	SW-SE	4	165	422	126	232
Dec.	956	29	20	34	14	88	126	217	0	12	119	3	NE	4	176	373	106	214
Annual	957	30	20	36	14	86	1,828	2,629	1,220	155	170	3	—	4	2,056	410	1,450	224
Rec. (yrs.)	10	10	10	10	10	3	30	30	30	30	30	4	4	10	10	3	3	3

TABLE XXVI

CLIMATIC TABLE FOR BITAM, GABON
Latitude 2°05′N, longitude 11°29′E, elevation 599 m

Month	Temperature (°C)				Relat. humid. (%)	Precipitation					Averages			
	mean		extreme			mean (mm)	max. (mm)	min. (mm)	days ≥ 0.1 mm	max. 24 h (mm)	cloud-iness (oktas)		sun-shine (h)	evap. (mm)
	max.	min.	max.	min.							07h	19h		
Jan.	29	20	33	16	86	49	116	1	5	50	7	4	118	50
Feb.	30	20	33	17	84	72	152	7	6	61	7	5	118	56
Mar.	30	20	34	16	84	182	336	89	13	96	7	5	117	54
Apr.	30	20	35	17	85	191	300	115	16	83	7	5	131	54
May	30	20	33	18	87	231	334	99	16	104	7	5	137	50
June	28	20	34	16	88	101	153	46	10	45	8	5	107	42
July	27	19	33	13	87	26	122	1	5	47	8	5	84	44
Aug.	27	19	32	14	85	37	93	3	5	67	8	6	66	50
Sept.	28	20	32	17	87	277	440	43	17	104	8	6	87	48
Oct.	29	20	32	17	88	297	427	105	22	100	8	6	107	44
Nov.	29	20	32	17	87	208	285	90	16	73	8	6	113	43
Dec.	29	20	32	17	87	75	134	13	8	70	7	4	120	45
Annual	29	20	35	13	86	1,747	2,159	1,174	139	104	7	5	1,304	580
Rec. (yrs.)	12	12	12	12	10	12	12	12	12	12	12	12	8	12

293

TABLE XXVII

CLIMATIC TABLE FOR NIOKA, CONGO
Latitude 2°09'N, longitude 30°39'E, elevation 1,678 m

Month	Temperature (°C)				Relat. humid. (%)	Precipitation					Wind		Averages			
	mean		extreme			mean (mm)	max. (mm)	min. (mm)	days ≥ 0.1 mm	max. 24 h (mm)	av. speed (km/h)	preval. direct.	cloud- iness (oktas)	sun- shine (h)	radia- tion (Ly/ day)	evap. (mm)
	max.	min.	max.	min.												
Jan.	27	12	31	8	64	25	117	0	5	50	6.4	ENE	3	244	504	147
Feb.	28	13	32	7	62	63	198	3	9	42	6.2	ENE	3	206	515	139
Mar.	27	14	32	11	72	100	171	28	13	59	7.3	ENE	4	201	478	144
Apr.	26	14	31	10	77	137	283	47	15	80	6.9	E	4	180	494	144
May	25	14	32	7	77	124	216	64	14	65	6.3	SSE	4	191	472	139
June	24	12	29	9	78	109	216	17	14	56	5.7	SSE	4	172	429	116
July	23	12	27	8	81	120	230	4	16	51	5.4	SSE	5	141	365	95
Aug.	23	13	27	8	83	175	282	45	21	80	5.1	SSE	5	118	377	99
Sept.	24	12	27	9	80	183	349	55	20	79	5.3	ENE	5	148	435	117
Oct.	25	13	27	10	79	131	280	25	17	50	5.9	ENE	5	162	445	127
Nov.	25	13	29	10	72	85	269	9	12	68	6.6	ENE	3	217	519	150
Dec.	26	13	30	8	71	52	143	1	8	72	6.7	ENE	3	245	518	151
Annual	25	13	32	7	75	1,304	1,682	930	164	80	6.2	—	4	2,225	462	1,568
Rec. (yrs.)	10	10	10	10	3	30	30	30	30	30	2	3	8	8	3	3

TABLE XXVIII

CLIMATIC TABLE FOR TSHIBINDA, CONGO
Latitude 2°19'S, longitude 28°45'E, elevation 2,055 m

Month	Temperature (°C)				Relat. humid. (%)	Precipitation					Wind		Averages			
	mean		extreme			mean	max.	min.	days ≥ 0.1	max. 24 h	av. speed	preval. direct.	cloud-iness	sun-shine	radi-ation[1]	diffuse rad.
	max.	min.	max.	min.		(mm)	(mm)	(mm)	mm	(mm)	(km/h)		(oktas)	(h)	(Ly/day)	(Ly/day)
Jan.	22	11	26	8	84	165	301	52	17	72	4	W	5	164	442	238
Feb.	22	12	25	8	86	175	354	50	17	74	4	W	5	136	452	245
Mar.	22	11	25	9	84	195	311	113	18	94	4	SE	5	162	492	234
Apr.	21	12	24	9	88	215	364	122	21	71	4	SE	5	146	463	232
May	21	12	23	9	89	164	295	61	17	68	4	SE	5	131	399	225
June	21	11	24	8	84	56	112	0	7	45	4	SE	4	182	397	188
July	21	9	23	5	76	34	170	0	4	63	4	SE	3	209	404	195
Aug.	22	10	25	7	75	57	165	0	7	73	5	SE	4	196	421	213
Sept.	22	11	27	8	74	145	252	33	15	84	5	SE	4	180	481	220
Oct.	22	11	25	8	83	214	424	99	19	104	4	SE	5	152	454	238
Nov.	22	11	24	8	85	201	398	92	21	91	4	ENE	5	147	484	240
Dec.	22	11	25	9	87	212	358	33	20	78	4	W	5	144	465	243
Annual	22	11	27	5	83	1,833	2,306	1,352	183	104	4		4	1,949	446	226
Rec. (yrs.)	8	8	8	8	3	30	30	30	30	30	2		8	8	4	4

[1] Radiation from Lwiro.

TABLE XXIX

CLIMATIC TABLE FOR KRIBI, CAMEROONS
Latitude 2°57'N, longitude 9°54'E, elevation 624 m

Month	Mean sta. press. (mbar)	Temperature (°C) mean		extreme		Relat. humid. (%)		Precipitation mean (mm)	max. (mm)	min. (mm)	days > 0.1 mm	max. 24 h (mm)	Wind av. speed (km/h)	preval. direct.	calm (%)	Averages cloud- iness (oktas)	evap. (mm)
		max.	min.	max.	min.	max	min										
Jan.	1,008	30	24	33	20	97	76	102	206	20	10	134	5	SW	7	4	67
Feb.	1,008	30	23	34	20	96	74	128	350	30	10	125	5	SW	9	5	69
Mar.	1,007	30	23	34	19	96	74	203	402	47	15	130	4	SW	21	5	70
Apr.	1,007	30	23	33	19	97	74	264	509	161	18	136	3	V	19	5	66
May	1,009	29	23	33	20	97	76	378	654	160	21	205	4	V	22	5	61
June	1,010	28	23	32	20	96	78	257	779	50	16	190	6	V	7	6	64
July	1,010	27	22	31	19	95	77	117	357	9	14	121	6	V	5	6	65
Aug.	1,012	27	22	32	19	96	79	234	773	25	21	122	4	S	14	6	59
Sept.	1,011	27	23	31	20	97	82	512	1,017	243	26	161	4	S	18	6	47
Oct.	1,010	28	22	32	20	98	82	540	927	248	26	175	4	W	22	6	44
Nov.	1,009	29	23	32	20	97	79	197	329	67	18	102	3	W	28	5	52
Dec.	1,009	29	23	32	19	97	76	96	233	7	10	117	5	W	8	4	64
Annual	1,009	29	23	34	19	97	77	3,017	4,070	2,147	205	205	5	—	15	5	728
Rec. (yrs.)	7	27	27	27	27	21	21	30	30	30	30	30	10	10	10	15	20

TABLE XXX

CLIMATIC TABLE FOR BONGABO, CONGO
Latitude 3°06′N, longitude 20°32′E, elevation 450 m

Month	Temperature (°C)				Relat. humid. (%)	Precipitation					Wind preval. direct.	Averages			
	mean		extreme			mean (mm)	max. (mm)	min. (mm)	days ≥ 0.1 mm	max. 24 h (mm)		cloud-iness (oktas)	sun-shine (h)	radi-ation (Ly/day)	evap. (mm)
	max.	min.	max.	min.											
Jan.	31	18	35	12	83	38	91	0	3	85	WSW	3	220	401	117
Feb.	32	19	37	10	78	63	146	12	5	75	WSW	3	202	440	124
Mar.	32	20	38	15	82	135	233	58	10	76	SW	4	199	466	152
Apr.	32	20	35	17	83	167	252	69	11	86	SW	4	193	499	155
May	31	20	35	17	85	189	365	104	13	90	SW	4	191	465	147
June	30	20	34	17	86	180	343	72	11	106	WSW	5	155	413	121
July	29	19	33	16	88	186	319	68	13	73	WSW	5	153	356	104
Aug.	29	20	33	17	87	250	376	81	16	90	WSW	5	142	389	117
Sept.	30	19	34	16	85	207	392	104	14	92	SW	4	162	439	132
Oct.	30	19	34	16	85	209	320	140	15	104	SW	4	175	443	132
Nov.	30	19	34	16	86	130	317	27	9	68	SW	4	165	395	114
Dec.	31	18	34	11	85	56	128	0	5	55	WSW	3	213	419	123
Annual	31	19	38	10	84	1,810	2,210	1,412	124	106	–	4	2,170	427	1,538
Rec. (yrs.)	9	9	9	9	3	20	20	20	20	20		8	8	3	3

TABLE XXXI

CLIMATIC TABLE FOR LOMI, CAMEROONS
Latitude 3°09'N, longitude 13°37'E, elevation 624 m

Month	Temperature (°C)				Relat. humid. (%)		Precipitation					Wind			Averages	
	mean		extreme		max	min	mean (mm)	max. (mm)	min. (mm)	days ≥ 0.1 mm	max. 24 h (mm)	av. speed (km/h)	preval. direct.	calm (%)	cloudiness (oktas)	evap. (mm)
	max.	min.	max.	min.												
Jan.	28	18	32	13	98	68	40	157	0	5	101	3	W	50	4	42
Feb.	29	18	35	12	98	61	62	196	0	5	104	3	W	50	5	50
Mar.	29	19	34	12	98	62	123	340	10	11	88	2	V	53	5	55
Apr.	30	19	34	14	98	63	182	325	64	14	111	2	E	62	5	50
May	29	19	33	15	98	67	179	265	101	17	97	3	E	53	5	46
June	28	19	32	15	98	72	141	274	17	13	86	3	W	51	5	36
July	26	19	31	13	98	72	85	237	5	10	82	3	W	57	6	33
Aug.	27	19	31	13	98	71	133	305	8	12	104	4	V	31	6	37
Sept.	28	19	32	16	98	68	268	581	124	18	125	4	V	30	6	35
Oct.	28	19	32	16	98	69	255	438	122	23	147	3	V	66	6	39
Nov.	28	19	33	15	98	65	131	236	34	15	59	2	V	75	5	38
Dec.	28	18	32	13	98	66	42	128	0	6	80	2	V	90	4	37
Annual	28	19	35	12	98	69	1,642	2,580	1,088	149	147	3	—	56	5	498
Rec. (yrs.)	22	22	22	22	14	14	30	30	30	30	30	10	10	10	15	7

TABLE XXXII

CLIMATIC TABLE FOR BAMBESA, CONGO
Latitude 3°27'N, longitude 25°43'E, elevation 621 m

Month	Temperature (°C)				Relat. humid. (%)	Precipitation					Wind		Averages			
	mean		extreme			mean (mm)	max. (mm)	min. (mm)	days ≥ 0.1 mm	max. 24 h (mm)	av. speed (km/h)	preval. direct.	cloud- iness (oktas)	sun- shine (h)	radi- ation (Ly/day)	evap. (mm)
	max.	min.	max.	min.												
Jan.	31	17	37	10	80	34	75	1	5	45	3	NE	3	234	440	129
Feb.	33	17	39	8	76	73	211	1	7	90	3	NE	3	217	475	131
Mar.	31	19	40	12	83	135	300	48	13	77	4	NE	4	195	464	147
Apr.	31	19	36	13	86	199	324	62	16	90	4	NE	4	184	468	143
May	30	19	33	16	85	201	325	115	17	90	4	NE	4	206	470	149
June	29	19	32	16	87	152	255	86	16	70	3	NE	4	176	427	125
July	28	18	32	15	89	184	298	87	17	83	3	NE	5	162	384	111
Aug.	28	19	32	16	89	205	382	93	18	118	3	NE	5	144	422	126
Sept.	29	19	33	16	87	209	381	86	18	85	3	NE	4	175	466	138
Oct.	30	19	33	15	87	220	358	122	20	82	3	NE	4	186	458	140
Nov.	30	19	33	14	86	128	243	45	13	90	3	NE	4	200	465	138
Dec.	30	17	35	10	85	42	111	2	6	46	3	NE	3	224	441	130
Annual	30	18	40	8	85	1,782	2,396	1,442	166	118	3	—	4	2,303	448	1,607
Rec. (yrs.)	10	10	10	10	3	30	30	30	30	30	2		10	10	3	3

TABLE XXXIII

CLIMATIC TABLE FOR SANTA ISABEL, FERNANDO PÓO
Latitude 3°46'N, longitude 8°46'E, elevation 12 m

Month	Mean press. (mbar)	Temperature (°C) mean		extreme		Relat. humid. (%) 08h00	Precipitation mean (mm)	days ≥ 0.1 mm	max. 24 h (mm)	Wind av. speed (km/h)	preval. direct.	Mean sunshine (h)
		max.	min.	max.	min.							
Jan.	1,011	31	19	35	16	89	32	4	35	4	SW	102
Feb.	1,010	32	21	35	18	87	64	5	79	5	SW	100
Mar.	1,009	31	21	36	19	88	107	10	53	5	SW	112
Apr.	1,010	32	21	36	19	91	182	12	76	5	SW/S	93
May	1,011	31	22	39	19	92	238	18	80	5	SW/S	81
June	1,013	29	21	35	19	92	281	19	88	4	SW	56
July	1,014	29	21	34	17	90	189	18	85	5	SW/W	37
Aug.	1,014	29	21	36	17	90	167	15	62	5	SW/W	50
Sept.	1,013	30	21	36	18	91	243	21	83	5	SW/W	40
Oct.	1,013	30	21	36	18	90	264	20	103	5	SW	72
Nov.	1,011	30	22	33	19	90	89	11	74	5	SW	90
Dec.	1,011	31	21	34	18	91	42	4	72	5	V	91
Annual	1,012	30	21	39	16	90	1,898	157	103	5	—	924
Rec. (yrs.)	6	6	6	6	6	6	6	16	16	6	6	6

TABLE XXXIV

CLIMATIC TABLE FOR DOUALA, CAMEROONS

Latitude 4°01'N, longitude 9°43'E, elevation 11 m

Month	Mean press. (mbar)	Temperature (°C)				Relat. humid. (%)		Precipitation					Wind			Averages		
		mean		extreme				mean (mm)	max. (mm)	min. (mm)	days ≥ 0.1 mm	max. 24 h (mm)	av. speed (km/h)	preval. direct.	calm (%)	cloud-iness (oktas)	sun-shine (h)	evap. (mm)
		max.	min.	max.	min.	max.	min.											
Jan.	1,009	31	23	34	19	98	64	57	183	1	7	93	4	SW	52	4	124	58
Feb.	1,008	32	23	35	20	97	61	82	185	5	10	72	4	SW	46	4	140	60
Mar.	1,008	32	23	34	20	97	62	216	426	58	17	193	3	SW	52	5	134	65
Apr.	1,008	32	23	36	20	98	63	243	349	130	18	123	3	V	68	5	149	60
May	1,010	31	23	35	19	98	65	337	599	141	22	160	2	V	70	6	132	56
June	1,012	29	23	33	20	98	71	486	862	226	24	217	4	V	60	6	88	46
July	1,012	27	22	31	20	98	77	725	1,154	277	29	223	3	V	54	6	41	35
Aug.	1,012	27	22	32	20	98	77	776	1,240	248	29	238	3	V	54	6	39	33
Sept.	1,011	28	23	32	20	98	73	638	980	315	28	193	3	SW	56	6	68	39
Oct.	1,010	29	22	33	20	98	68	388	602	259	26	167	2	SW	62	6	110	47
Nov.	1,009	30	23	34	19	98	67	150	298	36	16	120	2	SW	71	5	122	49
Dec.	1,008	31	23	34	19	98	65	52	184	4	8	76	2	SW	69	4	127	55
Annual	1,010	30	23	36	19	98	68	4,150	5,328	3,238	234	238	3	—	60	5	1,274	603
Rec. (yrs.)	30	27	27	27	27	26	26	30	30	30	30	30	10	10	10	15	25	30

TABLE XXXV

CLIMATIC TABLE FOR KINSHASA, CONGO
Latitude 4°20'S, longitude 15°16'E, elevation 358 m

Month	Mean sta. press. (mbar)	Temperature (°C) mean max.	mean min.	extreme max.	extreme min.	Relat. humid. (%)	Precipitation mean (mm)	max. (mm)	min. (mm)	days ≥ 0.1 mm	max. 24 h (mm)	Wind av. speed (km/h)	preval. direct.	Averages cloudiness (oktas)	sunshine (h)	radiation (Ly/day)	diffuse rad. (Ly/day)
Jan.	978	30	22	34	18	82	128	321	2	10	128	4	WSW	5	132	385	245
Feb.	978	31	22	35	19	80	139	330	49	10	105	5	WSW	5	134	427	248
Mar.	977	31	22	35	19	80	181	429	58	13	108	4	WSW	5	150	448	256
Apr.	977	32	22	34	20	82	209	379	59	15	131	4	WSW	4	166	445	235
May	978	30	22	34	19	83	134	280	22	11	111	4	WSW	5	140	374	220
June	980	28	19	33	15	81	5	38	0	1	29	4	WSW	5	139	332	198
July	981	27	17	32	13	76	1	34	0	0	34	5	WSW	5	125	319	198
Aug.	980	28	18	34	11	69	4	24	0	1	24	6	WSW	5	146	364	221
Sept.	979	30	20	36	16	69	33	100	2	4	73	5	WSW	5	129	375	234
Oct.	978	30	22	35	17	76	137	282	20	11	155	5	WSW	5	132	381	250
Nov.	977	30	22	34	19	81	236	348	84	16	147	5	WSW	5	142	418	245
Dec.	977	30	22	33	20	83	171	327	47	14	73	4	WSW	5	135	380	247
Annual	978	30	21	36	11	79	1,378	1,824	1,124	106	155	5	–	5	1,670	387	235
Rec. (yrs.)	6	10	10	10	10	3	30	30	30	30	30	1		9	9	7	7

TABLE XXXVI

CLIMATIC TABLE FOR LUKI, CONGO
Latitude 5°37'S, longitude 13°06'E, elevation 350 m

Month	Temperature (°C)				Relat. humid. (%)	Precipitation					Wind		Averages			
	mean		extreme			mean (mm)	max. (mm)	min. (mm)	days ≥ 0.1 mm	max. 24 h (mm)	av. speed (km/h)	preval. direct.	cloud- iness (oktas)	sun- shine (h)	radi- ation (Ly/day)	evap. (mm)
	max.	min.	max.	min.												
Jan.	29	22	34	19	86	130	347	12	10	105	3	WSW	5	124	365	111
Feb.	30	21	35	20	83	152	528	0	10	129	3	WSW	5	142	381	105
Mar.	30	22	34	19	84	171	298	20	13	101	3	WSW	5	156	405	126
Apr.	30	22	33	20	88	194	327	98	14	95	3	WSW	5	157	389	116
May	27	21	32	17	89	74	279	2	8	167	3	WSW	6	109	255	68
June	25	18	29	14	85	1	10	0	2	3	3	WSW	5	112	247	57
July	22	16	27	12	86	0	3	0	1	2	3	WSW	7	59	219	50
Aug.	23	17	29	13	85	2	11	0	3	3	4	WSW	7	62	210	49
Sept.	26	19	31	16	85	11	40	0	9	30	4	WSW	7	39	215	53
Oct.	28	20	34	18	85	54	162	9	15	69	4	WSW	7	70	266	77
Nov.	29	21	33	19	85	197	375	12	16	110	4	WSW	6	102	335	98
Dec.	29	21	33	19	86	150	352	11	13	107	3	WSW	5	114	381	118
Annual	28	20	35	12	86	1,136	1,888	574	114	167	3	–	6	1,246	306	1,028
Rec. (yrs.)	6	6	6	6	3	30	30	30	30	30	2		6	6	3	3

TABLE XXXVII

CLIMATIC TABLE FOR TABOU, IVORY COAST
Latitude 4°55'N, longitude 7°22'W, elevation 4 m

Month	Mean sta. press. (mbar)	Temperature (°C) mean		extreme		Relat. humid. (%)		Precipitation mean (mm)	max. (mm)	min. (mm)	days ≥1 mm	max. 24 h (mm)	Wind preval. direct.	calm[1] (%)	Aver. cloudiness (oktas)
		max.	min.	max.	min.	06h	12h								
Jan.	1,010	30	23	33	18	95	79	64	251	1	4	108	SW	28	5
Feb.	1,009	30	23	34	19	95	78	50	111	1	4	60	SW	28	5
Mar.	1,009	31	23	35	13	95	77	98	304	15	7	88	SSW	25	5
Apr.	1,009	31	24	35	20	94	77	153	324	25	11	142	SW	27	5
May	1,011	29	24	35	21	94	81	438	608	258	17	141	SSW	28	6
June	1,013	28	24	32	20	89	82	545	956	167	14	129	SSW	20	7
July	1,014	27	23	32	19	84	77	109	251	17	8	97	SW	6	7
Aug.	1,013	26	22	31	19	89	80	90	198	10	9	113	SW	13	7
Sept.	1,012	27	23	31	19	94	87	257	596	54	17	123	SSW	23	7
Oct.	1,011	28	23	31	21	94	84	229	575	127	14	180	SSW	22	7
Nov.	1,010	29	24	33	19	94	81	180	355	117	13	144	SSW	26	6
Dec.	1,010	30	23	33	20	95	79	170	520	0	9	231	SW	27	5
Annual	1,011	29	23	35	13	93	80	2,383	3,402	2,018	127	231	—	23	6
Rec. (yrs.)	7	19	19	19	19	10	10	30	10	10	15	16	5	5	

[1] Calm = <4 knots.

TABLE XXXVIII

CLIMATIC TABLE FOR LULUABOURG, CONGO

Latitude 5°53'S, longitude 22°25'E, elevation 660 m

Month	Mean sta. press. (mbar)	Temperature (°C)				Relat. humid. (%)	Precipitation					Wind		Averages			
		mean		extreme			mean (mm)	max. (mm)	min. (mm)	days ≥ 0.1 mm	max. 24 h (mm)	av. speed (km/h)	preval. direct.	cloud-iness (oktas)	sun-shine (h)	radi-ation (Ly/day)	evap. (mm)
		max.	min.	max.	min.												
Jan.	937	29	20	35	17	84	128	245	66	12	81	4.11	ESE	5	148	386	121
Feb.	937	29	20	35	16	82	123	259	39	12	72	4.54	ESE	5	132	419	123
Mar.	937	30	20	35	17	84	204	394	71	15	98	5.05	ESE	5	154	430	139
Apr.	938	30	20	35	18	84	177	305	104	15	67	4.93	ENE	4	162	419	130
May	938	31	20	35	16	78	89	195	13	8	58	4.31	ENE	3	218	433	143
June	939	31	18	34	14	66	16	69	0	2	65	3.88	ENE	2	257	399	119
July	938	30	18	35	13	77	17	73	0	2	60	3.80	ENE	3	226	279	123
Aug.	938	30	19	34	14	79	50	121	5	5	63		ENE	4	191	371	116
Sept.	937	30	19	34	15	82	118	200	20	10	61		ENE	4	183	445	141
Oct.	936	30	19	33	17	81	165	411	98	13	179		NNW	4	191	446	145
Nov.	937	29	20	34	17	84	238	413	126	16	92		ESE	5	160	447	137
Dec.	935	29	20	33	17	85	247	378	165	16	118		ESE	5	139	421	132
Annual	937	30	19	35	13	80	1,572	1,962	1,274	126	179	—	—	4	2,161	416	1,569
Rec. (yrs.)	6	9	9	9	9	3	20	20	20	20	20	1	3	9	9	3	3

TABLE XXXIX

CLIMATIC TABLE FOR MONROVIA, LIBERIA
Latitude 6°18'N, longitude 10°45'W, elevation 25 m

Month	Temperature (°C)				Relat. humid. (%)		Precipitation					Wind	
	mean		extreme				mean (mm)	max. (mm)	min. (mm)	days ≥1 mm	max. 24 h (mm)	av. speed (km/h)	preval. direct.
	max.	min.	max.	min.	09h	15h							
Jan.	31	21	33	19	93	79	51	101	15	4	99	6	W
Feb.	31	22	33	18	93	82	71	257	1	3	108	6	W
Mar.	32	22	36	20	91	83	120	304	27	8	182	6	W
Apr.	32	21	34	18	91	83	154	364	10	12	101	6	W
May	31	20	33	18	91	84	442	732	232	22	164	7	S
June	30	21	35	19	92	86	958	—	480	24	308	11	S
July	29	20	34	18	88	85	797	1,460	304	21	363	13	S
Aug.	29	21	31	19	89	84	354	712	101	17	223	13	SW
Sept.	29	21	32	18	93	86	720	948	546	24	271	11	S
Oct.	30	21	33	18	92	84	598	866	264	22	284	8	S
Nov.	31	21	33	20	92	82	237	397	91	16	78	8	S
Dec.	31	21	34	19	94	81	122	304	28	9	76	6	W
Annual	31	21	36	18	92	83	4,624	—		182	363	8	—
Rec. (yrs.)	10	10	10	9	7	7	10	10	10	6	13	6	6

TABLE XL

CLIMATIC TABLE FOR BATOURI, CAMEROONS
Latitude 6°25'N, longitude 14°24'E, elevation 650 m

Month	Mean sta. press. (mbar)	Temperature (°C) mean max.	mean min.	extreme max.	extreme min.	Relat. humid. (%) max.	min.	Precipitation mean (mm)	max. (mm)	min. (mm)	days ≥ 0.1 mm	max. 24 h (mm)	Wind av. speed (km/h)	preval. direct.	calm (%)	Averages cloud-iness (oktas)	sun-shine (h)	evap. (mm)
Jan.	937	30	17	34	11	98	53	31	94	0	3	93	2	W	74	3	161	81
Feb.	936	31	18	36	12	97	47	50	154	<1	5	59	3	W	60	4	165	97
Mar.	936	31	20	37	12	97	53	119	260	28	9	65	3	W	74	5	156	91
Apr.	936	31	20	35	15	98	57	153	272	54	12	120	4	W	76	5	174	74
May	938	30	19	35	14	98	60	184	348	72	14	81	3	V	76	5	192	66
June	939	29	19	34	15	99	65	173	373	56	14	104	2	W	75	5	139	49
July	939	27	19	32	14	99	69	112	325	26	10	94	2	W	75	6	105	44
Aug.	939	27	19	32	14	99	68	161	358	56	12	169	3	W	74	6	94	46
Sept.	938	28	19	32	15	99	64	217	375	79	18	101	4	W	67	6	112	47
Oct.	938	29	19	32	13	99	63	274	409	166	22	102	2	W	75	6	138	50
Nov.	937	29	18	34	14	99	58	117	200	20	11	94	4	V	70	5	178	60
Dec.	937	30	17	34	12	99	55	34	193	0	3	62	2	W	70	3	183	73
Annual	938	29	19	37	11	98	59	1,625	1,913	1,104	133	169	3	—	72	5	1,797	778
Rec. (yrs.)	16	27	27	27	27	26	26	25	25	25	25	25	10	10	10	15	22	20

TABLE XLI

CLIMATIC TABLE FOR GANDAJIKA, CONGO
Latitude 6°45'S, longitude 23°57'E, elevation 780 m

Month	Temperature (°C) mean max.	mean min.	extreme max.	extreme min.	Relat. humid. (%)	Precipitation mean (mm)	max. (mm)	min. (mm)	days ≥ 0.1 mm	max. 24 h (mm)	Wind av. speed (km/h)	preval. direct.	cloud-iness (oktas)	sun-shine (h)	radi-ation (Ly/day)	evap. (mm)
Jan.	29	19	35	16	83	157	288	32	13	95	7	NNW	5	155	422	125
Feb.	30	19	34	16	82	131	241	26	13	99	6	NNW	5	145	432	116
Mar.	30	19	34	16	81	181	412	52	15	87	6	NNW	4	181	469	143
Apr.	31	18	34	16	82	174	369	72	14	102	6	NNW	4	199	492	145
May	31	18	35	13	69	51	140	0	5	70	5	NNW	2	257	485	147
June	32	15	34	11	57	4	25	0	1	23	6	ESE	2	284	428	117
July	31	15	34	10	53	6	55	0	1	42	6	ESE	2	278	418	119
Aug.	32	17	37	12	66	35	94	0	4	73	6	ESE	3	228	399	120
Sept.	31	18	37	15	73	100	237	41	9	100	6	ESE	4	184	431	131
Oct.	30	18	34	16	78	139	258	29	12	106	7	NNW	4	203	453	139
Nov.	30	18	34	16	81	200	447	99	15	108	6	NNW	4	181	470	138
Dec.	29	19	34	15	82	217	378	109	17	119	5	NNW	5	159	462	138
Annual	31	18	37	10	74	1,395	1,916	1,155	119	119	6	—	4	2,454	447	1,578
Rec. (yrs.)	10	10	10	10	3	30	30	30	30	30	3		6	6	3	3

TABLE XLII

CLIMATIC TABLE FOR DARU, SIERRA LEONE
Latitude 7°59′N, longitude 10°52′W, elevation 90 m

Month	M.S.L. press. (mbar)	Temperature (°C)				Mean relat. humid. (%)	Precipitation					Mean cloudiness (oktas)
		mean		extreme			mean (mm)	max. (mm)	min. (mm)	days >1 mm	max. 24 h (mm)	
		max.	min.	max.	min.							
Jan.	1,011	31	19	36	9	78	10	41	0	1	32	4
Feb.	1,010	34	20	38	13	73	36	116	tr.	3	31	4
Mar.	1,010	34	21	37	18	74	101	237	35	7	46	5
Apr.	1,010	33	22	37	16	78	152	242	81	12	51	5
May	1,011	32	22	36	19	80	259	425	144	15	101	6
June	1,013	31	22	36	19	82	287	399	160	20	93	6
July	1,014	29	22	34	18	84	297	451	162	21	93	7
Aug.	1,014	28	22	33	19	85	371	539	122	24	157	7
Sept.	1,013	31	22	34	18	83	416	664	217	23	158	7
Oct.	1,012	31	21	36	18	81	336	638	203	22	93	6
Nov.	1,011	31	21	36	16	82	203	383	54	15	66	6
Dec.	1,011	30	21	35	10	82	56	156	tr.	5	54	5
Annual	1,012	31	21	38	9	80	2,530	2,881	2,179	168	158	6
Rec. (yrs.)	30	18	18	18	18	10	22	20	20	20	9	10

TABLE XLIII

CLIMATIC TABLE FOR KAMINA, CONGO
Latitude 8°44'S, longitude 25°00'E, elevation 1,105 m

Month	Mean sta. press. (mbar)	Temperature (°C) mean max.	Temperature (°C) mean min.	extreme max.	extreme min.	Relat. humid. (%)	Precipitation mean (mm)	max. (mm)	min. (mm)	days ≥ 0.1 mm	max. 24 h (mm)	Wind preval. direct.	Averages cloud-iness (oktas)	sun-shine (h)	radi-ation (Ly/day)
Jan.	899	27	18	31	15	85	201	341	91	12	87	ESE	5	122	381
Feb.	889	27	18	32	15	85	193	313	116	12	67	ESE	6	108	353
Mar.	889	28	18	32	10	84	202	338	98	13	85	ESE	5	150	428
Apr.	889	28	18	32	16	81	119	276	40	9	76	ESE	3	207	457
May	890	29	16	32	12	68	18	66	0	1	66	ESE	2	292	496
June	892	29	14	32	10	50	1	23	0	0	44	SE	1	309	461
July	891	29	14	32	10	43	1	15	0	0	10	SE	1	320	475
Aug.	890	30	16	34	10	47	5	26	0	1	48	SE	2	287	453
Sept.	889	30	14	35	13	63	38	89	6	3	79	SE	3	222	459
Oct.	889	29	18	34	12	73	121	265	16	8	70	ESE	4	195	440
Nov.	889	28	18	32	15	81	191	402	88	12	82	ESE	5	157	441
Dec.	889	27	18	31	15	85	253	373	159	15	165	ESE	5	126	411
Annual	890	29	17	35	10	70	1,343	1,681	1,072	86	165	—	3	2,495	438
Rec. (yrs.)	6	9	9	9	9	3	20	20	20	20	20		7	7	3

TABLE XLIV

CLIMATIC TABLE FOR LUBUMBASHI, CONGO
Latitude 11°39'S, longitude 27°28'E, elevation 1,290 m

Month	Mean sta. press. (mbar)	Temperature (°C)				Relat. humid. (%)	Precipitation					Wind		Averages				
		mean		extreme			mean (mm)	max. (mm)	min. (mm)	days ≥ 0.1 mm	max. 24 h (mm)	av. speed (km/h)	preval. direct.	cloud-iness (oktas)	sun-shine (h)	radi-ation (La/day)	evap. (mm)	diffuse rad. (Ly/day)
		max.	min.	max.	min.													
Jan.	870	27	17	31	13	83	256	427	149	24	116	5	ESE	5	129	451	145	252
Feb.	869	27	17	31	14	85	264	422	130	23	100	5	ESE	5	120	413	118	247
Mar.	870	27	17	31	12	81	210	378	89	21	112	6	ESE	4	174	449	143	234
Apr.	871	27	15	30	10	75	53	155	9	9	94	7	SE	3	234	465	143	181
May	873	27	12	31	3	68	3	41	0	2	23	7	SE	2	291	480	132	115
June	874	25	9	30	4	62	0	4	0	0	3	7	SE	1	295	468	114	103
July	874	25	8	29	4	54	0	0	0	0	0	6	ESE	1	315	477	117	96
Aug.	873	28	11	34	3	45	0	15	0	0	12	6	ESE	1	318	523	138	119
Sept.	871	31	14	36	9	42	3	31	0	1	27	9	ESE	1	294	555	146	155
Oct.	870	32	16	37	9	44	27	72	0	5	56	8	V	2	282	554	160	189
Nov.	870	29	17	36	13	74	166	396	43	17	88	5	ESE	4	194	493	154	207
Dec.	870	27	17	32	13	83	262	479	113	24	81	4	ESE	5	132	445	136	255
Annual	871	28	14	37	3	66	1,244	1,554	868	126	116	6	—	3	2,778	481	1,646	179
Rec. (yrs.)	6	10	10	10	10	3	30	30	30	30	30	3	3	10	10	5	5	5

Chapter 9

Eastern Africa

J. F. GRIFFITHS

Introduction

In an area covering more than 1.5 million km² astride the equator lie the republics of Kenya, Uganda and Tanzania (Fig.1). Within this zone are found most of the equatorial and tropical climatic regions ranging from the hot, humid coast through arid scrub land to the dense equatorial rain forests and the highland climes. The mountains, which rise to above 6,000 m, have on their slopes a vast variety of vegetation and climates, going through dry areas to wet, cloud forests, open moorland and the perpetual snow belt.

Kenya covers about 580,000 km² and has a population of nearly ten million. The two largest cities are Nairobi (300,000 people) and Mombasa (180,000), and coffee, tea, sisal, meats and pyrethrum are the chief exports. Uganda, the smallest of the three republics,

Fig.1. Station locations.

is only 240,000 km² in extent and has a population of seven million. The capital is Kampala (50,000) and its chief exports are coffee, cotton and tea. Tanzania (originally, Tanganyika and Zanzibar) is over 940,000 km² and has a population of ten million, of whom 130,000 live in the capital Dar-es-Salaam. The chief exports are sisal, cotton, coffee and diamonds.

Causes of the climate

In general, considering its equatorial position, East Africa does not experience much rainfall. TREWARTHA (1961) has given as the reason for this dryness: (*1*) the divergent character of both the northeast and the southwest monsoons; (*2*) the shallow depth of the southwest monsoon; (*3*) the strong meridional flow in all but the transition seasons; and (*4*) the stable stratification aloft together with a marked decline in the moisture content. In this zone, affected greatly by the I.T.C.Z., the front becomes very diffuse due to the topography of the area. The high mountains break up some of the classical patterns and superimpose their own upon the rather indeterminate I.T.C.Z. This fact, together with the influence of the great lakes, introduces such significant modifications to the flow that the seasons cannot be said to follow the classical (I.T.C.Z.) pattern with enough correlation and reliance to make the approach a practical one. Broadly speaking, there are two main synoptic subdivisions of the annual pattern, the period from early June to early October and the period from November to the end of April. May and late October are best considered simply as transitional stages.

From June to October a low pressure over Uganda and a high pressure ridge over the Tanzanian coast help bring about the rainfall patterns that are illustrated later in Fig.5. Then, in the second period a number of synoptic situations can exist, situations that are identified mainly by the upper air pressure fields and the pressure patterns in middle tropical latitudes (JOHNSON and MÖRTH, 1960). It is because these situations may occur at any time during the period that the variations in rainfall amount are so great.

Radiation, sunshine and cloudiness

During the past ten years great use has been made in East Africa of the Gunn–Bellani distillometer, a spherical radiation integrator, for the measurement of global radiation. In excess of 50 stations now have reliable records with this instrument and Fig.2 gives a representation of the pattern of annual means in East Africa using the complete data.

Tables I–III give the mean monthly global radiation values for some months at the 54 stations with consistent data. Values in excess of 500 cal./cm² day as an annual average occur in four distinct areas, northeast Uganda/northwest Kenya, eastern Kenya, central Tanzania and southern Tanzania. The lowest values are found in the region of Mount Elgon (312 cal./cm² day) but, if data were available, it is likely that less would be recorded in the area close to the Ruwenzori Mountains. There are only small areas with annual means below 400 cal./cm² day. Monthly means in excess of 550 cal./cm² day generally occur only in November–February, except in central Tanzania where September and October give high radiation values. Monthly means below 300 cal./cm² day are very rare.

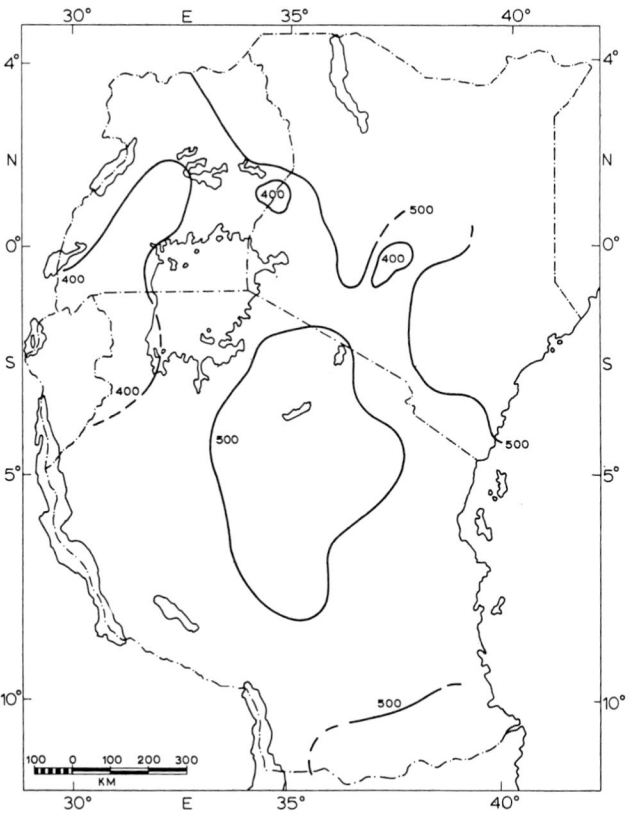

Fig.2. Mean annual global radiation (cal./cm² day).

TABLE I

MEAN MONTHLY AND ANNUAL GLOBAL RADIATION, KENYA (cal./cm² day)

Station	Lat.	Long. (E)	Alt. (m)	Jan.	Apr.	July	Oct.	Annual
Garissa	0°29′S	39°38′	128	472	450	391	410	429
Kabete	1°16′S	36°45′	1,820	627	517	348	545	506
Katumani	1°35′S	37°14′	1,600	545	485	390	495	490
Kedong	0°55′S	36°30′	1,900	536	490	401	523	483
Kericho	0° 4′S	35°20′	2,070	530	445	427	448	471
Kimakia	0°48′S	36°45′	2,500	536	465	293	487	452
Kitale	1°00′N	35°00′	1,896	607	467	425	469	493
Kitui	1°21′S	35°00′	1,090	577	537	399	531	509
Koru	0° 7′S	35°16′	1,620	553	473	440	445	482
Lodwar	3° 7′N	35°37′	506	518	456	498	528	512
Marigat	0°30′N	36°02′	1,000	598	527	525	548	560
Mombasa	4°02′S	39°37′	55	563	575	384	542	504
Muguga	1°13′S	36°38′	2,100	537	460	346	496	463
Mwea Tebere	0°42′S	37°22′	1,280	643	590	388	543	555
Nairobi	1°18′S	35°50′	1,890	547	458	321	472	452
Nakuru	0°16′S	36° 4′	1,811	585	471	458	488	508
Narok	1° 8′S	35°50′	1,890	520	448	404	493	467
Ol Joro Orok	0° 7′S	36°21′	2,380	436	420	347	403	411
Ruiru	1° 4′S	34°54′	1,610	450	415	370	455	408
S. Kinangop	0°37′S	36°42′		408	383	301	406	376
Thika	0°59′S	37° 4′	1,550	535	447	342	457	451
Voi	3°24′S	38°34′	560	493	451	361	445	449

TABLE II

MEAN MONTHLY AND ANNUAL GLOBAL RADIATION, TANZANIA (cal./cm² day)

Station	Lat. (S)	Long. (E)	Alt. (m)	Jan.	Apr.	July	Oct.	Annual
Arusha Chini	3°30′	37°18′	700	625	495	415	560	521
Bukoba	1°20′	31°49′	1,137	392	362	400	353	375
Dar-es-Salaam	6°53′	39°12′	55	468	336	368	450	419
Dodoma	6°10′	35°40′	1,119	485	424	420	497	451
Iringa	7°40′	35°45′	1,426	536	455	526	582	519
Kongwa	6°12′	36°25′	1,021	481	400	449	578	480
Lyamungu	3°14′	37°15′	1,250	570	328	312	482	412
Mbeya	8°50′	33°28′	2,400	385	395	529	512	451
Mwanza	2°28′	32°55′	1,139	504	465	487	474	473
Nachingwea	10°21′	38°46′	440	534	513	515	554	526
Ngomeni	5° 9′	38°54′	180	605	430	405	510	500
Sao Hill	8°29′	35°12′	2,000	475	430	435	640	478
Seatondale	7°47′	35°31′	1,550	445	433	503	610	502
Tabora	5° 5′	32°50′	1,181	511	460	497	504	486
Ukiriguru	2°42′	33° 1′	1,200	560	523	565	570	552
Zanzibar	6°13′	29°13′	15	454	375	408	442	461

TABLE III

MEAN MONTHLY AND ANNUAL GLOBAL RADIATION, UGANDA (cal./cm² day)

Station	Lat.	Long. (E)	Alt. (m)	Jan.	Apr.	July	Oct.	Annual
Atumatak	2°14′N	34°39′	1,280	568	513	457	531	523
Bugusege	1° 9′N	34°15′	1,433	366	284	263	290	312
Entebbe	0° 3′N	32°27′	1,146	474	440	402	435	439
Gulu	2°45′N	32°20′	1,109	474	397	362	440	426
Jinja	0°27′N	33°11′	1,173	494	443	352	451	436
Kabanyolo	0°28′N	32°37′	1,137	421	414	358	405	397
Kasese	0°11′N	30° 6′	959	457	410	387	434	437
Lira	2°17′N	32°56′	1,200	486	441	397	496	464
Masindi	1°41′N	31°45′	1,146	431	383	323	310	385
Mbarara	0°37′S	30°39′	1,443	393	390	366	366	379
Namalu	1°48′N	34°36′	1,220	448	374	346	416	399
Namulonge	0°32′N	32°37′	1,148	443	423	372	424	418
Nyakatonzi	0° 2′S	29°50′	1,030	434	471	418	484	462
Orichinga	0°52′S	30°47′	1,280	379	359	379	403	382
Tororo	0°41′N	34°10′	1,170	578	467	413	509	493
Wadelai	2°44′N	31°24′	640	451	434	368	449	430

Hourly analysis of radiation is only possible for the Nairobi station (GRIFFITHS, 1967) at which an Eppley pyranometer is installed. Since Nairobi is located close to the equator it is quite meaningful to group all the months together to show the mean diurnal variation, and this is depicted in Fig.3. On the same diagram mean values for the diffuse radiation and the ratio (diffuse/global) are given. It is apparent that, during the hours of high

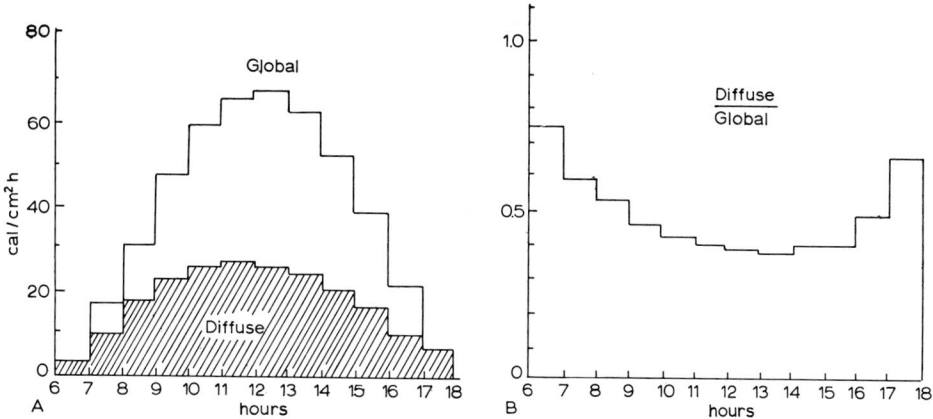

Fig.3. Mean annual radiation details for Nairobi (cal./cm² day).

sun, the ratio is steady at about 0.4. However, this ratio does show some variation during the year, as is clear from Fig.4 where the extremes are given.

In Table IV some sunshine statistics are presented for eighteen stations. It is seen that East Africa receives an average of about 7 h/day, 2,500 h/year, while in central Tanzania and northern Kenya the total reaches in excess of 3,000 h. Lyamungu, on the southern slopes of Kilimanjaro, receives just over 1,600 h/year. Monthly means naturally show a direct correlation with the rainfall seasons and variation within months gives rise to a standard deviation of approximately 15%. From Table IV, it can be seen that Dar-es-Salaam and Equator have very similar sunshine, and therefore radiation amounts, but very different mean annual temperatures, 26°C and 13°C respectively. Temperature does not necessarily depend on the incoming radiation load.

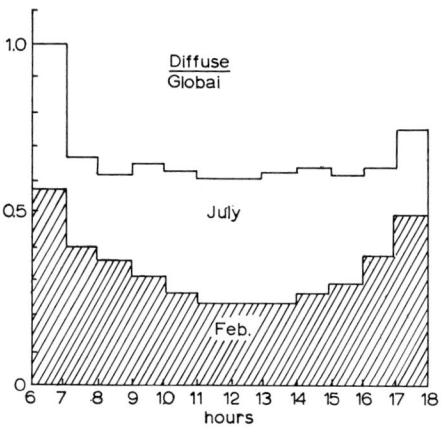

Fig.4. Radiation at Nairobi (cal./cm² day).

A paper by GLOVER and McCULLOCH (1958) showed that sunshine and radiation are significantly linked by the equation:

$$R/R_a = 0.29 \cos \gamma + 0.52n/N$$

where R is the short wave radiation received at station in latitude γ on a horizontal

TABLE IV

SUNSHINE HOURS FOR SELECTED STATIONS

Station	Alt. (m)	Sunshine (h/day)		
		mean	maximum	minimum
Dar-es-Salaam	50	7.6	9.0 (Nov.)	5.2 (Apr.)
Equator	2,760	7.5	9.1 (Feb.)	5.2 (July, Aug.)
Gulu	1,110	7.8	9.0 (Jan.)	6.2 (July)
Kabale	1,870	4.9	5.5 (July)	3.7 (May)
Kampala	1,310	6.5	7.7 (Jan.)	5.7 (July)
Kisumu	1,150	7.8	8.6 (Jan.)	5.9 (July, Aug.)
Kongwa	1,020	8.5	10.1 (Sept.)	6.9 (Jan.)
Lamu	30	8.7	10.1 (Oct.)	7.9 (Apr.)
Lodwar	510	8.7	10.7 (Sept.)	8.4 (July)
Lyamungu	1,250	4.3	6.4 (Jan., Feb.)	2.4 (June)
Mombasa	50	8.2	9.1 (Mar.)	6.8 (July)
Morogoro	580	5.1	6.2 (Feb.)	3.7 (May)
Nairobi	1,800	6.9	9.5 (Feb.)	4.2 (July, Aug.)
Naivasha	1,900	5.0	5.7 (Oct.)	4.2 (Dec.)
Nakuru	1,890	7.1	7.9 (Jan.)	6.6 (Apr.)
Namulonge	1,150	5.5	6.1 (Jan., Mar.)	4.9 (Aug.)
Nanyuki	1,950	6.0	7.3 (Jan.)	4.1 (Nov.)
Tabora	1,270	8.6	10.6 (July)	6.9 (Jan.)

plane, R_a is the same as R but with a completely transparent atmosphere, n/N is the percentage sunshine. For East Africa $N = 12.1$ (maximum error ± 0.6) and $\cos \gamma = 1$ (maximum error -0.015) so that:

$$R/R_a = 0.29 - 0.043\,n$$

The diurnal variation of sunshine shows many distinct patterns over the territory (GRIFFITHS, 1967) and Fig.5 illustrates the pattern at just two stations, Kabete and Equator. The clear skies of February are evident around Nairobi but it is seen that in July the early morning stratus burns off by about mid-day. At Equator, in both February and August, the day is characterized by continuous build-up of cumulus and cumulo-nimbus clouds. In view of this it appears strange that the annual means for all stations show remarkably little variation between the 09h00 and 15h00 local time readings. The only stations showing an afternoon build up of 2 oktas are Mbale, Kitale, Nanyuki and Iringa. A few stations exhibit a decrease in the afternoon, but never of more than

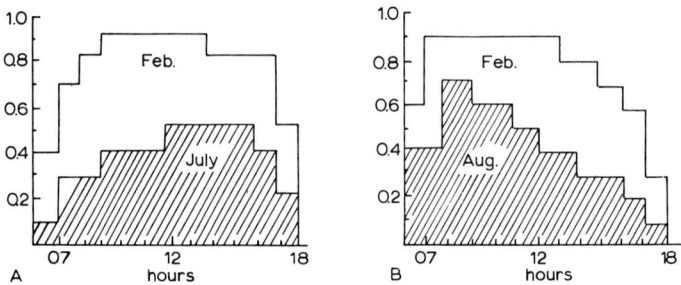

Fig.5. Diurnal variation of sunshine. A. Kabete; B. Equator.

one okta. Most of the annual means are in the range 4–6 with Kabale at 7 being the largest, and Isiolo and Lamu, both 3.5, the least. Mean monthly values below 2 oktas are generally reported only from central Tanzania in the June–October dry spell. The highest value is at Lyamungu at 09h00 in April–June when 7.5 is reached.

Temperature

In equatorial regions, such as East Africa, the variation of the mean monthly air temperature through the year is very small, usually being about 1°–2°C in southwest Uganda and the southwestern half of Lake Victoria, with a maximum of 5°–6°C in southern Tanzania. This fact makes it allowable, in a short section such as this, to concentrate on the mean annual values, correcting later for seasonal variation if required.

Nearly all stations report July or, sometimes, August as the coldest month. The warmest month shows a greater variation, from February in Uganda and extreme southwestern Kenya, to March in Kenya and parts of Tanzania, to November and December in central and southern Tanzania. A small region from Musoma to Tabora exhibits a maximum temperature in October.

As may be expected, the mean annual maximum and minimum temperatures in the zone are very closely correlated with station elevation. The lapse rate remains reasonably constant within the territories but the constant of the regression does change. The equations of best fit were calculated to be (GRIFFITHS, 1968):

maximum temperature $= 34 - 5.6\,h$
minimum temperature $= 24.5 - 6.3\,h$

where temperatures are in °C and h is the elevation in thousands of metres. The areas in which temperatures differ by more than 2°C from these given equations are shown in Fig.6. It should be noted that the coastal region is excluded from the pattern of the equations as this region is subjected to distinct cooling by the land–sea breeze cycle and presents a different population of values. The boundaries suggested in Fig.6 are not too well defined due to the paucity of reliable data in some regions but it is apparent that there is no obvious correlation between the deviations and latitude or longitude. A recent study by KENWORTHY (1966) has indicated that conditions at a given elevation in the east Kenya highlands are generally believed to be warmer, at the same elevation, than in the west Kenya highlands where cloudiness and mist are more common. The linear regression method she used would tend to indicate this fact but differences are hardly mathematically significant although from a practical viewpoint the lower maxima in the west Kenya highlands may be important.

In this zone there are few stations that have recorded a screen frost and even ground frosts seldom occur below 2,400 m, except during July and August in the southern highlands of Tanzania and, occasionally, in cold air drainage hollows (frost hollows) down to about 1,800 m.

Temperatures in excess of 40°C are rare, only Soroti (40.1°C), Mandera (40.1°C), Magadi (42°C) and Garissa (46°C) of the regularly reporting stations reaching this limit. There may be some doubt about the Garissa high readings of 1957 but it is likely that the area does reach temperatures above 40°C.

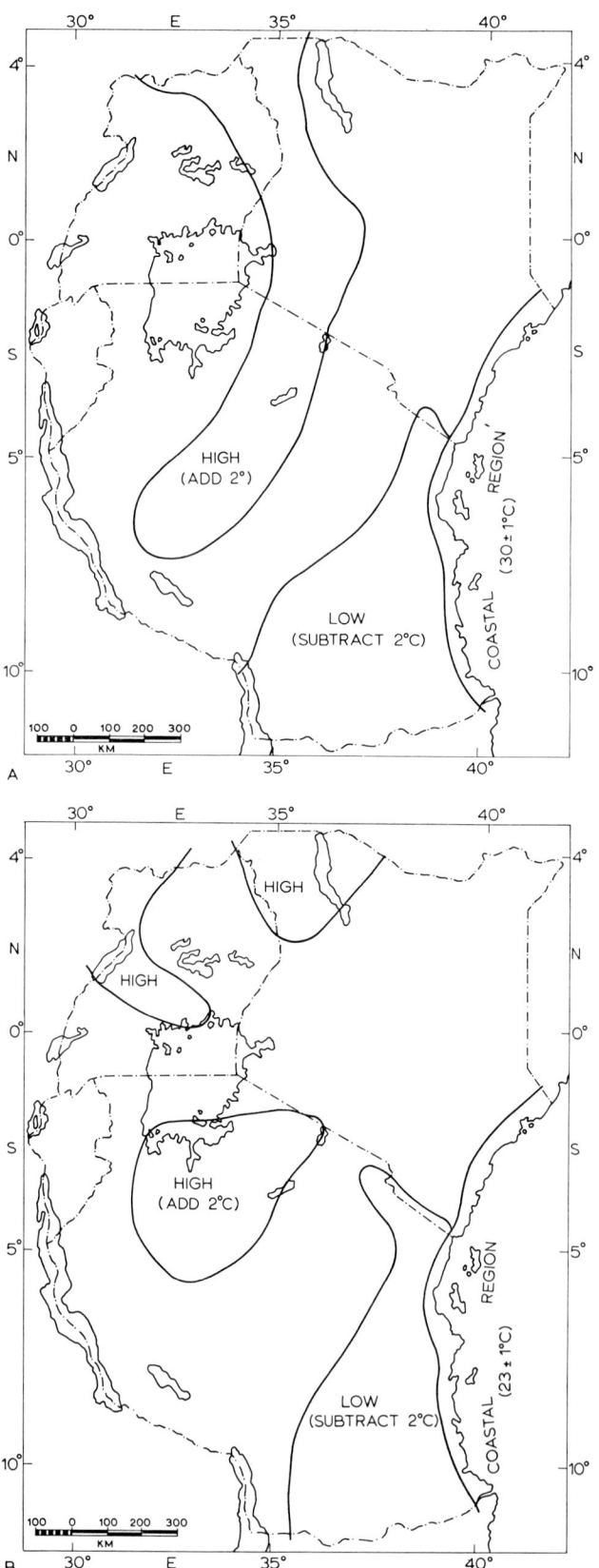

Fig.6A. Deviations of mean annual maximum temperature from altitude corrected mean.
B. Deviations of mean annual minimum temperature from altitude corrected mean.

The diurnal variation at most stations is in the range 10–13°C, except along the coast or near the lakes where 7–9°C is more usual. Lamu, with 5°C, has the smallest daily fluctuation. Values around 16°C are reached in extreme northern Uganda and in the Rift Valley from Nakuru to Narok.

Soil temperatures measurement are, unfortunately, relatively rare and many of the data are summarized in Table V.

TABLE V

SOIL TEMPERATURES AT SELECTED STATIONS (°C)[1]

Station	Alt. (m)	Mean air temp.	Mean soil temp.	Mean range at		Excess of soil over air temp.
				15 cm	120 cm	
Dar-es-Salaam	0	26	29	7	4	3
Entebbe	1,200	22	24	–	1	2
Kabete (Nairobi)	1,800	18	22	5	2	4
Muguga (near Nairobi)	2,100	16	21	6	2	5

[1] The mean temperatures from about 10 to 120 cm do not differ from the profile mean by more than approximately 1°C.

Rainfall

This zone is well known for the year to year variation in rainfall amounts in addition to the wide variation in the time of year at which the rain falls. Because of these facts a simple map, such as that of the mean annual rainfall (Fig.7), can prove extremely misleading. Due to the great variability in annual totals it is necessary to present the data in the form of probability maps. Such maps will show, for instance, the amount likely to be exceeded four years out of five (GRIFFITHS and STOCK, 1961) or the probability of receiving 30 inches (750 mm) in a year (GLOVER et al., 1954). From the former map Table VI has been calculated.

The implications of this table are disconcerting. Kenya receives a reliable 750 mm/year in only a seventh of the territory, compared with about half of Tanzania and three-quarters of Uganda.

Seasonal distribution

In a recent study (GRIFFITHS, 1968) the movement of the rain areas, on a month to month basis, was shown for the whole of East Africa. In this presentation the 50 mm in a month isohyet was used as the line of demarcation between wet and dry months. This chosen amount could be criticised but any other reasonable threshold will show, broadly, the same patterns. In Fig.8 the rainfall areas are indicated for eight months of the year. In April the whole zone is "wet" (more than 50 mm) and Fig.8A shows quite effectively how the area begins to "dry out" in May as the isohyets close in from both north and south,

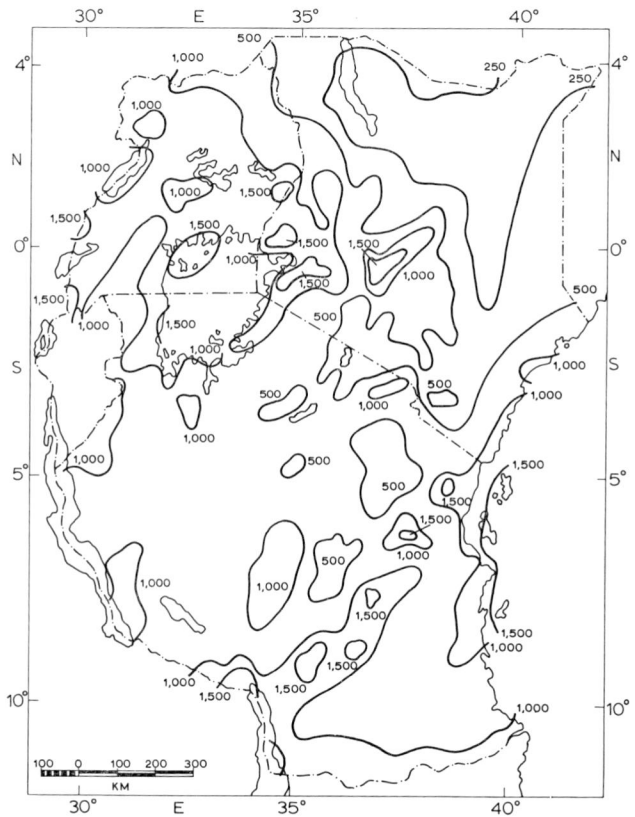

Fig.7. Mean annual rainfall (mm), generalized.

TABLE VI

PERCENTAGE OF LAND AREA RECEIVING SELECTED AMOUNTS OF ANNUAL RAINFALL IN 4 YEARS OUT OF 5

Rainfall (mm)	Kenya	Tanzania	Uganda	E. Africa
< 500	72	16	12	35
500–750	13	33	10	20
750–1,250	12	47	72	41
> 1,250	3	4	6	4

a process that continues in June. During July, August and September this reduction in "wet" area proceeds slowly, with local variations around Mount Kenya and the Aberdares, until September (Fig.8B) becomes, in area, the driest month of the year. The effect of the "monsoon" circulation at the coast is very much in evidence. The October pattern is a gradual enlarging of the two distinct areas until they coalesce. November is seen to be, like May, a transitional month.

By December (Fig.8C) the whole of Tanzania is receiving more than 50 mm while the northern boundary of the rain belt is retreating southwards. The isohyet continues to move southwards until the January limit is reached. The February and March lines (Fig.

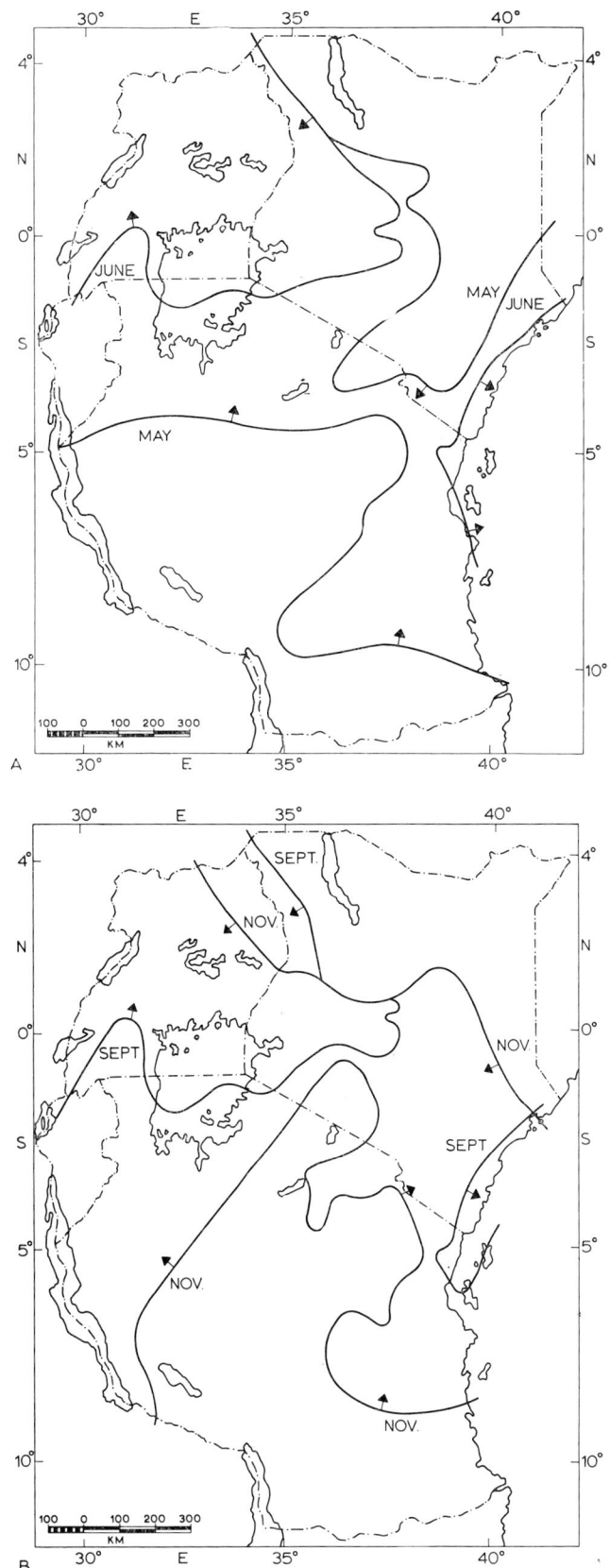

Fig.8. A and B (legend see p.324).

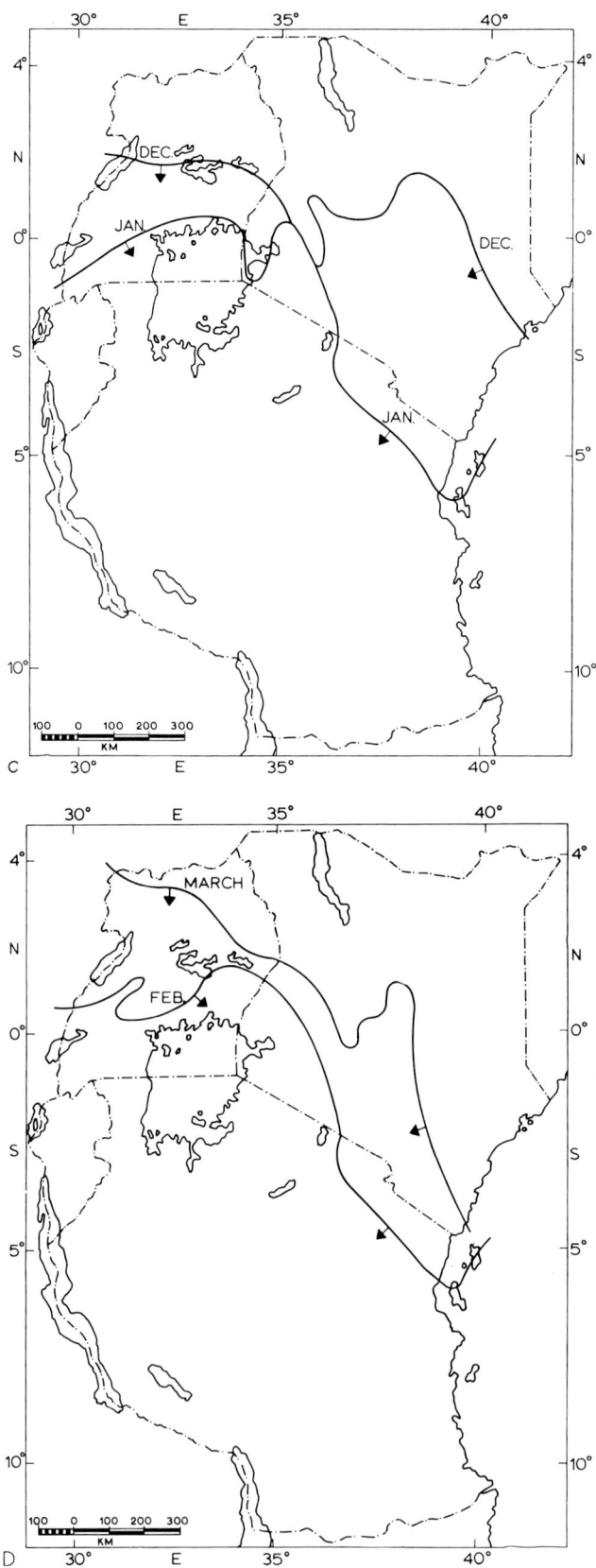

Fig.8. 50-mm isohyets. A. May and June; B. September and November; C. December and January; D. February and March.

8D) show a movement towards the northeast and a trend naturally into the "wet" pattern of April.

By making a composite map from the twelve monthly patterns the distribution of rainfall seasons is made evident, and this is shown in Fig.9. The extremely complex nature of the

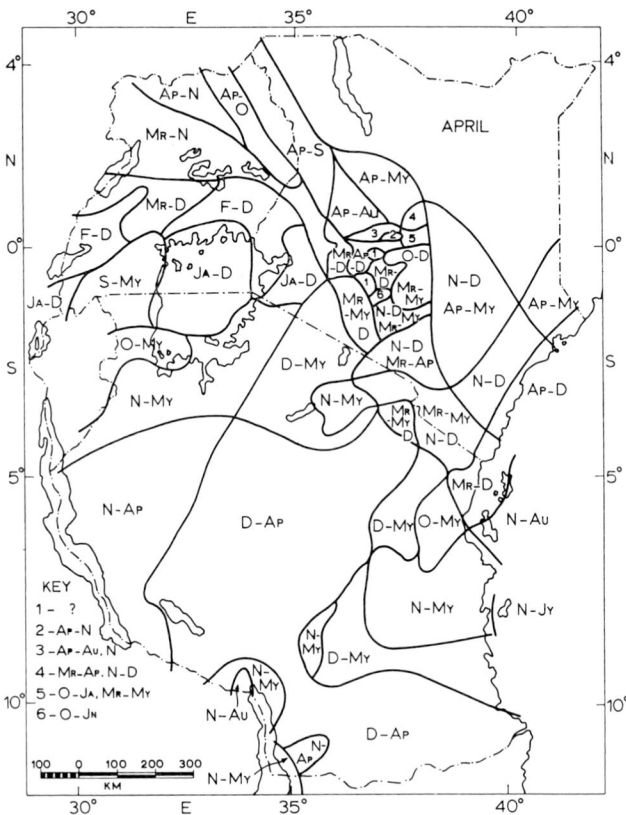

Fig.9. Rainfall regions.

rainfall climatology is very evident from this figure. There are 52 separate regions covering 30 different rainfall seasons. Table VII gives a breakdown of the areal distribution of these regimes.

Variation and periodicity

Perhaps the station that exhibits the greatest variation between years is Makindu (Table VIII). Many stations have recorded months with amounts ranging from zero to over 500 mm while Meru (Kenya) has recorded as high as 1,386 mm and as low as 15 mm in October. Annual falls in excess of 3,000 mm usually occur only in southern Tanzania, with Kyela (9°35′S 33°51′E, 540 m) holding the records with 4,972 mm in a year and 1,441 mm in a month (April).

Many stations in Africa and in the temperate regions show a single peak in the seasonal distribution of rainfall but in East Africa a pattern with two maxima is quite common. Of course, when the two maxima are caused by an intervening month(s) having just a few millimetres less, the periodicity is really trivial and so, in the finality, a definition of

TABLE VII

AREAL DISTRIBUTION OF GIVEN RAINFALL REGIMES

Single period		Double period						
No. wet months	% area	No. wet months	wet	dry	wet	dry	% area
12	1.8	7	4	1	3	4	0.2
11	3.7	7	4	2	3	3	1.0
10	3.5	6	5	2	1	4	0.2
9	6.9	5	2	2	3	5	2.3
8	3.2	4	2	2	2	6	1.3
7	12.3	4	1	2	3	6	1.4
6	16.4	4	2	3	2	5	2.0
5	22.7	3	2	3	1	6	3.5
2	2.6	unident.					0.2
1	14.8						
	Total 87.9					*Total* 12.1	

TABLE VIII

RAINFALL AT MAKINDU (mm)

	Jan.	Feb.	Mar.	Apr.	May	June	July	Aug.	Sept.	Oct.	Nov.	Dec.	Year
Maximum	214	175	650	822	203	41	8	7	29	327	518	603	1,964
Average	40	28	79	111	31	2	1	1	1	29	68	120	611
Minimum	0	0	0	0	0	0	0	0	0	0	0	0	67

double periodicity is bound to be subjective. Here, the criterion has been chosen that both maxima must exceed 50 mm while both minima must be less than 50 mm. In this case the pattern depicted in Fig.10 ensues, lending credence to the belief that the Kenya highlands cause a retardation of the normal movement of the I.T.C.Z. which, later, moves forward rapidly to "catch up" with the western and central sections.

A measure of the periodicity may be made by expressing the difference between the secondary maximum and the secondary minimum as a percentage of the annual mean. In this case a number of stations yield a value of more than 20% with Garba Tulla (27%) and El Wak (26%) being the most extreme. For stations with an annual mean of more than 1,000 mm the value of 22% for Kitui is outstanding. The monthly means for these three stations are given in Table IX.

Diurnal distribution

In regions such as East Africa, where agriculture plays a fundamental role in the economy and survival of the countries, a most important aspect of rainfall patterns is the time of day at which the rain occurs. A paper by THOMPSON (1957), together with a

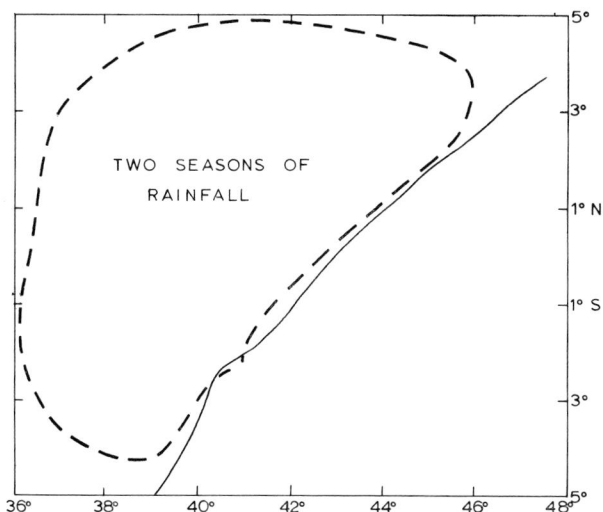

Fig.10. Area of eastern Africa with pronounced two-season rainfall.

TABLE IX

STATIONS WITH MARKED RAINFALL PERIODICITY (mm)

Stations	Jan.	Feb.	Mar.	Apr.	May	June	July	Aug.	Sept.	Oct.	Nov.	Dec.	Year
Garba Tulla	6	6	28	112	13	0	0	0	0	25	115	56	361
El Wak	0	0	37	82	20	0	2	4	3	51	95	16	310
Kitui	41	24	118	244	56	5	3	5	6	82	304	143	1,031

recent set of statistics (EAST AFRICAN METEOROLOGICAL DEPARTMENT, 1968), has shown "... the absence at many inland stations of the strong afternoon maximum of rainfall which should occur, on the simple continental theory of diurnal rainfall variation". For fuller details these papers should be consulted but, briefly, the findings are as given in the following paragraphs.

During the wet months (amounts in excess of about 200 mm) many stations do not show a distinct time of maximum. By this is meant that the percentage occurring in each hour varies only between about 2 and 7%, compared with the ideal of 4% (100/24) of a non-temporal distribution.

Considering the times of maxima it is found that they follow the pattern outlined below:

(*1*) 00h00–03h00—a rare occurrence, noted at Nairobi in March, Lyamungu in April.

(*2*) 03h00–06h00—a high maximum over northwest Lake Victoria during November to May (during the northeast monsoon), and also at Kigoma on Lake Tanganyika. Occurs at Malindi in March, April and September.

(*3*) 06h00–09h00—high maximum over northwest Lake Victoria in May to September (during the southeast monsoon), and also at Mombasa in August and October.

(*4*) 09h00–12h00—small amounts occur over Kenya and in central and southern Tanzania, except the coastal areas. There is a high maximum over northwest Lake Victoria.

(*5*) 12h00–15h00—maxima occur along the Tanzanian coast (February–November), Kitale and western Uganda.

(6) 15h00–18h00—heavy falls east of Lake Victoria, in the Kenya highlands, the Uganda Plateau and the southern highlands of Tanzania.

(7) 18h00–21h00—maxima east and northeast of Lake Victoria.

(8) 21h00–24h00—maximum at Nairobi during the short rains (October–December).

In the above tabulation months with low rainfall (below 50 mm) have not been considered. The pattern around Lake Victoria is understandable in view of the normal lake breeze circulation superimposed upon an easterly flow. In the afternoon the breezes blowing from the lake meet with the easterly flow, the resulting convergence giving rise to cumulus that develops into cumulonimbus. Some of this cloud is later advected across the lake and is reinforced by the land breeze (flowing in an easterly direction over the western lake) converging with the easterly upper air flow.

Greater than 20% of the average monthly fall occurs in very few stations and hours: Kericho (August, September, 15 h), Kisii (July, August, 17 h; October, 15–16 h; November, 15 h), Kisumu (September, 17–18 h), Kitale (July, August, 15 h; September, October, 14 h) and Nanyuki (June–September, 15–16 h). On an annual basis over 50% falls between 17 h and 21 h at Kisumu, 13 h and 17 h at Kitale, 14–18 h at Nakuru, 13–17 h at Nanyuki and 15–19 h at Tororo. For comparison, Mahe, Seychelles, has an annual variation by hours from only 3.5 to 5.1% while Amani in May varies from 3.1 to 5.5%. Lamu from 2.8 to 6.2% shows the least annual variation in East Africa.

Intense rainfall

Maximum daily falls vary appreciably with location but rarely does more than 200 mm fall at the coast, 150 mm over land above 2,000 m and 100 mm over plateaus. Some of the greatest falls are given in Table X.

Recording rain gauges are not very numerous in this zone but some initial studies showed

TABLE X

EXAMPLES OF HIGH MAXIMUM VALUES OF DAILY RAINFALL

Station	Date	Rainfall (mm)
Kenya[1]:		
Vanga	Oct., 1966	404
Vanga	Oct., 1953	380
Near Meru	Oct., 1961	362
Near Mazeras	Oct., 1938	356
Uganda[2]:		
Entebbe	May, 1958	283
Tanzania[3]:		
Tukuyu	April, 1955	432

[1] Falls in excess of 300 mm have occurred at Lamu, Kitui and Kwale.

[2] Falls in excess of 200 mm are rare.

[3] Falls in excess of 300 mm are usually confined to the southeastern slopes of Kilimanjaro and the Tukuyu district.

that falls in excess of 40 mm in a period of a quarter of an hour have been noted in all three countries. During one hour amounts of 80–100 mm have been recorded. The Entebbe fall in May, 1958, reported over 250 mm in a three hour spell.

Humidity

In this zone the dew point usually shows little variation ($\pm 1°C$) during the 24 h. In the hot, dry areas, however, changes of about 5°C are not unusual, due to the influx or advection of different air masses. The variation of the monthly mean at a given station is, like the temperature fluctuation, quite small. The average is about 3°–4°C but near the large lakes it is as low as 1°–2°C. Naturally, dew points are higher during the wetter months. At the coast the mean annual dew point averages about 23°C. Physical theory would then expect a lapse rate of about 4.7°C/1,000 m. Using this calculated lapse rate and comparing theoretical with observed values it is possible to obtain a plot of these deviations (Fig.11).

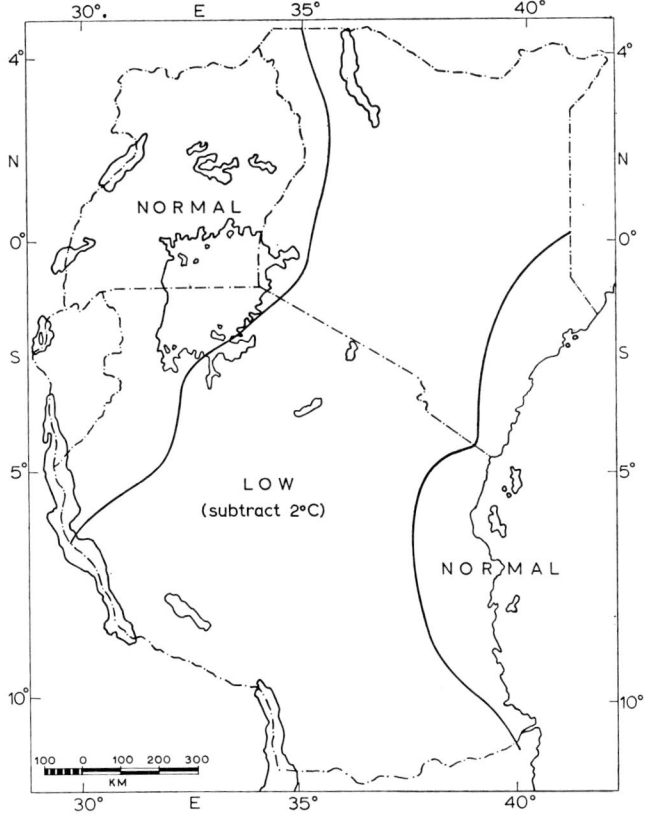

Fig.11. Deviation of mean annual dew point from altitude corrected mean.

A consideration of relative humidity values shows that at the 06h00 reading (sunrise) most stations have an annual mean value of 85–95%, the major exception being in northern Kenya with Lodwar at 65% and Mandera at 73%.

At 12h00, readings are generally around 50%, except at the coast or lakeside stations (65–70%) and in the very arid areas (Lodwar and Mandera, 35%). Mean values along the coast are close to 80% for many months of the year, the lowest value in the zone being Lodwar in February with 43%.

Evaporation

Evaporation, measured from 10- or 15-inch pans, ranges in annual totals from 1,100 mm at Kabale to a surprising 4,500 mm at Lodwar. Table XI gives data for the annual means at all long period stations.

The mean monthly totals, their pattern reflecting the distribution of the rainy seasons, vary from over 420 mm (Lodwar, October) to below 70 mm (Equator, August). Extremes for a month have been over 500 mm (Lodwar, November) and less than 60 mm (Equator, July).

TABLE XI

MEAN ANNUAL EVAPORATION (mm)

Evap.	Station	Evap.	Station
1,100	Kabale	2,100	Kisumu, Tororo, Voi
1,300	Equator	2,200	Gulu, Makindu, Dar-es-Salaam
1,400	Fort Portal, Mbarara	2,400	Mombasa
1,500	Nairobi	2,500	Tabora
1,600	Eldoret, Narok	2,800	Moshi
1,700	Nanyuki	3,900	Mandera
1,800	Entebbe	4,500	Lodwar
1,900	Nakuru		

Recently, studies of potential evapotranspiration for Uganda (RIJKS and OWEN, 1965) and Kenya (WOODHEAD, 1968) have been published. These two investigations, using Penman type equations, indicate annual values ranging from below 1,400 mm to above 2,600 mm. Based on his calculations WOODHEAD (1968) has suggested that the potential evapotranspiration in Kenya can be expressed as $E_0 = 2,422 - 0.358\,h$, where E_0 is in millimetres and h is the station elevation in metres. This equation gave an r^2 of 0.66 for a sample of 78 stations. However, some calculations have been made using radiation data of dubious accuracy.

Air flow

In equatorial zones, such as East Africa, the surface winds (measured at 10 m) rarely reach the high speeds often noted in the temperate zones. For example, the maximum gust recorded in all observations is only about 110 km/h, at Kisumu, while values above 70 km/h are rare and come only as short-lived gusts. These are usually noted just prior to, or during, intense convective thunderstorms and are of the greatest speed along the northeast of Lake Victoria.

Over most of the territory the average run of the wind is about 150 km/day, with little seasonal variation ($\pm 30\%$). In the northeast province of Kenya and along the north coast of Kenya, however, the ratio between the windiest and the calmest month is about 2.5–3. July is generally the calmest month in the highlands with October a windy month over the whole zone. The hours of darkness are almost calm but, as would be expected, most stations show a strengthening of the wind during the afternoon, especially along the coast (Mombasa 5 knots at 09h00 and 13 knots at 15h00), in the Rift Valley (Naivasha 3 and 7 knots, Nakuru 4 and 10 knots), and in northeastern Uganda (Lira 3 and 10 knots, Moroto 2 and 5 knots). Mean annual monthly speeds in excess of 15 knots are reported only from Equator (February, November, December 16 knots, March 17 knots) and Isiolo (July, 16 knots). Two of the calmest places are, apparently, Lyamungu (2 and 4 knots, no monthly mean above 5 knots) and Morogoro (2 and 4 knots).

Thunder and hail

The statistics relating to this phenomenon are published as "thunder heard at the station" and so will apply to a large area. Incidence ranges from over 200 days/year at Kampala, Entebbe and Kisumu, to below 5 days/year at Kongwa, Mafia, Pemba, Garissa, Isiolo, Wajir, Lamu and Malindi. The rarity of this occurrence at Pemba is surprising when Zanzibar, the neighbouring island, notes 61 days/year.

Entebbe records from 15 to 22 occasions every month while Kampala and Kisumu have from 10 to 23 each month. As would be expected the incidence per month is related to the rainfall of that month and most stations record their maximum at the time of the wettest month. However, on the coast, from Mtwara to Mombasa, this is not so, the maximum value occurring in March, a month earlier than the wettest month. This phenomenon extends a little inland, for Amani, Arusha, Morogoro, Moshi, Same and Voi give the same result.

According to SANSOM (1966) "the incidence of hail in parts of western Kenya, particularly in the Kericho and Nandi Hills area, is probably greater than anywhere else in the world, with hail occurring on well over 100 days per annum". It is possible that such a high value is also reached on the Peruvian altiplano. The hailstones are not usually large, average diameter 6–14 mm, and storms are generally local in character. August is the month of greatest frequency. The actual frequency at a point may reach 10 per annum, and no month is free from hail. Hail is also quite common in western Uganda, near the Ruwenzori Mountains. The point frequency is between 5 and 10 per annum with maximum incidence during September, October, January, February and March.

Lake Victoria

Of great importance to this region, as well as to other countries, is the vast Lake Victoria (70,000 km²), the source of the White Nile. It is true that much of the water leaving the lake never reaches the arid regions of the northern Sudan and Egypt, due to large evaporative loss especially in the sudd area, but, nevertheless, the rise and fall of the lake is most important. Recently the World Meteorological Organization has instituted a special hydro-meteorological study of the whole drainage basin, covering parts of Burundi,

Kenya, Rwanda, Tanzania and Uganda. However, for such a large water area, the drainage area is relatively small and the rainfall over the lake itself is of major importance.

Earlier studies in the 1920's suggested a correlation between lake levels and sunspots but the past decades have tended to show this was not real and only a sampling variation. BARGMAN et al. (1965) have recently suggested that the water level is dependent upon "dry" or "small rain" season (September–February) and not so much upon the "long rains" (March–August). Small variation in this amount apparently gives rise to large variations in lake level; it reached a maximum of 4 m above normal in 1962–1963. The fluctuations that can occur in the rainfall seasons are illustrated by KENWORTHY and GLOVER (1958) but the full details of this study have yet to be published (MÖRTH, 1967, 1968). It is also speculated that a 5-year cycle in the maxima of the "small rains" phenomenon may exist.

References

BARGMAN, D. J., LUMB, F. E. and MÖRTH, H. T., 1965. Lake levels in East Africa. *Proc. Army Conf. Tropical Meteorol., Univ. Miami, Florida, 1965*, pp.2–13.

EAST AFRICAN METEOROLOGICAL DEPARTMENT, 1968. Tables showing diurnal variation of precipitation in East Africa and Seychelles. *E. African Meteorol. Dept., Tech. Mem.*, 10:49 pp.

GLOVER, J. and MCCULLOCH, J. S. G., 1958. The empirical relation between solar radiation and hours of bright sunshine. *Quart. J. Roy. Meteorol. Soc.*, 84:172–175.

GLOVER, J., HENDERSON, J. P. and ROBINSON, P., 1954. Provisional maps of the reliability of annual rainfall in East Africa. *Quart. J. Roy. Meteorol. Soc.*, 80:602–609.

GRIFFITHS, J. F., 1967. *Sunshine and Radiation Data at Stations in East Africa*. E. African Meteorol. Dept., Nairobi, 19 pp.

GRIFFITHS, J. F., 1968. The climate of East Africa. In: E. W. RUSSELL (Editor), *Natural Resources of East Africa*. Hawkins, Nairobi, pp.77–87.

GRIFFITHS, J. F. and STOCK, G. D., 1961. *10% and 20% Probability Maps of Annual Rainfall in East Africa*. Survey of Kenya, Government Printers, Nairobi, 2 maps.

JOHNSON, D. H. and MÖRTH, H. T., 1960. Forecasting research in East Africa. In: D. J. BARGMAN (Editor), *Tropical Meteorology in East Africa*. Munitalp, Nairobi, pp.56–137.

KENWORTHY, J. M., 1966. Temperature conditions in the tropical highland climates of East Africa. *E African Geograph. Rev.*, 4(1):1–11.

KENWORTHY, J. M. and GLOVER, J., 1958. The reliability of the main rains in Kenya. *E. African Agr. J.*, 23(4):267–280.

MÖRTH, H. T., 1967. *Annual Report*. Res. Sect. E. African Meteorol. Dept., Nairobi, 6 pp.

MÖRTH, H. T., 1968. *Annual Report*. Res. Sect. E. African Meteorol. Dept., Nairobi, 8 pp.

RIJKS, D. A. and OWEN, W. G., 1965. *Hydro-meteorological Records from Areas of Potential Agricultural Development in Uganda*. Min. Mineral Water Resources, Entebbe, 13 pp.

SANSOM, H. W., 1966. Occurrence and distribution of hail in Africa. *Meteorol. Mag.*, 95:212–218.

THOMPSON, B. W., 1957. Diurnal variation of precipitation in British East Africa. *E. African Meteorol. Dept., Tech. Mem.*, 8:70 pp.

TREWARTHA, G. T., 1961. *The Earth's Problem Climates*. Univ. Wisc. Press, Madison, Wisc., 334 pp.

WOODHEAD, T., 1968. *Studies of Potential Evaporation in Kenya*. Min. Nat. Resources, Nairobi, 69 pp.

TABLE XII

CLIMATIC TABLE FOR EQUATOR, KENYA
Latitude 0°01'S, longitude 35°33'E, elevation 2,762 m

Month	Mean sta. press. (mbar)	Temperature (°C)				Dew point (°C)		Precipitation					Wind				Averages			
		mean		extreme		09h	15h	mean (mm)	max. (mm)	min. (mm)	days ≥ 0.1 mm	max. 24 h (mm)	av. speed (kts.) 09h 15h	preval. dir. 09h 15h	calm (%)	cloud-iness (oktas)	sun-shine (h)	evap. (mm)	thunder (days)
		max.	min.	max.	min.														
Jan.	734	20	8	23	3	7.1	5.3	33	171	0	5	45	17 15	E E	0	6	276	133	4
Feb.	734	21	8	24	5	7.0	4.5	34	139	2	6	44	16 16	E E	0	5	258	139	4
Mar.	734	21	8	25	5	7.9	5.6	72	234	0	10	52	17 17	E E	0	6	267	139	6
Apr.	734	19	9	24	5	9.5	8.2	168	311	11	18	50	14 15	E E	0	7	216	122	12
May	735	18	9	23	5	9.6	8.8	142	239	40	18	50	11 14	E E	1	6	239	97	14
June	735	17	8	21	5	8.7	8.5	123	220	31	16	46	8 12	E E	1	6	201	96	14
July	735	16	8	21	4	8.5	9.2	163	247	86	20	56	7 10	W W	4	6	164	80	16
Aug.	735	16	8	21	5	8.7	9.4	205	393	113	23	66	7 9	W W	2	6	167	68	18
Sept.	734	18	8	21	5	8.1	7.8	111	248	2	15	57	9 11	E E	1	5	222	98	14
Oct.	734	19	8	22	5	8.3	7.4	53	132	4	11	50	14 13	E E	0	6	248	115	7
Nov.	734	19	8	22	4	8.8	7.8	63	229	9	11	55	18 16	E E	0	6	225	117	4
Dec.	734	18	8	22	4	8.1	7.0	55	221	1	9	45	19 16	E E	0	6	254	132	3
Annual	734	18	8	25	3	8.3	7.4	1,222	1,513	798	162	66	13 14	—	1	6	2,737	1,336	116
Rec. (yrs.)	21	23	23	23	23	23	23	25	25	25	25	25	21 21	21	21	21	22	23	

TABLE XIII

CLIMATIC TABLE FOR ENTEBBE, UGANDA
Latitude 0°03'N, longitude 32°27'E, elevation 1,146 m

Month	Mean sta. press. (mbar)	Temperature (°C) mean max.	Temperature (°C) mean min.	Temperature (°C) extreme max.	Temperature (°C) extreme min.	Dew point[1] (°C)	Precipitation mean (mm)	Precipitation max. (mm)	Precipitation min. (mm)	Precipitation days ≥ 0.1 mm	Precipitation max. 24 h (mm)	Wind av. speed (kts.)	Wind preval. dir.	Wind calm (%)	Averages cloudiness (oktas)	Averages sunshine (h)	Averages evap. (mm)	thunder (days)
												09h 15h						
Jan.	888	27	17	31	13	17.8	100	358	17	9	103	4	S	0	6	233	148	15
Feb.	885	27	17	32	11	18.0	86	199	18	9	84	4	S	0	6	204	156	15
Mar.	886	27	18	31	14	18.5	141	309	62	15	85	5	S	0	6	205	173	18
Apr.	887	26	18	30	12	18.7	280	425	182	22	107	6	S	0	6	180	170	22
May	886	26	18	29	14	18.7	257	463	99	17	283	6	S	0	6	192	148	19
June	888	25	17	28	14	17.8	98	264	47	11	61	6	S	0	6	186	126	17
July	887	25	16	28	10	17.2	65	121	1	10	63	6	S	1	6	198	129	17
Aug.	887	25	16	29	12	17.4	91	184	13	9	112	5	S	1	6	195	134	16
Sept.	886	26	16	30	13	17.5	87	274	8	9	113	6	S	0	6	195	145	18
Oct.	886	26	17	30	14	17.8	108	265	20	13	75	5	S	1	6	201	163	20
Nov.	885	26	17	32	14	17.9	146	385	42	14	91	4	S	1	6	198	144	18
Dec.	885	26	17	30	14	17.9	126	339	5	14	68	4	S	1	6	211	142	17
Annual	886	26	17	32	10	17.9	1,585	2,303	1,128	152	283	5	—	<1	6	2,398	1,778	212
Rec. (yrs.)	17					17						7	7	7	17	31	6	

[1] Mean of 09h00 and 15h00.

TABLE XIV

CLIMATIC TABLE FOR KISUMU, KENYA

Latitude 0°06'S, longitude 34°45'E, elevation 1,146 m

Month	Mean sta. press. (mbar)	Temperature (°C)				Dew point (°C)		Precipitation					Wind				Averages			
		mean		extreme				mean (mm)	max. (mm)	min. (mm)	days ≥0.1 mm	max. 24 h (mm)	av. speed (kts.)		preval. direct.	calm (%)	cloud-iness (oktas)	sun-shine (h)	evap. (mm)	thunder (days)
		max.	min.	max.	min.	09h	15h						09h	15h						
Jan.	885	31	17	36	11	14.2	14.5	57	161	0	7	78	3	12	SW	1	5	267	209	10
Feb.	885	31	17	37	13	14.6	14.5	70	185	0	8	74	3	13	SW	0	5	246	201	11
Mar.	885	30	18	37	13	16.0	15.5	160	334	25	12	80	3	11	SW	1	6	263	202	16
Apr.	885	29	18	36	13	17.2	17.1	195	405	93	18	155	3	10	SW	1	6	231	164	21
May	886	28	17	32	14	17.2	17.2	177	358	77	17	81	3	8	SW	1	5	242	157	23
June	887	28	17	31	13	15.9	16.1	101	192	14	12	79	4	8	SW	0	5	225	153	18
July	887	28	17	31	12	15.3	15.2	68	147	27	10	90	4	8	SW	1	5	214	154	15
Aug.	887	28	16	32	12	15.1	15.3	96	220	17	12	102	4	8	SW	1	5	214	149	18
Sept.	886	29	16	34	12	14.7	15.3	79	151	16	11	69	4	9	S	0	5	228	166	20
Oct.	886	31	17	35	13	14.7	14.8	64	131	9	11	69	4	10	SW	0	5	239	187	18
Nov.	885	30	17	34	13	15.1	14.9	106	449	6	11	128	3	10	SW	1	6	219	173	17
Dec.	885	30	17	36	12	15.1	15.1	105	301	1	10	84	3	10	SW	1	5	254	185	13
Annual	886	29	17	37	11	15.4	15.5	1,278	1,884	942	139	155	3	10	—	1	5	2,842	2,100	200
Rec. (yrs.)	32	32	32	32	32	32	32	32	32	32	32	32	24	24	24	24				

335

TABLE XV

CLIMATIC TABLE FOR KABALE, UGANDA
Latitude 01°15'S, longitude 29°59'E, elevation 1,871 m

Month	Temperature (°C) mean max.	mean min.	extreme max.	extreme min.	Dew point (°C) 09h	15h	Precipitation mean (mm)	max. (mm)	min. (mm)	days ≥ 0.1 mm	max. 24 h (mm)	Wind av. speed (kts.) 09h	15h	preval. dir.	calm (%)	Averages cloudiness (oktas)	sunshine (h)	evap. (mm)	thunder (days)
Jan.	24	10	29	4	11.4	13.2	61	127	8	11	55	3	7	NE-SE	1	7	149	116	11
Feb.	24	10	29	6	11.7	13.6	91	217	10	13	76	2	7	NE-SE	0	7	157	95	10
Mar.	23	10	28	5	12.2	14.2	114	262	34	16	45	2	7	E-SE	0	7	155	100	12
Apr.	23	11	27	7	13.0	15.0	136	262	38	20	59	2	7	SE	0	7	129	85	11
May	22	11	26	6	13.1	14.9	92	255	22	15	59	3	7	SE	0	7	115	93	7
June	22	9	27	5	11.1	12.8	26	109	0	5	60	2	7	SE	0	6	171	92	3
July	23	9	28	3	10.0	11.2	20	96	0	3	50	3	8	SE	0	6	171	99	2
Aug.	23	10	29	3	11.1	11.5	55	100	5	8	91	3	8	SE	0	6	149	97	6
Sept.	24	10	28	5	12.1	12.9	95	150	14	14	49	3	8	SE	0	7	156	104	13
Oct.	23	10	27	6	12.5	13.6	98	136	22	18	43	3	8	SE	0	7	158	102	15
Nov.	23	10	27	6	12.5	14.2	107	248	46	18	51	3	8	E-SE	0	7	135	83	13
Dec.	23	10	26	5	12.1	13.9	91	257	15	15	55	3	7	E-SE	0	7	136	89	11
Annual	23		29	3	11.9	13.4	986	1,265	637	156	91	3	7	—	0	7	1,781	1,155	114
Rec. (yrs.)	32	32	32	32	32	32	45	45	45	45	45	25	25	25	25	31	6	5	

TABLE XVI

CLIMATIC TABLE FOR NAIROBI (DAGORETTI), KENYA
Latitude 01°18'S, longitude 36°45'E, elevation 1,798 m

Month	Mean sta. press. (mbar)	Temperature (°C) mean max.	mean min.	extreme max.	extreme min.	Dew point (°C) 09h	15h	Precipitation mean (mm)	max. (mm)	min. (mm)	days ≥ 0.1 mm	max. 24h (mm)	Wind av. speed (kts.) 09h	15h	preval. direct.	calm (%)	Averages cloudiness (oktas)	sunshine (h)	evap. (mm)	thunder (days)
Jan.	821	25	11	30	3	13.0	11.5	88	253	7	9	76	7	13	NE	1	5	273	155	3
Feb.	821	26	11	30	5	12.7	10.5	70	201	12	7	59	7	13	NE	0	5	263	163	3
Mar.	821	26	12	29	7	14.2	11.7	96	207	23	13	56	7	13	NE	1	6	270	168	3
Apr.	821	24	14	29	8	14.7	13.3	155	224	102	17	63	5	10	NE	1	6	219	126	5
May	823	23	13	26	7	14.0	13.7	189	380	85	18	85	4	7	E	5	7	183	97	5
June	823	22	11	26	4	12.2	11.3	29	82	2	5	25	3	7	E-S	3	6	177	90	1
July	823	21	9	26	2	11.2	10.0	17	85	2	5	47	3	6	SE	5	7	133	82	1
Aug.	823	22	10	28	3	11.2	10.7	20	42	1	5	23	3	7	SE	1	7	130	88	1
Sept.	822	24	10	28	4	11.9	10.7	34	62	9	7	54	3	9	E-SE	3	6	174	119	2
Oct.	822	25	12	28	5	12.9	10.7	64	164	12	8	45	6	11	E-NE	1	6	220	154	1
Nov.	822	23	13	28	6	13.9	12.7	189	623	41	16	64	8	12	E-NE	0	6	210	127	4
Dec.	821	23	12	27	6	13.7	12.7	115	379	18	11	112	8	13	NE	1	6	251	133	3
Annual	822	24	12	30	2	13.0	11.7	1,066	1,632	818	121	112	5	10	—	2	6	2,503	1,502	32
Rec. (yrs.)	8	8	8	8	8	8	8	9	9	9	9	9	8	8	8	8	8	8	8	8

337

TABLE XVII

CLIMATIC TABLE FOR GULU, UGANDA
Latitude 02°45'N, longitude 32°20'E, elevation 1,109 m

Month	Mean sta. press. (mbar)	Temperature (°C) mean max.	mean min.	extreme max.	extreme min.	Dew point (°C) 09h	15h	Precipitation mean (mm)	max. (mm)	min. (mm)	days ≥ 0.1 mm	max. 24 h (mm)	Wind av. speed (kts.) 09h	15h	preval. dir.	calm (%)	Averages cloud-iness (oktas)	sun-shine (h)	evap. (mm)	thunder (days)
Jan.	889	32	16	36	11	14.8	12.5	12	55	0	4	36	7	10	N/E	0	5	276	217	3
Feb.	888	32	17	37	12	15.7	13.5	43	229	0	6	77	7	10	N	0	5	244	214	6
Mar.	888	31	18	37	12	17.2	15.4	89	182	10	11	60	7	10	E	0	6	248	217	13
Apr.	889	29	18	37	14	18.8	17.9	173	319	69	17	78	8	8	S	0	6	228	186	18
May	890	28	18	33	15	18.9	18.7	172	393	88	17	77	7	8	S	0	6	242	165	19
June	891	27	17	32	15	18.1	18.2	148	370	53	14	83	6	7	S	1	6	231	166	16
July	891	27	17	29	13	17.4	17.9	166	387	28	17	83	6	7	N	0	6	192	141	17
Aug.	890	27	17	30	13	17.9	18.1	231	431	119	19	109	6	7	N	0	6	198	156	20
Sept.	890	28	17	31	14	18.2	17.9	127	323	36	17	68	6	8	N	0	6	243	166	16
Oct.	889	29	17	33	13	18.1	17.4	165	395	15	16	69	7	8	E	0	6	251	184	15
Nov.	889	30	16	34	12	17.2	16.0	97	320	13	11	106	7	8	E	0	5	246	166	11
Dec.	888	30	16	33	9	16.2	14.4	47	163	1	7	52	7	9	E	0	5	267	191	7
Annual	889	29	17	37	9	17.4	16.5	1,470	2,144	869	156	109	7	8	—	0	6	2,866	2,169	161
Rec. (yrs.)	31	32	32	32	32	32	32	52	52	52	52	52	25	25	25	25	32	6	5	

TABLE XVIII

CLIMATIC TABLE FOR VOI, KENYA
Latitude 03°24'S, longitude 38°34'E, elevation 560 m

Month	Temperature (°C) mean max.	mean min.	extreme max.	extreme min.	Dew point (°C) 09h	15h	Precipitation mean (mm)	max. (mm)	min. (mm)	days ≥ 0.1 mm	max. 24 h (mm)	Wind av. speed (kts.) 09h	15h	preval. direct. 15h	calm (%)	Averages cloud-iness (oktas)	evap.[1] (mm)
Jan.	32	20	37	16	19	17	32	152	0	6	51	5	9	NE	1	6	181
Feb.	33	20	37	15	19	17	30	190	0	4	126	4	9	NE	1	5	195
Mar.	33	21	37	17	20	17	73	413	0	7	89	4	7	E	1	6	205
Apr.	32	20	36	18	20	19	92	297	0	10	147	7	8	SE	0	6	170
May	30	20	35	16	18	17	29	111	0	7	60	9	9	S	0	6	167
June	29	18	33	13	16	15	7	77	0	1	41	9	11	S	1	6	174
July	28	17	32	13	15	14	3	27	0	1	18	9	11	S	0	6	172
Aug.	28	17	33	12	16	14	8	66	0	3	26	8	11	S	0	6	170
Sept.	29	18	33	13	16	14	15	138	0	4	44	8	11	SE	0	6	177
Oct.	31	19	35	14	17	15	27	150	0	5	52	6	10	SE	0	6	202
Nov.	31	20	35	15	19	17	96	261	0	10	107	4	8	NE	1	6	176
Dec.	31	21	35	16	20	18	126	591	0	14	254	4	7	NE	1	6	159
Annual	30	19	37	12	18	16	538	1,201	184	72	254	6	9		1	6	2,148
Rec. (yrs.)	25	25	25	25	25	25	59	59	59	59	59	25	25	25	25	25	6

[1] 15-inch pan.

339

TABLE XIX

CLIMATIC TABLE FOR MOYALE, KENYA
Latitude 03°32′N, longitude 39°03′E, elevation 1,113 m

Month	Temperature (°C)				Dew point (°C) 06h 18h		Precipitation					Wind 06h 12h				Aver. cloudiness[1] (oktas)
	mean		extreme				mean (mm)	max. (mm)	min. (mm)	days ≥ 1 mm	max. 24 h (mm)	av. speed (kts.)		preval. direct.	calm (%)	
	max.	min.	max.	min.												
Jan.	30	18	37	14	13	12	11	88	0	2	33	9	9	NE	11	3
Feb.	31	19	35	13	13	12	17	125	0	2	36	7	9	E	12	3
Mar.	30	19	35	11	16	15	55	162	0	7	54	7	8	E	10	4
Apr.	27	18	33	14	18	18	182	395	27	15	117	5	7	SE	13	6
May	25	17	30	13	17	18	118	397	8	14	155	7	6	SE	8	6
June	24	16	30	13	15	15	17	92	0	5	27	10	7	SE	3	6
July	24	15	28	12	14	14	17	89	0	5	28	10	8	SE	3	6
Aug.	24	16	29	11	14	14	17	94	0	4	72	10	9	SE	1	6
Sept.	26	16	30	14	14	14	25	135	0	3	46	10	8	SE	7	5
Oct.	26	17	32	14	16	16	96	388	9	11	145	6	7	SE	5	6
Nov.	27	17	32	14	17	16	86	267	5	10	55	5	7	SE	6	5
Dec.	28	18	32	14	15	14	41	138	0	5	36	6	7	SE	8	4
Annual	27	17	37	11	15	15	682	1,290	387	83	155	8	8		7	5
Rec. (yrs.)	27	27	27	27	27	27	48	48	48	34	48	27	27	27	27	27

[1] Mean of 06h00 and 12h00.

TABLE XX

CLIMATIC TABLE FOR MOMBASA, KENYA
Latitude 04°02′S, longitude 39°37′E, elevation 55 m

Month	Mean sta. press. (mbar)	Temperature (°C)				Dew point (°C)		Precipitation					Wind				Averages		
		mean		extreme		09h	15h	mean (mm)	max. (mm)	min. (mm)	min. ≥ 0.1 mm	max. 24 h (mm)	av. speed (kts). 06h 12h		preval. direct.	calm (%)	cloud-iness (oktas)	sun-shine (h)	evap. (mm)
		max.	min.	max.	min.														
Jan.	1,004	32	23	37	18	23	23	26	189	0	5	38	6	12	E	0	5	254	227
Feb.	1,004	32	24	36	21	23	23	15	83	0	3	37	5	13	E	0	5	255	226
Mar.	1,004	33	24	36	21	24	23	61	174	0	7	106	4	12	E	0	5	282	239
Apr.	1,005	31	24	35	22	24	23	200	608	15	15	101	5	12	S	1	5	231	192
May	1,007	29	23	33	19	23	23	319	1,043	46	19	139	7	13	S	1	6	201	164
June	1,010	29	21	32	18	22	21	112	389	4	14	43	7	14	S	1	5	231	158
July	1,010	28	20	31	18	21	20	89	299	6	14	37	6	13	S	1	5	211	147
Aug.	1,010	28	20	31	14	21	20	65	235	10	15	35	6	13	S	0	5	248	171
Sept.	1,009	29	21	32	18	21	20	68	323	7	12	150	6	13	S	0	5	255	197
Oct.	1,007	30	22	33	18	22	21	83	310	4	10	103	5	12	S	0	5	273	219
Nov.	1,006	31	23	36	20	23	23	93	703	3	9	86	3	12	E	0	5	276	213
Dec.	1,005	32	23	36	19	23	23	60	262	0	9	69	5	11	E	1	5	270	200
Annual	1,007	30	23	37	14	23	22	1,191	1,887	561	133	150	5	13	—	0	5	2,987	2,353
Rec. (yrs.)	17	17	17	17	17	17	17	73	73	73	73	17	17		17	17	17	14	6

TABLE XXI

CLIMATIC TABLE FOR KIGOMA, TANZANIA
Latitude 04°53'S, longitude 29°38'E, elevation 885 m

Month	Mean sta. press. (mbar)	Temperature (°C) mean max.	min.	extreme max.	min.	Dew point (°C) 09h	15h	Precipitation mean (mm)	max. (mm)	min. (mm)	days ≥ 0.1 mm	max. 24 h (mm)	Wind av. speed (kts.) 09h	15h	preval. direct.	calm (%)	Mean cloudiness (oktas)	Thunder (days)
Jan.	913	27	20	32	16	19.2	20.4	134	315	54	14	97	5	7	S	5	6	23
Feb.	913	27	20	33	16	19.3	20.5	118	269	42	12	80	4	8	W	4	6	21
Mar.	913	27	20	32	16	19.4	20.6	155	309	87	13	107	5	7	W	3	6	23
Apr.	913	27	20	33	17	19.3	20.6	151	313	60	16	94	5	8	W	2	7	18
May	914	28	19	32	16	18.4	19.5	51	147	0	8	46	6	8	W	3	6	12
June	915	28	18	31	14	16.2	17.2	6	47	0	1	46	8	9	S	1	4	6
July	915	28	17	31	13	14.4	16.0	2	29	0	0	20	8	10	S-W	0	3	2
Aug.	914	29	18	33	14	14.0	16.7	3	33	1	1	33	8	12	W	1	3	2
Sept.	913	30	20	35	15	15.6	18.5	15	86	0	3	48	7	11	W	1	4	6
Oct.	913	29	20	37	16	17.6	19.4	61	166	15	8	83	6	9	W	2	5	13
Nov.	913	27	20	33	16	18.9	20.0	130	263	42	17	85	5	8	W	4	6	22
Dec.	913	26	19	32	16	19.3	20.2	151	313	62	17	70	5	7	W	6	6	24
Annual	914	28	19	37	13	17.6	19.1	977	1,363	639	110	107	6	9	—	3	5	172
													09h 15h					
Rec. (yrs.)	29	29	29	29	29	29	29	29	29	29	29	29	27	27	27	27	29	

TABLE XXII

CLIMATIC TABLE FOR TABORA, TANZANIA
Latitude 05°02'S, longitude 32°49'E, elevation 1,265 m

Month	Mean sta. press. (mbar)	Temperature (°C) mean max.	mean min.	extreme max.	extreme min.	Dew point (°C) 09h	15h	Precipitation mean (mm)	max. (mm)	min. (mm)	days ≥ 0.1 mm	max. 24 h (mm)	Wind av. speed (kts.) 09h	15h	preval. direct.	calm (%)	Averages cloud-iness (oktas)	sun-shine (h)	thunder (days)
Jan.	874	28	17	34	14	17.2	17.0	132	228	57	16	74	3	5	E	17	6	211	14
Feb.	874	28	17	34	15	17.2	17.1	129	323	41	14	79	3	5	E	18	6	196	13
Mar.	874	28	17	33	15	17.3	17.4	166	378	25	15	84	4	5	E	13	6	229	14
Apr.	875	28	17	33	15	17.1	17.2	134	328	28	13	74	7	7	E	7	6	240	9
May	875	28	16	32	11	15.1	15.1	27	145	1	4	71	8	7	E	6	5	279	2
June	876	28	15	31	11	12.2	12.2	2	39	2	0	27	9	7	S	9	3	300	0
July	877	28	15	32	10	10.6	10.5	0	3	0	0	?	9	7	S	12	2	329	0
Aug.	876	29	16	32	12	10.7	10.5	1	11	0	0	6	11	7	S	8	3	313	0
Sept.	875	31	18	34	14	12.0	11.2	7	87	1	1	13	12	7	E-S	8	4	288	1
Oct.	874	32	19	35	16	12.9	11.8	17	68	0	3	39	10	6	E-S	13	5	288	2
Nov.	874	31	19	35	15	15.2	13.7	103	432	22	13	71	6	6	E	12	5	249	9
Dec.	874	28	18	34	15	16.9	16.3	174	371	34	20	87	3	5	E	15	6	220	15
Annual	875	29	17	35	10	14.5	14.2	892	1,390	354	99	87	7	6	—	12	5	3,142	79
Rec. (yrs.)	25	25	25	25	25	25	25	69	69	69	69	69	18	18	18	18	25	24	25

TABLE XXIII

CLIMATIC TABLE FOR DAR-ES-SALAAM, TANZANIA
Latitude 06°50′S, longitude 39°18′E, elevation 14 m

Month	Mean sta. press. (mbar)	Temperature (°C) mean max.	mean min.	extreme max.	extreme min.	Dew point (°C) 09h	15h	Precipitation mean (mm)	max. (mm)	min. (mm)	days ≥0.1 mm	max. 24h (mm)	Wind av. speed (km/h) 06h	12h	preval. direct.	calm (%)	Averages cloudiness (oktas)	sunshine (h)	evap. (mm)
Jan.	1,009	30	25	32	20	24	24	71	260	1	6	60	7	9	NE	1	5	251	208
Feb.	1,009	31	25	34	20	24	24	64	201	1	5	105	5	8	NE	0	5	241	203
Mar.	1,009	31	24	35	21	24	25	120	346	12	9	115	3	6	NE	4	5	217	188
Apr.	1,010	30	23	34	21	24	24	280	525	44	16	136	3	4	S	3	6	156	151
May	1,012	30	22	33	18	22	22	303	600	1	12	152	3	6	S	3	5	192	172
June	1,014	29	20	31	16	21	20	35	161	1	5	45	4	7	S	3	4	231	155
July	1,015	29	19	31	16	20	19	33	221	1	3	37	4	8	S	0	5	251	160
Aug.	1,014	29	19	31	15	20	19	25	108	1	3	25	3	9	S	1	4	242	179
Sept.	1,014	29	19	32	16	21	20	29	71	1	3	37	3	10	SE	0	4	243	195
Oct.	1,012	29	20	32	17	22	21	49	235	2	5	118	2	10	E	0	4	254	209
Nov.	1,010	30	22	34	19	23	23	79	331	5	7	70	3	9	E	2	4	270	207
Dec.	1,009	30	24	33	21	24	24	91	285	1	8	76	4	8	NE	2	5	267	210
Annual	1,011	30	22	35	15	22	22	1,179	1,531	438	84	152	4	8	—	2	5	2,815	2,237
Rec. (yrs.)	11	14	14	14	14	14	14	70	70	70	70	16	14	14	14	14	14	15	7

TABLE XXIV

CLIMATIC TABLE FOR MOROGORO, TANZANIA
Latitude 06°51'S, longitude 37°40'E, elevation 579 m

Month	Temperature (°C)				Dew point (°C)		Precipitation					Wind			Averages	
	mean		extreme				mean	max.	min.	days	max.	av.	preval.	calm	cloud-	sun-
	max.	min.	max.	min.	09h	15h	(mm)	(mm)	(mm)	> 0.1 mm	24 h (mm)	speed (kts.)	direct.	(%)	iness (oktas)	shine (h)
												06h 12h				
Jan.	32	21	36	17	21	20	94	301	4	10	63	2 4	E	19	5	177
Feb.	32	21	37	17	21	21	104	261	2	9	100	2 4	NE	17	6	165
Mar.	31	21	36	17	22	21	167	500	34	13	93	1 4	NE	26	6	183
Apr.	30	20	35	17	22	22	208	386	98	21	64	1 2	V	35	6	129
May	28	19	32	14	20	20	96	402	26	15	40	1 2	W	40	6	121
June	27	16	31	11	18	18	27	143	1	6	23	1 2	V	36	5	129
July	27	15	31	10	17	16	15	119	0	4	38	1 4	S	25	5	127
Aug.	28	16	33	9	17	16	10	66	0	5	34	2 5	S	20	5	130
Sept.	30	17	33	13	18	16	17	102	0	4	62	1 5	S	10	5	141
Oct.	31	18	35	14	18	17	27	168	1	5	34	1 6	S	8	5	177
Nov.	32	19	36	16	20	19	54	238	0	8	75	3 6	NE	13	5	186
Dec.	32	21	36	16	21	20	73	229	5	10	77	4 5	E	7	5	180
Annual	30	19	37	9	20	19	892	1,536	564	110	100	2 4	—	21	5	1,845
Rec. (yrs.)	15	15	15	15	15	15	57	57	57	57	57	14 14	14	14	14	16

TABLE XXV

CLIMATIC TABLE FOR MBEYA, TANZANIA
Latitude 08°56'S, longitude 33°28'E, elevation 1,736 m

Month	Mean sta. press. (mbar)	Temperature (°C) mean max.	mean min.	extreme max.	extreme min.	Dew point (°C) 09h	15h	Precipitation mean (mm)	max. (mm)	min. (mm)	days ≥ 0.1 mm	max. 24 h (mm)	Wind av. speed (kts.) 09h	15h	preval. direct.	calm (%)	Mean cloudiness (oktas)	Thunder (days)
Jan.	828	23	14	28	10	14.7	15.4	199	341	113	22	57	4	7	W	13	7	21
Feb.	828	23	14	27	10	14.7	15.6	165	269	37	20	69	3	7	W	12	7	19
Mar.	828	23	14	27	10	14.8	15.9	161	267	36	20	69	3	6	E	20	6	21
Apr.	829	23	13	27	9	14.3	15.8	116	303	45	17	88	4	7	E	13	6	14
May	830	22	11	27	6	12.4	13.9	17	54	0	4	40	4	9	S	3	4	3
June	831	21	9	26	3	10.0	11.5	1	9	1	0	7	4	11	S	3	3	0
July	831	21	8	26	2	8.5	10.2	1	6	0	0	6	5	11	S	4	3	0
Aug.	830	22	9	28	-1	8.5	10.3	1	14	0	0	14	6	11	S	1	3	0
Sept.	829	25	11	31	6	10.0	11.0	3	24	0	1	20	9	11	S	3	3	2
Oct.	829	27	12	31	7	11.4	11.9	15	69	0	3	30	13	11	S	5	4	7
Nov.	828	26	14	31	9	12.9	12.7	52	269	6	5	51	10	9	E-S	11	5	16
Dec.	828	24	14	31	10	14.3	14.7	152	397	8	17	59	6	7	E	10	6	20
Annual	829	23	12	31	-1	12.2	13.2	883	1,190	564	109	88	6	9	—	8	5	123
Rec. (yrs.)	30	30	30	30	30	30	30	31	31	31	31	31	24	24	24	24	30	24

TABLE XXVI

CLIMATIC TABLE FOR MTWARA, TANZANIA
Latitude 10°16'S, longitude 40°11'E, elevation 113 m

Month	Mean sta. press. (mbar)	Temperature (°C)				Dew point (°C)		Precipitation					Wind				Mean cloudiness (oktas)
		mean		extreme				mean	max.	min.	days	max.	av. speed (kts.)		preval.	calm	
		max.	min.	max.	min.	09h	15h	(mm)	(mm)	(mm)	≥ 0.1 mm	24 h (mm)	06h	12h	direct.	(%)	
Jan.	998	31	23	34	21	24	23	218	541	51	13	200	7	11	N	1	6
Feb.	998	31	23	35	20	24	24	151	452	17	12	169	6	10	N	3	6
Mar.	998	31	23	34	21	24	24	165	233	103	12	83	7	8	N	2	6
Apr.	999	31	22	34	21	24	23	197	416	15	14	152	9	9	SE	3	5
May	1,002	30	21	33	15	22	21	51	123	7	5	109	12	11	S	0	4
June	1,004	30	19	32	16	20	19	11	55	0	2	46	13	12	SE	0	4
July	1,005	29	19	32	16	19	18	15	51	1	3	26	13	13	SE	1	4
Aug.	1,004	30	19	33	15	20	19	11	43	2	3	23	11	13	SE	0	4
Sept.	1,003	30	19	33	16	21	19	65	468	4	3	91	7	13	NE	0	5
Oct.	1,002	31	21	34	18	21	20	24	65	7	4	31	7	13	NE	0	5
Nov.	1,000	32	22	35	19	23	22	33	119	1	5	38	6	12	NE	0	5
Dec.	998	31	23	34	20	23	23	218	441	4	8	184	7	11	N	1	5
Annual	1,001	31	21	35	15	22	21	1,159	1,504	780	84	200	9	11	—	1	6
Rec. (yrs.)	6	6	6	6	6	6	6	13	13	13	13	13	13	13	13	13	6

Chapter 10

Rwanda and Burundi

F. BULTOT

The factors of climate

Latitude and altitude

Rwanda extends approximately between 1° and 3°S, and Burundi between 3° and 4°S. These two territories are bordered to the west and northwest by a mountain chain running approximately north–south, with an altitude of between 2,000 and 2,500 m, called the spine of Rwanda (Fig.1, 2). To the east the land slopes gently, in contrast to the abrupt escarpment on the west of the area (along the valley of the Ruzizi especially). To the east of this spine the plateaus of Rwanda and Burundi are at an altitude of approximately 1,500 and 2,000 m. At the foot of the western slopes are situated Lake Kivu and Lake Tanganyika, at 1,460 and 771 m, respectively. The water from Lake Kivu flows towards Tanganyika via the Ruzizi along the channel between these two lakes.

The republics of Rwanda and Burundi cover an area of about 55,000 km² and have a population of about 5 million. The land is very mountainous with much territory above 1,000 m. Cash crops are mainly coffee and cotton with some mining of tin and tungsten.

Because these regions are so close to the equator, the total radiation balance at the ground has high values throughout the year. Dependent upon the season, a large part of this heat energy is taken up in the form of latent heat of evaporation of the soil or by the strong evapotranspiration of the vegetation which covers these regions. The balance is diffused by turbulence in the lower layers of the atmosphere. This then results in a very important vertical flux of water vapour and sensible heat which favours convective instability of the air. At the centre of this unstable air mass, when the thermal convection is not impeded by the advection of dry air in the upper layers of the atmosphere, cloud formations of large vertical extent develop, which give rise to thundershowers. These in their turn furnish the water necessary for the evaporation. There are two important aspects of the climatology that are related to the high elevation of Rwanda and Burundi. First, the air is colder, secondly, the wind speed is relatively high (at least during the day), in spite of the situation of these regions in the equatorial zone where there is little barometric variation and a high degree of continentality exists.

The general circulation and relief

The two subtropical anticyclones give rise to a prevailing flow of air with easterly component in the middle and upper layers of the African equatorial region (RIEHL, 1954;

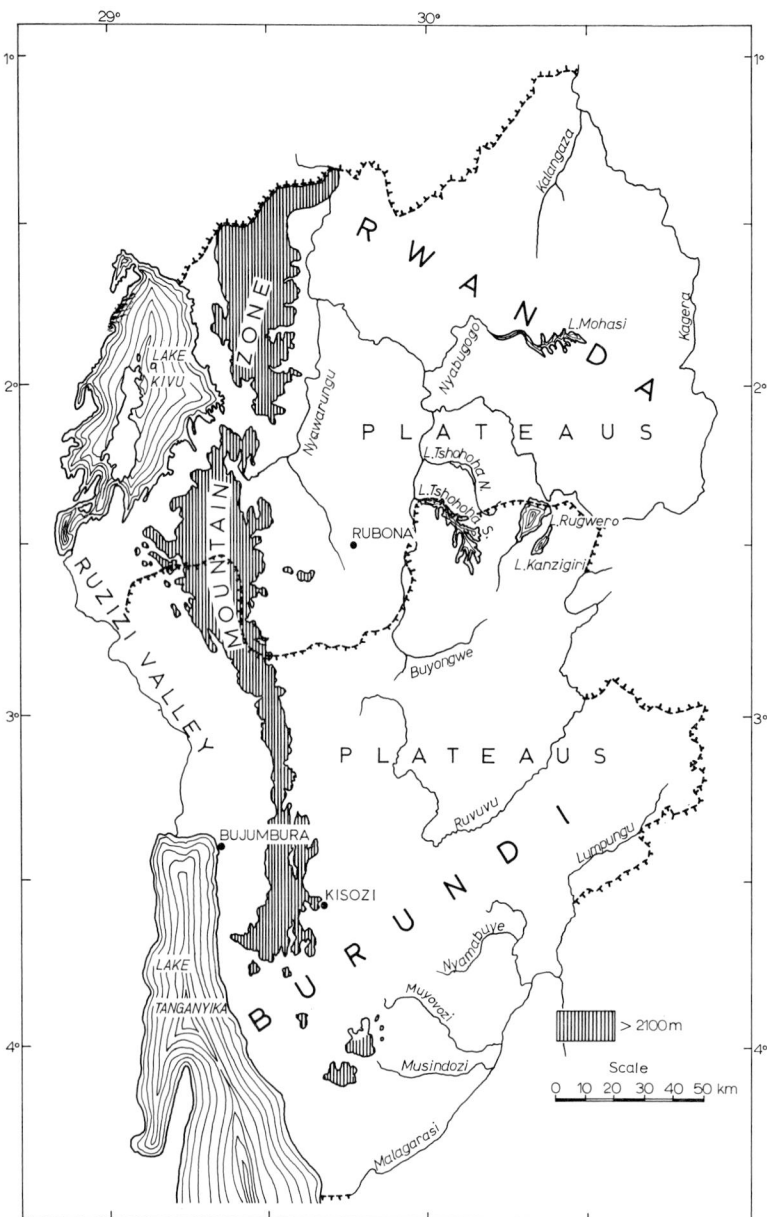

Fig.1. Station location, Rwanda-Burundi.

TSCHIRHART, 1959; QUOIDBACH and GOLBERT, 1969). When these upper air winds, always relatively dry even when they have been affected by a long trajectory over the Indian Ocean, are sufficiently attenuated, the vertical structure of the atmosphere exhibits the conditions required for convective clouds to be formed, especially during the warm hours of the day. In Rwanda and Burundi rainfall generally comes with convective clouds.

During the southern winter the South African anticyclone is reinforced and sends towards the equator a flow of dry air from the southeast, of directly continental origin, which impedes the development of clouds and causes almost a complete stop to all precipitation. During this time Rwanda and Burundi have a dry season of three to four months duration (Table I).

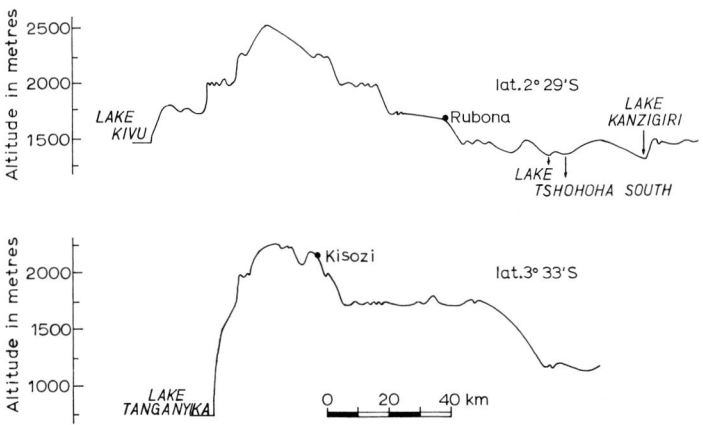

Fig.2. Elevation cross-sections, Rwanda-Burundi.

It should be noted also that the spine of Rwanda gives rise to a pronounced lifting of the air currents leading to orographic precipitation on the eastern slopes. On the western slopes, in contrast, the föhn prevents the development of clouds. This is why, at the elevation of Lake Kivu, and in spite of the large important vertical flux of water vapour that is

TABLE I

AVERAGE DATE OF START OF DRY AND WET SEASONS AND LENGTH OF DRY SEASON (1930–1959)

Regions	Start of dry season	Start of wet season	Length of dry season (days)
Plateau (Rubona)	June 1	Sept. 6	97
Mountain zone (Kisozi)	May 27	Sept. 14	110
Ruzizi Valley (Bujumbura)	May 24	Sept. 14	113

liberated there, the western slopes are relatively dry (BULTOT, 1950, 1969). In the Ruzizi plains the southeastern breeze, accelerated by the effect of the valley and moistened by its passage across Lake Tanganyika, gives rise to abundant rainfall as it strikes the western flanks of the spine of Rwanda which is particularly precipitous at this point. Because of the fractured relief and important differences in altitude, Rwanda and Burundi offer very great diversity of local climate.

The components of the radiation balance

Global solar radiation

On the plateaus of Rwanda and Burundi the mean monthly global radiation is between 450 and 500 cal./cm² day (Table II). The annual pattern of global radiation is determined by the solar position and cloud. The maximum values are observed in March and in September. In the mountain regions the global radiation is less (420–480 cal./cm² day), especially during the rainy months when the cloudiness is extreme over the plateau at this period. It is seen, moreover, that in spite of the high solar elevation global radiation remains low in February and March. The maximum monthly radiation occurs in September.

TABLE II

MEAN MONTHLY AND ANNUAL VALUES OF GLOBAL RADIATION (G), BALANCE OF TERRESTRIAL RADIATION (N), AND TOTAL RADIATION BALANCE (B) OVER A COVER OF *Paspalum notatum* (cal./cm² day)

Regions		Jan.	Feb.	Mar.	Apr.	May	June	July	Aug.	Sept.	Oct.	Nov.	Dec.	Ann.
Plateau	G	460	470	481	453	463	454	449	471	490	475	469	460	466
(Rubona)	N	127	127	127	123	123	154	174	170	160	142	130	126	140
1958–1959	B	227	235	243	226	234	196	167	188	212	224	231	228	218
Mountain zone	G	438	434	445	467	465	471	469	454	481	461	429	424	453
(Kisozi)	N	125	124	127	124	125	150	166	166	169	145	129	123	139
1958–1959	B	212	210	216	236	233	213	190	179	197	205	201	203	208
Ruzizi Valley	G	421	410	415	416	441	455	432	440	467	407	420	410	428
(Bujumbura)	N	108	106	106	104	114	138	152	157	137	121	109	108	122
1957–1958	B	216	210	214	216	226	212	176	177	218	188	210	208	206

In the Ruzizi Valley the global radiation is even lower because of the fact that the sunrise and sunset are affected by the two mountain chains which surround the valley. The maximum value also occurs in September. Finally, in the Ruzizi Valley and in the mountain zone the local radiation is higher in the dry season than in the wet season. On the plateau, to the contrary, there is very little practical difference between the two seasons. It is likely that in this region the atmospheric turbidity is sufficiently high during the dry season to compensate for the reduction in cloud (the period of grass and brush burning).

Diffuse solar radiation

From some measurements made at Rubona it appears that the solar diffuse radiation will attain, on average, some 40–50% of the global radiation in the wet season and some 20% in the dry season.

The balance of terrestrial radiation

The balance of terrestrial radiation (the upward flux minus the downward flux of long wave radiation) is approximately 120–150 cal./cm² day during the wet season and about 150–170 cal./cm² day in the dry season (Table II). Nevertheless, in the Ruzizi Valley in the vicinity of Lake Tanganyika, in spite of the high air temperature, the values of the balance of terrestrial radiation only reach 100–130 cal./cm² day in the rainy season and 130–160 cal./cm² day in the dry season. In this region the high value of the water vapour in the air because of the proximity of Lake Tanganyika, appreciably attenuates the terrestrial radiation.

Balance of total radiation

Mean monthly values of the balance of total radiation at the level of a cover of *Paspalum notatum* (the cover at the climatological station) are usually between 160–250 cal./cm² day on the plateaus of Rwanda and Burundi, 180–240 cal./cm² day in the mountains, and 170–230 cal./cm² day in the Ruzizi Valley (Table II). The balance of the total radiation reaches a minimum during the dry months of July and August, the period during which the energy in the terrestrial radiation band is at a maximum. The cover of *Paspalum notatum* has a coefficient of albedo of 0.23 (0.24 during the dry months). The savanna has a coefficient of 0.18 in the rainy season and 0.23 in the dry season (BULTOT, 1962). As mentioned earlier a large component of the total radiation balance is consumed in the form of latent heat of vaporization. On the plateau the evapotranspiration actually accounts for 80% of the heat used in the rainy season and 60–80% in the dry season; in the mountains 75–80% in the rainy season, 55–75% in the dry season; in the Ruzizi Valley 75–85% during the months with excessive rainfall (November–April) but only 15–20% during the course of dry months of June to August. As the heat exchange between the air and the soil is low from month to month (the temperature of the soil varies very little from one month to the next), it is as well to consider that the balance of the heat remaining is diffused into the air by turbulence.

Sunshine

On the plateau the mean monthly percentage of possible sunshine is between 40 to 50% in the wet season. It is around 60% during the dry season (Table III). At this time it at-

TABLE III

MEAN MONTHLY AND ANNUAL VALUES OF SUNSHINE HOURS (% OF POSSIBLE)

Regions	Jan.	Feb.	Mar.	Apr.	May	June	July	Aug.	Sept.	Oct.	Nov.	Dec.	Ann.
Plateau (Rubona) 1955–1959	46.8	47.0	48.8	44.8	44.1	61.4	63.4	60.5	56.3	51.1	47.7	46.4	51.5
Mountain zone (Kisozi) 1955–1959	39.5	36.9	44.2	42.1	40.5	60.8	64.1	62.1	56.0	48.5	41.4	36.0	47.6
Ruzizi Valley (Bujumbura) 1955–1959	39.8	37.6	45.4	42.9	51.7	71.6	69.7	67.4	57.9	44.5	38.2	37.8	50.3

tains a value of about 90% during the afternoon. In the mountains the amount of sunshine is of the same order as above during the dry season but is less in the wet season (35–45%); cloud is greater in amount in the mountains than on the plateau during the course of the rainy months. In the Ruzizi the sunshine is also approximately 35–45% during the rainy season but reaches 70% during the course of the dry months.

In Table IV it is seen that the sky is rarely covered during the entire day. Also it is quite rare for the sunshine to exceed 90% of that possible even during the dry season.

TABLE IV

RELATIVE FRQUENCY OF PERCENTAGE OF POSSIBLE SUNSHINE

Regions	% of possible sunshine	Jan.	Feb.	Mar.	Apr.	May	June	July	Aug.	Sept.	Oct.	Nov.	Dec.
Plateau	0	0	0	3	1	2	1	0	1	0	1	3	0
(Rubona)	1– 30	23	26	20	28	29	11	12	10	7	23	22	24
1956–1959	31– 60	51	38	35	44	40	28	20	35	32	41	44	52
	61– 90	24	34	40	26	29	56	66	48	61	35	30	23
	91–100	2	2	2	1	0	4	2	6	0	0	1	1
Mountain zone	0	2	3	3	2	0	0	0	0	1	1	0	2
(Kisozi)	1– 30	38	37	27	32	45	13	11	11	11	26	32	46
1946–1959	31– 60	47	42	42	41	31	33	21	32	26	36	49	38
	61– 90	12	18	28	23	22	51	59	52	61	36	18	14
	91–100	1	0	0	2	2	3	9	5	1	1	1	0

The components of the water balance

Rain

On the plateau the mean annual rainfall generally varies between 900 and 1,200 mm; in the mountains between 1,200 and 1,500 mm. On the plains of Kagera (in the north-eastern section of Rwanda) and the lower part of the Ruzizi, amounts of less than 900 mm are received: these are the driest regions. The eastern edges of Lake Kivu receive less than 1,200 mm. In Rwanda the rainiest months are April and May; in Burundi, March and April (Table V). Except in the mountains the mean monthly rainfall values do not exceed 200 mm.

The annual rainfall regime is evidently tied in with the seasonal evolution of the general atmospheric circulation. Fluctuations of short periods in the general circulation are also contributors, in part, to the origin of the great variability which characterizes the rainfall (Table V). At Kisozi, for example, on average, one time in ten the annual rainfall is less than 1,240 mm, while once in ten it exceeds 1,673 mm. The 10 and 90 percentiles of monthly rainfall amounts are even more extreme. In addition, in Table V, the extreme values observed during the 30-year period show how vast the variation can be.

The dry season, defined as a succession of days without precipitation or with very little precipitation, comes each year in approximately the same period and has a mean dura-

TABLE V

MEAN MONTHLY AND ANNUAL VALUES (mm), 10TH AND 90TH PERCENTILES AND EXTREMES, OF RAINFALL (1930–1959)

Regions		Jan.	Feb.	Mar.	Apr.	May	June	July	Aug.	Sept.	Oct.	Nov.	Dec.	Year
Plateau	min.	17.4	47.7	52.6	92.3	37.7	0.0	0.0	0.0	1.4	48.2	54.7	6.7	904.0
(Rubona)	P_{10}	26.9	66.0	59.3	127.1	77.2	0.6	0.0	1.9	17.7	50.0	62.9	38.7	983.0
	mean	110.8	155.7	139.5	182.7	164.4	23.2	7.3	26.8	62.8	102.0	110.3	93.2	1,138.7
	P_{90}	163.4	177.2	217.8	267.1	279.1	79.4	20.4	57.0	139.6	145.3	175.8	161.0	1,336.0
	max.	241.0	214.5	248.5	318.7	367.2	116.5	37.3	95.1	176.0	170.6	198.5	213.0	1,408.0
Mountain zone	min.	70.9	44.9	92.5	57.5	39.8	0.0	0.0	0.0	5.5	38.9	71.7	71.0	1,154.1
(Kisozi)	P_{10}	113.0	97.6	110.2	154.5	49.3	0.0	0.0	0.0	16.3	78.0	108.4	120.6	1,240.4
	mean	166.9	159.7	195.6	227.6	120.1	12.0	6.2	15.7	63.7	114.8	174.3	189.4	1,447.0
	P_{90}	229.8	231.4	293.7	318.3	199.4	39.9	21.5	51.5	120.4	174.1	251.6	280.1	1,673.2
	max.	294.7	247.6	385.8	324.0	313.3	56.3	35.9	74.9	177.0	194.0	348.2	349.3	1,708.8
Ruzizi Valley	min.	23.4	47.7	39.7	53.3	12.1	0.0	0.0	0.0	3.0	18.2	49.0	39.6	632.4
(Bujumbura)	P_{10}	43.4	51.7	74.6	73.4	12.8	0.0	0.0	0.0	9.3	25.8	54.1	47.6	684.7
	mean	93.7	109.3	121.4	125.1	56.6	10.9	5.4	10.6	37.0	63.7	99.6	113.6	846.9
	P_{90}	157.0	208.3	201.5	177.6	99.4	28.5	29.1	32.3	84.7	108.4	142.2	172.6	961.1
	max.	160.7	222.8	225.4	225.7	123.1	104.4	41.7	88.9	105.8	121.3	168.6	193.7	1,106.4

tion which increases from the northwest of Rwanda to the southeast of Burundi (BUL-TOT, 1969). In the northwest of Rwanda it is approximately 70–90 days; on the southeastern frontier of Burundi it is approximately 130 days. In the south of the Ruzizi the duration is approximately 110 days (Table I). The duration of the dry season is extremely variable from one year to another; the inter-decile interval is actually about 35–50 days (Table VI).

At Rubona the dry season begins, in eight cases out of ten, between the 19th of May and the 14th of June; it ends between the 21st of August and the 22nd of September. At

TABLE VI

DATES OF START OF DRY AND WET SEASONS AND LENGTH OF DRY SEASON (10TH AND 90TH PERCENTILES, EXTREMES) (1930–1959)

Regions	Start of dry season		Start of wet season		Length of dry season (days)		Start of dry season extremes		Start of wet season extremes		Length of dry season (day) extremes	
	P_{10}	P_{90}	P_{10}	P_{90}	P_{10}	P_{90}					min.	max.
Plateau (Rubona)	May 19	June 14	Aug. 21	Sept. 22	80	114	May 16	June 23	Aug. 4	Oct. 7	60	120
Mountain zone (Kisozi)	May 17	June 6	Aug. 28	Sept. 29	89	129	May 14	June 13	Aug. 17	Oct. 7	81	144
Ruzizi Valley (Bujumbura)	May 9	June 8	Aug. 26	Oct. 3	88	138	May 1	June 21	Aug. 17	Oct. 15	79	153

Kisozi, in eight cases out of ten, it starts between the 17th of May and the 6th of June and ends between the 28th of August and the 29th of September. From one year to another the date of commencement of the rainy and dry season actually deviates very little from mean values.

The latitudinal movement of the line of demarcation between the dry and wet zones is essentially discontinuous. The discontinuities are related to fluctuations, of short periods, in the atmospheric circulation (BULTOT, 1954). The rains cease very abruptly at the end of the season without any progressive diminution of the frequency (BODEUX, 1967). It is noted that, in the vicinity of the surface, the temperature and humidity of the air do not show any rapid change when passing from the dry season to the rainy season or vice versa (BULTOT, 1954). In the mountains, on the average, it rains two days out of three from November to April and one day in two from May to October (Table VII). On the plateau

TABLE VII

MEAN NUMBER OF RAIN DAYS WITH ⩾ 0.1 MM (1930–1959)

Regions	Jan.	Feb.	Mar.	Apr.	May	June	July	Aug.	Sept.	Oct.	Nov.	Dec.	Year
Plateau (Rubona)	15.0	15.1	17.7	21.6	18.4	4.2	2.1	4.8	11.2	16.0	20.1	17.2	163.4
Mountain zone (Kisozi)	20.8	18.8	21.9	22.8	16.9	3.4	1.2	2.6	8.3	14.3	21.7	21.8	174.5
Ruzizi Valley (Bujumbura)	14.5	14.2	16.8	17.9	10.3	2.6	1.1	1.9	7.6	12.0	18.5	18.8	136.2

the number of rain days is a little less, reducing gradually as one leaves the mountain chain. In the Ruzizi Valley from November to April the mean frequency of precipitation is approximately 0.50. It appears that the probable maximum rainfall is a little greater on the plateau than on the mountains. At Rubona the daily rainfall amount expected once in 10 years is, on the average, 77 mm and once in 50 years, 97 mm. At Kisozi the corresponding values are 71 and 86 mm (Table VIII). It is seen that the maximum probable precipi-

TABLE VIII

MAXIMUM PROBABLE AMOUNT OF RAIN IN 24 h (mm)

Regions	Period of 10 years[1]	Period of 25 years	Period of 50 years
Plateau (Rubona)	77	89	97
Mountain zone (Kisozi)	71	80	86

[1] Daily rainfall amount exceeded, on average, once in 10 years.

tation values are somewhat less than those relating to the Congo Basin and noticeably less than in the lower Congo in the vicinity of the Atlantic Ocean. In this latter region the values are raised to 117 and 143 mm. It is noted also that in the Ruzizi Valley the rainfall intensity has reached 21 mm in 10 min, 46 mm in 30 min, and 56 mm in 60 min. These are the values that can be expected to be exceeded, on average, once in 10 years (Table IX; PIRE et al., 1960).

TABLE IX

RAINFALL AMOUNT IN 10, 20 . . . 80 MIN, EXCEEDED, ON AVERAGE, ONCE IN 2 AND 10 YEARS (mm)

Region		10 min	20 min	30 min	40 min	50 min	60 min	70 min	80 min
Ruzizi Valley	2 years	16.3	27.4	33.5	38.0	39.9	40.6	41.5	45.1
(Bujumbura)	10 years	21.6	37.5	46.3	53.1	55.8	56.6	57.9	64.0

In six cases out of ten the precipitation falls between 11h00 and 19h00 (BODEUX, 1967). The rainfall intensity is also stronger during the diurnal showers than during the course of the nocturnal showers. In five cases out of ten the showers noted on the plateau were of less than 2 h duration, in seven cases out of ten less than 3 h, and in nine cases out of ten less than 5 h (BODEUX, 1967).

Hail

On the spine of the Rwanda, on the average, it is observed that more than five hailstorms per year occur. On the plateau less than three hail showers are noted annually and in Ruzizi less than two (BULTOT, 1959). Because of the generally high altitude of the level of freezing (BERRUEX, 1958) and the abundance of condensation nuclei, the hailstones do not become very large; it is only occasionally that their diameters exceed 13 mm (BULTOT, 1959).

Evaporation

Estimations of potential evapotranspiration on a mean monthly basis from a cover of *Paspalum notatum* (albedo 0.23–0.24) has been established by methods of the energy balance which are given in Table X (BULTOT, 1962, 1969). The values are approximately 85–105 mm on the plateau, from 75 to 95 mm in the mountains, and from 85 to 115 mm in Ruzizi. These values are confirmed by lysimeter measurements made in the basin of the Karuzi in Burundi (BODEUX, 1967). In spite of the drop in radiation balance in July

TABLE X

MEAN MONTHLY AND ANNUAL VALUES OF POTENTIAL EVAPOTRANSPIRATION FROM A COVER OF *Paspalum notatum* (mm)

Regions	Jan.	Feb.	Mar.	Apr.	May	June	July	Aug.	Sept.	Oct.	Nov.	Dec.	Year
Plateau (Rubona)	98	90	103	91	100	89	89	100	103	100	95	97	1,155
Mountain zone (Kisozi)	88	77	87	90	92	84	87	86	95	94	82	82	1,044
Ruzizi Valley (Bujumbura)	97	88	97	94	105	106	97	98	115	103	97	96	1,193

and August the potential evapotranspiration is not much less during this period than in the course of the rainy months. This is the result of the lower humidity and the higher wind speed in the dry season. The annual potential evapotranspiration does not differ much from one region to another (1,000–1,200 mm). Similarly the potential evapotranspiration varies relatively little from one year to the next in view of the small changes of the factors which are important (radiation balance, humidity, and wind speed).

The actual monthly evapotranspiration, which is related to the rainfall, naturally shows larger variation than the preceding factor and these values have been calculated separately for each of the available years during the period of observation. The median and 10 and 90 percentiles of the monthly values of the observed distributions are given in Table XI. The actual evapotranspiration over a cover of *Paspalum notatum* has been calculated by the water balance method of Thornthwaite using a retention value of water in the soil of 200 mm. The results are given in Table XI.

TABLE XI

MEDIANS AND 10TH AND 90TH PERCENTILES, BY MONTH, OF ACTUAL EVAPOTRANSPIRATION FROM A COVER OF *Paspalum notatum* (mm) (1930–1959)

Regions		Jan.	Feb.	Mar.	Apr.	May	June	July	Aug.	Sept.	Oct.	Nov.	Dec.	Year
Plateau	P_{10}	67	76	91	91	99	62	43	37	39	63	75	72	947
(Rubona)	med.	98	90	103	91	100	76	52	53	69	100	95	95	988
	P_{90}	98	90	103	91	100	89	71	79	103	100	95	97	1,053
Mountain zone	P_{10}	88	77	87	90	88	57	42	29	34	69	82	82	871
(Kisozi)	med.	88	77	87	90	92	70	50	39	63	94	82	82	922
	P_{90}	88	77	87	90	92	80	62	68	95	94	82	82	961
Ruzizi Valley	P_{10}	50	70	81	81	60	26	17	15	23	35	56	59	729
(Bujumbura)	med.	89	88	97	94	87	50	30	29	49	63	96	96	857
	P_{90}	97	88	97	94	103	79	62	55	87	102	97	96	950

In the rainy season in the mountain zone the actual evapotranspiration is, in eight cases out of ten, close or equal to the potential evaporation. On the plateau, in nine cases out of ten, it is in excess of 70 mm, while in Ruzizi it is in excess of 50 mm. During the rainy months, in spite of the large variability of rain, the actual evapotranspiration varies relatively little from one year to another. In the dry season, however, the actual evapotranspiration is considerably reduced. It is limited at that time by the amount of rainfall and therefore can show very important deviations from one year to another, particularly during the course of those transition months between the dry season and the rainy season. At the start of the dry season the evaporation rapidly dries the top layer of the soil. The evaporation is therefore appreciably reduced due to the hardening of this soil surface. At the end of the dry season the daily evaporation is around 0.5 mm (BODEUX, 1967). The median value of the actual annual evaporation of *Paspalum notatum* is between 900 and 1,100 mm in the mountains and on the plateaus. In the Ruzizi it is about 860 mm. It should be noted that the actual evapotranspiration from the typical vegetation cover is often greater than that from *Paspalum notatum*. The radiation balance for the savanna is a little greater than that of the *Paspalum notatum* during the wet months. On the plateau the actual evapotranspiration is generally between 80 and 90% of the rainfall amount; in the mountains it is about 65% of the reported rainfall; in the Ruzizi it is approximately equal to the amount of rainfall. It follows that the net mean horizontal flux of water vapour in Rwanda and Burundi is relatively limited.

Temperature and humidity of the air; temperature of the soil

Temperature of the air

Temperature is the element that is most dependent upon the radiation climate. On the average, it is very constant from one year to another. The mean daily temperature decreases approximately 0.65°C/100 m of elevation. At Rubona (1,706 m) it is 19.3°C, at Kisozi (2,155 m) 16.5°C; at Bujumbura (805 m) 23.9°C (Table XII). The mean daily temperature fluctuates little from one month to the next. The mean monthly extreme difference (annual range) is not more than 2°C.

TABLE XII

DAILY TEMPERATURES

Regions		Jan.	Feb.	Mar.	Apr.	May	June	July	Aug.	Sept.	Oct.	Nov.	Dec.	Year
Plateau	μ	19.4	19.3	19.4	19.2	19.0	18.5	18.9	19.9	20.1	19.8	19.2	19.1	19.3
(Rubona)	M	25.3	25.2	25.2	24.5	24.1	24.3	25.6	26.6	26.7	25.9	24.8	24.6	25.2
1950–1959	m	13.5	13.4	13.6	13.9	13.9	12.5	12.2	13.1	13.5	13.6	13.5	13.6	13.4
	MM	27.2	27.4	27.1	25.7	25.5	25.7	26.9	27.7	28.5	28.4	25.8	27.5	28.5
	mm	12.5	12.6	12.7	13.4	13.2	11.4	10.6	12.2	13.0	12.8	12.8	12.6	10.6
Mountain zone	μ	16.7	16.8	16.8	16.7	16.3	15.1	15.3	16.3	17.0	17.1	16.7	16.7	16.5
(Kisozi)	M	21.9	21.9	22.0	21.5	21.3	21.1	21.9	22.9	23.3	22.9	21.8	21.5	22.0
1951–1959	m	11.5	11.7	11.7	11.8	11.3	9.1	8.6	9.6	10.7	11.3	11.7	11.8	10.9
	MM	23.4	23.4	23.5	22.8	22.8	22.2	23.1	23.8	25.3	24.3	22.6	22.6	25.3
	mm	10.8	10.6	10.9	11.2	10.2	7.6	6.5	8.3	9.2	10.8	11.1	11.0	6.5
Ruzizi Valley	μ	23.7	23.8	23.8	23.7	23.9	23.3	23.1	24.1	25.0	24.8	23.7	23.5	23.9
(Bujumbura)	M	28.2	28.4	28.4	28.2	28.4	28.5	28.8	30.1	30.8	30.1	28.2	27.9	28.8
1950–1959	m	19.2	19.1	19.1	19.2	19.3	18.1	17.4	18.2	19.1	19.5	19.1	19.1	18.9
	MM	29.5	29.6	29.6	29.5	29.2	28.9	29.5	30.6	32.2	31.5	29.6	28.9	32.2
	mm	18.6	18.3	18.7	18.3	18.9	17.1	15.8	17.0	17.9	18.7	18.5	18.5	15.8

Note: μ = mean; M = mean maximum; m = mean minimum; MM and mm = extremes.

During the wet months the mean diurnal variation is between 9 and 12°C. This small value is due to the greenhouse effect characteristic of the equatorial region. This greenhouse effect, which is caused by the CO_2 and high water vapour content of the atmosphere, reduces the nocturnal radiation and maintains high minimum temperatures. In the dry season the temperature falls during the night due to the appreciable increase of the terrestrial radiation. This is the reason for a small lowering of the mean daily temperature at this period. The temperature can rise to about 32°C in the Ruzizi and fall as low as about 6°C in the mountains.

Locally, especially in the marshy or swampy valleys, the temperature in the dry season can approach the freezing point (BODEUX, 1967). At the grass level it often goes below 0°C (BODEUX, 1967). Temperature decreases rapidly between 16h00 and 20h00 (local mean time), then decreases more slowly until the minimum appears around 06h00. The increase is then rapid between 07h00 and 11h00 and more gradual following this. On the plateau the maximum occurs generally between 14h00 and 15h00, that is to say, about 2 h after the radiation balance has attained its maximum (BULTOT, 1967). In the mountains the maximum temperature is often found between 13h30 and 14h30. The difference between the radiation balance and this maximum temperature time is a little less in the mountains due, no doubt, to the strong turbulence of the air.

Humidity

The humidity of the air is essentially related to the actual evapotranspiration and the advection of water vapour from neighbouring humid regions. In comparing the monthly values of the humidity mixing ratios (Table XIII) the results show that in the lower Ruzizi the water vapour content of the air is great (14–16 g/kg in the rainy season and 11–13 g/kg in the dry season). In this region the important advection of water vapour from the region of Lake Tanganyika is a little offset by the small evapotranspiration. In the dry season, moreover, the water vapour content of the air is greater than that in the lower Congo near to the Atlantic Ocean. On the plateau the water vapour content of the air is 11–13 g/kg in the wet season and 9–11 g/kg in the dry season. In the mountains the water vapour content decreases slowly with altitude. At Kisozi (2,155 m) it is 10.5–12.5 g/kg in the wet season and 8.5–10.5 g/kg in the dry season. In this region the water vapour content of the air is limited by the temperature and, to a certain degree, by the turbulence of the air.

TABLE XIII

MEAN MONTHLY AND ANNUAL VALUES OF HUMIDITY MIXING RATIO, r (g/kg); WATER VAPOUR PRESSURE, e (mbar) AND RELATIVE HUMIDITY, U (%)

Region		Jan.	Feb.	Mar.	Apr.	May	June	July	Aug.	Sept.	Oct.	Nov.	Dec.	Year
Plateau	r	12.3	12.3	12.5	12.8	12.6	10.7	9.1	9.7	10.1	11.2	11.9	12.5	11.5
(Rubona)	e	16.1	16.1	16.3	16.7	16.5	14.1	12.0	12.8	13.3	14.7	15.6	15.3	15.1
1956–1958	U	79	78	78	83	72	70	59	60	60	71	76	80	73
Mountain zone	r	11.8	11.8	12.0	12.3	11.9	9.9	8.8	9.0	8.7	10.5	11.5	11.9	10.9
(Kisozi)	e	14.6	14.7	14.9	15.3	14.8	12.3	11.0	11.2	10.8	13.1	14.3	14.8	13.5
1956–1958	U	83	84	84	88	87	78	70	67	62	72	80	85	78
Ruzizi Valley	r	15.2	15.4	15.8	15.7	15.0	13.0	12.1	11.4	12.8	13.7	14.6	14.9	14.1
(Bujumbura)	e	22.0	22.3	22.9	22.8	21.8	19.0	17.7	16.6	18.6	19.9	21.2	21.7	20.5
1954–1956	U	79	79	81	82	78	67	62	55	59	65	75	78	72

In the wet season, when the actual evapotranspiration varies little from one year to the other, the mean monthly values of the atmospheric humidity deviate little from their mean values. The mean monthly water vapour pressure is generally between 12 and 17 mbar on the plateau, from 10.5 to 15.5 mbar in the mountains (about 2,000 m), and between 16.5 and 23 mbar in the Ruzizi (Table XIII). The mean monthly relative humidity is between 55 and 85% on the plateau and in the Ruzizi. It is a little greater in the mountains (60–90%). The difference between the daytime and nighttime values of the water vapour pressure is small. The water vapour pressure reaches a maximum during the day in the rainy season and at night in the dry season (BODEUX, 1967).

Soil temperature

The mean annual temperature range at 10 cm depth is approximately 2°C (Table XIV BULTOT, 1969); it is therefore very small. It is known that the annual temperature fluctuation reduces only slowly with depth. Meanwhile, from one month to another, the heat flux given up or absorbed by the soil is most often less than 100 cal./cm²; it would appear that this is almost negligible (less than 2%) in comparison with the mean monthly global radiation balance.

TABLE XIV

MEAN MONTHLY AND ANNUAL SOIL TEMPERATURES (°C) AT 10, 20 AND 50 CM DEPTH (1954–1959)

Region		Jan.	Feb.	Mar.	Apr.	May	June	July	Aug.	Sept.	Oct.	Nov.	Dec.	Year
Plateau	10 cm	22.6	23.0	23.5	22.2	22.1	23.0	23.3	23.7	23.7	22.7	22.4	22.5	22.9
(Rubona)	20 cm	22.5	22.7	23.2	22.0	21.9	22.8	23.0	23.5	23.5	22.8	22.3	22.3	22.7
	50 cm	22.4	22.5	23.1	22.1	21.8	22.7	22.8	23.2	23.2	22.6	22.2	22.2	22.6
Mountain zone	10 cm	17.1	17.4	18.2	17.7	17.0	16.8	17.8	18.6	19.1	18.4	17.4	17.1	17.7
(Kisozi)	20 cm	17.0	17.1	17.5	17.5	16.9	16.7	17.5	18.3	18.8	18.2	17.2	17.0	17.5
	50 cm	17.4	17.4	17.8	17.8	17.5	17.3	17.6	18.4	18.8	18.5	17.7	17.4	17.8

The mean diurnal temperature variation at 10 cm depth is usually between 7 and 10°C on the plateau and between 4 and 7°C in the mountains. It diminishes rapidly with depth; at 50 cm it is only some few tenths of a degree. The fluctuation of mean monthly values of the soil temperature is very small.

Atmospheric pressure and wind

Atmospheric pressure

The mean daily curve of the atmospheric pressure is the result of a semi-diurnal wave associated with the elastic properties of the atmosphere, and a daily wave which is correlated with the season and the temperature (VANDER ELST, 1955). The curve gives a maximum around 08h00–09h00 (local mean time) and a minimum around 15h00–16h00. The mean daily pressure variation is of the order of 3–5 mbar. The mean barometric pressure changes little from one month to the next; a small maximum appears, however, in June and July. The difference between the extreme mean monthly values does not exceed 2 mbar.

Surface winds

The mean monthly wind speed at a height of 2 m above the ground is relatively large. It is a maximum during the afternoon and a minimum at night. On the plateau it is approximately 8–10 km/h between 12h00 and 18h00; from 5 to 6.5 km/h between 18h00 and 06h00. In the mountains it is approximately 8–10 km/h between 12h00 and 18h00; and from 5 to 7.5 km/h between 18h00 and 06h00 (Table XV).

TABLE XV

MEAN WIND SPEED AT 2 m (km/h) (1958–1959)

Regions	Month	06h00 to 12h00	12h00 to 18h00	06h00 to 18h00	18h00 to 06h00	06h00 to 06h00
Plateau	Jan.	5.9	8.8	7.4	5.2	6.3
(Rubona)	Feb.	5.9	9.1	7.5	5.3	6.4
	Mar.	6.2	8.7	7.5	5.0	6.3
	Apr.	7.5	8.2	7.8	5.4	6.6
	May	6.8	8.8	7.3	5.2	6.3
	June	8.3	7.9	8.1	5.8	6.9
	July	8.7	8.4	8.5	6.2	7.4
	Aug.	8.8	9.5	9.2	6.4	7.8
	Sept.	8.7	10.1	9.4	6.2	7.8
	Oct.	7.6	10.0	8.8	6.1	7.4
	Nov.	7.1	10.1	8.6	5.3	6.9
	Dec.	6.3	9.6	7.9	4.9	6.4
	Year	7.3	9.1	8.2	5.6	6.9
Mountain zone	Jan.	7.3	9.4	8.3	5.2	6.8
(Kisozi)	Feb.	6.9	9.1	8.0	5.5	6.7
	Mar.	7.4	9.4	8.4	5.4	6.9
	Apr.	8.8	9.2	9.0	5.3	7.1
	May	8.3	8.7	8.5	5.7	7.1
	June	8.7	8.3	8.5	6.6	7.5
	July	9.7	9.2	9.4	7.2	8.3
	Aug.	10.1	10.0	10.0	7.3	8.7
	Sept.	9.8	9.9	9.9	6.5	8.2
	Oct.	9.5	10.1	9.8	5.6	7.7
	Nov.	8.8	9.8	9.3	5.2	7.3
	Dec.	7.8	9.2	8.5	4.8	6.7
	Year	8.6	9.4	9.0	5.9	7.4

It is noted that there is a greater wind speed in the dry season. At this time the wind attains its maximum speed at 10h00 and maintains this during the rest of the day. During the rainy months the wind speed is a little less, and reaches high wind speeds during a shorter period of the day than in the dry season, then it decreases rapidly during the night (BODEUX, 1967).

At 12h00 the prevailing directions on the plateau are from northeast to east in October–February, from southeast to east during March–May and in September, and from southeast to south from June to August (Table XVI). In the mountains the prevailing directions are northeast to easterly from October to March, easterly to southeasterly from

TABLE XVI

RELATIVE FREQUENCIES (%) OF WIND DIRECTION (1956–1959)

Regions	Month	06h00									12h00								
		calm	N	NE	E	SE	S	SW	W	NW	calm	N	NE	E	SE	S	SW	W	NW
Plateau (Rubona)	Jan.	1.6	4.0	1.6	1.6	5.6	4.8	8.9	33.1	38.8	0.0	8.9	26.6	25.0	18.5	8.1	4.8	1.6	6.5
	Feb.	1.8	0.9	1.8	2.7	1.8	3.5	11.5	36.3	39.7	0.0	8.8	26.5	27.5	18.6	8.0	4.4	2.7	3.5
	Mar.	4.8	5.6	1.6	2.4	1.6	4.0	5.7	29.9	44.4	0.0	6.5	21.8	25.8	27.4	7.3	4.8	3.2	3.2
	Apr.	1.7	2.5	1.7	3.4	10.9	10.1	10.1	29.3	30.3	0.0	5.9	22.7	21.8	32.8	9.2	3.4	0.8	3.4
	May	1.6	3.2	0.8	2.4	8.6	13.7	8.9	32.3	29.0	0.0	1.6	12.1	19.3	45.3	12.9	5.6	1.6	1.6
	June	0.8	1.7	0.8	0.0	5.8	9.2	5.8	36.7	39.2	0.0	0.8	2.5	15.8	46.7	25.0	7.5	1.7	0.0
	July	2.4	1.6	1.6	1.6	4.8	6.5	8.9	31.5	41.1	0.0	0.0	3.2	15.3	50.0	23.4	6.5	1.6	0.0
	Aug.	3.2	5.6	4.0	5.6	10.5	9.7	4.0	26.7	30.7	0.0	1.6	4.0	15.3	48.4	20.2	6.5	3.2	0.8
	Sept.	0.9	2.6	2.6	6.1	12.2	6.1	6.1	25.2	38.2	0.0	2.6	13.0	22.6	38.4	16.5	4.3	1.7	0.9
	Oct.	4.8	8.1	1.6	3.2	11.3	6.5	4.8	24.2	35.5	0.0	11.3	33.9	24.2	24.2	4.8	1.6	0.0	0.0
	Nov.	6.7	5.6	3.3	1.1	4.4	5.6	6.7	28.9	37.7	0.0	10.0	33.4	30.0	21.1	3.3	1.1	1.1	0.0
	Dec.	4.3	3.2	3.2	4.3	1.1	1.1	3.2	41.9	37.7	0.0	10.7	34.5	24.7	17.2	3.2	1.1	3.2	5.4
Mountain zone (Kisozi)	Jan.	29.0	1.6	0.8	2.4	3.2	15.3	29.9	6.5	11.3	1.6	7.3	36.3	25.0	12.9	2.4	7.3	2.4	4.8
	Feb.	15.9	3.5	0.9	0.0	1.8	22.1	37.2	7.1	11.5	0.0	9.7	37.2	19.5	16.8	4.4	3.5	2.7	6.2
	Mar.	21.8	2.4	2.4	1.6	9.7	21.8	26.6	5.6	8.1	0.8	8.1	30.6	26.7	20.2	4.8	3.2	2.4	3.2
	Apr.	10.8	1.7	1.7	8.3	24.2	29.2	20.8	2.5	0.8	0.8	2.5	21.7	38.2	26.7	4.2	1.7	2.5	1.7
	May	8.1	0.0	1.6	8.9	25.0	29.8	24.2	0.0	2.4	0.8	0.8	10.5	42.7	35.5	8.1	1.6	0.0	0.0
	June	0.8	0.0	0.0	1.7	11.7	44.1	41.7	0.0	0.0	0.0	0.8	5.8	29.2	45.1	15.8	2.5	0.8	0.0
	July	2.4	0.0	0.0	1.6	11.3	37.9	46.8	0.8	0.0	0.0	0.0	3.2	17.8	36.3	24.1	17.8	0.8	0.0
	Aug.	2.4	0.0	0.0	4.8	15.3	34.8	41.1	3.3	0.8	0.0	2.4	7.3	31.5	40.3	12.9	5.6	0.0	0.0
	Sept.	1.7	1.7	2.5	10.0	18.3	30.8	30.0	3.2	1.7	0.8	0.8	13.3	38.4	32.6	10.8	3.3	0.0	0.0
	Oct.	24.8	2.1	3.2	8.6	17.2	21.5	18.3	2.2	1.1	0.0	3.2	22.6	38.8	22.6	10.7	2.1	0.0	0.0
	Nov.	33.3	6.7	7.8	4.4	6.7	14.4	15.5	6.5	8.9	1.2	3.3	40.0	40.0	12.2	3.3	0.0	0.0	0.0
	Dec.	38.6	6.5	1.1	3.2	5.4	8.6	12.9	6.5	17.2	1.1	6.5	43.0	23.6	11.8	5.4	4.3	3.2	1.1

April to June and in September, and southeast to south in July. It is seen that during the nighttime the wind direction is noticeably influenced by the mountain breezes and these effects are felt relatively far out on the plateau. It is because of this that at Rubona at 06h00 the wind blows from a direction between northwest and west during more than 60% of the cases. At Kisozi at 06h00 it blows generally from southwest to south. In conclusion, during the day the territories of Rwanda and Burundi are swept by northeast to easterly currents during the rainy months. In the dry season these winds intensify and have a meridional component due to the reinforcement of the South African anticyclone. On the other hand one sometimes notices very violent gusts due to the turbulence of the air during the warm period of the day or when there is a passage of a squall line (Table XVII; CRABBE, 1968). This is why these gusts are generally only produced during the

TABLE XVII

MEAN NUMBER OF OCCASIONS PER MONTH ON WHICH WIND GUSTS REACH 10, 13 AND 17 M/SEC

Regions	Rainy season			Dry season		
	⩾ 10 m/sec	⩾ 13 m/sec	⩾ 17 m/sec	⩾ 10 m/sec	⩾ 13 m/sec	⩾ 17 m/sec
Plateau (Rubona)	12.3	6.2	1.6	2.0	0.7	0.3
Mountain zone (Kisozi)	4.6	1.4	0.3	0.2	–	–

rainy season and most often between 12h00 and 18h00 (CRABBE, 1968). Their directions are frequently between 0 and 180°. The highest wind speeds which have been registered are approximately 20–25 m/sec, that is approximately 75–90 km/h (Table XVIII; CRABBE, 1968).

TABLE XVIII

EXTREME WIND SPEEDS

Regions	Speed		Date	Local time	Direction	Period of observ.
	m/sec	km/h				
Plateau (Rubona)	24.0	86.4	5 Jan., 1959	15h25	ENE	1958–1959
Mountain zone (Kisozi)	21.7	78.1	5 Jan., 1956	16h15	N	1956–1958

Climatic classification

The aridity index of BUDYKO (1958), is equal to the ratio of B/Lr, where B, L and r are respectively the total radiation balance, the latent heat of vaporization and the mean annual precipitation (mm). The greater the index, the greater the aridity of the climate.

In the mountains the aridity index is slightly less than 1. On the plateau it increases from the west towards the east and takes a value generally between 1.0 and 1.4. Meanwhile, in the northeastern section of Rwanda it can be as high as 1.7. In the Ruzizi it is about 1.5 (BULTOT, 1969). These values are calculated from values of the total radiation balance taken at the top of a cover of *Paspalum notatum*. On the plateau and the mountains the Budyko index is not very large. In the low-lying regions of the Ruzizi and the Kagera (northeast of Rwanda), in comparison, the value of this index is at the limit of the range proposed for the tropical humid zone. We see then that if we take into account also the air temperature, the climate of Rwanda and Burundi (with the exception of the valleys of the Ruzizi and the Kagera) does not qualify for the term "tropical" in the strictest sense because the mean monthly temperature does not reach 20°C during eight months or more (BULTOT, 1964). Nevertheless, in these regions the thermal and precipitation regime are apparently those of the tropical regime and it would be inappropriate to consider these as temperate regions. In the end one can still class the climate of Rwanda and Burundi among the humid climates that have a monthly deficit of rainfall that is less than 25 mm during six months or more when calculated according to Thornthwaite's method.

References

BERRUEX, M., 1958. Contribution à la connaissance de l'atmosphère équatoriale. Une année de radio-sondages à Léopoldville. *Acad. Roy. Sci. Outre-Mer (Brussels), Classe Sci. Mén.*, 5(5): 78 pp.

BODEUX, A., 1967. Le bilan d'eau dans le bassin de la Karuzi au Burundi. *Arch. Mission Karuzi, Publ. Inst. Sociol., Univ. Bruxelles*, 3: 102 pp.

BUDYKO, M., 1958. The heat balance of the earth's surface. *U.S. Dept. Comm., Weather Bur. Publ.*, 259 pp.

BULTOT, F., 1950. Régimes normaux et cartes des précipitations dans l'est du Congo belge. *Publ. Inst. Natl. Etude Agron. Congo Belge, Sér. Tech.*, 1: 56 pp.

BULTOT, F., 1954. Saisons et périodes sèches et pluvieuses au Congo belge et au Ruanda-Urundi. *Publ. Inst. Natl. Etude Agron. Congo Belge, Sèr. Tech.*, 9: 70 pp.

BULTOT, F., 1956. Etude statistique des pluies intenses en un point et sur une aire au Congo belge et au Ruanda-Urundi. *Publ. Inst. Natl. Etude Agron. Congo Belge, Sér. Tech.*, 11: 90 pp.

BULTOT, F., 1959. Etude statistique des chutes de grêle au Congo belge et au Ruanda-Urundi. *Publ. Inst. Natl. Etude Agron. Congo Belge, Sér. Tech.*, 17: 43 pp.

BULTOT, F., 1962. Sur la détermination des moyennes mensuelles et annuelles de l'évaporation réelle et de l'écoulement dans le bassin congolais. *Bull. Séances Acad. Roy. Sci. Outre-Mer (Brussels)*, 4: 816–838.

BULTOT, F., 1964. Sur la délimitation de la zône tropicale humide. *Bull. Séances Acad. Roy. Sci. Outre-Mer (Brussels)*, 2: 406–412.

BULTOT, F., 1967. Estimation à partir d'un nombre limité de mesures des moyennes vraies journalières, diurnes et nocturnes de la température et de l'humidité de l'air au Congo, au Ruanda et au Burundi. *Publ. Inst. Natl. Etude Agron. Congo Belge, Sér. Tech.*, 20: 97 pp.

BULTOT, F., 1969. *Atlas Climatique de Bassin Congolais*. In preparation.

CRABBE, M., 1968. Coups de vent et périodes de vent fort au sol au Congo. *Bull. Séances Acad. Roy. Sci. Outre-Mer (Brussels)*, 6: 902–938.

DUPRIEZ, G., 1969. La température du sol en région equatoriale africaine. *Acad. Roy. Sci. Outre-Mer (Brussels), Classe Sci. Tech., Mém.*, 16(7): 60 pp.

PIRE, J., BERRUEX, M. and QUOIDBACH, J., 1960. L'intensité des pluies au Congo et au Ruanda-Urundi. *Acad. Roy. Sci. Outre-Mer (Brussels), Classe Sci. Tech., Mém.*, 6(1): 135 pp.

QUOIDBACH, J. and GOLBERT, G., 1969. Vents en altitude au Congo. *Meteorol. Serv. Kinshasa, Publ.*, 49: 13 pp.

RIEHL, H., 1954. *Tropical Meteorology*. McGraw-Hill, New York, N.Y., 392 pp.

TSCHIRHART, G., 1959. Les perturbations intéressant l'A.E.F. méridionale. *Monograph. Méteorol. Natl.*, 13: 32 pp.

VANDER ELST, N., 1955. La pression au Congo belge. *Acad. Roy. Sci. Outre-Mer (Brussels), Mém.*, 2(2): 142 pp.

TABLE XIX

CLIMATIC TABLE FOR RUBONA, RWANDA
Latitude 02°29'S, longitude 29°46'E, elevation 1,706 m

Month	Temperature (°C)				Relat. humid. (%)	Precipitation					Wind		Averages			
	mean		extreme			mean (mm)	max. (mm)	min. (mm)	days ≥ 0.1 mm	max. 24 h (mm)	aver. speed (km/h)	preval. direct.	cloud-iness (oktas)	sun-shine (h)	radi-ation (Ly/day)	evap. (mm)
	max.	min.	max.	min.												
Jan	25	14	27	13	79	111	241	17	15	66	6	NE	4	177	460	134
Feb.	25	13	27	13	78	156	215	48	15	79	6	NE	4	160	470	124
Mar.	25	14	27	13	78	140	249	53	18	76	6	NE	4	184	481	141
Apr.	25	14	26	13	83	183	319	92	22	80	7	SE	4	162	453	125
May	24	14	26	13	72	164	367	38	18	73	6	SE	4	164	463	136
June	24	13	26	11	70	23	117	0	4	68	7	SE	3	220	454	128
July	26	12	27	11	59	7	37	0	2	19	7	SE	3	236	449	134
Aug.	27	13	28	12	60	27	95	0	5	74	8	SE	3	226	471	147
Sept.	27	14	28	13	60	63	176	1	11	45	8	SE	3	204	490	146
Oct.	26	14	28	13	71	102	171	48	16	63	7	SE	4	193	475	140
Nov.	25	14	26	13	76	110	199	55	20	47	7	NE	4	175	469	131
Dec.	25	14	28	13	80	93	213	7	17	65	6	NE	4	177	460	133
Annual	25	13	28	11	73	1,139	1,408	904	163	79	7	—	4	2,278	466	1,619
Rec. (yrs.)	10	10	10	10	3	30	30	30	30	30	3		5	5	2	2

TABLE XX

CLIMATIC TABLE FOR BUJUMBURA, BURUNDI
Latitude 03°23'S, longitude 29°21'E, elevation 805 m

Month	Mean sta. press. (mbar)	Temperature (°C)				Relat. humid. (%)	Precipitation					Wind		Averages			
		mean		extreme			mean (mm)	max. (mm)	min. (mm)	days ≥ 0.1 mm	max. 24 h (mm)	aver. speed (km/h)	preval. direct.	cloud-iness (oktas)	sun-shine (h)	radi-ation (Ly/day)	evap. (mm)
		max.	min.	max.	min.												
Jan.	919	28	19	30	19	79	94	161	23	15	65	6	SW	5	159	421	129
Feb.	920	28	19	30	18	79	109	223	48	14	128	6	SW	5	140	410	117
Mar.	920	28	19	30	19	81	121	225	40	17	60	6	SSW	4	171	415	129
Apr.	920	28	19	30	18	82	125	226	53	18	54	6	SSW	5	153	416	125
May	921	28	19	29	19	78	57	123	12	10	49	8	SSW	4	196	441	140
June	922	29	18	29	17	67	11	104	0	3	83	7	SSW	3	242	455	145
July	921	29	17	30	16	62	5	42	0	1	33	8	SSW	2	269	432	139
Aug.	921	30	18	31	17	55	11	89	0	2	39	8	SSW	3	247	440	149
Sept.	920	31	19	32	18	59	37	106	3	8	30	5	WSW	4	202	467	162
Oct.	920	30	20	32	19	65	64	121	18	12	34	8	W	4	174	407	144
Nov.	920	28	19	30	19	75	100	169	49	19	64	7	W	5	141	420	129
Dec.	920	28	19	29	19	78	114	194	40	19	62	6	SW	5	148	410	128
Annual	920	29	19	32	16	72	848	1,106	632	138	128	7	—	4	2,242	428	1,636
Rec. (yrs.)	6	10	10	10	10	3	30	30	30	30	30	2	2	9	9	2	2

TABLE XXI

CLIMATIC TABLE FOR KISOZI, BURUNDI
Latitude 03°33'S, longitude 29°41'E, elevation 2,155 m

Month	Temperature (°C) mean max.	mean min.	extreme max.	extreme min.	Relat. humid. (%)	Precipitation mean (mm)	max. (mm)	min. (mm)	days ≥ 0.1 mm	max. 24 h (mm)	Wind aver. speed (km/h)	preval. direct.	Averages cloud-iness (oktas)	sun-shine (h)	radi-ation (Ly/day)	evap. (mm)
Jan.	22	12	23	11	83	167	295	71	21	61	7	NE	5	149	438	113
Feb.	22	12	23	11	84	160	248	45	19	69	7	NE	5	126	434	98
Mar.	22	12	24	11	84	196	386	93	22	72	7	NE	4	166	445	112
Apr.	22	12	23	11	88	228	324	58	23	103	7	SE	5	152	467	115
May	21	11	23	10	87	120	313	40	17	51	7	SE	5	150	465	118
June	21	9	22	8	78	12	56	0	3	28	8	SE-SW	3	217	471	111
July	22	9	23	7	70	6	36	0	1	31	8	SE-SW	3	237	469	118
Aug.	23	10	24	8	67	16	75	0	3	36	9	SE-SW	3	231	454	118
Sept.	23	11	25	9	62	64	177	6	8	45	8	SE	4	203	481	129
Oct.	23	11	24	11	72	115	194	39	14	67	8	SE	4	183	461	124
Nov.	22	12	23	11	80	174	348	72	22	70	7	NE	5	152	429	106
Dec.	22	12	23	11	85	189	349	71	22	60	7	NE	5	138	424	105
Annual	22	11	25	7	78	1,447	1,709	1,154	175	103	7	—	4	2,104	453	1,367
Rec. (yrs.)	9	9	9	9	3	30	30	30	30	30	2		6	6	2	2

one. During the former diurnal ranges are greater, 15°–20°C, compared with 10°C in the latter.

Frost is experienced above 2,200 m during the cool seasons and is not an uncommon occurrence in local areas, such as valleys in which there is cold air drainage. For example, the town of Awash, in the valley of the river Awash, often has frost yet is located at less than 1,000 m. Locations above about 2,500–2,700 m can have frosty nights almost any month of the year.

Soil temperatures were taken at Addis Ababa and Gondar for one year only. At Addis Ababa the mean annual maximum was 27.4°C (24.2°C July and 29.7°C March) at 30 cm and 24.8°C (22.9°C July and 26.7°C April) at 150 cm. The annual minimum was 8.0°C (5.3°C November and 9.8°C May) at 30 cm and 8.5°C (5.0°C December and 10.2°C April) at 150 cm. At Gondar at 30 cm the maximum was 33.4°C (27.1°C July and 40.1°C March) with the minimum 10.3°C (6.6°C January and 12.4°C October).

Rainfall

Annual rainfall amounts vary greatly over the zone (Fig.3). Some areas on the fringes of semi-arid and desert regions receive only 400–500 mm while others, in the mountainous areas, receive in excess of 2,000 mm. The wettest regularly reporting station is Gore Airport with an average of more than 2,200 mm and a high annual total of 2,786 mm in 1960.

There is, however, more uniformity in the seasonal distribution than there is in the totals.

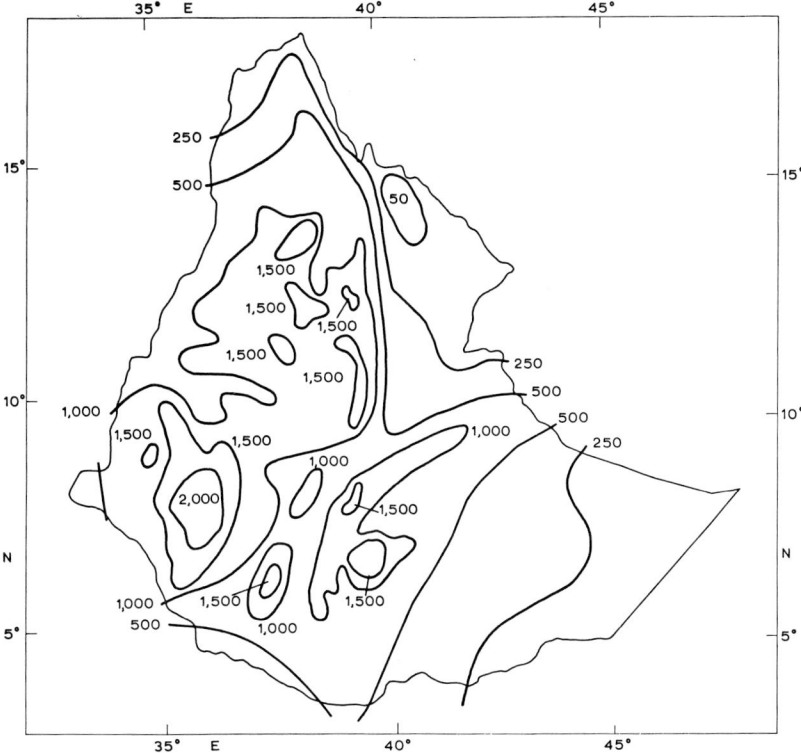

Fig.3. Mean annual rainfall (mm), simplified.

For most of the zone the heaviest rainfall is during the period June–September, for instance, Gondar 85%, Asmara 80%, Addis Ababa and Gambela 70%, Dire Dawa 60% and Jimma 55%. This percentage generally increases as one moves northwards, e.g., Moyale 11%, Neghelli 7% and Magalo 20%, for the rain associated with the I.T.C.Z. and related convective disturbances becomes more concentrated into this period. However, along the eastern escarpment a double-peaked pattern helps to reduce the June–September percentage; Quoram 52%, Harar 45% and Ghinda 16%. This is especially noticeable in the Eritrean province where there is a definite period of appreciable winter rains (see Table IV).

TABLE IV

MEAN MONTHLY AND ANNUAL RAINFALL (MM)

	Jan.	Feb.	Mar.	Apr.	May	June	July	Aug.	Sept.	Oct.	Nov.	Dec.	Ann.
Moyale	11	17	55	182	118	17	17	17	25	96	86	41	682
Neghelli	8	4	33	172	102	8	6	7	16	119	52	23	550
Magalo	14	7	92	92	95	4	21	34	54	107	6	7	532
Uondo	26	60	107	149	147	109	203	202	154	85	45	12	1,302
Adamitullo	12	24	35	60	66	56	109	94	83	16	9	13	577
Saiyo	11	33	68	139	198	192	194	216	142	79	50	18	1,342
Gore	29	51	85	136	276	307	276	313	314	163	76	33	2,059
Gambela	6	9	37	86	154	171	241	236	192	99	44	13	1,289
Daga Dima	73	53	147	118	108	142	170	140	140	97	41	14	1,243
Dembidollo	11	33	68	139	198	192	194	216	143	79	50	19	1,342
Bakaksa	40	57	137	193	257	178	204	186	201	126	98	26	1,702
Harar	11	32	60	109	121	101	142	137	98	46	23	10	889
Dire Dawa	20	29	43	83	30	23	108	165	70	12	17	10	582
Kurmuk	0	0	6	17	114	153	175	194	163	97	7	2	928
Bure	30	9	66	122	174	168	183	138	138	173	137	26	1,302
Dangila	5	10	25	62	122	224	319	301	207	78	40	6	1,399
Quoram	21	43	87	89	78	17	179	253	76	54	19	75	991
Gondar	0	5	9	57	77	182	369	356	122	47	18	3	1,246
Gallabat	0	0	5	17	74	166	193	239	164	30	2	0	890
Adi Ugri	0	1	15	31	34	64	193	161	49	7	10	1	565
Ghinda	152	89	80	74	58	15	48	52	30	77	52	99	826
Fil-Fil	162	204	89	120	15	0	42	0	15	104	120	252	1,123
Mt. Sabur	163	148	98	60	54	23	100	102	31	103	94	149	1,125

Annual rainfall shows very pronounced fluctuations from year to year, as illustrated by Table V for Addis Ababa. During this 60-year period the annual total has varied from 923 to 1,905 mm, or from 73 to 151% of the mean. Other stations show a similarly large variation, Adi Ugri 56–183%, Asmara 56–162%, Gambela 62–144%, Adamitullo 67–151% and Gore 71–122%. As is general the range tends to decrease as rainfall increases.

The seasonal variation is shown numerically for 23 stations in Table IV, and reference has been made earlier to the different single and double peak patterns—some have multiple peaks, such as Ghinda and Mount Sabur. The pattern of Table IV is simple to explain when it is realised that the stations are arranged in order of increasing latitude. However, it is more easily appreciated when presented in map form.

TABLE V

ANNUAL RAINFALL, ADDIS ABABA (mm), 1900–1959

Decade	Year 0	1	2	3	4	5	6	7	8	9
1900	1,165	1,241	985	1,433	1,107	1,104	1,543	1,047	1,132	1,263
1910	1,269	1,076	1,161	1,175	1,439	1,901	1,730	1,591	960	992
1920	1,076	1,039	1,061	1,321	1,905	1,476	1,755	1,271	1,342	1,244
1930	1,461	1,022	975	1,181	1,027	1,283	1,419	1,134	1,053	1,133
1940	937	1,106	1,154	1,054	1,083	1,006	1,138	1,261	1,413	1,351
1950	956	934	1,081	923	1,164	1,276	1,027	1,317	1,309	1,043

In Fig.4 the 50-mm isohyets are shown, the arrows point towards the wetter areas (GRIFFITHS and HEMMING, 1963). In December and January the only appreciable rainfall is experienced along the coastal belt and east facing slopes in Eritrea. This rainfall is associated with the convergence brought about by winter depressions moving northwest-

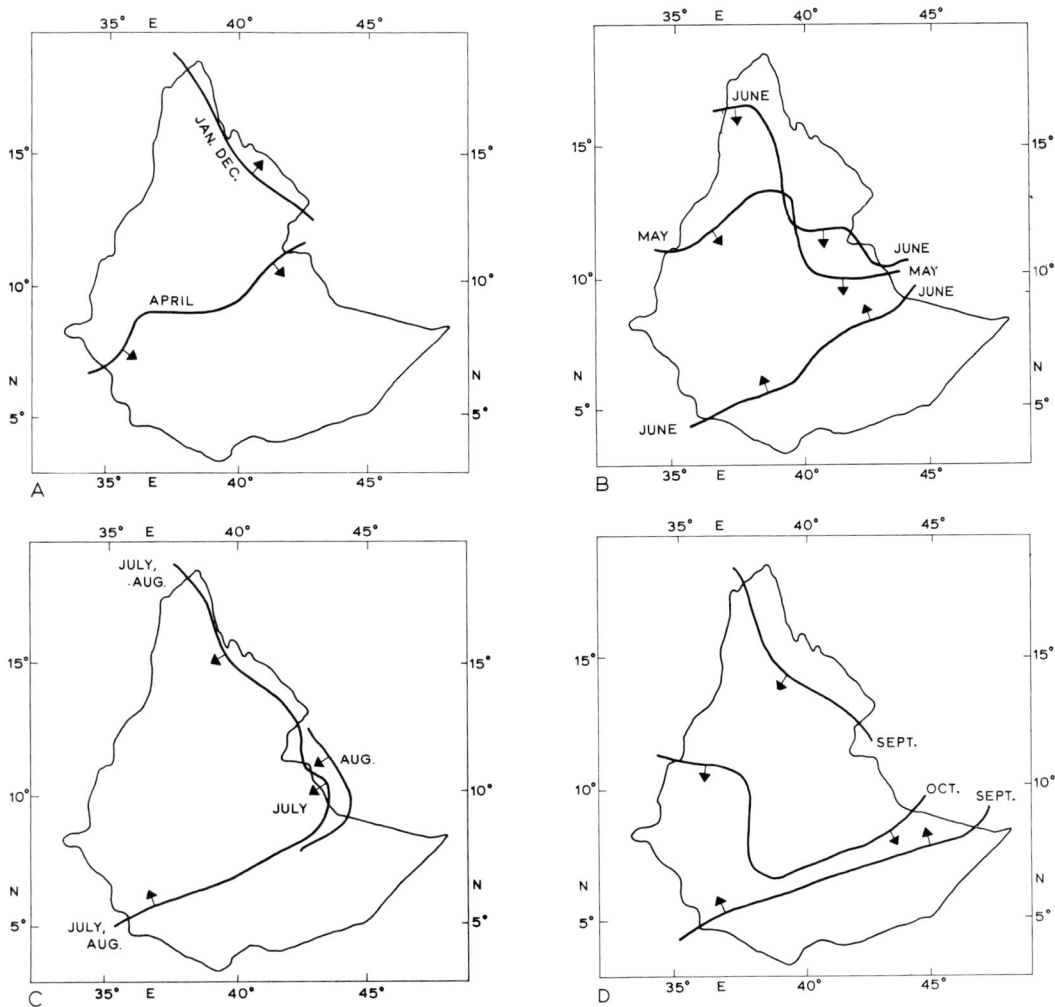

Fig.4. 50-mm isohyets. A. January, December and April; B. May and June; C. July and August; D. September and October.

wards from the Mediterranean and is dealt with in Chapter 4. During February and March the zone is dry, only rather isolated stations receiving more than 50 mm in these months, generally due to the impetus of local effects on the macroscale weather systems then prevailing. In April a wet region, associated with the motion of the I.T.C.Z. and the high ground, covers the southern half of the country. In May as the I.T.C.Z. movement continues this wet area enlarges by extension towards the Red Sea. In June the rain belt continues its northward shift and moves sufficiently far so as to leave a dry region in the southern portion. This pattern, with slight modifications persists through July, August and September. In October the rain belt takes a big leap southwards and leaves most of the north practically free from rain, except in the eastern Eritrean section where the winter rains begin to set in. In November the retreat continues and leads into the December pattern once again.

Monthly totals, like annual totals, can produce appreciable variation, as Table VI shows in the case of Addis Ababa. For instance, June can have totals as low as 47 or as high as 376 mm. The sudden transition to the wet season that usually occurs in July is well illustrated while September, normally at the end of the rainy season (mean fall 192 mm) can record times when the southward movement of the I.T.C.Z. is sufficiently delayed so as to bring heavy rains to the plateau. Monthly totals in excess of 400 mm are quite rare anywhere in this zone.

TABLE VI

GROUPING OF MONTHLY RAINFALL TOTALS, ADDIS ABABA (days), 1900–1940

	<100 mm	100–200 mm	200–300 mm	300–400 mm	400–500 mm	>500 mm
June	11	22	7	0	0	0
July	0	1	32	7	1	0
August	0	5	17	17	2	0
September	3	20	13	3	0	1

Daily rainfall is generally not excessive. Many stations have never recorded as much as 100 mm in a day and falls of even 50 mm in 24 h are unusual. Keren and Nacfa have only recorded two instances each in 27 and 18 years respectively. On the plateau rain can occur every day for long periods, for example, Addis Ababa reported rain every day from June 2 to September 14, 1948, and Lekempti from June 24 to October 11, 1952. Very persistent drizzle conditions (egnegne bilia—meaning "never stops") are experienced on the plateau during August and early September. At most stations 50% of the daily falls are less than 4 or 5 mm and about 10% (varying from 7 to 20%) are in excess of 20 mm (FANTOLI, 1965).

There are, unfortunately, very few records for periods of less than one day but Bahr Dar has recorded an astounding 204 mm in 2 h, an amount that is also the daily record for Ethiopia. Bahr Dar does experience greater intensity falls than other stations, 11% of the daily falls are in excess of 30 mm and 2.5% are over 50 mm (FANTOLI, 1965).

Thunderstorms

Thunderstorms are very frequent in the highlands of Ethiopia. On the plateau the average number of days with thunderstorms is approximately 90–100. In the eastern section, Dire Dawa, this number is reduced to about 25, mainly occurring in September as the I.T.C.Z. moves southwards. In Asmara about 115 thunderstorms occur each year, about half of these during the wet months of July and August (Table VII; ATTLEE, 1964). Many of these thunderstorms at Asmara are of long duration, the median value being about 4 h, on a yearly count, but 7 h during July. Thunderstorms of more than 6 h duration occurred in all months except December, January and February.

TABLE VII

THUNDERSTORM DATA, ASMARA, 1950–1959

	Jan.	Feb.	Mar.	Apr.	May	June	July	Aug.	Sept.	Oct.	Nov.	Dec.	Year
Average number	0	0	5	11	10	10	32	23	10	6	4	1	112
Percentage of total	0	0	5	10	9	9	29	21	8	5	3	1	—
Max. number	0	2	10	16	16	17	41	32	21	9	15	4	129
Min. number	0	0	1	8	0	6	21	14	3	1	0	0	94
Max. number of days	0	2	9	14	13	14	25	25	12	8	12	3	—

TABLE VIII

MEAN MONTHLY RELATIVE HUMIDITY (%)

Station	Time	Jan.	Feb.	Mar.	Apr.	May	June	July	Aug.	Sept.	Oct.	Nov.	Dec.	Ann.	Years rec.
Addis Ababa	07h00	61	64	58	65	63	76	86	86	79	56	59	62	68	12
	13h00	33	39	37	44	43	59	73	72	64	39	37	29	47	12
Agordat	09h30	75	72	69	47	32	36	57	70	58	35	54	62	56	1
	15h30	34	26	16	15	13	20	40	53	37	17	21	23	26	1
Asmara	05h30	71	72	68	72	69	70	92	94	84	78	78	80	77	5
	14h30	39	37	41	44	42	39	65	65	47	45	49	49	47	7
Axum	07h00	41	47	35	40	42	49	73	78	70	51	55	43	52	2
	13h00	25	34	32	36	34	46	69	76	66	39	49	23	44	2
Bahr Dar	08h30	54	46	47	44	70	74	86	88	86	77	72	64	67	4
	14h30	27	24	30	29	44	47	64	68	62	44	39	28	42	4
Dessie	07h00	57	59	54	45	46	37	54	61	59	51	51	49	50	3
	13h00	43	49	44	39	38	33	43	52	53	46	39	39	43	3
Dire Dawa	06h00	65	60	63	70	52	55	60	63	60	58	67	63	61	3
	15h00	33	40	34	45	25	30	30	36	33	35	33	30	34	3
Gambela	08h30	54	58	58	60	73	78	83	84	78	72	65	59	67	26
Harar	08h00	52	50	56	59	76	73	76	71	74	55	49	52	62	4
Jimma	07h00	53	61	63	66	74	78	77	79	78	67	53	52	67	2
	13h00	22	21	29	36	53	61	68	65	56	49	22	17	41	2
Macalle	07h00	45	51	51	43	39	51	72	81	60	44	45	49	53	2
	13h00	40	41	43	33	33	46	70	71	51	40	43	42	46	2

Humidity

Humidity measurements in Ethiopia are almost exclusively concerned with relative humidity. Unfortunately the measurements are generally of short period and are also made at different times during the day (Table VIII).

The early morning readings show an annual average of around 60–70% with the rainy months recording as high as 85–95%. The unusual patterns, such as illustrated by Dire Dawa and Agordat, make one very suspicious of the reliability of many of the data. The afternoon values show a very large increase during the wet period, reaching 65–80% compared with 20–40% in the dry spell.

Water vapour pressures are available for about 1 or 2 years during the Italian occupation. These values are given in Table IX for Addis Ababa. Most stations with two or more years of record show minima in December and January—single year records appear to be subject to inconsistent fluctuations. Maximum values generally occur in July or August, but Dessie (3 years of data) exhibits a September high that does not accord well with rainfall or humidity patterns.

TABLE IX

MEAN WATER VAPOUR PRESSURE (mm), ADDIS ABABA

Local time	Jan.	Feb.	Mar.	Apr.	May	June	July	Aug.	Sept.	Oct.	Nov.	Dec.	Year
08h00	6.1	7.2	7.2	7.0	7.6	8.6	9.1	9.3	9.1	6.9	4.8	4.9	7.3
11h00	5.9	6.5	6.6	6.4	7.4	8.7	9.4	9.7	9.4	6.5	4.3	4.4	7.1
14h00	5.1	6.1	5.9	5.9	6.4	8.0	9.2	9.7	9.0	6.3	4.1	4.0	6.6
19h00	5.5	6.0	6.4	5.9	6.3	8.2	9.4	9.8	9.0	6.4	4.4	4.3	6.8

Evaporation

Evaporation on the high land of Ethiopia nowhere reaches the large values recorded in the more arid regions (Chapters 3 and 4). Like so many climatological elements there are little data available for the zone, and those figures that have appeared refer either to a Piche evaporimeter or an unspecified instrument. The data available are given in Table X

TABLE X

MEAN MONTHLY EVAPORATION (mm)

	Jan.	Feb.	Mar.	Apr.	May	June	July	Aug.	Sept.	Oct.	Nov.	Dec.
Addis Ababa	5.5	5.9	7.8	4.7	7.6	4.1	2.2	2.0	3.3	6.1	5.8	6.6
Asmara	4.5	5.3	6.2	5.8	5.8	7.3	2.9	3.2	5.0	4.6	3.9	4.1
Bahr Dar	6.8	7.2	8.3	9.3	7.8	4.5	2.5	2.2	2.6	3.9	4.3	4.8
Combolcha	8.2	8.5	7.1	5.4	13.7	11.8	7.6	5.3	5.6	5.6	5.5	5.2
Debre Marcos	12.2	10.2	9.5	9.2	6.6	2.4	1.4	1.7	3.6	8.3	7.5	7.8
Faghena	1.3	1.7	1.9	3.2	7.1	13.5	10.1	8.9	10.9	5.4	2.6	1.3
Gallabat	13.7	16.1	18.7	18.8	14.4	8.8	4.5	3.1	4.2	6.4	10.2	12.1
Gambela	8.7	9.9	10.2	7.8	4.5	3.5	2.7	2.6	3.1	4.0	4.7	6.6
Keren	5.3	5.8	7.4	8.3	8.0	6.4	3.5	3.1	4.3	6.7	6.4	5.4

from which it seems that Gallabat, on the Sudanese border, has the extreme value, amounting to about 4,000 mm/year. Many of the plateau stations average around 1,800–2,000 mm. Evaporation is, naturally, less in the wet season while the extremely low values occurring in some months at Debre Marcos and Faghena (near Fil-fil, Eritrea) are associated, in part, with heavy cloud amounts.

Wind

The percentage of calm conditions during the year varies greatly with local conditions but, naturally, is greatest at the time of the early morning reading. Some areas have 60–85% calms at the 06h00 reading (Combolcha 83%), while others, like Tessenie have less than 20%. At most stations the 12h00 and 18h00 readings show less than 10% calms. Adua has less than 6% calms for a mean of the 08h00, 14h00 and 19h00 readings. Some stations have a greater percentage of calms during the winter period than during the summer (Awash 50% in December–March, 0% in June–August), while some have a complete reversal of this pattern (Macalle 50% in June–August, 6% in February).

Wind directions are generally dominantly east to southeasterly during the dry season but veer around to westerly or northwesterly in the rainy season (Table XI). Some stations are exceptions to this pattern. For example, Dire Dawa, with the local topography affecting the air flow, gives a northerly flow, bringing high temperatures and dust from the

TABLE XI

PREVAILING WIND DIRECTION AND PERCENTAGE CALMS (between brackets)

Station	Hour	Jan.	Mar.	May	July	Sept.	Nov.
Addis Ababa	06h00	E3(41)	E3(41)	NW1(57)	W3(34)	W2(43)	E2(51)
	12h00	SE4(8)	E3(5)	E4(10)	W3(15)	S4(11)	SE3(6)
	18h00	E7(1)	E6(3)	E7(6)	W2(16)	E/S2(20)	E8(1)
Asmara	06h00	E4(17)	E3(14)	E3(9)	NW6(8)	NW3(28)	E4(23)
	12h00	E3(5)	E3(1)	E3(1)	NW6(0)	NE6(13)	E3(3)
	18h00	E4(5)	E3(3)	E6(0)	NW5(1)	NE6(5)	E4(3)
Combolcha	06h00	W1(91)	W1(91)	W2(33)	W4(54)	W2(71)	W1(89)
	12h00	E6(23)	E6(25)	E6(21)	E4(26)	E5(39)	E4(28)
	18h00	E2(33)	E7(25)	E6(21)	E5(33)	E3(62)	E3(68)
Debre Marcos	06h00	E4(47)	E3(51)	E2(68)	E1(82)	E2(69)	E5(32)
	12h00	S3(25)	E2(31)	E2(34)	S2(46)	S3(27)	S4(14)
	18h00	W1(66)	S1(57)	W2(65)	W2(59)	W1(71)	S1(68)
Dire Dawa	06h00	S4(26)	S6(20)	S7(10)	S8(6)	S8(10)	S6(29)
	12h00	N5(7)	N4(10)	S2(24)	S6(9)	S4(15)	N5(12)
	18h00	N6(7)	N4(3)	S3(6)	S4(15)	S4(15)	N5(12)
Gore	06h00	SE2(22)	SE2(27)	E2(27)	NW1(48)	SW2(38)	SE3(26)
	12h00	E2(17)	E2(20)	E2(13)	W2(29)	NW1(30)	NE2(26)
	18h00	NW2(26)	W3(19)	NW3(30)	W2(23)	NW2(20)	W1(41)
Tessenie	06h00	E8(20)	E8(32)	E5(15)	S4(13)	E3(24)	E6(14)
	12h00	E5(10)	E3(0)	W3(1)	SW4(0)	W3(5)	E3(4)
	18h00	SW5(1)	NW3(5)	N3(7)	S3(4)	W3(15)	E3(4)

¹ The value after the direction is its frequency (in 10% units).

Danakil Desert, from October to April (save at 06h00 when a drainage wind from the south prevails) and then a southerly from May to September.

Wind speed is not reported from many stations. It averages about 4–6 knots with, generally, a slight increase during the transition period between the dry and wet spells.

Climate classification

In Fig.5 a representation of Ethiopian climate classified according to the Köppen system is given. This map was prepared from one supplied by the Ethiopian Climatological Service. The country clearly falls into three basic divisions—the arid and semi-arid (*BW* and *BS* climates), the hot, humid regions (*Aw*) and the tropical highlands (*Cw*, *Cf*).

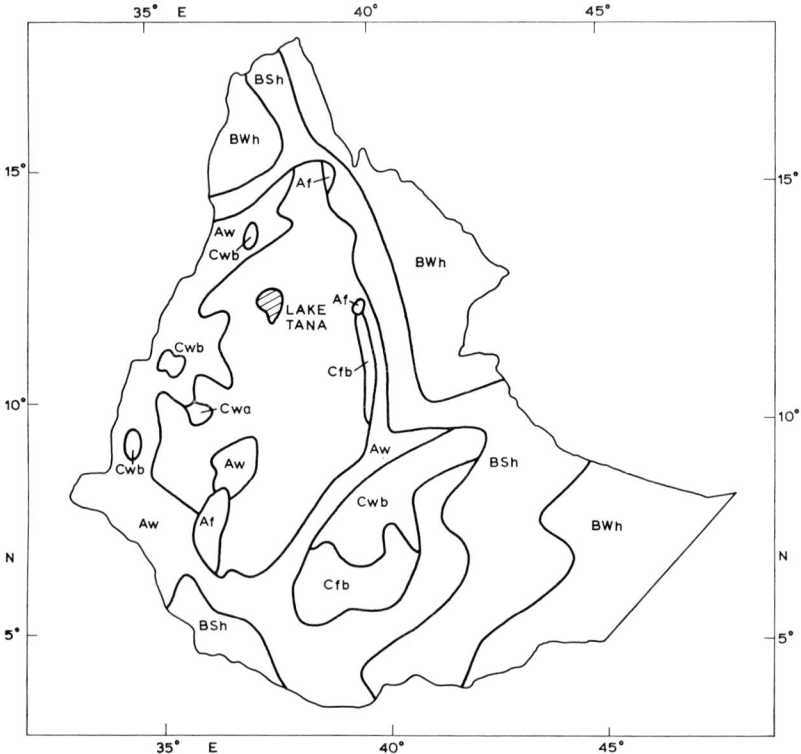

Fig.5. Ethiopian climatic regions using Köppen's classification.

This division accords reasonably well with that suggested by LISSICINE (1950) based on his knowledge of the country some 20 years ago (Fig.6). In his system the *Aw* region comprised the Sudan slopes (which he extended too far northwards), the south slopes and the eastern tableland. The *BW* and *BS* areas are the Ogaden, monsoon, low Somali tableland, coastal Danakil and Danakil and Awash. The *Cw* region is identifiable with the northern and Harar tablelands. The Galla tableland represents the *Aw* and *Af* tongue extending into the northern tableland.

Much reliable information still needs to be collected, collated and analysed for this zone. Publications are, generally, irregular in their appearance and, sometimes, dubious in

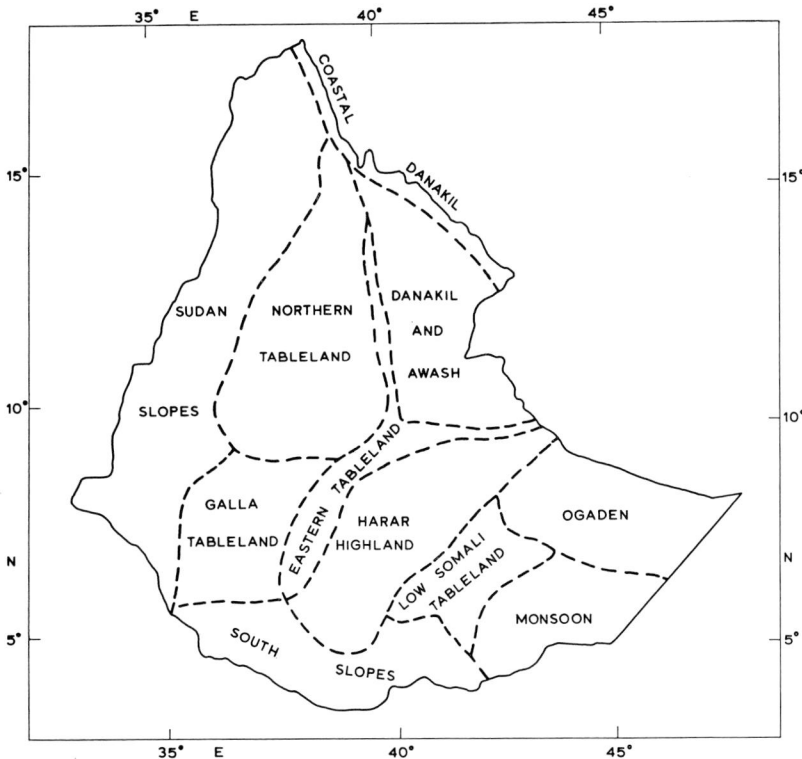

Fig.6. LISSICINE's (1950) classification.

their accuracy. It is to be hoped that a detailed study will be made during the next decade, for this is a fascinating and important area from many viewpoints, not the least of which is meteorology.

References

ATTLEE, G., 1964. *Weather at Asmara*. Civil Aviation Administration, Addis Ababa, 30 pp.

ATTLEE, G., 1965. *The Weather and Climate at Addis Ababa, Dire Dawa and Jimma*. Civil Aviation Administration, Addis Ababa, 36 pp.

FANTOLI, A., 1965. *Contributo all Climatologia dell'Etiopia*. Ministeri degli Afferi Esteri, Rome, 558 pp.

GRIFFITHS, J. F. and HEMMING, C. F., 1963. A rainfall map of eastern Africa and southern Arabia. *E. African Meteorol. Dept., Mem., Nairobi*, 3 (10): 42 pp.

LANDSBERG, H. E., LIPPMANN, H., PAFFEN, K. H. and TROLL, C., 1963. *World Maps of Climatology*. Springer, Berlin, 28 pp., 5 maps.

LISSICINE, V., 1950. *The Climate of Ethiopia and the Weather of Addis Ababa*. Civil Aviation Dept., Ethiopian Meteorological Service, Addis Ababa, 8 pp.

TABLE XII

CLIMATIC TABLE FOR NEGHELLI
Latitude 05°07'N, longitude 39°26'E, elevation 1,500 m

Month	Temperature (°C)				Relat. humid. (%)		Precipitation					Wind		Aver. cloudiness (oktas)
	mean		extreme		07h	13h	mean (mm)	max. (mm)	min. (mm)	days ≥2.5 mm	max. in 24 h (mm)	preval. direct.	calm[1] (%)	
	max.	min.	max.	min.										
Jan.	28	12	31	5	59	39	8	69	0	1	49	NE	0	2
Feb.	28	13	34	8	57	38	4	41	0	<1	41	N	8	2
Mar.	28	13	32	7	60	44	33	155	0	2	46	NE	0	4
Apr.	25	14	31	6	72	62	172	241	100	8	54	NE	0	5
May	24	12	30	6	79	66	102	204	35	7	53	NE	1	5
June	24	13	28	8	81	62	8	46	0	1	13	S	0	4
July	24	12	28	4	83	61	6	33	0	<1	9	S	0	5
Aug.	24	12	29	3	78	54	7	15	0	<1	15	S	0	5
Sept.	26	12	30	8	71	45	16	53	0	1	44	S	0	4
Oct.	25	13	29	8	77	61	119	237	32	10	57	E	0	4
Nov.	25	12	29	6	65	50	52	174	0	3	42	E	0	2
Dec.	26	11	30	7	56	40	23	89	0	2	21	NW	0	1
Annual	28	13	34	3	70	52	550	740	291	36	57	—	1	4
Rec. (yrs.)	9	10	9	10	3	3	11	11	11	11	7	4	4	4

[1] Mean of 08h00, 14h00 and 19h00.

TABLE XIII

CLIMATIC TABLE FOR JIMMA
Latitude 07°39'N, longitude 36°51'E, elevation 1,750 m

Month	Mean sta. press. (mbar)	Temperature (°C) mean max.	mean min.	extreme max.	extreme min.	Dew point[1] (°C)	Precipitation mean (mm)	max. (mm)	min. (mm)	days >1 mm	max. in 24 h (mm)	Wind av. speed (knots)	preval. direct.	calm (%) 06h	12h	Averages cloud-iness[2] (oktas)	sun-shine (h/day)	thunder-storms
Feb.	828	27	13	32	1	5.3	48	140	3	5	56	4	E	97	53	3	6.4	1
Mar.	826	27	13	31	6	5.6	82	203	3	7	51	5	SE	92	42	4	6.7	5
Apr.	828	26	14	30	8	7.0	180	264	63	9	52	4	E	87	56	5	6.3	7
May	830	25	14	30	8	9.4	150	225	88	10	76	3	E	87	47	4	6.4	8
June	830	24	14	28	11	9.4	220	306	171	12	52	4	SE	88	49	5	5.1	11
July	830	22	14	26	11	9.5	231	399	135	11	73	3	SSE	95	54	7	3.4	10
Aug.	830	22	14	30	10	9.4	214	263	138	14	75	4	SE	87	63	6	4.0	10
Sept.	830	23	14	27	9	9.4	192	287	58	12	75	3	E	83	54	5	5.7	8
Oct.	830	25	12	27	5	7.7	87	213	27	6	99	2	E	95	50	3	6.6	8
Nov.	828	26	10	32	2	5.1	39	123	1	4	35	3	SSE	97	64	2	6.2	3
Dec.	830	26	10	30	2	1.5	37	109	3	3	37	2	E	96	76	2	7.3	2
Annual	829	25	13	32	1	7.2	1,529	1,927	1,338	96	99	3	—	92	56	4	6.0	74
Rec. (yrs.)	2	6	6	6	6	4	15	15	15	15	15	10	10	10	10	5	3	7

[1] Mean of 08h00, 11h00, 14h00 and 19h00.
[2] Mean of 08h00 and 14h00.

TABLE XIV

CLIMATIC TABLE FOR ADDIS ABABA
Latitude 09°02'N, longitude 38°45'E, elevation 2,450 m

Month	Mean sta. press. (mbar)	Temperature (°C)				Relat. humid. (%)		Precipitation					Wind				Averages			
		mean		extreme		07h	13h	mean (mm)	max. (mm)	min. (mm)	days ≥1 mm	max. in 24 h (mm)	av. speed (knots)	preval. direct.	calm (%) 06h	12h	cloud-iness (oktas)	sun-shine (h/day)	evap. (mm/day)	thunder-storms
		max.	min.	max.	min.															
Jan.	766	23	6	28	-2	61	33	16	104	0	4	36	6	SSE	56	12	3	8.7	5.5	1
Feb.	764	24	7	30	0	64	39	44	174	0	4	73	5	E	51	10	4	8.5	5.9	1
Mar.	764	25	9	29	1	58	37	70	250	0	5	81	6	E	40	11	5	8.0	7.8	8
Apr.	765	25	10	31	3	65	44	86	316	0	7	61	7	E	41	10	5	7.1	4.7	7
May	765	25	9	33	2	63	43	95	302	3	7	78	6	E	64	16	5	7.0	7.6	7
June	765	23	10	34	6	76	59	136	376	47	11	53	5	S	52	23	6	5.2	4.1	15
July	765	20	11	31	7	86	73	282	475	123	14	72	4	S	53	39	7	2.2	2.2	17
Aug.	765	20	11	29	7	86	72	294	476	167	16	76	4	S	51	13	7	2.7	2.0	20
Sept.	766	21	10	27	6	76	64	192	570	51	13	74	5	S	57	21	6	4.6	3.3	15
Oct.	766	22	7	28	2	56	39	21	143	0	3	73	7	E	33	6	4	8.6	6.1	5
Nov.	766	22	4	27	0	59	37	15	96	0	1	26	8	SE	29	7	2	8.9	5.8	0
Dec.	766	22	5	27	0	62	29	6	69	0	2	51	7	E	40	8	2	8.6	6.6	0
Annual	765	23	8	34	-2	68	47	1,256	1,937	933	87	81	6	—	47	15	5	6.4	5.1	96
Rec. (yrs.)	2	14	14	14	14	12	12	42	62	62	14	30	10	10	10	10	4	10	4	10

TABLE XV

CLIMATIC TABLE FOR DIRE DAWA
Latitude 09°02'N, longitude 41°45'E, elevation 1,200 m

Month	Mean sta. press. (mbar)	Temperature (°C) mean		extreme		Relat. humid. (%)		Precipitation mean (mm)	max. (mm)	min. (mm)	days ≥ 1 mm	max. in 24 h (mm)	Wind av. speed (knots)	preval. direct.	calm (%)		Averages cloud-iness (oktas)	sun-shine (h/day)	thunder-storms
		max.	min.	max.	min.	06h	15h								06h	12h			
Jan.	886	29	15	35	5	65	33	20	85	0	1	51	4	N	43	10	15	7	0
Feb.	886	30	16	37	6	60	40	29	271	0	1	69	5	N	31	10	15	5	1
Mar.	884	32	18	37	9	63	34	43	171	0	4	63	5	N	23	14	13	7	4
Apr.	885	31	19	39	9	70	45	83	187	0	6	54	7	S	43	34	6	13	2
May	884	34	20	39	9	52	25	30	129	0	1	26	8	S	44	33	10	8	2
June	884	35	20	38	10	55	30	23	97	0	3	30	10	S	24	29	8	5	1
July	883	33	18	38	6	60	30	108	229	26	5	65	9	S	11	16	4	11	3
Aug.	884	31	17	37	5	63	36	165	242	83	8	50	8	S	5	17	4	8	4
Sept.	884	32	17	37	9	60	33	70	135	28	7	67	8	S	7	13	5	4	6
Oct.	887	33	17	36	8	58	35	12	42	0	2	25	6	N	46	30	16	4	1
Nov.	886	31	16	36	8	67	33	17	111	0	1	45	5	N	41	15	17	2	0
Dec.	887	29	14	34	6	63	30	10	68	0	1	52	4	N	60	30	18	3	0
Annual	885	32	17	39	5	61	34	582	769	367	40	69	7	—	32	21	11	6	2
Rec. (yrs.)	2	13	13	13	13	3	3	15	15	15	6	6	10	10	10	10	10	10	10

385

TABLE XVI

CLIMATIC TABLE FOR HARAR

Latitude 09°39'N, longitude 36°51'E, elevation 1,750 m

Month	Temperature (°C)				Dew point[1] (°C)	Precipitation					Wind			Averages	
	mean		extreme			mean (mm)	max. (mm)	min. (mm)	days ≥1 mm	max. in 24 h (mm)	av. speed (knots)	preval. direct.	calm (%)	cloud-iness (oktas)	sun-shine (h)
	max.	min.	max.	min.											
Jan.	25	13	28	7	0.2	11	78	0	2	77	5	SE–NW	11	3	254
Feb.	26	14	29	11	2.1	32	117	0	4	61	4	SE	9	3	231
Mar.	27	14	32	11	4.1	60	191	0	7	54	4	SE	11	4	202
Apr.	27	15	30	13	5.6	109	258	3	12	91	5	SE	10	5	236
May	27	15	31	13	7.6	121	332	18	12	93	3	SE	20	5	222
June	26	14	31	12	8.1	101	223	30	12	63	4	SE	8	6	198
July	24	14	29	11	9.0	142	314	54	14	69	4	SE	8	7	135
Aug.	23	14	28	11	7.8	137	268	35	15	51	4	SE	7	7	131
Sept.	24	14	29	12	6.4	98	186	40	14	48	4	SE	10	5	192
Oct.	26	14	29	10	2.7	46	127	0	5	71	3	SE	21	4	221
Nov.	26	13	28	8	−1.9	23	198	0	2	37	4	NW	10	2	285
Dec.	26	13	29	7	−3.8	10	94	0	1	25	6	NW	11	1	317
Annual	26	14	32	7	4.1	889	1,557	520	100	93	4	—	11	4	2,619
Rec. (yrs.)	10	10	10	10	4	22	22	22	22	15	8	8	8	4	2

[1] Mean of 08h00, 11h00, 14h00 and 19h00.

TABLE XVII

CLIMATIC TABLE FOR ADI UGRI
Latitude 14°54′N, longitude 38°49′E, elevation 2,022 m

Month	Temperature (°C)				Precipitation				Wind				Averages		
	mean		extreme		mean (mm)	max. (mm)	min. (mm)	max. in 24 h (mm)	preval. direct.		calm (%)		cloud-iness (oktas)		thunder-storms
	max.	min.	max.	min.					09h	15h	09h	15h	09h	15h	
Jan.	29	7	35	0	0	2	0	2	E	W	22	2	1	2	0
Feb.	30	8	36	0	1	13	0	13	E	W	15	1	1	3	0
Mar.	31	10	37	1	15	68	0	43	E	W	13	0	1	2	0
Apr.	31	11	39	3	31	68	0	40	E	W	8	6	2	4	1
May	31	11	39	4	34	90	8	40	E	W	21	4	2	5	1
June	29	11	39	2	64	151	3	51	W	W	31	2	3	6	2
July	24	10	32	2	193	384	21	85	W	W	41	3	5	7	3
Aug.	24	10	34	3	161	259	26	55	W	W	33	5	6	7	3
Sept.	30	10	34	1	49	126	14	45	W	W	36	4	4	5	2
Oct.	29	8	34	1	7	29	0	29	E	W/E	12	2	1	3	0
Nov.	28	7	33	0	10	102	0	34	E	E	29	1	1	2	0
Dec.	28	7	32	1	1	16	0	16	E	W	15	3	1	2	0
Annual	29	9	39	0	565	770	366	85	—		23	3	2	4	12
Rec. (yrs.)	17	17	17	17	27	27	27	27	6	6	6	6	5	6	5

387

TABLE XVIII

CLIMATIC TABLE FOR ASMARA
Latitude 15°17'N, longitude 38°55'E, elevation 2,300 m

| Month | Mean press. (mbar) | Temperature (°C) | | | | Relat. humid. (%) | | Precipitation | | | | | Wind | | | Aver. cloudiness (oktas) | |
| | | mean | | extreme | | | | | | | | | | calm (%) | | | |
		max.	min.	max.	min.	05h30	14h30	mean (mm)	max. (mm)	min. (mm)	days ≥1 mm	max. in 24 h (mm)	preval. direct.	06h	12h	09h	15h
Jan.	772	23	7	31	0	71	39	1	22	0	0	12	E	17	5	1	2
Feb.	771	24	9	31	0	72	37	1	31	0	<1	17	E	22	1	2	3
Mar.	770	25	10	31	1	68	41	10	36	0	3	25	E	14	1	2	4
Apr.	771	25	11	31	4	72	44	37	107	0	5	57	E	10	1	2	4
May	771	26	12	31	5	69	42	38	208	0	5	92	E	9	1	3	4
June	772	26	12	29	6	70	39	32	116	0	5	60	NE	19	0	4	5
July	771	22	12	29	6	92	65	170	421	27	17	70	NW	8	0	6	7
Aug.	772	22	12	27	6	94	65	127	363	61	14	107	NW	10	2	5	6
Sept.	772	24	10	27	5	84	47	33	119	1	5	64	NE	28	13	3	5
Oct.	772	22	9	30	3	78	45	7	23	0	2	22	E	24	3	2	3
Nov.	772	22	9	26	2	78	49	10	76	0	2	32	E	23	3	1	3
Dec.	772	22	8	26	3	79	49	2	20	0	1	13	E	23	3	2	3
Annual	771	23	10	31	0	77	47	468	910	314	60	107	—	17	3	3	4
Rec. (yrs.)	2	25	25	25	25	5	7	29	34	34	17	27	5	5	5	8	8

Chapter 12

Mozambique

J. F. GRIFFITHS

Introduction

The Portuguese province of Mozambique occupies an area of about 780,000 km² on the east coast of Africa. It extends from 10°25′ to 26°52′S (2,000 km) and the greatest longitudinal extent is from 30°20′ to 40°45′E (1,100 km). Much of the land south of Quelimane (18°S) is below the 200-m contour but in the north there is a large plateau of 500 m elevation with some small areas above 1,500 m. There is much swampy land in the south and the Zambezi is by far the largest river (Fig.1).

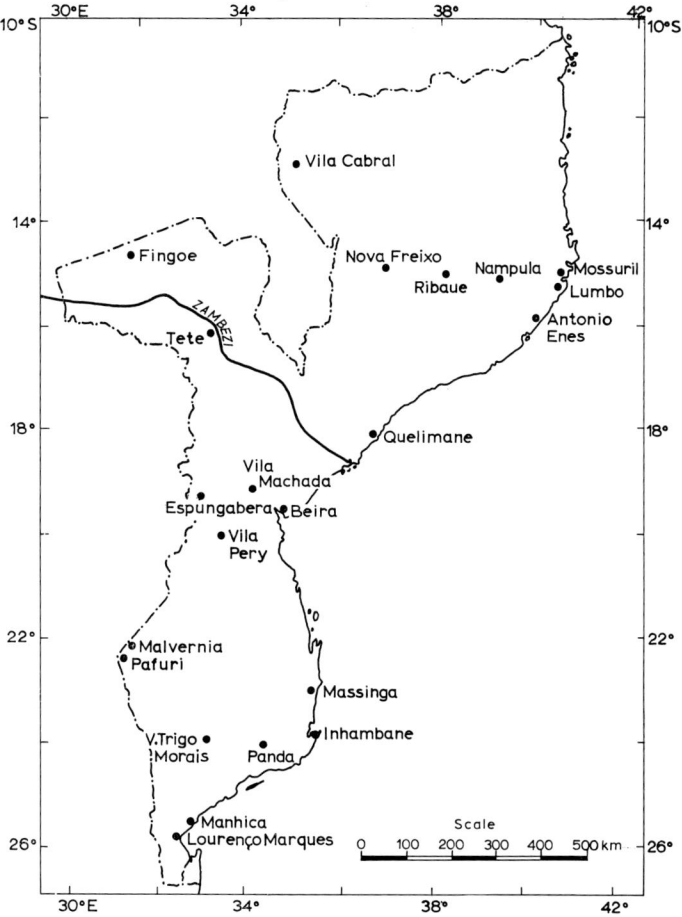

Fig.1. Station locations.

389

The population numbers nearly 7 million inhabitants with Lourenço Marques, the capital, being the largest city with nearly a quarter of a million people. Other large centres are Beira (60,000), Inhambane and Quelimane. The chief export of the country is cotton, followed by sugar, cashew nuts, copra and tea.

Causes of the climate

Summer

At the time of the summer (November–March) three pressure cells are the major determinants of the Mozambique climate. The two anticyclones are the Asian high (south of Lake Baikal) and the Indian Ocean high (centred about 35°S, halfway between Africa and Australia). The low pressure centre is a thermal phenomenon over the interior plateau of southern Africa. The air that leaves the Asian high is initially cold and dry but its trajectory over the northwest Indian Ocean soon gives it the warm, maritime characteristics of the Indian Ocean source air mass.

North of 20°S Mozambique is affected mainly by air from the Asian anticyclone (the northeast monsoon) but south of this latitude the air from the Indian Ocean high predominates (the southeast monsoon). The low pressure over the interior is less permanent at this time of the year and fluctuates greatly in position and intensity.

Winter

During the winter the I.T.C.Z. moves northwards, as does the Indian Ocean anticyclone (now at 30°S). The latter now extends westwards to link with the high pressure over the plateau area of southern Africa. Winds are thus predominantly south–north and air masses tend to parallel the coast.

Ocean currents

Mozambique experiences warm currents paralleling the coast throughout the year. This flow is known as the Mozambique Current but south of Lourenço Marques is called the Agulhas Current. In both seasons the flow is from northeast to southwest but in summer its speed is increased by the prevailing northeast winds to about 45 km/day, while in winter the prevailing southwesterlies help reduce the speed to about 11 km/day. Summertime temperature of the current is about 25°C and wintertime about 19°C. The current's effect is, therefore, much greater in summer than in winter.

Radiation, sunshine and cloud

A recent publication (DE ROCHA FARIA and DE MATA, 1965) has presented a map of the annual pattern of global radiation. This map is given here as Fig.2: it is calculated from sunshine data with extrapolations dependent upon the climatic regions of the country. Values increase towards Malawi and Zambia in the northwest as well as towards the

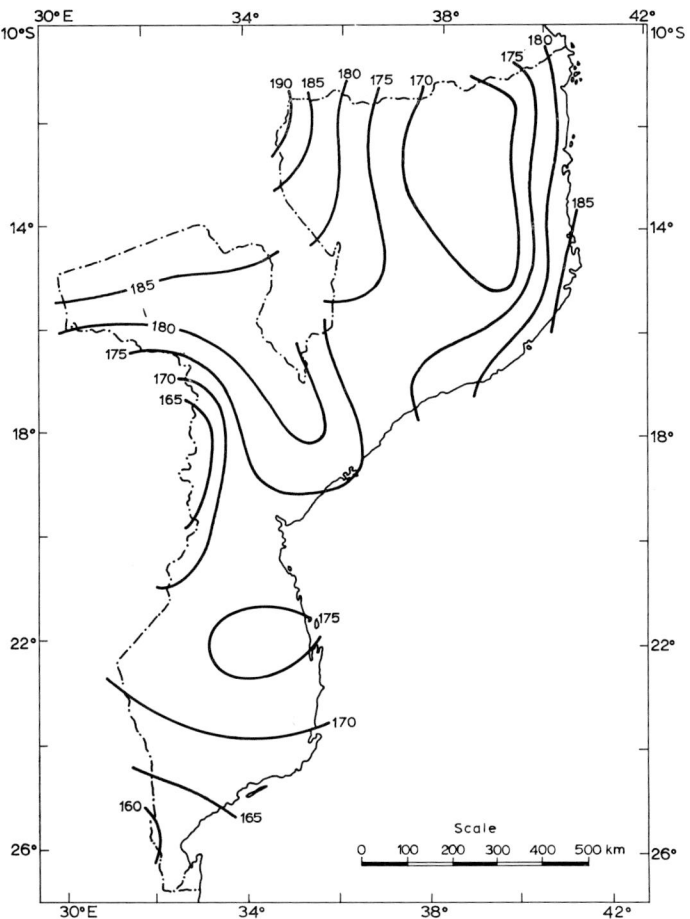

Fig.2. Mean annual global radiation (kcal./cm²).

northern coast. The complete range is only some 10%, or 175 kcal./cm² ±15 kcal./cm². The average value is thus about 480 cal./cm² day. Radiation measurements made during the past few years have shown these calculated values to be a little on the generous side. As can be noted from Table I the geographical variation is nevertheless similar to that

TABLE I

MEAN GLOBAL RADIATION (cal./cm² day)

	Jan.	Feb.	Mar.	Apr.	May	June	July	Aug.	Sept.	Oct.	Nov.	Dec.	Year
Beira	564	526	538	457	402	349	371	431	492	560	575	567	486
Inhambane	529	495	452	409	343	311	321	370	446	497	515	490	432
Lourenço Marques	569	539	513	400	356	322	337	391	463	479	505	538	451
Lumbo	501	487	494	466	442	401	415	471	545	604	604	583	501
Malvernia	537	484	496	400	356	312	305	357	474	559	526	504	442
Nampula	477	477	466	430	392	356	295	401	460	524	528	512	443
Tete	508	491	507	457	424	359	363	444	488	523	546	570	473
Vila Cabral	402	415	416	410	413	390	386	437	476	515	471	500	435
Vila Pery	508	524	484	441	385	350	364	415	476	516	509	502	456
Vila Trigo Morais	531	498	459	384	347	322	319	353	436	475	474	484	424

given in Fig.2. Radiation amounts are generally greatest during the summer months, in spite of the heavy cloud occurring then. All stations have some months in excess of 500 cal./cm² day with winter months having from 300 to 350 cal./cm² day. As would be expected the station nearest the equator shows the least variation from month to month, Vila Cabral—129 cal./cm² day.

Sunshine is not recorded at many stations so it is difficult to present a complete picture. Most stations have annual mean values of around 2,800–2,900 h. The mean monthly values differ little in the south for at the time of longer daylight there is an increase in the cloud amount. However, in the north Tete shows a variation from 193 h (February) to 287 h (October) while Mossuril goes from 169 h (February) to 307 h (October). The range at Beira is from 223 h (June) to 258 h (October).

Cloud amounts generally show a very pronounced seasonal variation. During the summer rainy season averages of 5–7 oktas are usual over the country with a tendency for greater cloud coverage towards the north. In the winter period some southern regions record less than 2 oktas. A few stations show little seasonal variation, for instance Antonio Enes and Massinga vary from 4 to 6 oktas. Manhica (2 oktas), Antonio Enes (5 oktas) and Massinga (5 oktas) are the extreme mean annual values.

Temperature

The mean annual temperature for the territory is about 24°C, with extremes of 20°–26°C. The maximum means occur along the northern coastal belt and in the vicinities of Tete and Pafuri while minimum values are found in the hills near southern Lake Nyasa and in the far south. The dramatic effect of the warm Mozambique Current is obvious when the mean temperature of 25.5°C at Lourenço Marques (26°S) is compared with that of 26°C at Dar-es-Salaam (6°S), some 2,000 km nearer the equator.

The hottest month varies from October to February, generally being later nearer to the coast. Around Quelimane the hottest month changes rapidly, from December in the north to February in the south. Mean temperatures are then approximately 26°–30°C. The mean maximum temperatures of the hottest month are given in Fig.3, where it is seen that the range is about 8°C (28°–36°C). The average maximum is generally 32°–34°C but absolute maxima in excess of 40°C have occurred in the inland area south of 15°S.

The coldest month over the whole country is July, with temperatures averaging about 16°–20°C, but rising to 24°C along the northeast coast. The mean minimum temperature of the coldest month is given in Fig.4. As would be expected the isotherms tend to parallel the coast with an additional effect due to altitude.

The annual range of temperature is shown in Fig.5. Values tend to increase with distance from the sea or large inland lakes and with increasing latitude. The modifying effect of the winds off the Indian Ocean and the Mozambique Current are quite evident, for the lowest values are reached where there is an abrupt change in the direction of the coast line direction at a sheltered spot.

Diurnal variation also increases with distance from a large body of water, averaging about 9°–10°C at the coast and reaching 15°C inland. At Pafuri, in the dry season, the daily range averages nearly 20°C while, at the other extreme, Beira in the rainy season (summer) fluctuates only 5°C.

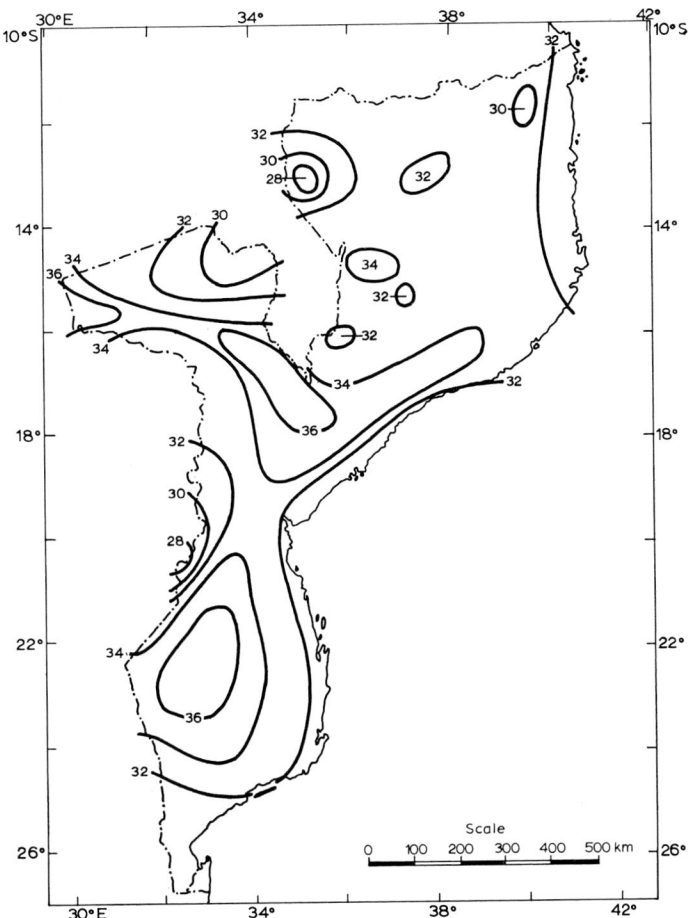

Fig.3. Mean daily maximum temperature (°C) of hottest month.

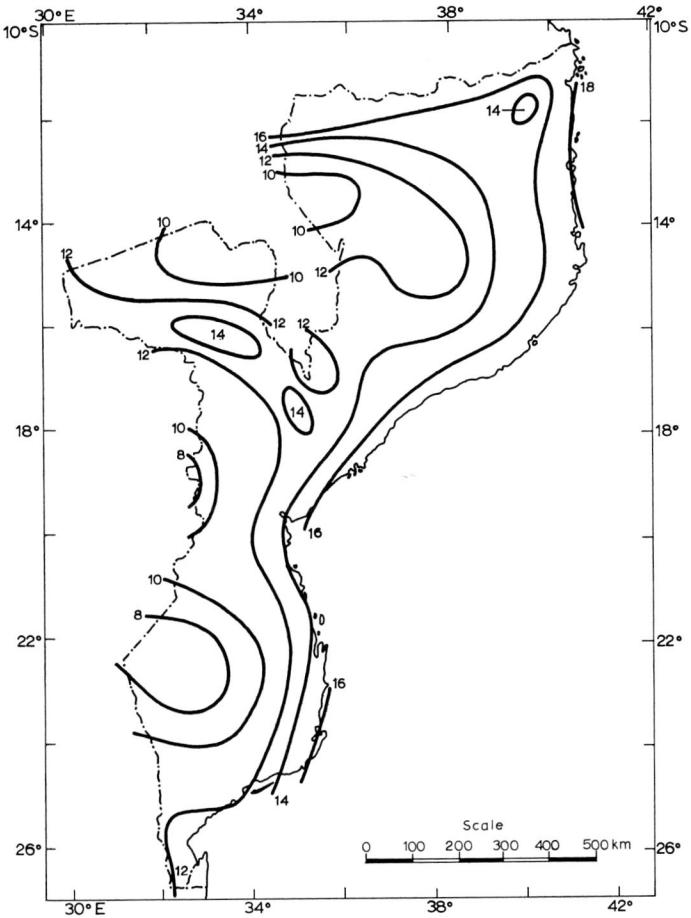

Fig.4. Mean daily minimum temperature (°C) of coldest month.

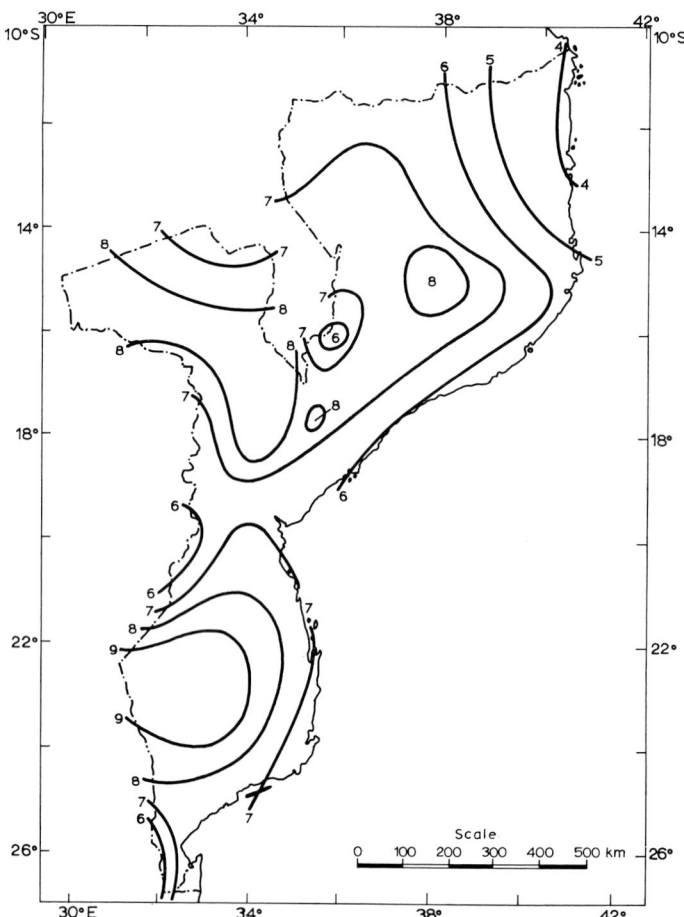

Fig.5. Mean annual temperature range (°C).

Rainfall

The prevailing winds in this zone have a pronounced easterly component so that the influence of the nearby island of Madagascar is quite definite. The warm, moist air from the Indian Ocean is, if the trajectory is right, made quite dry after its ascent over the highlands of Malagasy and has little time to acquire further moisture before meeting the coast line of Mozambique (PROTHERO, 1964). However, many moist air masses do affect the country, as explained earlier.

Mean annual rainfall varies between about 400 mm to in excess of 2,000 mm (Fig.6). The map shows a distinct belt of minimum rainfall running southwest to northeast through Tete and Nova Freixo. To the north and south of this rain shadow strip there is a definite increase in amount. South of Quelimane rainfall amounts decrease inland while to the north they increase as the spill-over of summer rain from the plateau is felt.

The rainy season really begins in November over most of the zone but is delayed until December in the northeast and the relatively dry Pafuri region. It is in January that the effect of the moisture laden northeast winds from the Asian high is most pronounced. However, convective showers also occur and, in consequence, the north–south rainfall gradient is less than might be expected. As the summer monsoon abates the southeast

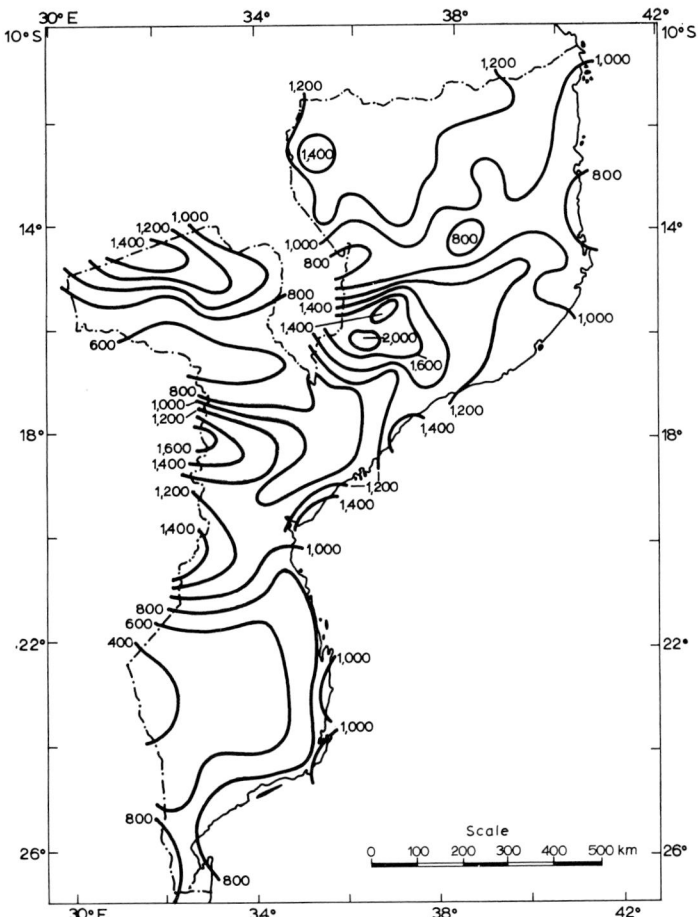

Fig.6. Mean annual rainfall (mm).

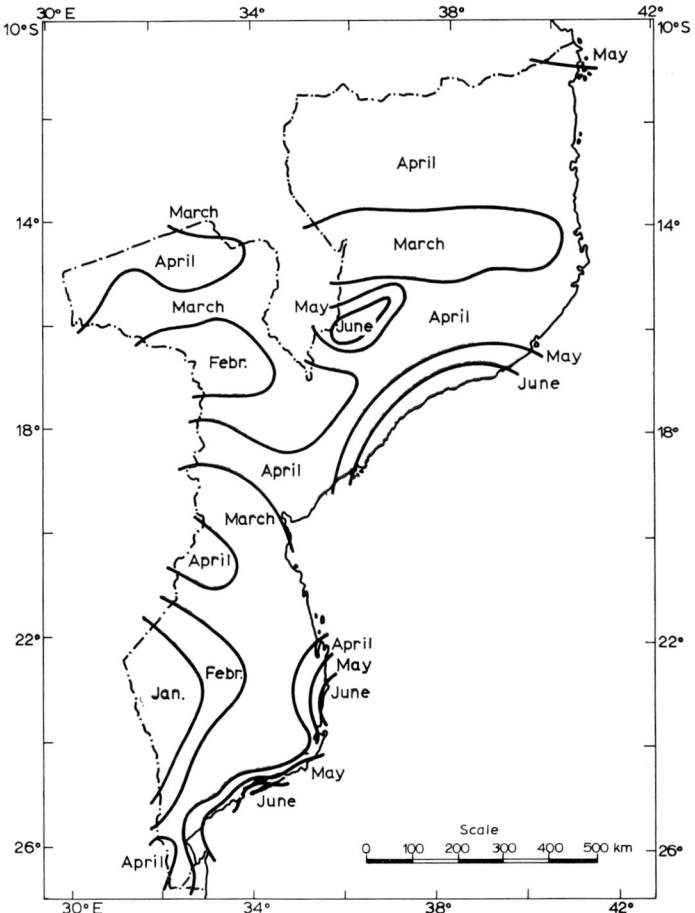

Fig.7. End of rainy season.

flow predominates and the end of the rainy season follows a fairly regular pattern (Fig. 7) illustrating both the influence of topography and the effect of the moist on-shore winds. The end of the rainy season shows a very rapid change south of Nova Freixo (4 month change in 100 km) and northeast of Lourenço Marques (4 months in 50 km). Fig.8 gives the length of the rainy season, a wide range from 2 to 8 months in duration.

January is generally the wettest month, except in the northeast section, north of 16°S. Here maxima are noted in March and April, perhaps owing to a slowing down in the retreat of the monsoon at that time. The whole country shows the single maximum pattern of seasonal rainfall, with December–February or January–March being by far the wettest quarter with 50–70% of the annual total.

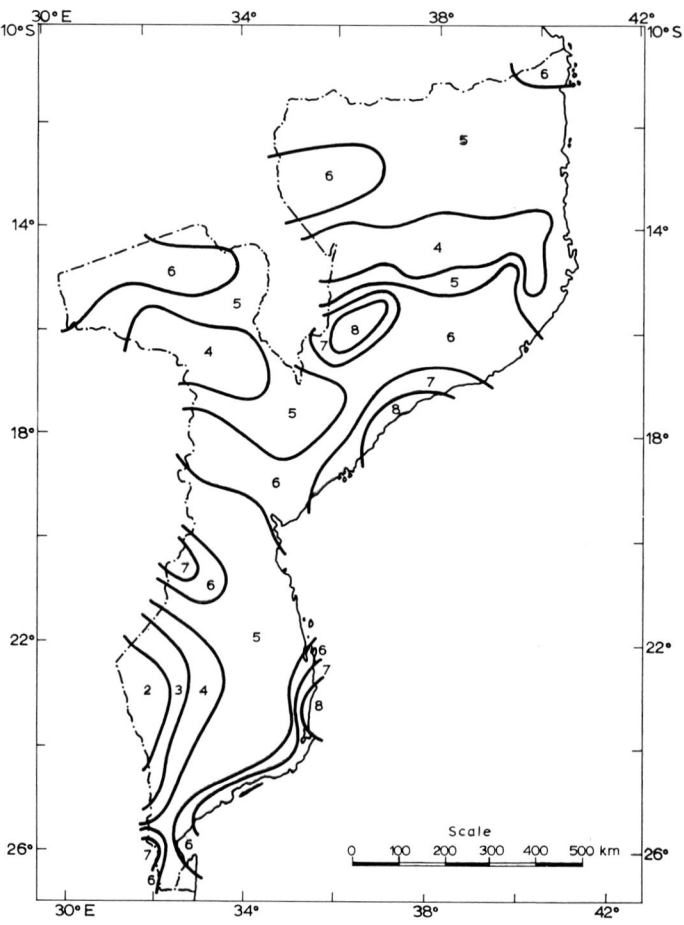

Fig.8. Length of rainy season (in months).

Daily falls in excess of 200 mm are rare, save along the coast, but most stations have reported over 100 mm in one day, even Pafuri with an annual mean of 380 mm. In late summer (January–April) severe storms often occur along the north and central coast. Many stations have had more than 100 mm in a day during each month from November to March. The heaviest fall is 775 mm in December at Vila Machada, with other large amounts being 415 mm at Espungabera (January) and 387 mm at Ribaue (March).

As is clear from the climatic tables rainfall variability is very large. Even annual amounts may fluctuate in a five to one ratio, for example, Quelimane from 530 to 2,501 mm and Lourenço Marques from 277 to 1,425 mm. Monthly totals show even greater variation. Almost every month at any station has recorded a value below 20 mm while falls of over 700 or 800 mm have occurred, especially in the Beira and Quelimane area.

Relative humidity and evaporation

The mean annual relative humidity averages about 70% over the zone (Fig.9) with extremes of about 75 and 60%, along the coast and near Pafuri, respectively. Naturally, the more humid areas are near the coast and there is little monthly variation there. In the afternoon during the dry season monthly means average about 30% in the Tete and Pafuri regions. The inland stations show a seasonal pattern strongly related to their rainy seasons.

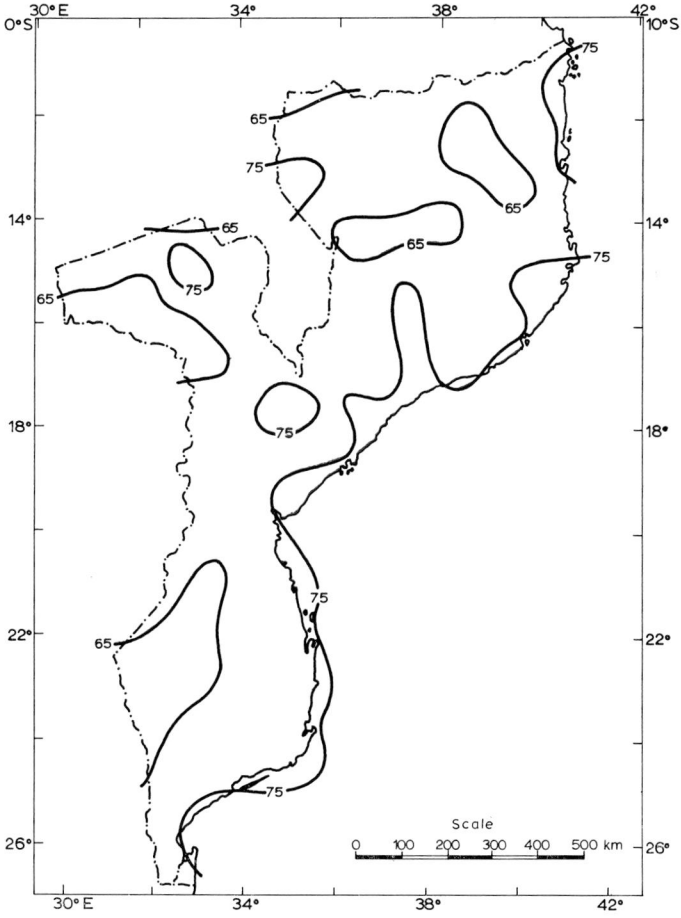

Fig.9. Mean annual relative humidity (%).

Annual evaporation varies greatly over the province, from a low 1,200 mm at Lourenço Marques to 3,000 mm at Pafuri and Tete. Along the coast values around 1,700 mm are usual but this total increases rapidly inland. At Lourenço Marques each month averages about 100 mm while at Nova Freixo the monthly means vary from 92 mm (February) to 359 mm (October).

Air flow

The prevailing air flow over the country is southeasterly, with some stations (Tete and Fingoe) having this dominant direction every month of the year. There is a tendency for winds to have a northerly component in summer (December to February) in the area north of 15°S, for a marked convergence zone exists then around this belt.

During April the winds have a more southerly component which becomes southwesterly at Mossuril due to local effects. This pattern persists through winter until the dominant easterlies return in October and bring the highest wind speeds.

Wind speeds are only available for a few stations but annual averages run from 6 km/h at Pafuri to 14 km/h at Lourenço Marques and Beira, with monthly means varying from 4 km/h (Pafuri, May and June) to 17 km/h (Beira, October). Occasionally "cyclones" are noted along the north coast with resultant high gusts recorded.

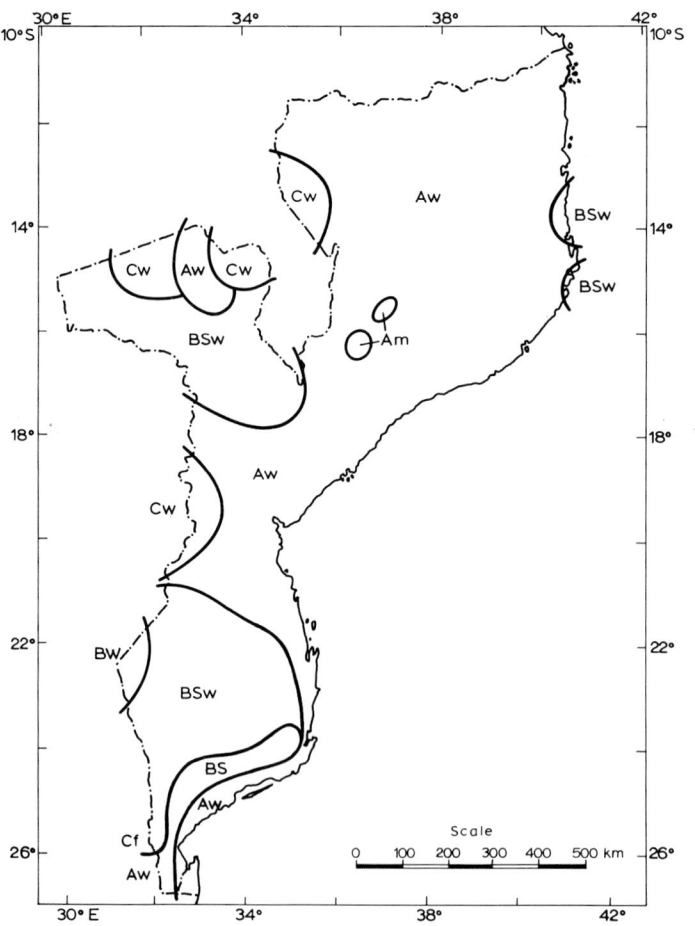

Fig.10. Climatic zones according to Köppen.

Climatic zones

Classifications of Mozambique, using Köppen's system have appeared in recent publications (Driscoll, 1959; De Rocha Faria and De Mata, 1965). Although based on data from different stations and different years they agree in all essentials, giving the pattern shown in Fig.10. The country has seven different regions, although two (*Am* and *Cf*) are trivial. The greater percentage of the country exhibits the *Aw* type of climate (tropical, summer rains), but the semi-arid (*BS*) and the tropical highland (*Cw* in this case) areas are also important. In the northeastern corner the *Aw* region becomes *Awi* due to the small annual temperature range. A small area of true desert (*BW*) exists around Pafuri.

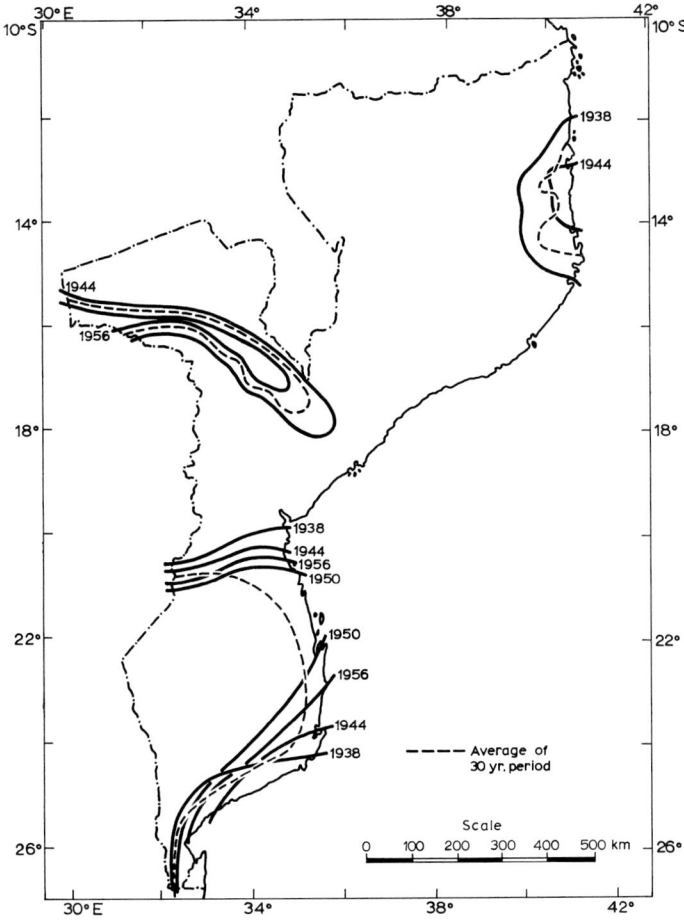

Fig.11. Fluctuations in *BS* boundary.

Driscoll (1959) has made an interesting study of the fluctuations of the *Aw/BS* boundary at intervals of 6 years, beginning in 1938. These are shown in Fig.11. It is evident that large areal changes take place, even if the shape of the areas is retained. In 1950 and 1956 no *BS* area existed in the northern coastal region.

References

DE ROCHA FARIA, J. M. and DE MATA, L. A., 1965. *Algunas Notas sobre o Clima de Mocambique* Servicio Meteorologico de Mocambique, Lourenço Marques, 9 pp., 23 maps.

DRISCOLL, D. M., 1959. *Temperature and Rainfall Distribution in Mozambique.* Thesis, Pennsylvania State University, University Park, Pa., 40 pp.

PROTHERO, R. M., 1964. Annual, seasonal and monthly rainfall over Mozambique. In: *Liverpool Essays, Geographers and the Tropics.* Liverpool University, Liverpool, pp.81–109.

TABLE II

CLIMATIC TABLE FOR NOVA FREIXO
Latitude 14°48'S, longitude 36°52'E, elevation 587 m

Month	Temperature (°C)				Relat. humid. (%)		Precipitation			Wind		Averages	
	mean		extreme		09h	21h	mean (mm)	days > 1 mm	max. 24 h (mm)	preval. direct.	calm (%) ≤ 1 km/h	cloud-iness[1] (oktas)	evap. (mm)
	max.	min.	max.	min.									
Jan.	31	20	39	10	75	77	246	14	135	NE	33	6	117
Feb.	31	20	40	10	75	79	205	13	60	V	32	6	92
Mar.	31	20	37	8	74	78	146	10	145	S	25	5	130
Apr.	31	18	36	8	69	73	25	3	37	S	25	4	136
May	29	15	39	7	66	69	7	1	30	S	27	3	153
June	28	12	33	3	65	67	2	0	22	S	25	3	170
July	28	12	34	3	63	62	1	0	7	S	26	3	204
Aug.	29	14	37	6	59	57	2	0	19	S	26	2	249
Sept.	32	17	37	9	56	50	5	0	90	S, NE	25	2	281
Oct.	35	20	42	10	51	45	15	1	95	NE	22	2	359
Nov.	35	21	42	10	54	53	50	5	56	NE	23	4	263
Dec.	33	20	44	10	69	71	186	12	76	NE	32	5	150
Annual	31	18	44	3	65	65	889	59	145	—	2	4	2,307
Rec. (yrs.)	30	30	30	30	30	30	30	30	30	10	10	15	8

[1] Mean of 09h00 and 21h00.

TABLE III

CLIMATIC TABLE FOR MOSSURIL
Latitude 14°57'S, longitude 40°40'E, elevation 15 m

Month	M.S.L. press. (mbar)	Temperature (°C) mean max.	mean min.	extreme max.	extreme min.	Relat. humid. (%) 09h	21h	Precipitation mean (mm)	max. (mm)	min. (mm)	days > 1 mm	max. 24 h (mm)	Wind preval. direct.	calm (%) ≤ 1 km/h	Averages cloud-iness (oktas) 09h	21h	sun-shine (h)	evap. (mm)
Jan.	1,008	32	24	38	19	72	86	214	333	123	13	127	NE	24	6	5	199	115
Feb.	1,008	33	24	37	15	74	86	205	466	40	11	203	V	25	6	5	177	94
Mar.	1,009	32	23	36	20	75	86	146	524	41	11	163	SW	27	6	4	169	99
Apr.	1,012	31	22	35	18	75	85	102	387	30	7	100	SW	21	5	3	236	104
May	1,014	30	20	35	13	73	84	24	139	0	3	96	SW	18	3	2	251	118
June	1,017	28	18	32	12	74	84	37	109	11	5	88	SW	16	3	2	198	117
July	1,018	28	17	31	13	73	82	18	28	2	4	29	SW	20	3	3	227	120
Aug.	1,017	28	18	34	13	71	82	15	72	0	2	43	SW	21	4	2	258	128
Sept.	1,016	30	19	35	14	65	81	9	48	0	1	45	SW	20	4	1	268	138
Oct.	1,014	31	21	36	16	60	80	6	5	0	1	70	NE	20	4	1	307	169
Nov.	1,012	33	23	37	19	60	80	28	102	2	5	76	NE	15	5	2	292	176
Dec.	1,010	33	26	39	21	65	82	34	247	51	8	108	NE	22	6	4	241	150
Annual	1,013	31	21	39	12	70	83	939	1,216	70	69	203	–	21	5	3	2,823	1,524
Rec. (yrs.)	5	30	30	30	30	30	30	30	10	10	30	30	30	30	15		9	9

TABLE IV

CLIMATIC TABLE FOR FINGOE
Latitude 15°10′S, longitude 31°53′E, elevation 857 m

Month	Temperature (°C)				Relat. humid. (%)		Precipitation			Wind		Average cloudiness (oktas)	
	mean		extreme				mean (mm)	days ≥1 mm	max. 24 h (mm)	preval. direct.	calm (%) ≤1 km/h		
	max.	min.	max.	min.	09h	21h						09h	21h
Jan.	29	19	39	11	75	72	244	16	92	SE	2	7	6
Feb.	28	19	37	11	77	73	259	15	174	SE	1	7	6
Mar.	28	18	37	10	76	71	168	12	97	SE	1	6	5
Apr.	28	17	35	9	70	65	35	4	75	SE	1	5	3
May	26	14	33	6	65	61	4	1	14	SE	2	3	2
June	26	12	34	6	62	60	8	2	28	SE	1	4	3
July	25	11	31	4	62	54	5	1	20	SE	<1	3	2
Aug.	26	12	36	5	56	48	4	1	30	SE	<1	2	2
Sept.	30	15	38	8	52	44	1	0	6	SE	<1	2	2
Oct.	33	16	40	10	48	45	8	1	48	SE	<1	2	2
Nov.	32	19	40	10	61	54	94	8	75	SE	<1	4	5
Dec.	30	19	39	13	71	68	232	13	146	SE	1	6	6
Annual	28	16	40	4	65	60	1,064	74	174	–	1	4	4
Rec. (yrs.)	30	30	30	30	30	30	30	30	30	30	30	30	

403

TABLE V

CLIMATIC TABLE FOR TETE
Latitude 16°11′S, longitude 38°35′E, elevation 140 m

Month	M.S.L. press. (mbar)	Temperature (°C)				Relat. humid. (%)		Precipitation					Wind		Averages		
		mean		extreme				mean (mm)	max. (mm)	min. (mm)	days ≥1 mm	max. 24 h (mm)	av. speed (km/h)	preval. direct.	cloud- iness[1] (oktas)	sun- shine (h)	evap. (mm)
		max.	min.	max.	min.	09h	21h										
Jan.	1,009	34	22	43	17	73	55	145	368	17	9	132	5	SE	7	201	172
Feb.	1,008	33	23	40	18	76	55	167	404	18	10	104	4	SE	7	193	133
Mar.	1,011	33	22	39	17	72	49	81	295	2	5	100	6	SE	6	239	192
Apr.	1,013	33	21	39	15	70	42	13	66	0	1	30	6	SE	5	240	221
May	1,015	31	18	39	11	68	39	2	13	0	1	4	5	SE	3	262	218
June	1,019	29	15	38	9	69	39	4	15	0	1	13	5	SE	3	196	200
July	1,019	28	15	36	8	66	38	2	6	0	1	6	6	SE	4	235	226
Aug.	1,017	31	17	39	8	64	32	2	21	0	<1	18	8	SE	3	272	283
Sept.	1,014	34	20	42	11	59	28	2	10	0	<1	8	10	SE	3	267	349
Oct.	1,011	37	22	44	14	53	26	4	28	0	1	17	11	SE	3	287	456
Nov.	1,010	36	23	45	15	58	34	52	152	7	4	67	10	SE	5	247	368
Dec.	1,009	34	23	43	16	67	46	130	310	45	9	130	7	SE	7	221	244
Annual	1,013	34	20	45	8	66	40	604	1,049	416	42	132	7	–	5	2,860	3,062
Rec. (yrs.)	9	20	20	20	20	20	20	20	20	20	20	20	16	16	18	14	17

[1] Mean of 09h00 and 15h00.

TABLE VI

CLIMATIC TABLE FOR BEIRA
Latitude 19°50'S, longitude 34°51'E, elevation 8 m

Month	M.S.L. press. (mbar)	Temperature (°C)				Relat. humid. (%)			Precipitation					Wind				Averages				gales ≥ 36 km/h
		mean		extreme					mean (mm)	max. (mm)	min. (mm)	days ≥ 1 mm	max. 24 h (mm)	av. speed (km/h)	preval. direct.		calm (%) ≤ 1 km/h	cloud-iness (oktas)		sun-shine (h)	evap. (mm)	
		max.	min.	max.	min.	09h	15h	21h							09h	21h		09h	21h			
Jan.	1,010	31	26	40	19	74	66	80	265	852	11	12	196	14	E	SE	3	6	4	245	171	2
Feb.	1,010	32	24	38	19	75	66	80	225	773	26	12	219	14	E	SE	2	6	3	224	154	1
Mar.	1,012	31	25	37	18	77	65	80	244	677	22	12	196	14	E	SE	2	5	3	243	156	2
Apr.	1,015	30	22	37	16	77	64	81	105	330	27	7	184	12	E	S	3	4	2	245	135	1
May	1,018	28	19	37	13	79	64	82	58	142	4	6	101	12	SE	S	4	3	2	253	120	1
June	1,021	26	17	33	9	80	64	83	42	133	2	5	88	12	SE	S	4	3	1	223	102	1
July	1,022	25	16	35	9	82	65	84	37	115	0	4	94	12	SE	SE	4	4	1	231	101	1
Aug.	1,020	26	17	35	10	78	66	83	30	133	0	3	65	13	E	SE	2	4	2	253	118	1
Sept.	1,018	28	19	40	12	73	66	82	27	108	0	3	63	15	E	SE	1	4	2	243	139	3
Oct.	1,015	29	21	42	13	68	66	80	29	145	1	3	102	17	E	SE	1	5	2	258	170	4
Nov.	1,013	30	22	43	16	88	67	79	133	545	6	7	218	16	E	SE	1	6	3	229	170	3
Dec.	1,011	31	23	41	17	71	67	80	234	780	38	10	222	14	E	SE	2	6	4	237	166	2
Annual	1,015	29	20	43	9	75	66	81	1,429	2,288	821	84	222	14	–	–	2	5	2	2,883	1,701	22
Rec. (yrs.)	30	30	30	30	30	30	30	30	30	48	48	30	30	30	30	30	30	30	30	30	30	30

405

TABLE VII

CLIMATIC TABLE FOR PAFURI
Latitude 22°26'S, longitude 31°20'E, elevation 290 m

Month	Temperature (°C)				Relat. humid. (%)		Precipitation					Wind		Averages		
	mean		extreme				mean	max.	min.	days	max.	av.	preval.	cloud-	sun-	evap.
	max.	min.	max.	min.	09h	15h	(mm)	(mm)	(mm)	$\geqslant 1$ mm	24 h (mm)	speed (km/h)	direct.	iness[1] (oktas)	shine (h)	(mm)
Jan.	35	21	43	11	63	44	90	324	0	5	83	6	S	5	235	259
Feb.	34	22	44	13	67	50	68	142	0	7	97	6	S	5	199	187
Mar.	34	20	40	12	65	44	39	186	0	4	44	6	S	5	213	231
Apr.	33	18	41	10	64	41	19	56	0	2	52	5	N	3	224	214
May	30	13	40	4	62	36	4	13	0	1	11	4	N	2	259	206
June	28	9	36	1	63	36	8	33	0	1	27	4	N	2	264	173
July	28	9	39	1	61	33	1	3	0	<1	3	4	N	2	254	208
Aug.	30	11	39	1	57	31	<1	6	0	<1	6	5	E	3	250	254
Sept.	32	15	43	4	57	32	8	59	0	1	55	7	V	3	229	307
Oct.	35	19	46	9	57	31	14	57	0	1	28	8	E	3	208	361
Nov.	34	20	47	9	58	27	49	98	12	3	58	7	E	5	224	307
Dec.	35	21	44	13	61	44	79	179	29	7	56	7	E	5	217	276
Annual	32	17	47	1	61	37	380	636	147	32	97	6	–	4	2,776	2,983
Rec. (yrs.)	15	15	15	15	12	12	15	15	15	15	15	8	8	8	6	8

[1] Mean of 09h00 and 15h00.

TABLE VIII

CLIMATIC TABLE FOR PANDA
Latitude 24°03'S, longitude 34°43'E, elevation 150 m

Month	Temperature (°C)				Relat. humid. (%)		Precipitation			Wind		Aver. cloudiness (oktas)	
	mean		extreme				mean (mm)	days ≥1 mm	max. 24 h (mm)	preval. direct.	calm (%) ≤1 km/h		
	max.	min.	max.	min.	09h	21h						09h	21h
Jan.	34	20	42	10	67	71	116	7	107	SE	0	5	3
Feb.	33	20	41	10	69	72	136	8	110	SE	0	5	4
Mar.	32	19	41	11	70	72	74	6	140	SE	0	5	3
Apr.	31	18	40	10	71	73	46	4	85	SE	0	3	3
May	29	16	38	9	73	73	34	4	78	S	0	2	2
June	27	15	35	8	75	75	25	3	90	S	0	2	2
July	26	14	34	9	74	73	19	3	33	S	0	2	2
Aug.	28	15	38	9	71	71	12	2	28	NE	0	2	2
Sept.	30	16	41	8	67	69	26	2	50	NE	0	3	2
Oct.	32	17	43	11	64	69	31	2	94	NE	0	4	3
Nov.	33	18	43	11	65	70	67	5	105	NE	0	5	4
Dec.	33	19	44	11	67	71	108	6	83	SE	0	5	4
Annual	31	17	44	8	69	72	695	52	140	–	0	4	3
Rec. (yrs.)	30	30	30	30	30	30	30	30	30	12	12	12	

TABLE IX

CLIMATIC TABLE FOR LOURENÇO MARQUES
Latitude 25°58′S, longitude 32°36′E, elevation 64 m

Month	M.S.L. press. (mbar)	Temperature (°C) mean max.	mean min.	extreme max.	extreme min.	Relative humidity (%) 09h	15h	21h	Precipitation mean (mm)	max. (mm)	min. (mm)	days > 1 mm	max. 24 h (mm)	Wind av. speed (km/h)	preval. direct. 09h	21h	calm (%) ≤ 1 km/h	Averages cloudiness (oktas) 09h	21h	sunshine (h)	evap. (mm)	gales (> 36 km/h)
Jan.	1,013	30	22	43	16	73	65	79	130	368		9	123	15	E	V	1	7	5	223	109	1
Feb.	1,013	30	22	41	17	75	66	80	124	373	6	8	201	14	E	V	1	7	5	210	91	2
Mar.	1,015	30	21	40	15	77	66	81	97	560	1	9	127	13	E	V	2	6	4	225	95	1
Apr.	1,017	29	19	40	12	76	64	81	64	356	2	6	161	13	E	V	2	5	3	229	88	1
May	1,019	27	16	38	8	74	60	80	28	145	0	3	68	13	E	V	2	4	2	253	94	1
June	1,023	25	14	34	7	73	59	80	27	250	0	2	166	13	NE	V	3	3	2	246	91	0
July	1,023	25	14	35	7	73	59	79	13	87	0	2	52	13	NE	V	2	3	2	256	96	1
Aug.	1,022	26	15	38	9	70	60	80	13	75	0	2	40	15	NE	V	1	4	2	252	106	1
Sept.	1,020	27	16	45	10	67	63	80	38	138	0	4	77	16	E	V	1	7	3	228	106	2
Oct.	1,017	28	18	45	12	68	66	82	46	150	4	6	102	16	E	V	1	7	5	210	108	3
Nov.	1,015	28	20	44	13	69	67	80	86	379	9	8	200	15	E	V	1	7	6	198	104	2
Dec.	1,013	30	21	44	16	71	66	80	103	244	10	8	87	15	E	V	1	7	6	220	107	2
Annual	1,017	28	18	45	7	72	63	80	768	1,425	277	67	201	14	–		1	5	4	2,748	1,196	17
Rec. (yrs.)	30	30	30	30	30	30	30	30	30	51	51	30	30	30	30	30	30	30	30	30	30	30

Chapter 13

Malawi, Rhodesia and Zambia

J. D. TORRANCE

Introduction

The three states, Malawi, Rhodesia and Zambia, together cover an area of about 1,250,000 km², between 8° and 22.5°S, and between 22° and 36°E. At its closest, this group is 250 km from the nearest sea, the Mozambique Channel portion of the Indian Ocean. Several major lakes are found in the region, notably the lakes Malawi, Kariba and Bangweulu, as well as small parts of lakes Tanganyika and Mweru. The region lies wholly within tropical latitudes, but, since it varies in altitude from sea level to over 1,500 m for some of the highland plateaus, or over 2,500 m for some mountain areas, it is subject to a wide variety of climatic conditions. Of prime importance throughout the region is the division of the year into a rainy season lasting 4–6 months during the summer half of the year, and a virtually rainless dry season taking up most of the remaining months of the year. The limited areas in which winter rainfall occurs assume a special economic significance in the growing of tea, soft fruit, and timber.

Savannah woodlands, interspersed with open grasslands to some extent, are characteristic of much of the region. Vegetation tails off to a semi-arid acacia scrub in the dry southwest of Rhodesia, but the woodlands merge into extensive forests in the wetter areas in the north of Zambia and Malawi.

Despite the generally favourable climatic conditions, occupation of the region has not been able to proceed uniformly, due to the occurrence of the tsetse fly. This has determined the routes by which immigration into the region could proceed, as well as the areas in which cattle, the mainstay of the early indigenous peoples, could survive. Apart from the lake shores, the early occupation was concentrated on the plateaus above 1,000 m, and even today, when vast areas have been cleared of the tsetse fly menace, some regions remain thinly settled. The present population of about 9,000,000 persons, is shared about equally amongst the three states. Thus Malawi, with less than one tenth of the combined land area, has a population density averaging 33 per square kilometre, compared with Rhodesia's 8 per square kilometre for one third the area, and Zambia's 4 per square kilometre for its two fifths of the combined area.

The population in Malawi is concentrated in the southern province and at a few centres on the lake shore; in the other two states the rural population is more evenly distributed, with, however, an increasing trend towards an urban concentration.

Economic development, starting slowly in the 1890's, has proceeded rapidly since the 1950's, and today the mining, manufacturing, and agricultural industries are firmly established. The more important minerals include copper, cobalt, zinc and lead from

409

Zambia; and gold, copper, chrome, coal, asbestos and iron from Rhodesia, with tin, nickel and mica also contributing to the economy. Industry includes heavy metal products, furniture, plastics, textiles, clothing and footwear, chemicals, and foodstuffs, mainly in Rhodesia. The production of electrical power should not be overlooked, in particular that gained from the Zambezi River and Lake Kariba, delivered as far north as the Copper Belt in Zambia, and to the south beyond Bulawayo. The greatest contrasts appear in agriculture, where traditional subsistence farming methods have not yet been fully ousted by the more profitable modern systems of production used for maize, tobacco, cotton, sugar, tea, coffee, citrus, timber, and cattle ranching. Irrigation of winter wheat and vegetables is gaining ground. One of Malawi's most valuable exports is that of manpower, since few minerals are being exploited, and the density of population does not allow substantial surpluses in food crops.

Economic development is rounded off by the communications systems. Frequent internal air services exist, linking the main centres with airports in East Africa, Mozambique, and South Africa, and thence overseas. A railway network covers Rhodesia, and with the through lines in Zambia and Malawi there are connections to the Congo, Angola,

Fig.1. Geographic and station locations.

Mozambique, Botswana, and South Africa. The proportion of main highways engineered to modern standards and tarred to 7 m width is being extended as rapidly as possible, amounting in early 1969 to some 1,800 miles in Rhodesia, 1,100 miles in Zambia, and 100 miles in Malawi. Finally, there are the steamer services on Lake Malawi, and one on Lake Tanganyika between Zambia and Tanzania.

While material development of a country is often rated supreme, the well-being of the inhabitants and improvement of their capabilities takes on special significance in the younger countries in the process of changing from a subsistence economy to a modern industrial society.

There is intense competition for development funds, and it is encouraging that the largest items of government expenditure are devoted to health and education services and agriculture, and that increasing attention is being paid to the preservation of natural resources.

In the ensuing discussion of climatic conditions in this region, all the place names mentioned will be found in Fig.1.

Causes of the climate

Malawi, Rhodesia and Zambia form a compact group lying between 8° and 22.5°S, and between 22° and 36°E, a land-locked group rather nearer to the east coast of Africa than the west. Much of the area lies on plateaus between 1,000 and 1,500 m above sea level, but these are deeply dissected by major river valleys, the Limpopo and Sabi in the south of Rhodesia, the Zambezi affecting both Rhodesia and Zambia, and the Luangwa in Zambia, and the Shire–Lake Malawi system in Malawi.

Throughout the year the group lies on the equatorward side of the Southern Hemisphere subtropical high-pressure belt, and the vagaries of the climate depend almost more on this factor than on any other one, though the effects of topography and the restricting presence of the South African mountain ranges forming the Great Escarpment must not be overlooked. Firstly, the high-pressure belt acts as a buffer against the travelling depressions and anticyclones of the middle latitudes, and though these do affect the weather considerably, their influence is exercised indirectly. Pressures rise and fall in resonance with the changes further south, but the amplitude decreases rapidly equatorwards; pressure peaks and troughs occur almost simultaneously over most of the latitude range with which we are concerned, and only in the extreme south is there much sign of west–east "travel" of pressure features.

The second feature associated with the location to the north of the high-pressure belt is the comparative steadiness of the plateau-level pressure distribution patterns which persist from day to day with very little change, despite considerable changes in upper air flow patterns and often quite marked changes in the weather. The seasonal changes follow a predictable pattern, and the winter anticyclonic pattern is replaced in midsummer by a weak pressure trough near the Zambezi Valley with weak gradients to the north and persistent easterly winds to the south. Fluctuations in the position and intensity of the trough, and whether they are linked directly to the travelling low-pressure systems further south, account for most weather changes.

The third consequence of being situated on the equatorward side of the subtropical high-pressure belt is the accessibility to the tropical cyclones of the southwest Indian Ocean, the effects of which depend on proximity and may vary from drought in some areas to floods in others.

Now that attention has been directed to the major weather controls, it is convenient to review the seasonal changes in rather more detail. In the winter half year, when the high-pressure belt spreads a little further north, the southeast trade winds are prevalent and weather in general is fine. The trades reach the region via the south of Madagascar or across Madagascar. Apart from the lowest layers there is little moisture in the air, and above the temperature inversion at about 600–700 mbar the air is extremely dry. In the case of Rhodesia, the winds in the middle levels originate from the Transvaal anticyclone, a separate cell in the high-pressure belt, and because of its continental situation, doubly dry.

With the southward movement of the sun, surface winds tend to back, and to strengthen as pressure falls over the interior of the continent. About mid-September, recurved southeast trades from the South Atlantic appear in the extreme northwest of Zambia, and become moister, leading to early thunderstorm conditions. By October or November, a portion of the Indian Ocean southeast trades reaches Malawi (and Zambia to some extent) by having recurved around the northern end of Madagascar, and in so doing become appreciably moister. These northeasters in due course merge into, or are replaced by, the northeast monsoon from India. The air-mass properties and weather depend very largely on the track. The branch arriving overland via Somalia and East Africa is dry, though with lapse rates steep enough to give afternoon thunderstorms. If the air has an oceanic track, it is much moister and gives more general thunderstorms.

During January and February the rainy season is at its height, and a characteristic configuration of air masses can be distinguished, forming part of the Inter-Tropical Convergence Zone (I.T.C.Z.), with a more or less permanent centre of low pressure in south-

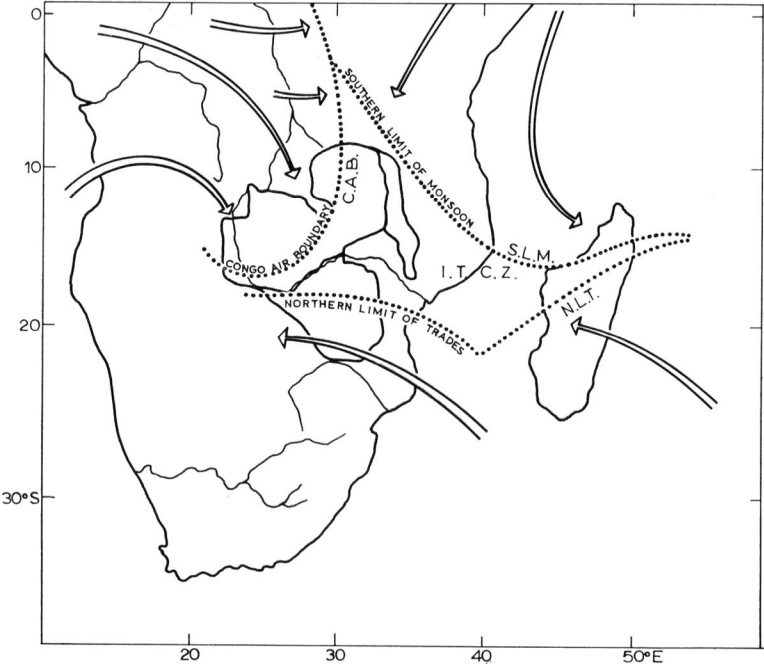

Fig.2. Intertropical Convergence Zone, mean position, January.

ern Zambia (see Fig.2). It is convenient, if not strictly proven, to postulate a northern and a southern boundary to the I.T.C.Z. in this region. The distinctions probably disappear north of about 5°S and east of about 50°E. These boundaries are preferred localities for convergence and disturbed weather, but the effects are not continuous along their length, and are often completely absent. In local forecasting terminology, the northern boundary of the I.T.C.Z. is referred to as the southern limit of the monsoon (S.L.M.), and the southern boundary as the northern limit of the trades (N.L.T.). Connected to these is the Congo air boundary (C.A.B.), though strictly not a part of the I.T.C.Z. since the air streams which it separates are both of Southern Hemisphere origin—the Indian Ocean southeast trades and the recurved South Atlantic air now known as Congo air. Thus there are four air masses involved with the I.T.C.Z. in this part of Central Africa: the northeast monsoon north of the I.T.C.Z., moist or dry according to its recent track; the southeast trades south of the I.T.C.Z., generally dry; Congo air northwest of the Congo air boundary, very moist with much rain and thunderstorms; and transitional or modified air between the two boundaries of the I.T.C.Z.

The rainy season usually comes to an end in March in Rhodesia, and somewhat later in Zambia and Malawi, due to the withdrawal northwards of the I.T.C.Z. This may take place in the form of temporary withdrawals and lesser advances, as the southeasterly airstream to the south of the I.T.C.Z. strengthens with rising pressure or weakens with falling pressure, in accordance with the movements of high and low pressure systems along the South African coasts. Each strengthening brings drier air and the rainfall becomes limited to thunderstorms and showers, which gradually become more infrequent. On occasion the end of the rainy season may occur as early as mid-February, or it may be delayed as late as mid-April. Sometimes the season terminates abruptly with a major outbreak of cold dry air from the south or southeast spreading well into Zambia, bringing a complete clearing in the weather as far north as about 10°S, and displacing the I.T.C.Z. far north beyond all hope of return. In Malawi any strengthening of the southeast winds intensifies orographic rainfall, and the wettest month of the year is usually March in the southern highlands, and on the windward escarpments in the north of Malawi in April or May.

The main features of the general circulation described above have superimposed on them the transitory and shorter-lived synoptic-scale weather and synoptic changes, and these will now be described.

The most important of all these are the low and high pressure systems which pass South Africa in succession at intervals of a few days. The lows are members of a family of temperate depressions, and move towards east-southeast or southeast according to the zonal index. When pressure is falling along the Natal coast, due to the eastward advance of one of these lows, winds in Rhodesia and Zambia tend to back to perhaps northeast, or even north or northwest in Rhodesia, and air temperature and dew points tend to rise, with a corresponding increase in cloudiness.

The intervening highs usually do not affect Rhodesia much, but a major outbreak of cold air forming a large migratory anticyclone is highly significant. The mountain ranges of South Africa constrain the movements of these systems, and the gap along the Natal and southern Mozambique coasts between the mountain ranges and the Indian Ocean anticyclone offers a favoured route for the northward advancement of cold air. Such airstreams customarily enter the interior via the major river valleys, the Limpopo and slightly less often the Zambezi and Shire valleys. When pressure starts rising in such cases, the northerly component in the Rhodesian winds is replaced by a southerly component and winds freshen considerably. The first effect in Rhodesia may be for coastal ("Channel") air from the Mozambique Channel eddies to be drawn in, and the rising dew points and falling temperatures combine with orographic ascent to give broken stratiform cloud along the Eastern Border mountains. This air soon gives way (usually by gradual changes, less often by well-defined cold frontal weather) to cold but nearly saturated southerly air from the migratory anticyclone. Low cloud spreads to blanket the southeastern half of Rhodesia, i.e., all rising ground up to the central watershed.

The diurnal temperature range falls to under 3°C, and waves of light rain or drizzle are common. These conditions, including the cold southeast winds, are known by the native name guti. Such weather may last for a few hours only, but quite often it lasts for 2 or 3 days with only slight breaks in the afternoons. Beyond the main watershed the same situation produces only a drop in temperatures with the freshening winds, with little cloud other than fair-weather cumulus clearing towards sundown. In Malawi, conditions similar to guti also develop when cold moist southerly air reaches the highland areas in the south of the country. Here the orographic cloud and rain or drizzle are known as chiperoni, and affect the Cholo, Shire, and Angoni highlands, and sometimes the east-facing escarpments along Lake Malawi. Over the lake itself, weather is fine, but the Mwera winds may be strong and even reach gale force. In Zambia the only areas likely to experience low cloud from this cause are the Chipata–Petauke Ridge, the Lusaka Plateau, and the Muchinga Escarpment, approximately Kabwe/Mpika. Even so, the low cloud is short-lived.

These invasions of cold air from the southeast occur throughout the year, often at about weekly intervals. In winter, the changes from fine weather to overcast are more dramatic, but the cloud layer tends to be shallow. In summer, when the weather is already cloudy and fairly cool, the lifting and displacement of the existing moist airstreams by the undercutting cold air produces a spell of general rain, and multiple cloud layers. However, dew points fall during the replacement phase, and weather clears as soon as the winds weaken. In summer these falling dew points result in a spell of fair weather, with little or no rainfall in Rhodesia.

Other synoptic patterns are more seasonal. In winter there are occasionally cold air outbreaks which come overland across the Cape Province and Botswana, and arrive in the southwest of Rhodesia and Zambia with dew points well below 0°C. The daytime maximum temperatures may fail to reach 15°C, and nighttime minimum temperatures may fall below 0°C. Extremely low temperatures are observed at ground level, the record being −9°C at Matopos near Bulawayo; and because of the absence of condensed moisture, these are known as black frosts. Such spells may last 1–5 days, but they seldom reach the northeastern halves of Rhodesia and Zambia because of the progressive backing of the wind from southwest to southeast. Often several years will pass without such severe spells, but in some other year two or three spells will occur.

Also in winter, there are occasionally outbreaks of thunderstorms which are associated with upper troughs. They occur when surface northeast winds give warmer and perhaps moister air than usual, coinciding with cool upper air flowing through a slow eastward-moving upper trough. Hail may occur. In August, September, and October, closed low-pressure systems sometimes form over South Africa, and produce a similar sequence of events.

In the summer half-year, the presence of any low-pressure area over the interior has to be watched with extreme alertness, either for instability aloft, or for fostering convergence in low-level airstreams. The presence of a semi-permanent low-pressure area in the vicinity of Mongu–Maun–Livingstone has already been mentioned in connection with the I.T.C.Z. This often develops a trough towards a depression off the south coast which then swings counter-clockwise with the eastward movement of the depression, to approach Rhodesia and give pre-frontal or frontal storms at the change-over to cool southeasters which come with the ensuing rise in pressure. Again, a persistent trough often develops eastwards from the Mongu low to the Mozambique Channel, separating moist westerlies over Zambia from drier easterlies over Rhodesia, and this is good for persistent rain and thunderstorms to about 100 km south of the trough. Indeed, the Rhodesian wet season depends largely on whether this or other troughs take up their position at about 12°S or at about 16°S. In the exceptional year the trough may establish itself or move frequently to the Limpopo Valley, and then heavy rainfall is general over Rhodesia, and at times over Transvaal. Small lows may develop at any time in this trough and result in local increases in rainfall and thunderstorm activity.

Not least in importance among the low-pressure systems are the tropical cyclones of the southwest Indian Ocean. While these most often follow a parabolic track east of Madagascar, a sufficient number cross Madagascar or enter the Mozambique Channel from the north to be a distinct feature of the Malawi and Rhodesian weather. The cyclone season is from December to April. Weather effects vary tremendously from case to case. A cyclone following the west coast of Madagascar or the centre of the channel is noted for causing a clearing in the weather and a break in the rains over Rhodesia, which may last for up to 10 days. This is due to the prevalence of southeast winds which become very dry in the upper levels, no doubt being part of the subsident outflow from the cyclone. However, the picture changes rapidly, even dramatically at times, when the cyclone approaches the Mozambique coast. In Rhodesia the strengthening southeasterlies cause orographic cloud and rain along the Eastern Border mountains, and possibly some orographic cloud elsewhere under the cover of the dry upper southeast winds. In Zambia the picture is very different, and cyclones usually give increased rainfall. Winds on the north side of the trough line freshen from the west, and cloudiness and rainfall tend to increase in the east of the country and over Malawi as this moist Congo air spreads eastwards. With its broken topography, Malawi has orographic cloud and rainfall with any strong winds, whatever the direction, and this applies especially to the southern highlands.

Should the cyclone move inland, as happens several times in a decade, the centre loses its violence rapidly, but the general convergence and rainfall may continue for several days and some extremely heavy downpours have been recorded. Movement inland usually occurs as the result of a rapid rush of cold air northwards up the Mozambique Channel, when the cyclone is caught up in the strengthening southeasterly winds and carried inland, usually along one of the major river valleys.

415

Rainfall

The rainfall regime of Central Africa is divided very clearly into two, a dry season and a rainy season. This applies, with only minor exceptions, to the whole region, though the proportion between the lengths of the dry and rainy seasons changes from about 7 to 5 months in the south of Rhodesia to about 5 to 7 in the north of Zambia.

The dry season is virtually rainless, the two exceptions being, firstly, the mountain highlands of Rhodesia and southern Malawi which obtain orographic rain at any time of the year, and secondly, short-lived outbreaks of high-level instability and thunderstorms which occur on occasion in the winter months over Rhodesia. The dry season commences about March or April in Rhodesia and southern Malawi, and about April or May in Zambia and northern Malawi, and continues until October or November in most areas. The end of the dry season is seldom clear-cut, as sporadic thunder activity slowly becomes more general with the continued rise in dew-points. The earliest thunderstorms start in Zambia in September, in the Mwinilunga and Kawambwa areas, and some time later start spreading towards the southeast. Meanwhile, thunder activity also starts in Rhodesia after mid-October, first over the central plateau and later over low ground. Southern Malawi also starts about this time, and storms spread towards the west. Thus the last area to start receiving rain is usually that about the Zambezi–Lunsemfwa–Luangwa confluences.

While the commencement of the rainy season is limited to afternoon thunderstorm activity, increasing moistness of the air soon becomes evident in the middle levels of the atmosphere also, and extensive middle cloud becomes common once the rainy season has set in, more particularly north of the I.T.C.Z. South of the I.T.C.Z., where the main airstream is the dryish southeast trades, rainfall tends to be organised into spells of a few days of rain alternating with dry spells of a few days duration. These spells are linked to the development or movement of pressure systems further south, high pressure and upper southeast winds promoting subsidence and decreased rainfall, while falling pressure and closed lows or troughs put a northerly component into the winds and bring moister air further south, increasing the rainfall in Rhodesia. In these wet spells, a characteristic weather sequence is that of early-morning altostratus and patchy rain, with or without stratus; cumulus clouds start forming as soon as there are any gaps in the middle cloud, and as this latter breaks and disperses, so the cumulus grow rapidly into cumulonimbus. Showers and storms are most numerous in the afternoon, but many last into the night. The altostratus is mainly cumulogenitive in origin, and is re-established by the afternoon and evening thunderstorms. Most places in Rhodesia manage to average over 5 hours of bright sunshine a day throughout the rainy season, but north of 15°S, where the air is much moister, cloud cover is more extensive and persistent, and the rainy spells are longer, and the dry spells shorter.

Despite the day-to-day control exercised by the pressure systems further south, the character of the rainy season is largely set by the behaviour of the I.T.C.Z., which reaches its southernmost latitudes and turning point in this region. The typical configuration of the I.T.C.Z. was shown in Fig.2. Congo air is recurved South Atlantic southeast trade air, which after moistening over the Atlantic and the Congo rain forests, and after several hundred metres of orographic lifting, arrives in Zambia nearly saturated with S.A.L.R., a wet-bulb potential temperature of 297°A. It is the moistest air mass to affect Central

Africa, and has the typical daily sequence of altostratus–cumulus–cumulonimbus–altostratus clouds mentioned earlier. Northeast monsoon air is usually rather modified by the time it enters Malawi or Zambia, generally with a steep lapse rate favouring convective activity, but its moistness depends on its previous track, whether over the East African land mass, or over the Indian Ocean. The southeast trades have a limited depth of moist air, and during the rainy season are regarded as a dry air mass, giving fair weather, or limited shower activity only.

The various boundaries attributed to the I.T.C.Z. may be quite inactive at times, as when there are similar wind directions on both sides, or very active under conditions of wind convergence. The boundaries move about, or become contorted, under the influence of the pressure systems to the south, or the occasional tropical cyclones. However, the I.T.C.Z. tends to take up a favoured position each year, to which it keeps returning after each displacement, and this has a profound influence on the nature of the rainy season in each country. In some years this position is about 10°–12°S, and with the dryish southeast trades covering most of the area to the south, rainfall conditions are poor over most of this area. A more usual position is about 15°–17°S, but on occasion the I.T.C.Z. moves as far south as the Limpopo Valley, giving exceptional rains over Rhodesia.

When a tropical cyclone enters the north of the Mozambique Channel, it is likely to draw Congo air across Zambia into Malawi, giving this area much wetter weather; but as the cyclone moves southwards, the southeast winds over Rhodesia strengthen and veer, and then displace the I.T.C.Z. northwards, with a decrease in rainfall over Rhodesia. If the tropical cyclone moves inland, as it sometimes does, heavy orographic rain occurs on all windward slopes and in the immediate vicinity of the cyclone itself. However, the cyclone rapidly loses its vigour over land, especially if it cannot follow a river valley or other low ground.

The end of the rainy season can be quite different in different years. It can come suddenly in Rhodesia and southern Zambia when an extra-strong invasion of cool air from the southeast drives away the moist northerly winds, and causes an almost overnight clearing. This may happen as early as the first week in February, or as late as mid-April, but mid-March is more common. In other years the season merely peters out with the scale of thunderstorm and shower activity diminishing steadily, and this is the more usual version in Zambia, so that the end of the season in northern Zambia may come 4–6 weeks later than in Rhodesia. In Malawi, conditions are quite different: here the strengthening southeast winds intensify rainfall along the southeast-facing escarpments bordering Lake Malawi, and at the northern end of the lake, the month of heaviest rainfall is April.

The distribution of rainfall is shown in Fig.3. Although there is a general increase in rainfall from south to north, there are important deviations from this trend. Rainfall is generally less over low-lying ground such as the major river valleys, the Limpopo, Sabi, lower Zambezi, and Luangwa valleys; and considerably higher over areas of high ground, or rapidly rising ground, such as to the south of Gwelo and Fort Victoria, and the Eastern Border mountains in Rhodesia, and the Shire and Zomba highlands of Malawi, and the escarpment bordering Lake Malawi. In Zambia the high ground between Kalomo and Mazabuka to the northwest of Lake Kariba also has enhanced rainfall, but the heavy rainfall areas around Solwezi and Lake Bangweulu appear to be related more to the availability of Congo air (these places being more or less continu-

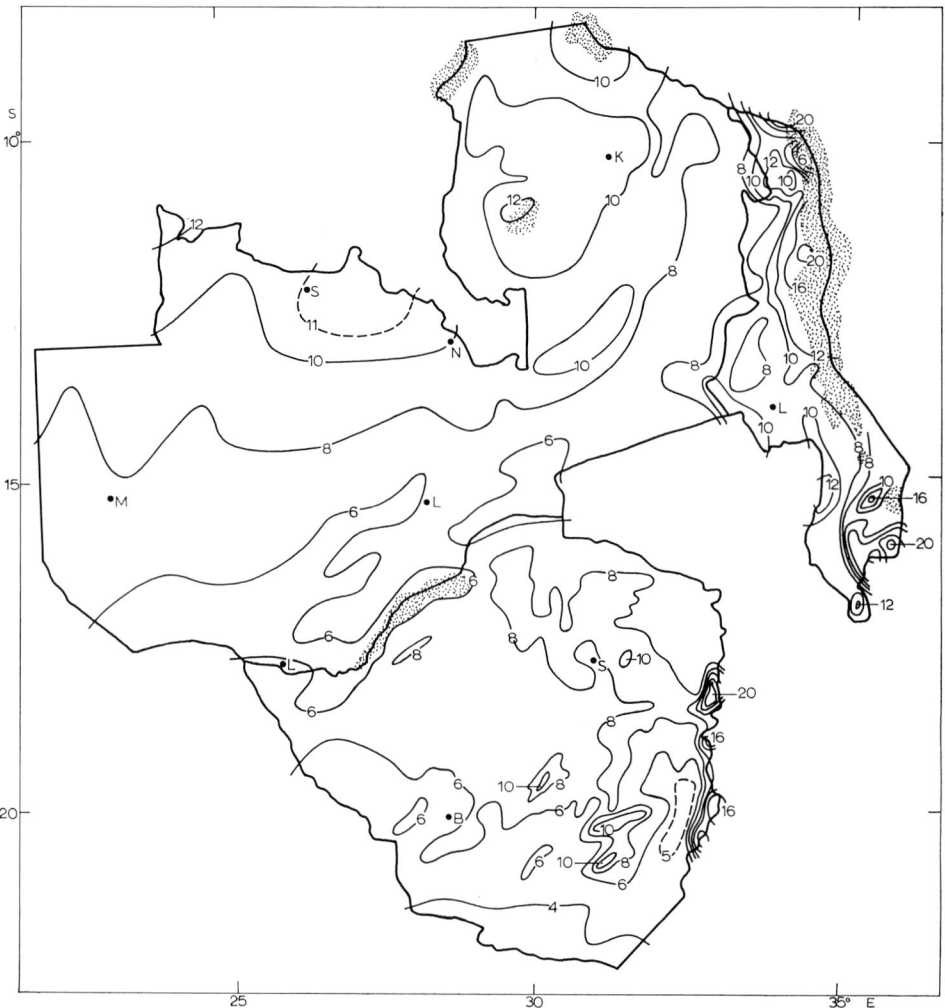

Fig.3. Mean annual rainfall (in hundreds of millimetres): Malawi, Rhodesia, Zambia.

ously in Congo air, northwest of the Congo air boundary) than to pronounced orographic features.

Rainfall reliability is presented most easily in terms of the coefficient of variability (standard deviation divided by the mean), as mapped in Fig.4. This coefficient exceeds 45% in the south and southeast of Rhodesia, dropping to under 25% in the northwest, and to as low as 15% over much of Zambia and Malawi. Analyses of the amount of rain which will be exceeded in 1 year out of 5, or in 4 years out of 5, show distribution patterns essentially similar to the distribution of annual rainfall, differing only in degree. In round figures the rainfall of a bad season may be less than 50% of normal, or more than 50% more in a wet season.

The distribution of rainfall within the season is similar at nearly all stations, the months of heaviest rainfall being December or January. Only in Malawi does this not apply, in the case of stations on southeast facing mountains and escarpments which have a March maximum, or even April at the north end of the lake. Thus, for two plateau stations, one to the east and one to the west of the Vipya Plateau, we find the distribution in Table I. The maximum 24-h falls vary considerably. In Zambia where conditions are least af-

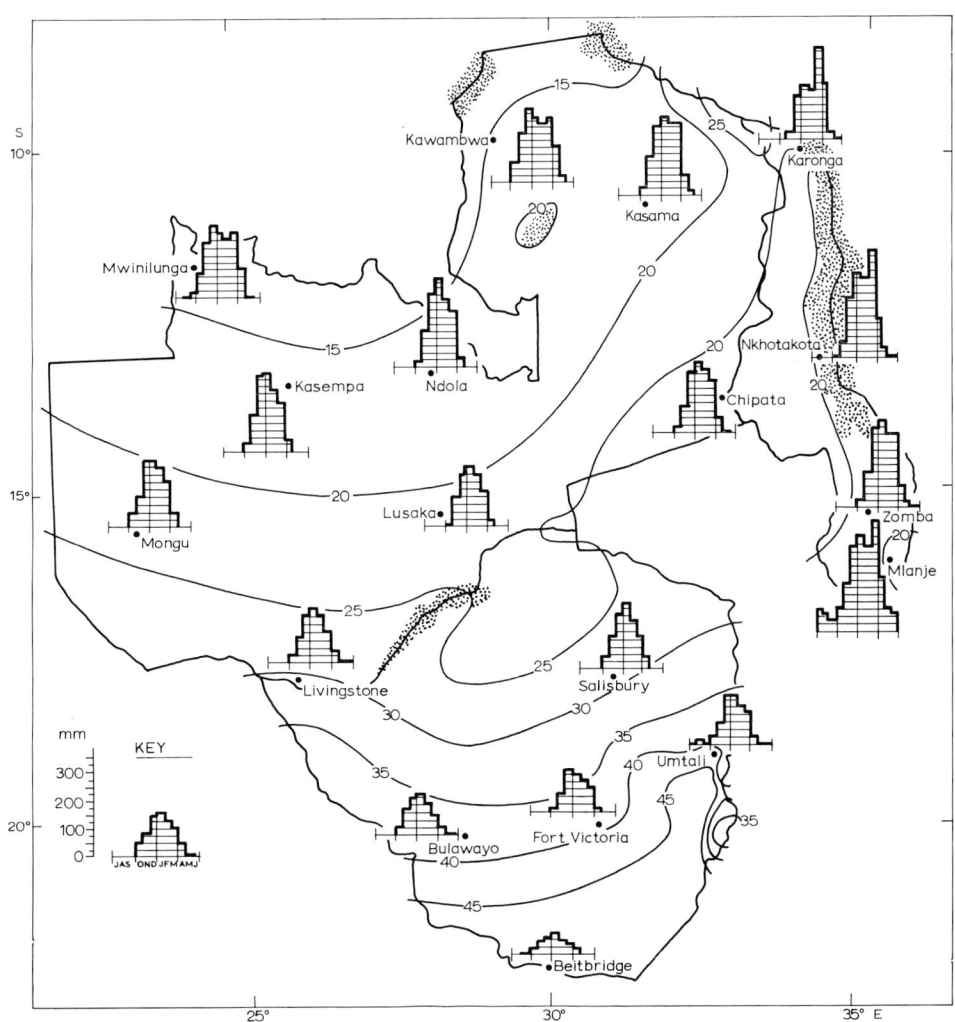

Fig.4. Percentage coefficient of variability of annual rainfall and seasonal distribution of rainfall. The year runs from July to June, to avoid splitting the rainy season.

fected by orography and tropical cyclones, maximum falls show good organisation. For a 30-year return period the maximum 24-h fall is likely to be between 10 and 20% of the annual mean, the wetter stations tending to the lower percentage and the drier stations to the higher percentage. Closely enough, the 30-year maximum 24-h fall is given by (65 mm + 5% of the annual mean), and the 100-year mean maximum fall by (75 mm + 6% of the annual mean). The record fall for the whole country is 307.6 mm in 24 h at Sesheke. In Rhodesia much heavier 24-h falls are found, notwithstanding the generally

TABLE I

SEASONAL VARIATION OF RAINFALL FOR TWO PLATEAU STATIONS (mm)

Station	Dec.	Jan.	Feb.	Mar.	Apr.	May
Mzuzu 11°27'S 34°01'E, 1,258 m	196.9	217.9	212.3	225.8	239.0	61.5
Mzimba 11°55'S 33°36'E, 1,355 m	162.6	235.2	191.5	171.7	37.3	1.8

lower average rainfall, particularly south of the main watershed. Here many places have 24-h maximum falls of over 175 or 200 mm, and in some cases this may be more than 30% of the annual mean. Beitbridge holds the record in this sense, for a 24-h fall of 161.3 mm in 1968, amounting to 47.5% of the annual mean. The record 24-h fall is 398.3 mm from a night thunderstorm at Gutu in 1946, closely followed by Chikore Mission in the Eastern Border mountains which received 363.2 mm during the passage of a tropical cyclone in January 1942.

However, most of these 24-h maximum falls south of the main watershed have occurred when moist Congo air has been undercut and replaced by a cool southeast maritime air mass. The approximation for these falls, corresponding with that given for Zambia, for a 30-year return period, is (65 mm + 5 to 7% of the annual mean), obviously a less precise estimate.

In Malawi the position is even more complex, not only because of the bigger contrasts in altitude, but because Malawi is more readily influenced by tropical cyclones moving in from the Mozambique Channel. One such, in December 1946, gave Zomba 509.0 mm in 24 h, and a further 200 mm in the next 12 h, but the 24-h record for the country is held by Nkhotakota for a fall of 570.2 mm in February 1957, apparently a severe local storm.

The numbers of rain days exceeding 1.0 mm of rain are given in the climatological tables at the end of the chapter. As is only to be expected, the number of falls increases with the mean annual rainfall, but there is also a change in the frequency distribution with increasing mean annual rainfall. In the wetter areas of Zambia, there are far fewer really heavy falls than in Rhodesia, the extra rainfall coming from more falls in the 15–40 mm class. It appears that because the air is so much moister, precipitation from shower or thunderstorm clouds commences at an earlier stage of development and storms are more numerous but less violent. A similar result was obtained from detailed analyses of rainfall intensity in the Kafue Basin. Here intensities increased with increasing annual mean rainfall up to about 915 mm, but decreased above this figure in the region north of the favoured position of the Congo air boundary. A typical expression derived for intensity – duration relationships of rainfall up to about 1,000 mm/year, was as follows:

$$I = 26 \times \frac{(0.16R - 83)(\log d + 2) + 10}{(t + 15)}$$

where I is intensity (mm/h); R is annual total rainfall (mm); d is return period in years; and t is time of duration (min).

Considering that the bulk of the rainfall in this region comes from thunderstorms, the incidence of hail is not very high, and damaging storms form but a fraction of all hail occurrences. The incidence of hail follows a definite seasonal pattern. Few storms occur during the dry season, but from October onwards the number of thunderstorms increases rapidly, and so does the number of hail storms. Hail reaches its maximum incidence in November, when upper lapse rates are steepest, and surface temperatures are still near peak values. December shows a marked decline in the number of hail storms, although the number of thunderstorms has increased; and for the remainder of the rainy season hail is infrequent. There may be a slight increase at the end of the rainy season, when there is a temporary rise in temperatures. Apart from the greatest number of hail storms being in November, these are most likely to be the severest of the year. Most

TABLE II

MEAN ANNUAL PERCENTAGE OF STATIONS REPORTING HAIL (RHODESIA)[1]

Lat. (°S) \ Long. (°E)	25–26	26–27	27–28	28–29	29–30	30–31	31–32	32–33
16–17	—	—	—	∅	32	28	8	17
17–18	∅	—	∅	∅	24	27	28	21
18–19	∅	∅	18	20	13	30	41	45
19–20	—	∅	20	35	23	23	23	29
20–21	—	—	27	35	20	11	13	16
21–22	—	—	∅	18	9	∅	∅	—
22–23	—	—	—	∅	∅	∅	—	—

[1] Based on 11 years of data, July 1956 to June 1967, for an average number of 1,125 stations. A dash means either a region outside Rhodesia or a region not containing any reporting stations; ∅ indicates less than 10 reporting stations.

hailstones are less than 6 mm in diameter, but occasionally stones as large as 20 mm diameter are observed. The expectancy of any one place receiving hail is about once in every two or three years, though there is some evidence to the effect that the mountain areas of the Eastern Border are more likely to have more, or heavier hail than this. Typical hail figures for Rhodesia are given in Table II and Table III, data for the other two countries not being available.

TABLE III

SEASONAL VARIATION IN THE MEAN PERCENTAGE OF STATIONS REPORTING HAIL (RHODESIA)[1]

July	Aug.	Sept.	Oct.	Nov.	Dec.	Jan.	Feb.	Mar.	Apr.	May	June	Year
∅	0.7	1.8	3.1	6.8	3.5	1.8	1.5	0.9	1.1	1.4	0.8	23.4

[1] Based on 11 years of data, July 1956 to June 1967, for an average number of 1,125 stations; ∅ means less than 0.1.

Evaporation

The high levels of solar radiation are reflected in the high rates of evaporation which are experienced in this region. The annual total is in the vicinity of 1,800–2,000 mm, or averaging about 5 mm/day. The comparatively low temperatures of the winter season are offset by the largely uninterrupted incidence of sunshine. Rising temperatures in September and October, accompanied also by the windiest conditions of the year, result in increased evaporation rates in these months, reaching values of 9–10 mm/day. During the rainy season, the evaporation rate drops to about 4 mm/day in most localities, thanks to the high humidity and cloudiness and low windspeeds.

Evaporation figures appear in the station climatological tables. The standard evaporation pan in use in this region is the American Class A pan, though modified by screening to prevent losses by animals and birds, and painted black inside. The combined effect of these modifications is to reduce evaporation by about 10% compared with unmodified pans.

As can be seen from the tables, evaporation is greater than rainfall in all but 3 or 4 months of the year, so that nearly all stations showed a marked moisture deficit over the year as a whole. With a dry season as long as several months, it is questionable whether it is reasonable to carry over deficits from one month to another as is so commonly done in assessing the moisture balance. A more realistic approach appears to be to compare rainfall and evaporation in individual months and take stock of the surpluses, if any, summing them over a period of years to obtain the mean. The results obtained by this method show better agreement with the observed run-off and river flow statistics than does any balance obtained from mean values directly. Tables IV and V show comparative figures for several stations, using both methods the contrasts being very evident.

TABLE IV

30-YEAR MEAN RAINFALL MINUS MEAN PENMAN EVAPORATION (mm)*

Station	Oct.	Nov.	Dec.	Jan.	Feb.	Mar.	Apr.	Oct.–Apr.	Nov.–Mar.
Malawi:									
Blantyre	−208	−121	−36	34	38	−15	−107	−415	−100
Fort Johnston	−189	−148	−28	16	20	−33	−125	−487	−173
Karonga	−199	−164	−11	39	37	179	67	−52	80
Lilongwe	−213	−123	4	55	53	−7	−102	−333	−18
Makanga	−218	−128	−50	−29	4	−78	−125	−624	−281
Mlanje	−112	−18	116	162	144	249	60	601	653
Mzimba	−224	−147	−5	78	60	18	−119	−339	4
Nkhotakota	−227	−149	42	125	160	205	−33	123	383
Zomba	−186	−68	116	130	117	88	−80	117	383
Rhodesia:									
Beitbridge	−191	−172	−169	−151	−146	−148	−126	−1,103	−786
Bulawayo	−202	−109	−70	−51	−56	−108	−120	−716	−394
Salisbury	−189	−86	8	52	14	−54	−106	−361	−66
Umtali Airport.	−188	−82	2	24	−19	−97	−99	−459	−172
Zambia:									
Chipata	−205	−105	42	77	78	11	−136	−238	103
Kasama	−197	−49	91	128	120	105	−83	115	395
Kasempa	−165	−37	118	128	85	24	−97	56	318
Livingstone	−197	−119	−27	11	−1	−72	−116	−521	−208
Mongu	−169	−90	38	49	28	−26	−142	−312	−1
Mwinilunga	−93	47	109	90	86	90	−36	293	422
Ndola	−188	−49	100	157	99	45	−105	59	352

* Based on 30 years, 1931–1960; a minus sign indicates a deficit of rainfall below evaporation.

Of the standard evaporation formulae tested, the most successful is undoubtedly that of Penman. While it fails to achieve the high evaporation rates of September–November, and slightly over-estimates in winter, the form of the annual curve matches observed conditions quite closely, and gives reasonable agreement on annual totals. The potential

TABLE V

MEAN OF THE SURPLUSES (IF ANY) ACCUMULATED FROM THE SUM OF INDIVIDUAL SEASONAL RAINFALLS
MINUS THE MEAN EVAPORATION (mm)*

Station	Annual rainfall	Seasonal rainfall	Surplus
Malawi:			
Blantyre	834	812	169
Fort Johnston	758	741	157
Karonga	1,081	1,036	453
Lilongwe	845	834	244
Makanga	749	745	111
Mlanje	1,796	1,574	751
Mzimba	869	862	280
Nkhotakota	1,442	1,385	699
Zomba	1,367	1,313	615
Rhodesia:			
Beitbridge	333	315	0
Bulawayo	589	570	134
Salisbury	831	804	242
Umtali Airport	765	721	170
Zambia:			
Chipata	1,026	1,010	354
Kasama	1,252	1,243	539
Kasempa	1,105	1,100	415
Livingstone	779	772	161
Mongu	990	985	327
Mwinilunga	1,346	1,230	538
Ndola	1,229	1,225	551

* Based on 30 years 1931–1960. Seasonal rainfall October–April.

evapotranspiration calculated from the Penman formula is shown in Fig.5. As would be
expected, amounts are least in the extreme north of Zambia where the rainy season is
longest, and in the mountain areas of Malawi and Rhodesia, and greatest in the major
river valleys, especially the Limpopo and Sabi in Rhodesia, the Zambezi below Livingstone, and the Shire.

An empirical formula has been developed for local use, and appears to give even closer
agreement with observed pan evaporation values. This formula uses only mean temperature and mean vapour pressure deficit, both of which are readily available from the
standard climatological observations taken several times a day. It takes the form:

$$E = Kn(aT + bV + c)$$

where E is the total evaporation for the month; n is the number of days in the month;
T is the mean temperature of the month (from the mean of fixed-hour observations
throughout the 24 h or from thermograms); V is the mean vapour pressure deficit of the
month (from mean temperature and the mean dew point, which is given very closely by
one quarter of the sum of the dew points at 06h00, at 08h00, and twice at 14h00 local

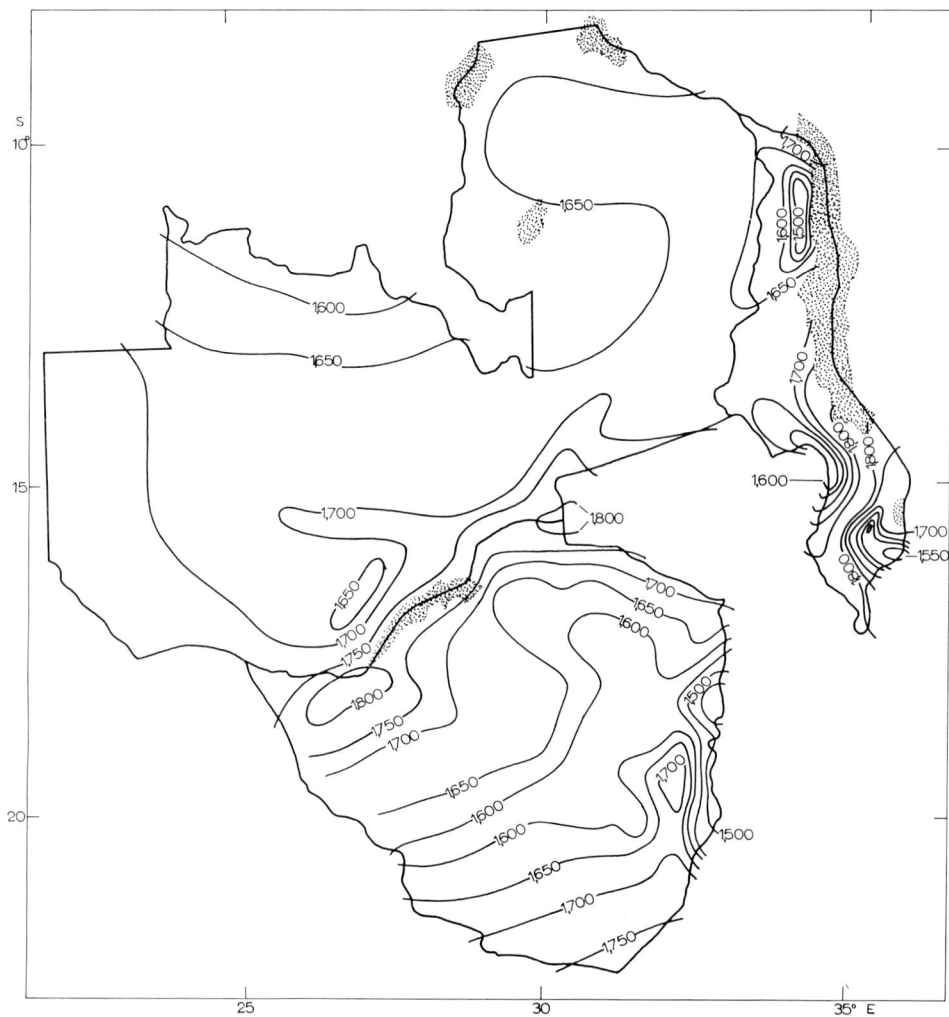

Fig.5. Potential evapotranspiration based on Penman formula. Annual total in millimetres.

time); K is a constant depending only on the latitude and altitude of the station; and a, b, c, are constants.

For temperatures in degrees centigrade, altitudes in thousands of metres above sea level (H), vapour pressure deficits in millibars, and evaporation in millimetres, the numerical value of the constants are: $a = 12$; $b = 10$; $c = -87$;

and $K = 3.0 \{6.5 \sin \theta + (H + 0.61)^2 + 2.5\} \cdot 10^{-3}$

Temperature

Rhodesia, Zambia, and Malawi owe much to their generally high altitude above sea level, in reducing tropical heat to temperate levels. With considerable parts of these countries above 1,000 m in elevation, temperatures are some 8°–9°C lower than they would be at sea level. Further relief is given by the rainy season which occupies the summer half of the year, its cloudiness interrupting the seasonal rise of temperatures before they can reach peak intensity. The highest temperatures occur about six weeks after the spring equinox, i.e., the end of October or early November; but then after a drop of about 4°C, temperatures remain very steady for the next four months, before dropping to the winter minimum. All in all, these give a climate which is difficult to improve upon—one or two cool months, a rapid rise to a one to two months hot season, and a four to five month period with mean temperatures near the optimum of 18°–20°C. In the lower areas, especially the major river valleys, the Limpopo, the Sabi, Zambezi, Luangwa, and Shire, temperatures are appreciably higher, but even here, many of these areas experience periodic invasions of cool air which bring welcome relief. The mean annual temperatures are shown in Fig.6.

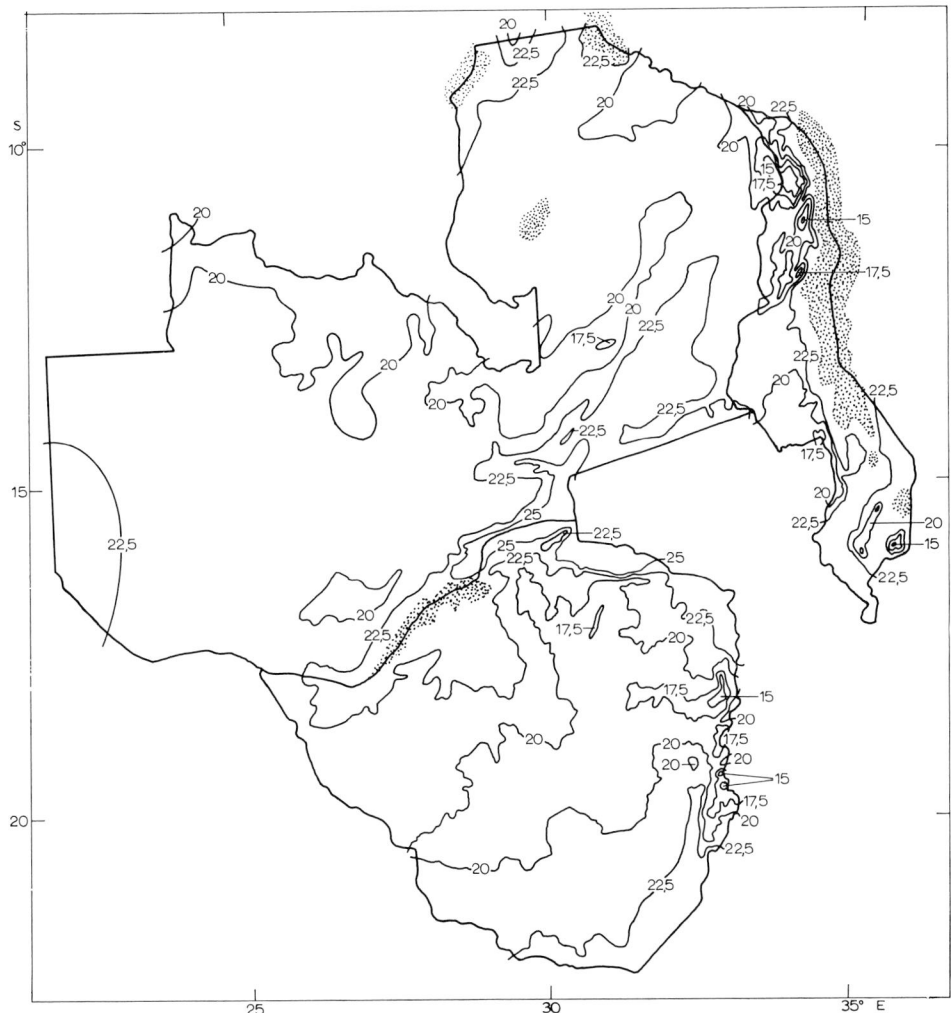

Fig.6 Annual mean temperature (°C): Malawi, Rhodesia, Zambia.

Because of the inland situation, the daily range of temperatures is pronounced, generally averaging about 10°C in the rainy season months, but as much as 20°C in the dry season in the southern parts of Rhodesia and Zambia. The maximum daily range observed to date is 30.9°C at the Matopos Research Station near Bulawayo on a day with near-record minimum temperatures of −9.4°C in the screen, and −12.3°C at 1 cm above ground. This serves to show that, while these countries lie wholly within the tropics, frost is far from unknown. Frost temperatures at screen level are observed each winter as far north as Solwezi (12.2°S 26.4°E, 1,333 m), regularly; and Mzuzu (11.5°S 34.0°E, 1,253 m) from time to time. In the main, for areas above the 800-m contour, frost conditions are light, of 1° or 2°C intensity only, on about 5 occasions per winter over most of Rhodesia and the southern part of Zambia; but conditions depend so much on local exposure and air drainage factors that this figure may be doubled or quadrupled for low-lying places, or reduced to zero at places on sloping ground.

Really severe frost is limited to occasional incursions of very cold dry air which reach Zambia and Rhodesia from the southwest across Botswana. These spells may last 1–4 days, and may occur two or three times in a season, or not at all for some years; but when they do occur, frost is widespread and severely damaging. The frequency of occurrence of such frosts drops off sharply to the north of a line Umtali–Mwinilunga, since on these occasions the winds back fairly rapidly from southwest through south to southeast, thereby limiting the northeastward penetration.

Temperature statistics appear in the climatological tables at the end of the chapter. All show the same lack of symmetry in the annual variation as described earlier, and all of them tend to repeat the annual cycle faithfully each year. Departures from the average seldom exceed 2°C, but there are exceptional years on record, as for example 1940 when the October mean temperature was lower than September's.

Day-to-day temperature changes tend to be small, especially in the north of Zambia and Malawi which are remote from the invasions of cool maritime air which affect Rhodesia and southern Malawi, and to some extent southern Zambia. Table VI shows this very clearly in the interdiurnal variability of maximum temperatures. Apart from the random 1°–2°C changes of settled weather, the main pattern for day to day changes is a series of moderate rises, followed by a sharp fall with the arrival of maritime air. These periodic invasions of cool maritime air are one of the characteristic features of the weather, and give rise to what is known locally as guti in Rhodesia, or chiperoni in Malawi, a combination of cold gusty southeast winds, 8/8 low stratus and stratocumulus, and intermittent drizzle or rain, over rising ground. In Rhodesia this zone is bounded by the water-

TABLE VI

INTERDIURNAL VARIABILITY OF MAXIMUM TEMPERATURE (tenths of °C)*

Station	Jan.	Feb.	Mar.	Apr.	May	June	July	Aug.	Sept.	Oct.	Nov.	Dec.	Year
Karonga	13	12	9	7	6	6	6	8	9	9	11	12	9
Kasama	18	16	13	8	9	9	8	9	11	9	16	16	12
Mwinilunga	21	19	16	11	8	8	8	9	11	16	21	17	13
Ndola	18	16	13	10	10	9	10	11	11	12	17	17	13
Chipata	16	17	12	11	11	11	11	12	14	11	15	19	13
Mongu	18	16	14	11	10	9	9	10	11	16	23	21	14
Lusaka	17	15	12	11	11	12	12	12	14	17	22	18	14
Blantyre Airport	16	14	12	12	14	15	15	16	17	17	21	18	16
Salisbury	14	13	12	12	11	12	13	14	15	16	19	16	14
Livingstone	18	16	13	11	11	10	11	12	12	16	21	20	14
Bulawayo	19	19	16	16	15	15	16	19	23	25	24	22	19
Chipinga	18	18	17	19	20	18	20	31	30	30	30	25	23

* Stations listed in order of increasing latitude; based on 15 years records, July 1941 June 1956.

shed from Plumtree through Bulawayo and Gwelo to Enkeldoorn and Marandellas, and thence eastwards to Inyanga. During such spells the diurnal temperature range may be reduced to less than 2°C. The change from fair weather with peak temperatures ahead of the guti to the overcast conditions gives the greatest 24-h temperature changes, of the order of 15°C fall in the guti and chiperoni areas, the record being 20°C at Chipinga.

Soil temperature data appear in several of the station climatological tables. As is to be expected, soil temperatures are greatly influenced by the soil type and its moisture content. Sand soils show the greatest ranges, with the diurnal cycle still evident at 30 cm depth, whereas clay soils have a smaller diurnal range which hardly penetrates to 30 cm. The effect of moisture is illustrated by Table VII of temperatures at 5 cm depth at 14h00, together with the rainfall for that month.

TABLE VII

SOIL TEMPERATURES AND RAINFALL AT TRELAWNEY*

Soil temp. (°C)	Rainfall (mm)	Year
35.3	39.4	1952
34.1	58.9	1965
33.6	84.8	1957
33.6	151.4	1966
32.9	147.6	1958
32.3	91.9	1961
32.3	122.4	1959
32.3	183.6	1967
31.6	72.9	1953
31.2	156.5	1963
30.8	157.7	1964
30.2	213.9	1955
29.7	284.7	1960
29.2	288.5	1954
27.7	185.7	1956
26.3	322.3	1962

* Depth 5 cm; December, 14h00.

Water temperatures are given in Table VIII for a number of representative sites, covering both lakes and rivers in Malawi and Rhodesia. No information is available in respect of Zambia.

In the case of the Zambezi River, two sets of figures are given, both taken at Chirundu about 80 km north of the Kariba Dam. One series gives the temperatures in the river before the closure of the river at Kariba, but though these no longer apply to the Zambezi River they are probably representative of other major rivers in this region, e.g., the Kafue. The second series gives temperatures in the river subsequent to the construction of the Kariba Dam. Whether the water reaches the river from Lake Kariba via the turbines of the hydroelectric station or through the discharge gates, it is water drawn from below the surface of the lake and so less affected by surface meteorological conditions. This latter series of temperatures shows the annual temperature range reduced to nearly half its former value.

TABLE VIII

WATER TEMPERATURES (°C)

	Nkhata Bay[1]	Fort Johnston[2]	Chirundu[3]		Birch-enough[4]	Lake McIlwaine[5]	Inyanga[6]
			prior	after			
Jan.	27.1	27.8	27.7	25.7	25.7	23.5	17.3
Feb.	27.3	28.1	27.9	25.9	25.1	23.4	17.2
Mar.	27.4	27.1	27.3	26.1	24.5	23.3	16.6
Apr.	26.9	26.0	26.4	25.7	22.8	21.8	15.1
May	26.0	24.4	23.5	24.1	19.4	19.7	13.4
June	24.9	22.8	20.3	22.7	16.4	17.2	11.5
July	23.9	21.7	19.3	21.5	16.1	16.2	10.9
Aug.	23.7	22.4	20.2	21.7	17.0	16.3	11.5
Sept.	24.1	24.0	23.7	22.4	19.9	18.7	13.7
Oct.	25.2	26.3	25.6	23.9	22.8	21.3	15.5
Nov.	26.6	27.3	26.9	25.1	24.6	22.6	16.8
Dec.	26.8	27.9	27.6	25.4	25.6	23.0	17.2
Annual	25.8	25.5	24.7	24.1	21.7	20.6	14.7
Av. air temp. (°C)	23.5	24.3	25.2	25.2	22.7	19.1	14.7
Lat. (S)	11°36′	14°29′	16°00′	16°00′	19°58′	17°55′	18°17′
Long. (E)	34°18′	35°16′	28°54′	28°54′	32°20′	30°48′	32°45′
Alt. (m)	481	482	395	395	498	1,372	1,859
No. years	6	17	9	8	16	4	11

Remarks
[1] Lake Malawi; deep water off floating jetty.
[2] Shire River, at exit to Lake Malawi; deep water flowing strongly.
[3] Zambezi River, near confluence with Kafue River, prior to Kariba Dam; after damming, partly natural flow from Kafue, partly subsurface discharge from Lake Kariba.
[4] Sabi River; depth varies with season, sometimes shallow.
[5] Deep water.
[6] Mare River; fast flowing mountain stream.

The annual mean temperature of surface waters appears to be somewhat higher than the annual mean air temperature, in the case of lakes, but a little lower in the case of running water in rivers. The form of the annual curve of water temperature is quite different from the mean air temperature curve, lacking the latter's peak values in October caused by the highest maximum temperatures. Instead, the trend of water temperatures is much more like that of the minimum air temperatures, with about two thirds the range, and closely in phase.

Water temperatures from Lake Malawi show that the annual range increases from about 3°C at Nkhata Bay in the northern part of the lake, to about 6°C at Fort Johnston at the south end of the lake. The seasonal curves cross in mid-September and mid-March, with Fort Johnston warmer in summer and cooler in winter than Nkhata Bay.

Radiation, sunshine and cloudiness

Rhodesia, Zambia and Malawi are well-served with sunshine recorders, from which it is possible to deduce the main variations in radiation. As regards direct measurement, however, for many years Bulawayo was the only station to have a Moll solarimeter, serving as a control station for the network of secondary radiation instruments. Bimetallic actinographs have failed to maintain their calibrations, and a network of Gunn-Bellani radiation integrators has been established over Rhodesia and the southern half of Malawi. The seasonal variation in the number of hours of sunshine broadly follows that of radiation, but with some differences. When expressed as a percentage of the maximum possible, all stations show a maximum about July and a minimum in January or February, ranging from about 85–90% to 30–35% in Zambia, and 80–85% to 40–45% in Rhodesia.

When expressed as hours per day this simplicity is reduced and some stations show an annual curve with one maximum and one minimum, while others show two maxima and two minima. The number of hours of sunshine per day is reduced in winter by the fewer hours of daylight, and six months later by the great cloudiness, giving what is effectively a semi-annual component of variation. Harmonic analysis applied to the monthly means shows that the amplitude of the annual component changes from 3.5 h in the extreme northwest of Zambia to 0.5 h in the extreme southeast of Rhodesia, and that the amplitude of the semi-annual component is about 70% of the annual component from central Malawi to the Limpopo Valley, varying between 1–2 and 0.2 h. As regards phase angle, most stations in Zambia and Rhodesia have their maximum about mid-July for the annual component, to mid or late August in Malawi. In the case of the semi-annual component the maximum changes from about 30th October in the extreme north of Zambia and Malawi, to about 30th August in the extreme south of Rhodesia. This tends to delay the maximum until as late as September or October in Malawi. Although the changes from station to station are quite systematic, the fit between the computed and observed curves is not always very close.

In Rhodesia even the rainy season months average at least 5 h/day of sunshine, compared with Zambia where some stations receive less than 4 h/day. Fig.7 shows the number of months averaging less than 5 h/day: the gradient is very steep between Kabwe and Solwezi, but not quite so sharply defined in the northeast.

It is significant that the favoured position of the Congo air boundary during the rainy season lies approximately Mongu–Mankoya–Kabwe–Mpika–Mbala with moist and highly unstable Congo air to the northwest of this boundary.

Daily totals of sunshine hours have a *J*-distribution in the dry-season months, the peak occurring at maximum possible on about 20% of occasions in Malawi, about 40% for most plateau stations, but as high as 60% at Livingstone and other stations protected from orographic cloud formation. In general, sunshine totals of less than 4 h/day account for well under 10% of occasions. In January the position is quite different, and apart from the arid Beitbridge area which still shows a *J*-distribution peaking just below the maximum possible, nearly all stations show little variation of frequency with different durations. Lilongwe, close to the favoured position of the I.T.C.Z., is an exception and has its highest frequencies (15%) for overcast and lowest frequencies (under 5%) for cloudless conditions.

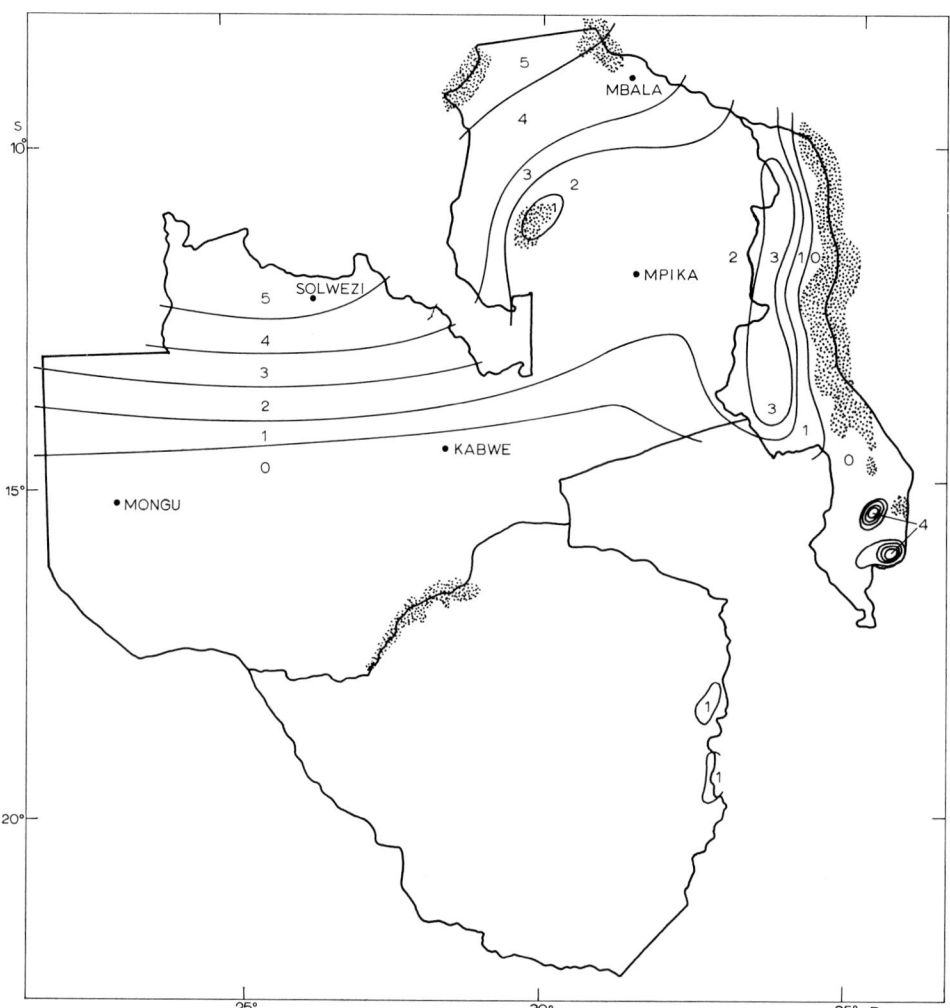

Fig.7. Number of months per year averaging less than 5.0 h sunshine per day: Malawi, Rhodesia. Zambia.

The seasonal migration of the sun, from just south of Rhodesia at the summer solstice, to far north of Zambia at the winter solstice, results in the usual twice-annual reversal of gradient of solar radiation. In most months the isopleths run more or less east–west, except over Malawi, where the comparative absence of convective clouds over the lake during the day ensures an enhanced receipt of insolation over the shores and immediate vicinity. However, this is more than compensated for by high cloudiness over the escarpments west of the lake.

Fig.8 shows the seasonal variation of radiation in the vicinity of 30°E, as deduced from recorded sunshine, using the well-known Ångström formula. The two months of transition when the gradient reverses from north to south, or from south to north, are October and April. October, shortly before the coming of the rains, and still relatively cloud-free, shows the highest monthly mean values. The onset of the rains in November results in a rapid decrease in insolation, and in the middle of the rainy season, insolation in Zambia is almost as low as that in Rhodesia in winter. This gives rise to the paradox

430

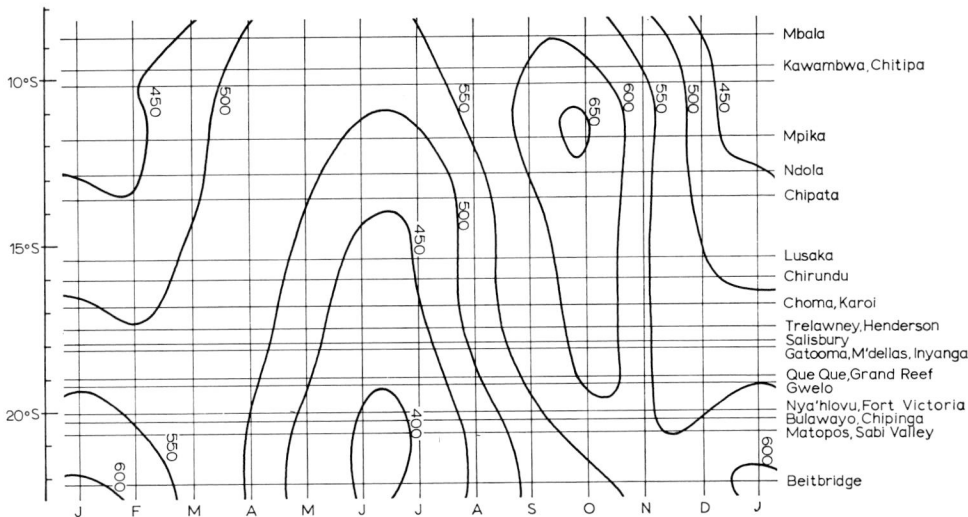

Fig.8. Seasonal variation of radiation between 27° and 33°E (Ly/day).

that Mbala has its lowest mean maximum temperatures in January, technically mid-summer.

As is to be expected from the tropical location, and the altitude above sea level, the intensity of insolation can be high, much higher than is apparent from the air temperature levels. When out of doors, being in the shade or in the sun may make a considerable difference to personal comfort, and to the degree of clothing required. Maximum daily and hourly values so far recorded at Bulawayo are shown in Table IX. Such high values occur during the rainy season when for some reason there is little cloud. One feature of the calendar is worth mentioning in this context, the seasonal smoke haze which results from extensive veld-burning activities in many countries of tropical Africa. The haze becomes noticeable about June or July, and is usually at its worst in September or October. This persistent haze reduces radiation considerably, though the greenhouse effect of the haze itself contributes to a feeling of oppression. When winds change from northeast to southeast, ahead of incoming maritime air, the haze thickens noticeably, and sometimes visibility may be reduced to 5 km or less at ground level. At one time

TABLE IX

MAXIMUM VALUES OF RADIATION AT BULAWAYO* (cal./cm²)

Jan.	Feb.	Mar.	Apr.	May	June	July	Aug.	Sept.	Oct.	Nov.	Dec.	Year
Maximum hourly values:												
102	99	96	85	79	70	74	83	91	95	99	101	102
114	102	100	89	84	74	77	86	94	101	103	108	114
Maximum daily values:												
778	760	702	604	531	472	501	587	675	725	765	780	780
813	795	730	634	556	488	527	631	701	782	801	812	813

* Based on 11 years records, January 1956–December 1967, from a Moll solarimeter. First lines: average of the yearly extreme values; second lines: absolute of the yearly extreme values.

cases were reported of haze being so dense that sunshine could not burn a Campbell–Stokes sunshine card, or again of having thunder clouds overhead without being able to distinguish them through the haze. However, such density of haze is seldom observed nowadays. Thick haze, as described above, is at its worst in the early morning, with visibility improving during the day as convection lifts and distributes the haze particles to higher layers of the atmosphere. Marked improvement in visibility occurs with each invasion of fresh maritime air from the southeast.

Surface winds

Throughout the winter months the airflow over Zambia, Malawi and Rhodesia is easterly, an off-shoot of the Indian Ocean southeast trades. With the southward migration of the sun, winds tend to back towards northeast, being most consistently northeast in October. Thereafter, winds become more variable, tending to veer again in Rhodesia and southern Malawi, and to back still further in the north and west of Zambia. In January some of the stations in Zambia show northwest as the predominant direction. The southern half of Rhodesia reverts to its usual east-southeast for the wet season. The end of the rainy season is marked by a strengthening of the southeast winds, either by higher speeds or a direction nearer south than at any other time of the year, with a return to the east-southeast to east-northeast winds in May or June.

Local modifications to this general pattern are common. Thus Blantyre Airport, which is situated on the northwest slopes of the Shire highlands, tends to have the winds deflected to south or southwest when other places are blowing from the southeast; Salisbury and Karoi, north of the main watershed in Rhodesia, have a prevailing northeast wind in contrast to the east-southeast prevailing wind over most of Rhodesia; Lusaka, Kafue Flats, and Mongu have much higher speeds in easterly winds than most places; places like Mbala, Mongu (in the wet season), and Kariba have diurnal variations of wind direction and speed resulting from their proximity to Lake Tanganyika, Barotse flood plains, and Lake Kariba respectively. Even more generally, many places in valleys or locally low-lying ground tend to have little or no wind at night.

Two patterns of diurnal variations in wind speed have been recognised. The more general one shows a minimum speed about dawn, speeds rising to a maximum about 10h00 or 11h00, and then moderating as winds become more variable in the afternoon. There is often a sunset lull, and then a fairly light wind throughout the night. The variation of windspeed during the day can be explained in terms of the profile of upper wind speeds: the profile usually has a pronounced maximum speed at about 1,000 m above ground, and as diurnal heating and mixing of the air takes place, so the momentum is brought down and shared by the surface wind, causing a rise in speeds. As air from yet higher levels is brought to the surface, so speeds drop off again.

The second main pattern in diurnal variation of speeds starts off similarly, but reaches its maximum speed at about 15h00. All places with this pattern are in the southeast and east of Rhodesia and Malawi, where the prevailing wind direction is southeast, the same as the upper wind directions. In part the continued freshening appears to be due to the constancy of upper wind directions, but the major cause appears to be the daytime steepening of the barometric gradients, here directed from southeast to northwest. This

TABLE X

DIURNAL VARIATION OF SURFACE WIND, AT BULAWAYO, 1932–1946

S.A. Standard Time	January		April		July		October	
	dir.*	speed (knots)	dir.	speed (knots)	dir.	speed (knots)	dir.	speed (knots)
Midnight	116	5.8	124	6.4	128	8.0	117	8.0
01h00	117	5.8	121	6.3	129	8.0	116	7.7
02h00	116	5.8	121	6.1	129	7.9	115	7.4
03h00	118	5.7	121	6.0	129	7.9	115	7.1
04h00	118	5.8	121	5.8	127	7.7	115	6.9
05h00	115	5.6	119	5.6	126	7.6	112	6.6
06h00	116	5.6	118	5.4	125	7.5	108	6.4
07h00	99	7.2	110	5.6	123	7.1	89	8.3
08h00	91	8.3	98	7.5	108	8.7	75	9.7
09h00	85	8.4	92	8.1	99	9.8	70	9.7
10h00	83	8.3	90	7.8	94	9.5	68	9.1
11h00	89	8.0	91	7.4	97	8.9	76	8.6
12h00	92	7.8	96	7.0	101	8.6	82	8.3
13h00	100	7.9	104	7.0	104	8.3	93	8.3
14h00	106	8.0	110	7.0	106	8.3	100	8.3
15h00	114	8.2	117	7.2	111	8.4	105	8.7
16h00	117	8.3	121	7.0	109	8.3	109	8.9
17h00	116	8.0	124	6.0	116	7.1	112	8.7
18h00	115	6.9	129	5.5	126	6.7	115	7.9
19h00	121	6.0	133	6.1	131	7.3	115	7.9
20h00	121	6.3	131	6.5	129	7.5	118	8.3
21h00	117	6.1	129	6.6	131	7.8	114	8.3
22h00	118	6.0	126	6.5	129	7.8	116	8.2
23h00	116	6.0	126	6.5	129	7.9	119	8.2
Mean	109	6.9	117	6.6	118	7.5	103	8.1

* Directions in degrees from true north.

derives from unequal depths of air being heated during the day over low and high ground so that pressure falls most over high ground, and the gradients are steepened on the coastal side, and weakened further inland. Tables X and XI give data from representative stations.

A feature of this part of Central Africa is the persistence of the same barometric distribution day after day. Pressure may rise and fall, but the orientation and configuration of the isobars (or more strictly, the 850-mbar geopotentials which appear on the standard synoptic charts) vary comparatively little, the pressure gradient being directed in all areas from southeast to northwest for most of the winter season, and similarly over most of Rhodesia even during the rains. In the rainy season, the pattern is more complex, and quasi-stationary troughs and low-pressure areas take up favoured positions. It is observed that winds blow across the isobars at an angle of about 40°, from high to low pressure. When pressure is rising rapidly, the isallobaric component takes charge and

TABLE XI

DIURNAL VARIATION OF SURFACE WIND AT SALISBURY, 1936–1946

S.A. Standard Time	January		April		July		October	
	dir.*	speed (knots)	dir.	speed (knots)	dir.	speed (knots)	dir.	speed (knots)
Midnight	62	4.3	65	5.4	69	6.3	58	7.0
01h00	60	4.1	62	5.0	73	6.2	58	6.9
02h00	60	3.9	64	4.7	73	6.1	57	6.8
03h00	60	4.0	64	4.7	74	5.9	57	6.6
04h00	60	3.9	62	4.6	74	5.8	54	6.6
05h00	60	3.9	60	4.6	74	5.9	54	6.4
06h00	55	4.9	57	4.9	74	6.0	53	7.5
07h00	52	6.5	60	6.3	79	6.6	52	9.8
08h00	52	7.3	62	7.5	84	8.5	51	11.1
09h00	47	7.2	63	7.1	90	8.8	48	10.8
10h00	44	6.9	70	6.5	97	8.2	48	9.7
11h00	38	6.4	80	6.0	103	7.5	51	8.5
12h00	38	6.4	90	5.6	100	6.9	57	7.5
13h00	45	6.0	90	5.1	100	6.6	61	7.1
14h00	60	5.9	86	4.8	99	6.1	68	6.7
15h00	78	6.0	85	4.6	96	5.8	67	6.6
16h00	94	5.6	83	4.3	93	5.7	67	6.7
17h00	96	5.2	87	4.1	89	5.7	68	6.7
18h00	91	4.7	76	4.5	81	6.1	63	6.5
19h00	77	4.6	76	5.1	77	6.4	60	6.9
20h00	74	4.3	73	5.2	75	6.4	59	7.2
21h00	70	4.3	71	5.1	72	6.3	61	7.2
22h00	69	4.5	69	5.2	70	6.3	60	7.2
23h00	63	4.6	67	5.3	68	6.3	60	7.2
Mean	60	5.2	69	5.3	82	6.5	57	7.5

* Directions in degrees from true north.

winds may cross the isobars even more sharply. In contrast, when a trough or low pressure area is involved, the winds tend to blow more closely along the isobars.

Wind speeds are, on the whole, comparatively light. Few places average as much as 10 knots over a period as long as a month. On hourly values, wind speeds of over 20 knots are infrequent, and most of these are from the southeast, during periods of rapidly rising pressure. On the other hand, squalls from thunderstorms can be severe, and speeds of over 50 knots are likely sometime during the year.

The squalls vary widely, from the case of the 50-knot squall rising from near-calm in a few minutes and equally suddenly returning to calm, to cases where squalls may last for half an hour or longer with speeds of over 30 knots for much of this period. Table XII gives mean values and extreme values of surface winds.

In common with other mountainous areas, disturbed wind flow must be expected in the vicinity of mountains during periods of strong wind flow. However, records of such

TABLE XII

SURFACE WIND MAXIMUM GUST VALUES* (knots)

	Jan.	Feb.	Mar.	Apr.	May	June	July	Aug.	Sept.	Oct.	Nov.	Dec.	Year	Period
Malawi:														
Blantyre	46	44	44	47	49	44	43	44	49	63	50	65	65	1945/61
Lilongwe	40	39	45	37	38	32	33	36	39	41	46	47	47	1952/61
Rhodesia:														
Bulawayo	55	44	47	41	56	43	46	46	52	49	56	48	56	1936/61
Chipinga	54	50	36	47	34	37	36	35	48	51	52	43	54	1953/61
Fort Victoria	46	39	44	37	45	42	37	38	46	46	47	49	49	1940/61
Gwelo	58	54	43	47	38	43	37	42	47	49	48	49	58	1941/61
Salisbury	45	49	46	43	39	38	37	41	45	52	69	54	69	1936/61
Umtali Airport	63	43	37	53	37	31	33	35	45	64	48	52	63	1948/61
Zambia:														
Kasama	49	67	50	48	32	41	35	37	37	37	51	62	67	1939/61
Livingstone	48	51	38	38	35	32	35	35	40	45	51	52	52	1940/61
Lusaka	50	53	38	52	41	40	43	44	45	61	58	47	61	1938/61
Mongu	52	43	46	38	34	38	36	40	45	51	70	43	70	1957/61
Ndola	45	58	47	40	33	36	39	42	38	44	54	55	58	1943/61
Maxima	63	67	50	53	56	44	46	46	52	64	70	65	70	

* Data from Dines anemographs.

events are largely lacking, apart from very strong southeast winds recorded at Blantyre Airport at night preceding the onset of a chiperoni, believed to be a standing wave; and subsident northwest winds along the Eastern Border mountains of Rhodesia when pressure is falling, though these are generally light.

South Angolan Plateau

Much of the southern half of the Portuguese province of Angola lies above the 1,000-m contour. In view of this the high temperatures of the tropical regions are modified and reduced sufficiently to place the area in the temperate type (Köppen *C*) of climate. Because this occurs the area is considered in the same context as the Rhodesia, Malawi and Zambia region.

The Angolan region extends from about 11° to 18°S and is bordered on the west by the semi-arid belt (cf. Chapter 15) or a thin strip on the wetter slopes, a Köppen *A* climate, before it becomes steppe type country (Fig.9).

Angola covers an area of about 1.25 million km² and has a population of nearly 5 million people. Luanda, on the coast, is the capital and has a population of almost 250,000. There are a number of large towns on the plateau, the main one being Nova Lisboa, Angola's second most populous city. Important exports include coffee (from the north), diamonds (northeast) and sisal (Ganda district of the plateau). The highland area raises mainly corn and beans for local consumption.

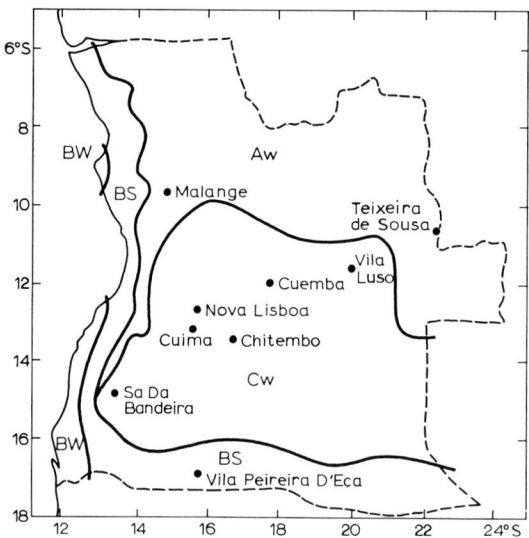

Fig.9. Angola. Station location and Köppen classification zonation.

The climate of the area is greatly influenced by the altitude and by the trajectory of the moist air masses stemming from the South Atlantic high. During the winter period (May–September) there is no continuing flow of maritime air over the plateau, skies are clear and rainfall is negligible. In summer, however, the region is located near the convergence zone between the air masses from the Indian Ocean and the South Atlantic so that rainfall, associated with topography, convection and convergence, is general.

Radiation measurements within the area are available only from Vila Luso and from Malange on the northwestern edge. Both stations have annual mean values of global radiation of about 440 cal./cm² day but, due to the short period of records at present, it is difficult to analyse the monthly variation.

Sunshine measurements are made at only a few stations on the plateau. In the central region the mean annual number of hours is about 2,300 but, in the drier areas, this increases to about 2,700 h. The sunniest months are in the winter (May–September) when mean values as high as 9 h/day are recorded. The summer months, the period of overhead sun, show a very different picture for the heavy cloud results in averages of about 4–5 h/day.

Cloud amounts show much the same pattern, inversely, as the sunshine hours. During the winter an average of only 1–2 oktas is general. In the summer this value increases to 5–6 oktas (Table XIII).

Temperatures in such a region are, naturally, very dependent upon latitude and elevation, with a decrease of about 0.7°C/100 m. The mean annual maximum temperature at about 1,700 m averages approximately 26°C, while minima are 12°C. In the more arid southern portion these averages can be increased by as much as 4°C. The hottest month is either September or October with the coldest being June or July. The annual range is quite small, being about 5°C in the north and 9°C in the south.

Maximum temperatures rarely exceed 35°C, except at elevations below 1,400 m, and temperatures above 40°C are rare at any station. Minimum temperatures below zero have been recorded from most areas but they are not common. Chitembo is the coldest

TABLE XIII

MEAN MONTHLY CLOUDINESS (oktas)

Station	Jan.	Feb.	Mar.	Apr.	May	June	July	Aug.	Sept.	Oct.	Nov.	Dec.	Year
Chitembo	5	5	5	3	2	1	1	2	2	3	4	5	3
Cuemba	6	6	6	4	2	1	1	2	3	5	6	6	4
Cuima	5	5	5	3	1	0	0	1	2	3	5	5	3
Nova Lisboa	6	6	6	5	2	1	1	1	3	5	6	6	4
Sa da Bandeira	6	6	6	4	1	1	1	1	2	4	5	5	4
Teixeira de Sousa	5	5	4	3	2	1	1	1	2	2	4	5	3
Vila Luso	6	6	6	4	1	0	0	1	2	4	6	6	3

station (1,500 m) with an average of five days per year with temperatures below zero; it also had an absolute minimum reading of $-8°C$ in July.

The average rainfall on the plateau is approximately 1,100 mm/year, increasing towards the west and the north until the tropical zone is reached. The limits range from about 700 mm to 1,500 mm. In all cases October–April is the rainy season but the wettest month varies between December and March, although the variation among monthly means in this period is usually small. A weak minimum often occurs in January as the upper-air trough weakens. The winter (May–September) is almost dry, the five months contributing about 2–3% of the annual total. The percentage decreases as the border with Southwest Africa is approached. Daily falls in excess of 100 mm are very rare, although Vila Pereira d'Eca has recorded 206 mm on one day in March.

Relative humidity (measured at 09h00) shows a distinct reduction from north to south, not only on the annual basis but also monthly. The annual values range from 45 to about 70% while monthly means vary from 25 to 80%. Relative humidity measured at this time of day is not very enlightening as it is a period of rapid change in the parameter. However, the over-all pattern is likely to be correct. In the afternoon during the winter monthly values are around 20% or lower.

Evaporation, measured using Piche evaporimeters exposed in an instrument shelter, varies from about 1,600 to 2,400 mm/year but it is likely that higher values are reached in the extreme south. Mean monthly measurements of 100–150 mm occur during the summer with values around 200 mm, even to more than 300 mm, being general in winter.

Wind speed averages about 3–6 km/h in all months of the year with easterlies in effect all the year in the southern section but only from April to September in the north where westerlies are dominant in December–February. The percentage of calms is high, about 20% in all months.

Conclusion

The main elements of the climate have been discussed in some detail in the preceding pages. However, climate as a whole depends on the interrelationships of the constituent elements, and it is therefore necessary to take an over-all view of the climates of Malawi, Rhodesia, and Zambia. All have the same division into the rainy season and the dry season, yet the factors of altitude, latitude, and distance from the sea introduce many subtle variations.

In layman's language, four main climatic types are easily distinguished. First, the mountain climates, for the high plateaus in the centre and north of Malawi, and the Eastern Border mountains of Rhodesia. Altitude gives lower temperature levels, greater cloudiness and rainfall. Second, there are the lake climates, with generally higher humidity, and distinctive patterns of cloudiness, rainfall and wind. The main lake areas are Tanganyika, Mweru, Bangweulu, Kariba, and above all, Lake Malawi which is bigger than all the others put together and has correspondingly greater weather contrasts. The lakes tend to be free of convective cloud during the day, with increased cloudiness along the escarpments, and in the case of Lake Malawi at least to have the maximum incidence of rain along the lake shore during the night and early morning. Lake and land breezes are common. Third, there are the major river valleys which tend to be hot and relatively dry. Here the Luangwa, the Zambezi Valley between Livingstone and Lake Kariba, and

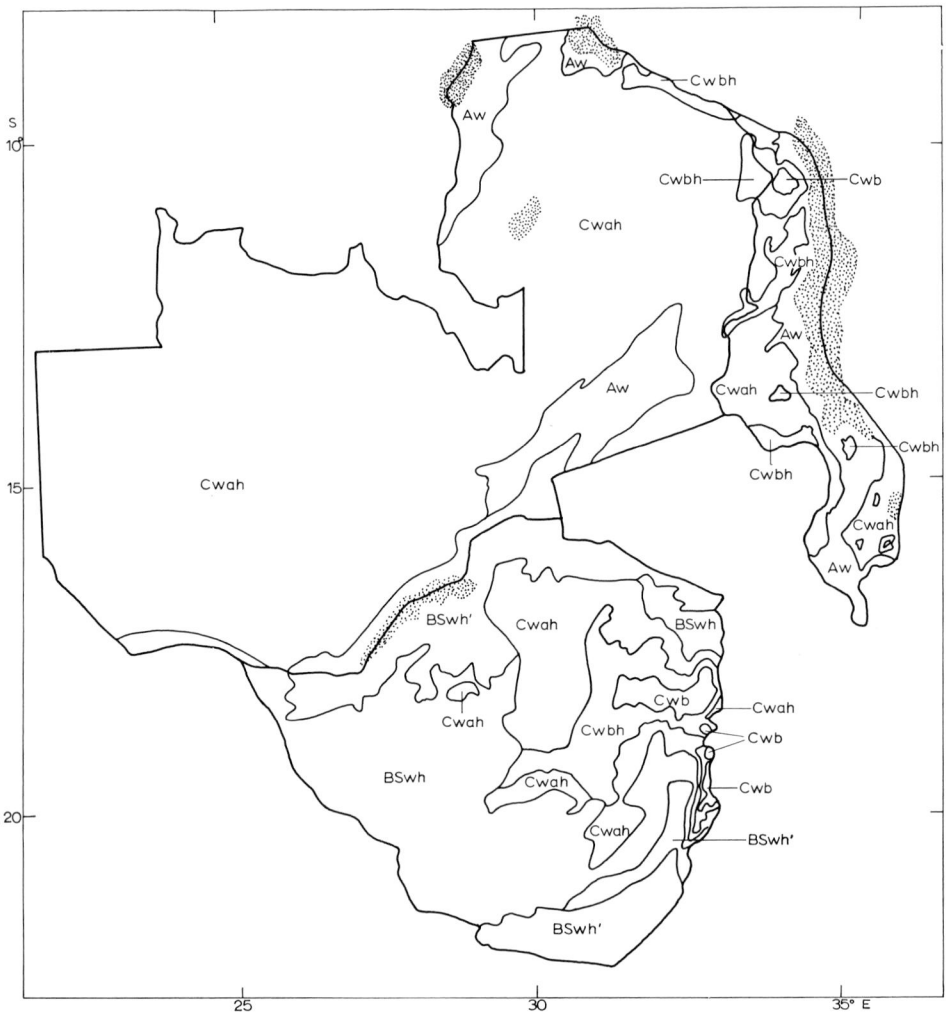

Fig.10. The climates of Malawi, Rhodesia and Zambia according to the Köppen classification.

downstream of Lake Kariba, and the Limpopo–Sabi lowveld are those most affected. However, the Rhodesian lowveld in the southeast does enjoy the periodic cool spells of invading maritime air which give guti weather over higher ground. Fourth in this list of simplified climates are the general plateau climates of Rhodesia and Zambia, applicable above about 1,000 m elevation. These enjoy a mild to warm summer, moderate to heavy rainfall, and a cool winter. Again, some regional differences are evident: rainfall is much heavier north of the line Mongu–Kabwe–Chipata; frost is more frequent in the south-western portions of this climatic division; and there is the periodic guti weather over the southeastern half of Rhodesia giving cool cloudy spells. Because of the comparative lack of relief over the greater part of Zambia, the climate is more nearly uniform there than elsewhere, and Malawi, with its major lake and rugged topography, has the most variable weather conditions.

If a more technical climatic classification is required, then there is no doubt that the Köppen classification provides a realistic grouping of climates which adequately matches the observed natural regions. Fig.10 shows this classification applied to Malawi, Rhodesia and Zambia. Only one modification to the standard symbology has been adopted, the use of *h'* to indicate an annual mean temperature greater than 22°C, in addition to the usual *h* denoting an annual mean temperature greater than 18°C. The greater part of Zambia, the plateau area of Malawi, and most of the plateau area of Rhodesia are *Cwh* zones, mainly *Cwah* with the mean temperature of the warmest month greater than 22°C, and much smaller areas *Cwbh*, with the mean temperature of the warmest month below 22°C. *Aw* climates are found in the extreme north of Zambia and along the shores of Lake Malawi, and the Luangwa Valley; but the remaining low-altitude areas are all *B* climates showing a deficiency of rainfall. Small blocks of *Cwb* are found in the mountains of the Eastern Border of Rhodesia, and the various highlands areas of Malawi.

The *Cw* delineations correspond quite closely with those areas which have been found suitable for agricultural production, tending to intensive development in the *Cwb* areas, whereas the *B* areas in general are given over to cattle ranching. However, where water can be provided from storage facilities, these areas have proved equally capable of intensive agricultural production.

Malawi, Rhodesia and Zambia

TABLE XIV

CLIMATIC TABLE FOR KARONGA, MALAWI
Latitude 9°56'S, longitude 33°56'E, elevation 482 m

Month	Mean sta. press. (mbar)	Temperature (°C) mean max.	mean min.	extreme max.	extreme min.	Humidity dew point (°C)	relative (%)	Precipitation mean (mm)	max. (mm)	min. (mm)	days ≥1 mm	max. 24 h (mm)	Wind av. speed (m/sec)	preval. direct.	calm (%)	Mean daily cloudiness (oktas)	Average number thunderstorms
Jan.	957	30	22	35	18	21.4	81	183	432	38	12	103	1.3	E	11	6	26
Feb.	957	30	22	34	18	21.5	83	163	345	50	13	132	1.3	ENE	12	6	25
Mar.	957	29	21	34	18	21.8	85	316	599	119	18	137	1.3	ESE	14	6	25
Apr.	959	29	21	32	17	21.4	87	187	475	44	12	111	2.2	SE	6	5	17
May	961	28	19	32	14	19.3	78	35	132	—	5	48	2.3	SE	5	4	3
June	963	27	16	31	11	16.6	71	6	82	—	1	17	2.0	SE	6	5	—
July	963	27	15	30	11	15.4	69	1	4	—	—	3	2.5	SE	4	3	—
Aug.	963	28	16	32	11	16.3	69	2	14	—	—	13	2.2	SE	8	2	—
Sept.	961	30	17	34	12	17.1	65	1	11	—	—	11	2.2	ESE	5	2	—
Oct.	959	32	19	37	15	18.1	60	4	57	—	—	45	2.7	ESE	5	3	1
Nov.	957	33	21	37	17	19.8	64	39	210	—	3	131	2.8	ESE	7	5	9
Dec.	957	31	22	36	19	21.0	76	144	421	31	12	116	1.6	ESE	7	6	25
Annual	960	29	19	37	11	19.1	74	1,081	1,826	649	76	137	2.0	ESE	7	5	131
Rec. (yrs.)	12	20	20	20	20	10	10	30	30	30	30	30	6	6	6	6	9

440

TABLE XV

CLIMATIC TABLE FOR KASAMA, ZAMBIA

Latitude 10°13'S, longitude 31°08'E, elevation 1,382 m

Month	Mean sta. press. (mbar)	Temperature (°C) mean max.	mean min.	extreme max.	extreme min.	Humidity dew point (°C)	relative (%)	Precipitation mean (mm)	max. (mm)	min. (mm)	days ≥1 mm	max. 24 h (mm)	Wind av. speed (m/sec)	preval. direct.	calm (%)	Mean daily cloudiness (oktas)	Average sunshine (h/day)	evap. (mm)	thunder storms
Jan.	864	26	16	31	14	16.8	81	267	429	142	21	103	1.7	NNW	9	7	4.1	142	25
Feb.	864	26	16	30	13	17.0	82	251	378	97	19	81	1.6	NNW	7	7	4.2	121	24
Mar.	864	26	16	30	13	17.1	80	259	354	122	18	93	1.6	ENE	7	6	5.4	139	23
Apr.	865	26	16	29	11	16.2	76	69	181	3	7	90	2.1	E	2	5	7.8	150	10
May	866	26	13	29	7	13.3	66	8	81	—	1	27	2.6	ESE	1	3	9.1	157	1
June	867	24	10	28	4	10.1	60	—	—	—	—	1	2.8	ESE	1	2	9.7	152	—
July	867	25	10	29	4	8.8	55	—	1	—	—	—	3.0	ESE	1	2	10.2	168	—
Aug.	866	28	11	33	3	9.1	48	1	12	—	—	12	3.2	ESE	1	2	10.0	207	—
Sept.	865	30	14	34	6	10.0	43	1	7	—	—	7	3.4	ESE	—	2	9.5	239	1
Oct.	864	31	16	35	12	11.4	41	17	78	—	2	37	2.8	E	1	4	8.5	259	5
Nov.	864	29	17	35	13	14.9	60	135	282	13	13	81	2.0	ENE	4	6	7.3	173	19
Dec.	864	27	16	33	14	16.8	78	237	402	69	19	87	1.6	NNE	8	7	5.4	138	26
Annual	865	27	14	35	3	13.4	64	1,245	1,574	830	100	103	2.4	ENE	3	5	7.6	2,045	134
Rec. (yrs.)	25	25	25	25	25	10	10	30	30	30	30	30	21	17	3	4	22	5	12

TABLE XVI

CLIMATIC TABLE FOR MWINILUNGA, ZAMBIA
Latitude 11°45'S, longitude 24°26'E, elevation 1,361 m

Month	Mean sta. press. (mbar)	Temperature (°C) mean max.	mean min.	extreme max.	extreme min.	Humidity dew point (°C)	rela- tive (%)	Precipitation mean (mm)	max. (mm)	min. (mm)	days ≥1 mm	max. 24 h (mm)	Wind av. speed (m/sec)	preval. direct.	calm (%)	Mean daily cloud- iness (oktas)	Average sun- shine (h/day)	thunder- storms (days)
Jan.	864	26	16	31	12	17.1	84	225	372	116	20	68	1.3	NW	39	7	4.0	24
Feb.	864	26	16	31	12	17.1	85	221	366	102	19	85	1.2			6	3.9	22
Mar.	865	26	16	31	11	17.1	82	227	411	121	19	77	1.1			6	4.3	22
Apr.	866	27	15	31	8	15.9	77	95	347	7	9	59	1.2	ENE	13	4	7.7	15
May	867	27	10	31	2	12.1	66	8	77	—	1	52	1.2			2	9.6	2
June	868	25	6	29	—1	8.1	59	1	17	—	—	16	1.3			1	9.4	—
July	868	26	6	30	0	6.6	53	—	1	—	—	1	1.8	ESE	24	1	9.6	—
Aug.	867	28	9	33	—1	7.6	46	1	8	—	—	6	1.7			2	9.4	1
Sept.	866	31	13	35	4	10.7	45	15	75	—	2	30	1.5	NE		3	8.4	4
Oct.	865	30	15	34	8	14.9	60	92	245	9	9	100	1.5		8	5	7.2	16
Nov.	865	27	16	33	11	16.8	79	196	385	79	18	68	1.2			7	4.5	24
Dec.	865	26	16	32	12	17.2	84	261	414	150	23	99	1.3			7	4.1	25
Annual	866	27	13	35	—1	13.4	68	1,342	1,717	1,056	120	100	1.4			4	6.8	155
Rec. (yrs.)	25	25	25	25	25	10	10	30	30	30	30	30	5	5	5	5	10	10

TABLE XVII

CLIMATIC TABLE FOR MZIMBA, MALAWI
Latitude 11°53'S, longitude 33°37'E, elevation 1,349 m

Month	Mean sta. press. (mbar)	Temperature (°C)				Humidity		Precipitation					Wind			Mean daily cloud-iness (oktas)	Average		thunder-storms (days)
		mean		extreme		dew point (°C)	rela-tive (%)	mean (mm)	max. (mm)	min. (mm)	days ≥1 mm	max. 24 h (mm)	av. speed (m/sec)	preval. direct.	calm (%)		sun-shine (h/day)	
		max.	min.	max.	min.													
Jan.	867	25	16	30	13	17.0	82	228	498	79	15	196	2.0	ENE	25	7	4.3	23
Feb.	867	25	16	29	12	16.9	84	194	386	78	12	63	1.7	WNW	27	7	4.1	19
Mar.	867	25	16	29	11	16.8	82	173	342	21	11	79	2.2	ESE	15	7	5.2	19
Apr.	868	25	15	29	10	15.9	80	41	148	—	3	81	3.7	ESE	3	5	7.4	7
May	870	24	13	30	6	13.5	73	2	15	—	—	8	4.0	ESE	1	4	8.6	2
June	871	23	11	30	2	11.4	72	1	21	—	—	20	4.1	ESE	1	3	8.7	—
July	872	22	10	28	2	10.2	69	1	8	—	—	8	4.3	ESE	1	3	9.0	—
Aug.	871	23	11	30	1	10.4	65	1	6	—	—	4	4.8	ESE	1	3	9.4	—
Sept.	870	26	14	32	4	11.4	59	2	17	—	—	9	5.2	ESE	1	3	9.6	2
Oct.	868	28	17	33	8	12.7	53	5	38	—	—	29	5.1	E	2	3	10.2	2
Nov.	867	28	17	33	13	15.1	61	58	139	—	4	70	3.9	E	5	6	8.5	9
Dec.	867	26	17	32	11	16.4	76	163	279	57	11	117	2.4	E	19	7	5.5	22
Annual	869	25	14	33	1	14.0	71	869	1,309	622	56	196	3.6	ESE	8	5	7.5	103
Rec. (yrs.)	15	20	20	20	20	10	10	30	30	30	30	29	5	5	5	6	14	12

TABLE XVIII

CLIMATIC TABLE FOR NOVA LISBOA, ANGOLA
Latitude 12°48'S, longitude 15°45'E, elevation 1,700 m

Month	Mean sta. press. (mbar)	Temperature (°C)				Relative humid. (%)		Precipitation					Wind			Average		
		mean		extreme		15h00	21h00	mean (mm)	max. (mm)	min. (mm)	days ≥1 mm	max. 24 h (mm)	av. speed (km/h)	preval. direct.	calm (%)	cloud-iness* (oktas)	sun-shine (h)	evap. (mm)
		max.	min.	max.	min.													
Jan.	829	25	14	31	9	61	85	209	422	58	16	86	7	W	14	6	141	93
Feb.	830	25	14	31	8	58	83	179	373	24	14	79	7	W	13	6	139	94
Mar.	830	25	15	30	10	63	87	231	500	88	17	89	6	V	15	6	142	83
Apr.	831	25	14	29	7	54	81	144	422	50	10	86	6	E	19	5	171	97
May	832	26	11	29	5	37	66	16	113	0	2	56	6	E	15	2	243	154
June	833	25	8	28	2	29	53	0	0	0	0	0	6	E	16	1	269	173
July	833	25	8	29	2	24	45	0	1	0	0	1	6	E	16	1	268	208
Aug.	832	27	10	31	5	22	39	1	9	0	0	6	7	E	13	1	256	256
Sept.	831	29	13	32	8	30	51	19	71	0	3	18	8	E	14	3	201	228
Oct.	831	27	14	32	11	49	74	124	216	35	13	53	8	N	12	5	165	157
Nov.	831	25	14	31	8	63	86	231	331	82	18	70	7	N	15	6	134	98
Dec.	830	25	15	30	9	62	86	233	477	79	17	76	7	N	16	6	140	99
Annual	831	26	12	32	2	46	70	1,386	2,350	962	110	89	7	—	15	4	2,268	1,740
Rec. (yrs.)									20	20								

* Mean of 09h00, 15h00 and 21h00.

TABLE XIX

CLIMATIC TABLE FOR NKHOTAKOTA, MALAWI

Latitude 12°55'S, longitude 34°17'E, elevation 500 m

Month	Temperature (°C)				Humidity		Precipitation					Mean daily cloud-iness (oktas)	Average number thunder-storms
	mean		extreme		dew-point (°C)	rela-tive (%)	mean (mm)	max. (mm)	min. (mm)	days >1 mm	max. 24 h (mm)		
	max.	min.	max.	min.									
Jan.	28	21	33	18	21.6	83	287	664	52	16	146	6	25
Feb.	28	21	32	18	21.4	84	308	840	101	15	570	6	23
Mar.	28	21	33	17	21.2	81	371	836	165	15	216	5	19
Apr.	28	20	32	15	20.3	78	132	310	8	9	135	4	10
May	27	18	31	13	17.4	73	35	185	—	3	127	3	1
June	26	16	29	11	14.8	70	11	126	—	1	37	3	—
July	25	15	29	10	12.2	65	6	51	—	1	26	3	—
Aug.	27	16	32	9	14.4	64	2	23	—	1	21	2	—
Sept.	29	18	34	12	16.3	62	3	25	—	—	19	2	—
Oct.	32	21	36	17	18.1	57	5	43	—	1	25	2	2
Nov.	32	22	37	18	19.8	61	58	291	—	3	108	5	9
Dec.	30	22	36	18	21.4	75	224	427	85	12	147	6	26
Annual	28	19	37	9	18.2	71	1,442	2,519	927	77	570	4	115
Rec. (yrs.)	20	20	20	20	10	10	30	30	30	30	30	6	5

TABLE XX

CLIMATIC TABLE FOR NDOLA, ZAMBIA
Latitude 13°00′S, longitude 28°39′E, elevation 1,269 m

Month	Mean sta. press. (mbar)	Temperature (°C) mean max.	Temperature (°C) mean min.	Temperature (°C) extreme max.	Temperature (°C) extreme min.	Humidity dew point (°C)	Humidity relative (%)	Precipitation mean (mm)	Precipitation max. (mm)	Precipitation min. (mm)	Precipitation days ≥1 mm	Precipitation max. 24 h (mm)	Wind av. speed (m/sec)	Wind preval. direct.	Wind calm (%)	Mean daily cloudiness (oktas)	Average sunshine (h/day)	Average evap. (mm)	thunderstorms (days)
Jan.	874	26	17	32	12	17.3	80	289	527	58	20	86	1.3	NNE	29	7	4.4	109	22
Feb.	874	26	17	30	11	17.3	82	252	417	124	19	99	1.3	NNE	32	7	4.3	103	22
Mar.	875	27	16	31	10	17.1	77	184	319	57	15	77	1.3	E	29	6	5.8	166	17
Apr.	876	27	13	31	7	15.4	71	39	125	3	5	69	1.5	E	35	4	8.0	163	6
May	878	26	9	30	1	12.1	63	5	41	—	—	40	1.5	ESE	27	3	8.7	161	1
June	879	24	6	29	0	8.8	58	—	1	—	—	1	1.8	ESE	25	2	8.9	147	—
July	879	25	6	29	−2	7.6	52	—	—	—	—	—	2.3	ESE	21	1	9.3	171	—
Aug.	878	27	9	31	−1	7.7	45	1	14	—	—	14	2.6	ESE	17	1	9.5	162	—
Sept.	877	30	12	34	3	8.9	40	1	7	—	—	6	2.7	E	17	2	9.3	241	1
Oct.	876	32	15	36	9	11.2	40	19	55	—	4	30	2.6	E	19	4	8.9	245	6
Nov.	875	29	17	35	11	15.6	62	130	222	14	12	61	1.7	ENE	26	6	6.4	182	18
Dec.	875	27	17	33	12	17.1	79	249	427	108	19	106	1.3	NE	25	7	4.5	134	24
Annual	876	27	13	36	−2	13.0	62	1,169	1,621	782	94	106	1.8	E	25	4	7.3	1,984	117
Rec. (yrs.)	25	20	20	20	20	20	10	30	30	30	30	30	17	14	3	5	20	5	12

TABLE XXI

CLIMATIC TABLE FOR KASEMPA, ZAMBIA
Latitude 13°27'S, longitude 25°50'E, elevation 1,234 m

Month	Mean sta. press. (mbar)	Temperature (°C) mean max.	mean min.	extreme max.	extreme min.	Humidity dew point (°C)	rela- tive (%)	Precipitation mean (mm)	max. (mm)	min. (mm)	days ≥1 mm	max. 24 h (mm)	Wind av. speed (m/sec)	preval. direct.	calm (%)	Mean daily cloud- iness (oktas)	Average sun- shine (h/day)	thunder- storms (days)
Jan.	877	27	16	32	11	17.4	81	273	528	107	20	171	0.7	NNE	28	6	5.6	19
Feb.	877	27	16	31	11	17.4	82	223	378	104	17	133	0.7			7	4.8	19
Mar.	878	27	16	31	11	16.9	78	161	361	58	13	162	0.9			5	6.8	15
Apr.	879	27	13	31	4	15.2	72	35	126	—	3	124	1.0	E	17	3	8.6	5
May	881	26	9	31	—1	11.4	64	3	14	—	—	14	1.2			2	9.5	1
June	882	25	6	29	—1	7.7	57	—	5	—	—	5	1.3			2	9.3	—
July	882	25	6	30	—6	6.3	51	—	—	—	—	—	1.5	E	18	1	9.8	—
Aug.	881	28	8	33	—2	7.0	45	—	9	—	—	8	1.7			1	9.9	—
Sept.	880	31	12	36	2	8.7	41	3	69	—	—	33	1.7			2	9.4	1
Oct.	878	32	14	36	7	12.4	45	34	107	—	4	47	1.4	E	14	4	8.9	6
Nov.	878	28	16	36	9	16.2	69	141	266	24	13	87	1.0			6	6.5	20
Dec.	877	27	16	33	8	17.3	82	266	443	99	19	104	0.8			7	4.5	24
Annual	879	27	12	36	—6	12.8	64	1,139	1,499	853	89	171	1.2	E		4	7.8	110
Rec. (yrs.)	25	22	22	22	22	22	10	30	30	30	30	30	5	5	5	5	4	8

TABLE XXII

CLIMATIC TABLE FOR CHIPATA, ZAMBIA
Latitude 13°34′S, longitude 32°35′E, elevation 1,029 m

Month	Mean sta. press. (mbar)	Temperature (°C) mean max.	mean min.	extreme max.	extreme min.	Humidity dew point (°C)	rela- tive (%)	Precipitation mean (mm)	max. (mm)	min. (mm)	days ≥1 mm	max. 24 h (mm)	Wind av. speed (m/sec)	preval. direct.	calm (%)	Mean daily cloud- iness (oktas)	Average sun- shine (h/day)	thunder- storms (days)
Jan.	899	27	18	36	13	18.0	80	256	433	81	18	139	1.5	ESE	12	6	4.6	20
Feb.	900	27	18	33	14	18.3	83	236	410	67	16	97	1.5			7	5.1	19
Mar.	900	27	18	34	12	17.7	77	164	328	9	14	94	1.9			5	5.8	16
Apr.	902	28	17	33	11	16.3	71	45	153	—	5	70	2.2	SE	2	4	7.9	5
May	903	25	13	32	8	13.3	64	5	26	—	1	23	2.3			3	9.2	1
June	905	24	12	31	6	10.4	60	1	4	—	—	3	2.4			2	8.2	—
July	906	25	12	31	6	9.2	53	—	5	—	—	5	2.4	ESE	2	3	8.6	—
Aug.	905	26	14	34	3	9.6	47	1	25	—	—	22	2.7			2	8.6	—
Sept.	903	30	17	36	9	10.8	43	1	17	—	—	17	3.3			2	8.5	1
Oct.	901	32	20	37	13	12.6	42	9	69	—	1	43	3.3	E	1	3	8.7	3
Nov.	900	31	19	38	13	15.2	53	94	205	—	8	60	2.5			5	7.1	14
Dec.	900	28	18	35	13	17.6	74	208	379	95	16	81	1.9			6	5.2	21
Annual	902	27	16	38	3	14.1	62	1,020	1,271	702	79	139	2.3			4	7.3	100
Rec. (yrs.)	25	30	30	30	30	10	30	30	30	30	30	30	5	5	5	5	15	12

TABLE XXIII

CLIMATIC TABLE FOR LILONGWE, MALAWI

Latitude 13°58'S, longitude 33°42'E, elevation 1,134 m

Month	Mean sta. press. (mbar)	Temperature (°C) mean max.	mean min.	extreme max.	extreme min.	Humidity dew-point (°C)	rela-tive (%)	Precipitation mean (mm)	max. (mm)	min. (mm)	days ≥1 mm	max. 24 h (mm)	Wind av. speed (m/sec)	preval. direct.	calm (%)	Mean daily cloud-iness (oktas)	Average sun-shine (h/day)	radi-ation (cal./cm²)	thunder-storms (days)
Jan.	889	27	17	32	13	18.3	82	208	428	67	14	83	2.0	E	21	7	5.2	425	20
Feb.	889	27	17	31	12	18.4	85	207	379	17	12	89	1.8	SE	23	7	5.3	453	17
Mar.	890	27	16	32	9	17.9	81	132	356	30	9	77	1.9	SE	16	6	5.8	457	15
Apr.	891	27	14	30	4	16.4	77	37	115	4	4	93	2.2	SE	11	5	7.9	473	5
May	893	26	10	31	3	13.3	71	5	17	—	1	17	2.2	SE	11	4	8.2	449	1
June	895	24	8	30	−1	10.6	67	1	18	—	1	18	2.4	SE	9	3	7.7	434	—
July	895	24	6	29	−3	9.1	61	—	2	—	—	2	2.6	SE	5	3	8.0	395	—
Aug.	894	25	8	31	−2	9.5	58	2	41	—	—	24	2.9	ESE	6	3	8.5	470	—
Sept.	893	25	10	33	2	11.2	54	3	79	—	—	79	3.2	E	6	3	8.9	575	—
Oct.	891	30	15	36	9	13.1	50	5	38	—	1	21	3.2	E	8	3	9.8	562	3
Nov.	890	30	17	34	12	15.7	59	70	188	—	4	75	2.8	E	13	6	7.8	495	9
Dec.	889	28	18	34	11	17.8	76	175	290	73	12	99	2.1	E	18	6	5.5	432	19
Annual	891	32	13	36	−3	14.3	68	845	1,197	465	58	99	2.4	ESE	12	5	7.4	468	89
Rec. (yrs.)	20	20	20	20	20	10	10	30	30	30	30	30	10	10	10	6	15	6	12

TABLE XXIV

CLIMATIC TABLE FOR SA DA BANDEIRA, ANGOLA
Latitude 14°56'S, longitude 13°34'E, elevation 1,760 m

Month	Mean sta. press. (mbar)	Temperature (°C) mean max.	mean min.	extreme max.	extreme min.	Relative humid. (%) 15h00	21h00	Precipitation mean (mm)	max. (mm)	min. (mm)	days ≥1 mm	max. 24 h (mm)	Wind av. speed (km/h)	preval. direct.	calm (%)	Average cloud-iness* (oktas)	sun-shine (h)	evap. (mm)
Jan.	825	25	13	30	5	57	80	140	440	14	12	72	7	E	15	6	165	123
Feb.	825	25	13	31	5	57	81	153	291	11	12	71	7	E	15	6	162	119
Mar.	826	25	13	30	2	60	83	172	380	33	14	74	6	E	17	6	174	104
Apr.	827	25	13	29	3	55	78	94	227	5	8	120	6	E	16	4	204	115
May	827	25	10	30	1	35	63	6	30	0	1	29	6	E	13	1	272	177
June	828	24	8	28	−1	28	55	1	4	0	0	4	6	E	20	1	284	183
July	828	24	8	28	−1	23	46	0	0	0	0	0	6	E	20	1	283	215
Aug.	827	26	11	30	0	20	41	0	0	0	0	0	7	E	13	1	283	270
Sept.	827	28	13	31	5	24	49	4	28	0	1	14	8	E	14	2	240	289
Oct.	826	28	13	34	4	41	66	70	221	8	8	73	7	E	15	4	214	227
Nov.	825	26	13	33	5	51	74	118	240	12	12	53	7	E	16	5	208	164
Dec.	825	25	13	31	4	57	75	153	272	41	14	86	7	E	17	5	202	146
Annual	826	26	12	34	−1	42	66	908	1,442	495	82	120	7	—	16	4	2,691	2,132
Rec. (yrs.)	30	30	30	30	30	30	30	30	30	30	30	30				30		

* Mean of 09h00, 15h00 and 21h00.

TABLE XXV

CLIMATIC TABLE FOR MONGU, ZAMBIA
Latitude 15°15'S, longitude 23°10'E, elevation 1,052 m

Month	Mean sta. press. (mbar)	Temperature (°C) mean max.	mean min.	extreme max.	extreme min.	Humidity dew point (°C)	relative (%)	Precipitation mean (mm)	max. (mm)	min. (mm)	days ≥1 mm	max. 24 h (mm)	Wind av. speed (m/sec)	preval. direct.	calm (%)	Mean daily cloudiness (oktas)	Average sunshine (h/day)	evap. (mm)	thunderstorms (days)
Jan.	896	28	19	34	13	18.5	77	217	419	68	17	85	2.4	NNE		6	5.4	166	21
Feb.	896	28	19	33	14	18.8	80	211	483	73	16	114	2.3	NNW		6	5.5	141	20
Mar.	896	28	18	34	12	18.9	75	145	341	6	12	89	2.5	ENE		5	6.6	168	20
Apr.	898	29	17	33	9	15.4	65	37	165	—	4	51	2.8	E		3	8.9	176	8
May	900	28	13	33	2	10.6	56	1	22	—	—	8	3.3	E		2	9.7	173	1
June	902	26	10	32	0	7.0	50	—	16	—	—	14	3.3	E		1	9.7	159	—
July	902	26	9	32	−2	4.9	42	—	—	—	—	—	3.8	E		1	9.8	185	—
Aug.	900	29	12	36	2	4.7	34	—	11	—	—	11	4.0	E		1	10.0	231	—
Sept.	898	33	16	37	7	6.6	31	2	28	—	—	28	4.0	E		1	9.4	287	2
Oct.	897	34	18	39	7	11.5	40	35	135	—	4	41	3.1	ENE		4	8.4	287	9
Nov.	897	31	18	38	12	16.5	64	102	264	17	11	71	2.4	NE		6	6.8	183	19
Dec.	896	29	18	37	13	18.1	75	222	380	92	17	84	2.4	NNE		6	5.7	157	23
Annual	898	29	16	39	−2	12.6	57	972	1,379	604	81	114	3.0	ENE		3	8.0	2,313	123
Rec. (yrs.)	25	22	22	22	22	22	10	30	30	30	30	30	7	7		5	12	7	11

TABLE XXVI

CLIMATIC TABLE FOR ZOMBA, MALAWI
Latitude 15°23'S, longitude 35°19'E, elevation 949 m

Month	Mean sta. press. (mbar)	Temperature (°C) mean max.	mean min.	extreme max.	extreme min.	Humidity dew point (°C)	relative (%)	Precipitation mean (mm)	max. (mm)	min. (mm)	days >1 mm	max. 24 h (mm)	Wind av. speed (m/sec)	preval. direct.	calm (%)	Mean daily cloudiness (oktas)	Average sunshine (h/day)	thunderstorms (days)
Jan.	908	27	19	33	11	19.0	82	298	609	29	18	103	1.1	ESE		6	4.4	16
Feb.	908	27	19	32	12	18.8	81	270	670	90	16	134	1.0	SE		6	4.8	18
Mar.	909	26	18	32	11	18.4	81	246	581	21	17	120	1.0	E		6	4.8	13
Apr.	911	26	17	31	12	17.2	79	72	260	5	7	85	1.0	E		5	6.1	5
May	913	24	14	30	9	14.6	76	19	90	—	3	67	0.9	E		4	6.0	1
June	915	22	13	28	7	12.4	74	13	53	—	2	49	0.9	E		4	5.3	—
July	915	22	12	29	7	11.6	69	6	18	—	2	13	1.0	ENE		4	5.3	—
Aug.	914	24	13	32	7	11.8	64	8	39	—	1	24	1.1	E		3	7.1	—
Sept.	913	27	15	33	8	13.1	58	8	108	—	1	71	1.4	E		2	7.3	1
Oct.	911	30	18	35	8	14.6	56	24	108	—	2	67	1.4	E		3	8.1	4
Nov.	909	29	19	36	12	16.7	65	120	286	18	9	75	1.3	E		5	6.5	12
Dec.	908	27	19	34	13	18.7	79	283	981	97	16	509	1.1	E		6	4.5	21
Annual	911	26	16	36	7	15.6	72	1,367	2,099	729	94	509	1.1	E		4	5.9	91
Rec. (yrs.)	15	30	30	30	30	30	25	30	30	30	30	30	6	5		6	17	12

TABLE XXVII

CLIMATIC TABLE FOR LUSAKA, ZAMBIA
Latitude 15°25'S, longitude 28°19'E, elevation 1,274 m

Month	Mean sta. press. (mbar)	Temperature (°C) mean max.	mean min.	extreme max.	extreme min.	Humidity dew point (°C)	rela- tive (%)	Precipitation mean (mm)	max. (mm)	min. (mm)	days >1 mm	max. 24 h (mm)	Wind av. speed (m/sec)	preval. direct.	calm (%)	Mean daily cloud- iness (oktas)	Average sun- shine (h/day)	thunder- storms (days)
Jan.	873	26	17	35	14	17.6	82	218	414	97	17	83	2.3	ENE	7	7	5.0	19
Feb.	873	26	17	31	12	17.7	86	196	530	46	16	72	2.3	ENE	11	6	5.1	17
Mar.	874	26	16	33	12	16.9	79	106	250	5	10	56	2.9	E	3	5	6.5	9
Apr.	876	26	15	32	10	14.8	71	21	65	—	2	32	3.7	E	—	4	8.6	3
May	877	25	12	30	8	11.1	63	4	37	—	—	25	3.8	E	—	3	9.1	1
June	879	23	10	28	4	8.2	59	—	6	—	—	6	3.9	E	—	2	8.9	—
July	879	23	10	28	4	6.8	34	—	2	—	—	1	4.2	ESE	—	2	9.2	—
Aug.	878	26	12	34	4	7.0	46	—	4	—	—	4	4.3	E	—	2	9.7	—
Sept.	876	29	15	35	7	8.3	41	—	6	—	—	4	4.5	E	—	1	9.5	1
Oct.	875	31	18	38	11	10.4	40	15	137	—	2	92	4.2	E	1	3	9.0	5
Nov.	874	29	18	38	12	14.6	59	91	184	1	8	72	3.2	E	5	6	6.8	13
Dec.	874	27	17	34	14	17.0	78	186	304	60	16	75	2.5	E	7	6	5.6	21
Annual	876	26	15	38	4	12.5	62	837	1,134	518	71	92	3.5	E	3	4	7.7	89
Rec. (yrs.)	25	23	23	23	23	23	10	30	30	30	30	30	23	20	3	5	23	12

TABLE XXVIII

CLIMATIC TABLE FOR BLANTYRE AIRPORT, MALAWI
Latitude 15°41'S, longitude 34°58'E, elevation 766 m

Month	Mean sta. press. (mbar)	Temperature (°C) mean max.	Temperature (°C) mean min.	Temperature (°C) extreme max.	Temperature (°C) extreme min.	Humidity dew point (°C)	Humidity relative (%)	Precipitation mean (mm)	Precipitation max. (mm)	Precipitation min. (mm)	Precipitation days ≥1 mm	Precipitation max. 24 h (mm)	Wind av. speed (m/sec)	Wind preval direct.	Wind calm (%)	Mean daily cloudiness (oktas)	Average sunshine (h/day)	Average thunderstorms (days)
Jan.	927	28	20	35	15	19.4	79	200	405	30	14	152	2.4	SE	10	6	6.0	16
Feb.	927	28	20	35	14	19.6	80	179	315	40	12	95	2.4	SSE	11	6	6.2	18
Mar.	928	27	19	36	14	18.8	80	125	337	3	11	80	2.8	SSE	8	6	6.1	13
Apr.	930	28	17	32	13	17.3	75	43	97	1	5	37	3.0	SSE	5	5	7.7	5
May	932	26	15	32	10	14.4	70	9	48	—	1	46	3.1	SSE	4	3	8.1	1
June	934	24	13	31	8	11.9	69	4	26	—	—	25	3.3	SSE	3	3	7.1	—
July	935	24	13	29	8	11.1	63	3	14	—	1	14	3.7	SSE	3	4	7.3	—
Aug.	934	26	14	34	8	11.5	57	1	11	—	1	6	3.8	SE	3	3	8.0	—
Sept.	932	29	17	35	10	12.8	52	5	35	—	1	35	3.9	SE	2	3	8.1	1
Oct.	931	31	19	38	13	14.5	50	20	71	—	2	46	4.0	ESE	2	3	8.7	6
Nov.	929	31	20	38	15	17.0	60	81	197	11	8	55	3.2	ESE	5	5	7.3	16
Dec.	928	29	20	36	16	18.9	74	164	336	47	12	76	2.7	SE	7	6	6.1	19
Annual	931	27	17	38	8	15.6	67	834	1,145	408	68	152	3.2	SE	5	4	7.2	95
Rec. (yrs.)	25	22	22	22	22	20	10	20	22	22	22	22	16	16	16	6	17	12

TABLE XXIX

CLIMATIC TABLE FOR MLANJE, MALAWI
Latitude 16°05'S, longitude 35°38'E, elevation 652 m

Month	Mean sta. press. (mbar)	Temperature (°C) mean max.	min.	extreme max.	min.	Humidity dew point (°C)	rela- tive (%)	Precipitation mean (mm)	max. (mm)	min. (mm)	days ≥1 mm	max. 24 h (mm)	Wind av. speed (m/sec)	preval. direct.	calm (%)	Mean daily cloud- iness (oktas)	Average sun- shine (h/day)	radi- ation (cal./cm²)	thunder- storms (days)
Jan.		29	19	36	13	20.2	83	313	627	114	16	83	1.3	SE	6	6	5.6	538	20
Feb.		29	19	34	13	20.4	85	319	666	86	15	140	1.3	SSW	10	6	5.8	495	19
Mar.		28	18	34	12	19.8	84	308	541	114	18	145	1.3	SSE	7	6	5.5	452	13
Apr.		28	17	33	10	18.5	81	125	472	—	11	120	1.3	SSE	8	4	6.7	465	5
May		26	13	33	7	15.9	78	59	165	4	6	76	1.2	ESE	12	4	7.1	425	1
June		24	12	30	5	13.8	79	64	165	4	8	46	1.1	SE	13	4	5.9	380	—
July		24	11	30	4	13.3	73	38	110	—	5	30	1.4	E	8	4	6.1	380	—
Aug.		26	11	34	2	13.6	67	33	107	2	4	38	1.6	SE	8	4	7.4	473	2
Sept.		29	14	36	7	14.7	62	28	120	—	3	112	1.7	ESE	5	3	7.5	533	7
Oct.		32	16	38	6	16.1	56	58	233	—	4	148	1.7	E	6	3	8.7	576	7
Nov.		31	18	39	11	18.3	68	183	386	23	8	109	1.6	ESE	5	5	7.4	565	15
Dec.		30	19	36	13	20.7	81	268	490	51	15	155	1.4	SE	6	5	5.8	541	23
Annual		28	16	39	2	17.1	75	1,796	2,349	1,292	113	155	1.4	SE	8	5	6.6	485	105
Rec. (yrs.)		20	20	20	20	10	10	27	27	27	21	23	7	7	7	6	10	4	10

455

TABLE XXX

CLIMATIC TABLE FOR LIVINGSTONE, ZAMBIA
Latitude 17°49'S, longitude 29°49'E, elevation 985 m

Month	Mean sta. press. (mbar)	Temperature (°C)				Humidity		Precipitation					Wind			Mean daily cloud- iness (oktas)	Average		thunder- storms (days)
		mean max.	mean min.	extreme max.	extreme min.	dew point (°C)	rela- tive (%)	mean (mm)	max. (mm)	min. (mm)	days ≥1 mm	max. 24 h (mm)	av. speed (m/sec)	preval. direct.	calm (%)		sun- shine (h/day)	evap. (mm)	
Jan.	903	29	19	38	11	18.7	75	186	360	75	15	87	1.6	ENE	25	6	6.1	183	20
Feb.	903	29	19	36	13	18.8	79	175	449	21	14	70	1.6	ENE	23	6	6.3	149	19
Mar.	904	30	17	34	8	17.5	70	101	398	—	8	68	1.5	E	17	4	7.6	196	11
Apr.	906	30	15	36	8	14.8	61	28	149	—	2	59	1.5	E	18	3	9.0	182	4
May	908	28	11	34	2	9.8	52	5	70	—	—	39	1.6	E	16	2	9.5	165	1
June	910	25	7	32	−3	6.6	52	—	9	—	—	7	1.7	E	19	1	9.4	132	—
July	910	25	7	31	−2	5.2	44	—	—	—	—	—	1.8	E	15	1	9.6	153	—
Aug.	909	28	10	36	−1	5.4	36	—	8	—	—	7	2.1	E	12	1	10.1	199	—
Sept.	907	32	15	39	4	7.1	32	2	50	—	—	25	2.4	E	12	1	8.7	265	1
Oct.	905	35	19	41	11	10.7	34	26	101	—	2	40	2.3	E	14	3	8.9	304	8
Nov.	904	33	19	40	9	15.6	57	92	274	24	8	126	1.9	ENE	17	5	7.2	217	17
Dec.	903	30	19	38	10	17.9	71	164	328	23	12	101	1.6	NE	19	6	5.9	161	21
Annual	906	30	15	41	−3	12.3	55	779	1,186	410	61	126	1.8	E	17	3	8.2	2,303	102
Rec. (yrs.)	25	30	30	30	30	10	10	30	30	30	30	30	21	19	19	6	28	4	12

TABLE XXXI

CLIMATIC TABLE FOR SALISBURY, RHODESIA
Latitude 17°50′S, longitude 31°01′E, elevation 1,470 m

Month	Mean sta. press. (mbar)	Temperature (°C)				Humidity		Precipitation					Wind			Mean daily cloudiness (oktas)	Average		evap. (mm)	thunder-storms (days)
		mean		extreme		dew point (°C)	rela-tive (%)	mean (mm)	max. (mm)	min. (mm)	days ≥1 mm	max. 24 h (mm)	av. speed (m/sec)	preval. direct.	calm (%)		sun-shine (h/day)	radi-ation (cal./cm²)		
		max.	min.	max.	min.															
Jan.	854	26	16	32	8	15.7	75	213	514	74	15	76	2.6	ENE	8	6	6.3	514	173	14
Feb.	854	26	16	31	9	15.7	75	173	414	18	13	156	2.6	ENE	3	6	6.4	507	136	13
Mar.	856	26	14	32	8	14.8	72	101	298	9	9	68	2.8	E	5	4	6.9	558	174	7
Apr.	857	25	12	32	6	12.7	64	39	93	—	4	50	2.8	ENE	3	3	8.2	535	155	4
May	859	23	9	29	2	9.4	58	11	42	—	2	31	2.8	ENE	3	3	8.6	483	139	1
June	860	21	7	27	0	6.7	54	5	22	—	1	14	3.0	E	3	2	8.4	439	115	—
July	860	21	7	28	−1	5.7	50	1	11	—	—	11	3.3	E	2	2	8.8	434	133	—
Aug.	860	23	8	31	−1	5.9	45	3	45	—	—	28	3.6	ENE	1	2	9.4	517	168	1
Sept.	858	27	12	33	3	7.3	42	5	19	—	1	19	3.9	ENE	1	1	9.4	586	220	2
Oct.	857	29	15	35	7	9.8	44	30	94	—	4	38	3.8	ENE	2	2	9.1	597	260	5
Nov.	856	27	15	35	8	13.1	57	100	236	33	10	71	3.3	ENE	3	5	6.9	533	195	11
Dec.	855	26	16	33	9	14.9	68	186	429	71	14	96	2.9	ENE	6	6	6.1	499	172	13
Annual	857	25	12	35	−1	10.9	58	868	1,291	550	73	156	3.1	ENE	3	3	7.9	517	2,040	71
Rec. (yrs.)	25	30	30	30	30	30	20	30	30	30	30	30	28	28	5	6	30	7	10	20

457

TABLE XXXII

CLIMATIC TABLE FOR UMTALI, RHODESIA
Latitude 18°58'S, longitude 32°40'E, elevation 1,117 m

Month	Mean sta. press. (mbar)	Temperature (°C) mean max.	mean min.	extreme max.	extreme min.	Humidity dew point (°C)	relative (%)	Precipitation mean (mm)	max. (mm)	min. (mm)	days ≥1 mm	max. 24 h (mm)	Wind av. speed (m/sec)	preval. direct.	calm (%)	Average sunshine (h/day)	evap. (mm)	thunderstorms (days)
Jan.	891	28	17	36	11	17.2	77	171	469	42	13	116	2.2	ESE	12	7.3	177	13
Feb.	891	27	17	35	11	17.4	79	134	365	14	12	85	2.1	ESE	16	7.0	139	12
Mar.	892	26	16	33	11	16.9	76	99	346	11	9	82	2.0	ESE	13	7.2	165	5
Apr.	895	26	15	35	8	15.2	70	26	86	—	4	66	1.9	E	14	8.1	143	3
May	896	24	11	31	3	12.0	63	10	60	—	2	28	1.7	ESE	16	8.1	120	1
June	898	21	9	29	1	9.4	59	9	26	—	2	17	1.5	ESE	18	7.5	97	1
July	898	21	9	29	0	9.1	57	7	19	—	2	14	1.9	E	20	7.5	117	—
Aug.	898	23	10	32	2	9.5	55	11	55	—	2	38	2.5	E	13	8.3	155	1
Sept.	896	26	13	36	4	11.1	54	10	61	—	2	55	3.3	E	7	8.8	225	1
Oct.	894	29	15	39	6	12.9	56	27	101	—	3	46	3.7	E	5	8.7	258	5
Nov.	893	28	16	39	8	15.3	66	91	169	17	9	69	3.0	E	7	7.3	223	11
Dec.	892	28	17	37	11	16.7	73	161	274	32	13	90	2.4	E	11	7.1	188	14
Annual	894	26	14	39	0	13.6	65	756	1,239	401	73	116	2.3	ESE	13	7.7	2,007	67
Rec. (urs.)	20	20	20	20	20	20		30	30	30	30	30	13	13	6	20	10	20

TABLE XXXIII

CLIMATIC TABLE FOR BULAWAYO, RHODESIA

Latitude 20°09'S, longitude 28°37'E, elevation 1,344 m

Month	Mean sta. press. (mbar)	Temperature (°C) mean max.	Temperature (°C) mean min.	Temperature (°C) extreme max.	Temperature (°C) extreme min.	Humidity dew-point (°C)	Humidity relative (%)	Precipitation mean (mm)	Precipitation max. (mm)	Precipitation min. (mm)	Precipitation days ≥1 mm	Precipitation max. 24 h (mm)	Wind av. speed (m/sec)	Wind preval. direct.	Wind calm (%)	Mean daily cloudiness (oktas)	Average sunshine (h/day)	Average radiation (cal./cm²)	evap. (mm)	thunderstorms (days)
Jan.	867	27	16	36	9	15.3	74	134	308	—	10	132	3.5	ESE	6	5	7.1	564	185	11
Feb.	867	27	16	34	8	15.6	76	112	368	—	9	90	3.5	ESE	3	5	7.4	537	146	9
Mar.	869	26	15	34	9	13.4	71	65	183	1	5	102	3.6	ESE	4	3	7.7	528	172	4
Apr.	870	26	13	33	3	11.8	63	21	87	—	3	47	3.3	ESE	5	3	8.5	486	143	3
May	872	24	10	31	−1	8.0	56	9	34	—	1	24	3.5	ESE	2	2	9.1	452	128	1
June	874	21	7	28	−2	5.2	58	3	33	—	—	22	3.8	ESE	2	2	9.1	401	107	1
July	874	21	7	28	0	4.3	50	—	2	—	—	2	4.0	ESE	2	2	9.2	422	120	—
Aug.	873	24	9	32	0	4.8	43	1	10	—	1	10	4.2	ESE	3	1	9.7	491	161	2
Sept.	871	27	12	36	3	6.6	42	5	29	—	1	12	4.3	ESE	3	1	9.5	545	209	2
Oct.	870	30	15	36	7	9.7	44	25	116	—	3	49	4.0	ESE	4	2	8.6	574	246	6
Nov.	868	28	16	37	9	12.7	60	89	241	8	8	106	3.4	ESE	6	4	7.4	529	189	13
Dec.	868	27	16	35	11	14.6	69	124	273	3	10	90	3.2	ESE	7	5	7.0	529	182	12
Annual	870	26	13	37	−2	10.2	59	589	1,093	199	50	132	3.7	ESE	4	3	8.4	505	1,990	62
Rec. (yrs.)	25	30	30	30	30	30	10	30	30	30	30	30	25	30	7	10	30	8	9	20

TABLE XXXIV

CLIMATIC TABLE FOR BEITBRIDGE, RHODESIA
Latitude 22°13′S, longitude 30°00′E, elevation 456 m

Month	Mean sta. press. (mbar)	Temperature (°C) mean max.	Temperature (°C) mean min.	Temperature (°C) extreme max.	Temperature (°C) extreme min.	Humidity dew point (°C)	Humidity relative (%)	Precipitation mean (mm)	Precipitation max. (mm)	Precipitation min. (mm)	Precipitation days ≥1 mm	Precipitation max. 24 h (mm)	Wind av. speed (m/sec)	Wind preval. direct.	Wind calm (%)	Mean daily cloudiness (oktas)	Average sunshine (h/day)	Average evap. (mm)	Average thunderstorms (days)
Jan.	962	33	21	43	13	18.7	62	85	452	5	5	161	2.3	ESE	3	5	7.9	267	5
Feb.	962	33	21	42	14	18.8	64	51	137	—	4	68	2.1	ESE	4	5	7.7	200	5
Mar.	964	32	20	41	12	17.8	60	40	157	—	3	97	2.1	E	5	4	7.8	217	2
Apr.	966	31	17	39	4	15.9	58	17	77	—	1	77	1.7	ESE	7	4	8.0	165	2
May	968	28	12	37	3	11.2	52	4	30	—	1	27	1.3	E	8	3	8.9	128	1
June	971	25	8	34	−1	7.4	56	5	38	—	—	33	1.3	ESE	13	2	8.4	100	—
July	971	25	8	34	−1	7.1	51	2	26	—	—	26	1.3	E	11	2	8.5	117	—
Aug.	970	27	11	37	2	8.3	46	1	16	—	—	3	1.6	E	9	2	8.8	154	1
Sept.	968	30	15	40	6	11.5	46	7	77	—	1	27	2.1	ESE	6	2	8.4	204	4
Oct.	965	32	19	43	9	14.7	48	20	78	—	3	51	2.5	ESE	3	3	8.0	256	5
Nov.	963	33	20	44	11	16.7	53	42	129	—	4	83	2.4	E	2	5	7.5	235	5
Dec.	962	33	21	43	14	17.9	57	64	211	3	5	85	2.2	ESE	3	5	7.3	248	7
Annual	966	29	16	44	−1	13.8	54	337	640	110	27	161	1.9	ESE	6	3	8.1	2,291	32
Rec. (yrs.)	25	27	27	27	27	10	10	30	30	30	30	30	6	9	9	6	10	9	20

Chapter 14

Madagascar

J. F. GRIFFITHS AND R. RANAIVOSON

Introduction

Madagascar, extending 1,650 km from 12 to 25°S, is almost completely within the tropical zone (Fig.1). A dorsal mountain ridge reaching 1,200–1,500 m in height, with three isolated massifs above 2,600 m, runs north–south the length of the island. The geographical location, the relief, the influence of the ocean and the wind regimes are the main causes of the very varied climatic conditions that are found on the island.

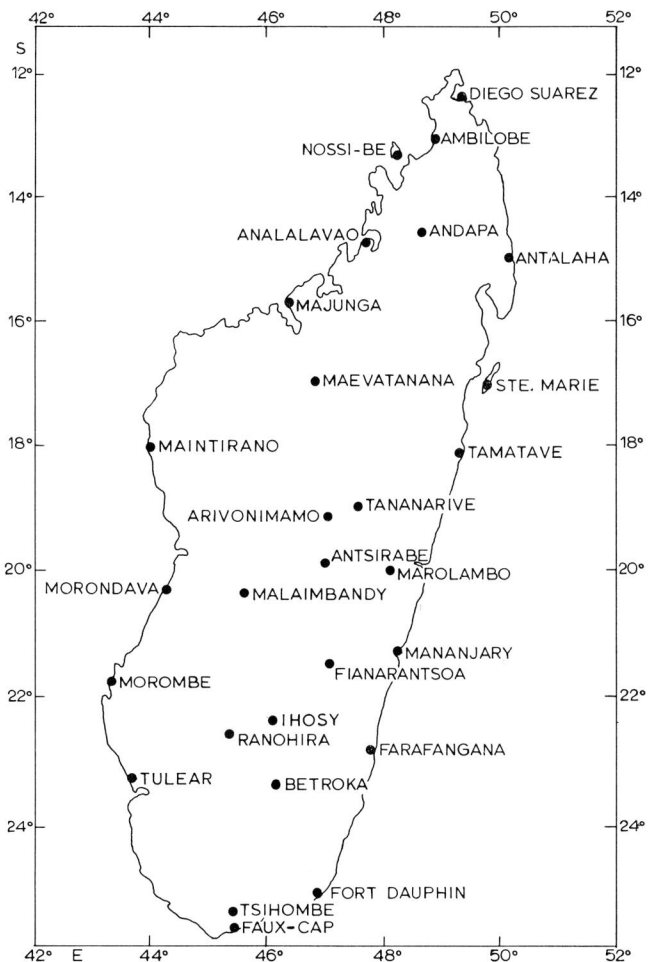

Fig.1. Station locations in Madagascar.

The island has an area of nearly 600,000 km² and a population of 7 million people. Evergreen rain forest covers much of the eastern slopes, the east coast and the northwest, but the southwest has lush vegetation and mangrove swamps abound along the west coast. The rest of the country has a savanna type of vegetation (called Savoka); it is of generally poor fertility, perhaps from burning. The major crops are coffee, vanilla, sugar and rice.

Climatic causes

Two seasons can be distinguished in Madagascar, the winter from May to October and the summer from November to April. Two short intermediate seasons separate these

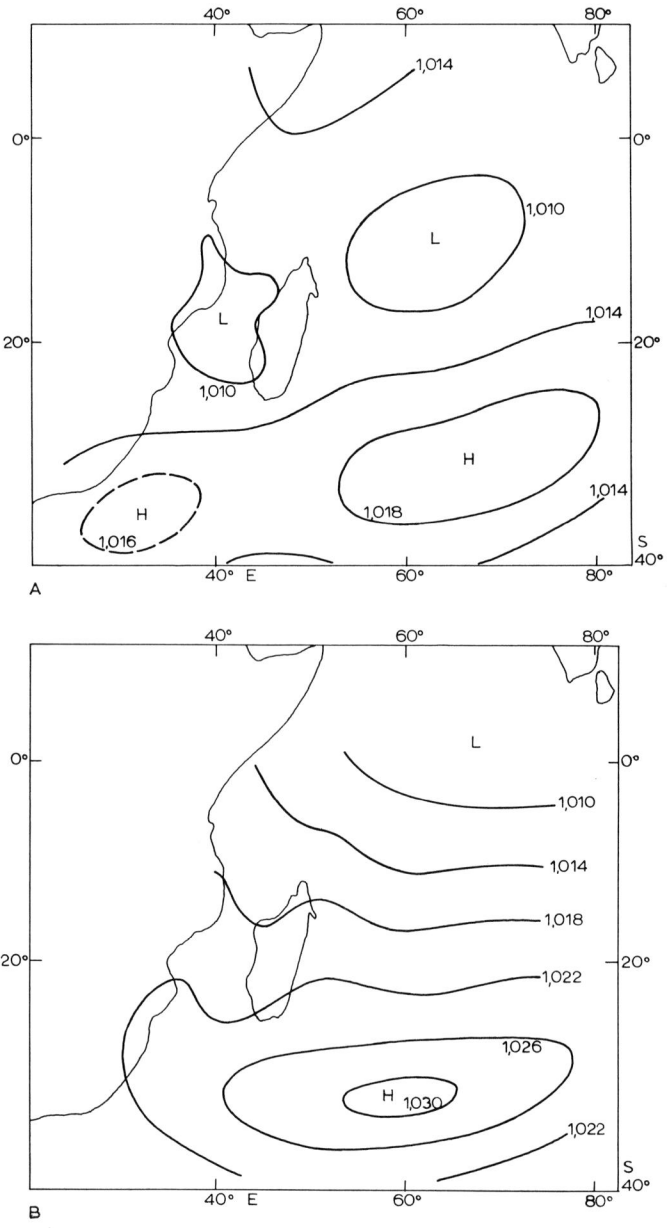

Fig.2. Mean pressure patterns. A. January; B. July.

but they are each of less than one month duration. During winter, or the cool season, the main activity stems from the tropical anticyclonic belt which is often subject to perturbations from the passage of moving pressure systems from the west to the east. These high pressures produce a deep southeast trade wind and variable patterns over Madagascar. In this season that part of the island to the east of the mountain range experiences a humid climate "of the wind" (windward), while the western portion has the aridity of a climate "under the wind" (leeward).

During summer, the hot season, the situation is more complex: the oceanic anticyclone weakens and subdivides and a ridge of the Arabian anticyclone intermittently affects the north of the Mozambique Channel, while the intertropical convergence zone extends its influence over Madagascar. The trade-wind circulation becomes less regular and convective instability develops almost daily in all regions. It is during this season that the depressions and tropical cyclones spawned in the southwest Indian Ocean can, if conditions are right, affect Madagascar.

Fig.2 gives the mean position of the pressure centres in the southwest Indian Ocean in January and July.

Cloud and sunshine

The average annual cloud amount (based on three observations per day) is approximately 4 oktas, with stations on the east coast and the highlands reaching 5 oktas and those on the southwest coast recording only 3 oktas.

Cloud amounts are, of course, subject to considerations of wind regime, air mass and topography. Therefore, in Madagascar, a well pronounced seasonal variation exists (Table I). Amounts are generally lower in the winter and the spring than in the wet summer spell. In some locations (the southwest of the island) monthly means can get as low as 1 okta, but other areas (northeast coast and some highland situations) never go below

TABLE I

MEAN MONTHLY AND ANNUAL CLOUD AMOUNTS (OKTAS)

	Jan.	Feb.	Mar.	Apr.	May	June	July	Aug.	Sept.	Oct.	Nov.	Dec.	Year	No. of Years
Antalaha	6	5	6	5	5	5	5	5	5	5	5	5	5	10
Diego-Suarez	6	6	6	5	3	4	4	3	3	3	4	5	4	10
Fianarantsoa	6	6	6	5	5	5	5	4	4	4	5	5	5	12
Fort Dauphin	5	4	5	4	4	4	4	3	3	3	5	6	4	4
Ihosy	6	6	6	4	4	4	3	3	3	3	4	6	4	4
Maevatanana	6	6	5	4	2	2	2	2	1	2	4	5	4	10
Maintirano	6	6	5	3	2	2	2	3	2	3	4	5	4	10
Mananjary	5	6	6	6	5	6	6	5	3	3	4	5	5	4
Morondava	5	5	2	2	2	1	1	1	2	2	3	4	3	4
Nossi-Be	6	6	5	4	3	3	3	3	3	3	4	5	4	10
Tamatave	5	5	6	5	5	5	6	5	5	5	5	6	5	10
Tananarive	7	6	6	5	4	4	5	4	4	3	6	6	5	10
Tulear	4	4	3	3	2	2	2	2	1	2	3	4	3	10

4 or 5 oktas. The latter stations show very little seasonal variation in their cloud amount compared with the rest of the island for the moist northeasterly flow persists all through the year.

The diurnal variation of annual values (Fig.3) shows dramatically the early morning cloud formed over the highland and its relatively rapid dissipation. Nevertheless, over the rest of the island the general build up of convective cloud is seen in the difference between the 12h00 and 17h00 maps. From November to March this increase is large, reaching a maximum in December. During May–September the eastern half of the island exhibits a morning maximum but on the west side amounts of cloud remain low throughout the day, except when there is a marked anticyclonic strengthening.

A short period study showed that Majunga had few low clouds during winter and spring but Tamatave and Fort Dauphin recorded a high percentage in all seasons. At Diego-Suarez only the summer afternoons had an appreciable percentage of low cloud.

Sunshine, naturally, shows a picture very related to cloudiness. Along the west coast annual means of 70–84% of the possible sunshine hours are measured, the amount generally increasing towards the south. Along the east coast averages are about 60% with the

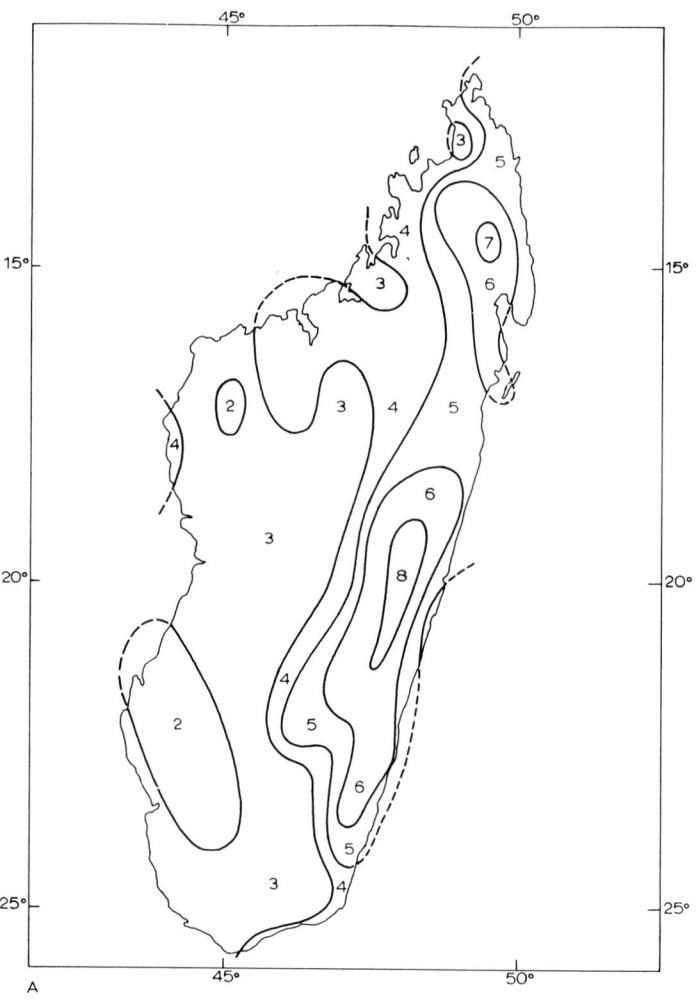

Fig.3. Mean annual cloudiness in oktas. A. 07h00; B. 12h00; C. 17h00.

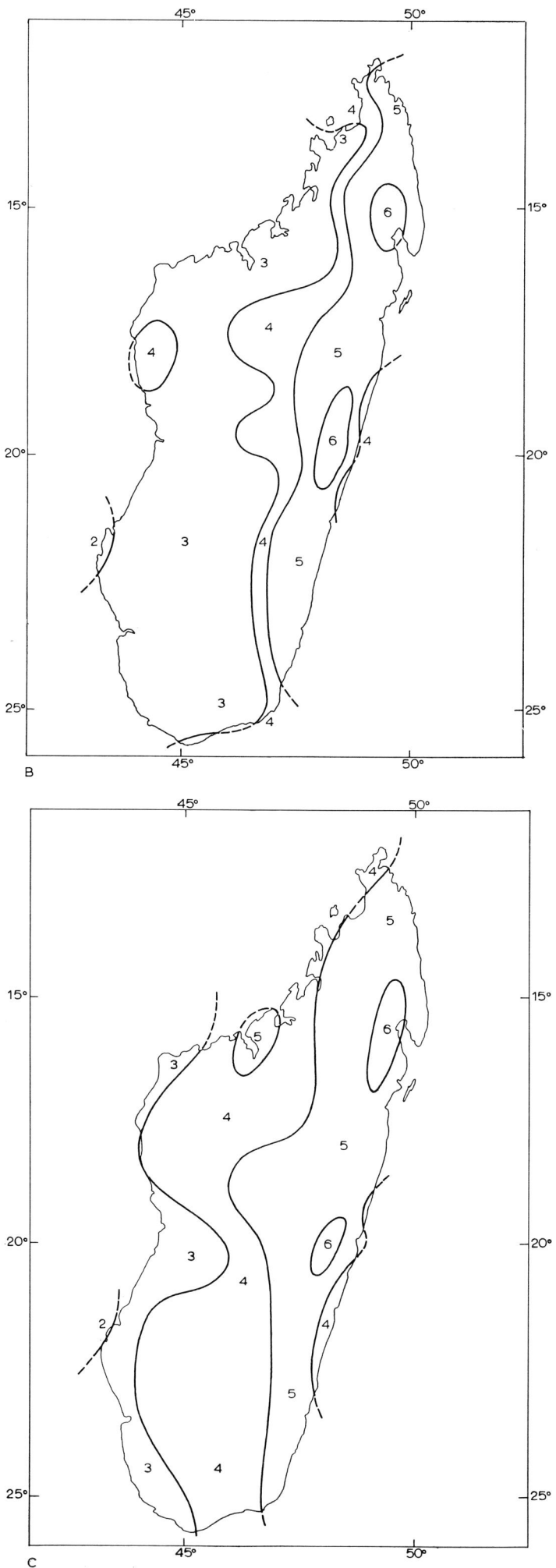

B

C

exception of the extreme northern part where Diego-Suarez has over 70%. On the plateau averages are also about 60% but local relief and location play an important role. For example, Andapa has only 39% and Ranohira 72%.

TABLE II

SUNSHINE HOURS FOR SELECTED MONTHS

	Jan.	Apr.	July	Oct.	Year
Antalaha	205	243	224	260	2,777
Diego-Suarez	188	325	260	348	3,279
Fort Dauphin	226	215	201	251	2,702
Maintirano	273	305	301	327	3,534
Majunga	183	291	303	339	3,280
Nossi-Be	205	252	278	309	3,059
Tamatave	226	199	170	231	2,445
Tananarive	204	236	216	272	2,690
Tulear	305	302	291	324	3,610

Over the whole country October is the sunniest month (Table II), many areas recording a mean of over 300 h. February and March are generally the months with the least sunshine but Tamatave has a weak July minimum. The June minimum at Tulear does not accord well with cloud amounts and is suspect. As with cloud amounts the smallest variation between months occurs along the east coast, while Majunga, on the west coast, exhibits the greatest fluctuation, from 173 h in March to 339 h in October.

Temperature

The mean annual temperature at sea level varies from about 23 to 26°C. The value is a function of latitude, being greater in the north than in the south, but, for the same latitude, the west coast is generally warmer than the east coast by from 1° to 3°C (Fig.4). Inland the mean annual temperature is very dependent upon the elevation and values of around 20°C are reached at 1,000 m altitude. The mean lapse rate is close to 0.5°C/100 m. The annual range is relatively small, due to the oceanic nature of the island's climate, and varies from about 4°C in the north to 8°C in the extreme south.

Extremes

Table III gives values of the absolute extremes of temperature recorded on the island. Readings below 10°C are rare on the coast, except in the southwest, as are readings in excess of 40°C. Inland stations show the greatest variation. It is clear that the winter of 1964 was unusually cold over much of the island.

In Fig.5 the mean annual maximum temperature is given. It follows, roughly, the same pattern as the mean annual temperature, with the west coast being warmer than the east and with a decrease away from the equator.

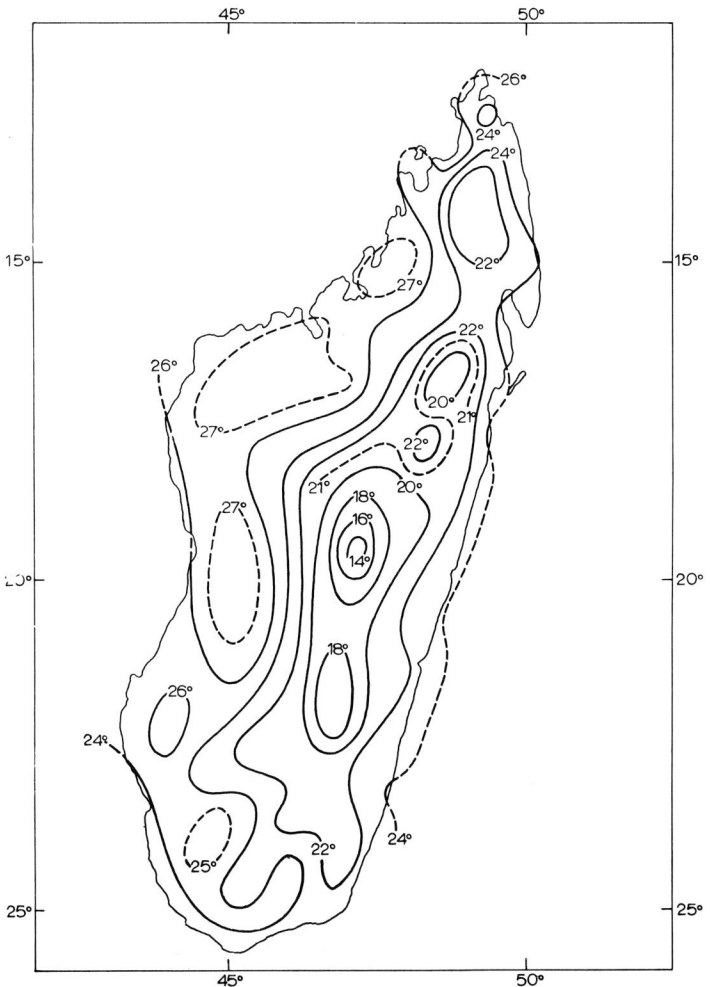

Fig.4. Mean annual temperature (°C).

In the extreme north of the island's east coast two maxima occur of approximately equal magnitude, in April and December. They are separated by a primary minimum in August and a secondary in January. For the remainder of the east coast there is a single maximum (January or February) and a minimum in July or August.

Along the northern half of the west coast double maxima again occur, one in March–April and the other in October–December; they are approximately equal. The primary minimum is now in July with the secondary still in January. In the southwest the single maximum (January–March) and the single minimum (June–July) is typical. On the plateau the maximum generally appears in November with the minimum in July.

The mean minimum temperature reaches its lowest value in July or August over the whole of Madagascar. Generally, stations with an August minimum are in the north. The mean monthly minimum attains its highest value in November–March, but it occurs most often in February. Fig.6 gives a map of the mean annual minimum temperature.

TABLE III

TEMPERATURE EXTREMES (°C)

Station	Absolute minimum		Absolute maximum	
	value	date	value	date
East coast:				
Diego-Suarez	14.6	Aug. 1967	36.8	Dec. 1936
Tamatave	11.3	June 1964	36.5	Jan. 1953
Fort Dauphin	8.8	Aug. 1966	35.4	Feb. 1956
Plateaux:				
Tananarive-S.C.M.	1.6	Aug. 1963	31.6	Oct. 1941
Nanokely	−8.5	July 1963,		
		Aug. 1964	28.8	Oct. 1950
Antsirabe	−5.4	June 1964	31.7	Nov. 1959
Fianarantsoa	0.0	June 1964	36.7	Nov. 1933
Betroka	0.0	July 1957,		
		Aug. 1956	40.0	Nov. 1955
Nossi-Be (Sambirano):				
Nossi-Be	13.2	July 1963	39.0	Apr. 1931
Ambilobe	10.5	July 1964,	45.0	Nov. 1928,
		Aug. 1964		Dec. 1928
West coast and lowlands:				
Analalava	14.0	Aug. 1964	39.4	Apr. 1921
Majunga	13.0	June 1961	39.1	Nov. 1932
Maintirano	9.1	July 1963	36.8	Jan. 1966
Morondava	6.9	July 1958	38.7	Jan. 1937
Morombe	5.1	Aug. 1948	39.8	Feb. 1940
Tulear	6.0	Aug. 1935	40.4	Feb. 1962
South:				
Tsihombe	4.3	Aug. 1953	42.4	Jan. 1936
Tranoroa	3.2	July 1934	46.5	Nov. 1936

Mean diurnal variation

The daily range is smaller at coastal stations of the east, west and north than it is in the interior and on the southwestern coast.

The diurnal range reaches its maximum during the cold season along the whole of the west and northeast coastal areas. The extreme values observed are 8.5°C at Maintirano and 14.2°C at Tsihombe. In contrast, on the east coast the maximum is attained during the warm season with values of about 7°–8°C. Inland and on the plateau the maximum is reached in October and is about 15°C.

The minimum diurnal range is recorded during the warm season on the north, northwest and southwest coast. On the east coast the minimum is reached during the cold season or at the end of the warm season. On the plateau the minimum is attained in Febru-

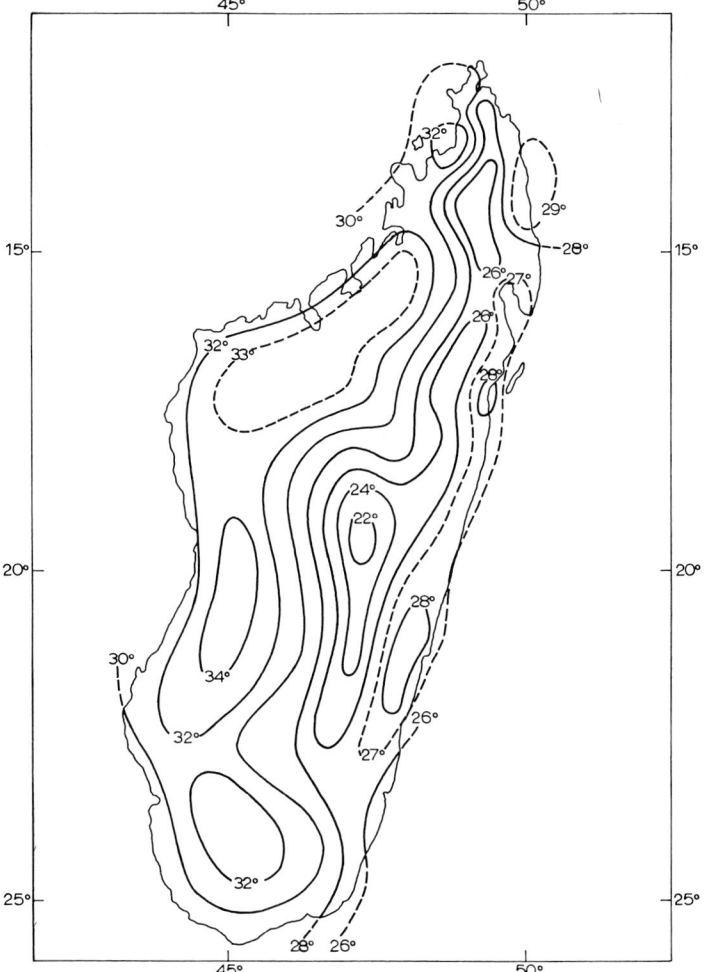

Fig.5. Mean annual maximum temperature (°C).

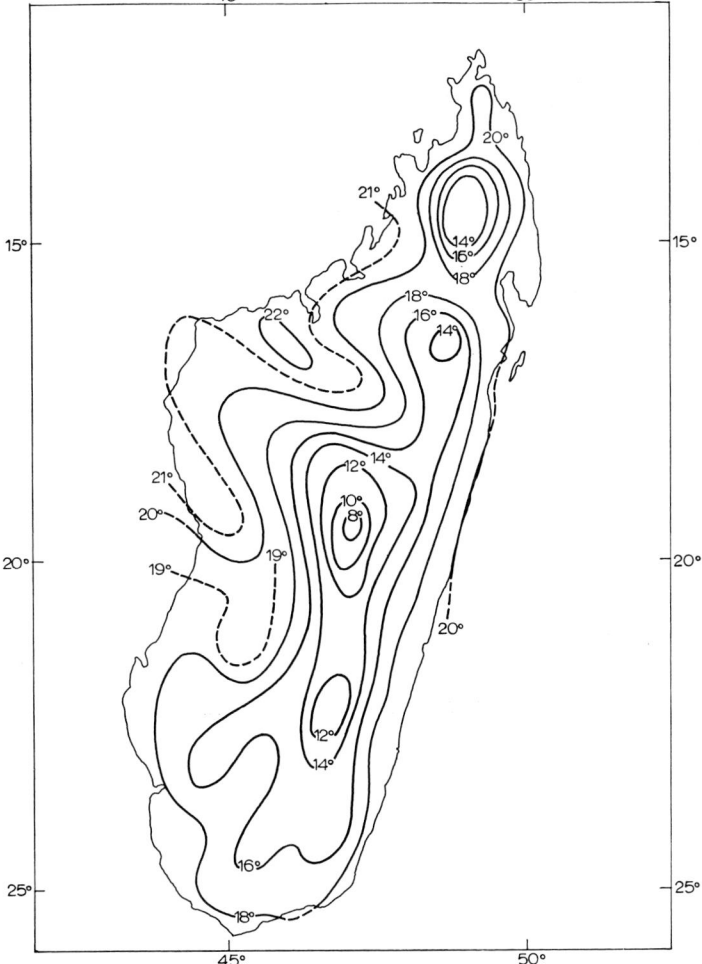

Fig.6. Mean annual minimum temperature (°C).

ary or March. It should be noted that in most areas the seasonal change in diurnal variation is quite small, with 4° or 5°C being maximal.

Fig.7 gives a map of the mean annual diurnal temperature variation.

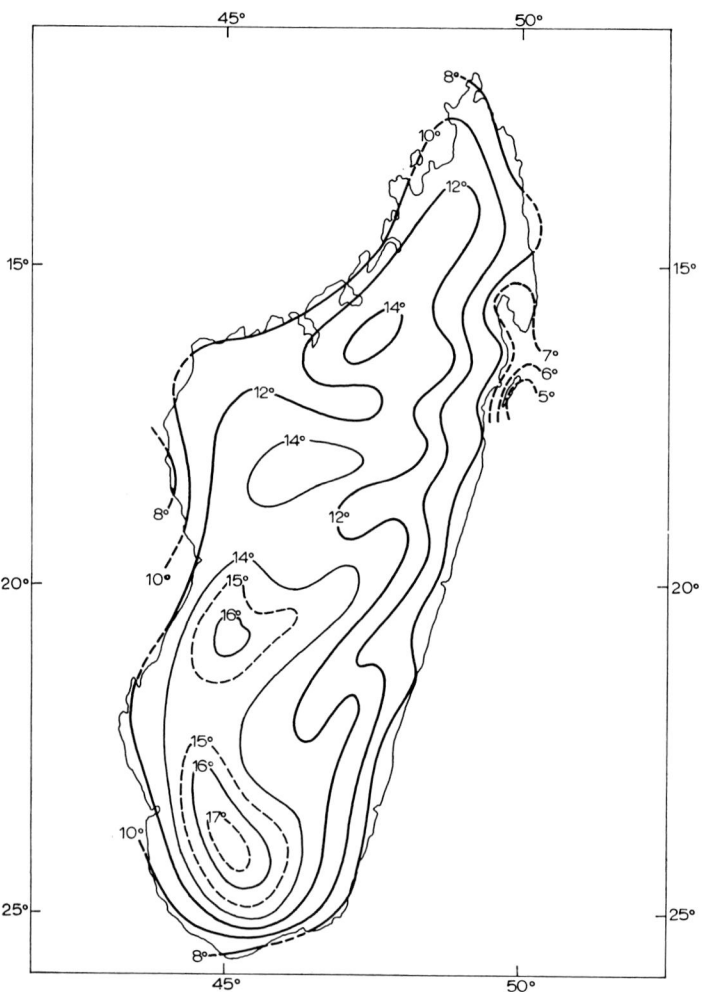

Fig.7. Mean annual diurnal temperature variation (°C).

Altitude changes

As was mentioned earlier, the lapse rate of temperature of the mean annual value is around 0.5°C/100 m. An interesting set of data covering one year for Tananarive and Tsiafajavona (2,600 m) showed that the lapse rate reached a minimum in January of 0.65°C/100 m and a maximum in September of 0.85°C/100 m. The gradient at 07h00 was down to 0.56°C/100 m and between 15h00 and 16h00 it rose to 1.03°C/100 m. The rapid and pronounced change was borne out by observations of cloudiness and thunderstorms.

Rainfall

The essential characteristics of the rainfall regime are:

(*1*) The annual value varies from a mean of 340 mm on the southwest coast to a mean of 3,700 mm in the Bay of Antongil; it is possible that a station in the forested region of the eastern slopes reaches 3,800 mm.

(*2*) The mean number of rain days varies between 30 and 250-per year.

On the west coast, the western plains and the plateau, from 90 to 95% of the annual total is received between October and April. For these regions a definite dry season and rainy season cycle is identified.

On the east coast and the eastern slopes only 30–50% of the annual total falls during the same period. For these areas there is no definite dry season, only a reduction in the rainfall during September and October. Table X at the end of the chapter, give the relevant data concerning rainfall amount and days for 18 stations while Fig.8 gives the mean annual isohyetal pattern.

From the above mentioned table it is seen that annual totals can vary between a low of 120 mm to an amount approaching 5,000 mm.

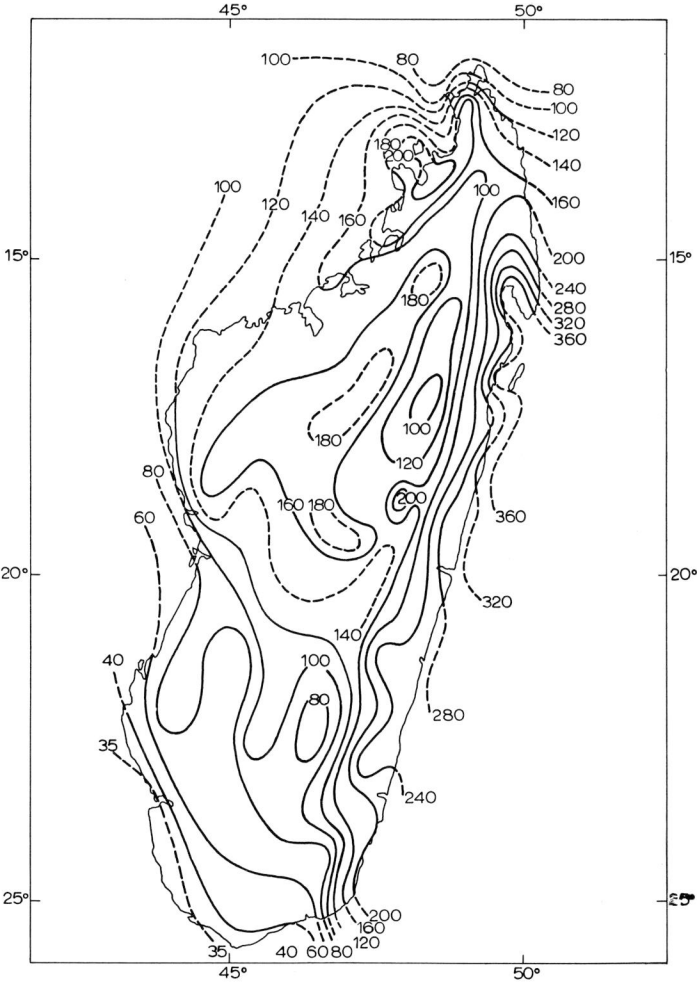

Fig.8. Mean annual rainfall (cm).

The maximum rainfall reported during 24 h exceeded 500 mm and occurred at Diego-Suarez during March. Falls in excess of 300 mm are confined to the summer months (December–March) and to few stations (Diego-Suarez, Tamatave, Mananjary, Nossi-Be, Majunga, Maintirano and Ambodifototra). Stations along the east coast can record nearly 100 mm or more in a day during any month of the year, but on the west coast such falls are extremely rare during April–November. However, Tulear, with a mean annual total of only 350 mm, has recorded 102 mm on an October day, while Tsihombe had 120 mm on one June day. Generally, falls of over 100 mm/day are rare on the plateau.

In amount certain stations on the east coast can show the greatest annual variation, about 2,500 mm, but Maintirano has the greatest percentage variation from (45 to 240% of normal), followed closely by Morombe with 27–210%.

Tamatave and the Île Ste.-Marie have never recorded less than 200 rain days in a year, very different from the maximum of 47 days at Morombe. The first two stations also have never had less than 6 rain days in any one month. The average amount per rain day is about 10 mm, but between 16 and 22°N on both the east and west coasts this increases to 15 mm. The lowest values are reached at Fianarantsoa (7.3 mm) and Tsihombe (6.8 mm).

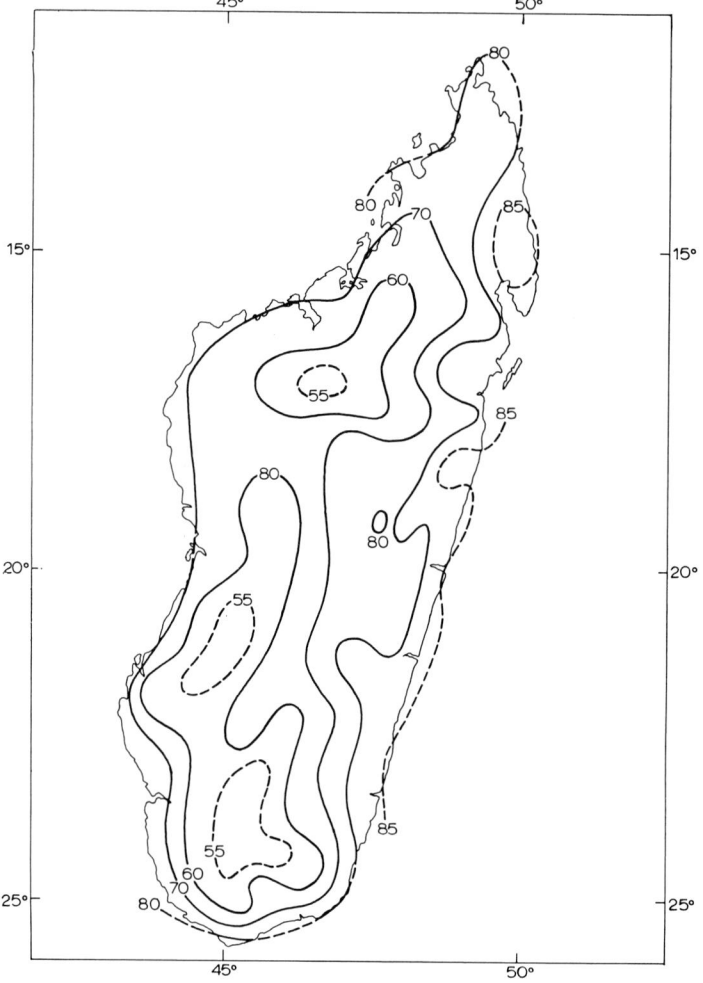

Fig.9. Mean annual relative humidity (%).

Relative humidity

Over the eastern half of Madagascar the direct exposure to the moist trade winds makes for a high relative humidity. The eastern coast averages about 10% higher than the west coast. The lowest annual values exist in those regions where dry, subsiding air reaches the lower land (Fig.9).

The variation in mean monthly values is low, less than 10% on the east coast and much of the plateau. The extreme variation is found at Majunga with 22% (from 62 to 84%). The significant changes are all related to the dry and wet season pattern.

The daily variation of relative humidity is small (about 15–20%) along the east coast and

TABLE IV

RELATIVE HUMIDITY (%)

Station	Relat. humid. (abs. min.)	Date
East coast:		
Diego-Suarez	23	July 1950
Antalaha	39	July 1945
Sainte-Marie	39	Oct. 1960
Tamatave	37	May 1950
Marolambo	36	Nov. 1943
Mananjary	25	June 1965
Farafangana	20	July 1966
Fort Dauphin	28	Sept. 1941
Plateaux:		
Andapa	30	Dec. 1966
Tananarive-Ville	7	Nov. 1957
Arivonimamo	5	Aug. 1951 and 1956
Nanokely	27	Aug. 1944
Antsirabe	7	Aug. 1963
Fianarantsoa	14	Sept. 1958
Betroka	20	Sept. 1949
Nossi-Be—Sambirano:		
Ambilobe	32	Sept. 1944
Nossi-Be	25	Aug. 1962
West coast and lowlands:		
Analalava	14	Aug. 1964
Majunga	15	Sept. 1966
Maevatanana	23	Sept. 1946
Maintirano	13	Aug. 1946
Morondava	11	Sept. 1947
Malaimbandy	23	Sept. 1945 and Oct. 1946
Morombe	10	Oct. 1966
Tulear	10	Nov. 1941
Extreme south:		
Tranoroa	24	Oct. 1941
Tsihombe	29	Sept. 1950
Faux-Cap	19	May 1960

in the forested regions. On the plateau this reaches about 30% and inland, to the west, will exceed 35–40%.

From time to time there are outstandingly rapid changes in the relative humidity that are observed in the cool season. These are due to the establishment of a dry, westerly regime, a pattern caused by the influence of the African continent following a reduction in the depth of the trade wind temperature inversion.

In Table IV values of the extreme minima of relative humidity show that even on the east coast low values can be experienced.

Evaporation

The basic details of evaporation measurements are given in Table V. It is seen that along the eastern coast from north of Antalaha to Fort Dauphin and then round the south coast to Tulear the rate of annual evaporation increases steadily, but with the common characteristic that there is little variation in monthly totals. For example, Antalaha is 65 mm $\pm$ 20% per month, Tamatave 70 mm $\pm$ 10%, Fort Dauphin 125 mm $\pm$ 20% and Tulear 150 mm $\pm$ 10%. October is the month of maximum evaporation and February and/or June that of least amount. On the plateau the monthly values show greater variation, the least being about half the greatest, but the maximum and minimum occur at about the same time as above. This seasonal pattern appears to hold also for the west coast.

TABLE V

EVAPORATION DATA (mm)

Station	Annual	Monthly min.	max.
Antalaha	755	54	77
Diego-Suarez	2,412	82	311
Fianarantsoa	923	57	116
Fort Dauphin	1,470	102	153
Maintirano	1,173	71	122
Majunga	1,863	78	215
Nossi-Be	1,076	57	143
Tamatave	838	63	80
Tananarive	1,172	80	143
Tulear	1,819	135	162

The section from Majunga to Diego-Suarez exhibits a very pronounced seasonal variation, with February values being only 1/3 to 1/4 of those in the month with the greatest evaporation. The value at Diego-Suarez is, like Tulear's amount, much in excess of the mean annual rainfall. The October average of 311 mm is by far the greatest for any month anywhere on the island.

Wind flow

The trade winds

The principal wind of Madagascar is the southeasterly trade wind which stems from the semi-permanent anticyclone of the Indian Ocean and exhibits a remarkable regularity from June to August. The trade winds are very humid and bring abundant precipitation to the coast and the easterly slopes. The depth of the trade wind varies between 2,000 and 4,000 m. The lower layers of the trade wind are strongly diverted by the topography toward the north in the region between Tamatave to Antalaha and towards the south from Mananjary to Fort Dauphin. The wind speed has a very marked diurnal variation, especially at Diego-Suarez, which varies in August from 64 km/h (14h00) to 26 km/h (05h00) (Fig.10).

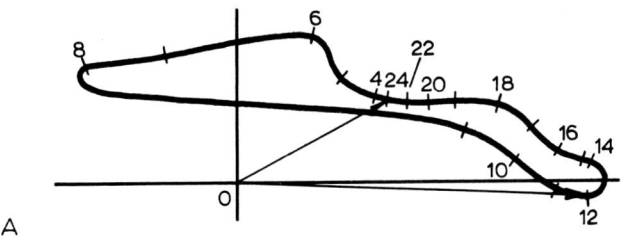

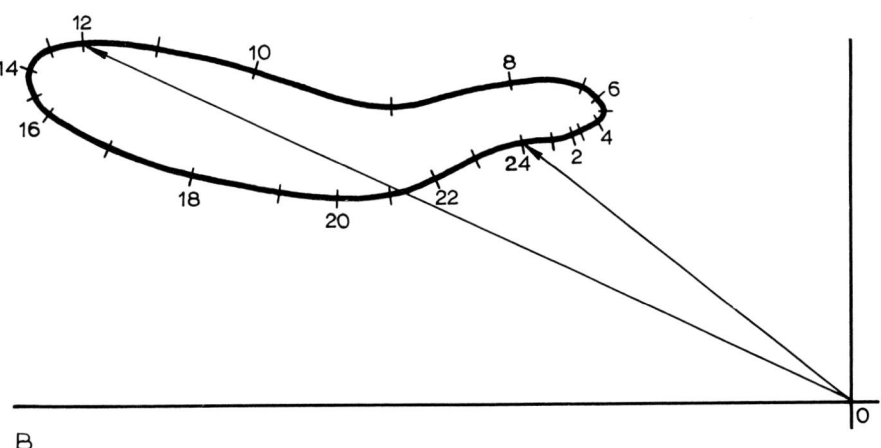

Fig.10. Daily surface variation at Diego-Suarez. A. January; B. August. (Scale: 5 mm = 2 km/h.)

Westerly winds

The trade winds are surmounted by subsiding, dry westerly winds. At the time of the passage of polar fronts to the south of Madagascar the trade winds sometimes vanish over a large part of the island and are replaced by westerly winds. In winter, when they arrive at the plateau surface, these winds bring to the regions they affect a period of generally clear weather or a few clouds with morning mists on the plateau. In summer these westerlies take on moisture as they cross the Mozambique Channel and, on reaching the plateau, favour the development of thunderstorms in regions where there is convergence with the southeast flow.

Northwest winds

In summer the Arabian anticyclone sometimes develops a ridge over the north of the Mozambique Channel. It then institutes outbreaks in the northwest and west central regions so that the western part of the plateau experiences some weak or moderate northwest winds (called monsoons by some authors). This very unstable wind of equatorial origin favours the development of thunderstorm centres (squall lines) over regions that it influences. Following a cyclonic development this wind is reinforced and is accompanied by heavy rains. The limit between the northwest winds and those of the southeast is called the inter-tropical convergence zone (I.T.C.Z.) or inter-tropical front (I.T.F.) It is in this zone that the cyclonic perturbations are formed.

Land and sea breezes

These breezes are observed, to a greater or lesser extent, around the whole coast. They are especially well defined on the west coast, sheltered from the trade winds, and where the hinterland is such that a large diurnal temperature variation results.

The land–sea breeze cycles are much better developed in the summer and transition seasons than during the winter. The winter season exhibits a well established southeasterly flow making such local circulations felt only in moderation and in the lower layers (less than 300–500 m).

General pattern

In winter the easterlies and in summer the westerlies are very noticeable over much of the island, as Table VI shows. The effect of the curving southwesterly flow and the reinforcing by the sea breeze is very much in evidence at Tulear in July. The summer mon-

TABLE VI

PERCENTAGE AND DIRECTION OF WINDS IN SUMMER AND WINTER

Station	Easterlies July (%)	Westerlies Jan. (%)
Diego-Suarez	90	43
Tamatave	—	32
Farafangana	65	—
Fort Dauphin	85	0
Tulear	29	52
Majunga	62	55
Tananarive	85	20

soon regime is dominated by westerlies only in the north and on the west coast. The shading effect of the mountains plus the sea breeze is particularly noticeable at Fort Dauphin.

Wind velocity

Wind speed and direction at the surface have a most pronounced daily variation as illustrated in Fig. 10–13. It is seen that some stations, Diego-Suarez (Fig. 10) and Tamatave (Fig. 13) have very distinct seasonal variation. Wind speeds in winter are uniformly higher than in summer. Wind speeds up to 30 km/h are rather frequent at all lowland stations, occurring about 20–30% of the observations at coastal sites, up to 50% at

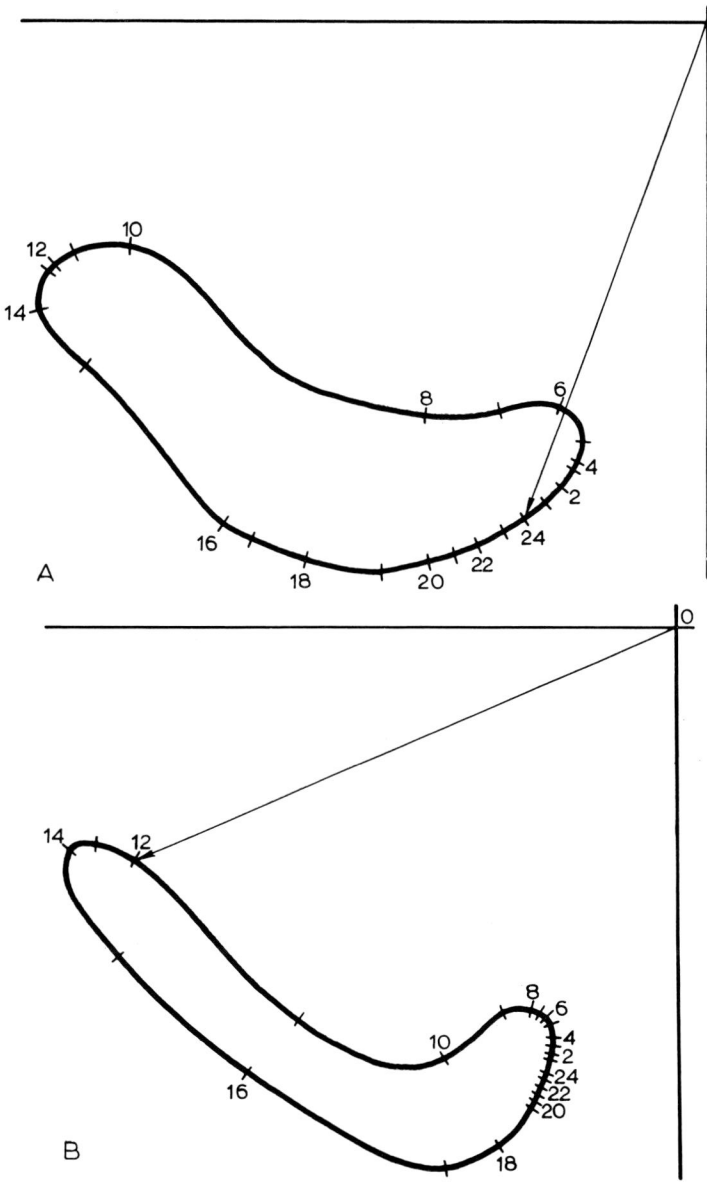

Fig. 11. Daily surface wind variation at Fort Dauphin. A. January; B. August. (Scale: 10 mm = 2 km/h.)

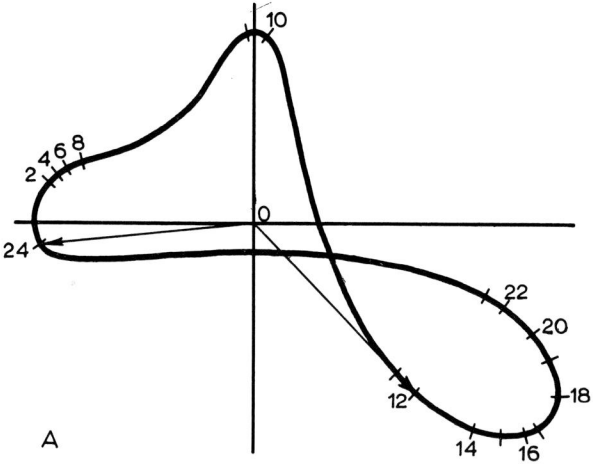

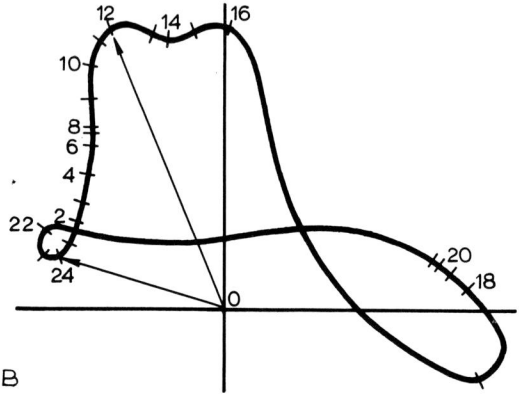

Fig.12. Daily surface wind variation at Majunga. A. January; B. August. (Scale: 5 mm = 2 km/h.)

Diego-Suarez. This is the "windiest" station with speeds of above 60 km/h for 15% of the time, compared with 2% at other stations.

Hail

Hail is not a rare phenomenon in Madagascar. Table VII gives the distribution during the course of the year of 3,026 incidences of hail reported over the whole of the island. The damages caused to the crops are noticeably important in the case of rice where the harvest takes place in November and in April.

The frequency of the phenomenon is mainly a function of the altitude. Table VII also gives the frequencies of the incidences of hail on the plateau of the provinces of Tananarive and Fianarantsoa.

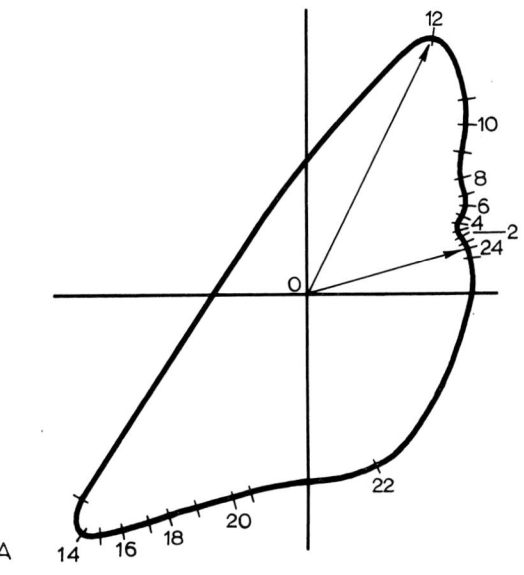

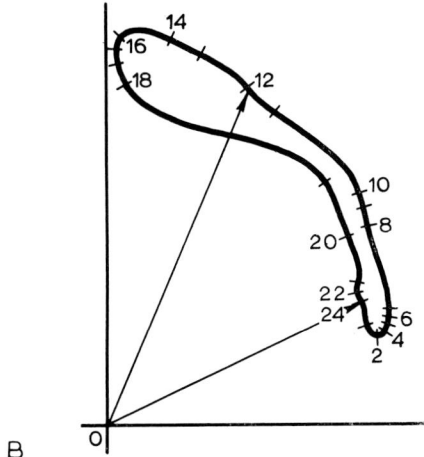

Fig.13. Daily surface wind variation at Tamatave. A. January; B. August. (Scale: 5 mm = 2 km/h.)

TABLE VII

YEARLY DISTRIBUTION (%) OF HAIL THROUGHOUT MADAGASCAR AND FREQUENCY (%) IN TANANARIVE
AND FIANARANTSOA

	Distribution	Frequency
Jan.	7.4	5.6
Feb.	5.1	2.7
Mar.	8.6	3.7
Apr.	10.6	18.0
May	3.8	3.4
June	4.0	1.6
July	0.3	1.4
Aug.	1.0	1.3
Sept.	2.0	1.8
Oct.	16.7	20.0
Nov.	28.4	26.9
Dec.	12.1	13.6

Cyclones

Cyclones are especially prevalent during the warm season. They form generally in the I.T.C.Z., either in the Indian Ocean or in the Mozambique Channel. It is principally in the northern half and on the east coast that they are the most violent. As a matter of fact, there is not an area of the island that is sheltered from their influence. Their intensity usually diminishes when they travel over land, but they can be regenerated on reaching the sea again.

During a cyclone the winds, with a speed that can reach 200 km/h, the heavy falls of rain and very high tides often cause considerable damage. The areas of intense rainfall can extend for several hundred kilometers from the centre of the storm and cause destruction over the entire region.

TABLE VIII

YEARLY DISTRIBUTION (%) OF CYCLONIC DISTURBANCES (1848–1966)

Jan.	28
Feb.	30
Mar.	18
Apr.	6
May–Nov.	3
Dec.	15

Table VIII shows the yearly distribution of 244 cyclonic disturbances which have affected Madagascar between 1848 and 1966:

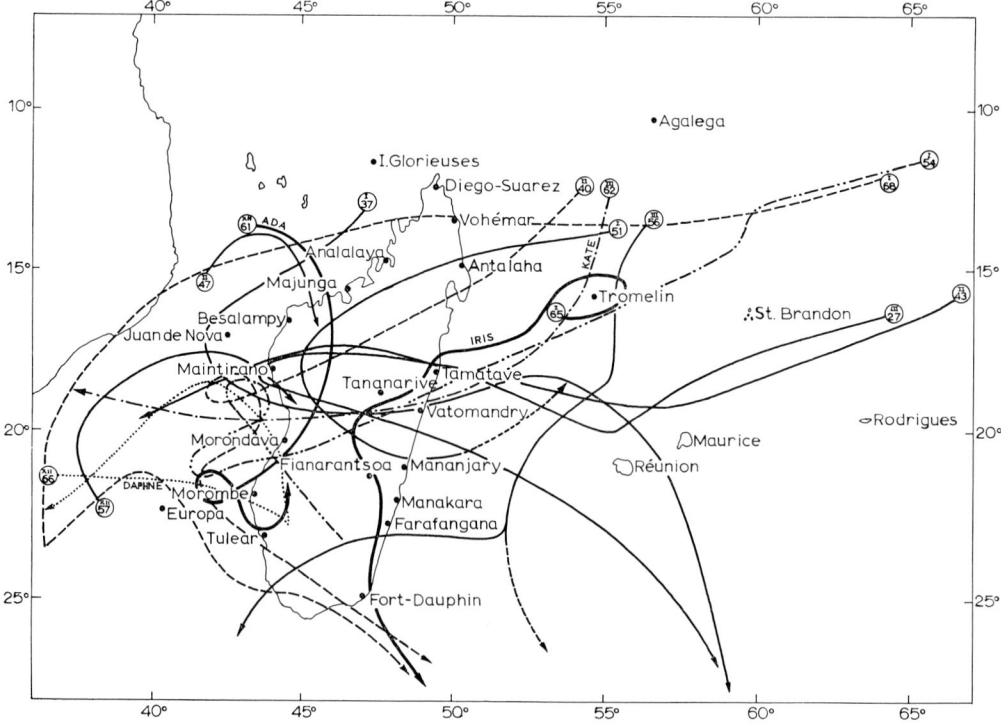

Fig.14. Basic trajectories of cyclones.

An earlier study (1888–1927) classified the 95 cyclones into 52 violent and 43 weaker disturbances, most crossing the island in the north or the south avoiding the central highlands. The cyclones usually form north of the island between 8 and 10°S.

Fig.14 gives the basic trajectories of some cyclones or depressions that have affected Madagascar.

Thunderstorms

The average annual number of thunderstorms varies from less than 50 in the central section of the eastern coast to over 130 in the western central plateau and the central western coast. The most frequent quarter for thunderstorms is in the summer (December–February) when, on average, about half the year's total is experienced (Table IX). During

TABLE IX

DISTRIBUTION OF THUNDERSTORM DAYS

Station	Alt. (10 m)	Jan.	Feb.	Mar.	Apr.	May	June	July	Aug.	Sept.	Oct.	Nov.	Dec.	Total
Diego-Suarez	11	16	15	14	6	1	0	0	0	0	1	4	13	70
Nossi-Be	1	12	15	13	7	2	0	0	0	0	2	8	16	75
Analalava	6	22	19	18	10	1	0	0	0	0	3	12	21	106
Antalaha	1	12	19	19	11	2	0	0	0	0	3	7	15	98
Majunga	2	22	21	21	11	2	0	0	0	1	6	14	22	120
Maevatanana	8	24	22	20	9	1	0	0	1	1	9	16	23	126
Sainte-Marie	0	11	12	11	6	1	0	0	0	0	2	5	12	60
Maintirano	2	24	23	22	11	1	1	0	1	3	10	19	24	139
Tamatave	1	20	18	20	7	1	1	1	1	2	11	17	20	47
Tananarive	131	22	17	19	12	3	1	1	2	2	14	18	21	132
Antsirabe	151	15	12	12	8	2	0	1	0	1	11	16	16	94
Marolambo	40	15	14	13	8	2	1	1	0	1	7	13	17	92
Morondava	1	21	20	16	4	1	0	0	1	1	6	13	21	104
Malaimbandy	16	23	20	18	8	2	0	1	1	2	11	20	24	130
Mananjary	1	9	9	9	6	2	1	1	0	0	3	6	11	57
Fianarantsoa	111	14	11	8	6	2	0	1	2	1	6	13	15	79
Morombe	1	21	16	16	4	2	1	1	0	2	4	8	17	92
Ihosy	80	14	10	9	5	2	0	0	0	1	7	11	15	74
Farafangana	1	8	10	9	7	3	1	1	0	1	3	8	11	62
Betroka	80	18	12	11	7	3	1	1	2	1	7	15	18	96
Tulear	1	19	15	13	6	3	2	1	1	1	5	11	17	94
Fort Dauphin	1	11	10	9	5	4	3	2	2	1	5	8	10	70
Tsihombe	6	12	10	6	4	2	2	1	1	1	3	8	10	60

the winter (June–August) thunderstorms are extremely rare in the northern half of the island although the southern tip records a few, spawned by the air mass interactions at that time of year. January, the time of maximum thermal instability, is the month with the greatest number of thunderstorms, many stations reporting over 20, although December values are nearly as high.

Climatic regions

East coast

This region has a hot and humid climate. It is exposed directly to the trade winds and receives more than 2,500 mm of rainfall with a maximum of 3,700 mm in the Bay of Antongil and a minimum (900–1,600 mm) in the north and south extremes.

The rains are especially abundant from January to April; they reach their minimum in September or October (although these months experience more than 7–15 rain days). There also exists a secondary minimum in May between the summer and winter rains. The mean annual temperature is in the vicinity of 24°C; the absolute extremes of temperature are 36.8°C at Diego-Suarez and 8.8°C at Fort Dauphin.

The plateau

This region comprises the interior of the island above 700 m. It rises to more than 2,800 m in the massif of Tsaratanana. In the period between May and September the zone above 1,500 m is sometimes subject to hail and two cases of snowfall have been observed on Andringitra, on the 8th of August, 1961, and the 29th of July, 1963. The climate of the plateau is generally temperate. Around 1,200 m the mean annual temperature varies between 18 and 22°C. The local variations of climate are very important, being related to the exposure and the altitude. The maximum temperature observed is 40°C at Betroka and the minimum is –8.4°C at Nanokely.

The rainfall amounts vary from 1,250 to 1,900 mm, but Andringitra and Tsaratanana receive more than 2,500 mm. In the depression of Lake Alaotra, which is noticeably warmer than the local areas, the annual mean is of the order of 1,000 mm. The rains are almost entirely limited to the period from October to April; nevertheless a zone of 50–100 km wide at the edge of the eastern forest receives 30–40 days of mist during the dry season. The start of the rainy season generally occurs during the second decade of October but may be as late as the first decade of December. The end of the rainy season can lie between the third decade of March and the third decade of May. There is also a tendency for the existence of a clear minimum in precipitation either during the third decade of January or the first decade of February.

Nossi-Be — Sambirano

The climate of this part of the island is very similar to that of the east coast; hot and humid with annual precipitation also abundant (2,000–2,500 mm) of which about 15% falls in the winter. The months of December to March are the rainiest. The maximum monthly has been observed in January 1941 at Hell-Ville with a 1,001.5 mm.

The mean annual temperature is about 25°C. The absolute maxima are 39.0°C at Hell-Ville and 45.0°C at Ambilobe; the absolute minima are 13.2°C at Fascene and 10.5°C at Ambilobe.

West coast (to the south of Nossi-Be) and coastal plains of the west

The climate of this region is warm and dry. The mean annual temperature varies between 24°C (south) and 27°C (north). The absolute maximum has been 40.4°C at Tulear and the absolute minimum 5.1°C at Morombe.

The mean annual precipitation diminishes from the north to the south, reaching 1,910 mm at Analalava and only 340 mm at Tulear. The dry season is particularly well marked and extends from May to October. The maximum precipitation is observed in January in the northern half and in February in the southern half of this region.

Extreme south

This region is characterized by a large variability of climate, which is expected as this is a semi-arid zone. It receives from 340 to 750 mm of rain each year. The distribution is very irregular in the course of the year. One can find, nevertheless, evidence of a "little rainy season" of variable duration (4–17 decades) beginning in October or in January and finishing either in January or at the beginning of May. The droughts can extend over

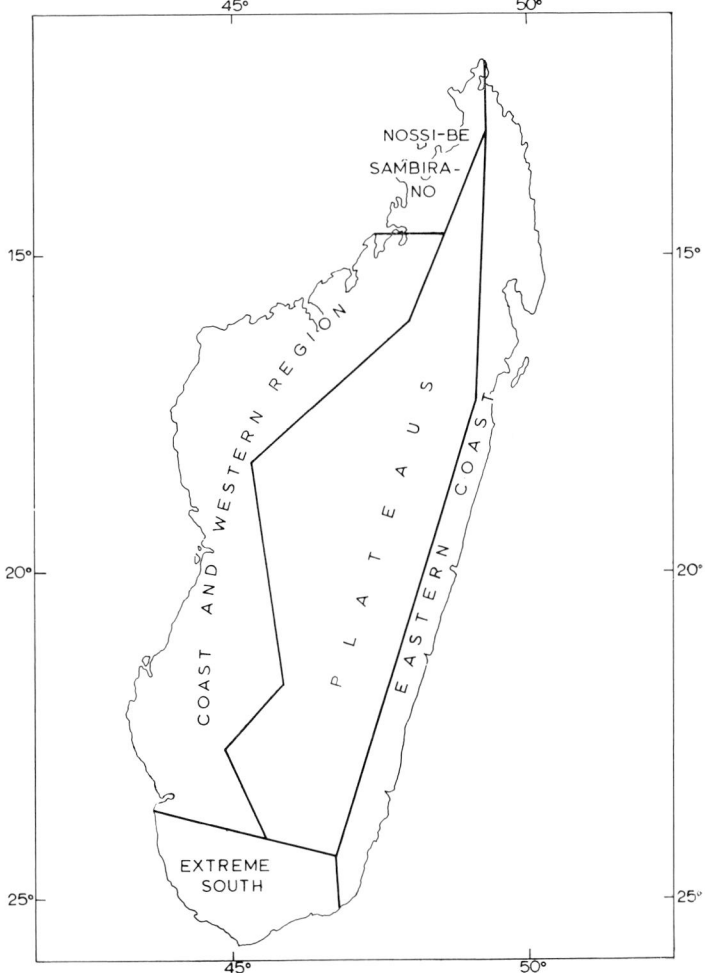

Fig.15. Major climatic regions.

many months (4 months in 1943). The mean annual temperature for this region is about 24°C. Absolute maximum is 46.5°C at Tranoroa and the absolute minimum is 2.0°C at Ampotaka-Marolinta.

Fig.15 depicts the various climatic zones.

TABLE X

RAINFALL DATA FOR DIFFERENT STATIONS

Month	Monthly rainfall (mm)				Days with rain		
	mean	max.	min.	max. in 24 h	mean	max.	min.
Diego-Suarez (12°21'S 49°18'E, 105 m)							
Jan.	276.5	516.9	94.7	230.5	20	27	10
Feb.	211.4	468.6	38.0	177.4	18	24	12
Mar.	187.2	884.8	27.0	508.1	14	24	6
Apr.	55.7	196.1	0.0	97.0	6	16	0
May	8.1	42.5	0.0	42.5	3	8	0
June	8.1	34.8	0.0	22.9	4	11	0
July	6.5	22.8	0.0	13.7	4	12	0
Aug.	7.2	44.0	0.0	37.1	4	11	0
Sept.	4.7	36.1	0.0	34.4	3	11	0
Oct.	10.6	60.7	0.0	25.8	4	12	0
Nov.	27.8	171.7	2.0	73.9	6	13	1
Dec.	111.1	489.0	6.1	254.7	12	22	4
Year	914.9	1,812.3	384.1	508.1	98	131	75
Antalaha (15°00'S, 50°20'E, 24 m)							
Jan.	260.1	484.9	85.6	200.7	18	25	11
Feb.	246.2	729.5	89.7	282.0	17	27	9
Mar.	266.5	635.8	53.4	185.2	17	25	11
Apr.	280.5	871.1	74.4	212.7	18	24	11
May	150.4	537.4	8.8	191.2	17	29	6
June	162.1	366.8	60.9	134.3	20	26	11
July	148.3	288.5	42.6	111.6	22	28	8
Aug.	131.8	396.6	17.4	96.9	21	29	5
Sept.	103.7	476.1	30.0	108.8	17	25	8
Oct.	76.0	203.7	32.7	97.5	15	23	6
Nov.	113.5	328.8	16.2	127.9	15	25	4
Dec.	211.2	478.1	26.1	119.5	17	25	11
Year	2,150.3	3,169.6	1,496.5	282.0	214	254	150
Ambodifototra (Ile Ste-Marie, 17°05'S, 49°49'E, 3 m)							
Jan.	382.8	865.6	77.8	206.6	21	29	14
Feb.	444.3	1,204.6	218.9	269.6	20	24	13
Mar.	574.2	1,205.3	259.6	301.5	24	29	17
Apr.	454.1	1,027.2	120.1	221.3	23	28	19
May	320.9	706.2	135.4	158.6	24	30	16
June	343.8	641.4	113.1	127.7	24	29	14
July	281.2	505.1	85.8	136.0	25	30	21
Aug.	187.9	425.1	60.2	85.2	23	30	12
Sept.	109.4	340.3	28.0	95.4	18	26	8
Oct.	84.6	260.0	33.1	114.1	14	25	6
Nov.	130.9	415.9	23.1	168.0	15	21	8
Dec.	285.2	580.6	66.3	169.5	19	27	8
Year	3,599.3	4,892.5	2,429.4	301.5	250	275	202

TABLE X *(continued)*

Month	Monthly rainfall (mm)				Days with rain		
	mean	max.	min.	max. in 24 h	mean	max.	min.
Tamatave (18°07'S, 49°24'E, 5 m)							
Jan.	419.7	850.2	137.3	233.4	21	26	15
Feb.	441.3	1,065.4	121.8	247.1	20	27	10
Mar.	528.4	1,068.9	107.6	441.5	22	28	16
Apr.	404.4	934.5	80.2	376.3	21	27	14
May	302.5	991.2	83.5	154.1	20	28	7
June	299.6	771.0	87.9	180.0	22	28	15
July	257.2	473.7	90.9	129.2	23	29	17
Aug.	208.2	407.9	69.4	133.7	23	29	14
Sept.	134.2	364.6	36.1	122.4	18	26	9
Oct.	87.3	249.9	14.7	104.1	15	23	8
Nov.	184.4	577.6	32.7	217.5	16	25	8
Dec.	258.9	516.8	53.4	134.9	19	26	10
Year	3,526.1	4,911.2	2,398.0	441.5	240	273	203
Mananjary (21°12'S, 48°22'E, 6 m)							
Jan.	398.1	936.3	73.9	384.2	21	30	13
Feb.	369.6	834.5	133.7	235.0	20	28	15
Mar.	497.7	1,377.1	100.4	430.8	22	29	15
Apr.	245.4	713.1	92.6	187.6	18	24	7
May	194.7	415.9	47.2	190.0	18	26	11
June	229.6	591.7	25.1	197.0	18	28	8
July	158.4	378.3	24.2	113.5	18	25	11
Aug.	136.0	474.6	23.6	152.5	17	28	6
Sept.	102.7	242.7	17.6	86.3	14	22	8
Oct.	79.1	280.5	3.5	124.5	11	20	5
Nov.	172.5	498.1	6.4	160.1	14	23	4
Dec.	209.7	406.9	35.3	154.0	17	26	8
Year	2,793.5	3,776.2	1,912.4	430.8	208	236	162
Fort Dauphin (25°02'S, 46°57'E, 8 m)							
Jan.	201.9	562.0	27.3	218.6	15	26	6
Feb.	183.6	436.8	54.9	111.6	15	23	9
Mar.	235.7	588.0	19.7	282.7	17	28	5
Apr.	113.0	262.1	15.7	111.1	13	22	4
May	117.3	288.0	2.0	93.8	12	18	4
June	134.9	379.0	15.2	148.0	13	21	6
July	108.5	305.9	20.5	102.7	13	24	7
Aug.	93.5	325.1	9.5	161.3	11	20	3
Sept.	61.4	264.1	4.3	124.3	9	15	2
Oct.	72.7	207.9	0.7	86.1	8	14	1
Nov.	90.7	222.1	8.1	97.9	12	18	7
Dec.	123.9	314.0	56.1	78.0	14	24	6
Year	1,537.1	2,059.3	988.3	282.7	152	193	120

TABLE X *(continued)*

Month	Monthly rainfall (mm)				Days with rain		
	mean	max.	min.	max. in 24 h	mean	max.	min.
Andapa (14°39′S, 49°37′E, 471 m)							
Jan.	362.9	575.8	143.6	114.7	23	29	13
Feb.	338.9	980.2	110.6	251.5	21	26	9
Mar.	297.3	478.8	83.9	107.2	21	31	9
Apr.	180.5	478.0	37.8	265.0	18	27	7
May	75.1	183.5	12.3	49.6	17	29	7
June	83.6	334.9	36.0	58.8	18	27	6
July	105.7	373.0	31.4	204.9	20	28	2
Aug.	102.3	296.6	6.0	50.5	20	28	3
Sept.	67.1	154.1	7.5	114.6	16	26	4
Oct.	60.1	136.2	20.5	114.6	13	23	5
Nov.	97.6	365.1	4.0	129.4	13	19	2
Dec.	271.3	711.8	63.4	196.8	19	25	5
Year	2,042.4	3,284.3	1,195.2	265.0	219	272	136
Tananarive Observatoire (18°55′S, 47°33′E, 1,381 m)							
Jan.	304.5	598.1	42.6	133.3	22	29	10
Feb.	235.0	665.5	94.7	132.5	18	26	11
Mar.	220.6	611.6	22.9	121.6	19	28	9
Apr.	47.1	149.1	0.2	66.7	10	19	1
May	15.8	49.3	0.4	18.1	9	23	1
June	8.8	23.8	0.0	21.0	10	22	0
July	8.7	41.3	1.4	15.2	10	20	1
Aug.	8.9	24.2	0.5	19.9	9	23	1
Sept.	13.9	120.3	0.0	106.5	6	14	0
Oct.	49.3	170.7	1.4	132.2	7	13	1
Nov.	154.0	431.9	1.0	100.1	14	24	2
Dec.	292.2	540.9	103.3	110.0	20	28	10
Year	1,358.8	1,943.8	950.2	133.3	154	227	105
Antsirabe-Ecole (19°52′S, 47°01′E, 1,506 m)							
Jan.	293.4	561.8	64.9	107.6	23	30	11
Feb.	240.7	443.5	93.8	99.8	19	26	10
Mar.	217.8	445.7	76.2	111.3	19	27	9
Apr.	77.3	203.8	3.7	88.6	10	20	2
May	30.5	97.7	tr	40.2	6	12	0
June	12.5	55.0	0.0	24.8	4	11	0
July	16.7	83.7	0.0	35.5	4	11	0
Aug.	15.0	84.2	0.0	64.0	3	7	0
Sept.	23.5	99.7	0.0	42.3	4	12	0
Oct.	76.7	199.8	8.8	75.8	9	18	3
Nov.	157.8	335.5	28.9	64.5	15	25	6
Dec.	267.6	444.6	87.2	86.6	22	27	11
Year	1,429.5	1,961.9	1,014.3	111.3	138	176	101

TABLE X *(continued)*

Month	Monthly rainfall (mm)				Days with rain		
	mean	max.	min.	max. in 24 h	mean	max.	min.
Fianarantsoa (21°27′S, 47°06′E, 1,106 m)							
Jan.	290.6	610.6	70.5	127.9	22	31	6
Feb.	205.5	582.7	71.4	166.6	20	26	11
Mar.	173.7	424.9	46.0	79.0	21	30	10
Apr.	44.3	191.8	8.8	45.6	13	25	4
May	26.7	97.6	0.0	47.0	11	20	0
June	20.3	77.8	2.0	33.8	11	22	2
July	18.5	42.3	2.6	19.3	11	23	1
Aug.	17.4	62.8	0.0	26.1	10	17	0
Sept.	23.8	91.3	0.0	36.0	8	14	0
Oct.	33.8	127.5	3.6	69.7	7	15	1
Nov.	130.5	246.6	13.3	100.5	14	25	6
Dec.	236.7	467.8	106.9	95.6	19	31	6
Year	1,221.8	1,804.0	825.0	166.6	167	208	68
Betroka (23°17′S, 46°05′E, 795 m)							
Jan.	207.6	524.9	41.9	147.0	13	23	4
Feb.	133.7	406.1	16.4	90.0	11	22	2
Mar.	94.5	305.5	19.6	78.5	9	20	5
Apr.	27.4	115.0	0.0	63.9	4	9	0
May	12.2	46.7	0.0	29.0	3	9	0
June	10.8	47.5	0.0	25.0	2	7	0
July	7.2	59.8	0.0	24.9	1	5	0
Aug.	6.0	41.1	0.0	27.4	1	6	0
Sept.	15.3	110.2	0.0	47.2	2	7	0
Oct.	33.4	113.6	0.0	52.2	4	9	0
Nov.	97.1	197.1	11.5	86.9	9	15	3
Dec.	201.9	383.0	67.7	123.0	14	23	6
Year	847.1	1,475.3	590.1	147.0	73	95	40
Nossi-Be (Hell-Ville) (13°19′S, 48°19′E, 11 m)							
Jan.	463.8	1,001.5	176.8	190.2	22	28	10
Feb.	425.2	920.0	132.0	234.0	20	26	2
Mar.	286.6	658.7	115.7	172.8	18	26	5
Apr.	141.2	386.8	17.0	186.2	12	18	5
May	58.3	230.0	11.7	63.2	7	11	4
June	48.6	160.8	5.1	55.0	6	12	2
July	32.6	85.8	0.0	57.7	6	13	0
Aug.	40.4	116.1	3.8	70.2	8	16	3
Sept.	49.4	150.5	7.3	94.0	8	18	4
Oct.	95.7	250.6	4.9	111.5	11	19	2
Nov.	188.9	375.1	13.2	159.5	15	22	5
Dec.	361.7	940.0	143.8	332.2	20	27	10
Year	2,192.4	2,738.8	1,613.6	332.2	153	180	124

TABLE X *(continued)*

Month	Monthly rainfall (mm)				Days with rain		
	mean	max.	min.	max. in 24 h	mean	max.	min.
Majunga (15°40'S, 46°21'E, 22 m)							
Jan.	465.8	1,125.0	147.8	274.0	20	27	13
Feb.	369.7	781.1	30.4	180.4	18	24	7
Mar.	282.4	1,033.9	46.1	320.5	15	20	6
Apr.	56.8	236.9	0.8	87.7	5	12	1
May	7.9	58.2	0.0	58.1	1	5	0
June	2.6	41.7	0.0	32.2	1	4	0
July	1.0	6.7	0.0	6.7	1	4	0
Aug.	2.1	15.9	0.0	13.9	1	4	0
Sept.	2.6	15.9	0.0	14.0	1	5	0
Oct.	23.7	117.7	0.0	84.3	3	6	0
Nov.	109.6	274.5	10.6	83.8	8	15	2
Dec.	242.6	436.5	60.6	117.3	15	20	7
Year	1,566.8	2,692.3	1,002.7	320.5	89	109	67
Maintirano (18°03'S, 44°02'E, 23 m)							
Jan.	301.8	923.0	84.8	271.7	17	24	11
Feb.	220.3	582.7	36.0	260.8	15	19	4
Mar.	158.4	684.6	12.0	284.1	13	23	4
Apr.	31.9	204.4	0.0	61.6	4	11	0
May	8.7	53.8	0.0	36.2	1	7	0
June	4.4	31.3	0.0	25.4	1	5	0
July	3.7	30.8	0.0	28.6	1	4	0
Aug.	3.5	37.5	0.0	16.9	1	7	0
Sept.	8.5	71.5	0.0	61.1	2	7	0
Oct.	16.7	73.9	0.0	41.7	3	7	0
Nov.	63.1	244.8	0.0	115.8	6	11	0
Dec.	177.2	827.4	38.6	300.7	12	20	7
Year	998.2	2,427.2	454.3	300.7	76	103	19
Morondava (20°17'S, 44°19'E, 8 m)							
Jan.	227.8	613.7	28.6	248.2	13	18	7
Feb.	209.1	841.9	21.6	313.0	11	18	3
Mar.	116.6	355.5	5.0	130.0	8	16	1
Apr.	13.2	79.8	0.0	54.2	1	4	0
May	7.0	45.8	0.0	45.8	1	6	0
June	5.7	66.0	0.0	60.3	1	4	0
July	1.2	21.5	0.0	20.0	1	3	0
Aug.	1.6	15.1	0.0	15.1	1	3	0
Sept.	6.7	44.7	0.0	44.7	1	5	0
Oct.	8.9	67.0	0.0	67.0	1	3	0
Nov.	17.1	69.0	0.0	40.2	3	7	0
Dec.	128.6	454.8	26.1	263.0	8	16	2
Year	743.5	1,422.3	340.1	313.0	50	69	34

TABLE X *(continued)*

Month	Monthly rainfall (mm)				Days with rain		
	mean	max.	min.	max. in 24 h	mean	max.	min.
Morombe (21°45′S, 43°22′E, 5 m)							
Jan.	123.3	513.0	8.9	217.4	7	13	2
Feb.	134.4	538.9	0.0	242.2	6	18	0
Mar.	59.0	489.0	0.0	170.4	4	12	0
Apr.	4.5	36.5	0.0	29.8	1	5	0
May	7.2	32.3	0.0	32.3	2	5	0
June	6.8	44.2	0.0	31.6	1	6	0
July	2.1	38.8	0.0	31.2	1	4	0
Aug.	0.5	10.1	0.0	5.4	1	3	0
Sept.	5.3	67.4	0.0	34.4	1	5	0
Oct.	3.6	48.8	0.0	39.6	1	2	0
Nov.	22.3	96.4	0.0	62.1	2	7	0
Dec.	84.7	348.6	0.2	112.1	5	13	1
Year	453.7	946.2	120.0	242.2	32	47	16
Tulear (23°23′S, 43°44′E, 9 m)							
Jan.	70.5	337.8	5.5	103.6	7	15	1
Feb.	71.3	191.0	2.4	70.0	6	15	1
Mar.	42.3	359.6	0.0	57.9	5	15	0
Apr.	6.5	39.8	0.0	29.9	1	5	0
May	17.9	139.0	0.0	66.7	2	7	0
June	10.7	44.8	0.0	25.9	2	8	0
July	4.0	21.0	0.0	19.5	1	5	0
Aug.	3.1	51.5	0.0	48.0	1	2	0
Sept.	9.5	47.6	0.0	31.0	1	5	0
Oct.	13.5	102.9	0.0	102.3	1	4	0
Nov.	34.4	127.4	0.0	83.4	2	8	0
Dec.	57.1	192.7	0.0	105.1	5	11	0
Year	340.8	665.9	129.4	105.1	34	60	16
Tsihombe (25°18′S, 45°30′E, 64 m)							
Jan.	77.7	388.8	2.2	158.3	9	18	2
Feb.	90.0	246.2	0.9	117.8	8	19	1
Mar.	59.5	299.8	2.6	166.8	7	22	2
Apr.	18.9	70.3	0.1	50.9	5	11	1
May	24.2	85.1	0.0	42.1	6	12	0
June	30.5	230.3	0.0	119.9	6	14	0
July	13.5	40.3	0.0	19.4	5	11	0
Aug.	8.0	45.9	0.0	27.5	4	9	0
Sept.	15.1	60.0	0.0	25.5	3	11	0
Oct.	15.4	75.8	0.0	38.2	3	8	0
Nov.	30.6	107.1	0.4	68.8	6	11	2
Dec.	106.0	288.8	9.0	144.4	10	19	3
Year	489.4	895.8	203.9	166.8	72	104	50

TABLE XI

CLIMATIC TABLE FOR DIEGO-SUAREZ
Latitude 12°21'S, longitude 49°18'E, elevation 105 m

Month	M.s.l. press. (mbar)	Temperature (°C)				Relat. humid. (%)	Precipitation					Wind[1]			Averages		
		mean		extreme			mean (mm)	max. (mm)	min. (mm)	days	max. in 24 h	av. speed (km/h)	preval. direct.	calm (%)	cloud-iness (oktas)	sun-shine (h)	evap. (mm)
		max.	min.	max.	min.												
Jan.	1,011	30	23	36	20	82	276	517	95	20	231	14	W	18	6	188	113
Feb.	1,010	30	23	36	20	84	211	468	38	18	177	13	W	20	6	190	82
Mar.	1,011	30	23	35	21	83	187	885	27	14	508	15	E	16	6	253	108
Apr.	1,012	31	23	36	19	77	56	196	0	6	97	19	ESE	8	5	325	164
May	1,014	30	21	35	16	71	8	42	0	3	42	21	ESE	3	3	290	228
June	1,016	29	20	34	16	72	8	35	0	4	23	23	ESE	3	4	256	222
July	1,017	28	20	34	15	68	6	23	0	4	14	25	ESE	2	4	260	241
Aug.	1,017	28	19	34	15	67	7	44	0	4	37	27	ESE	1	3	289	274
Sept.	1,016	29	20	32	17	68	5	36	0	3	34	28	ESE	1	3	317	302
Oct.	1,015	30	21	34	18	68	11	61	0	4	26	29	ESE	1	3	348	311
Nov.	1,013	31	23	37	19	72	28	172	2	6	74	24	ESE	2	4	290	226
Dec.	1,012	31	23	37	20	78	111	489	6	12	255	16	E	12	5	273	141
Annual	1,014	30	22	37	15	74	915	1,812	384	97	508	21	—	7	4	3,279	2,412
Rec. (yrs.)	9	9	9	35	35	9	30	30	30	30	30	9	9	10	9	14	9

[1] Mean of 07h00, 12h00 and 17h00 local time.

TABLE XII

CLIMATIC TABLE FOR NOSSI-BE (FASCENE)
Latitude 13°20'S, longitude 48°17'E, elevation 10 m

Month	M.s.l. press. (mbar)	Temperature (°C)				Relat. humid. (%)	Precipitation					Wind[1]				Averages		
		mean		extreme			mean (mm)	max. (mm)	min. (mm)	days	max. in 24 h	av. speed (km/h)	preval. direct.	calm (%)	cloud-iness (oktas)	sun-shine (h)	evap. (mm)
		max.	min.	max.	min.												
Jan.	1,011	31	23	36	20	87	464	1,001	177	22	190	7	W	42	6	205	68
Feb.	1,010	31	23	36	20	88	425	920	132	20	234	6	WSW	49	6	182	57
Mar.	1,011	31	23	39	20	88	287	659	116	18	173	6	WSW	51	5	213	64
Apr.	1,012	31	22	39	19	87	141	387	17	12	186	5	NE	52	4	252	66
May	1,014	31	20	35	15	84	58	230	12	7	63	5	NE	49	3	281	78
June	1,016	29	19	35	14	84	49	161	5	6	55	5	NE	46	3	252	76
July	1,017	29	17	32	13	82	33	86	0	6	58	6	NE	39	3	278	90
Aug.	1,017	29	18	33	14	79	40	116	4	8	70	7	NE	37	3	293	106
Sept.	1,016	31	19	34	15	76	49	150	7	8	94	7	NE	30	3	295	126
Oct.	1,015	32	20	37	15	75	96	251	5	11	111	8	NE	28	3	309	143
Nov.	1,013	32	22	36	18	79	189	375	13	15	160	7	NE	37	4	271	119
Dec.	1,012	31	23	36	20	85	362	940	144	20	332	6	NE	38	5	228	83
Annual	1,014	31	21	39	13	83	2,192	2,739	1,614	153	332	6	—	42	4	3,059	1,076
Rec. (yrs.)	9	9	9	39	39	9	30	30	30	30	30	9	9	9	10	9	12

[1] Mean of 07h00, 12h00 and 17h00 local time.

TABLE XIII

CLIMATIC TABLE FOR ANTALAHA
Latitude 15°00'S, longitude 50°20'E, elevation 5 m

Month	M.s.l. press. (mbar)	Temperature (°C) mean max.	mean min.	extreme max.	extreme min.	Relat. humid. (%)	Precipitation mean (mm)	max. (mm)	min. (mm)	days	max. in 24 h	Wind[1] av. speed (km/h)	preval. direct.	calm (%)	Averages cloud-iness (oktas)	sun-shine (h)	evap. (mm)
Jan.	1,011	30	23	37	19	85	260	485	86	18	201	10	E	20	6	205	60
Feb.	1,010	30	22	39	20	85	246	729	90	17	282	10	E	23	5	204	54
Mar.	1,011	30	22	37	19	86	266	636	53	17	185	9	SSE	20	6	190	56
Apr.	1,013	29	22	35	18	85	281	871	74	18	213	12	SSE	21	5	243	59
May	1,015	28	20	32	16	85	150	537	9	17	191	12	SSE	5	5	253	63
June	1,018	26	19	31	14	86	162	367	61	20	134	12	SSE	7	5	242	58
July	1,019	25	18	30	14	85	148	289	43	22	112	13	SSE	8	5	224	56
Aug.	1,019	25	18	30	14	85	132	397	17	21	97	13	SSE	4	5	256	68
Sept.	1,019	26	18	32	14	83	104	476	30	17	109	13	SSE	5	5	266	72
Oct.	1,017	27	19	34	15	82	76	204	33	15	98	13	SSE	9	5	260	77
Nov.	1,015	28	21	35	17	84	113	329	16	15	128	11	E	7	5	237	68
Dec.	1,012	29	22	37	18	85	211	478	26	17	120	10	E	14	5	197	64
Annual	1,015	28	20	39	14	85	2,150	3,170	1,497	213	282	12	—	17	5	2,777	755
Rec. (yrs.)	9	15	15	36	36	9	30	30	30	30	30	14	14	14	10	8	16

[1] Mean of 07h00, 12h00 and 17h00 local time.

TABLE XIV

CLIMATIC TABLE FOR MAJUNGA
Latitude 15°40'S, longitude 46°20'E, elevation 22 m

Month	M.s.l. press. (mbar)	Temperature (°C)				Relat. humid. (%)	Precipitation					Wind[1]			Averages		
		mean		extreme			mean (mm)	max. (mm)	min. (mm)	days	max. in 24 h	av. speed (km/h)	preval. direct.	calm (%)	cloud-iness (oktas)	sun-shine (h)	evap. (mm)
		max.	min.	max.	min.												
Jan.	1,011	31	24	37	18	82	466	1,125	148	20	274	12	NW	7	6	183	112
Feb.	1,010	31	24	36	20	84	370	781	30	18	180	12	NW	8	6	173	78
Mar.	1,010	31	24	38	17	82	282	1,034	46	15	321	12	E	7	6	221	90
Apr.	1,012	32	23	37	18	74	57	237	1	5	88	11	E	3	3	291	128
May	1,014	32	20	36	15	68	8	58	0	1	58	12	ESE	3	2	317	166
June	1,017	31	19	34	13	66	3	42	0	1	32	12	ESE	3	2	297	215
July	1,018	30	18	34	14	63	1	7	0	1	7	14	ESE	3	2	303	184
Aug.	1,018	31	18	36	15	62	2	16	0	1	14	14	ESE	2	2	320	208
Sept.	1,016	32	20	36	16	63	3	16	0	1	14	16	ESE	2	2	318	206
Oct.	1,015	32	22	37	16	66	24	118	0	3	84	16	NW	4	2	339	201
Nov.	1,013	32	23	39	16	72	110	274	11	8	84	15	NW	5	4	290	158
Dec.	1,011	31	24	38	18	80	243	436	61	15	117	12	NNW	6	5	228	117
Annual	1,014	31	21	39	13	72	1,567	2,692	1,003	88	321	13	—	4	4	3,280	1,863
Rec. (yrs.)	9	9	9	36	36	9	30	30	30	30	30	9	9	9	10	16	15

[1] Mean of 07h00, 12h00 and 17h00 local time.

TABLE XV

CLIMATIC TABLE FOR MAINTIRANO
Latitude 18°03'S, longitude 44°02'E, elevation 23 m

Month	M.s.l. press. (mbar)	Temperature (°C)				Relat. humid. (%)	Precipitation					Wind[1]			Averages		
		mean		extreme			mean (mm)	max. (mm)	min. (mm)	days	max. in 24 h	av. speed (km/h)	preval. direct.	calm (%)	cloud-iness (oktas)	sun-shine (h)	evap. (mm)
		max.	min.	max.	min.												
Jan.	1,010	31	23	37	19	85	302	923	85	17	272	13	SW	29	6	273	80
Feb.	1,009	31	24	35	20	85	220	583	36	15	261	11	SW	25	6	235	71
Mar.	1,010	31	23	35	20	84	158	685	12	13	284	12	SW	32	5	271	77
Apr.	1,012	31	23	35	18	81	32	204	0	4	62	11	SW	33	3	305	88
May	1,015	29	20	34	13	78	9	54	0	1	36	12	SW	23	2	305	100
June	1,017	27	18	32	11	77	4	31	0	1	25	13	SW	18	2	293	96
July	1,018	27	18	32	9	77	4	31	0	1	29	13	SW	20	2	301	101
Aug.	1,018	28	19	34	11	78	3	38	0	1	17	14	SW	18	3	317	106
Sept.	1,016	29	20	35	15	77	8	72	0	2	61	15	W	25	2	312	114
Oct.	1,015	30	22	37	17	77	17	74	0	3	42	15	W	32	3	327	122
Nov.	1,013	31	23	37	17	77	63	245	0	6	116	14	W	32	4	311	117
Dec.	1,011	32	23	36	20	81	177	827	39	12	301	13	W	33	5	284	101
Annual	1,014	30	21	37	9	80	998	2,427	454	76	301	13	—	27	4	3,534	1,173
Rec. (yrs.)	8	25	25	35	35	15	30	30	30	30	30	14	14	14	10	5	25

[1] Mean of 07h00, 12h00 and 17h00 local time.

TABLE XVI

CLIMATIC TABLE FOR TAMATAVE
Latitude 18°07'S, longitude 49°24'E, elevation 5 m

Month	M.s.l. press. (mbar)	Temperature (°C)				Relat. humid. (%)	Precipitation					Wind[1]			Averages		
		mean		extreme			mean (mm)	max. (mm)	min. (mm)	days	max. in 24 h	av. speed (km/h)	preval. direct.	calm (%)	cloud-iness (oktas)	sun-shine (h)	evap. (mm)
		max.	min.	max.	min.												
Jan.	1,011	30	23	37	20	84	420	850	137	21	233	14	E	13	5	226	80
Feb.	1,011	30	23	35	20	85	441	1,065	122	20	247	13	SSE	12	5	185	71
Mar.	1,012	29	22	36	19	87	528	1,069	108	22	442	14	S	10	6	184	71
Apr.	1,015	28	21	33	17	86	404	934	80	21	376	14	SSW	9	5	199	70
May	1,017	27	19	30	15	86	302	991	84	20	154	14	SSW	4	5	197	69
June	1,020	25	18	29	11	86	300	771	88	22	180	14	SSW	6	5	172	63
July	1,021	24	17	29	13	86	257	474	91	23	129	14	S	4	6	170	65
Aug.	1,021	25	17	28	12	85	208	408	69	23	134	12	E	4	5	188	66
Sept.	1,020	26	17	29	13	84	134	365	36	18	122	12	E	9	5	216	71
Oct.	1,018	27	18	30	13	83	87	250	15	15	104	11	E	11	5	231	74
Nov.	1,015	29	20	32	16	83	184	578	33	16	217	12	E	14	5	242	69
Dec.	1,013	29	22	35	16	85	259	517	53	19	135	11	E	16	6	235	69
Annual	1,016	27	20	37	11	85	3,526	4,911	2,398	240	442	13	—	9	5	2,445	838
Rec. (yrs.)	31	12	12	35	35	12	30	30	30	30	30	12	12	12	10	17	11

[1] Mean of 07h00, 12h00 and 17h00 local time.

TABLE XVII

CLIMATIC TABLE FOR TANANARIVE

Latitude 18°54′S, longitude 47°32′E, elevation 1,310 m

Month	Mean sta. press. (mbar)	Temperature (°C) mean max.	mean min.	extreme max.	extreme min.	Relat. humid. (%)	Precipitation mean (mm)	max. (mm)	min. (mm)	days	max. in 24 h	Wind[1] av. speed (km/h)	preval. direct.	calm (%)	Averages cloud-iness (oktas)	sun-shine (h)	evap. (mm)
Jan.	870	25	16	30	12	82	255	427	58	19	83	7	ESE	13	7	204	92
Feb.	870	26	16	30	11	81	187	346	54	14	89	6	SE	16	6	205	81
Mar.	871	25	16	29	12	83	263	604	102	19	134	7	SE	14	6	194	80
Apr.	873	24	15	29	9	80	42	110	4	7	67	7	ESE	15	5	236	87
May	874	22	12	28	3	78	8	88	1	5	19	7	ESE	13	4	231	89
June	875	21	10	26	3	79	9	39	1	7	32	7	ESE	11	4	212	80
July	876	20	10	25	3	78	17	52	1	9	29	7	ESE	9	5	216	82
Aug.	876	20	10	29	2	76	13	64	1	7	33	7	E	8	4	239	100
Sept.	876	22	11	29	3	73	16	113	0	5	33	7	E	8	4	249	118
Oct.	875	25	12	32	6	71	47	152	<1	5	68	7	E	11	3	272	143
Nov.	873	26	15	31	8	75	170	361	73	14	91	7	E	12	6	224	126
Dec.	871	25	16	30	10	81	366	504	252	22	105	6	E	19	6	208	94
Annual	873	24	13	32	2	78	1,393	1663	1111	133	134	7	—	12	5	2,690	1,172
Rec. (yrs.)	13	13	13	30	30	13	13	13	13	13	30	13	13	13	10	19	13

[1] Mean of 07h00, 12h00 and 17h00 local time.

TABLE XVIII

CLIMATIC TABLE FOR FIANARANTSOA
Latitude 21°26'S, longitude 47°07'E, elevation 1,106 m

Month	Mean sta. press. (mbar)	Temperature (°C)				Relat. humid. (%)	Precipitation					Wind[1]			Averages	
		mean max.	mean min.	extreme max.	extreme min.		mean (mm)	max. (mm)	min. (mm)	days	max. in 24 h	av. speed (km/h)	preval. direct.	calm (%)	cloud-iness (oktas)	evap. (mm)
Jan.	891	26	17	34	12	83	291	611	71	22	128	7	E	50	6	81
Feb.	891	26	17	32	11	84	206	583	71	20	167	7	E	49	6	71
Mar.	891	25	16	31	9	86	174	425	46	21	79	7	E	52	6	64
Apr.	893	24	15	30	9	84	44	192	9	13	46	5	E	56	5	67
May	895	22	12	29	4	83	27	98	0	11	47	5	E	58	5	64
June	897	20	10	27	0	84	20	78	2	11	34	5	E	60	5	59
July	898	20	10	26	1	85	18	42	3	11	19	6	E	56	5	57
Aug.	898	20	10	30	1	82	17	63	0	10	26	7	E	47	4	67
Sept.	897	23	11	31	3	78	24	91	0	8	36	8	E	48	4	93
Oct.	895	25	13	35	6	77	34	128	4	7	70	9	E	47	4	116
Nov.	893	26	15	37	6	79	130	247	13	14	100	8	E	56	5	104
Dec.	892	26	16	35	11	83	237	468	107	19	96	7	E	57	5	80
Annual	894	24	13	37	0	82	1,222	1,804	825	167	167	7	—	53	5	923
Rec. (yrs.)	15	15	15	35	35	9	30	30	30	30	30	9	9	9	12	9

[1] Mean of 07h00, 12h00 and 17h00 local time.

TABLE XIX

CLIMATIC TABLE FOR TULEAR
Latitude 23°23′S, longitude 43°44′E, elevation 9 m

Month	M.s.l. press. (mbar)	Temperature (°C) mean max.	mean min.	extreme max.	extreme min.	Relat. humid. (%)	Precipitation mean (mm)	max. (mm)	min. (mm)	days	max. in 24 h	Wind av. speed (km/h)	preval. direct.	calm (%)	Averages cloud-iness (oktas)	sun-shine (h)	evap. (mm)
Jan.	1,010	32	23	39	16	78	71	338	5	7	104	14	SW	18	4	305	162
Feb.	1,010	32	23	40	16	78	71	191	2	6	70	13	SW	22	4	285	140
Mar.	1,011	32	22	39	14	76	42	360	0	5	58	14	SW	18	3	296	161
Apr.	1,014	31	20	37	10	76	6	40	0	1	30	13	SW	15	3	302	143
May	1,017	29	17	36	8	74	18	139	0	2	67	13	SSW	12	2	306	148
June	1,019	27	15	33	7	75	11	45	0	2	26	13	SSW	9	2	277	135
July	1,020	27	14	32	6	74	4	21	0	1	19	13	SSW	8	2	291	154
Aug.	1,019	27	15	35	6	74	3	51	0	1	48	14	SSW	8	2	298	152
Sept.	1,018	29	16	38	8	74	10	48	0	1	31	15	SSW	7	1	307	159
Oct.	1,016	29	18	39	10	76	14	103	0	1	102	15	SSW	12	2	324	159
Nov.	1,013	30	20	40	12	75	34	127	0	2	83	15	SW	17	3	313	161
Dec.	1,011	31	22	38	12	79	57	193	0	5	105	14	SW	20	4	306	145
Annual	1,015	30	19	40	6	76	341	666	129	34	105	14	—	14	3	3,610	1,819
Rec. (yrs.)	11	11		36	36	11	30	30	30	30	30	11	11	11	10	11	11

TABLE XX

CLIMATIC TABLE FOR FORT DAUPHIN
Latitude 25°02'S, longitude 46°58'E, elevation 7 m

Month	M.s.l. press. (mbar)	Temperature (°C) mean max.	mean min.	extreme max.	extreme min.	Relat. humid. (%)	Precipitation mean (mm)	max. (mm)	min. (mm)	days	max. in 24 h	Wind[1] av. speed (km/h)	preval. direct.	calm (%)	Averages cloud-iness (oktas)	sun-shine (h)	evap. (mm)
Jan.	1,012	29	23	34	18	82	202	562	27	15	219	21	NE	9	5	226	120
Feb.	1,012	30	23	35	18	80	184	437	55	15	112	21	ENE	15	4	232	123
Mar.	1,013	28	22	35	16	82	236	588	20	17	283	20	ENE	9	5	200	117
Apr.	1,015	27	20	33	15	81	113	262	16	13	111	20	NE	11	4	215	109
May	1,018	26	18	31	11	80	117	288	2	12	94	17	NE	14	4	236	114
June	1,021	24	16	29	10	81	135	379	15	13	148	16	NE	14	4	210	102
July	1,022	23	16	29	9	81	108	306	21	13	103	17	NE	14	4	201	104
Aug.	1,021	24	16	29	9	79	94	325	10	11	161	21	NE	8	3	239	130
Sept.	1,020	26	17	31	10	78	61	264	4	9	124	23	NE	7	3	230	140
Oct.	1,017	27	19	32	13	79	73	208	1	8	86	26	NE	12	3	251	153
Nov.	1,015	27	20	33	15	81	91	222	8	12	98	23	NE	13	4	232	129
Dec.	1,013	29	22	35	16	81	124	314	56	14	78	21	ENE	12	5	230	129
Annual	1,017	27	19	35	9	80	1,537	2,059	988	152	283	21	—	12	4	2,702	1,470
Rec. (yrs.)	10	13	13	36	36	13	30	30	30	30	30	9	9	9	10	13	13

[1] Mean of 07h00, 12h00 and 17h00 local time.

Chapter 15

South Africa

B. R. SCHULZE

General

The region to be discussed in this chapter comprises the southern tip of Africa from about 17°S southwards, excluding the territories of Rhodesia and Mozambique. The newly independent African states of Botswana (Bechuanaland), Lesotho (Basutoland) and Swaziland, as well as the mandated territory of Southwest Africa, are therefore included in this climatic survey.

The area described in this zone covers over 2.8 million km², with a total population of nearly 18 million people, of whom about 90% live in the Republic of South Africa. Johannesburg is the largest city, with over 1 million inhabitants, while Cape Town (725,000) is the biggest port. Economically the chief exports are minerals (gold, diamonds

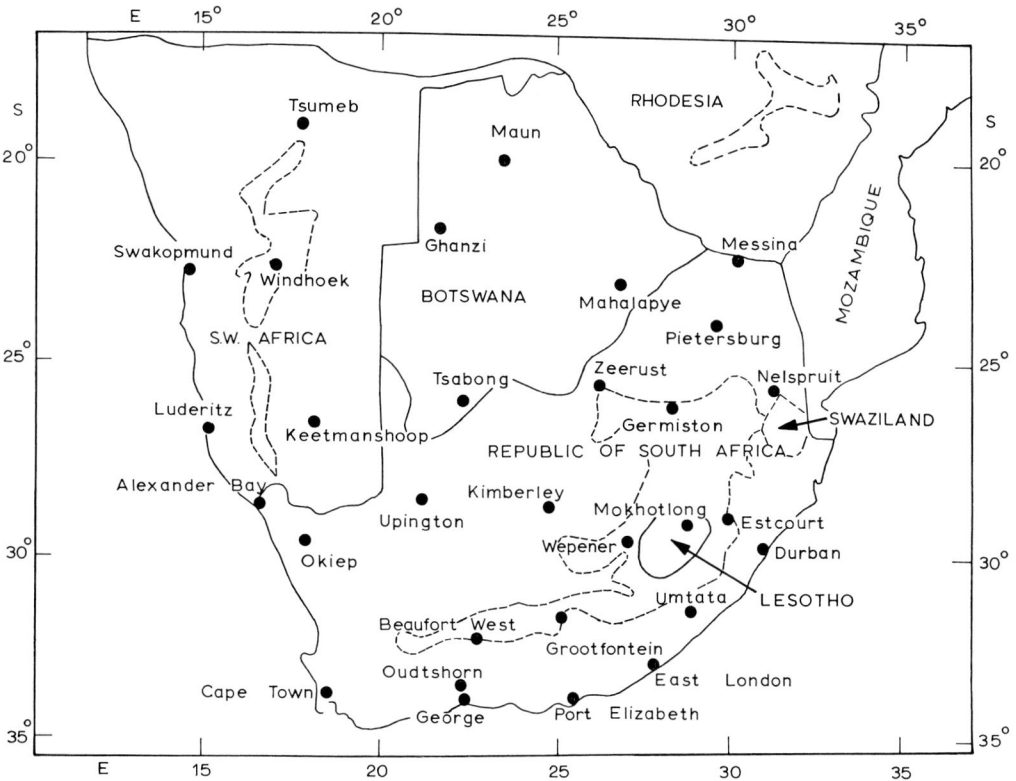

Fig.1. South Africa, showing the position of climate stations. Continuous lines: international boundaries, broken lines: 1,500 m contour.

and uranium) but crops, such as citrus and deciduous fruits, sugar and tobacco, are also very important. The Republic exports a lot of wine and has a considerable trade in canned pilchards and crayfish. One of the chief items of exports is wool (karakul pelts in South-west Africa) while dairy produce and cattle are confined to the domestic market.

The period for which averages and frequencies appear in the main climatological tables refers in all cases to the years 1931–1960. However, certain stations manned by professional personnel have not been in existence for this full period of 30 years; in such cases, whenever possible, 30-year averages were obtained from neighboring cooperative stations, suitable adjustments having been made to reduce one series to another. Also, due to changes and improvement in the observational procedure it was not always possible to obtain averages for the full 30-year period; this applies especially to data at 14h00 South African Standard Time and to the frequency of hydrometeors. The times stated always refer to South African Standard Time which is 2 hours in advance of G.M.T.

The 30 stations employed were selected in the first place to give an even spread over the region as a whole, in order to be representative of all the main types of climate, and secondly for the reliability of the data.

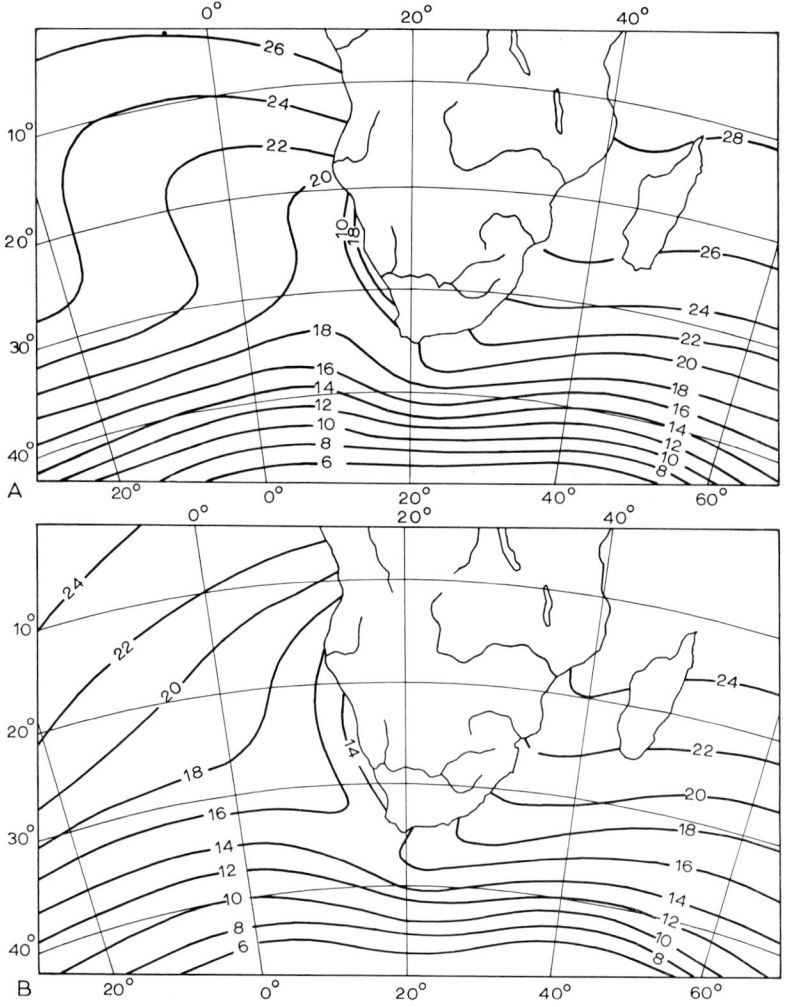

Fig.2. Mean surface temperature (°C). A. January; B. July. (After TALJAARD, 1958.)

Fig.1 shows the location of the climatic stations, the position of the different territories mentioned above, and a rough representation of the height contours in steps of 500 m. It will be seen that the physical structure is that of a high plateau rising in nearly all directions from about 1,000 m in Botswana and the northwestern Republic and culminating in the great escarpment which in Lesotho rises to above 3,000 m. From the great escarpment there is a more or less abrupt fall, sometimes in the form of terraces towards the coast.

This tapering sub-continent of Africa projects barely to 35°S into the vast southern ocean, is washed on the west coast by the cold, northward-flowing Benguela Current, and on the east and south by the much warmer waters of the Mozambique and Agulhas currents flowing southeastwards and eastwards from the Indian ocean. At 30°S South Africa is about 1,300 km wide as against South America's 2,100 km and Australia's 3,900 km for the same latitude, and is therefore, comparatively speaking, largely under the influence of maritime air which, in conjunction with its high plateau structure, exercises a moderating influence on its climate.

The distribution of mean sea surface temperature in January and July is shown in Fig.2, and illustrates the considerable temperature anomaly brought about by the warm waters on the eastern and southern coasts and on the west coast by the cold current and the upwelling of cold waters under the influence of the southeasterly trade winds. The sea temperature reaches a maximum in late February or early March, a lag behind the summer solstice of at least two months, whilst over the high plateau soil temperature at a depth of 2.5 cm shows a lag of about 3 weeks. Minimum temperatures are similarly retarded in respect of the winter solstice.

The general circulation

The average pressure distribution for January and July is shown in Fig.3. South Africa lies almost completely within the high pressure belt of the Southern Hemisphere, which, at the surface is centred on about 30°S. This is the main circumstance dominating the South African climate which is largely arid to semi-arid, except where influenced by other factors (to be mentioned later). Above a relatively shallow layer of maritime air in the high pressure belt, there exists, on the average, a temperature inversion (TALJAARD and SCHUMANN, 1940; TALJAARD, 1955) due to subsidence in the upper atmosphere. This inversion is found at approximately plateau level and is strongest on the west coast (about 7°C) probably due to the cold Benguela Current. On the east coast it is less pronounced and the inversion lies at about 2–2.5 km in summer as against 1 km in winter. The high pressure belt is subject to a seasonal displacement of about 4° latitude, its centre being furthest south in February and furthest north in July–August. The effect of the land mass which is differently heated in summer and winter is to cause the high pressure belt to be separated into two cells—the Atlantic and the Indian Ocean high. Fig.3A shows the appearance of a shallow low pressure over the land in summer, promoting the influx of moist tropical air, whilst in winter the high pressure is intensified over land, inhibiting the entry of maritime air onto the land. Furthermore, the core of the Indian Ocean high pressure cell lies much further eastwards in summer than in winter. In summer it would therefore appear that surges of air from the South Atlantic around

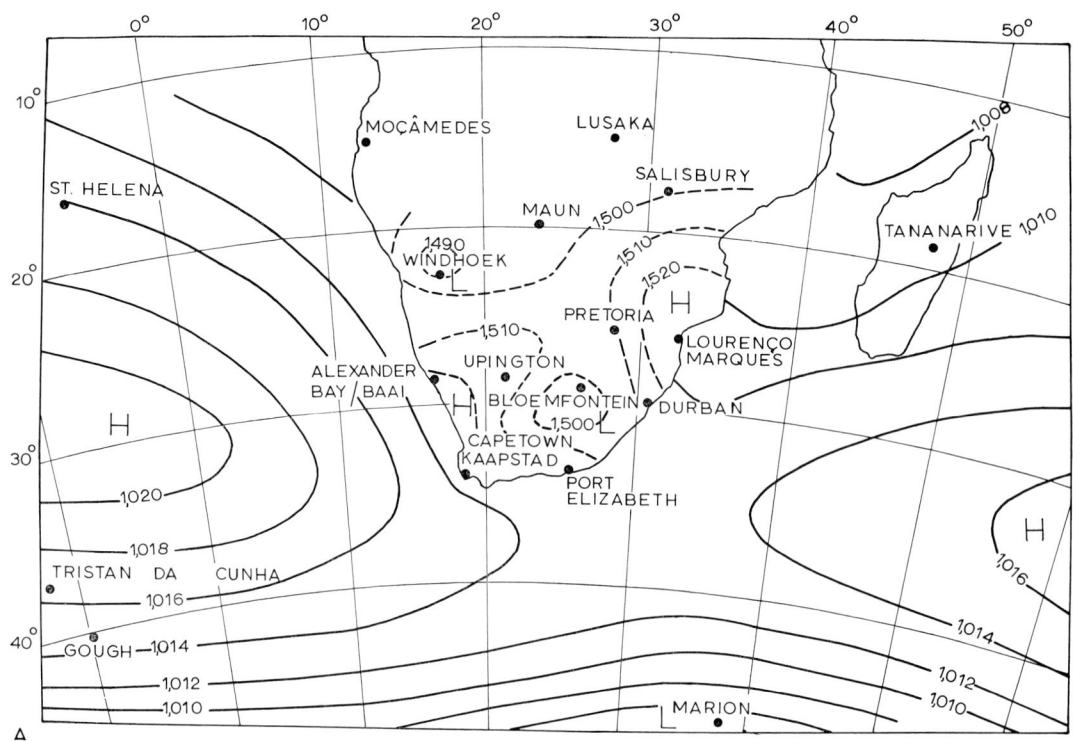

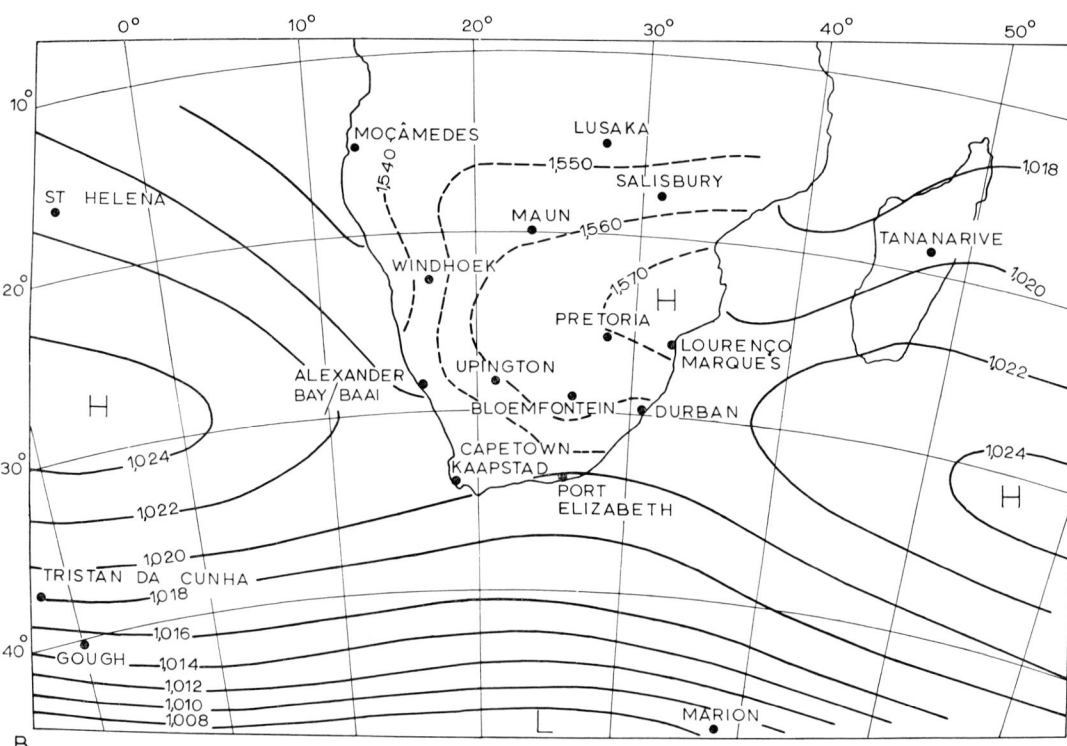

Fig.3. Mean sea-level isobars (full lines) and mean contours of the 850-mbar pressure surface (broken lines) at 14h00 South African Standard Time (12h00 G.M.T.), (18 year average). A. January; B. July.

the South African coast, thus "feeding" the Indian Ocean cell, are much more likely and frequent in summer than in winter. In this connection TREWARTHA (1962) has expressed the view that "the Indian Ocean cell is more in the nature of composite eastward moving individual cells of high pressure than it is a permanent element".

Another important fact in respect of the average pressure distribution is that the anticyclonic belt does not extend vertically into the upper atmosphere, but slants towards the north, with the result that the centre of the pressure belt at the 500-mbar level is at about 22°S in summer to 18°S in winter. The circumpolar westerly winds to the south of the high pressure belt, which at the surface occur from about 35°S southwards, are therefore found at much lower latitudes in the upper air and it can be said with confidence that weather changes in South Africa are largely dominated by perturbations (waves) in the Southern Hemisphere's westerly circulation, though to a lesser extent in summer than in winter. On the surface these disturbances are revealed as a series of cyclones and anticyclones.

Cyclones affecting South Africa usually originate in the South Atlantic Ocean between 30° and 40°S. Their centres travel east-southeastwards and are followed by anticyclones travelling eastwards and very often, especially in summer, moving northeastwards around the South African coast. Fig.4 shows the tracks of cyclone and anticyclone centres,

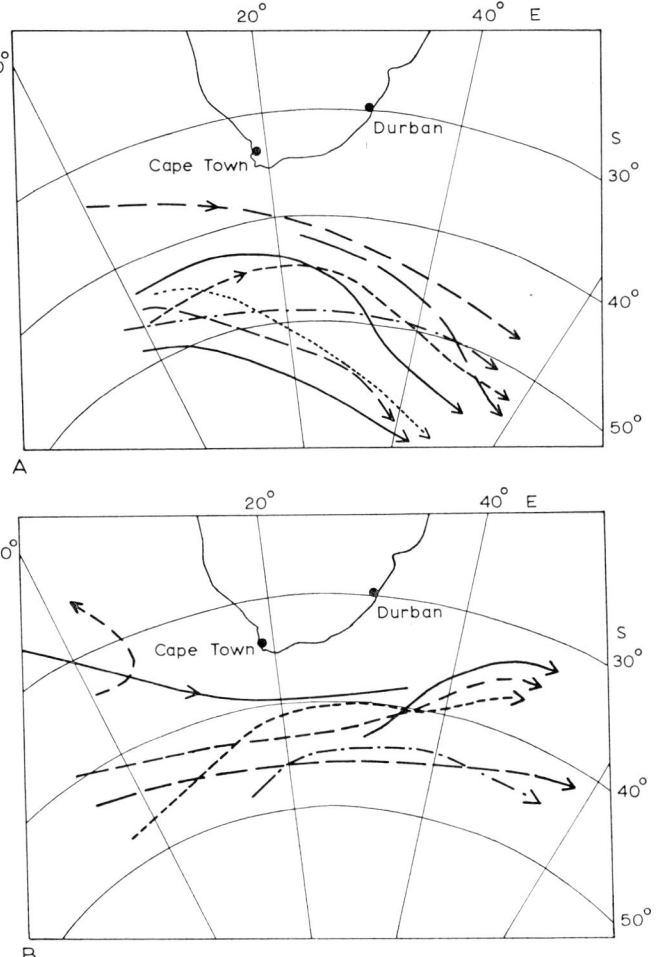

Fig.4A. Tracks of cyclone centres, April 1958; B. tracks of anticyclone centres, July 1957.

simplified after TALJAARD and VAN LOON (1962, 1963) and TALJAARD (1964, 1965). Though these figures refer only to two particular months, they serve to give an idea of the movement of the pressure systems.

Some examples of typical weather situations which recur from time to time will serve towards a better understanding of the general climatic conditions pertaining to South Africa. Unfortunately the frequency of these types in different seasons has not yet been determined, though in this connection VOWINCKEL (1955) gives a table of frequencies of certain types of weather for the high plateau. For each of the situations following here, the surface chart and the 700-mbar chart are shown; on the surface chart the iso-clinics on the plateau are the contours of the 850-mbar pressure level.

(*1*) The most common type of weather situation is shown in Fig.5, the main feature of which is an anticyclone over the whole country. This situation occurs mostly in winter, but as shown here also occurs in summer and sometimes persists for periods up to 14 days with progressively increasing temperature and drought. In late summer this type of weather situation often coincides with the appearance of a tropical cyclone near Madagascar or in the Mozambique Channel. In winter, when the southern cyclonic disturbances reach further to the north, rain, largely orographic, occurs during northwesterly winds against the western, southwestern, and southern escarpment as the cold front approaches the land. This is, in fact, the "normal" condition in winter and explains the Mediterranean climate of the southwestern Cape. Quite often a subsidiary (or coastal) low appears on the west coast and moves around to the south coast, under which conditions hot "berg" winds blowing at more or less right angles to the coast usually start on the west coast and eventually occur on the south and southeastern coasts. These hot föhn-like winds constitute one of the most unpleasant features of the coastal climate; they may sometimes persist for some days on end, until, when the cold front passes over the land, the wind suddenly switches to southwesterly, accompanied by a considerable drop in temperature, followed by fog and low stratus on the western and southwestern coasts. In the interior fine and dry conditions persist. This situation agrees closely with VOWINCKEL's (1955) type 1, for which he gives a frequency of 60–70% in mid-winter and about 8% in mid-summer.

(*2*) Fig.6 shows a common situation mainly in late winter and spring and exemplifies an influx of cold air over the whole country—this might be termed the "normal" cold snap situation. Depending on the intensity of the low and its nearness to the coast this type could cause bad weather and gales along the southwestern, southern and south-eastern coasts. As the cold front moves across the coast pre-frontal rain may be expected over the southern Cape Province whilst showers typical of a cold air mass occur after the passage of the cold front, usually clearing rapidly from the west. Snow is likely to fall on the high mountain regions in the south and southeast (Lesotho). The high pressure in the wake of the cyclone usually rushes around the coast and orographic cloud and drizzle results against the southeastern and eastern escarpments. In the northern interior the air is usually dry and the weather normally remains fine.

(*3*) Fig.7, again, shows a wave disturbance in the westerly air stream which has developed into a "cut-off" low pressure cell over South Africa. Warm, moist equatorial air is drawn in a broad stream from the north and northwest, converges over South Africa and gives rise to extensive and copious rains over a large portion of the country. This, as in the former case (Fig.6), is invariably followed by an anticyclone moving around the coast

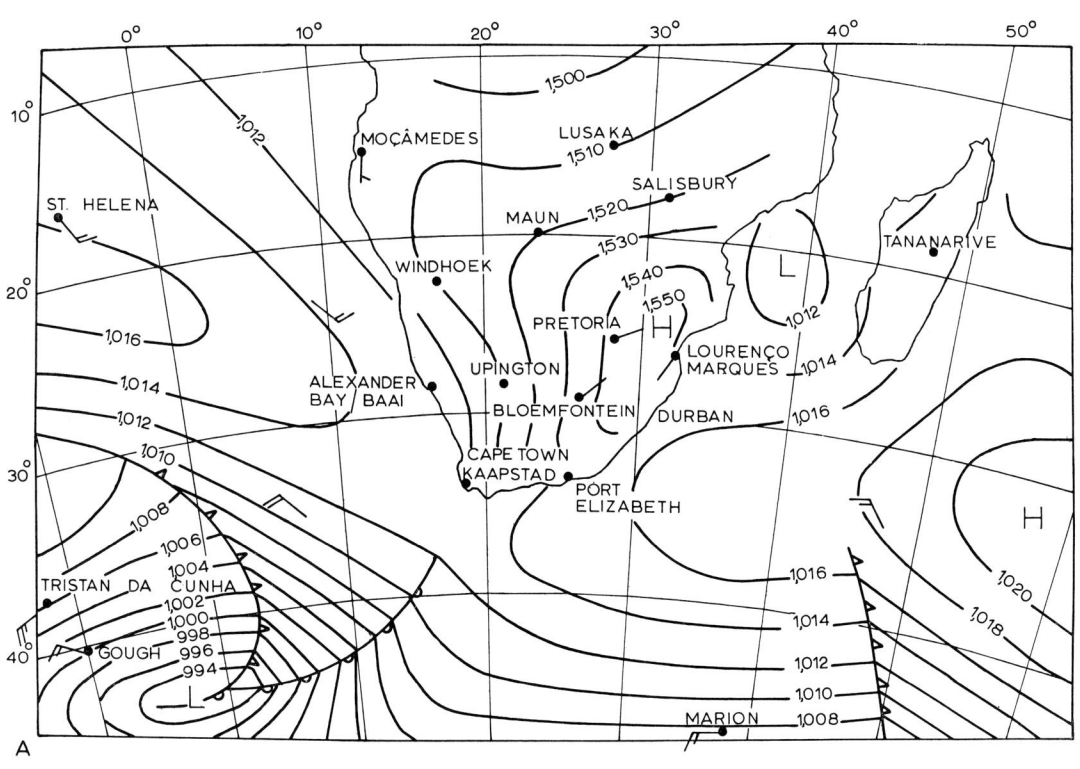

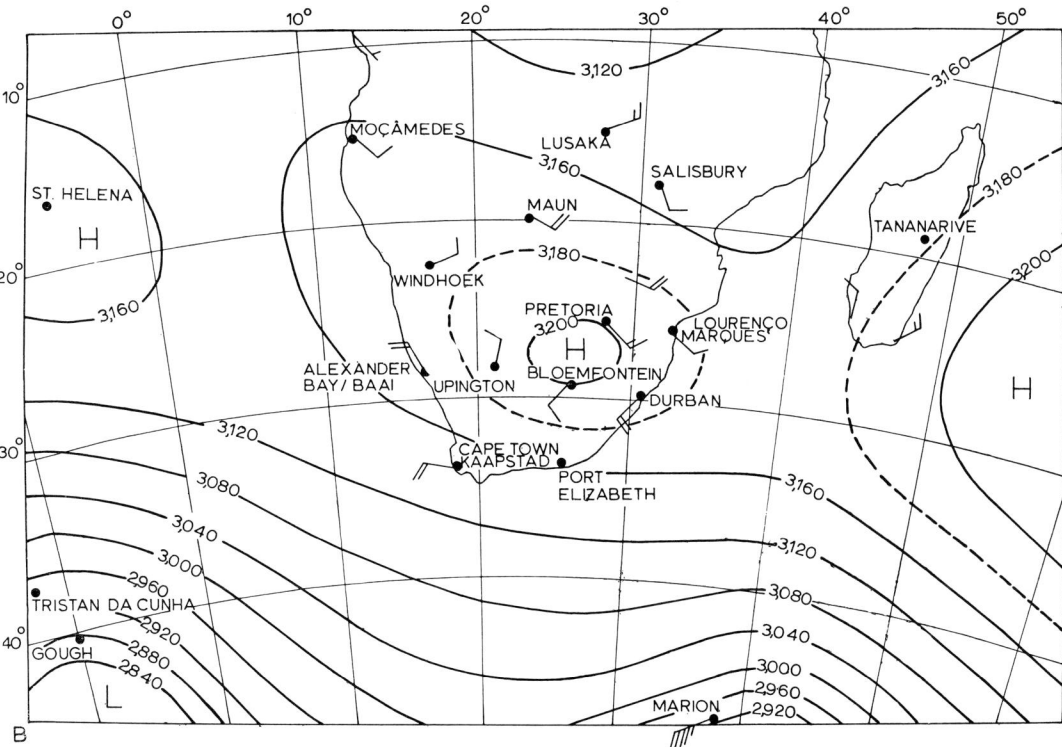

Fig.5A. Surface synoptic chart, January 10, 1961—summer drought; B. contours of 700-mbar level (m), January 10, 1961.

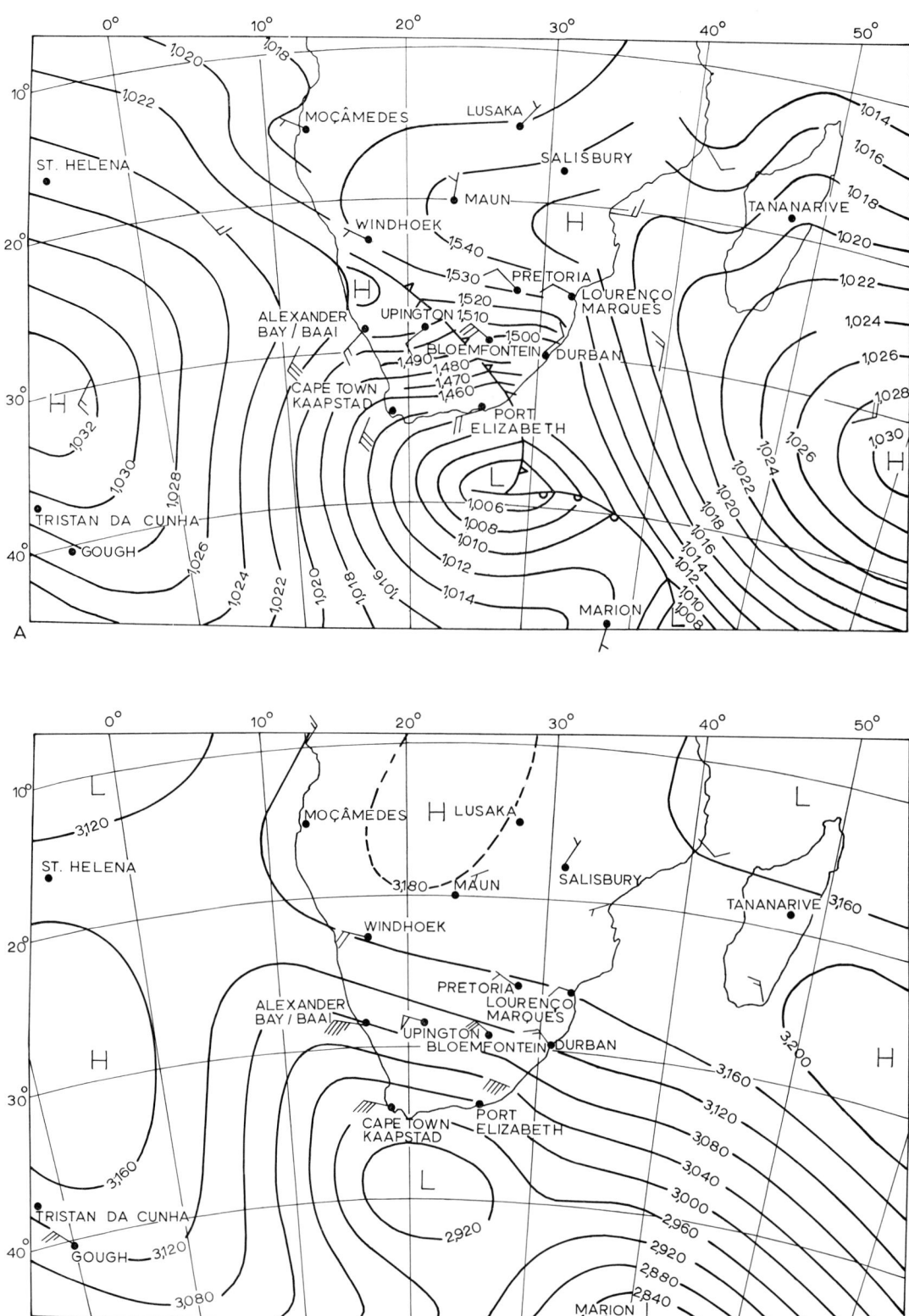

Fig.6A. Surface synoptic chart, August 11, 1964—cold front; B. contours of 700-mbar level (m), August 11, 1964.

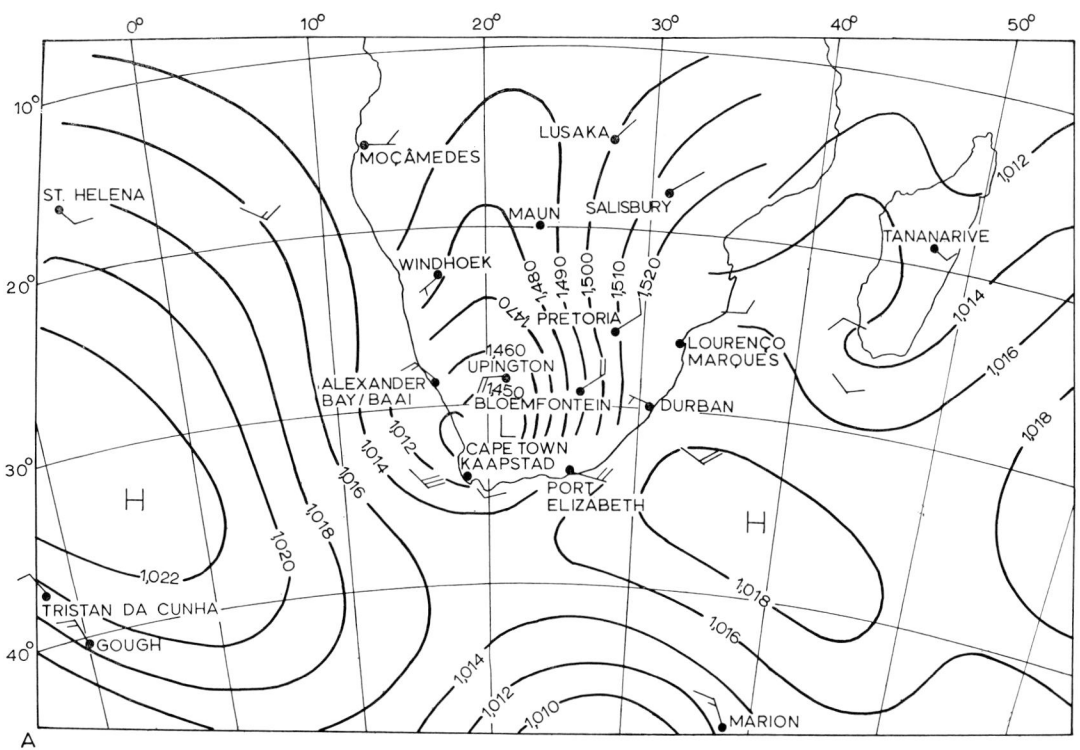

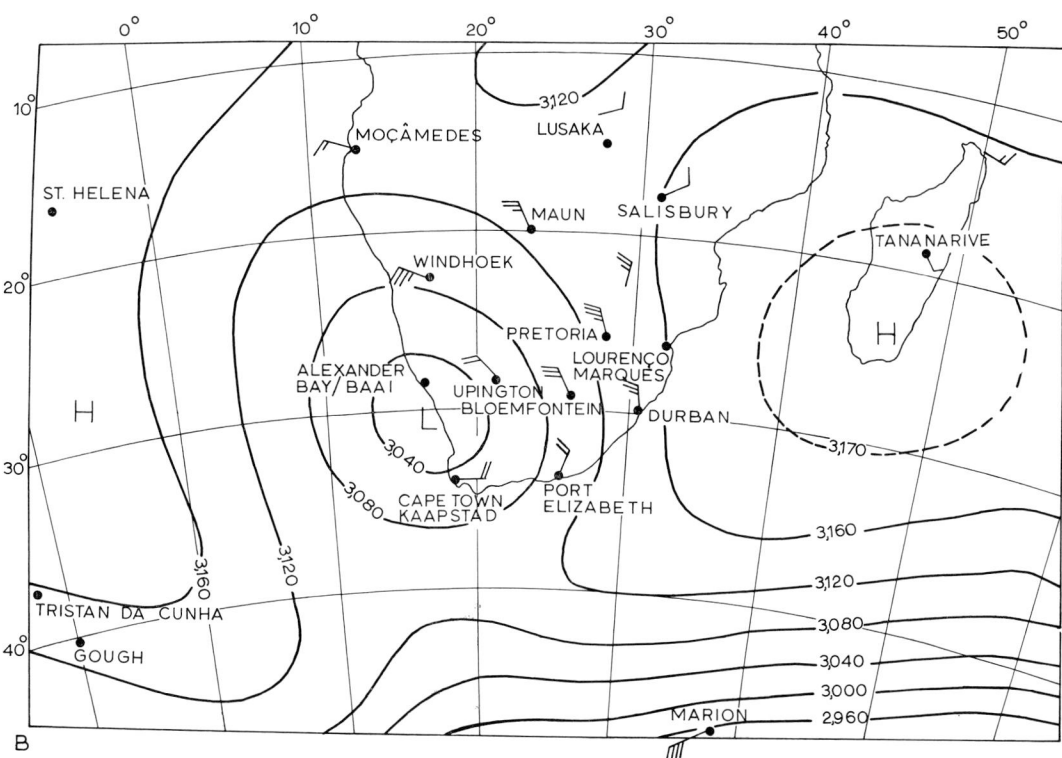

Fig.7A. Surface synoptic chart, December 19, 1960—cut off low; B. contours of 700-mbar level (m), December 19, 1960.

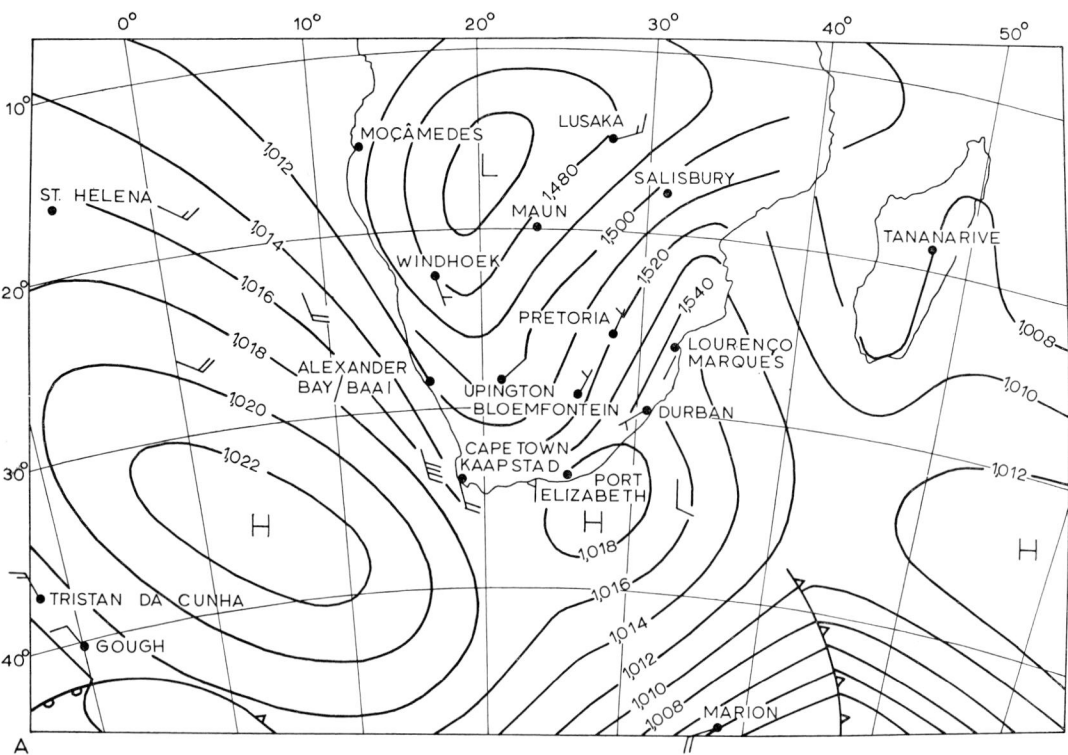

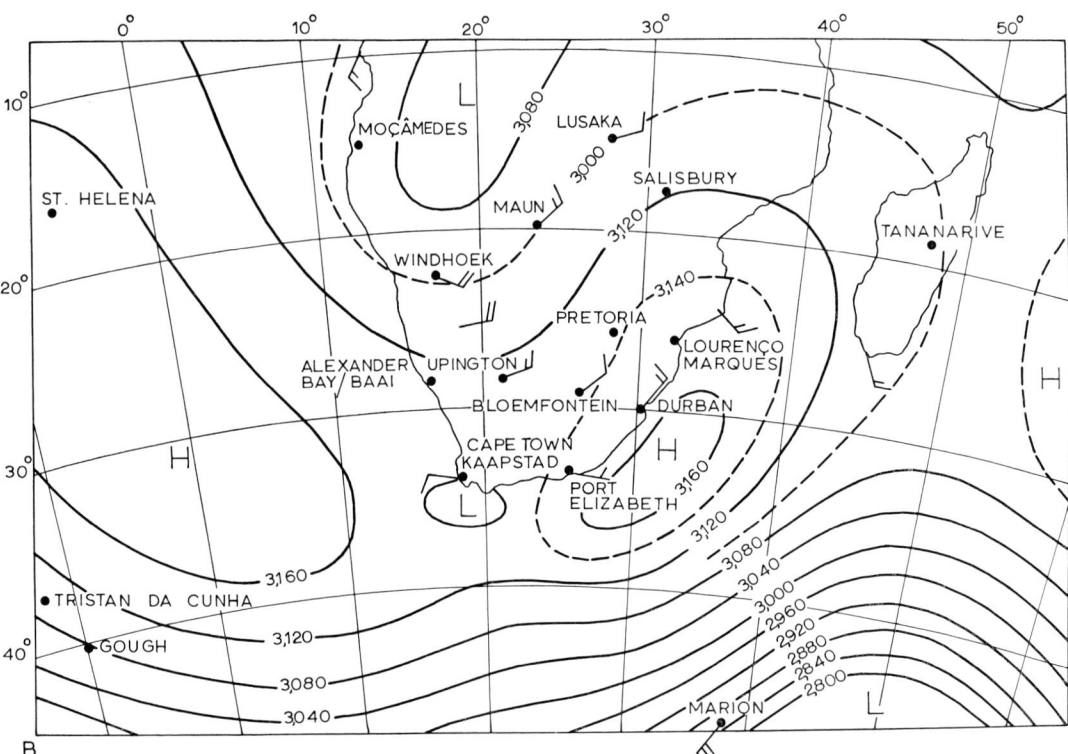

Fig.8A. Synoptic surface chart, February 9, 1955—copious rains in east and central South Africa; B. contours of 700-mbar level (m), February 9, 1955.

from the southwest towards the northeast, which, whilst gathering moisture as it proceeds over the warm Agulhas and Mozambique currents, forces moist southeasterly to easterly air against the escarpment, causing orographic rain and at the same time promotes convergence and uplifting of the southward moving equatorial air. This weather situation is usually short-lived, lasting from 2 to 3 days as the disturbance travels eastwards, and ceases when the following high (or anticyclone) is established over the land. This type of distribution occurs in summer and in winter in which latter season extensive snowfalls sometimes result.

(*4*) A typical summer situation, though of rather infrequent occurrence, but on the other hand highly significant in that it spells extensive and protracted rainy weather over the northern and eastern portions of the interior, is shown in Fig.8. In this situation the wave in the westerly airstream is far to the south, and instead of a "cut-off" low (or cold pool), an equatorial trough is established over the western interior, a condition which may be described as a wave in the easterlies. It is found that in such a situation a succession of high pressure cells move around the coast whilst the equatorial trough remains stationary; this condition may in extreme cases persist for more than 14 days. This situation agrees closely with VOWINCKEL's (1955) equatorial type No.6 for which he gives a frequency of between 20 and 30% for each of the summer months November–March, and practically no occurrence in the winter months June–September, and represents what might be called the "tropical" weather type in South Africa, in contradistinction to the "temperate" weather types which are due primarily to wave disturbances in the circumpolar westerly airstream.

The weather situations exemplified in Fig.5–8 broadly typify the general run of events in South Africa. Needless to say, they are subject to countless more or less minor variations. A somewhat more detailed account may be found in a recent publication by HAYWARD and STEYN (1967).

The climatic elements

The main surface climatic elements, namely temperature, relative humidity, precipitation and cloudiness are given in the tables for 30 stations.

The average annual precipitation

The main features of the distribution of average annual precipitation are shown in Fig.9. A detailed map on the scale 1 : 250,000 is available in *Climate of South Africa*, Part 4: "Rainfall maps" (SOUTH AFRICA WEATHER BUREAU, 1957). First it will be seen that over the interior plateau precipitation decreases (longitudinally) fairly regularly from the eastern escarpment westwards, and secondly, the very marked effect of orographic features is apparent around the coast, from the southwest to the northeast. The latter are most pronounced in the southwestern Cape Province where the average over the coastal flats is of the order of 400 mm, whilst more than 2,000 mm are recorded on the adjacent mountain ranges (in certain situations the increase with height is of the order of 200 mm/100 m). In the southern Cape Province the west–east orientated mountain ranges show the effect of altitude very clearly, but to a somewhat lesser extent, the increase with altitude there being very much less.

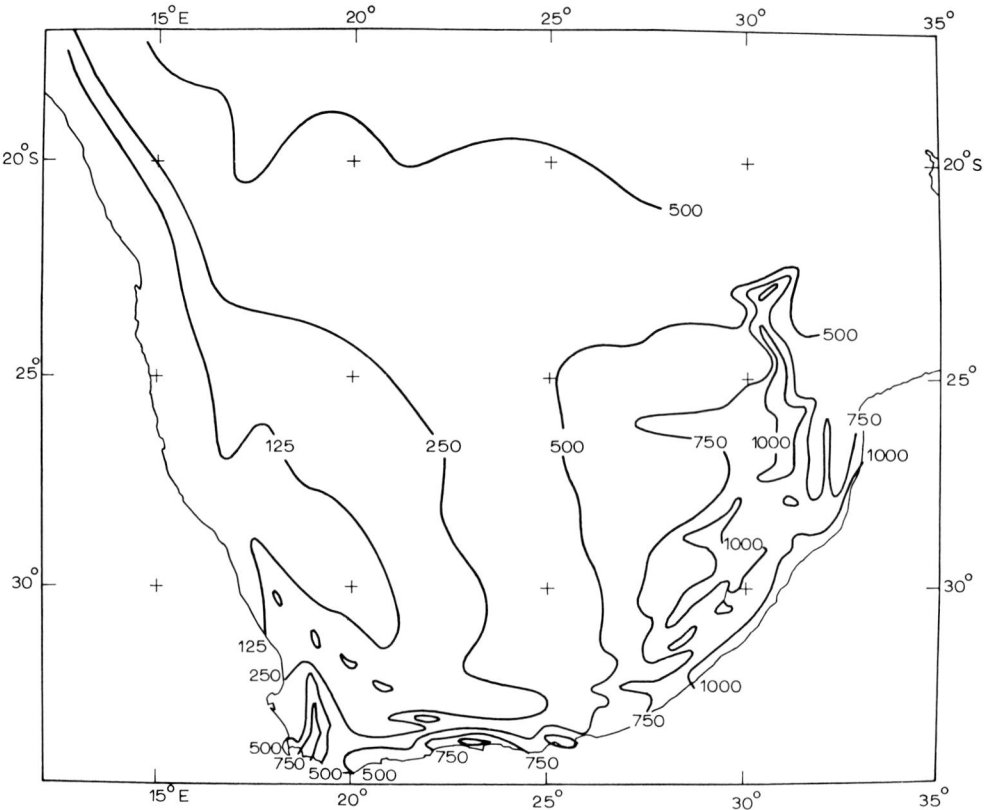

Fig.9. Mean annual rainfall (mm), simplified.

Against the eastern escarpment, again, the increase with altitude is considerable, being of the order of 110 mm/100 m in the vicinity of latitudes 26°–23°S.

The two highest rainfall regions in South Africa are to be found against the northeastern Transvaal escarpment and in the westward facing mountains of the southwestern Cape Province. At Broederstroom (23°48′S 29°59′E, elevation 1,554 m) for example, the mean annual rainfall is 2,088 mm calculated over a period of 35 years; and at Jonkershoek (34°00′S 19°01′E, elevation 1,219 m) in the southwestern Cape an average of 3,200 mm is recorded, though this average refers only to a period of 5 years. Rainfall is lowest on the coast of Southwest Africa between Luderitz and Swakopmund where the average is less than 25 mm.

There is considerable variation in annual rainfall from year to year; for example, the maximum in Broederstroom was 3,027 mm in 1917, and the minimum 1,033 mm in 1941. The maximum for Jonkershoek was 3,874 mm in 1950, and the minimum 2,921 mm in 1949. As examples taken from the low rainfall areas we find that the maximum for Port Nolloth on the west coast was 158 mm in 1925 and the minimum 15 mm in 1895 (SOUTH AFRICA WEATHER BUREAU, 1954).

In order to give an idea of the frequency of annual amounts within specified limits, we have recourse to the annual "district" values of rainfall (SOUTH AFRICA WEATHER BUREAU, 1949). The districts are shown in Fig.10 and the results for some of the districts appear in Table I.

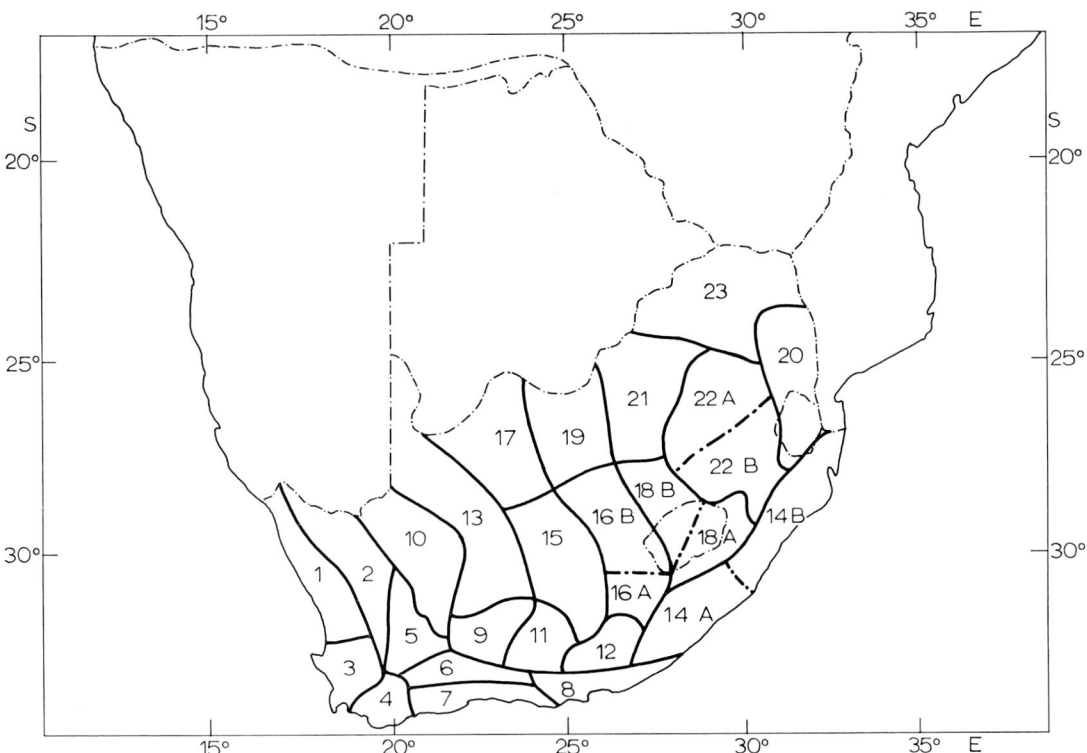

Fig.10. Rainfall districts.

It will be seen that on the Natal coast (district 14B) annual rainfall is reasonably close to the normal in about 8 out of 10 years, whilst unusually wet or dry years are exceptional. The position in the northwestern interior (district 13) is quite different: here extremely wet or dry years occur much more frequently, in other words the variability of annual rainfall increases considerably in the interior from east to west, but a fairly moderate degree of variability is maintained around the escarpment from the east and westwards as far as the Cape.

TABLE I

FREQUENCY (%) OF ANNUAL DISTRICT RAINFALL[1]

District	Class intervals (% of average)									Period (years)
	21–40	41–60	61–80	81–100	101–120	121–140	141–160	161–180	180	
14B			10	41	41	5	3			61
8		2	8	43	36	11				61
7			5	49	36	10				61
3			13	38	38	5	6			61
22A			9	43	38	8	2			58
16B			20	31	28	19	0	2		61
13	3	12	19	17	21	17	7	2	2	58
2		9	26	22	21	14	3	3	2	58

[1] Districts are shown in Fig.10.

Fig.11 shows the relative variability (%) (mean deviation/mean) of annual rainfall based on 60 individual stations (not district values) and bears out what has been said above. The variability is least on the southern and southwestern coastal regions and on the eastern highlands, and increases rapidly westwards over the interior, attaining a maximum of 80% on the desert coast of Southwest Africa. The relative variability of monthly rainfall is, obviously, much greater than that of annual rainfall.

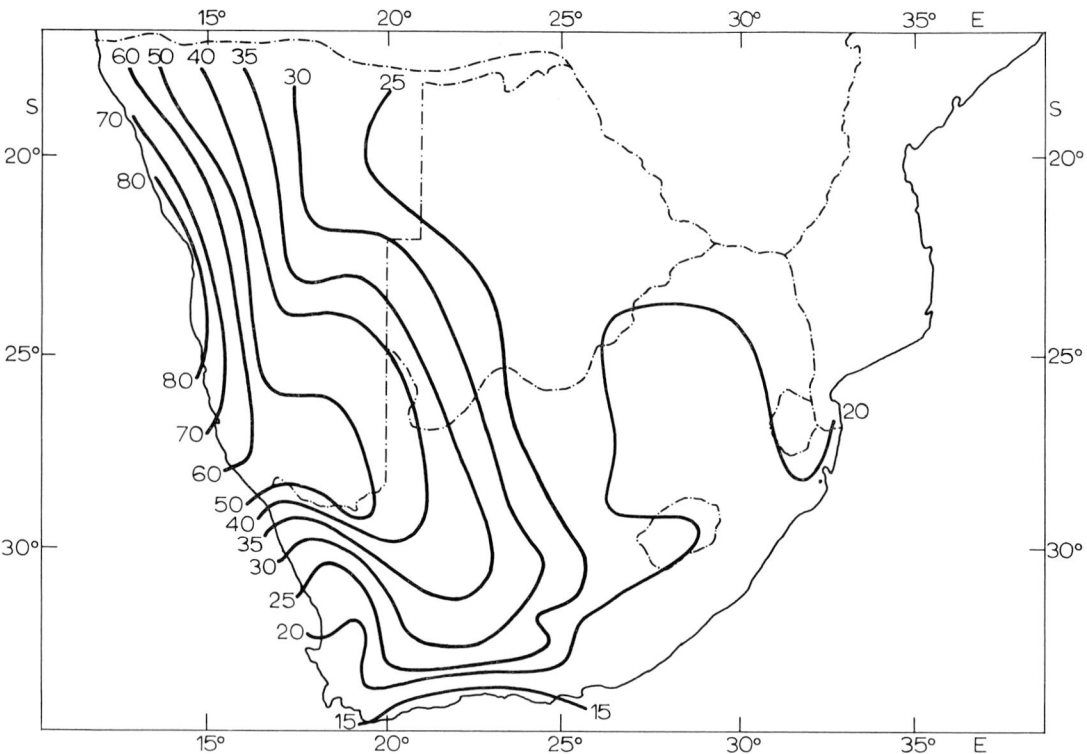

Fig.11. The relative variability of annual rainfall (%).

In the first 60 years of this century the years 1909, 1917, 1921, 1925, 1934, 1939, 1943, 1950, and 1955 showed exceptional precipitation (more than 130% of the normal) over large tracts of South Africa. Similarly, extremely dry years, having 70% or less of the normal rainfall were 1903, 1908, 1912, 1919, 1922, 1926, 1927, 1932, 1945, 1949, and 1951. It is noticeable that there is no regularity in the occurrence of either wet or dry years. This is also borne out by smoothed time series (SOUTH AFRICA WEATHER BUREAU, 1949) which show that long-term irregular fluctuations undoubtedly exist, but that these differ as to the time of occurrence of maxima and minima in different regions of South Africa. In other words, whereas a certain region may experience excessive precipitation, another may suffer drought during the same season.

Over the major part of South Africa rainfall occurs mainly in the summer half-year from October to March. It is only over a limited area in the western and southwestern Cape Province where the reverse is the case. Along the southern coastal areas precipitation occurs in all seasons, but shows two maxima more or less in spring and autumn. Fig.12 shows this clearly and we notice the gradual increase in purely summer rainfall

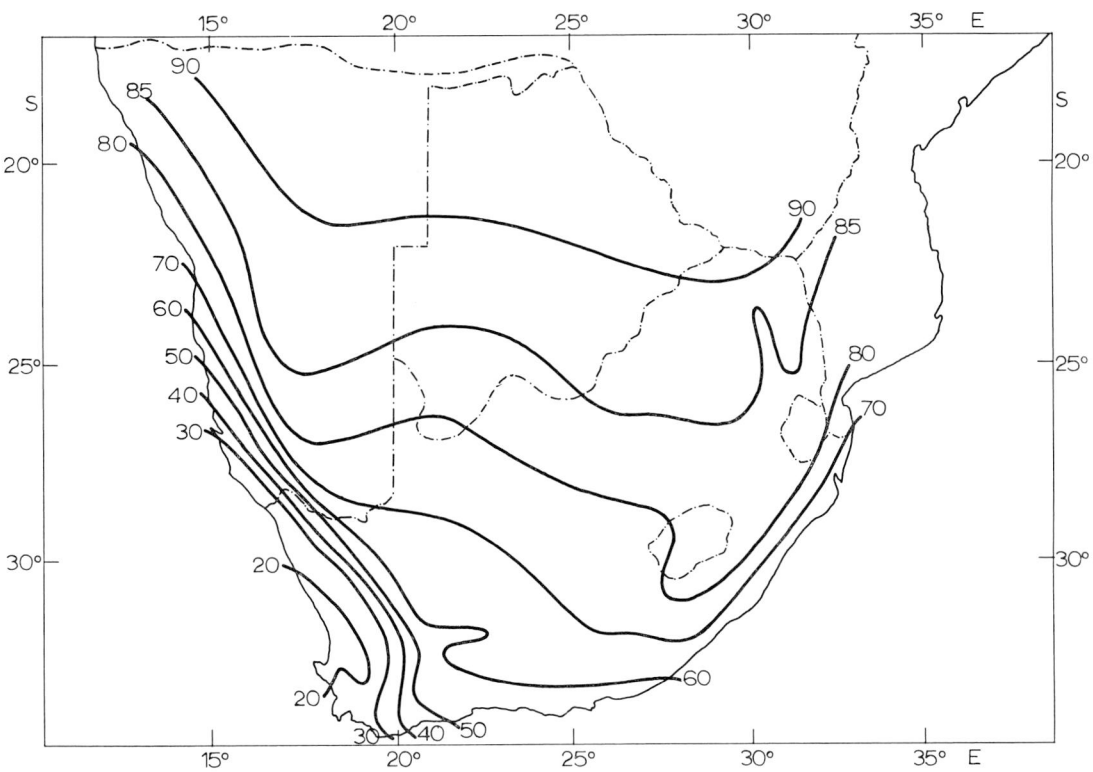

Fig.12. Seasonal rainfall (October–March) as the percentage of the normal annual rainfall.

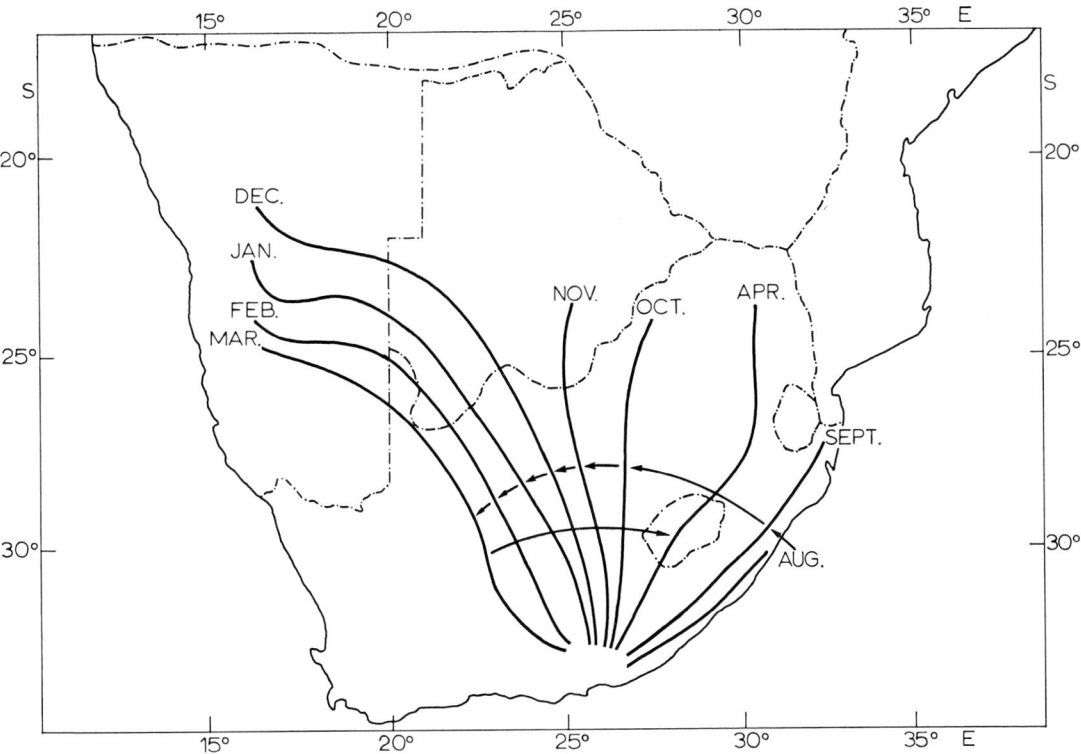

Fig.13. Advance and retreat of the 50-mm isohyet over the summer rainfall zone.

515

when proceeding from south to north. In the north practically all rain falls in the summer season.

Whereas the height of the rainy season in the southwestern winter rainfall zone falls in June and July, in the summer rainfall zone the peak of the rainy season occurs earlier (late spring and summer) than in the western interior where the maximum is in March. In this connection it is interesting to observe the progress of the 50-mm isohyet over the summer rainfall zone as shown schematically in Fig.13. In winter it lies on the south-eastern coast, starts moving westwards in September, swivelling around a "nodal point" north of Port Elizabeth, reaches its furthermost western position in March, and recedes suddenly eastwards as far as the eastern escarpment in April. This sudden cessation in April is a marked feature of the summer rainfall regime over South Africa.

The seasonal distribution of rainfall can best be shown by a series of monthly maps (COOKE, 1946) showing the rainfall as a percentage of the annual average precipitation as shown by bi-monthly data in Fig.14. It appears that the summer rainy season pro-gresses from the south and southeast northwards to the Transvaal highveld up to No-vember, due mainly to cyclonic action and anticyclones moving up the east coast. There-after the "tropical" rainfall regime takes over, and the rainfall increases south and westwards, culminating in about January on the eastern high plateau, and only in March in the western interior. In April there is a sudden cessation of the summer rains, whilst the winter rainy season starts developing on the western and southwestern coastal areas. This quasi-anticlockwise progression of the rainy season over South Africa is naturally connected with seasonal changes in the general circulation of the atmosphere.

The frequency of rainy days

In certain favoured situations, mainly against the eastern and southeastern escarpment and in the mountainous regions of the southwestern Cape Province, rain occurs on an average of 120–140 days/year. In the interior, proceeding westwards, the frequency decreases to an insignificant 10 days or less on the west coast. These figures refer to days with measurable precipitation of 0.25 mm (0.01 inches) or more. The distribution is essentially similar to the quantitative rainfall distribution shown in Fig.9.

For agricultural purposes it is perhaps more important to know the frequency of days with a fall of at least 10 mm (0.40 inches), especially in the summer rainfall region where small amounts are mostly ineffective. A rough estimate shows that days with 10 mm or more are about one quarter as frequent as rain days with 0.25 mm or more.

During rainy spells (which imply cloudy weather) small falls may also be effective since evaporation is then retarded. Fig.15 shows the average frequency of occurrence of spells of rainy weather with at least four consecutive rain days. It will be seen that this condi-tion is infrequent except against the eastern escarpment where it is largely due to oro-graphic rain.

The annual march of precipitation

In South Africa four main types of annual variation may be discerned, namely:
(*1*) The "Mediterranean" type with a very pronounced maximum in winter, in the south-western Cape Province.

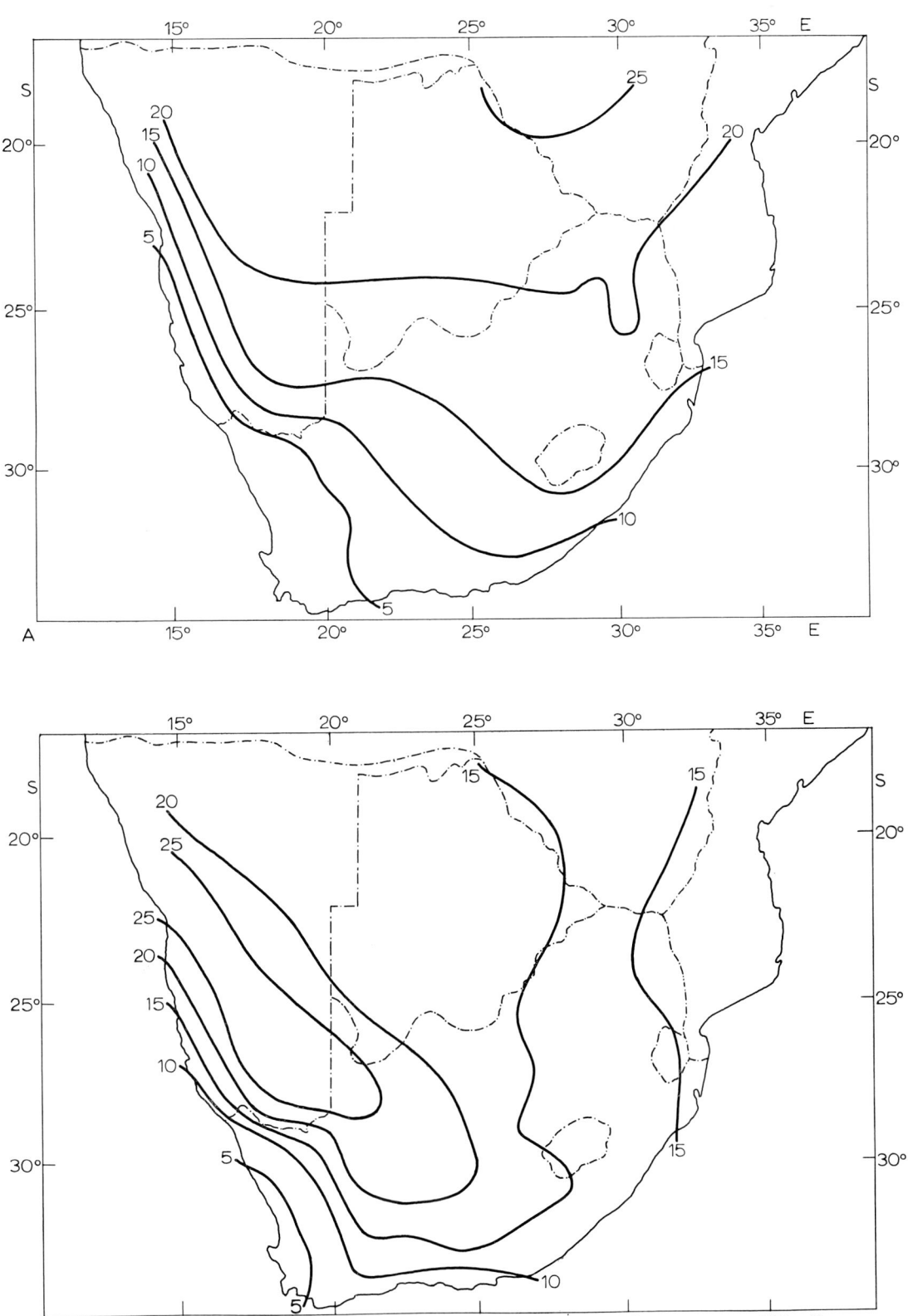

Fig.14. A and B (legend see p.519).

517

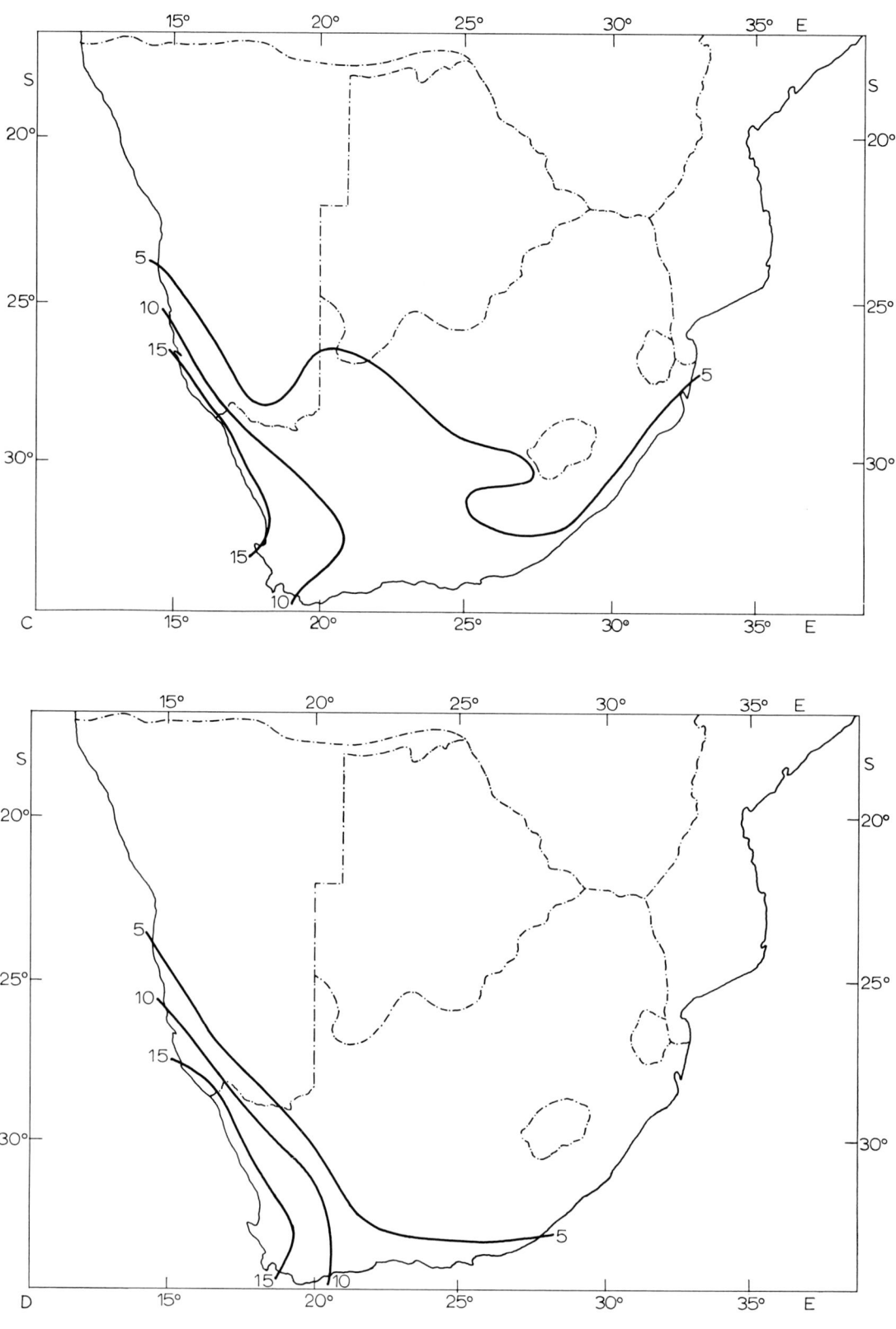

Fig.14. C and D (legend see p.519).

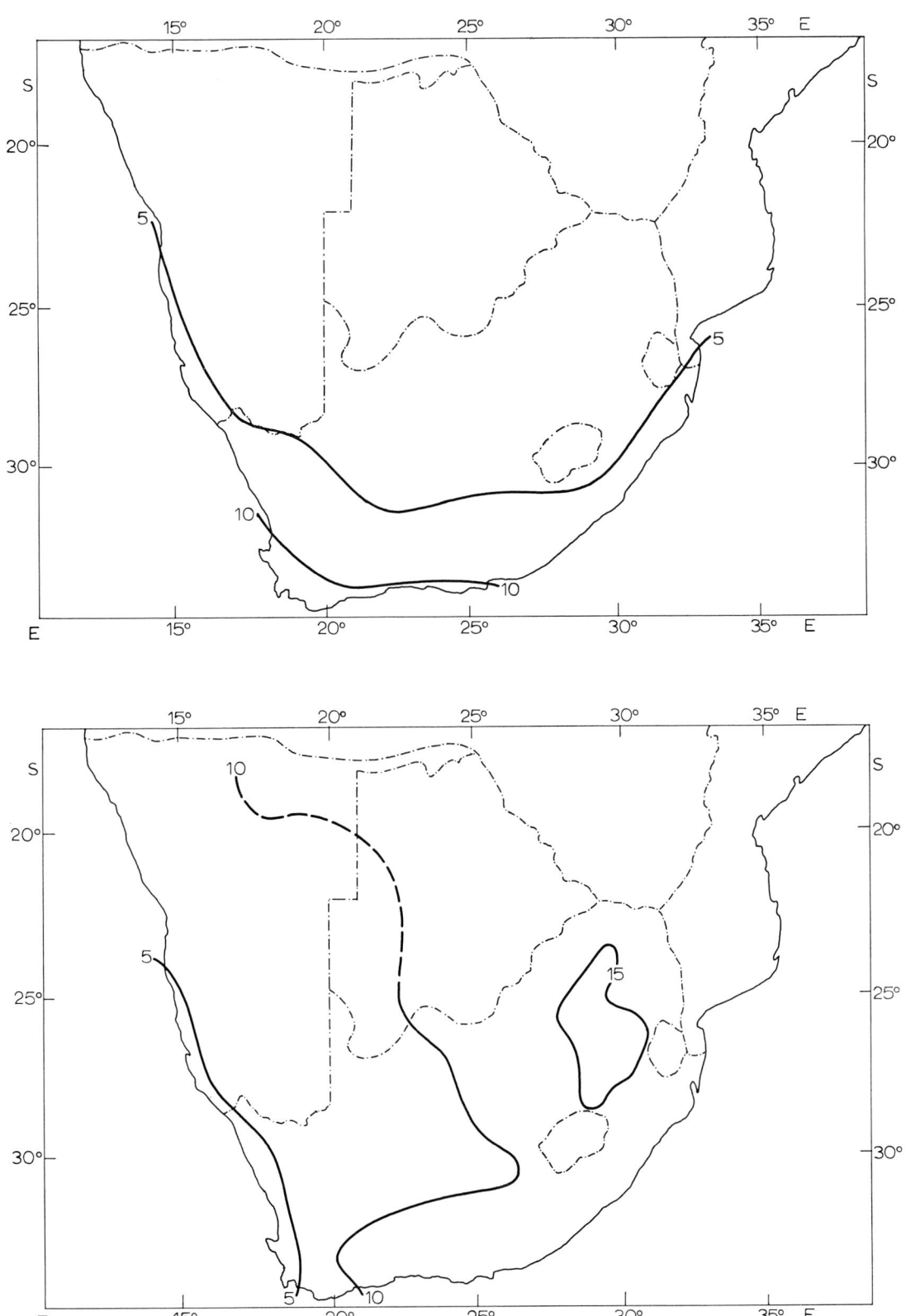

Fig.14. Rainfall for selected months as a percentage of the normal annual rainfall: A. January; B. March; C. May; D. July; E. September; F. November.

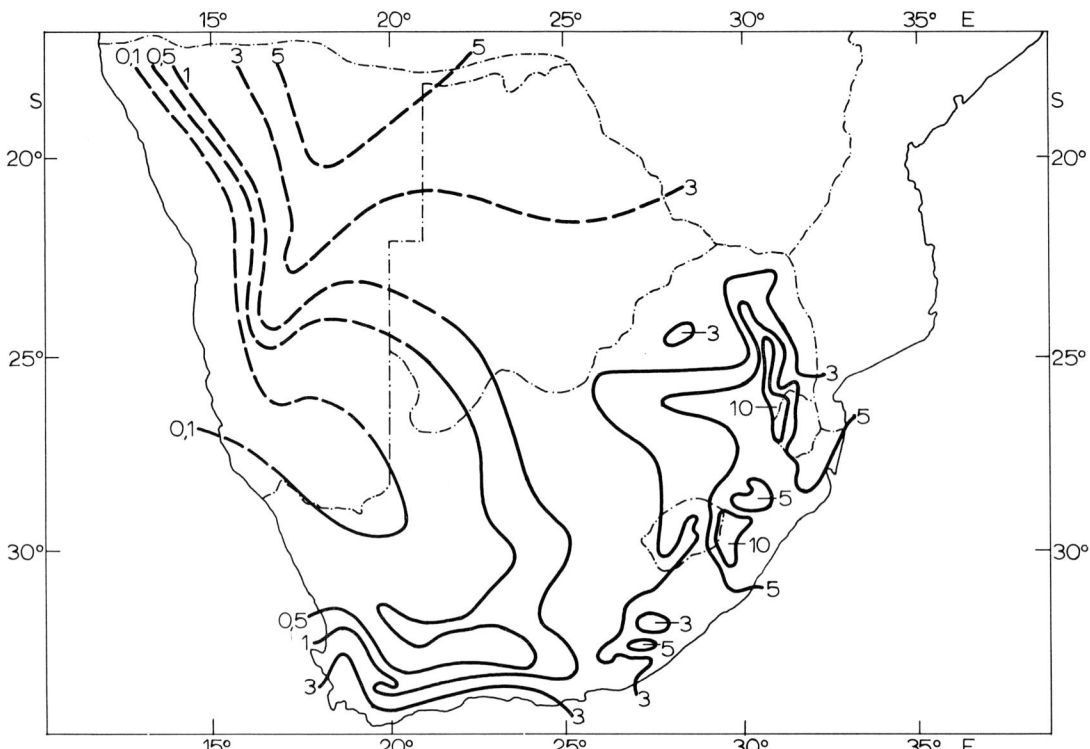

Fig.15. Average annual number of periods with at least four consecutive rain days.

(*2*) The type with rainfall in all seasons, but showing a double maximum in autumn and spring, occurring in the southern Cape Province as far east as East London.

(*3*) The "monsoonal" type with a single pronounced maximum in midsummer, occurring on the eastern plateau and against the eastern escarpment.

(*4*) The type showing a maximum in late summer or autumn, occurring on the western interior plateau.

The transition from one region to another is gradual rather than abrupt. The four types, showing also the annual variation of the number of rain days, are illustrated in Fig.16.

Periods of drought

South Africa, like other countries in similar latitudes is periodically visited by severe and sometimes prolonged droughts. This is a phenomenon that cannot be rigidly defined by meteorological parameters only, and is primarily an affliction of cultivated regions as has been pointed out by LANDSBERG (1958, p.247). Nevertheless, rainfall statistics provide useful information on the occurrence and duration of dry periods.

If we may assume, as has been done in a previous publication (SOUTH AFRICA WEATHER BUREAU, 1949), that a drought in a certain district is reached when its 12-monthly moving totals of precipitation fall below 75% of the annual average, and continues until good rains cause the 12-monthly moving totals to rise above this level, we arrive at periods of drought of varying length (months). The frequency of droughts thus calculated, appears in Table II whilst the location of the districts is shown in Fig.10.

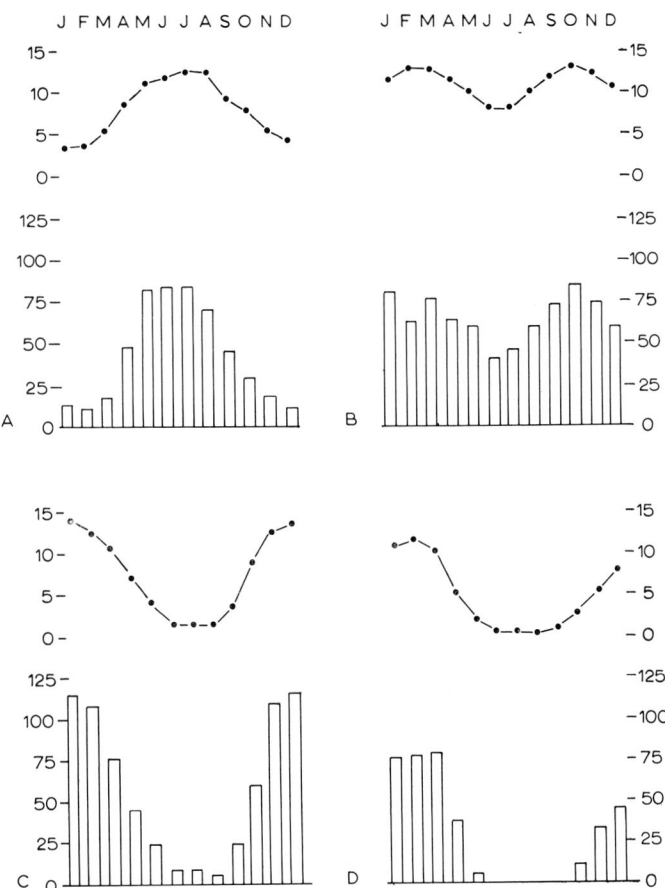

Fig.16. Annual pattern of rainfall (amounts and days), adjusted to 30-day months: A. Cape Town; B George; C. Germiston (Johannesburg); D. Windhoek (Southwest Africa).

This table shows the contrast in drought conditions between districts bordering on the coast or in the eastern highveld, and those in the western high plateau.

An investigation (REPUBLIC OF SOUTH AFRICA, 1965) into rainless periods at a few individual stations has shown that a complete drought can last for 169 days in the interior, and that a dry period during which no rain of any consequence has fallen (i.e., a period begun after, and ended before a day on which 10 mm was precipitated) has been observed to last for 331 days. Presumably this period is exceeded in the western interior (southern Southwest Africa), though this is not proven.

Nature of precipitation

Over the summer rainfall zone precipitation is mainly due to thunderstorms and instability showers; in the southwestern and southern coastal regions, however, precipitation is largely of a frontal nature, being less intense than over the interior. Right around the escarpment, from the southwestern Cape Province to the eastern Transvaal light orographic rain and drizzle is a common feature whenever an anticyclone skirts the coast, forcing moist maritime air against the mountain ranges.

TABLE II

FREQUENCY OF DROUGHTS OF DIFFERENT DURATION IN MONTHS, BASED ON 56½ YEAR RECORDS

Duration (months)	Distr.*:3	8	13	14B	16A	19	22A
1	8	7	8	2	14	8	4
2	3	0	6	3	1	1	3
3	1	0	2	2	4	1	0
4	2	0	1	1	0	1	1
5	1	1	2	0	0	2	
6	2	0	2	0	0	0	
7		0	2	0	1	1	
8		0	0	1	1	3	
9		0	0			1	
10		0	1			1	
11		0	1			1	
12		0	1				
13		1	0				
14		1	0				
15			2				
16			1				
17			1				
18			1				
19			1				
20			1				
21			1				
% no. of drought months	6.2	5.8	24.5	3.8	10.0	13.0	2.1

* For district numbers see Fig.10.

Fig.17 and 18 show approximately the average number of days on which thunder and hail occur (REPUBLIC OF SOUTH AFRICA, 1965; SCHULZE, 1967). As may be expected, the highest frequency, in both cases, is found on the eastern high plateau. In the mountainous regions of the southwestern Cape Province hail is largely of the soft or "graupel" type, whereas true (or hard) hail is the usual form in the summer rainfall zone, and especially on the high plateau. There is no doubt that the eastern high plateau is subject to extremely severe hailstorms, comparable to those in the midwestern states of the U.S.A., and it is interesting to note that the maximum frequency of hail days is also of the same order. Considerable damage is caused by hailstones depending on the severity of the storm and its locality.

Snow (REPUBLIC OF SOUTH AFRICA, 1965, pp. 302,303) occurs spasmodically in South Africa, mainly from April to November and most frequently in June and July. It is usually confined to the high mountain ranges in southern and southeastern South Africa (Lesotho) where, on the average, it occurs on about 5–9 occasions per year. Very occasionally severe snowstorms (STEWART, 1904) affect large tracts of South Africa, and the northernmost limit of snow over the plateau appears to be latitude 23°S.

Depending on the requisite conditions in the general circulation over South Africa, heavy individual showers and copious rain continued over several days sometimes give

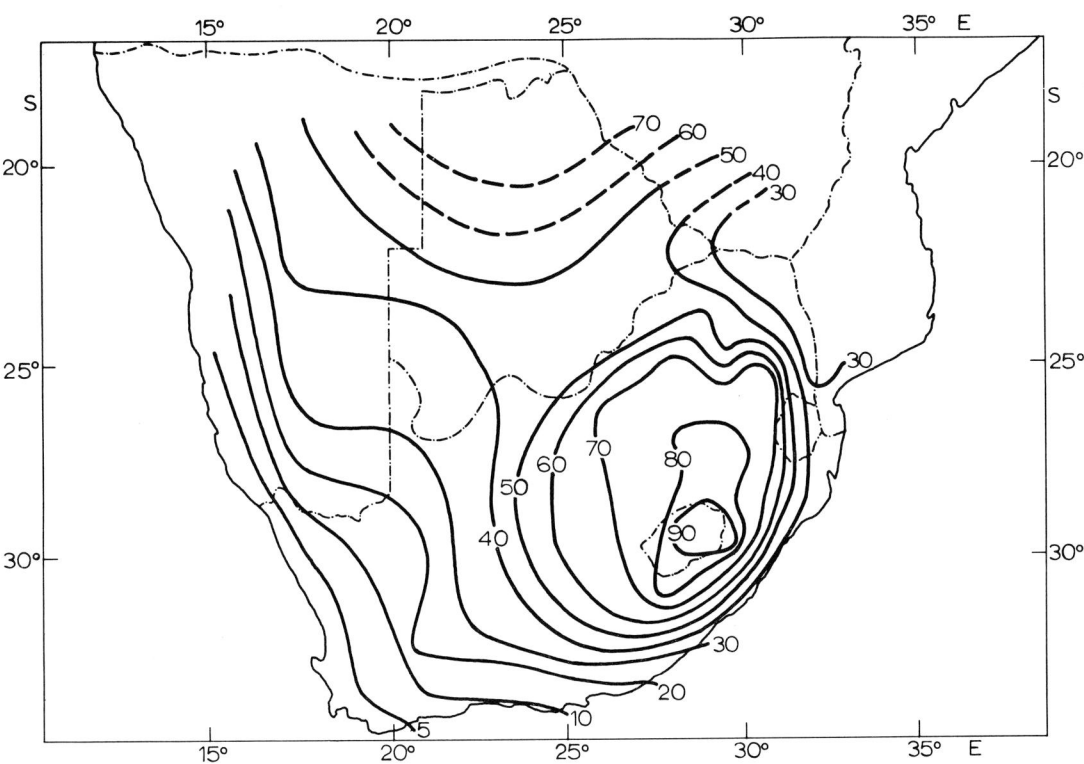

Fig.17. Average annual number of days with thunder (generalized).

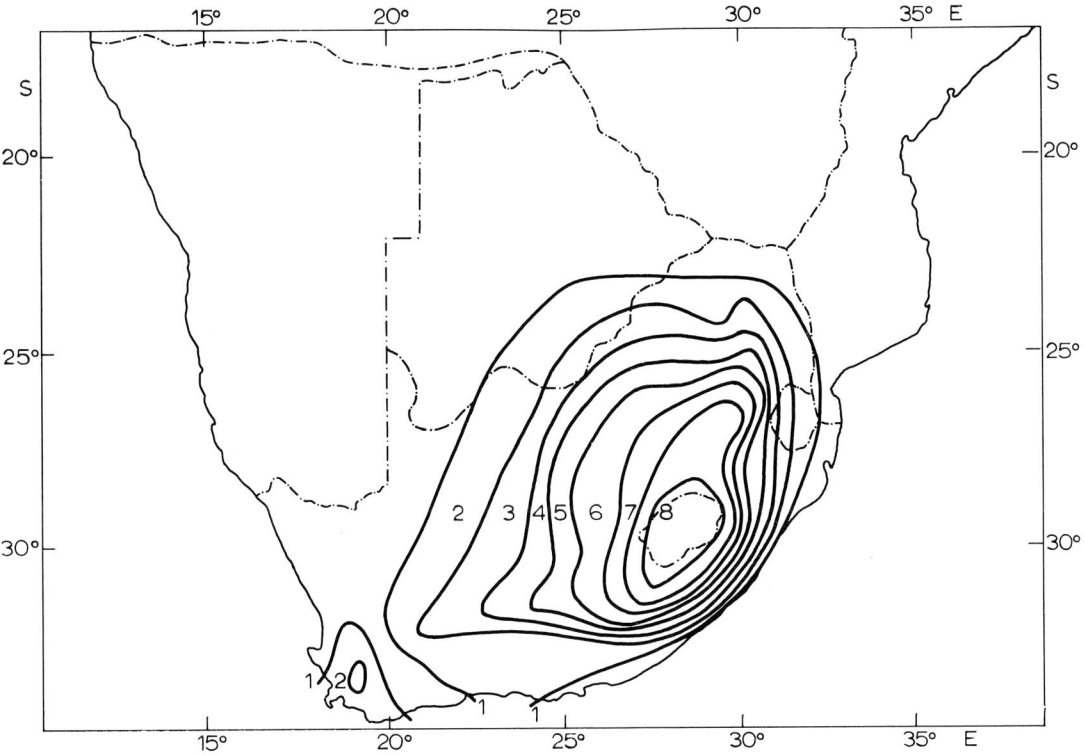

Fig.18. Average annual number of days with hail (generalized).

523

rise to severe flooding (STEWART, 1918; FRITH, 1940; MEINEKE, 1960; TRIEGAARDT, 1961; KOCH, 1963) and consequent damage to bridges and crops. Thus some exceptional a-mounts recorded on a single day are: 121 mm at Molteno Reservoir (Cape Town); 208 mm at George (southern Cape); 230 mm at East London; 382 mm at Port St. Johns; 315 mm at Gingindlovu (Natal); 475 mm at Kaapsche Hoop (eastern Transvaal); 282 mm at Krugersdorp (near Johannesburg); 108 mm at Bloemfontein, and 123 mm at Tsumeb (S.W.A.).

Great intensities in short time periods (REPUBLIC OF SOUTH AFRICA, 1965, pp. 299,305) have been recorded, and the maximum intensity in a 15-min period thus far observed was of the order of 45 mm (or about 7 inches/h).

Diurnal variation of precipitation

The occurrence of precipitation shows a marked diurnal variation; in the southwestern and southern Cape Province precipitation is most frequent in the early morning or at night, but further eastwards (from about East London) and over the interior summer rainfall zone the pattern changes and rain falls more often than not during the afternoon and early evening. This latter is partly due to the convectional showers brought about by diurnal heating of the surface air. The actual amounts falling during the course of an average day also show this tendency over the interior summer rainfall area, though, on the coastal belt, as far eastwards as Durban the density (or rain per "rain-hour") shows very little variation.

Very little information is available on the diurnal occurrence of hail. However, over the eastern plateau the indications are that hail falls mostly during the hours 12h00–22h00 (REPUBLIC OF SOUTH AFRICA, 1965, p. 302; SCHULZE, 1967) with a pronounced maximum at about 17h00–18h00.

Surface temperature

If we compare South Africa with other countries in similar latitudes, e.g., northern Africa and Australia, we find that South Africa enjoys a cooler climate. This is due to two main factors: namely its greater elevation and the tapering shape of the sub-continent, which, projecting into the vast southern oceans makes it more accessible to cool maritime air.

The coolest regions are found on the edge of the great escarpment from the southwest to the northeast, and the hottest regions are the low-lying areas of the western interior, especially the valley of the Orange River system, and the eastern and northern lowveld of the Transvaal province (Limpopo Valley and the Kruger National Game Reserve). Thus far the two coldest stations known are Belfast on the eastern Transvaal highveld (1,870 m) and Sutherland in the Roggeveld Mountains northeast of Cape Town (1,456 m), their mean annual temperatures being respectively 12.4° and 12.6°C while their absolute extremes are 33.9° and –13.2°C for Belfast, and 36.7° and –11.7°C for Sutherland. The two warmest stations are Komatipoort (140 m) on the Mozambique–Transvaal border, and Goodhouse (203 m) in the lower Orange River Valley; means for these two stations are respectively 23.1° and 23.3°C, while extremes range from 48° and 2°C in the former case to 48° and 1°C in the latter.

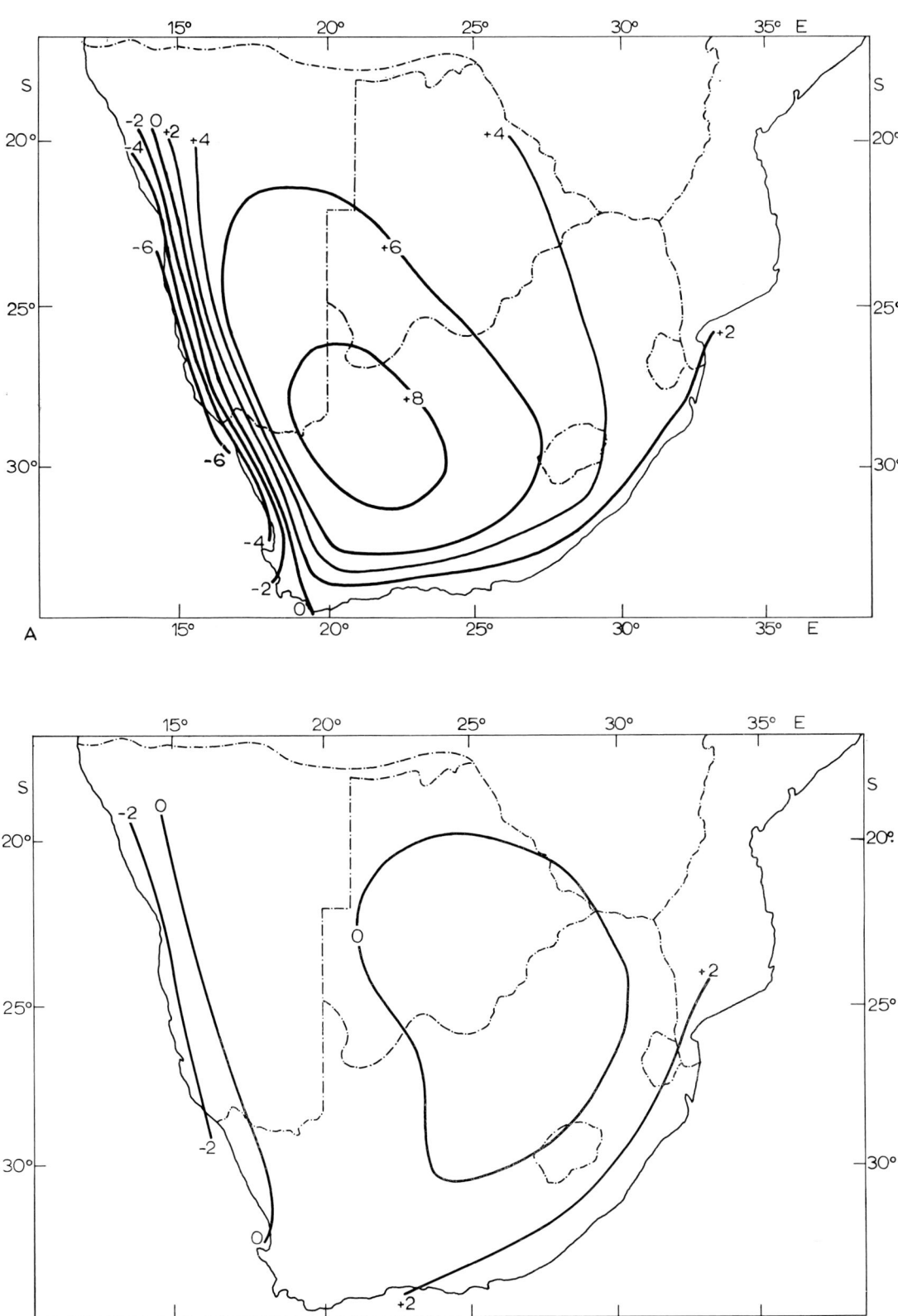

Fig.19. Temperature anomaly (°C) for: A. January; B. July.

The effect of the warm Agulhas ocean current on the eastern and southern coasts, and the cold Benguela Current on the west coast upon the temperature is strikingly shown in Fig.19, the temperature anomaly for January. The considerable anomaly of $+8°C$ over the western interior in summer is on a par with that found for South America. In July the anomaly is much reduced and the contrast between summer and winter (January and July) is mainly due to the considerable heating of the land mass especially in the western interior where clear skies predominate even in summer, while the slight negative anomaly in winter is due mainly to terrestrial radiation during the predominantly clear winter nights.

With regard to long-term climatic change (SCHUMANN and THOMPSON, 1934; HOFMEYR and SCHULZE, 1963; REPUBLIC OF SOUTH AFRICA, 1965) there seems to be some superficial evidence of upward and downward trends of 30 years' duration in mean annual temperature. However, this aspect of climate requires lengthier periods of records before coming to a satisfactory conclusion.

The annual march of temperature

BILHAM (1938) mentions in his treatise on the *"The Climate of the British Isles"* that the seasonal change from the cold winter to the warmth of summer is perhaps the most familiar of all meteorological periodicities. On the South African high plateau, with its semi-arid climate, the diurnal variation is at least equally familiar, and its amplitude is of the same order as, and very often greater than, that of the annual variation of the mean temperature.

The basic data (monthly means and extremes) on temperatures for a selected number of stations in the Republic of South Africa and including Southwest Africa, Botswana and Lesotho are given in the climatic tables at the end of the chapter; and in order to obtain a general view of the annual temperature change over South Africa, diagrams for six stations are shown in Fig.20. These diagrams indicate the march by months of: (*1*) mean temperature; (*2*) mean daily maximum temperature; (*3*) mean daily minimum temperature; (*4*)m ean monthly maximum; (*5*) mean monthly minimum; (*6*) absolute maximum; and (*7*) absolute minimum temperatures. In these diagrams a thick black vertical line connects the mean daily maximum and minimum temperatures for each month, the length of this line thus indicating the mean diurnal range of temperature.

Certain points of interest regarding the regular (periodic) temperature variations, as shown on these diagrams may be observed. We cite here some of the main points:
(*1*) The greatest range of temperature occurs in the central regions of South Africa, namely the northern Karroo and the Kalahari, decreasing towards the tropics and the coastal regions.
(*2*) At coastal stations the absolute minimum temperatures are generally fairly stable, whereas absolute maximum temperatures are subject to large fluctuations. In the interior, however, and especially towards the north, the opposite is the case, with stable maximum temperatures and large fluctuations in the minimum temperatures. This agrees with the fact that the coastal belt is subject to occasional hot bergwind (föhn), whereas the interior suffers from occasional influences of cold sub-antarctic air.
(*3*) The daily range of temperature, as indicated by the length of the vertical black lines, is very much influenced by the incidence of cloud. The daily range increases from summer

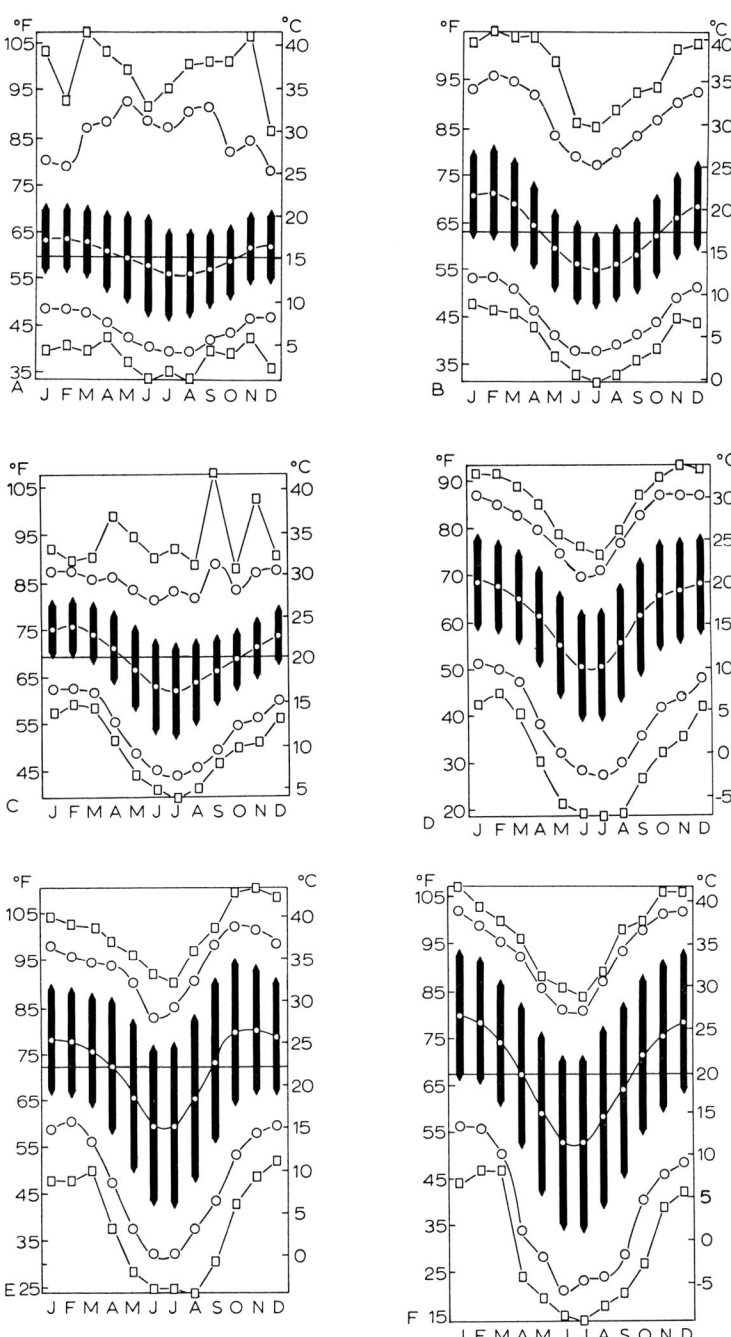

Fig.20. Examples of the annual march of temperature: A. Alexander Bay; B. Cape Town; C. Durban; D. Germiston; E. Maun; F. Tsabong. (For further explanation see text.)

to winter in the summer rainfall areas; in the southern Cape Province and Great Karroo there is little variation throughout the year, while in the winter rainfall area the range is largest in summer, decreasing towards the winter when the variation is least. The effect of the eastern escarpment is to moderate the temperature range, due, of course, to the frequent cloudy weather often accompanied by rain and drizzle.

(*4*) South of latitude 23.5°S the annual variation of mean temperature conforms approximately to a sine curve with a maximum in January and minimum in July. As one moves further north this curve changes gradually into a curve with a double period, for the northerly stations have two maxima, in February and October, and two minima, in December–January and in June–July. The December–January minimum is almost negligible, due to the fact that these stations lie on the southern fringe of the tropics. One would expect the two maxima, which are due entirely to solar radiation, to be equally high and equally spaced about the summer solstice; but this is not the case, the reason being that the rainfall (and cloud) regime starts only in October, and reaches its height in January and February. As a result the highest temperatures occur in October—which is actually too early—and the secondary maximum is decreased. South of the tropic the October–November maximum is still somewhat in evidence (due to the rainfall regime), as far south as the northern Orange Free State, especially as regards the extreme maxima. It may be noted from the main table that in practically the whole of Transvaal the hottest days, individually, occur in November.

In the Great Karroo, due mainly to the very clear or only slightly cloudy conditions which exist throughout the year, we find an almost perfect sine curve in the mean temperature variation; on the coasts, however, the annual mean temperature variation is reduced, due to the influence of the oceans, the maximum falling in February, and the minimum in late July or August. (This is especially noticeable on the west coast—see the climatic tables at the end of the chapter.)

Regional distribution of monthly mean temperature

Maps showing the regional distribution of monthly mean temperatures are similar in essence to the map of mean annual temperature, although the values of the isotherms differ from month to month.

The coolest areas during all months (or coldest in winter) are found solely along the edge of the great escarpment, from Sutherland in the southwestern Cape Province to north of Belfast in eastern Transvaal, and, of course, right on the west coast. Here it may be mentioned that the mean temperature in summer on the west coast may be compared with that of the highlands of Lesotho (about 2,300 mm), while in the winter Lesotho is some 7°–8°C colder than the west coast. On the other hand the warmest (or hottest) regions are found in the Orange River Valley, the Limpopo Valley and the eastern Transvaal lowveld. (In summer the Great and Little Karroo must also be classed as hot regions, although in winter they are colder than the south coast.)

Another point of interest is that, in summer, the western interior Orange River Valley is warmer than the eastern Transvaal lowveld, whereas in winter it is colder than the latter region.

The form and characteristics of the mean annual temperature curve

It will be seen from Fig.20 (temperature diagrams) that the annual curves of mean temperature vary from place to place. They vary in four respects, namely: (*1*) the general level of temperature (as given by the annual mean temperature); (*2*) the annual range; (*3*) the time of year when the maximum and minimum temperatures occur; and (*4*) the curve is very seldom symmetrical.

In order to draw a comparison between the different temperature regimes regionally, we use Köppen's (and Johansson's) (KÖPPEN and GEIGER, 1936) method of "relative temperatures" by means of which four main types of annual curves can be identified in South Africa. In the southern interior of the Cape Province (about 32°S) the annual curve is almost perfectly symmetrical; this is also the case on the west coast with a phase shift of about one month; on the east coast it is both asymmetrical and out of phase, while over the northern interior we have the "continental" type showing very marked asymmetry.

It is found that asymmetry increases northwards over the continent, and that it is greater over the eastern highveld than over the western interior on the same latitude. The large values are mainly due to the fact that spring temperatures are much higher than those indicated by a symmetrical curve. Over the northern interior the phase shift is negative, indicating that the maximum and minimum of the annual curves are advanced (occur too early), while on the coast the opposite is the case. Over the interior the maximum of the curve is advanced much more than the minimum, hence also the large values of skewness. Along the coasts (especially the west coast) however, both the maxima and minima of the curves are retarded resulting in large values for phase shift and small values for asymmetry. The large contrasts in phase shift between coast and interior are, of course, a direct consequence of the different thermal properties of water and land.

It is also interesting to note that the line of no phase shift in the southwest agrees fairly with the transition period between summer and winter rainfall.

The *interdiurnal variation of temperature* as obtained from 27 stations over the period 1941–1950 is shown is Fig.21. It is evident that the greatest variability is found against

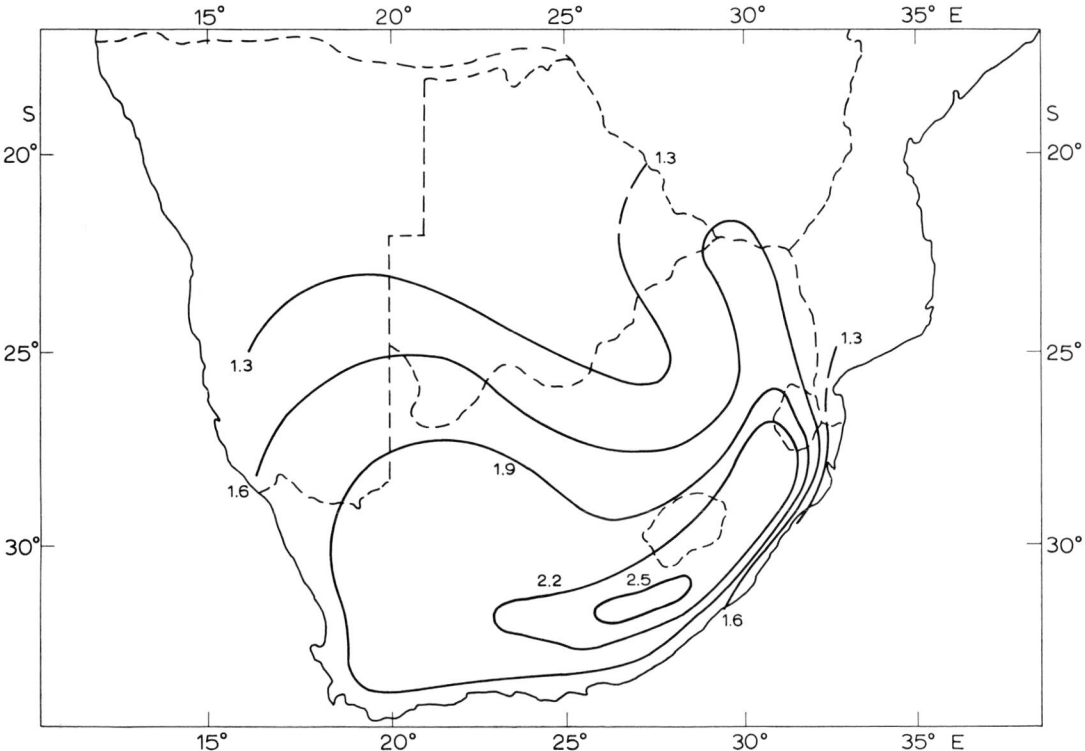

Fig.21. Mean interdiurnal temperature variation for the year (°C).

the southeastern escarpment. The annual march of interdiurnal variation shows that, on the whole, temperature is most variable in spring and least in autumn; however, on the west coast the maximum variability occurs in winter. Table III gives a few examples. This indicator of interdiurnal variation, however, gives us only a general picture of the average day to day change in temperature. It is of greater interest to classify the day to day rises and falls of mean daily temperature separately under certain temperature

TABLE III

INTERDIURNAL VARIATION OF TEMPERATURE (°C)[1]

Station	Jan.	Feb.	Mar.	Apr.	May	June	July	Aug.	Sept.	Oct.	Nov.	Dec.	Year
Alexander													
Bay	1.3	1.4	1.7	1.7	2.1	*2.5*	2.2	1.9	2.1	1.4	1.3	1.3	1.7
Cape Town	1.7	*1.9*	*1.9*	1.6	*1.9*	1.6	1.6	1.7	1.8	1.8	1.8	*1.9*	1.8
Durban	1.2	1.2	1.2	1.1	1.1	1.1	1.2	1.2	1.4	1.4	1.4	*1.6*	1.3
Grootfontein	1.8	1.8	1.7	2.1	1.9	2.2	2.6	*2.9*	*2.9*	2.4	2.2	2.3	2.2
Johannes-													
burg	1.5	1.5	1.3	1.4	1.4	1.5	1.4	1.6	*1.8*	*1.8*	1.7	1.7	1.5
Maun	1.1	1.1	1.1	1.1	1.3	1.2	1.2	1.3	1.2	1.4	*1.5*	1.2	1.2

[1] Numbers in italics are maximum values.

intervals, in order to gain some idea of the frequency of large, as against small, changes of temperature. This aspect of the temperature regime is of importance in the question of human efficiency, because it reflects the number of times one is subjected to varying changes of temperature.

Table IV shows such a classification for temperature steps of 2.5°C in respect of four stations.

Cold and warm spells

In considering the question of temperature variation one must take into acccount the fact that a fall in temperature, for example, is not necessarily followed by a rise on the following day. A rise or fall in temperature usually lasts for a series of days—not necessarily for an equal number of days—and these periods of rise and fall are referred to as, respectively, warm and cold spells. We shall now analyze their frequency under both length of spell in days, and total temperature rise or fall exceeding certain values. It is found that cold spells decrease in frequency more rapidly with duration (in days) than do warm spells; furthermore, however intense a cold spell may be, it will very much more often than not last for only two or three days.

The annual number of cold spells with temperature falls exceeding 5° and 10°C respectively are shown in Fig.22 and 23, which indicate that a maximum of cold spells occur against the southeastern escarpment, decreasing in all directions in frequency. It is interesting to note that the greatest fall in temperature found during a cold spell of whatever duration was 19.7°C (35.6°F) which was experienced in the eastern Cape on September 23, 1947. During this spell the temperature fell for three days.

TABLE IV

FREQUENCY (%) PER SEASON AND PER ANNUM WITH WHICH MEAN DAILY TEMPERATURE FALLS (F) OR RISES (R) FROM
ONE DAY TO THE NEXT BY AMOUNTS EXCEEDING THE VALUES INDICATED[1]

	Season	0°C	2.5°C	5.0°C	7.5°C	10°C	0°C	2.5°C	5.0°C	7.5°C	10°C
		Johannesburg					*Durban*				
Summer	F	40.8	9.4	1.1			38.5	8.2	0.7		
	R	49.2	6.8	0.1			51.5	2.9			
Autumn	F	43.5	7.4	1.4	0.2		44.1	5.4	0.6		
	R	48.4	4.7	0.3	0.1		47.6	2.1			
Winter	F	39.2	7.8	2.4	0.2	0.1	45.0	5.1	0.4		
	R	52.7	6.1	0.3	0.1		46.9	5.2	0.3		
Spring	F	39.6	11.5	2.8	1.0		41.0	8.1	1.0	0.5	0.1
	R	51.4	11.0	0.4			50.0	5.8	0.7	0.2	0.1
Year	F	163.1	36.2	7.8	1.5	0.1	168.6	26.8	2.7	0.5	0.1
	R	201.7	28.6	1.1	0.2		196.0	16.0	1.0	0.2	0.1
		Cape Town					*Windhoek*				
Summer	F	41.4	13.5	2.1	0.1		41.4	5.5	0.5		
	R	48.6	12.1	1.7	0.0		48.6	3.6	0.1		
Autumn	F	44.4	13.2	2.3	0.3		44.8	4.0	0.5		
	R	47.5	12.2	0.9	0.1		47.2	1.6	0.1		
Winter	F	45.8	10.5	0.7	0.0		41.1	4.4	1.3	0.3	
	R	46.2	10.7	1.6	0.0		50.9	3.9	0.3		
Spring	F	43.4	12.2	1.5	0.2		41.7	7.2	1.4	0.1	
	R	47.3	12.5	1.7	0.3		49.3	6.0	0.2		
Year	F	175.0	49.5	6.6	0.7		169.0	21.1	3.7	0.4	
	R	189.6	47.5	5.9	0.4		196.0	15.1	0.7		

[1] Computed from records for the ten years 1941–1950.

The largest rise in temperature experienced was 20°C (36°F) which occurred at Grootfontein on the 26th of August, 1944, lasting four days before the temperature started
falling again.

It must of course be borne in mind that cold or warm spells have different effects in
different seasons; thus a cold spell in summer, if not too severe, may have a beneficial
result, while in winter the reverse is most certainly the case. The opposite is probably
true in respect of warm spells, since a prolonged hot spell in summer is usually conducive
to severe desiccation, and therefore harmful to all vegetation.

It is of interest to compare the number of cold spells in summer (October–March) with
the number occurring during the winter half-year. In summer the greatest number of
cold spells generally occurs over the southeastern and eastern escarpment, whereas
during winter they occur more frequently over the western interior. Thus it seems that
in winter cold air enters South Africa more or less directly from the west (by way of

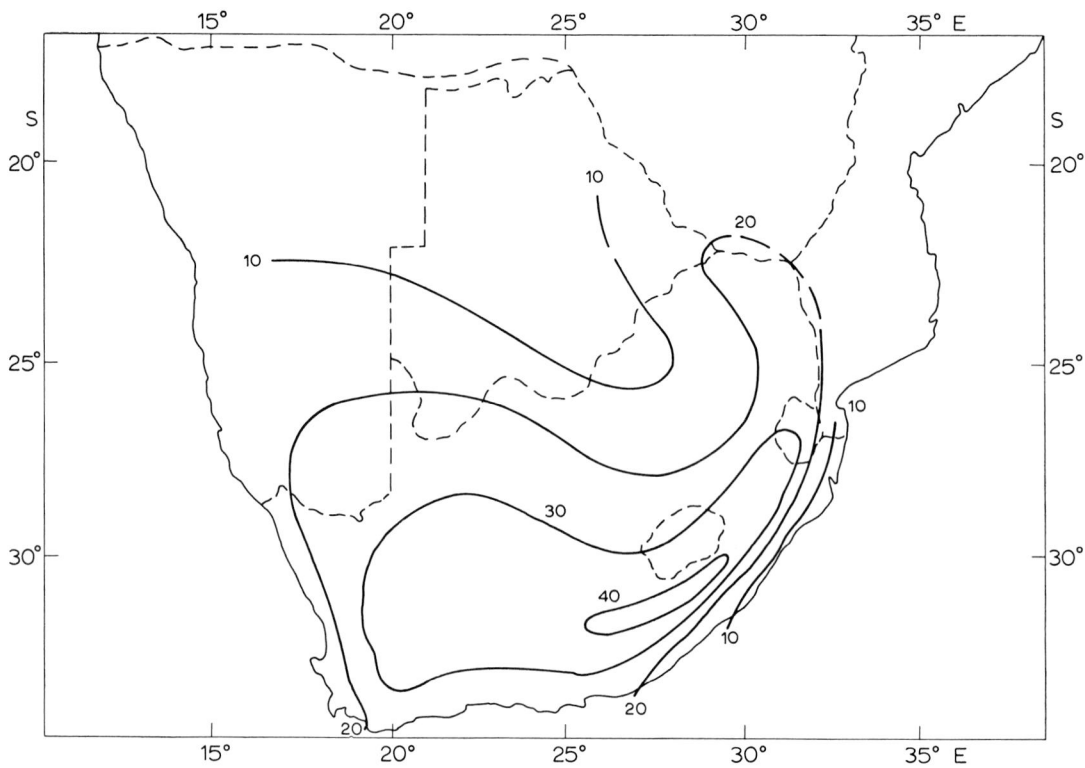

Fig.22. Annual frequency of cold spells (temperature fall >5°C).

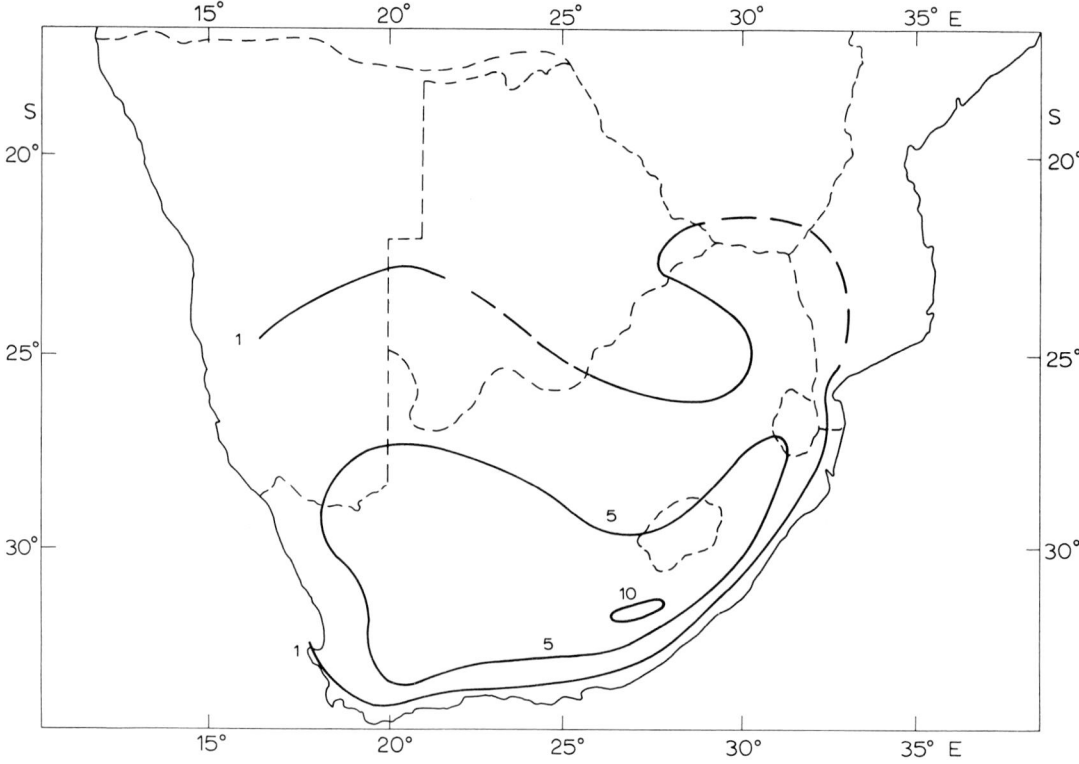

Fig.23. Annual frequency of cold spells (temperature fall exceeding 10°C).

Namaqualand), while in summer it moves around the escarpment, entering the country from the southeast and east. This is in accordance with the seasonal shift of the subtropical high pressure belt.

Extreme temperatures and the frequency of occurrence of maximum and minimum temperatures above or below certain values

Although the data on which the following section is based does not always refer to a standard period of years, the results are sufficiently consistent to give a very generalized picture of the occurrence of certain conditions of temperature in different regions of South Africa.

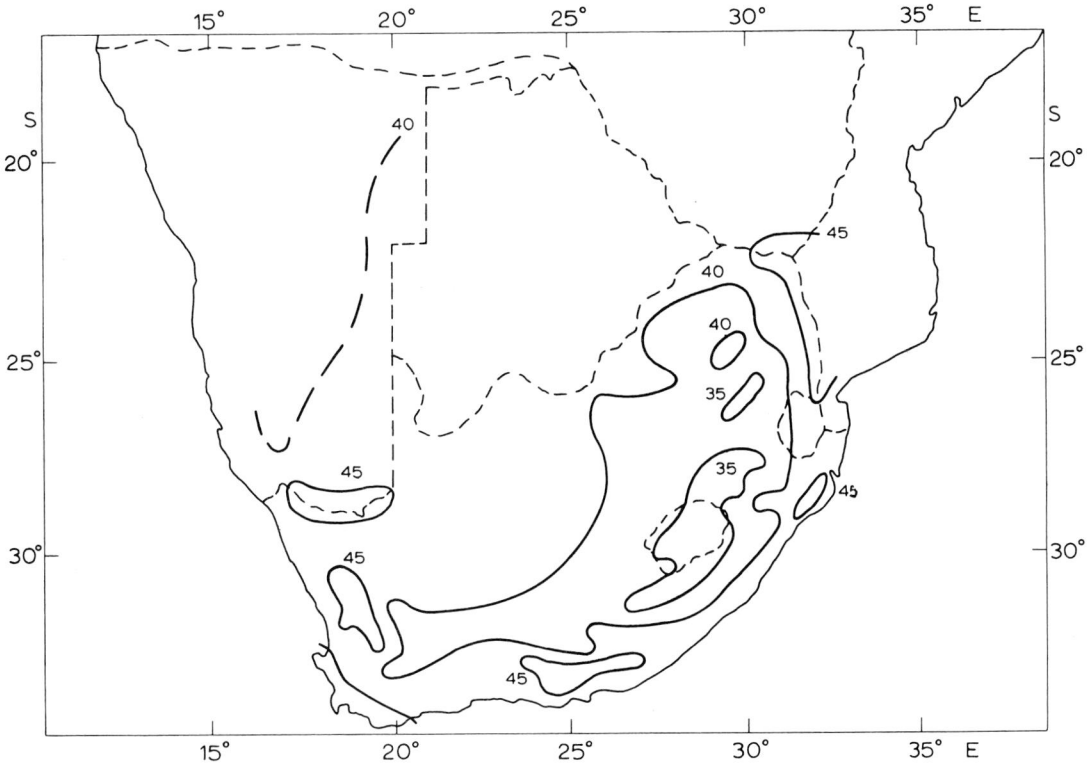

Fig.24. Absolute maximum temperature (°C).

Fig.24 represents the hottest day that is likely to be encountered. Areas with hot days over 45°C (113°F) are indicated in the low-lying regions on the seaward side of the great escarpment. In these areas the high temperatures are mainly due to the occurrence of hot berg winds. All these areas may be considered as the focal points in regard to very hot days. As to the time of occurrence of these extreme maximum temperatures it may be noted that they occur in early summer (October, November) in northern Natal, northern and eastern Transvaal and further north; on the south and west coasts they are most frequent in April; in the southwestern Cape in February, and over the remainder of the country in January.

Fig.25 shows the maximum temperature on the coldest day yet experienced. On the eastern, southeastern and southern escarpment, days with maximum temperatures barely

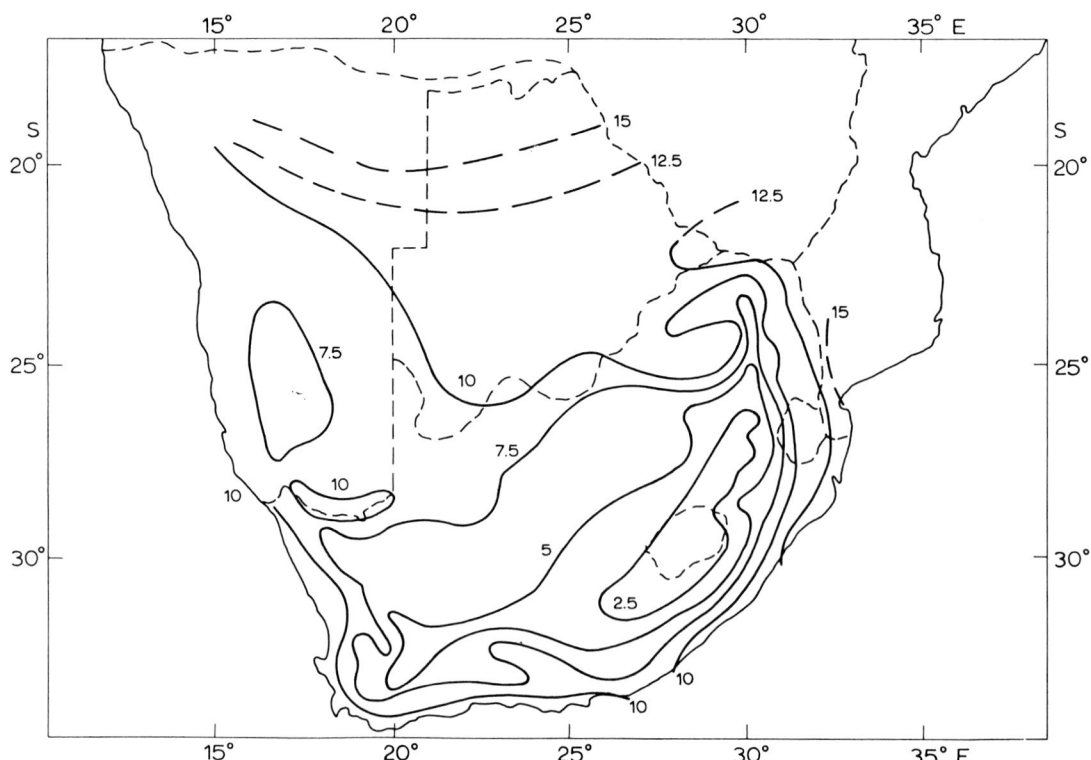

Fig.25. Lowest of daily maximum temperature (°C).

above freezing point have been recorded, e.g., 0.6°C (33°F) at Mokhotlong (Lesotho), Sutherland and Harrismith. It is interesting to note that the coldest day in the lower Orange River Valley is on the whole colder than in the eastern Transvaal lowveld, although the hottest days are much the same. This is quite understandable when one considers that cold air from the southern Atlantic reaches the western interior first, but is considerably modified over the warm Agulhas Current before reaching the eastern Transvaal.

Fig.26, in contradistinction to Fig.25, gives the temperature of the warmest night yet observed. If one accepts a night with minimum temperature above 20°C as a "tropical night" then a very small area in South Africa is entirely free from tropical nights—that is, the highlands of Lesotho and the southeastern Transvaal highveld. In two areas of the western interior minima of over 30°C (86°F) have been recorded, due to eastern föhn-like winds—trying conditions indeed, but mitigated somewhat by the fact that in these areas under such conditions the air is usually very dry. (A night with minimum temperature over 27.5° or even 25°C as observed on the eastern seaboard may be much more trying on account of the higher humidity.)

In these figures the extreme values at different places have no relation to one another in time, often having occurred in different years and on different dates; the purpose, however, of these maps is to give an idea of the extremes of temperature which may be expected in any given locality.

Regarding warm days (Fig.27) it may be noted that there is no weather station in South Africa at which a temperature of 30°C (86°F) has not been reached, although at some stations, for example Belfast on the eastern highveld, this only occurs about once in two

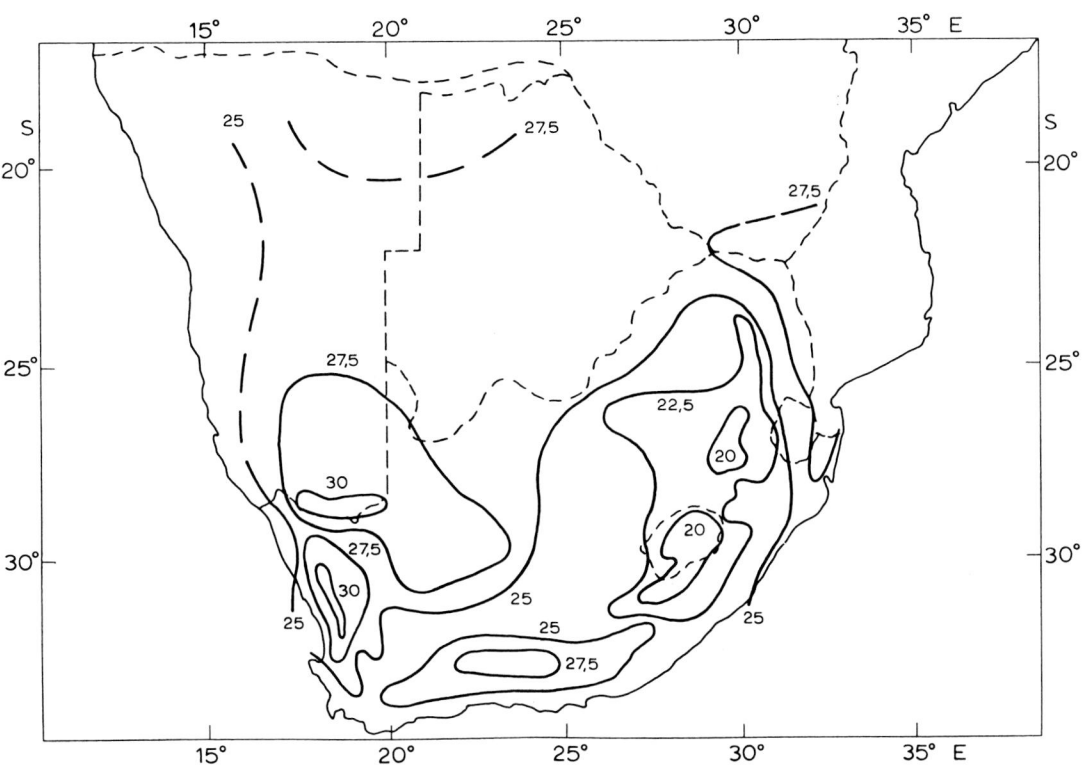

Fig.26. Highest of daily minimum temperature (°C).

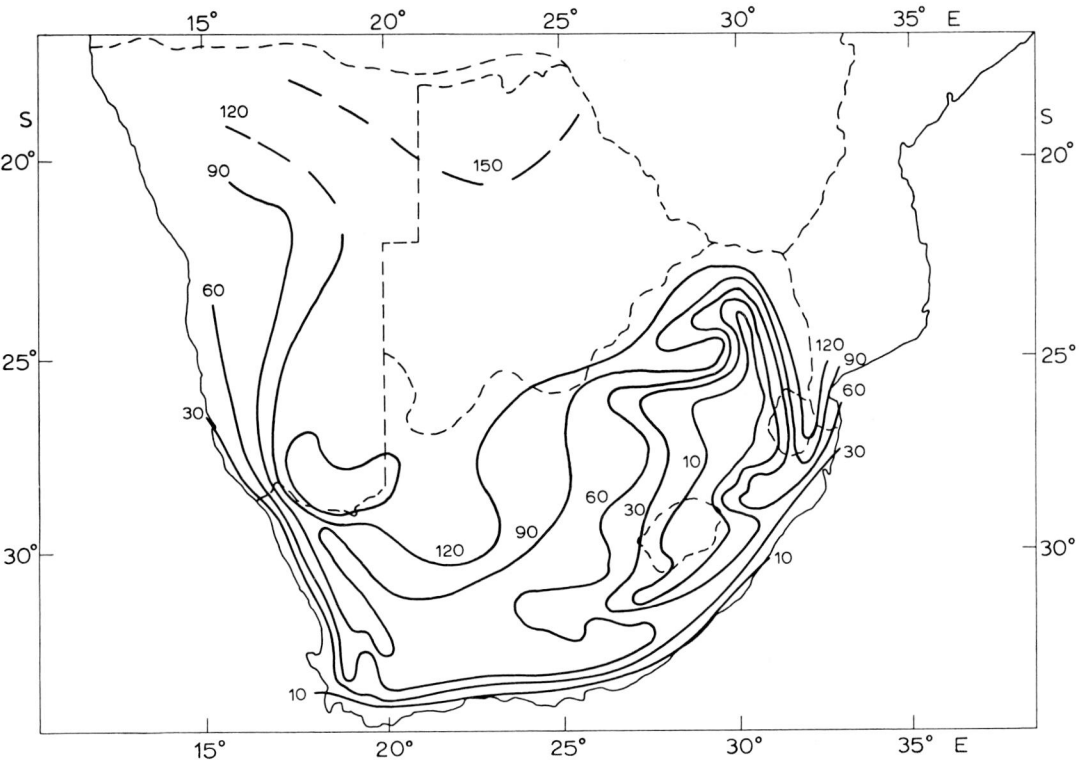

Fig.27. Average annual frequency of days with maximum temperature >30°C.

535

years. As against this, the western and northern interior are subject to such daily maximum temperatures for over 180 days/year.

Cold days (i.e., maximum temperature below 10°C) are relatively infrequent, and occur mainly on the edge of the great escarpment, from Okiep round to eastern Transvaal. The greatest number of such days (20 per annum) occur at Sutherland in the Roggeveld Mountains. The coastal belt, as well as the Transvaal lowveld, Botswana and further northwards are practically free from such days.

Tropical nights are of especial significance in that they affect human efficiency by causing lack of sleep. This type of condition is most frequent (60 or more per year) in low-lying areas, especially on the east coast and in the Transvaal lowveld. Tropical nights occur mainly after mid-summer when the air is most humid and cloudiness is at its height, which condition reduces outward radiation of heat. This is also the reason why the frequency is less in the lower Orange River Valley, since here the air as a rule is much drier and the cloudiness less. On the high plateau such enervating nights occur less than five times per year, and on the higher areas in eastern Transvaal and Lesotho less than once per year or not at all.

In considering frosty nights (Fig.28) it must be pointed out that in South Africa it very rarely happens that the diurnal minimal temperature occurs during the daytime, so that frequency of frosty nights is synonymous with frosty days, the day being considered as a 24-h period. From this map (which, incidentally gives the *number* of frosty nights per annum, and *not* the length of the frost period) we see that the coastal belt is practically free of frosty nights, and that the greatest frequency of this condition is to be found on the edge of the great escarpment.

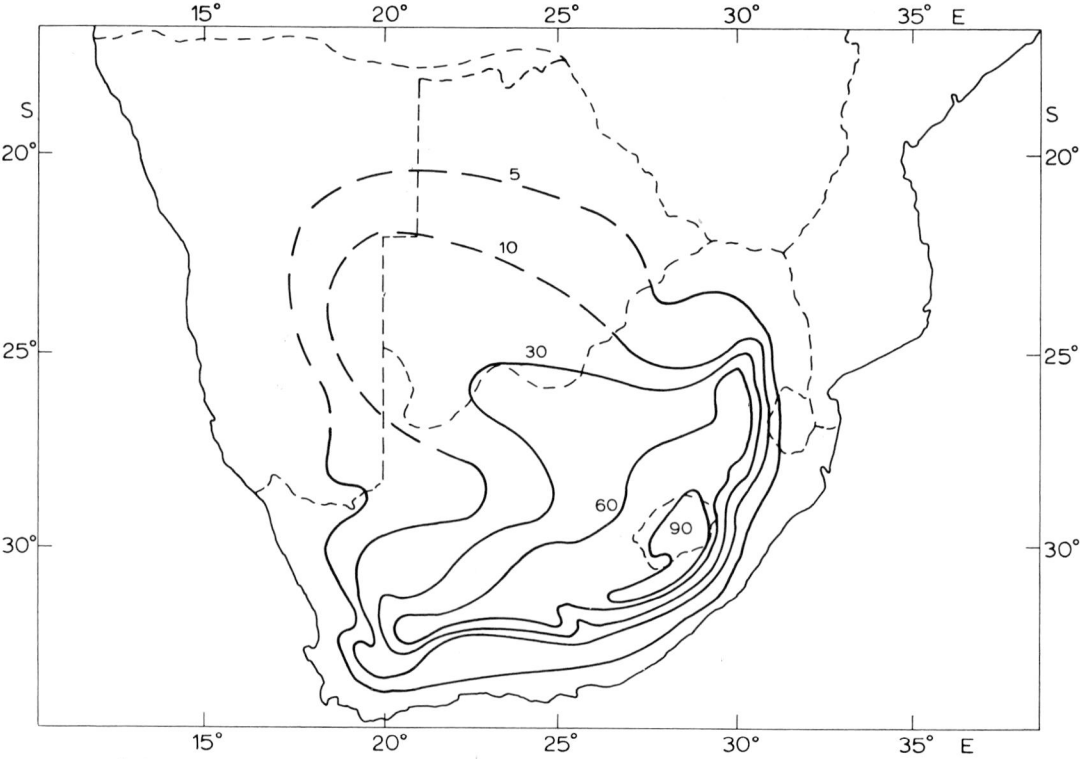

Fig.28. Average annual frequency of days with minimum temperature <0°C.

Frost in South Africa

Frost, mainly in the form of hoar frost, is a common phenomenon in South Africa during the winter months, April–September, but especially from mid-May to mid-September. In general it is severest on the high plateau, especially in valleys, and is least found on the coastal plateaus. Occasionally, during an influx of very cold dry air from the south, a so-called "black frost" occurs.

Frost which is very similar in appearance to hoar frost may also occur when a deposit of dew formed during the earlier part of a night, later freezes.

Conditions most conducive to frost are: (*1*) a relatively dry atmosphere and clear sky, promoting outward radiation of heat. This condition is almost constantly present in the interior of South Africa during the winter, but infrequently along the coastal belt; (*2*) a relatively non-conductive surface layer (grass, loosely tilled soil, etc.) which prevents the conduction of heat from the lower layers of the soil, although this condition is entirely dependent upon the nature of the surface in different areas; (*3*) absence of wind, promoting stratification of the air and a strong inversion of the temperature as is generally the case in the interior. This condition is, however, greatly influenced by topography, since chilled air (being denser) will flow down any slope, however slight, and become stagnant at the bottom. Furthermore the influence of topography is shown by the fact that in South Africa, north facing slopes receive more heat than south facing ones, and are thus less prone to frost.

There are many instances of differences in the incidence of frost, due to situation on a slope or in a valley, even in sites which are within a mile of one another. For example, the north facing Muckleneuk and Magaliesberg ridges in Pretoria seldom have frost, while in the valleys it is almost a nightly occurrence in winter.

We see, therefore, that a regional representation of the duration and dates of the frost period can only be very general, giving only a rough picture of the general situation. However, a generalized picture of the average duration of the frost period is shown in Fig.29; in which figure the criterion for frost is the occurrence of a minimum temperature below 0°C (32°F), the thermometer being exposed at a height of 1.2 m (4 ft.) in a Stevenson screen.

Both the earliest and the latest appearances of frost, on the average, occur on the higher lying valleys on the edge of the great escarpment, the earliest (before April 10) being in Lesotho.

The whole interior high plateau south of latitude 23°S is subject to at least one day with frost every year.

The very appreciable difference between the air temperature immediately above the ground and that at the height of a few metres, depending on the nature of the surface and the presence of cloud (or humid air) and wind, has already been noted. Light frost is therefore liable to occur even though the minimum temperature in the Stevenson screen is somewhat above 0°C. From observations made at a number of stations in South Africa it has been found that the average difference is roughly 3°C (5.4°F), and if we should employ a screen minimum of 3°C as a criterion for light ground frost, the average dates of first and last appearances of frost will be about 18 days earlier and the same amount later, respectively, so that the average duration of the frost period will be lengthened by approximately 35 days.

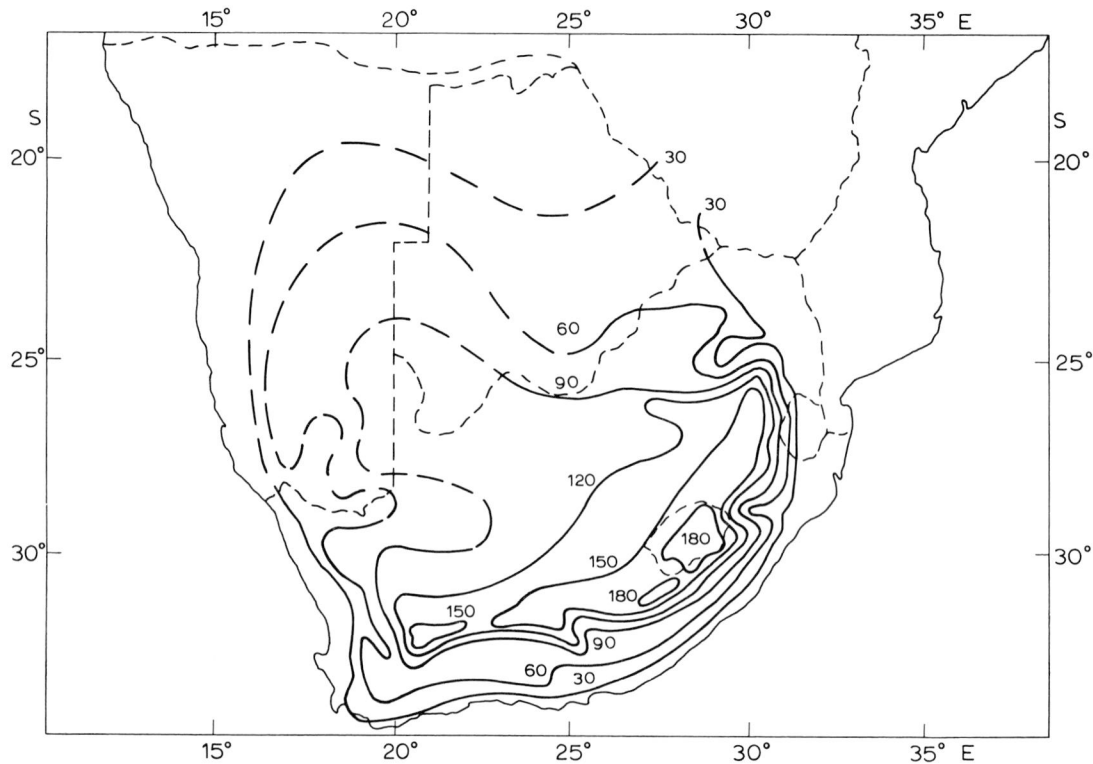

Fig.29. Average duration (days) of frost periods.

Readings of the so-called "grass minimum" thermometer reveal that frost on the high plateau is possible even in January as shown by the minimum values for Bethlehem (28°10′S 28°18′E, height 1,631 m) in Table V, in respect of data over 10 years. On the other hand, the maximum values show that even in mid-winter frost does not necessarily occur on all nights.

The average frequency of occurrence of frosty nights in July (mid-winter) is approximately 25 in Lesotho and about 20–25 on the edge of the great escarpment.

TABLE V

AVERAGE (M), HIGHEST (H) AND LOWEST (L) "GRASS MINIMUM" TEMPERATURES (°C) FOR BETHLEHEM (28°10′S 28°18′E; 1,631 m)

	Jan.	Feb.	Mar.	Apr.	May	June	July	Aug.	Sept.	Oct.	Nov.	Dec.	Year
M	10.2	9.6	7.6	2.7	−2.5	−7.1	−5.6	−4.7	0.5	5.2	7.8	9.9	2.8
H	15.3	15.3	14.3	10.1	11.3	4.6	5.8	6.3	9.5	13.0	15.5	15.5	15.5
L	−1.2	3.7	0.0	−7.6	−10.4	−15.9	−15.5	−12.5	−11.0	−7.5	−2.4	3.4	−15.9

Diurnal temperature variation

The diurnal temperature variation is well-marked all over South Africa, especially on the interior plateaus. In the dry season the amplitude usually exceeds the average annual variation of temperature by a wide margin. In the southwestern Cape winter rainfall zone the diurnal amplitude is largest in summer, while the reverse is the case in the summer rainfall zone. This can be seen in the main table which shows the average aperiodic range for each month.

During settled anticyclonic conditions over the interior the diurnal curve will often pursue an almost normal trend for one or two weeks in succession until disturbed by the passage of a cold front. Along coastal regions, as also along the seaward side of the great escarpment the diurnal curve is quite often disturbed by hot föhn-like berg-winds on individual, or a series of days, which may on occasions send the temperature rocketing up to 48°C. This condition is more in evidence on the western and southern coastal regions. In the summer rainfall zone with its predominantly convectional type of rain, the normal course of the diurnal march is disturbed during the passage of thunderstorms during which we have the characteristic sudden drop in temperature. This temperature decrease can on occasions be of the order of 10–14°C within as many minutes; such drops in temperature, needless to say, bring welcome relief on hot summer afternoons.

Humidity

In general the air is dry over the South African plateau and the humidity increases rapidly from the great escarpment to coastal areas. At 14h00 (South African Standard Time) when the air is driest and usually well mixed through turbulence, the coastal areas show an average annual relative humidity between 70 and 80% while on the plateau the humidity decreases from about 50% on the eastern escarpment to less than 30% in the western interior (Namaqualand, the Kalahari Desert and Southwest Africa).

Normally one would expect the relative humidity to show an annual variation inverse to that of air temperature. This is only the case in the western interior desert areas and on the western and southwestern coasts which latter have their main rainy season in winter. In the eastern or summer rainfall areas (as far west, or further west than Kimberley) the month of maximum humidity is in summer and the beginning of autumn; on the southern coastal belt we find two rather ill-defined maxima of humidity in February and October, in agreement with the annual march of rainfall in that region. The variation (at 14h00) from wettest to driest month is least on the coasts, being of the order of 10% or less, while over the western and northern interior the variation is of the order of 20–25%.

The *diurnal variation of relative humidity* is considerable over the interior plateau, the amplitude being of the order of 40–50%. Extremely low humidities of less than 5% have been noted on the high plateau of Southwest Africa. On the coasts the amplitude is of course reduced due to sea breezes, though under hot wind or föhn conditions very large variations on single days can be of the order of 50–60%. The maximum relative humidity is of course 100%, and this is reached quite often mainly on summer or autumn mornings under which conditions copious deposits of dew occur over the interior.

The average montly values of relative humidity contained in the main table throw no light on the frequency with which certain categories of humidity occur. To give some idea of this aspect, values pertaining to six main cities are given in Table VI, showing percentage frequency of *daily mean* (24 h) relative humidity by months and for the year. Fig.30, based on the yearly values serves to indicate how variable relative humidity is, and especially the change in humidity from the coasts and across the interior of the sub-

TABLE VI

PERCENTAGE FREQUENCY OF DAILY (24-h mean) RELATIVE HUMIDITY WITHIN SPECIFIED LIMITS[1]

Month	Frequency range									
	1–10	11–20	21–30	31–40	41–50	51–60	61–70	71–80	81–90	91–100
Durban										
Jan.	—	—	—	—	—	—	11.3	34.0	*50.0*	4.7
Feb.	—	—	—	—	0.7	0.0	7.1	34.0	*54.0*	4.3
Mar.	—	—	—	—	—	1.9	12.3	32.2	*49.0*	4.5
Apr.	—	—	—	—	—	3.3	7.3	*49.3*	38.7	1.3
May	—	—	—	—	2.6	7.7	18.1	*46.4*	24.5	0.6
June	—	—	—	—	4.7	10.0	38.7	*40.6*	6.0	—
July	—	—	0.6	1.3	5.2	20.0	*36.8*	29.0	7.1	—
Aug.	—	—	—	—	3.9	10.3	15.5	*43.2*	24.5	2.6
Sept.	—	—	—	—	—	2.0	17.3	*44.7*	34.7	1.3
Oct.	—	—	—	—	—	1.3	2.6	30.3	*58.7*	7.1
Nov.	—	—	—	—	—	0.0	9.3	41.3	*44.0*	5.3
Dec.	—	—	—	—	—	—	6.5	29.6	*59.3*	4.5
Year	—	—	0.1	0.1	1.4	4.8	15.3	37.9	37.4	3.0
Bloemfontein										
Jan.	—	3.2	10.3	*21.9*	18.7	19.4	15.5	4.5	3.9	2.6
Feb.	—	—	0.7	2.8	15.6	*36.2*	22.0	14.9	5.0	2.8
Mar.	—	—	4.6	9.8	18.3	18.3	*26.1*	13.1	7.2	2.6
Apr.	—	—	3.3	8.7	12.7	24.0	19.4	*24.6*	6.0	1.3
May	—	—	1.9	11.0	18.7	*30.3*	20.6	12.9	4.5	—
June	—	—	1.3	10.0	*34.7*	24.0	17.3	8.7	4.0	—
July	—	0.7	12.4	15.0	*29.4*	18.9	13.7	5.9	3.3	0.7
Aug.	—	5.2	18.1	*32.9*	23.2	13.5	5.8	1.3	—	—
Sept.	—	16.0	*30.7*	22.6	16.7	8.0	3.3	1.3	1.3	—
Oct.	—	5.8	18.1	*27.7*	18.7	11.6	11.0	3.9	1.9	1.3
Nov.	—	2.7	9.3	22.0	*24.0*	14.7	12.0	12.0	2.7	0.7
Dec.	—	2.6	9.7	21.3	*28.4*	16.1	10.3	7.1	4.5	—
Year	—	3.0	10.1	17.3	21.6	19.5	14.7	9.1	3.7	1.0
Cape Town (Wingfield)										
Jan.	—	—	—	—	0.6	18.7	34.8	*35.5*	9.7	0.6
Feb.	—	—	—	—	0.7	12.1	29.8	*39.7*	15.6	2.1
Mar.	—	—	—	0.6	0.6	10.3	27.1	*38.8*	21.9	0.6
Apr.	—	—	—	—	0.7	6.0	9.3	30.0	*42.0*	12.0
May	—	—	—	—	—	2.6	9.0	32.3	*34.8*	21.3
June	—	—	0.7	0.7	2.0	4.0	14.0	26.6	*40.0*	12.0
July	—	—	—	0.6	0.6	3.2	7.1	23.2	*48.4*	16.8
Aug.	—	—	—	—	1.3	5.2	18.1	32.2	*38.7*	4.5
Sept.	—	—	—	—	1.3	10.0	18.0	*34.7*	32.7	3.3
Oct.	—	—	—	—	1.9	7.7	26.5	*32.9*	29.0	1.9
Nov.	—	—	—	—	4.7	13.3	28.7	*37.3*	15.3	0.7
Dec.	—	—	—	—	1.3	15.5	*40.6*	34.2	8.4	0.0
Year	—	—	0.1	0.3	1.3	9.0	21.9	33.1	28.1	6.3

[1] Values are for the five year period 1951–1955. Monthly maximum values are shown in italics.

TABLE VI *(continued)*

Month	Frequency range									
	1–10	11–20	21–30	31–40	41–50	51–60	61–70	71–80	81–90	91–100
Port Elizabeth										
Jan.	—	—	—	—	—	0.6	16.8	*42.6*	34.8	5.2
Feb.	—	—	—	—	—	0.7	10.6	38.3	*41.9*	8.5
Mar.	—	—	—	—	—	1.3	11.6	36.1	*41.3*	9.7
Apr.	—	—	—	—	—	6.0	10.0	38.0	*42.0*	4.0
May	—	—	—	—	0.6	8.4	22.6	29.7	*35.5*	3.2
June	—	—	—	2.0	6.7	6.7	21.3	*32.0*	28.0	3.3
July	—	—	—	—	5.2	14.2	20.6	*30.3*	28.4	1.3
Aug.	—	—	—	—	1.3	6.5	18.1	*40.6*	29.0	4.5
Sept.	—	—	—	—	1.3	1.3	14.0	*41.3*	36.0	6.0
Oct.	—	—	—	—	—	3.2	10.3	*38.7*	38.7	9.0
Nov.	—	—	—	—	—	3.3	18.0	*42.7*	28.7	7.3
Dec.	—	—	—	—	—	1.9	20.6	*51.6*	24.5	1.3
Year	—	—	—	0.2	1.3	4.5	16.3	38.5	34.0	5.3
Pretoria										
Jan.	—	—	—	1.3	1.3	18.7	31.6	*34.2*	10.3	2.6
Feb.	—	—	—	—	2.1	12.8	29.1	*36.2*	15.6	4.2
Mar.	—	—	—	—	4.5	11.0	34.8	*36.1*	12.3	1.3
Apr.	—	—	—	—	6.7	12.7	*34.6*	25.3	18.7	2.0
May	—	—	—	1.9	7.1	26.4	*34.8*	22.0	5.2	2.6
June	—	—	—	2.0	19.3	28.7	*33.3*	14.7	2.0	—
July	—	—	2.6	14.2	25.2	*30.3*	20.6	3.2	3.9	—
Aug.	—	—	10.3	23.2	*31.6*	22.0	12.3	0.6	—	—
Sept.	—	2.7	8.7	*30.0*	28.0	16.6	10.7	2.7	—	0.7
Oct.	—	0.6	3.2	*21.9*	17.4	18.1	15.5	16.8	4.5	1.9
Nov.	—	—	—	9.3	12.7	20.0	*27.4*	22.6	6.7	1.3
Dec.	—	—	—	0.6	5.2	21.3	*34.2*	21.9	13.6	3.2
Year	—	0.3	2.1	8.8	13.5	19.9	26.6	19.6	7.7	1.6
Windhoek										
Jan.	0.6	11.0	*21.3*	*21.3*	16.1	13.6	9.7	3.2	3.2	—
Feb.	—	0.7	7.8	9.9	15.6	*19.9*	10.6	19.2	15.6	0.7
Mar.	—	3.9	9.0	*21.3*	18.7	15.5	8.4	10.3	11.0	1.9
Apr.	—	2.0	12.0	16.0	*24.7*	20.6	12.0	8.0	4.0	0.7
May	—	3.2	21.9	*35.6*	21.4	7.7	7.7	1.9	0.6	—
June	—	5.3	26.7	*41.3*	18.0	5.3	3.3	—	—	—
July	0.6	23.2	*42.0*	29.7	4.5	—	—	—	—	—
Aug.	18.3	*37.2*	32.7	8.5	3.3	—	—	—	—	—
Sept.	17.3	*56.7*	17.3	3.3	3.3	2.0	—	—	—	—
Oct.	10.3	*37.4*	22.6	10.3	8.4	5.2	4.5	1.3	—	—
Nov.	9.3	*32.0*	22.0	14.0	8.7	6.7	2.7	3.3	1.3	—
Dec.	—	16.8	*26.4*	18.7	17.4	11.6	5.2	2.6	1.3	—
Year	4.7	19.2	21.9	19.3	13.3	8.9	5.3	4.1	3.0	0.3

continent; on the coasts humidity is normally in the categories 70–90%; at Pretoria on the eastern plateau the maximum frequency is in the category 60–70%; further westwards (Bloemfontein and Windhoek) the maximum categories are, respectively, 40–50% and 20–30%. This example is illustrative of the considerable difference in climate existing between coastal areas on the one hand, and the interior plateau when proceeding from

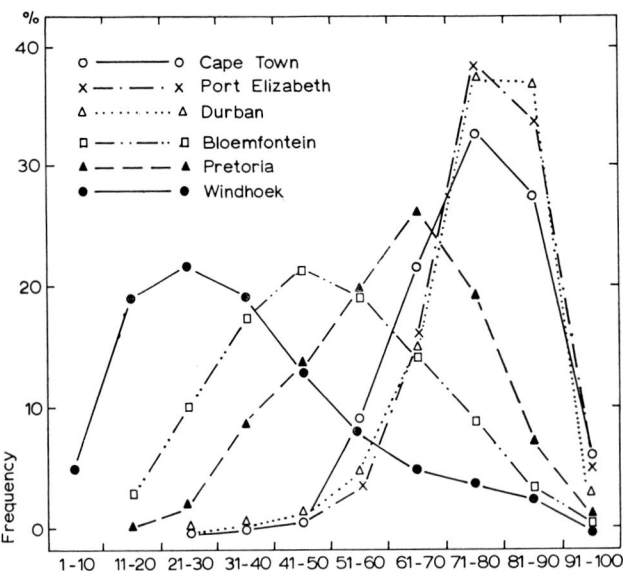

Fig.30. Percentage frequency of daily mean relative humidity within specified limits for the year.

east to west on the other. Whereas at the coast mean daily relative humidity is almost exclusively confined within narrow limits (70–90%), this is not the case in the interior where, at Windhoek for instance, all categories are represented, though, of course, not equally. The *saturation deficit* is extensively used in formulae for estimating evaporation, and expresses the difference between the actual vapour pressure and the saturation vapour pressure of the air. Fig.31 and 32 show the distribution over South Africa for the months

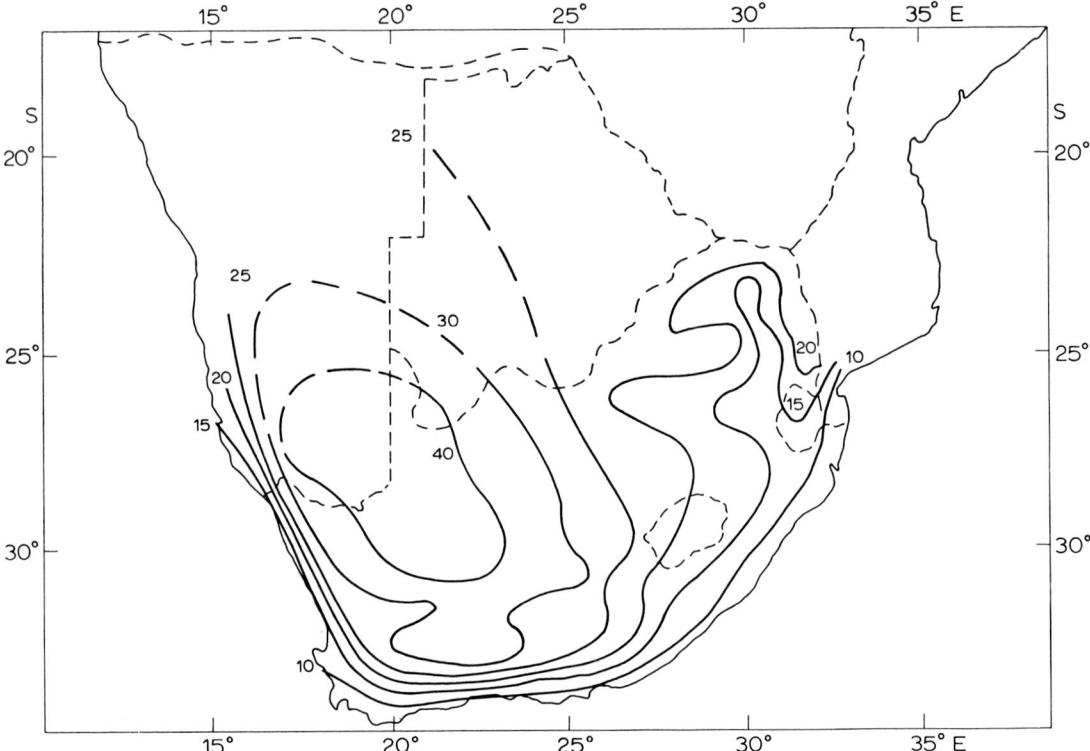

Fig.31. Average saturation deficit (mbar) at 14h00 in January.

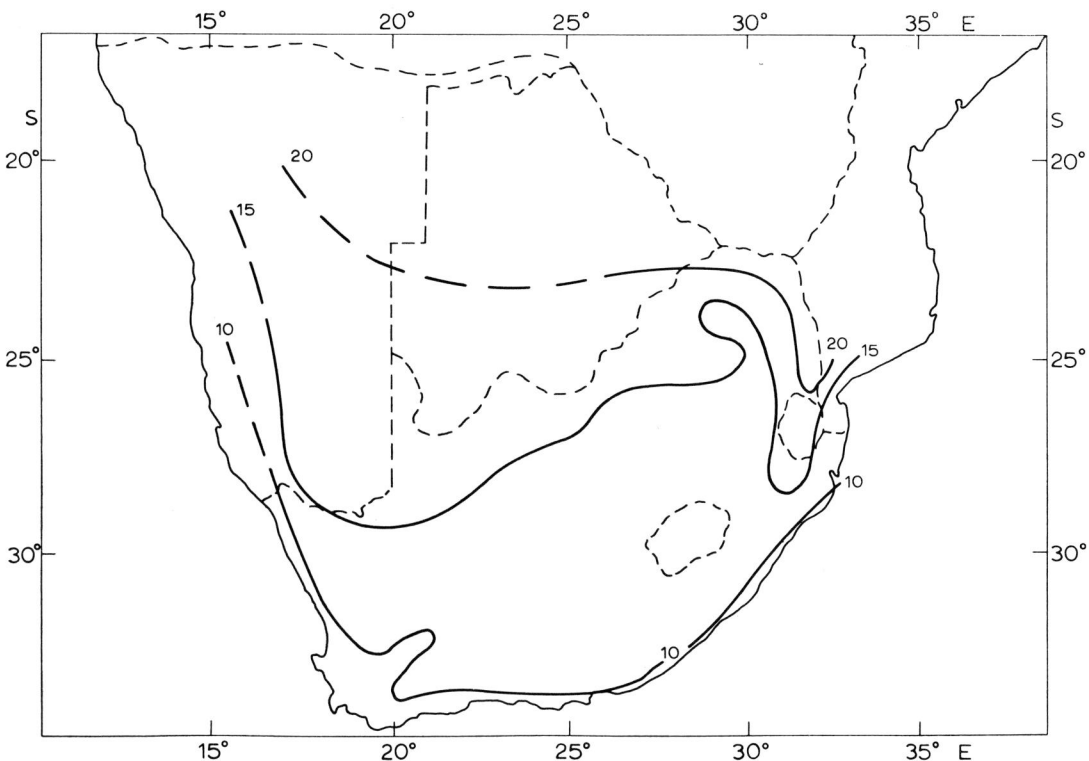

Fig.32. Average saturation deficit (mbar) at 14h00 in July.

January and July. It will be seen that the saturation deficit is least in winter when both the temperature and the possible vapor content are at a minimum. The map for January emphasizes the dryness of the atmosphere over the western interior. Here, although the average temperature is more or less of the same order as in the eastern Transvaal low-veld, the saturation deficit is very much higher.

Saturation deficit is subject to large diurnal variation; at 08h00 when the temperature is near the daily minimum value, the deficit is very much less than at 14h00. This fact may profitably be used in irrigation practice which would be more advantageous when performed during late evening when the wind speed and particularly the evaporation deficit decrease rapidly.

Evaporation

Evaporation loss from a free water surface has been measured in South Africa by means of the British Symon's evaporation pan, and readings date back some 35 years. These were placed at most of the irrigation dams by the Department of Water Affairs. It is only very recently that the American "class A" pan was installed at a number of weather stations, at some of which Symon's pans were installed for purposes of comparison. The average data gained from the "class A" pans are embodied in the main table. Over the greater part of South Africa the average annual values gained from the Symon's pan are roughly 75% of the evaporation from "A" pans; only on the southern and south-western coastal areas is the relation somewhat closer, namely of the order of 85%.

Fig.33 shows the regional distribution of average annual evaporation according to the "A" pan. In this map data from both Symon's and "A" pans are embodied, making careful use of the known relationships between the respective data. This map shows that evaporation is greatest on the western interior plateau, especially in southern Southwest Africa, and least along the eastern escarpment, in the mist belt of Natal and along the southeastern, southern and southwestern coasts. Large, well-defined river basins to the east of the eastern escarpment, such as the Tugela River Valley, show a slightly higher evaporation than the neighbouring highlands.

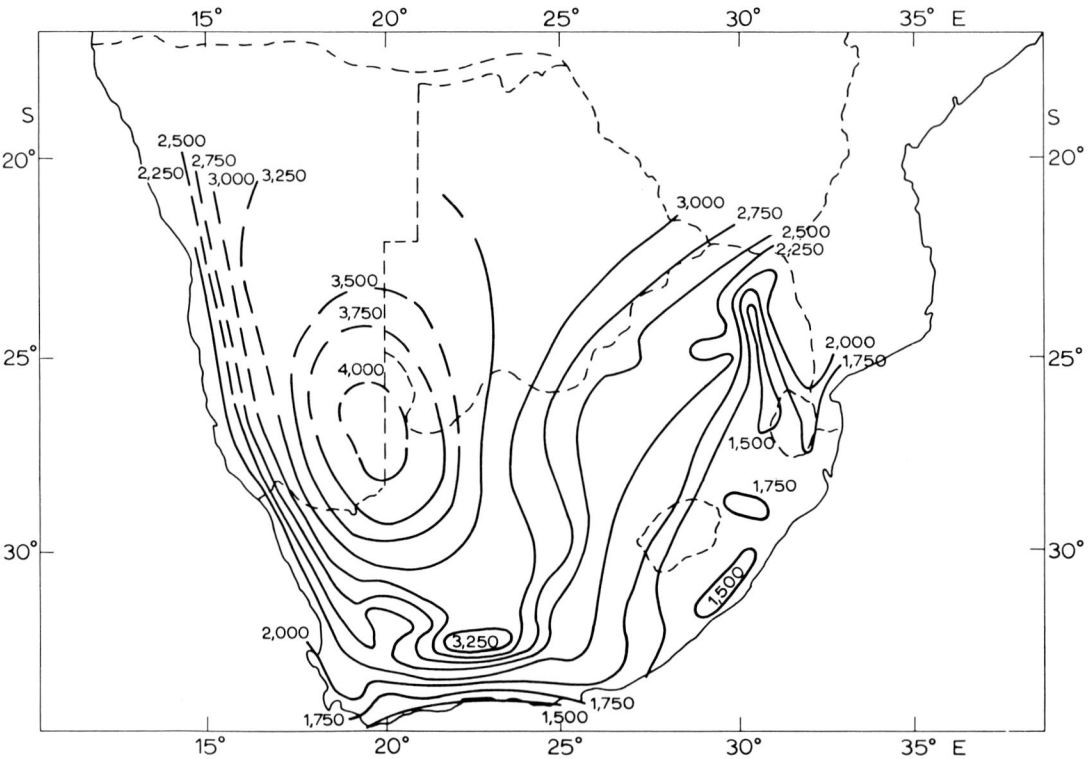

Fig.33. Average annual evaporation (mm) from Class A pans.

Regarding the annual march of evaporation, it may be said that the maximum occurs during mid-summer and the minimum during mid-winter over the southern regions of South Africa (approximately south of the 28th parallel) as may be gathered from the data in the main table. In the northern parts of the country (Transvaal, Botswana and northern Southwest Africa) the maximum falls decidedly in October. Hence the parallelism between (maximum) temperature and evaporation is apparent. The maximum annual range occurs in southern Southwest Africa (see Keetmanshoop); it is, however, interesting to note that the annual range at Cape Town is of the same order on account of the dry hot summer and the cool moist winter.

Surface winds

Fig.34 and 35 show wind roses for January and July from which two important facts are apparent; namely: (*1*) the prevailing winds at coastal stations blow either way ap-

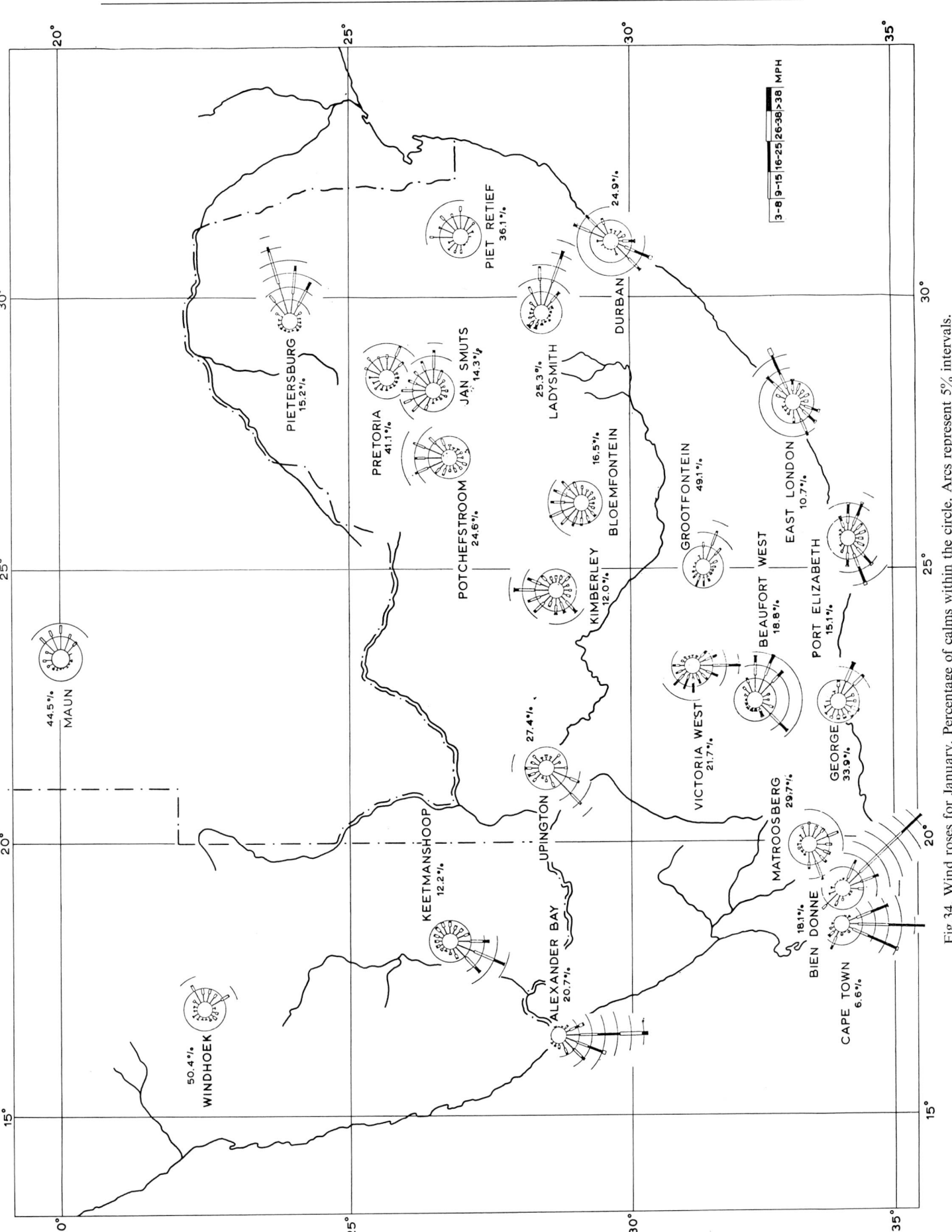

Fig.34. Wind roses for January. Percentage of calms within the circle. Arcs represent 5% intervals.

South Africa

Fig.35. Wind roses for July. Percentage of calms within the circle. Arcs represent 5% intervals.

WINDHOEK 49.6%

KEETMANSHOOP 10.8%

MAUN 37.2%

ALEXANDER BAY 35.8%

UPINGTON 44.5%

KIMBERLEY 14.2%

PIETERSBURG 15.7%

PRETORIA 57.2%

JAN SMUTS 10.9%

POTCHEFSTROOM 32.1%

PIET RETIEF 43.8%

LADYSMITH 42.4%

DURBAN 37.2%

BLOEMFONTEIN 31.7%

GROOTFONTEIN 35.3%

BEAUFORT WEST 28.9%

VICTORIA WEST 35.3%

EAST LONDON 5.6%

PORT ELIZABETH 28.5%

GEORGE 31.4%

MATROOSBERG 39.8%

BIEN DONNE 33.3%

CAPE TOWN 15.5%

3-8 | 9-15 | 16-25 | 26-38 | >38 MPH

proximately parallel to the coast line; and (2) on the whole the winds along the coast are stronger than in the interior, especially the northern interior. This arises from the fact that an established anticyclone is the most common form of pressure distribution over the interior, while depressions most commonly skirt the coastal areas.

In the eastern and southeastern interior there is a well-marked seasonal change in wind direction to be observed (see Grootfontein, Ladysmith and Piet Retief): in winter the prevailing winds are mainly off-shore (northwesterly) and in summer in the opposite direction; this indicates that there is a monsoonal effect though no regular monsoon is in evidence as is the case in India. The southern and eastern coastal stations, if one were to compute the resultant air movement, also show an on-shore component in summer and an off-shore component in winter. Over the central interior (see Potchefstroom, Bloemfontein and Kimberley) there is little seasonal change in direction, the winds being mainly from the northern sector; here the winds from the southern sector are mainly due to the passage of thunderstorms. In the western interior (see Keetmanshoop and Upington) there is again a marked seasonal change, viz. mainly north to northeast in winter and south to southwest in summer, in conformity with an established winter anticyclone over the interior and a shallow depression over the interior in summer.

In the northern interior, north of the high-pressure belt, the surface winds tend to be from the eastern sector all the year round, as is to be expected (see Pietersburg, Maun and Windhoek). They are stronger in summer when the high-pressure belt is at its furthest southerly position.

It must be realized that these generalities described above are modified by the topographical situation of the station. For example, Jan Smuts Airport, at nearly 1,800 m is much windier than Pretoria, which lies some 50 km to the north of it and about 300 m lower in an east to west orientated valley; the former shows (in winter) 11% calms, or light airs, as against Pretoria's 57%.

Strong winds exceeding gale force and lasting for some hours on end are mainly confined to the western, southwestern, southern and southeastern coasts. Maximum wind speeds of one hour's duration with an average speed of 65 to just over 100 km/h have occurred in the interior, usually during the passage of a thunderstorm, but are very unlikely to occur in the interior to the north of the 23rd parallel. Maximum instantaneous wind gusts of the order of 130 to 160 km/h have been noted during the passage of thunderstorms. Whirlwinds or dust-devils are a common feature in the interior on hot days.

Tornadoes are fortunately of rare occurrence, and usually last for a short time only; tremendous damage is done if they happen to strike densely populated areas as has occurred on the Rand.

Duststorms associated with thunder conditions and similar to the "haboob" of Egypt occur in the more arid regions of the western interior; statistics on their frequency are unfortunately not available.

Sandstorms of great severity occur in the Namib Desert on the coast of Southwest Africa. In a particular storm of this nature, for example, the railway line between Swakopmund and Walvis Bay was blocked by 3–4 m high drifts of sand.

Annual variation of wind speed

On the western and southwestern coastal belt the strongest winds occur in mid-summer and over the remainder of the country mainly in spring (September–November). Autumn and early winter are the seasons with least wind over practically the whole of South Africa. Data on mean wind speed are included in the climatic tables (pp. 556–586).

Diurnal variation

At coastal stations the daily maximum of wind speed occurs on the average in the afternoon both in winter and in summer. Over the interior, however, all stations in winter show the maximum speed in the early afternoons, but in summer the diurnal curve of wind speed is as a rule much distorted; at a number of stations the diurnal curve shows a tendency towards a double maximum, namely, in the forenoon and in the afternoon. Fig.36, which shows the diurnal variations of wind vectors for Kimberley, shows the maximum speed at 09h00 or 10h00 from the north-northeast, and a secondary maximum late in the afternoon at about 16h00 or 17h00 from a westerly direction.

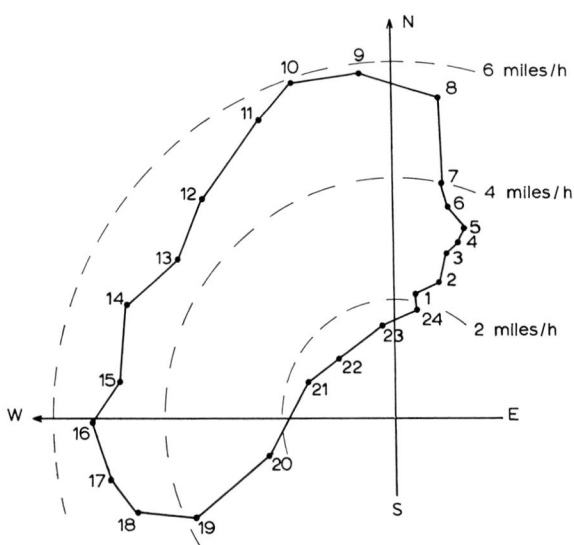

Fig.36. Hourly wind vectors for Kimberley in January.

Land and sea breezes are common diurnal phenomena around the coast, though not very noticeable in summer on the western and southwestern coasts. Average hourly wind resultants for Alexander Bay and Durban as shown in Fig.37 will illustrate this point. At Alexander Bay in summer the resultant direction remains almost due south throughout the day while the speed shows a very pronounced variation with maximum at 17h00. On the other hand, in winter there is a very well-marked and abrupt change in direction from the northeast at night and during the forenoon to southwest in the afternoon; one also notices the double maximum in the speed curve which sinks to a calm at the change in direction. At Durban the sea breeze is in evidence in both seasons, though of shorter duration in winter; the velocity, however, is not nearly as remarkable as on the west coast where the speed of the sea breeze on occasions exceeds 50 km/h.

Further statistics and information on surface winds appear in: *Weather on the Coasts of Southern Africa* (Meteorological Services of the Royal Navy and the South African

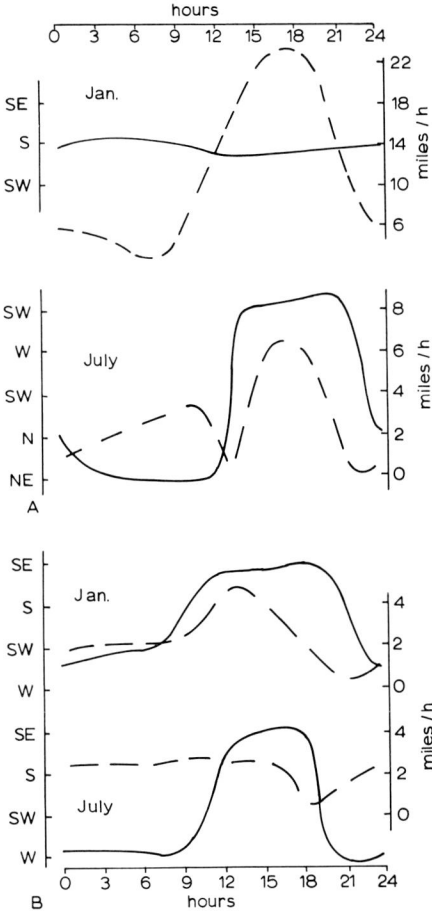

Fig.37. Diurnal variation of wind speed and direction; A. Alexander Bay (west coast); B. Durban (east coast). Solid line is direction; broken line is speed.

Air Force); *Climate of South Africa*, Part 6; "Surface Winds" (Union of South Africa Weather Bureau, Govt. Printer, Pretoria, 1960); *Climate of South Africa*, Part 8: "General Survey" (Republic of South Africa, Govt. Printer, Pretoria, 1965).

Sunshine duration

Throughout South Africa the sunshine duration is obtained from the charts of Campbell-Stokes recorders. Some 80 stations equipped with this instrument are at present in existence, though not all for an equal period of years. Nevertheless the processed data are sufficient to give an adequate overall picture of conditions in this country.

South Africa, straddled by the high pressure belt of the Southern Hemisphere, is a land enjoying abundant sunshine. The average annual sunshine duration is shown in Fig.38 expressed as a percentage of the possible duration; from this it will be seen that the western interior receives well over 80% of the possible sunshine, and the southern and eastern coastal regions, on the seaward side of the great escarpment, between 50 and 60%. Even in extreme years the average is hardly likely to fall below 40%, even on the foggy

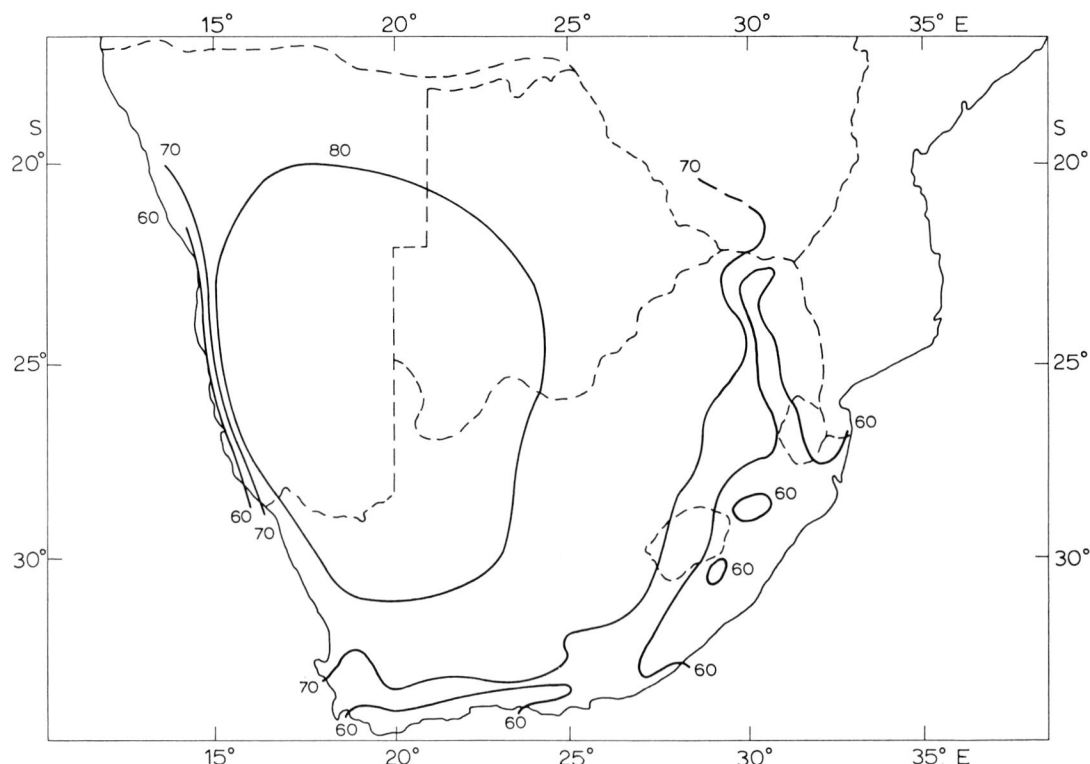

Fig.38. Average annual duration of sunshine (% of possible).

west coast; thus far, in 20 years of records, the minimum annual value at Durban, for instance, was 47%.

Of importance is the frequency of occurrence of days falling within certain categories of sunshine duration. Fig.39 and 40 show the distribution of days with less than 10% of the possible duration, which may be termed "very cloudy or overcast days", and the frequency of days with over 90% sunshine or almost "cloudless days" over South Africa. The most notable aspects are the cloudless skies of the desert or semi-deserts of the western interior, and, on the other hand, the role played by the great escarpment, especially in the east, in mitigating these stringent conditions.

Annual variation of sunshine duration

On account of the varying length of day through the year it is advisable to consider the annual variation (%) relative to the mean monthly day length. In the main table the actual mean monthly sunshine hours per day are listed.

On the east coast and east of the escarpment the maximum sunshine duration is reached in May and June, and the minimum before mid-summer. On the central high plateau the maximum and minimum occur in August (after mid-winter) and in February (after mid-summer). In the western and southwestern interior the minimum (relative) duration occurs in March when the rainfall (and cloudy) season is at its height. In the southern Cape Province to the south of the great escarpment a double maximum is indicated, in agreement with the cloud and rainfall regime. The winter rainfall zone (southwestern Cape Province) with its dry hot summer naturally shows the maximum of relative sun-

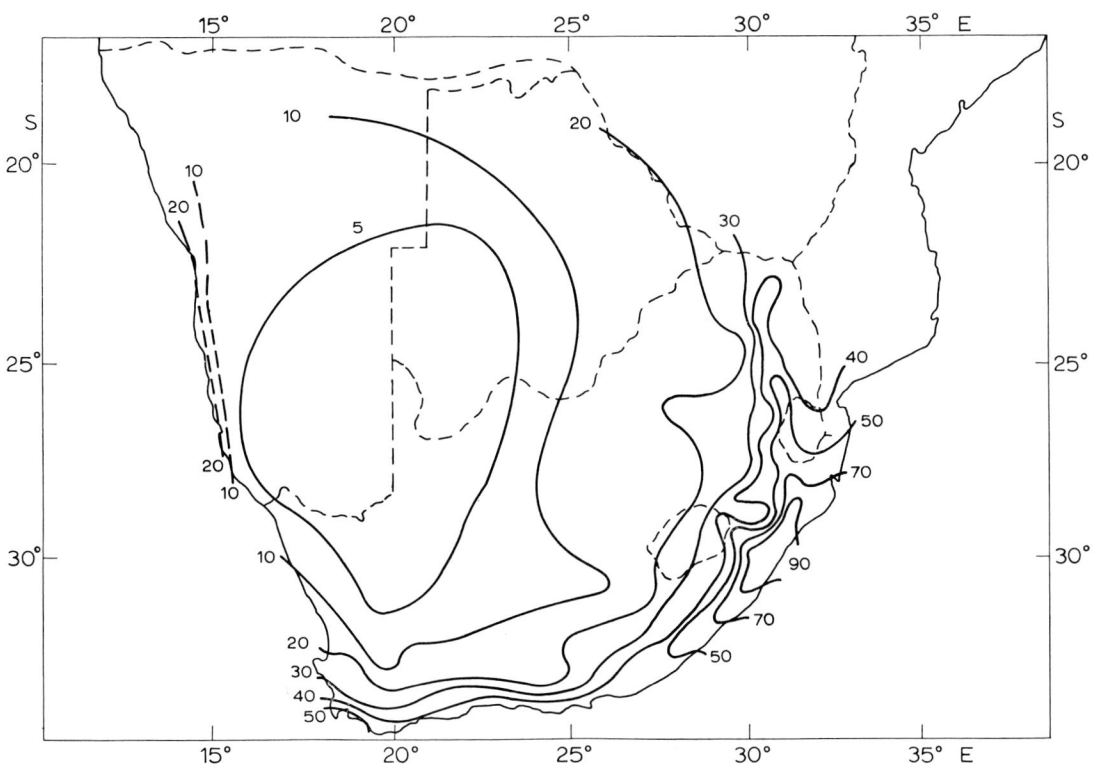

Fig.39. Average annual number of days with 10% or less of the possible sunshine duration.

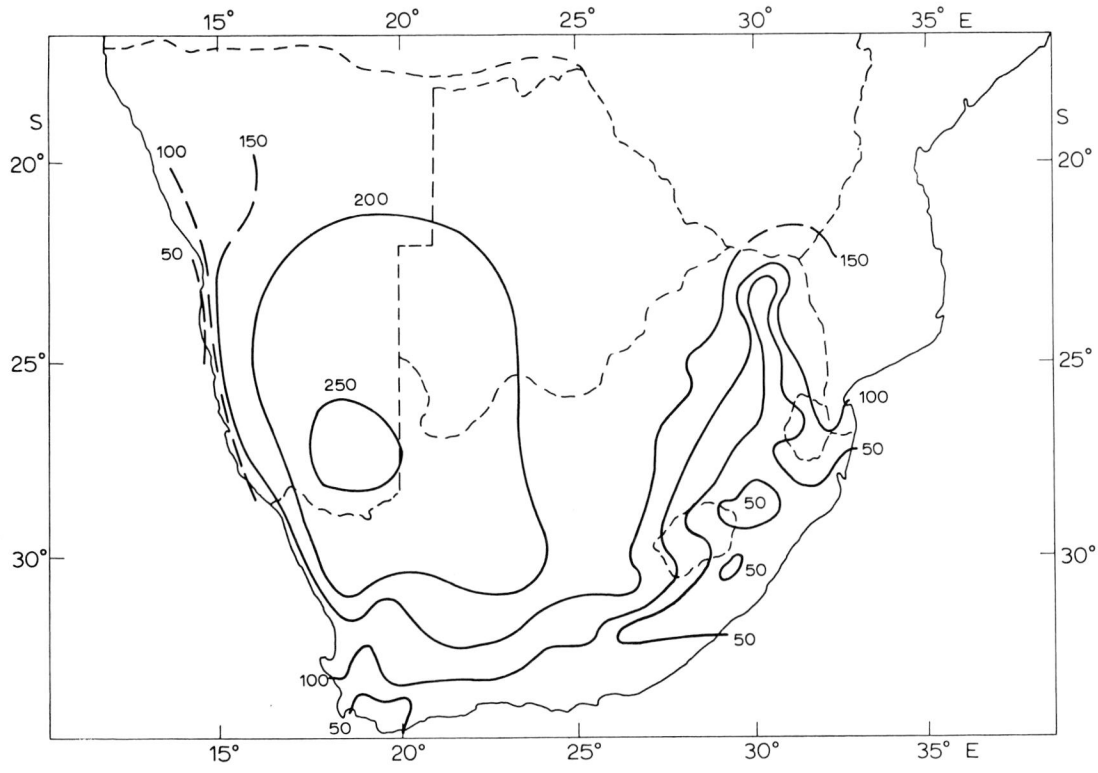

Fig.40. Average annual number of days with 90% or more of the possible sunshine duration.

551

shine duration in January or February, and the minimum in May or June. Further to the north, on the west coast at Walvis Bay or Swakopmund, the position is reversed and the maximum relative duration occurs in winter; somewhere along the west coast, therefore, there should be a region where the relative duration shows no annual variation— this happens to be very nearly the case at Alexander Bay.

Diurnal variation

The diurnal variation of sunshine duration is inversely connected with the mean daily march of cloudiness and to some extent with the type of cloud, i.e., whether stratiform or cumuliform. Data on the diurnal variation of sunshine show some interesting characteristics: on the coast at Swakopmund and to a lesser extent at Alexander Bay, Cape Town and as far east as Port Elizabeth the sunshine duration is less in the forenoon than in the afternoon, in other words, the mornings are cloudier than the afternoons. At Swakopmund and Walvis Bay, where the usual morning fog and stratus clouds obscure the sun with decreasing effect as the day progresses, full sunshine occurs normally as late as 11h00, or thereafter. Further eastwards, however, at East London and further northwards to Durban and beyond, afternoon cloudiness mainly due to convectional cumulus causes the mornings to be more sunny than the afternoons. This condition is enhanced on the interior plateau especially in summer, due again to cumulus formation during the afternoons, and is most noticeable in the northwestern interior (northern Southwest Africa and Botswana). In the southern and southwestern interior, where in any case the average cloud amount is small, both mornings and afternoons are equally sunny, as is also the case in winter over most of the interior of South Africa.

A more elaborate discussion and statistics on sunshine duration are contained in the Weather Bureau publication *Climate of South Africa*, Part 8: "General Survey".

Solar radiation

Measurements of solar radiation by the Weather Bureau were first instituted in 1951 in Pretoria. Since that year, several other stations have been equipped with similar instruments; the result is that no strictly comparable data over an equal period of years are as yet available, though the data given in the climatic tables (pp. 556–586) already serve to provide a reasonable idea of this very important element.

The instruments used at all stations listed are Kipp solarimeters measuring both total and diffuse sky radiation; the data apply to a horizontal surface and are given according to the International Pyrheliometric Scale (Ångström scale $+1.5\%$). It is to be noted that the data for Pretoria and Bloemfontein are included in the climatic tables (at the end of the chapter) under the nearby stations Germiston and Kimberley, respectively.

The data reveal that in the western interior (southern Southwest Africa and the Kalahari Desert) total radation is at a maximum, averaging annually more than 550 Ly/day, while diffuse radiation (about 100 Ly/day) in this locality shows a minimum. This is, of course, due to the predominantly clear and dry atmosphere in these regions. Proceeding from this region, the average annual total radiation decreases southwards to about 450 Ly/day and eastwards (at Durban) to about 400 Ly/day, whereas the diffuse radiation shows an increase mainly on account of the greater cloudiness on the coastal belt.

Perusal of the monthly data in the climatic tables will indicate that the annual march of total radiation varies inversely to, and diffuse radiation in the same sense as, cloudiness. The greatest annual range is found in northern Botswana (at Maun) with its very cloudy summer and clear winter, while the smallest annual range occurs in southern Southwest Africa where skies are more or less equally clear throughout the year. It is also worthy of note that, during the cloudiest months, the diffuse radiation on the east coast at Durban very nearly amounts to half of the total radiation; the opposite extreme is found in Keetmanshoop (southern Southwest Africa) where the diffuse radiation is only about one sixth of the total radiation.

As far as is indicated by the present available data the maximum total radiation on a single day is of the order of 940 Ly/day in Southwest Africa, and about 800 Ly on the east coast. The minimum on a single day varies from about 100 Ly on the east coast to approximately 300 Ly in the western desert. Regarding diffuse radiation, maximum and minimum values to be expected on a single day are of the order of 400 and 30 Ly.

On account of the relatively short period of radiation records, a frequency distribution of daily total and diffuse radiation has been attempted only for Pretoria in respect of the months December and June. The results are shown in Table VII from which it will be seen that only diffuse radiation in summer shows a near normal distribution. Total radiation is markedly negatively-skewed in both summer and winter, while diffuse radiation in winter is positively-skewed.

TABLE VII

FREQUENCY WITHIN GIVEN LIMITS OF DAILY TOTAL (T) AND DIFFUSE (D) RADIATION FOR DECEMBER AND JUNE AT PRETORIA

	Radiation intervals (Ly)									Total
	0–100	101–200	201–300	301–400	401–500	501–600	601–700	701–800		
Dec. T.	0	9	20	27	28	55	86	54		279
Dec. %	0	3.2	7.2	9.7	10.0	19.7	30.8	19.4		100
	Radiation intervals (Ly)									Total
	0–50	51–100	101–150	151–200	201–250	251–300	301–350	351–400	401–450	
June T	1	2	3	2	7	16	110	126	3	270
June %	0.4	0.7	1.1	0.7	2.6	5.9	40.8	46.7	1.1	100
Dec. D	0	11	25	38	43	23	14	1	0	155
Dec. %	0	7.1	16.1	24.5	27.7	14.8	9.1	0.7	0	100
	Radiation intervals (Ly)									Total
	0–25	26–50	51–75	76–100	101–125	126–150	151–175			
June D	0	22	91	19	7	9	2			150
June %	0	14.7	60.7	12.7	4.7	6.0	1.3			100

Angolan Desert

In the south and west of Angola, occupying a narrow strip of land (nowhere more than about 150 km wide), lies a region of semi-arid and arid country. This region forms a natural climatic continuation of the dry Southwest Africa area and is considered in this vein here.

Along the coast the truly desert conditions stretch northwards to 12°S while even around Luanda (9°S) an arid area exists. The semi-arid belt stretches right into the Cabinda enclave but ends there very abruptly, as Table VIII shows. The rainfall gradient between Cabinda and Landana is approximately 11 mm for every kilometre. The sudden drop from a reasonable May total to a completely dry June, north of about 7°S, is very striking.

TABLE VIII

MONTHLY AND ANNUAL MEAN RAINFALL (mm)

Station	Lat. S	Jan.	Feb.	Mar.	Apr.	May	June	July	Aug.	Sept.	Oct.	Nov.	Dec.	Year
Mossamedes	15°12′	7	11	18	13	0	0	0	1	0	1	2	3	56
Lobito	12°20′	19	38	81	63	5	0	0	0	1	13	20	27	267
Luanda	8°49′	39	37	67	121	12	0	0	1	2	6	26	27	338
Banana	6°00′	28	167	152	140	107	0	0	1	2	20	95	70	772
Cabinda	5°33′	59	109	85	117	56	0	0	1	6	34	114	89	670
Landana	5°13′	86	185	192	185	95	0	0	1	3	57	182	59	1,045

The number of wet months (over 50 mm) is still only 5 or 6, even as far north as 15°S, but at elevations above about 1,200 m the temperatures become sufficiently low for the region to be considered more temperate than tropical. The large plateau area is included in Chapter 13, on the south Savanna Plateau. In the semi-arid region precipitation averages about 600–800 mm/year. The wet months, even in the far south (Vila Pereira d'Eca), are still November–April, the same as Cabinda in the north. The slight secondary minimum of January that appears in many stations in the south becomes a very marked one in the north. In the Cabinda–Caxito region an unusual three-peaked type of rainfall pattern exists, with maxima in November, February and April. Comparison with neighbouring areas would suggest that this is due to a drier March than expected. The pattern is not evident at Luanda or Landana (30 km north of Cabinda) and the reason for this unusual distribution is not yet identified.

The highest fall in 24 hours is about 70–140 mm, increasing toward the north. This range of values holds also in the southern belt although Vila Pereira d'Eca has recorded one fall in excess of 200 mm.

Along the coast the annual temperature range varies from about 5° to 8°C increasing southwards, with a mean diurnal range of 7°C. The maximum temperatures are reached in February–April with the minima occurring in June–August. Temperatures are lower than at the corresponding latitude on the east coast because of the cool Benguela Current. For instance, concerning mean annual temperatures, Cabinda is 26°C, Tanga is 27°C, Moçamedes is 21°C and Mozambique is 26°C, Walvis Bay is 17°C and Vilanculos 25°C, Port Nolloth is 14°C and Durban 21°C.

The cool current is also instrumental in the reduction of the number of sunshine hours. Cabinda has only 1217 h/year (less than 30% of possible) with 147 h in March and only 62 in September and October, Luanda has 2340 h, 233 in May and 145 in September, Lobito 1958 h, 208 in January and 114 in August, Moçamedes 2157 h, 234 in March and 102 in July. Winds are prevailingly southwesterly and southerly throughout the year with a large percentage of calms at Moçamedes, Lobito and Cabinda (approximately 20%) but fewer at Luanda (4%). Wind speed at Luanda averages 13 km/h with the monthly means only varying 2 km/h around this.

References

BILHAM, E. G., 1938. *The Climate of The British Isles*. MacMillan, London, 347 pp.

COOKE, H. B. S., 1946. Some observations on rainfall distribution in South Africa. *S. African Geograph. J.*, 28: 34–38.

FRITH, E., 1940. A heavy rainfall in South Africa. *Quart. J. Roy. Meteorol. Soc.*, 66: 363.

HAYWARD, L. Q. and STEYN, E. E., 1967. *Aeronautical Climatological Summaries: Descriptive Memoranda for the Airports Johannesburg/Jan Smuts, Cape Town/D. F. Malan, Bloemfontein/J. B. M. Hertzog*. Government Printer, Pretoria, 73 pp.

HOFMEYR, W. L. and SCHULZE, B. R., 1963. Temperature and rainfall trends in South Africa during the period of meteorological records. *Proc. UNESCO-W.M.O. Symp. Climatic Change*, pp. 81–84.

KOCH, C., 1963. An illustrated account of a major flood in the Kuiseb River. *Kreis*, 2/3: 14 pp.

KÖPPEN, W. und GEIGER, R., 1936. *Handbuch der Klimatologie*. Bornträger, Berlin, Band I, B, 556 pp.

LANDSBERG, H. E., 1958. *Physical Climatology*, 2nd ed. Gray, Du Bois, Pa., 446 pp.

MEINEKE, E. N., 1960. Floods in the southeastern coastal area, May, 1959. *J. S. African Civil Engrs.*, 2A: 191–199.

REPUBLIC OF SOUTH AFRICA, 1965. *Climate of South Africa, 8. General Survey*. Government Printer, Pretoria, 330 pp.

SCHULZE, B. R., 1967. Hail and thunderstorm frequency in South Africa. *Notos*, 14: 67–71.

SCHUMANN, T. E. W. and THOMPSON, W. R., 1934. A study of South African rainfall and secular variations. *Univ. Pretoria Publ., Ser. 1*, 28: 46 pp.

SOUTH AFRICA WEATHER BUREAU, 1949. *Climate of South Africa, 5. District Rainfall*. Government Printer, Pretoria, 114 pp.

SOUTH AFRICA WEATHER BUREAU, 1954. *Climate of South Africa, 2. Rainfall Statistics*. Government Printer, Pretoria, 188 pp.

SOUTH AFRICA WEATHER BUREAU, 1957. *Climate of South Africa, 4*. Government Printer, Pretoria, 20 pp.

STEWART, C. M., 1904. The blizzard of June 1902. *S. African Soc. Advan. Sci.*, pp.118–120.

STEWART, C. M., 1918. Cape Colony floods of May 1916. *Repts. Director Irrigation, Cape Town, App. C*, pp.136–142.

TALJAARD, J. J., 1955. Stable stratification in the atmosphere over South Africa. *Notos*, 4: 217.

TALJAARD, J. J., 1958. *South African Air Masses and Weather*. University of Witwatersrand, Johannesburg, 221 pp.

TALJAARD, J. J., 1964. Cyclogenesis, cyclones and anticyclones in the Southern Hemisphere during autumn 1958. *Notos*, 13: 31–36.

TALJAARD, J. J., 1965. Cyclogenesis, cyclones and anticyclones in the Southern Hemisphere during the period June–December, 1958. *Notos*, 14: 73–84.

TALJAARD, J. J. and SCHUMANN, T. E. W., 1940. Upper air temperatures and humidities at Walvis Bay, South Africa. *Bull. Meteorol. Soc.*, 21.

TALJAARD, J. J. and VAN LOON, H., 1962. Cyclogenesis, cyclones and anticyclones in the Southern Hemisphere during the winter and spring of 1957. *Notos*, 11: 3–20.

TALJAARD, J. J. and VAN LOON, H., 1963. Cyclogenesis, cyclones and anticyclones in the Southern Hemisphere during summer 1957–1958. *Notos*, 12: 37–50.

TREWARTHA, G. T., 1962. *The Earth's Problem Climates*. University of Wisconsin Press, Madison, Wisc., 334 pp.

TRIEGAARDT, D. O., 1961. Flood rains in the Karoo. *Notos*, 10:

VOWINCKEL, E., 1955. Beitrag zur Witterungsklimatologie Südafrikas. *Arch. Meteorol. Geophys. Bioklimatol.*, 7: 11–17.

TABLE IX

CLIMATIC TABLE FOR LUANDA, ANGOLA
Latitude 8°49'S, longitude 13°13'E, elevation 45 m

Month	Mean sea level press. (mbar)	Temperature (°C) mean max.	mean min.	extreme max.	extreme min.	Relative humidity (%) 09h	15h	Precipitation mean (mm)	max. (mm)	min. (mm)	days >1 mm	max. in 24h (mm)	Wind av. speed (km/h)	preval. direct.	calm (%)	Averages cloud-iness* (oktas)		sun-shine (h)	evap. (mm)
Jan.	1,005	30	24	33	19	80	78	26	163	0	2	96	13	W	3	7	4	219	82
Feb.	1,005	31	24	35	20	79	76	35	152	0	3	88	14	W	2	7	5	208	84
Mar.	1,005	31	24	35	20	80	77	97	299	0	7	94	13	W	3	7	5	213	82
Apr.	1,005	31	24	35	21	84	79	124	404	15	9	158	12	W	4	7	5	199	61
May	1,006	29	23	36	18	83	80	19	100	0	2	59	12	W	3	7	3	233	63
June	1,009	27	20	32	15	83	80	0	6	0	0	6	12	W	3	6	2	223	60
July	1,010	24	18	30	14	84	80	0	1	0	0	1	11	SW	4	7	2	175	54
Aug.	1,009	24	18	29	14	85	80	1	15	0	<1	14	11	W	4	7	3	150	48
Sept.	1,009	26	20	29	17	83	80	2	8	0	1	8	12	W	2	7	3	145	54
Oct.	1,007	28	22	32	18	82	80	6	25	0	2	20	15	W	2	7	4	164	73
Nov.	1,006	29	23	34	20	81	80	34	159	0	3	54	15	W	2	7	4	199	79
Dec.	1,006	30	23	33	19	80	79	23	135	0	3	63	13	W	4	7	4	212	79
Annual	1,007	28	22	36	14	82	79	367	864	62	32	158	13	—	3	7	5	2,341	819
Rec. (yrs.)	30	20	20	20	20	20	20	30	30	30	30	30							

* 1st column: 09h00; 2nd column: 15h00 and 21h00.

TABLE X

CLIMATIC TABLE FOR TSUMEB, SOUTHWEST AFRICA
Latitude 19°14'S, longitude 17°43'E, elevation 1,311 m

Month	Temperature (°C)				Relat. humid. (%)	Precipitation					Averages		
	mean		extreme			mean (mm)	max. (mm)	min. (mm)	days > 1 mm	max. in 24 h (mm)	cloud-iness (tenths)		sun-shine (h/day)
	max.	min.	max.	min.							08h	14h	
Jan.	31	18	39	10	56	119	335	24	12	75	4	5	8.5
Feb.	30	18	38	10	57	139	371	9	12	123	5	5	5.6
Mar.	30	17	38	7	65	79	254	2	9	79	4	5	8.9
Apr.	29	15	36	7	57	40	186	4	5	121	2	3	8.8
May	27	10	35	1	45	6	45	0	1	19	1	2	9.4
June	25	7	30	−4	37	0	3	0	0	3	1	1	10.3
July	25	7	31	−4	35	0	2	0	0	2	1	0	10.8
Aug.	28	10	34	1	27	0	0	0	0	0	1	1	10.7
Sept.	32	15	38	3	22	1	20	0	0	11	1	1	10.5
Oct.	34	18	39	7	27	19	58	0	3	33	3	3	9.2
Nov.	33	18	40	12	38	53	132	7	6	69	3	4	9.4
Dec.	32	18	40	8	48	97	207	2	11	81	4	4	9.5
Annual	30	14	40	−4	43	553	969	235	59	123	2	3	9.3
Rec. (yrs.)	30	30	30	30	5	30	30	30	30	30	13	13	1

TABLE XI

CLIMATIC TABLE FOR WINDHOEK, SOUTHWEST AFRICA
Latitude 22°34'S, longitude 17°06'E, elevation 1,728 m

Month	Mean sta. press. (mbar)	Temperature (°C) mean		extreme		Relat. humid. (%)	Precipitation mean (mm)	max. (mm)	min. (mm)	days >1 mm	max. in 24 h (mm)	Aver. wind speed (km/h)	Averages cloud-iness (tenths) 08h	14h	sun-shine (h/day)	rad.	diff. rad.	evap. (mm)
		max.	min.	max.	min.													
Jan.	830	30	17	36	8	40	77	229	4	8	86	6	4	6	9.3	641	189	353
Feb.	831	28	16	35	7	46	73	223	9	9	46	6	4	6	9.0	575	185	262
Mar.	832	27	15	34	4	51	81	312	5	8	78	5	4	6	9.1	527	153	249
Apr.	833	26	13	31	2	43	38	170	0	3	76	5	3	4	9.1	492	104	246
May	834	23	9	29	−2	32	6	52	0	1	20	6	1	2	10.0	447	72	228
June	836	20	7	26	−3	31	1	19	0	0	19	8	1	1	10.3	409	62	193
July	835	20	6	25	−3	27	1	11	0	0	11	7	1	1	10.5	441	62	206
Aug.	835	23	9	30	−4	22	0	2	0	0	1	8	1	1	11.0	506	82	272
Sept.	833	29	11	33	−1	18	1	12	0	0	10	8	1	2	10.7	585	114	333
Oct.	832	29	15	35	2	19	12	41	0	2	25	8	2	4	10.3	624	154	389
Nov.	831	30	15	36	0	32	33	151	0	4	62	8	3	5	9.9	669	154	358
Dec.	830	30	16	36	3	31	47	134	0	6	44	7	3	5	9.2	647	164	378
Annual	833	26	12	36	−4	33	370	745	91	41	86	7	2	3	9.9	547	125	3,467
Rec. (yrs.)	30	30	30	30	30	10	30	30	30	30	30	5	23	23	5	8	8	4

TABLE XII

CLIMATIC TABLE FOR SWAKOPMUND, SOUTHWEST AFRICA*

Latitude 22°41'S, longitude 14°31'E, elevation 12 m

Month	Temperature (°C)				Relative humid. (%)		Precipitation					Averages		
	mean		extreme				mean (mm)	max. (mm)	min. (mm)	days >1 mm	max. in 24 h (mm)	cloudiness (tenths)		sunshine (h/day)
	max.	min.	max.	min.	08h	14h						08h	14h	
Jan.	20	15	25	4	91	82	1	5	0	0	3	9	5	7.5
Feb.	21	16	29	9	93	83	2	18	0	0	17	9	5	6.7
Mar.	20	15	40	11	94	83	2	11	0	0	11	8	5	6.8
Apr.	18	13	40	7	95	85	2	9	0	1	9	6	5	7.9
May	18	11	38	5	89	79	0	5	0	0	5	6	4	8.1
June	20	11	36	5	81	73	0	4	0	0	4	5	3	7.7
July	18	9	36	3	84	75	0	3	0	0	1	6	3	7.6
Aug.	16	9	40	4	93	82	0	1	0	0	1	7	5	7.1
Sept.	16	10	29	5	95	84	0	0	0	0	0	8	5	6.3
Oct.	16	11	41	5	92	82	0	4	0	0	3	9	5	7.3
Nov.	18	13	24	8	93	83	1	18	0	0	18	9	5	7.0
Dec.	19	14	27	8	93	84	0	4	0	0	2	9	5	6.9
Annual	18	12	41	3	91	81	10	29	0	1	18	8	5	7.2
Rec. (yrs.)	15	15	15	15	15	15	15	15	15	15	15	15	15	5

* Sunshine duration at Walvis Bay.

TABLE XIII

CLIMATIC TABLE FOR KEETMANSHOOP, SOUTHWEST AFRICA
Latitude 26°34'S, longitude 18°07'E, elevation 1,066 m

Month	Mean sta. press. (mbar)	Temperature (°C) mean max.	mean min.	extreme max.	extreme min.	Relat. humid. (%)	Precipitation mean (mm)	max. (mm)	min. (mm)	days >1 mm	max. in 24 h (mm)	Av. wind speed (km/h)	Averages cloudiness (tenths) 08h	14h	sunshine (h/day)	rad. (Ly/day)	evap. (mm)	diff. rad.
Jan.	890	35	18	42	8	31	22	87	3	3	33	14	2	3	11.6	718	465	126
Feb.	890	34	19	42	9	37	30	114	0	4	65	12	3	4	10.6	646	373	139
Mar.	892	32	17	40	7	40	35	182	0	4	56	12	3	3	10.0	553	328	111
Apr.	893	29	14	37	2	38	13	54	0	2	23	12	2	2	10.2	500	251	74
May	895	25	10	39	−1	36	5	35	0	1	30	14	2	2	9.9	411	185	92
June	898	22	7	32	−3	39	2	31	0	0	14	15	2	2	9.7	368	170	54
July	897	21	6	31	−4	35	1	8	0	0	4	15	2	1	9.9	392	206	59
Aug.	896	24	7	34	−3	31	1	11	0	0	10	15	2	1	10.5	456	246	77
Sept.	894	27	10	36	−1	26	2	45	0	0	23	17	2	2	10.8	556	323	97
Oct.	892	30	13	40	1	27	5	21	0	1	21	15	2	3	11.3	660	396	115
Nov.	891	33	15	41	5	28	14	56	0	2	33	16	2	3	11.8	725	465	110
Dec.	890	34	17	42	3	28	17	114	0	2	99	16	2	3	12.1	741	495	121
Annual	893	29	13	42	−4	33	147	333	43	19	99	15	2	2	10.7	561	3,903	98
Rec. (yrs.)	30	30	30	30	30	15	30	30	30	30	30	5	20	20	10	4	4	4

TABLE XIV

CLIMATIC TABLE FOR MAUN, BOTSWANA
Latitude 19°59'S, longitude 23°25'E, elevation 942 m

Month	Mean press. (mbar)	Temperature (°C) mean max.	mean min.	extreme max.	extreme min.	Relat. humid. (%)	Precip. mean (mm)	max. (mm)	min. (mm)	days > 1 mm	max. in 24 h (mm)	Av. wind speed (km/h)	cloud-iness (tenths) 08h	14h	sun-shine (h/day)	rad. (Ly/day)	evap. (mm)	diff. rad.
Jan.	910	32	19	40	9	71	110	380	14	10	90	6	5	7	7.9	553	262	188
Feb.	910	31	19	39	9	74	102	339	8	10	103	5	5	7	7.4	508	208	193
Mar.	912	31	17	39	10	67	85	275	0	7	120	5	4	6	8.3	526	213	157
Apr.	914	31	14	37	3	58	26	93	0	3	61	5	2	4	9.4	483	211	100
May	916	28	10	36	−3	50	22	34	0	1	26	5	1	2	10.0	453	188	72
June	918	25	6	33	−6	46	1	10	0	0	10	6	1	1	10.0	417	178	67
July	918	25	6	32	−5	40	0	1	0	0	1	6	1	1	10.1	425	221	79
Aug.	916	29	9	36	−4	33	0	0	0	0	0	6	1	1	10.7	500	277	84
Sept.	914	33	13	39	−1	30	1	12	0	0	8	9	1	2	10.5	559	330	119
Oct.	911	35	18	43	6	34	15	61	0	3	33	7	3	3	9.4	579	401	167
Nov.	911	34	19	43	9	52	46	116	1	5	55	7	4	5	8.8	565	312	187
Dec.	910	32	19	42	11	66	80	233	16	8	71	6	5	6	6.9	551	257	207
Annual	913	30	14	43	−6	51	471	776	285	47	120	6	3	4	9.1	510	3,058	135
Rec. (yrs.)	30	30	30	30	30	10	30	30	30	30	30	6	30	20	10	5	3	5

TABLE XV

CLIMATIC TABLE FOR GHANZI, BOTSWANA
Latitude 21°42'S, longitude 21°39'E, elevation 1,131 m

Month	Temperature (°C)				Relative humidity (%)		Precipitation					Averages			
	mean		extreme		08h	14h	mean (mm)	max. (mm)	min. (mm)	days >1 mm	max. in 24 h (mm)	cloud-iness (tenths) 08h 14h		sun-shine (h/day)	evap. (mm)
	max.	min.	max.	min.											
Jan.	32	18	42	7	67	41	98	389	5	9	130	5	7	9.5	317
Feb.	32	18	38	7	73	40	94	227	17	7	124	5	7	10.0	257
Mar.	30	16	39	8	74	44	74	274	3	6	108	4	6	10.1	239
Apr.	29	13	36	−1	72	38	39	185	0	4	52	3	4	9.4	236
May	26	8	33	−6	66	31	8	45	0	1	34	2	2	10.2	229
June	23	4	32	−7	66	32	1	6	0	0	6	1	1	10.2	206
July	24	4	31	−6	60	27	0	1	0	0	1	1	1	10.2	175
Aug.	27	6	38	−3	51	23	0	3	0	0	3	1	1	10.3	241
Sept.	31	10	38	−1	45	20	2	21	0	0	11	1	1	10.2	343
Oct.	33	15	39	1	47	24	21	111	0	3	83	3	4	9.0	396
Nov.	33	17	42	6	55	32	43	115	0	6	56	4	6	10.0	366
Dec.	33	18	41	7	63	37	66	141	6	7	81	5	6	8.6	300
Annual	29	12	42	−7	62	32	446	767	200	43	130	3	4	9.8	3,305
Rec. (yrs.)	30	30	30	30	30	20	30	30	30	30	30	30	30	1	3

TABLE XVI

CLIMATIC TABLE FOR MAHALAPYE, BOTSWANA
Latitude 23°04′S, longitude 26°48′E, elevation 1,001 m

Month	Mean sta. press. (mbar)	Temperature (°C)				Precipitation					Aver. cloud-iness (tenths)	
		mean		extreme		mean (mm)	max. (mm)	min. (mm)	days > 1 mm	max. in 24 h (mm)		
		max.	min.	max.	min.						08h	14h
Jan.	903	32	19	42	9	84	226	16	7	85	5	6
Feb.	903	31	18	39	10	95	424	18	7	128	5	6
Mar.	905	29	17	38	9	77	239	6	5	110	4	6
Apr.	906	28	13	37	0	30	153	0	3	126	4	4
May	908	26	8	34	−6	10	104	0	2	35	2	2
June	911	23	4	31	−4	6	50	0	1	37	2	2
July	910	23	4	31	−7	3	40	0	0	38	2	2
Aug.	909	26	7	35	−4	2	19	0	0	18	1	2
Sept.	907	29	11	39	−3	7	61	0	1	29	3	2
Oct.	905	32	16	40	2	28	95	0	3	63	4	4
Nov.	905	32	18	41	8	72	171	0	6	66	5	6
Dec.	903	32	18	41	9	97	264	12	8	125	5	6
Annual	906	29	13	42	−7	511	928	193	43	128	4	4
Rec. (yrs.)	10	30	30	30	30	30	30	30	30	30	30	15

TABLE XVII

CLIMATIC TABLE FOR TSABONG, BOTSWANA
Latitude 26°03'S, longitude 22°27'E, elevation 962 m

Month	Temperature (°C)				Relative humidity (%)		Precipitation					Averages		
	mean		extreme				mean (mm)	max. (mm)	min. (mm)	days >1 mm	max. in 24 h (mm)	cloud-iness (tenths)		sun-shine (h/day)
	max.	min.	max.	min.	08h	14h						08h	14h	
Jan.	35	18	42	7	59	29	37	76	1	4	35	3	5	10.7
Feb.	33	18	39	8	66	34	50	132	9	5	109	4	5	10.2
Mar.	31	16	38	6	73	37	46	106	3	5	47	3	5	10.1
Apr.	28	11	36	−4	75	37	31	122	0	4	46	3	3	9.6
May	25	6	32	−7	77	34	11	59	0	2	19	2	2	9.5
June	22	1	30	−9	78	31	8	54	0	1	38	2	1	9.7
July	22	1	30	−11	71	27	2	15	0	0	8	1	1	9.7
Aug.	25	3	33	−10	64	26	1	4	0	0	2	1	1	10.7
Sept.	28	7	39	−7	52	24	11	121	0	1	60	2	2	10.7
Oct.	31	12	40	−3	48	23	13	48	0	2	24	3	3	11.1
Nov.	33	15	41	4	50	25	22	131	0	3	35	3	4	11.1
Dec.	34	17	42	6	52	25	39	89	0	4	61	3	4	10.7
Annual	29	10	42	−11	64	29	271	507	133	31	109	3	3	10.6
Rec. (yrs.)	20	20	20	20	20	20	20	20	20	20	20	20	20	2

TABLE XVIII

CLIMATIC TABLE FOR MESSINA, SOUTH AFRICA*

Latitude 22°20′S, longitude 30°03′E, elevation 549 m

Month	Temperature (°C)				Relative humidity (%)		Precipitation					Averages			
	mean		extreme				mean	max.	min.	days	max.	cloudiness (tenths)		sunshine	evap.
	max.	min.	max.	min.	08h	14h	(mm)	(mm)	(mm)	>1 mm	in 24 h (mm)	08h	14h	(h/day)	(mm)
Jan.	32	21	42	15	68	47	78	487	2	6	167	6	6	7.9	274
Feb.	32	21	41	15	71	47	55	132	0	5	71	6	6	8.2	224
Mar.	31	20	42	14	72	44	40	241	1	4	94	5	6	7.3	241
Apr.	30	18	39	7	72	39	15	104	0	2	48	4	5	8.3	203
May	28	14	36	6	70	32	4	23	0	1	23	3	3	9.2	203
June	25	11	34	3	71	36	4	41	0	1	41	2	3	8.9	137
July	25	11	34	4	71	34	3	27	0	0	21	3	3	8.8	155
Aug.	27	13	36	4	65	29	1	11	0	0	10	2	2	9.4	198
Sept.	29	16	41	9	62	33	7	56	0	1	30	3	3	9.0	251
Oct.	31	19	43	11	60	34	21	83	0	2	56	4	4	8.5	312
Nov.	32	20	43	11	61	38	42	122	0	5	63	6	6	8.2	307
Dec.	32	21	41	15	65	43	70	141	4	5	107	6	7	8.6	292
Annual	29	17	43	3	67	38	340	685	76	32	167	4	5	8.5	2,797
Rec. (yrs.)	30	30	30	30	30	5	30	30	30	30	30	30	5	8	4

* Sunshine duration at Macuville.

TABLE XIX

CLIMATIC TABLE FOR PIETERSBURG, SOUTH AFRICA

Latitude 23°51'S, longitude 29°27'E, elevation 1,230 m

Month	Mean sta. press. (mbar)	Temperature (°C) mean max.	mean min.	extreme max.	extreme min.	Relat. humid. (%)	Precipitation mean (mm)	max. (mm)	min. (mm)	days >1 mm	max. in 24 h (mm)	Av. wind speed (km/h)	Averages cloudiness (tenths) 08h	14h	sunshine (h/day)	evap. (mm)
Jan.	877	27	16	35	8	71	84	218	17	8	65	12	6	6	8.0	244
Feb.	877	27	16	34	6	73	71	214	6	7	109	12	6	6	7.5	198
Mar.	879	26	15	34	6	73	54	139	8	6	57	10	6	6	7.5	206
Apr.	880	25	12	31	2	71	33	159	0	3	122	9	4	5	8.1	167
May	881	22	8	30	−1	65	12	70	0	2	57	9	3	3	8.6	163
June	884	20	4	27	−4	62	6	47	0	1	29	10	2	2	8.9	124
July	884	20	4	28	−4	59	3	33	0	1	14	11	2	3	8.6	140
Aug.	883	22	6	32	−2	56	1	8	0	0	7	11	2	2	8.9	180
Sept.	881	25	10	34	−1	57	13	56	0	2	33	11	3	3	8.7	234
Oct.	880	27	14	36	5	60	34	82	10	4	55	13	4	4	8.7	295
Nov.	878	27	15	37	6	66	76	173	0	7	77	14	6	6	8.2	272
Dec.	877	27	16	36	9	70	98	252	18	9	86	12	6	6	8.1	239
Annual	880	25	11	37	−4	65	485	792	280	50	122	11	4	4	8.3	2,462
Rec. (yrs.)	28	30	30	30	30	30	30	30	30	30	30	7	30	30	13	4

TABLE XX

CLIMATIC TABLE FOR NELSPRUIT, SOUTH AFRICA
Latitude 25°27′S, longitude 30°58′E, elevation 665 m

Month	Temperature (°C)				Relat. humid.* (%)	Precipitation					Averages	
	mean		extreme			mean (mm)	max. (mm)	min. (mm)	days < 1 mm	max. in 24 h (mm)	cloud-iness (tenths) 08h	sun-shine (h/day)
	max.	min.	max.	min.								
Jan.	29	19	38	11	77	126	332	51	10	127	6	6.5
Feb.	29	19	41	12	80	130	404	33	9	234	6	6.8
Mar.	28	17	38	9	81	100	238	22	8	118	5	6.6
Apr.	27	15	36	4	80	53	145	1	5	63	4	7.5
May	25	10	34	2	75	19	62	0	3	48	2	8.3
June	23	7	33	0	71	10	84	0	2	33	2	8.3
July	23	7	33	−2	71	11	56	0	2	49	2	8.1
Aug.	25	9	37	0	71	12	98	0	1	64	3	8.1
Sept.	27	12	41	2	69	31	86	1	4	75	4	7.4
Oct.	28	15	41	6	71	53	155	1	6	75	5	6.9
Nov.	28	17	41	8	73	109	228	32	10	77	6	6.4
Dec.	29	18	42	8	75	151	360	53	10	104	6	5.8
Annual	27	14	42	−2	75	805	1,244	408	70	234	4	7.2
Rec. (yrs.)	30	30	30	30	30	30	30	30	30	30	30	13

* At 08h00.

TABLE XXI

CLIMATIC TABLE FOR ZEERUST, SOUTH AFRICA
Latitude 25°33′S, longitude 26°05′E, elevation 1,207 m

Month	Temperature (°C)				Relative humidity (%)		Precipitation					Aver. cloud-iness (tenths)	
	mean		extreme				mean (mm)	max. (mm)	min. (mm)	days > 1 mm	max. in 24 h (mm)		
	max.	min.	max.	min.	08h	14h						08h	14h
Jan.	31	17	41	8	67	41	100	233	12	10	80	5	6
Feb.	30	17	38	8	73	46	100	232	19	9	77	5	6
Mar.	28	14	36	5	77	48	83	289	1	7	104	5	6
Apr.	26	10	33	1	77	42	41	141	0	5	61	3	4
May	23	5	31	−5	78	35	19	99	0	2	45	2	3
June	21	1	28	−6	75	33	10	135	0	1	48	2	2
July	21	1	28	−8	75	33	6	82	0	1	44	2	2
Aug.	24	4	31	−7	64	28	3	31	0	1	27	1	2
Sept.	27	9	36	−6	53	28	17	111	0	2	71	3	2
Oct.	30	13	38	3	55	32	46	103	4	5	41	4	4
Nov.	31	15	39	4	63	38	67	157	4	7	70	4	5
Dec.	31	16	40	5	63	39	98	274	7	8	106	5	6
Annual	27	10	41	−8	68	37	590	960	420	58	106	3	4
Rec. (yrs.)	30	30	30	30	30	22	30	30	30	30	30	30	22

568

TABLE XXII

CLIMATIC TABLE FOR GERMISTON, SOUTH AFRICA*

Latitude 26°15'S, longitude 28°09'E, elevation 1,665 m

Month	Temperature (°C)				Relat. humid. (%)	Precipitation					Av. wind speed (km/h)	Averages					
	mean		extreme			mean (mm)	max. (mm)	min. (mm)	days >1 mm	max. in 24 h (mm)		cloudiness (tenths)		sunshine (h/day)	rad. (Ly/day)	evap. (mm)	diff. rad.
	max.	min.	max.	min.								08h	14h				
Jan.	26	14	34	6	70	117	568	36	12	91	11	2	6	8.2	581	234	202
Feb.	25	14	33	7	71	101	335	45	9	101	11	5	6	7.8	528	196	189
Mar.	24	13	32	5	70	78	191	16	8	76	10	4	6	7.4	489	183	160
Apr.	22	10	29	−1	65	46	105	1	5	49	9	3	4	8.3	422	150	113
May	19	6	26	−6	58	25	145	0	3	73	10	2	3	9.0	367	150	78
June	17	4	24	−7	54	9	59	0	1	31	12	2	2	9.0	341	119	68
July	17	4	24	−7	53	8	66	0	1	30	12	2	2	9.1	356	132	74
Aug.	20	6	27	−7	47	6	32	0	1	25	13	2	2	9.7	437	183	88
Sept.	23	9	30	−3	49	25	117	0	3	48	16	2	3	9.3	497	216	115
Oct.	25	12	32	0	56	63	199	11	7	65	16	4	4	8.7	541	272	161
Nov.	25	13	34	2	65	110	232	7	10	73	15	5	6	9.1	569	241	181
Dec.	26	14	33	6	68	120	233	19	11	89	13	5	6	9.0	560	231	205
Annual	22	10	34	−7	61	708	1,034	517	71	101	12	3	4	8.7	474	2,307	136
Rec. (yrs.)	30	30	30	30	30	30	30	30	30	30	7	30	30	10	11	4	11

* Solar radiation at Pretoria.

TABLE XXIII

CLIMATIC TABLE FOR LÜDERITZ BAY, SOUTHWEST AFRICA
Latitude 26°38'S, longitude 15°06'E, elevation 23 m

Month	Temperature (°C)				Relative humid. (%)		Precipitation					Averages		
	mean		extreme				mean (mm)	max. (mm)	min. (mm)	days >1 mm	max. in 24 h (mm)	cloudiness (tenths)		sunshine (h/day)
	max.	min.	max.	min.	08h	14h						08h	14h	
Jan.	21	14	33	10	88	75	1	13	0	0	13	3	2	4.5
Feb.	22	14	30	5	90	71	3	36	0	0	24	4	2	4.7
Mar.	22	14	34	8	89	74	4	56	0	0	31	3	2	7.6
Apr.	20	13	35	8	88	72	1	8	0	0	7	3	2	5.6
May	19	12	33	7	85	73	3	22	0	1	20	4	2	4.6
June	19	11	32	0	76	68	2	13	0	0	12	3	2	3.4
July	18	10	31	3	78	69	1	6	0	0	5	3	2	5.2
Aug.	17	10	33	5	84	72	1	5	0	0	3	4	3	4.9
Sept.	17	11	35	7	86	74	1	5	0	0	2	4	3	6.5
Oct.	18	12	35	8	85	74	0	2	0	0	2	4	3	5.5
Nov.	20	13	38	8	85	75	0	3	0	0	3	4	3	4.9
Dec.	21	13	31	4	85	75	1	7	0	0	7	3	2	3.5
Annual	20	12	38	0	85	73	18	59	1	1	31	3	2	5.1
Rec. (yrs.)	20	20	20	20	20	20	20	20	20	20	20	20	20	3

TABLE XXIV

CLIMATIC TABLE FOR UPINGTON, SOUTH AFRICA
Latitude 28°26'S, longitude 21°16'E, elevation 809 m

Month	Mean sta. press. (mbar)	Temperature (°C) mean max.	mean min.	extreme max.	extreme min.	Relat. humid. (%)	Precipitation mean (mm)	max. (mm)	min. (mm)	days >1 mm	max. in 24 h (mm)	Aver. wind speed (km/h)	Averages cloud-iness (tenths) 08h	14h	sun-shine (h/day)	evap. (mm)
Jan.	921	36	20	43	9	32	25	139	0	3	68	9	2	3	11.6	483
Feb.	921	34	21	42	9	37	40	123	0	4	63	9	3	4	10.5	399
Mar.	923	32	17	39	7	43	37	125	0	4	60	8	3	3	9.7	323
Apr.	925	28	13	37	2	47	27	167	0	2	119	6	2	3	9.7	251
May	927	24	8	33	−3	50	11	74	0	2	43	6	3	3	9.1	162
June	931	21	4	30	−8	52	3	10	0	1	9	6	2	2	9.1	132
July	930	20	3	30	−7	46	5	73	0	1	28	8	2	2	9.2	183
Aug.	929	23	5	34	−7	39	4	25	0	1	16	8	2	2	10.0	231
Sept.	927	26	9	37	−3	31	3	41	0	1	27	9	2	2	10.6	300
Oct.	924	30	12	41	−1	32	11	88	0	1	36	8	3	3	10.8	386
Nov.	922	32	16	42	7	33	16	70	0	2	31	10	2	3	11.6	472
Dec.	921	34	18	42	8	31	22	87	0	2	28	10	2	3	11.8	483
Annual	925	28	12	43	−8	39	204	566	88	24	119	8	2	3	10.3	3,805
Rec. (yrs.)	30	30	30	30	30	13	30	30	30	30	30	5	30	20	10	4

TABLE XXV

CLIMATIC TABLE FOR ALEXANDER BAY, SOUTH AFRICA
Latitude 28°34'S, longitude 16°32'E, elevation 21 m

Month	Mean sea level press. (mbar)	Temperature (°C) mean max.	mean min.	extreme max.	extreme min.	Relat. humid. (%)	Precipitation mean (mm)	max. (mm)	min. (mm)	days >1 mm	max. in 24 h (mm)	Av. wind speed (km/h)	Averages cloudiness (tenths) 08h	14h	sunshine (h/day)	rad. (Ly/day)	diff. rad.	evap. (mm)
Jan.	1,013	24	15	37	9	77	1	8	0	0	7	21	6	2	10.4	710	155	297
Feb.	1,013	24	15	38	10	77	2	25	0	0	16	18	6	2	9.9	649	137	244
Mar.	1,014	24	14	42	8	77	4	39	0	1	17	14	6	2	9.2	557	114	229
Apr.	1,015	23	12	41	6	75	4	15	0	1	7	11	5	2	8.9	432	103	165
May	1,017	22	10	36	5	76	10	46	0	2	39	8	5	3	7.9	330	95	124
June	1,020	22	10	33	3	69	7	28	0	1	20	11	4	2	8.5	298	67	114
July	1,020	21	9	33	3	71	6	26	0	2	10	11	4	3	7.9	317	77	130
Aug.	1,020	20	9	36	2	73	9	34	0	2	21	13	5	3	8.3	386	100	155
Sept.	1,018	21	10	42	4	72	2	8	0	1	7	16	5	2	9.1	495	124	193
Oct.	1,017	21	11	40	5	74	2	7	1	1	3	19	6	3	9.6	599	156	244
Nov.	1,015	23	13	39	8	74	2	20	0	0	19	19	5	2	10.4	699	144	274
Dec.	1,013	23	14	39	9	76	3	18	0	1	17	19	6	2	10.4	712	172	297
Annual	1,016	22	12	42	2	74	52	95	22	12	39	14	5	2	9.2	515	120	2,466
Rec. (yrs.)	30	14	14	14	14	14	14	14	14	14	14	10	14	14	9	4	4	6

TABLE XXVI

CLIMATIC TABLE FOR KIMBERLEY, SOUTH AFRICA*

Latitude 28°48'S, longitude 24°46'E, elevation 1,197 m

Month	Mean sta. press. (mbar)	Temperature (°C) mean max.	mean min.	extreme max.	extreme min.	Relat. humid. (%)	Precipitation mean (mm)	max. (mm)	min. (mm)	days >1 mm	max. in 24 h (mm)	Av. wind speed (km/h)	Averages cloud-iness (tenths) 08h	14h	sun-shine (h/day)	rad. (Ly/day)	diff. rad.	evap. (mm)
Jan.	874	33	18	40	6	29	55	171	9	6	58	14	3	5	9.7	655	173	363
Feb.	875	31	17	38	6	34	64	235	2	9	54	13	3	5	9.5	590	162	290
Mar.	877	29	15	36	5	36	72	220	18	8	68	10	3	4	8.9	501	142	246
Apr.	878	25	11	34	−1	38	44	141	3	5	52	10	2	3	9.0	436	100	185
May	880	21	6	30	−5	36	19	73	0	3	30	12	3	3	8.6	350	84	127
June	883	19	3	28	−7	34	13	104	0	1	67	12	2	3	8.8	315	68	99
July	882	19	3	26	−7	32	6	40	0	1	27	13	2	2	9.1	338	69	130
Aug.	881	22	5	31	−6	27	11	117	0	1	58	15	2	2	9.7	430	80	185
Sept.	879	25	8	34	−4	24	11	63	0	1	27	14	2	3	9.7	522	114	254
Oct.	877	28	12	38	−1	25	31	135	2	4	59	15	3	4	9.7	598	146	338
Nov.	876	30	14	39	2	25	47	131	0	5	49	16	3	4	10.2	664	165	373
Dec.	875	32	16	39	6	27	58	172	3	6	65	15	2	4	10.5	675	177	378
Annual	878	26	11	40	−7	31	431	710	179	50	68	13	3	4	9.5	506	123	2,968
Rec. (yrs.)	30	30	30	30	30	30	30	30	30	30	30	10	30	30	14	7	7	4

* Solar radiation at Bloemfontein.

TABLE XXVII

CLIMATIC TABLE FOR ESTCOURT, SOUTH AFRICA
Latitude 29°01′S, longitude 29°52′E, elevation 1,181 m

Month	Mean sta. press. (mbar)	Temperature (°C)				Relat. humid. (%)		Precipitation					Av. wind speed (km/h)	Averages			
		mean		extreme				mean (mm)	max. (mm)	min. (mm)	days >1 mm	max. in 24 h (mm)		cloud-iness (tenths)		sun-shine (h/day)	evap. (mm)
		max.	min.	max.	min.	08h	14h							08h	14h		
Jan.	877	27	15	38	6	75	51	108	292	22	11	76	11	6	6	7.4	206
Feb.	877	27	15	37	8	78	52	115	244	39	11	81	8	6	5	7.4	170
Mar.	878	26	14	35	4	81	52	89	198	18	9	69	7	5	5	7.4	165
Apr.	879	24	11	33	1	79	45	47	194	0	5	51	8	4	4	7.7	127
May	880	21	6	31	−2	75	38	23	98	0	3	56	7	3	3	8.0	107
June	882	19	3	27	−5	71	33	7	49	0	1	25	6	2	2	8.6	97
July	882	19	2	27	−5	70	30	13	71	0	2	23	9	3	2	8.7	109
Aug.	881	21	5	31	−3	67	30	15	139	0	2	53	9	3	3	7.9	140
Sept.	880	24	8	35	−2	66	32	30	195	0	4	83	12	4	3	8.2	168
Oct.	878	25	11	38	−1	68	39	63	198	14	8	66	13	5	5	7.3	196
Nov.	877	26	13	38	3	71	44	98	215	19	10	78	14	6	5	7.2	193
Dec.	876	27	14	37	4	73	48	117	239	62	13	61	12	6	6	7.0	203
Annual	879	24	10	38	−5	73	41	725	1,251	439	79	83	10	4	4	7.7	1,881
Rec. (yrs.)	19	30	30	30	30	30	22	30	30	30	30	30	5	30	30	6	4

Sunshine duration and windspeed at Ladysmith.

TABLE XXVIII

CLIMATIC TABLE FOR MOKHOTLONG, LESOTHO
Latitude 29°17'S, longitude 29°05'E, elevation 2,375 m

Month	Temperature (°C)				Precipitation					Aver. cloudiness (tenths)	
	mean		extreme		mean (mm)	max. (mm)	min. (mm)	days > 1 mm	max. in 24 h (mm)		
	max.	min.	max.	min.						08h	14h
Jan.	24	9	33	2	96	151	55	13	33	4	6
Feb.	24	9	35	1	85	153	24	12	45	4	6
Mar.	22	7	28	− 1	63	141	22	10	33	4	5
Apr.	20	4	27	− 6	34	75	5	6	31	3	4
May	16	−1	26	−12	26	131	0	3	78	3	4
June	14	−4	23	−12	5	21	0	1	9	2	2
July	14	−5	23	−12	10	48	0	2	23	2	3
Aug.	17	−2	24	−13	15	71	0	2	33	2	3
Sept.	20	2	27	− 8	20	121	0	3	35	2	3
Oct.	22	6	31	− 7	57	128	17	8	76	4	5
Nov.	22	7	31	− 4	83	179	32	12	34	4	5
Dec.	23	9	33	0	92	177	32	12	35	4	6
Annual	20	3	35	−13	586	806	285	84	78	3	4
Rec. (yrs.)	25	25	25	25	25	25	25	25	25	25	10

TABLE XXIX

CLIMATIC TABLE FOR OKIEP, SOUTH AFRICA
Latitude 29°36'S, longitude 17°52'E, elevation 927 m

Month	Mean sta. press. (mbar)	Temperature (°C) mean max.	mean min.	extreme max.	extreme min.	Relat. humid. (%) 08h	14h	Precipitation mean (mm)	max. (mm)	min. (mm)	days >1 mm	max. in 24 h (mm)	Averages cloud-iness (tenths) 08h	14h	sun-shine (h/day)	evap. (mm)
Jan.	913	30	15	39	7	49	25	4	41	0	1	11	2	2	12.5	404
Feb.	913	31	16	39	6	53	26	7	63	0	1	23	2	2	11.5	396
Mar.	914	30	15	37	4	57	28	10	50	0	1	30	2	2	10.5	335
Apr.	915	25	12	37	3	63	32	14	61	0	1	33	2	2	9.2	213
May	916	21	9	32	0	64	35	23	69	0	3	24	3	3	7.1	124
June	919	18	7	28	−1	65	36	26	123	0	3	18	2	2	8.4	127
July	919	17	6	26	−3	70	40	20	82	0	4	18	3	3	8.6	150
Aug.	918	19	7	31	−2	64	37	24	89	0	3	19	2	3	8.9	178
Sept.	917	21	8	33	0	61	35	15	74	0	3	34	3	3	9.9	226
Oct.	915	25	10	35	0	53	28	9	59	0	1	11	3	2	10.6	282
Nov.	914	27	12	38	2	52	27	6	67	0	1	51	3	2	11.9	386
Dec.	913	29	14	38	1	46	25	4	27	0	1	19	2	2	12.2	432
Annual	916	24	11	39	−3	58	31	162	327	49	23	51	2	2	10.1	3,253
Rec. (yrs.)	7	20	20	20	20	20	12	67	67	67	20	20	20	12	3	4

TABLE XXX

CLIMATIC TABLE FOR WEPENER, SOUTH AFRICA
Latitude 29°44'S, longitude 27°02'E, elevation 1,440 m

Month	Temperature (°C)				Relat. humid.[1] (%)	Precipitation					Averages			
	mean		extreme			mean (mm)	max. (mm)	min. (mm)	days >1 mm	max. in 24 h (mm)	cloud-iness (tenths)		sun-shine (h/day)	evap. (mm)
	max.	min.	max.	min.							08h	14h		
Jan.	30	15	38	3	49	85	178	22	9	90	4	6	10.0	267
Feb.	28	14	37	3	57	98	228	24	10	121	4	6	9.3	231
Mar.	26	12	35	1	60	92	231	25	9	67	4	5	7.7	180
Apr.	23	7	32	−4	61	54	147	1	6	59	4	5	8.5	129
May	19	3	27	−7	60	29	89	1	4	46	3	4	7.5	94
June	17	−2	25	−11	57	9	39	0	2	19	3	3	7.8	69
July	17	−1	23	−11	53	15	86	0	2	33	3	3	7.8	84
Aug.	20	1	28	−10	45	16	79	0	2	33	2	3	9.2	124
Sept.	23	5	32	−7	40	22	125	0	3	57	3	4	9.3	185
Oct.	26	9	34	−4	43	56	177	3	6	95	4	5	9.8	241
Nov.	27	11	37	−1	45	71	152	4	7	61	4	5	9.9	267
Dec.	29	14	38	2	47	79	159	5	8	68	4	6	9.7	277
Annual	24	7	38	−11	51	626	1,048	406	68	121	3	5	8.9	2,148
Rec. (yrs.)	30	30	30	30	30	30	30	30	30	30	30	30	5	4

[1] Deduced from records at Bloemfontein.

TABLE XXXI

CLIMATIC TABLE FOR DURBAN, SOUTH AFRICA
Latitude 29°50'S, longitude 31°02'E, elevation 5 m

Month	Mean sea level press. (mbar)	Temperature (°C) mean max.	mean min.	extreme max.	extreme min.	Relat. humid. (%)	Precipitation mean (mm)	max. (mm)	min. (mm)	days > 1 mm	max. in 24 h (mm)	Av. wind speed (km/h)	Averages cloudiness (tenths) 08h	14h	sunshine (h/day)	rad. (Ly/day)	diff. rad.	evap. (mm)
Jan.	1,014	27	20	33	14	81	118	383	10	11	177	12	6	6	6.5	520	206	203
Feb.	1,014	28	21	38	15	82	128	358	22	9	151	11	5	5	6.7	480	188	170
Mar.	1,015	27	20	32	14	83	113	267	23	9	83	11	5	5	6.2	434	152	180
Apr.	1,016	26	18	37	11	81	91	315	8	7	146	9	4	4	6.8	365	112	127
May	1,018	24	14	35	7	77	59	260	5	4	161	8	3	4	7.4	266	83	99
June	1,022	22	11	32	5	73	36	356	0	3	240	8	3	3	6.9	275	70	84
July	1,022	22	11	33	4	73	26	109	1	3	55	9	3	3	6.9	285	76	89
Aug.	1,020	22	12	36	5	77	39	136	2	4	82	12	4	3	6.9	324	103	122
Sept.	1,020	23	15	42	8	79	63	143	7	6	95	13	5	5	5.8	402	144	142
Oct.	1,017	23	17	40	8	81	85	251	25	10	78	14	6	7	5.2	413	178	170
Nov.	1,015	25	18	39	10	81	121	278	21	11	135	15	6	7	5.7	459	215	173
Dec.	1,014	26	19	35	13	81	124	363	41	12	100	13	6	6	6.0	495	233	196
Annual	1,017	25	16	42	4	79	1,003	1,397	631	89	240	11	5	5	6.4	393	147	1,755
Rec. (yrs.)	30	30	30	20	20	20	30	30	30	30	30	10	30	30	10	7	7	4

TABLE XXXII

CLIMATIC TABLE FOR GROOTFONTEIN, SOUTH AFRICA
Latitude 31°29′S, longitude 25°02′E, elevation 1,263 m

Month	Temperature (°C)				Relat. humid. (%)		Precipitation					Av. wind speed (km/h)	Averages			
	mean		extreme				mean (mm)	max. (mm)	min. (mm)	days >1 mm	max. in 24 h (mm)		cloud-iness (tenths)		sun-shine (h/day)	evap. (mm)
	max.	min.	max.	min.	08h	14h							08h	14h		
Jan.	30	12	38	0	64	30	47	126	0	5	71	10	4	4	10.4	300
Feb.	29	12	38	2	70	32	65	183	4	7	71	10	4	4	9.4	254
Mar.	26	10	34	0	76	38	59	123	6	6	62	9	4	4	9.0	206
Apr.	23	6	32	−4	75	39	29	84	2	4	54	9	4	4	8.2	147
May	19	3	28	−9	74	37	21	69	0	3	40	11	3	4	7.7	102
June	16	−1	24	−13	75	35	7	29	0	2	23	14	3	3	8.0	91
July	15	−1	24	−11	73	34	13	75	0	2	39	14	3	2	7.6	114
Aug.	18	1	31	−11	66	34	10	65	0	2	32	16	3	2	8.6	155
Sept.	21	3	37	−9	60	29	16	67	0	2	44	13	3	3	9.1	196
Oct.	24	6	34	−6	60	27	27	85	0	3	39	13	4	5	9.7	249
Nov.	26	9	36	−2	61	28	40	150	1	5	49	13	4	4	9.3	287
Dec.	29	11	38	1	61	29	43	109	0	5	55	11	3	4	10.7	292
Annual	23	6	38	−13	68	33	377	623	183	46	71	12	3	4	9.0	2,393
Rec. (yrs.)	30	30	30	30	30	20	30	30	30	30	30	5	30	30	9	4

TABLE XXXIII

CLIMATIC TABLE FOR UMTATA, SOUTH AFRICA
Latitude 31°35'S, longitude 28°47'E, elevation 696 m

Month	Temperature (°C) mean		extreme		Relat. humid. (%)		Precipitation					Averages			
	max.	min.	max.	min.	08h	14h	mean (mm)	max. (mm)	min. (mm)	days >1 mm	max. in 24 h (mm)	cloudiness (tenths) 08h	14h	sunshine (h/day)	evap. (mm)
Jan.	28	16	43	7	74	58	91	241	34	9	72	6	6	6.1	163
Feb.	28	16	39	7	80	58	87	241	23	10	54	6	6	6.1	137
Mar.	27	15	38	6	84	58	97	240	14	9	52	5	5	6.8	132
Apr.	26	11	37	2	85	50	41	151	1	6	35	5	5	6.5	104
May	24	7	34	−2	87	40	27	173	0	3	55	4	4	6.1	81
June	22	3	32	−6	83	33	16	180	0	2	45	3	3	6.5	74
July	21	3	30	−4	83	32	17	190	0	3	28	3	3	6.7	81
Aug.	23	5	34	−3	81	37	20	100	0	2	39	4	3	7.6	102
Sept.	24	8	38	−2	78	41	43	239	3	5	57	4	4	7.3	114
Oct.	25	11	41	3	71	51	58	155	3	8	69	6	6	6.0	147
Nov.	26	13	39	4	73	56	76	235	8	10	76	6	6	5.9	150
Dec.	27	14	42	4	72	60	81	178	0	9	68	6	6	5.6	165
Annual	25	10	43	−6	79	48	654	979	344	76	76	5	5	6.4	1,450
Rec. (yrs.)	18	18	18	18	18	10	68	68	68	18	18	18	10	2	4

TABLE XXXIV

CLIMATIC TABLE FOR BEAUFORT WEST, SOUTH AFRICA
Latitude 32°21'S, longitude 22°35'E, elevation 857 m

Month	Mean sta. press. (mbar)	Temperature (°C)				Relat. humid. (%)	Precipitation					Aver. wind speed (km/h)	Averages			
		mean		extreme			mean (mm)	max. (mm)	min. (mm)	days >1 mm	max. in 24 h (mm)		cloud-iness (tenths)		sun-shine (h/day)	evap. (mm)
		max.	min.	max.	min.								08h	14h		
Jan.	911	32	16	41	4	46	14	55	0	2	27	14	3	3	10.9	437
Feb.	912	31	16	42	7	50	34	162	1	3	61	14	4	3	10.4	366
Mar.	913	29	14	39	4	54	32	103	0	4	47	12	4	4	9.0	279
Apr.	914	25	11	36	2	52	17	68	0	3	45	12	4	4	8.2	193
May	915	21	8	32	-2	52	14	76	0	2	44	14	4	4	8.0	155
June	919	19	5	27	-6	51	7	35	0	1	33	14	3	3	7.9	150
July	918	18	5	28	-6	51	10	58	0	2	29	15	3	3	8.1	170
Aug.	917	20	6	32	-5	49	12	80	0	2	29	16	4	3	8.7	185
Sept.	916	23	8	37	-3	46	12	55	0	1	42	15	4	4	8.8	259
Oct.	914	26	10	39	-1	46	16	74	0	2	50	15	4	4	9.6	323
Nov.	912	28	13	41	4	46	28	116	0	3	53	15	4	4	10.7	399
Dec.	912	31	15	42	6	46	26	232	0	3	97	14	3	3	11.2	414
Annual	914	25	11	42	-6	49	222	387	64	28	97	14	4	4	9.3	3,330
Rec. (yrs.)	30	25	25	25	25	25	30	30	30	30	30	10	25	25	9	4

TABLE XXXV

CLIMATIC TABLE FOR EAST LONDON, SOUTH AFRICA
Latitude 33°02'S, longitude 27°52'E, elevation 125 m

Month	Mean sea level press. (mbar)	Temperature (°C) mean max.	mean min.	extreme max.	extreme min.	Relat. humid. (%)	Precipitation mean (mm)	max. (mm)	min. (mm)	days > 1 mm	max. in 24 h (mm)	Av. wind speed (km/h)	Averages cloudiness (tenths) 08h	14h	sunshine (h/day)	evap. (mm)
Jan.	1,014	25	18	36	9	82	69	177	17	9	107	17	6	6	7.6	198
Feb.	1,014	26	18	43	11	82	78	183	29	8	122	17	6	6	7.3	185
Mar.	1,016	25	17	35	11	82	99	243	20	9	116	16	6	5	7.1	155
Apr.	1,017	23	15	36	7	78	69	242	9	6	119	15	5	5	7.2	107
May	1,018	23	13	36	4	72	48	152	7	5	89	15	4	5	7.3	86
June	1,022	21	11	33	3	66	35	136	0	2	109	16	4	4	7.9	94
July	1,021	21	10	33	2	66	32	199	0	3	122	17	3	3	7.8	94
Aug.	1,021	21	11	37	3	71	42	101	4	5	66	19	4	4	7.6	127
Sept.	1,019	21	12	41	5	77	97	292	16	7	113	18	5	5	7.5	130
Oct.	1,017	21	14	41	7	77	111	465	33	9	265	18	6	6	6.8	165
Nov.	1,016	23	15	40	9	81	93	227	1	8	122	20	6	6	7.6	180
Dec.	1,015	24	17	36	9	80	87	224	16	10	127	18	6	6	7.4	193
Annual	1,017	23	14	43	2	76	860	1,349	500	81	265	17	5	5	7.4	1,714
Rec. (yrs.)	30	21	21	21	21	21	21	21	21	21	21	10	21	21	10	4

TABLE XXXVI

CLIMATIC TABLE FOR OUDTSHOORN, SOUTH AFRICA
Latitude 33°35'S, longitude 22°12'E, elevation 335 m

Month	Temperature (°C)				Relat. humid. (%)		Precipitation					Aver. cloudiness (tenths)	
	mean		extreme				mean (mm)	max. (mm)	min. (mm)	days > 1 mm	max. in 24 h (mm)		
	max.	min.	max.	min.	08h	14h						08h	14h
Jan.	32	15	44	6	69	35	18	119	0	2	107	3	3
Feb.	32	15	43	7	73	38	19	72	0	3	49	3	3
Mar.	30	14	43	6	79	39	27	106	2	4	40	3	3
Apr.	26	10	38	3	85	42	24	84	2	3	37	3	4
May	22	7	34	−2	86	47	21	72	0	3	26	4	4
June	20	4	30	−3	87	46	14	36	0	3	30	3	4
July	19	3	31	−3	83	44	21	73	0	3	40	3	4
Aug.	21	5	36	−2	85	44	21	66	0	3	44	3	4
Sept.	23	7	38	0	78	40	20	49	1	4	27	4	4
Oct.	26	10	40	2	71	41	24	69	0	4	35	3	5
Nov.	28	12	42	4	68	40	29	97	0	3	44	4	4
Dec.	30	14	43	4	65	38	16	57	0	2	35	3	3
Annual	26	10	44	−3	77	41	254	406	153	37	107	3	4
Rec. (yrs.)	30	30	30	30	30	20	30	30	30	30	30	30	20

TABLE XXXVII

CLIMATIC TABLE FOR CAPE TOWN, SOUTH AFRICA
Latitude 33°54'S, longitude 18°32'E, elevation 17 m

Month	Temperature (°C)				Relat. humid. (%)	Precipitation					Aver. wind speed (km/h)	Averages					evap. (mm)
	mean		extreme			mean (mm)	max. (mm)	min. (mm)	days >1 mm	max. in 24 h (mm)		cloudiness (tenths)		sunshine (h/day)	rad. (Ly/day)	diff. rad. (mm)	
	max.	min.	max.	min.								08h	14h				
Jan.	26	16	38	7	72	12	56	0	2	25	22	3	3	10.9	732	150	322
Feb.	26	16	38	5	74	8	61	1	2	30	21	3	2	10.5	627	146	257
Mar.	25	14	39	5	77	17	53	4	3	30	17	4	3	9.1	525	124	213
Apr.	22	12	39	2	81	47	150	4	6	44	16	5	4	6.9	369	112	135
May	19	10	35	−1	78	84	163	13	9	62	14	5	5	5.9	261	97	74
June	18	8	30	−2	80	82	173	18	9	55	13	5	4	6.0	223	80	63
July	17	7	29	−2	84	85	202	14	10	49	16	5	5	5.7	241	87	71
Aug.	18	8	32	−1	82	71	156	18	10	47	17	5	5	6.4	306	110	91
Sept.	19	9	35	0	80	43	123	3	7	38	18	5	5	7.2	437	143	135
Oct.	21	11	33	1	77	29	102	4	5	49	20	5	4	8.9	562	167	193
Nov.	23	13	34	4	74	17	59	2	3	20	21	4	4	9.9	667	177	259
Dec.	25	15	38	5	72	11	37	0	2	26	20	4	3	11.1	722	171	328
Annual	22	12	39	−2	78	506	756	347	68	62	18	4	4	8.2	473	130	2,141
Rec. (yrs.)	30	30	30	30	25	30	30	30	30	30	9	25	25	10	9	9	4

TABLE XXXVIII

CLIMATIC TABLE FOR GEORGE, SOUTH AFRICA
Latitude 33°58'S, longitude 22°25'E, elevation 221 m

Month	Mean sea level press. (mbar)	Temperature (°C) mean max.	Temperature (°C) mean min.	Temperature (°C) extreme max.	Temperature (°C) extreme min.	Relat. humid. (%)	Precipitation mean (mm)	Precipitation max. (mm)	Precipitation min. (mm)	days >1 mm	max. in 24 h (mm)	Av. wind speed (km/h)	Cloudiness (tenths) 08h	Cloudiness (tenths) 14h	Sunshine (h/day)	evap. (mm)
Jan.	1,015	24	15	41	8	81	81	183	16	8	131	9	5	6	7.8	150
Feb.	1,014	24	15	37	8	83	59	192	16	8	48	8	6	5	7.0	145
Mar.	1,016	24	14	41	8	82	78	190	24	9	83	7	5	6	6.5	109
Apr.	1,017	22	12	39	5	81	63	228	13	7	70	7	5	6	6.5	79
May	1,018	21	10	35	3	75	61	155	14	7	97	8	5	6	6.3	61
June	1,021	19	8	31	2	70	38	89	4	5	33	10	4	5	6.6	81
July	1,021	19	7	30	1	72	47	121	2	6	72	10	4	4	6.7	63
Aug.	1,020	19	8	33	2	74	59	267	9	7	110	10	5	5	6.6	91
Sept.	1,020	19	9	38	2	78	71	128	20	8	55	8	5	6	6.7	94
Oct.	1,018	20	10	41	4	81	86	173	16	10	89	9	6	6	7.0	114
Nov.	1,016	22	12	34	5	81	73	198	6	8	97	10	6	6	7.0	135
Dec.	1,015	23	13	39	4	80	60	137	17	8	78	9	6	6	7.4	160
Annual	1,018	21	11	41	1	78	776	993	523	91	131	9	5	5	6.8	1,282
Rec. (yrs.)	30	20	20	20	20	20	20	20	20	20	20	10	20	20	11	4

585

TABLE XXXIX

CLIMATIC TABLE FOR PORT ELIZABETH, SOUTH AFRICA
Latitude 33°59'S, longitude 25°36'E, elevation 58 m

Month	Mean sea level press. (mbar)	Temperature (°C) mean max.	mean min.	extreme max.	extreme min.	Relat. humid. (%)	Precipitation mean (mm)	max. (mm)	min. (mm)	days >1 mm	max. in 24 h (mm)	Aver. wind speed (km/h)	Averages cloudiness (tenths) 08h	14h	sunshine (h/day)	rad. (Ly/day)	diff. rad.	evap. (mm)
Jan.	1,014	25	16	39	7	80	37	134	9	5	88	17	5	4	8.5	598	209	249
Feb.	1,014	25	17	40	8	81	33	91	10	5	73	16	5	4	8.2	586	171	223
Mar.	1,015	24	16	40	7	82	48	154	7	6	109	14	5	4	7.5	454	146	183
Apr.	1,016	23	13	38	5	80	44	129	1	5	51	14	5	4	7.6	342	106	130
May	1,017	22	10	35	0	78	65	236	5	6	57	12	5	4	6.9	263	79	94
June	1,021	20	8	32	0	76	58	183	0	5	70	10	4	4	6.9	237	67	86
July	1,021	19	7	32	0	76	56	110	1	6	62	12	4	4	7.1	254	73	79
Aug.	1,020	20	8	37	0	78	59	172	5	6	133	15	4	4	7.6	322	94	102
Sept.	1,019	20	10	40	0	80	68	295	12	8	135	16	5	4	7.4	413	146	132
Oct.	1,017	21	12	41	4	81	61	200	17	8	91	18	6	5	7.7	505	175	180
Nov.	1,016	22	14	40	6	80	61	200	1	7	54	20	6	4	8.3	610	210	231
Dec.	1,015	24	15	38	7	78	42	168	6	5	100	18	5	4	8.9	634	211	259
Annual	1,017	22	12	—	—	79	632	814	469	72	135	15	5	4	7.7	435	141	1,948
Rec. (yrs.)	30	30	30	30	30	24	30	30	30	30	30	9	30	24	10	4	4	4

References Index

LANDSBERG, H. E., 31, 34, 520, 555
LANDSBERG, H. E., LIPPMANN, H., PAFFEN, K. H. and
  TROLL, C., 17, 19, 34, 40, 53, 93, 110, 145, 151,
  184, 186, 193, 201, 370, 381
LASSOW, G. B., *see* HOWE, G. M. et al.
LEBEDEV, A. V., 32, 34
LEBRUN, A. and VANDER ELST, N., 280, 290
LEE, D., 279, 290
LISSICINE, V., 380, 381
LIPPMANN, H., *see* LANDSBERG, H. E. et al.
LUMB, F. E., *see* BARGMANN, D. J. et al.

McCORMACK, J. G., 186
McCULLOGH, J. S. G., *see* GLOVER, J. and
  McCULLOGH, J. S. G.
McINDOE, K. G., 283, 290
MEINEKE, E. N., 524, 555
METEOROLOGICAL OFFICE, 39, 40, 53, 151
MILLER, A. A., 110, 175
MÖRTH, H. T., 332
MÖRTH, H. T., *see* JOHNSON, D. H. and MÖRTH, H. T.
MURPHEY, R., 38, 53

NAKAMURA, K., 32, 34

OBASI, G. O. P., 186
OLIVER, R. and FAGE, J. D., 1, 34
OWEN, W. G., *see* RIJKS, D. A. and OWEN, W. G.

PAFFEN, K. H., *see* LANDSBERG, H. E. et al.
PEDGLEY, D. E., 142, 151
PIRE, J., BERRUEX, M. and QUOIDBACH, J., 269, 290,
  357, 365
PROTHERO, R. M., 394, 400

QUOIDBACH, J. and GOLBERT, G., 260, 290, 350, 365
QUOIDBACH, J., *see* PIRE, J. et al.

REED, L. J., *see* HOWE, G. M. et al.
REPUBLIC OF SOUTH AFRICA, 521, 522, 524, 526, 555
RIEHL, H., 260, 290, 349, 365
RIJKS, D. A. and OWEN, W. G., 330, 332
ROBINSON, P., *see* GLOVER, J. et al.
RODWELL, E. E., 32, 34

SANSOM, H. W., 331, 332
SANSOM, H. W., *see* FRISBY, E. M. and SANSOM, H. W.
SCHUEPP, W., 266, 290
SCHULZE, B. R., 522, 524, 555
SCHULZE, B. R., *see* HOFMEYR, W. L. and SCHULZE,
  B. R.
SCHUMANN, T. E. W. and THOMPSON, W. R., 526, 555
SCHUMANN, T. E. W., *see* TALJAARD, J. J. and SCHU-
  MANN, T. E. W.
SELLERS, W. D., 16, 34
SELTZER, P., 40. 51, 53
SERVICE MÉTÉOROLOGIQUE RÉPUBLIQUE DU SÉNÉGAL,
  195, 201
SERVICIO METEOROLOGICO DE ANGOLA, 35
SERVICIO METEOROLOGICO NACIONAL, LISBOA, 35
SIERRA LEONE METEOROLOGICAL SERVICE, 224, 234
SOUTH AFRICA WEATHER BUREAU, 511, 512, 514, 520,
  555
STANHILL, G., 184, 186
STEWART, C. M., 522, 524, 555
STOCK, G. D., *see* GRIFFITHS, J. F. and STOCK, G. D.
STEYN, E. E., *see* HAYWARD, L. Q. and STEYN, E. E.
STRUNING, J. O. and FLOHN, H., 32, 34

TALJAARD, J. J., 502, 503, 506, 555
TALJAARD, J. J. and SCHUMANN, T. E. W., 503, 555
TALJAARD, J. J. and VAN LOON, H., 506, 555
TERJUNG, W. H., 31, 34
THOMPSON, B. W., 8, 9, 17, 34, 326, 332
THOMPSON, W. R., *see* SCHUMANN, T. E. W. and
  THOMPSON, W. R.
TREWARTHA, G. T., 225, 234, 314, 332, 505, 555
TRIEGAARDT, D. O., 524, 555
TROLL, C., 32, 34
TROLL, C., *see* LANDSBERG, H. E. et al.
TSCHIRHART, G., 260, 261, 262, 290, 350, 365

VANDENPLAS, A., 274, 290
VANDER ELST, N., 277, 278, 290, 361, 365
VANDER ELST, N., *see* LEBRUN, A. and VANDER ELST,
  N.
VAN LOON, H., *see* TALGAARD, J. J. and VAN LOON, H.
VOWINCKEL, E., 506, 511, 555

WINSTANLEY, D., 32, 34
WOODHEAD, T., 330, 332
WORLD METEOROLOGICAL ORGANIZATION, 29, 34, 35

Geographical Index

Subject Index